CONTEMPORARY
Black
Biography

ISSN-1058-1316

CONTEMPORARY

Black
Biography

Profiles from the International Black Community

Volume 93

GALE
CENGAGE Learning

Detroit • New York • San Francisco • New Haven, Conn • Waterville, Maine • London

Contemporary Black Biography, Volume 93

Kepos Media, Inc.: Derek Jacques, Janice Jorgensen, and Paula Kepos, editors

Project Editor: Margaret Mazurkiewicz

Image Research and Acquisitions: Leitha Etheridge-Sims

Manufacturing: Dorothy Maki, Rita Wimberley

Composition and Prepress: Mary Beth Trimper, Gary Leach

Imaging: John Watkins

For product information and technology assistance, contact us at
Gale Customer Support, 1-800-877-4253.
For permission to use material from this text or product,
submit all requests online at **www.cengage.com/permissions.**
Further permissions questions can be emailed to
permissionrequest@cengage.com

Gale
27500 Drake Rd.
Farmington Hills, MI, 48331-3535

ISBN-13: 978-1-4144-7173-0
ISBN-10: 1-4144-7173-4

ISSN 1058-1316

This title is also available as an e-book.
ISBN 13: 978-1-4144-7269-0
ISBN-10: 1-4144-7269-2
Contact your Gale sales representative for ordering information.

Printed in Mexico
1 2 3 4 5 6 7 15 14 13 12 11

Advisory Board

Contents

Introduction ix

Cumulative Nationality Index 175

Cumulative Occupation Index 193

Cumulative Subject Index 219

Cumulative Name Index 269

Benjamin Banneker 1
    First noted African-American scientist
Buju Banton 4
    Troubled dancehall reggae star
Elgin Baylor..8
    All-time NBA great for the Lakers
Jacqueline A. Berrien...12
    *Respected chair of the U.S. Equal Employment
    Opportunity Commission*
Daquan Chisholm 15
    Student innovator of safer helmets for police officers
Kevin Clash..17
    Ebullient voice of Elmo
George Clinton..21
    Godfather of funk
CoCo Brother..26
    Gospel radio and television personality
De'Jaun Correia 29
    Young anti–death penalty activist
Donald Lee Cox 31
    Field marshal for the Black Panther Party
David Crosthwait...33
    Innovative climate-control engineer
John Dabiri...35
    Renowned biophysicist and Genius Grant recipient
Meri Nana-Ama Danquah.......................................38
    Ghanain-American memoirist and public speaker

Jason Derülo...41
    R&B singer-songwriter sensation
Dave Duerson..43
    *Football player whose suicide called attention to NFL
    head injuries*
Percival Everett...46
    Acclaimed experimental novelist
Fabolous 50
    Grammy-nominated rap sensation
Curt Flood 53
    Radically altered Major League Baseball
Thais Francis 56
    Budding dramatist
Michael Franti 58
    Leader of the hip-hop band Spearhead
Doug E. Fresh 61
    Pioneering hip-hop performer
Roscoe C. Giles...64
    Prominent Chicago surgeon and civil rights activist
Peter J. Gomes..67
    Beloved Harvard minister
Edward O. Gourdin...71
    *First African American appointed to the Massachusetts
    Superior Court*
Tanya Hamilton 74
    Promising filmmaker
Tony Hansberry II 77
    *Student who developed a new surgical technique at the
    age of 14*
Elvin Hayes...79
    One of the top all-time NBA players
Derek Jeter 83
    New York Yankees superstar
Lonnie G. Johnson 87
    *Inventor of wildly popular toy and alternative energy
    breakthrough*
Talib Kweli 91
    Socially conscious rapper

LaChanze...94
  Tony Award–winning actress
Lunsford Lane...98
  Entrepreneurial former slave and memoirist
Ollie Matson...101
  Legendary NFL Hall-of-Fame running back
Benjamin Matthews 103
  *Operatic champion of the African-American musical
  tradition*
Jan Matzeliger 105
  Ingenious shoemaker and inventor
George McJunkin...107
  *Autodidact who changed the understanding of human
  history*
Tracy McMillan..109
  Bestselling memoirist and television screenwriter
Omar Benson Miller 111
  Versatile character actor
Frederick A. Morton Jr. 114
  Enterprising founder of Caribbean music television
Abdias do Nascimento..117
  *Renowned Brazilian activist, politician, and man of
  letters*
Sophia A. Nelson 120
  Republican media pundit
Eleanor Holmes Norton 123
  Admired legal scholar and DC delegate to Congress

Stephanie Rawlings-Blake...............................127
  Determined Baltimore mayor
Dana Redd..130
  Revitalizing mayor of Camden, New Jersey
Cedric Richmond 133
  Louisiana congressman
Cecilia Rouse..136
  Esteemed economist and presidential advisor
Danzy Senna 139
  Author of nuanced portraits
Terri Sewell 142
  *First African-American woman to represent Alabama in
  Congress*
Slick Rick 145
  Influential and controversial hip-hop artist
Wole Soyinka..148
  Powerful Nigerian writer and Nobel laureate
Tom Stith..153
  College basketball star at St. Bonaventure University
David E. Talbert 156
  Author of popular plays
Mike Tyson..159
  Notorious heavyweight boxing champion
Denzel Washington..164
  Iconic film actor
Kanye West 169
  Outspoken rap musician and producer

Introduction

Contemporary Black Biography provides informative biographical profiles of the important and influential persons of African heritage who form the international black community: men and women who have changed today's world and are shaping tomorrow's. *Contemporary Black Biography* covers persons of various nationalities in a wide variety of fields, including architecture, art, business, dance, education, fashion, film, industry, journalism, law, literature, medicine, music, politics and government, publishing, religion, science and technology, social issues, sports, television, theater, and others. In addition to in-depth coverage of names found in today's headlines, *Contemporary Black Biography* provides coverage of selected individuals from earlier in this century whose influence continues to impact on contemporary life. *Contemporary Black Biography* also provides coverage of important and influential persons who are not yet household names and are therefore likely to be ignored by other biographical reference series. Each volume also includes listee updates on names previously appearing in *CBB*.

Designed for Quick Research and Interesting Reading

- **Attractive page design** incorporates textual subheads, making it easy to find the information you're looking for.

- **Easy-to-locate data sections** provide quick access to vital personal statistics, career information, major awards, and mailing addresses, when available.

- **Informative biographical essays** trace the subject's personal and professional life with the kind of in-depth analysis you need.

- **To further enhance your appreciation** of the subject, most entries include photographic portraits.

- **Sources for additional information** direct the user to selected books, magazines, and newspapers where more information on the individuals can be obtained.

Helpful Indexes Make It Easy to Find the Information You Need

Contemporary Black Biography includes cumulative Nationality, Occupation, Subject, and Name indexes that make it easy to locate entries in a variety of useful ways.

Available in Electronic Formats

Diskette/Magnetic Tape. Contemporary Black Biography is available for licensing on magnetic tape or diskette in a fielded format. Either the complete database or a custom selection of entries may be ordered. The database is available for internal data processing and nonpublishing purposes only. For more information, call (800) 877-GALE.

On-line. Contemporary Black Biography is available on-line through Mead Data Central's NEXIS Service in the NEXIS, PEOPLE and SPORTS Libraries in the GALBIO file and Gale's Biography Resource Center.

Disclaimer

Contemporary Black Biography uses and lists websites as sources and these websites may become obsolete.

We Welcome Your Suggestions

The editors welcome your comments and suggestions for enhancing and improving *Contemporary Black Biography*. If you would like to suggest persons for inclusion in the series, please submit these names to the editors. Mail comments or suggestions to:

The Editor

Contemporary Black Biography

Gale, Cengage Learning

27500 Drake Rd.

Farmington Hills, MI 48331-3535

Phone: (800) 347-4253

Benjamin Banneker

1731–1806

Farmer, astronomer, mathematician, surveyor, almanac author

Banneker, Benjamin, photograph. North Wind Picture Archives via AP Images.

Benjamin Banneker, a free person of color who lived in rural Maryland during the latter two-thirds of the 18th century, is often called the first African-American scientist. As the son of a freed slave and a biracial free woman of color, Banneker faced harshly circumscribed educational and career opportunities. A self-taught mathematician and astronomer, Banneker worked on his family's farm until his later years, at which point he committed himself to scientific study and calculations. His aptitude in astronomy and math attracted attention, and he assisted in the surveying of the nation's new capital city, Washington, DC, in 1791. He exchanged letters with secretary of state Thomas Jefferson, and he began publishing a yearly almanac based on his astronomical calculations in 1792.

Banneker's achievements and intellectual abilities were used as evidence of the equality of the races by 18th- and 19th-century abolitionists and 20th-century civil rights advocates, and in some cases his biography was exaggerated or mythologized. Subsequent historical research has corrected certain myths while verifying the remarkable nature of Banneker's self-education and achievement.

Educated Himself on Family Farm

Benjamin Banneker was born in 1731 into a Maryland household of mixed British and African heritage. His grandmother Molly Welsh (or Walsh) came to the United States as an indentured servant after being falsely accused by her English employers of stealing a pail of milk. After fulfilling the seven years of her sentence in 1690, she set out to establish her own small farm. Alone in what was then the wilderness of rural Baltimore County, and in spite of her personal opposition to the institution of slavery, she purchased two slaves to help her in this project.

One of these slaves refused to work, claiming to be the son of a West African king. His name was Bannaka (or some phonetic equivalent thereof). Banneker's definitive biographer, Silvio A. Bedini, has found reason to believe that Bannaka may have been part of the Wolof tribal group in an area near present-day Ghana and Nigeria, and that his claims of royal lineage are plausible, if ultimately unverifiable. Once the agricultural output on her farm enabled Welsh to repay the loan she had assumed to purchase the land, she freed her slaves,

At a Glance . . .

Born Benjamin Banneker on November 9, 1731, in Baltimore County, MD; died on October 9, 1806 in Baltimore County, MD; son of Mary and Robert Banneker (a farmer). *Religion*: Christian.

Career: Farmer, 1731–91; astronomer, mathematician, 1791–1806; almanac author, 1792–97.

and in violation of the miscegenation laws of the time, she married Bannaka—who was by then commonly known as "Banneky"—most likely in the year 1696.

Welsh took the Banneky name and withdrew from her white neighbors. The couple had four daughters, the oldest of whom, Mary, was born in 1700. In 1730 Mary married a freed slave named Robert. Robert took his wife's last name, which at some point had been recast as Banneker. The couple had their first of four children, and their only son, Benjamin, in 1731.

Banneker's grandmother taught him to read, reportedly using the only book she owned, the Bible. According to some sources, Banneker's grandfather, although deceased by the time of his grandson's birth, may have passed along tribal knowledge not only of agriculture but also of engineering and astronomy, which his wife in turn presumably passed along to her grandson. Banneker's formal education, at any rate, was limited to a short period of attendance at an integrated Quaker school, where he was taught no more than the basics of mathematics.

Unable to continue his schooling because his labor was required on the family's 100-acre tobacco farm, Banneker read widely in his spare time, borrowing books from neighbors, who increasingly marveled at his intellectual precocity, and he pursued mathematical and mechanical studies. He taught himself to play musical instruments including the flute and the violin, and at age 22 he carved and assembled the mechanical components for a chiming clock, reportedly without ever having seen any form of timepiece other than a pocket watch. The clock kept correct time for decades before being destroyed in a fire that consumed his home shortly after his death.

Surveyed the District of Columbia

When his father died in 1859, Banneker assumed responsibility for the household, working diligently to support his mother and sisters. He never married, and after his mother died and the family dispersed, he continued to farm and live alone, growing his own food

and caring for himself. While his obvious intellectual abilities brought him to the attention of educated citizens in Baltimore County during his early and middle years, it was with the arrival of the wealthy Ellicott family in the area in 1771 that he made his most fruitful personal connections.

George Ellicott, one of two Ellicott brothers who relocated to Baltimore County and played an instrumental role in the area's development, was an amateur astronomer, and he helped Banneker develop his skills in this field. In addition to encouraging Banneker, Ellicott lent him books, instruments, and a desk. Through astronomical observations Banneker almost correctly predicted a solar eclipse in 1788; his failure to achieve perfect accuracy with his prediction, he later discovered, was due to an error in his source materials. But it was not until he was 59 or 60, when he cut back on his farming due to rheumatism, that Banneker was able to take up his scientific studies in earnest.

Banneker was chosen, on the strength of his astronomical and mathematical skills, to serve as the assistant to Major Andrew Ellicott, a cousin of the Baltimore County Ellicotts, who was charged with surveying the District of Columbia in 1791 in preparation for establishing the nation's new capital city. This episode in Banneker's life has been frequently mythologized, with some biographers claiming that he was involved in the selection of building sites and Pierre L'Enfant's design for the city. In fact, according to Bedini, Banneker's contributions, while significant, were mostly limited to calculations and did not bring him into contact with L'Enfant.

Compiled and Published Almanac, 1792–97

Banneker had, since before his involvement in the surveying of Washington, begun to compile his astronomical observations and calculations into an ephemeris, or table of celestial data that could be used to produce an almanac. In August of 1791 he sent the ephemeris, along with a letter, to secretary of state Thomas Jefferson. In the letter, Banneker appealed to Jefferson's reported sympathy for black Americans and suggested that if his views as expressed in the Declaration of Independence were sincere, then it was incumbent upon him to pursue all means of ending "any state of degradation, to which the unjustifiable cruelty and barbarism of men may have reduced him."

Jefferson responded politely, professing agreement with Banneker's basic contentions but stopping short of full acknowledgment of the issues he had raised and giving no indication that he had examined the ephemeris. He did note that he had sent the ephemeris to the French Academy of Science as a testament to the capabilities of those of African descent. No such copy of Banneker's ephemeris has been located.

Beginning in 1792, Banneker found a publisher for an almanac based on his ephemeris, and the almanac appeared yearly until 1797. The almanac's publication was a pioneering demonstration of African-American intellectual capability. Its scientific content, rooted in Banneker's diligent astronomical and mathematical operations, included information on the weather, the tides, and lunar and solar cycles. The publication also included a variety of general-interest items, including proverbs, poems, facts, speeches, essays, and other texts, many of which related to the abolitionist cause and other humanitarian concerns. The 1793 edition contained, among other items, Banneker's correspondence with Jefferson, and each of the yearly editions included a profile of Banneker himself. In his lifetime, the almanac spread Banneker's fame and made him an important figure within abolitionist circles; for scholars today, the scope and reliability of Banneker's calculations demonstrate the degree of his achievement as a self-taught scientist.

Banneker continued to live alone on his farm in his later years, surviving after he was no longer able to farm, and after his almanac ceased publication due to declining sales, by leasing and selling off his property piecemeal. He sold off what remained of the family farm in a deal with the Ellicotts that granted him a yearly pension. He died on October 9, 1806.

Sources

Books

Bedini, Silvio A., *The Life of Benjamin Banneker: The First African-American Man of Science*, 2nd ed., Maryland Historical Society, 1999.
Cerami, Charles A., *Benjamin Banneker: Surveyor, Astronomer, Publisher, Patriot*, John Wiley and Sons, 2002.

Periodicals

Journal of American History, December 1972, pp. 696–98.
Journal of Negro History, April 1918, pp. 99–118; July 1972, pp. 304–6.
Journal of Southern History, November 1972, pp. 645–47.
Social Studies of Science, April 1997, pp. 307–15.

Online

Africans in America, PBS, http://www.pbs.org/wgbh/aia/home.html (accessed July 15, 2011).
Corrigan, Mary Beth, "Review of Cerami, Charles A., *Benjamin Banneker: Surveyor, Astronomer, Publisher, Patriot*," H-Maryland, H-Net Reviews, April 2003, http://www.h-net.org/reviews/showrev.php?id=7440 (accessed July 15, 2011).

—Mark Lane

Buju Banton

1973—

Reggae musician

Banton, Buju, photograph. AP Images/Yesikka Vivancos.

Jamaican singer Buju Banton rose to stardom on the dancehall reggae scene as a teenager in the 1990s, producing a string of hit "slack" singles notable for their explicit sexuality and homophobia. His 1992 song "Boom Bye Bye," which seemed to advocate violence against gay men, drew the ire of the international gay and lesbian community and sparked boycotts of his music. In the aftermath of the controversy, Banton changed his tune—quite literally—offering a more spiritual, socially conscious message in the spirit, and sound, of roots reggae of the 1970s. Banton's 1995 album *'Til Shiloh* was hailed as a masterpiece, earning him comparisons to Bob Marley, and helped steer dancehall away from the violent lyrics that had characterized the genre for a decade. After 2004, however, Banton's career was derailed by legal troubles. In 2011 the singer was convicted in the United States of federal drug-trafficking charges and sentenced to 10 years in prison. Nonetheless, he remained wildly popular in Jamaica, where fans insisted on his innocence, organizing a "Free Buju" movement.

Became Teenage Dancehall Sensation

Buju Banton was born Mark Anthony Myrie on July 15, 1973, in Kingston, Jamaica, and grew up in the city's Salt Lane ghetto, the youngest of 15 children of a street vendor. He was a direct descendant of Maroons, runaway slaves who set up free communities in the interior of the island and fought for their freedom from British colonial authorities in the 18th century. As a boy, his mother gave him the nickname "Buju," a Maroon slang word for breadfruit, in reference to his chubby build. Later he would take the surname "Banton" in homage to DJ Burro Banton, his mentor and his first musical influence.

In 1986, at age 13, Banton began working as a DJ and "toaster," a rapper or MC, with local sound systems—a sort of mobile disco—and soon he was writing his own songs. That year, fellow DJ Clement Irie introduced the young singer to producer Robert French, and Banton released his first single, "The Ruler." In 1990 Banton began working with producer and engineer Dave

"Rude Boy" Kelly, releasing a string of singles on Donovan Germain's Penthouse label, including "Man Fi Dead" and "Jackie and Joyce."

In the aftermath of Bob Marley's death in 1981, Jamaican music was dominated in the 1980s and 1990s by "dancehall" reggae—so called for the venues in which it became popular—and by ragga (also called digital dancehall), styles that were less political in their message than Marley's roots reggae and which made ample use of electronic instrumentation. Dancehall music was characterized by the violence associated with Jamaica's "bad bwai" (bad boy) culture. "Slackness," a popular form of dancehall, was notorious for its sexually explicit language, and Banton's early songs exemplified the genre. In 1991 Banton had his first major hit with "Love Mi Browning," a tribute to his light-skinned girlfriend. After receiving complaints from darker-skinned Jamaican women, he followed up with "Love Black Woman."

Banton also had success recording with his Penthouse label mates, including Beres Hammond, who would become a longtime collaborator, and Wayne Wonder. He teamed with Winston Riley to record the dancehall classics "Stamina Daddy" and "Gold Spoon," and with Frankie Paul, known as the "Stevie Wonder of Jamaica," on the duet "Bring You Body Come to Me." In 1992 Banton's duet with Don T, "Big It Up," was the first release on Kelly's Mad House label; it was followed by such hits as "Batty Rider," "Woman Nuh Fret," and "Bogle." That year, Banton broke Bob Marley's record for the most No. 1 hits in a single year. His debut album, *Mr. Mention,* did not disappoint, becoming the fastest-selling album in Jamaican history. That summer Banton landed a recording contract with a major label, Mercury Records, which promised to introduce the reggae artist to a wider international audience.

Success Disrupted by Controversy

Just as Banton was poised on the brink of stardom, controversy threatened to end his career. Following the release of *Mr. Mention,* the Shang label issued a reggae compilation that included one of Banton's earlier songs, "Boom Bye Bye," a violent, homophobic track recorded in 1988 that seemed to advocate the murder of gay men. The song sparked an outcry in the international gay and lesbian community and was banned on some radio stations in New York, where Banton's music had begun to make inroads.

In a carefully worded statement issued by Mercury, Banton said, "I do not advocate violence against anyone and it was never my intention to incite violent acts with 'Boom Bye Bye.' However," he continued, "I must state unequivocally, that I do not condone homosexuality, as the lifestyle runs contrary to my religious beliefs," referring to Rastafarianism. The statement did little to quell the outrage, and Banton was removed from the lineup of the WOMAD (World of Music, Arts and Dance) Festival. His steadfast refusal to repudiate the song would haunt Banton throughout his career, with gay rights groups routinely calling for boycotts of his music.

In the spring of 1993, Mercury released Banton's major label debut, *Voice of Jamaica.* Heavier on social commentary than on sexual boasting, the album seemed to attest that Banton had been chastened by his experiences of the past year. On the single "Willy (Don't Be Silly)," he championed safe sex, pledging to donate the profits to a charity supporting children with AIDS. Other socially minded tracks included "Operation Ardent," an indictment of police brutality, and "Deportees (Things Change)," in which he criticized Jamaican emigrants who failed to share their overseas earnings with their poor families at home. The single "Make My Day" brought Banton some international recognition, reaching number 72 in Great Britain. In Jamaica, the album was among the top sellers of the year.

Hailed as the Next Bob Marley

Banton's next album, *'Til Shiloh* (1995), provided further evidence of the singer's transformation, bearing the mark of his deepening Rastafarian faith. The album showed an introspection and social awareness that surprised fans who had expected more bad bwai dancehall fare. Banton also employed live musicians in place of the digital instrumentation that was standard in the genre, marking a return to roots reggae. The record's standout track is "Murderer," a scathing attack on dancehall's culture of violence, inspired by the shooting deaths of two fellow DJs, Panhead and Dirtsman. Critics lauded the album as Banton's best work, calling

him the successor to Bob Marley, and credited "Murderer" with singlehandedly turning the lyrical mood of dancehall away from violence. The *New York Times* called *'Til Shiloh* "one of the most important reggae albums of the 1990s," while *Billboard* described the album as "luminous."

He continued in a roots- and Rasta-inspired vein on *Inna Heights* (1997), a deeply spiritual album of 19 tracks punctuated by four "inter linguas," brief spoken-word meditations on Banton's music and philosophy. The record reached No. 1 on the *Billboard* Top Reggae Albums charts, his only album to do so, and earned Banton his first of five Grammy Award nominations. Critic Josh Kun of *Rolling Stone* noted that "*Inna Heights* goes a long way toward further establishing Banton as a ghetto messenger of peace and social justice—a role few expected he would ever be grown-up enough to play."

After a three-year hiatus, Banton released *Unchained Spirit* (2000), his first recording for the California-based label Epitaph. The album featured a more eclectic mix of musical genres, incorporating elements of hip-hop, jazz, gospel, and traditional Rastafarian drumming, and featuring guest appearances by Luciano, Peter "Gramps" Morgan, Stephen Marley (son of Bob Marley), and the punk rock group Rancid. A duet with Beres Hammond, "Pull It Up," earned Record of the Year honors at the 12th Annual Tamika Reggae Awards in New York that year.

Career Derailed by Legal Troubles

In 2003 Banton returned on Atlantic Records with *Friends for Life,* a more pop-friendly record that featured less of the roots/dancehall blend that he had become famous for. His career was interrupted later that year when he was arrested on marijuana possession charges after police raided his home in Jamaica and found several fully grown marijuana plants. He was convicted and received a 60-day sentence. More seriously, he was barred from entering Great Britain and the United States for one year, forcing him to cancel a number of tour dates. Banton's troubles with the law continued in 2005, when he faced trial for his alleged role in an assault on six gay men in Kingston. Though he was later acquitted, gay rights activists questioned whether justice for the victims was possible in such a virulently homophobic culture—an intolerance perpetuated, they pointed out, by songs such as Banton's "Boom Bye Bye."

Unhappy with his treatment at the major record companies, Banton decided to form his own label, Gargamel Music, and released the album *Too Bad* in 2006, followed by *Rasta Got Soul* in 2009, both of which earned Grammy nominations. As he was readying his next album, Banton was arrested again in December of 2009, charged with conspiracy to distribute more than five kilograms of cocaine. Federal agents from the U.S. Drug Enforcement Agency alleged that the singer had conspired with two other men to buy a shipment of cocaine from an undercover officer.

Banton maintained his innocence, claiming that he had been set up; he had only spoken of cocaine with the agent, he said, to impress him, believing that the man had connections to the music industry. Banton's most ardent fans in Jamaica talked of a conspiracy against the singer, which they believed was the handiwork of the U.S. government or gay activists who still held a grudge against Banton.

In September of 2010, the judge in Banton's case declared a mistrial when the jury was unable to reach a decision. A week later, his tenth studio album, *Before the Dawn,* hit stores; he had recorded the 10 songs in Jamaica before his arrest, and worked with producers and engineers by telephone from jail to complete the album. Banton was released on bond in November, and a new trial was scheduled for February of 2011. In the meantime, Banton was permitted to perform one concert to raise money for his defense and security expenses; he played to a sold-out arena in Miami on January 16.

A day before his second trial was set to begin in Tampa, Banton received the Grammy Award for best reggae album for *Before the Dawn,* marking his fifth nomination and first win. Days later, on February 22, he was found guilty of conspiracy to possess with intent to distribute cocaine, as well as possession of a firearm and use of communication wires to facilitate a drug-trafficking offense. Letters in support of the singer's innocence were written to the court by several of Banton's children, a Jamaican government official, actor Danny Glover, and Stephen Marley, among others. In June the judge threw out the gun conviction and sentenced Banton on the remaining charges to 10 years in prison, the minimum allowable penalty.

Selected discography

Mr. Mention, Penthouse, 1992 (includes "Man Fi Dead," "Love Mi Browning," "Love Black Woman," "Batty Rider," and "Woman Nuh Fret").

Voice of Jamaica, Mercury, 1993 (includes "Willy—Don't Be Silly," "Operation Ardent," "Deportees—Things Change," and "Make My Day").

'Til Shiloh, Loose Cannon/Polygram, 1995 (includes "Murderer").

Inna Heights, Jet Star, 1997.

Unchained Spirit, Epitaph, 2000 (includes "Pull It Up").

Friends for Life, Atlantic, 2003.

Too Bad, Gargamel, 2006.

Rasta Got Soul, Gargamel, 2009.

Before the Dawn, Gargamel, 2010.

Sources

Books

Thompson, Dave, *Reggae and Caribbean Music,* Backbeat Books, 2002.

Periodicals

Billboard, December 28, 1996.
Gleaner (Jamaica), December 13, 2009.
Miami Herald, June 23, 2011.
New York Times, May 28, 1999; August 17, 2000.
Rolling Stone, March 5, 1998, p. 68.
Vibe, October 1993, p. 75.
Washington Post, March 4, 1998; August 16, 2000.

Online

Huey, Steve, "Buju Banton," All Music, http://www. allmusic.com/artist/buju-banton-p37281 (accessed June 12, 2011).

Other

Associated Press, December 4, 2003; September 30, 2005; September 26, 2010; February 3, 2011.

—Deborah A. Ring

Elgin Baylor

1934—

Athlete, sports executive

Baylor, Elgin, photograph. AP Images.

Elgin Baylor is a former professional basketball player who is often ranked among the best players of all time. Drafted in 1958 by the team that became the Los Angeles Lakers, the small forward spent 14 seasons in the National Basketball Association (NBA) and was part of the Lakers' powerhouse roster of the 1960s. His prowess in dunking, bank shots, and rebounds marked a turning point in the league, for Baylor was the first African-American player to emerge as a top scorer in the NBA. A former Laker from this era, Tommy Hawkins, asserted in *Investor's Business Daily* that "pound for pound, Elgin Baylor is the greatest player who ever played the game. . . . Elgin worked hard. He loved to play basketball and was always working on his shots. Elgin doesn't get the credit he deserves."

Emerged as a Teenage Hoops Prodigy

Baylor was born in Washington, DC, in 1934. He attended segregated schools in the city and emerged as a standout athlete at Phelps Vocational High School in the early 1950s but struggled with his grades and

eventually dropped out. For several months during 1952 and 1953 he worked in a furniture store while playing basketball in a local recreation league. Friends persuaded the talented athlete, who had grown to six feet, five inches, to reenroll in the newly built Spingarn High School. In his senior year there Baylor set a new scoring record for high school basketball in the city and took home the award for best player in the DC schools, but there was little interest from college recruiters because his grades were still abysmal.

Another pal steered Baylor to the College of Idaho, which offered him an athletic scholarship to play both football and basketball. After the school's athletic program was reorganized in 1955 Baylor lost his scholarship. He moved to Seattle and started playing for an Amateur Athletic Union (AAU) team, and his prowess brought him to the attention of Seattle University coaches. He spent two years at the school, and in 1958 the Chieftains—as the team was known at the time—advanced all the way to the men's finals in the National Collegiate Athletic Association (NCAA) championships, which was a first for the school. Baylor and his teammates traveled to Louisville, Kentucky, to face the

University of Kentucky Wildcats, but he played with a cracked rib from an earlier title game. Although the Chieftains initially had an 11–point lead, they lost the championship by a final score of 84–72. Baylor won the Most Outstanding Player of the NCAA Final award, and was soon fielding offers from professional teams and even the Harlem Globetrotters.

A month later Baylor was the No. 1 pick in the 1958 NBA Draft, taken by the last-place Minneapolis Lakers. He was offered a salary of $20,000 per year—an impressive sum at the time—and dropped out of college to begin his professional career. He spent the first few weeks of the season racking up an astonishing number of points per game, passing the 500 mark in early December, which made him the league's new leading scorer. This was a racial breakthrough in basketball: while the NBA had eased its way into integration over the past decade, Baylor's fellow minorities were men like Chuck Cooper, Earl Lloyd, and Nat "Sweetwater" Clifton. "Each was his team's blue-collar worker—rebounders and defenders who did what now is called 'the dirty work' in basketball," explained Ron Thomas in his 2004 book *They Cleared the Lane: The NBA's Black Pioneers.* "The first black player

with carte blanche to shoot didn't come along until Elgin Baylor arrived in Minneapolis."

Won Rookie of the Year

Baylor finished his first professional season as the NBA's third-leading scorer and won its Rookie of the Year award after the team advanced all the way to the finals, where they were trounced by the Boston Celtics. The Lakers spent one more year in Minneapolis before moving to Los Angeles for the start of 1960—61 season. Baylor's prowess, always widely commented upon by sportswriters, made him one of the NBA's rising stars, and that celebrity helped generate excitement in Los Angeles for this new professional franchise. His abilities helped the Lakers advance consistently to the finals over the next decade, and turned the team into a basketball powerhouse. During his 14 seasons he averaged 27.4 points per game and was voted into the First Team on the All-Star balloting 10 times. His teammates Jerry West and Wilt "The Stilt" Chamberlain also emerged as legendary Lakers during this era.

Baylor was known for his running bank shot, bouncing the ball off the rim as he sped toward it. Basketball analysts also cite him as one of the first masters of the "aerial game," wowing fans with what appeared to be an ability to levitate briefly. "He got up high but he stayed up," said Chick Hearn, the broadcast announcer for the Lakers for four decades, in *They Cleared the Lane.* "The other guy went up with him but Elgin wouldn't shoot until the guy came down. . . . He was doing things in the sixties that people are getting credit for in the nineties." Famously, Baylor brooked conventional wisdom and did not release the ball at the peak of ascent; instead he shot it on his descent, a move that Michael Jordan later made famous during his championship years with the Chicago Bulls.

On November 15, 1960, Baylor scored an astonishing 71 points in a single game—a new NBA high. "They kept throwing the ball to me, and I had to shoot," he told *Ebony* about the feat in his characteristically unpretentious fashion. Fifty years later, only three other players ever racked up more points in a game— Chamberlain, who set the NBA record in 1962 while playing for the Philadelphia Warriors, was one of them, along with Kobe Bryant, another legendary Laker. Baylor set a record (later surpassed by others) for points scored during a playoff half in a game against Boston in 1962. Baylor scored 33 points in the first half of Game 5. He scored 61 points altogether for the entire game, which five decades later remained a record for the league for points scored in a championship final. The Lakers won with a score of 126–121, but lost the series.

Transitioned to Management Role

Baylor's knee began to give him problems during the

1963–64 season. During the 1965 NBA playoffs, he blew it out completely but returned to the court for the 1965–66 season, after some had warned he might never play again. His point-per-game (PPG) totals continued to increase, and at the end of the 1967–68 season he nearly won the NBA title as leading scorer with an average of 26.0 PPG, but lost it to the most recent Rookie of the Year winner—and fellow DC native and Spingarn player—Dave Bing of the Detroit Pistons. *Sports Illustrated* put Baylor on its October 24, 1966, cover and opened its feature story with an array of full-color shots of Baylor in action. Writer Frank Deford's prose reflected attitudes of the era. "On and off the court, he glides with such regal mien, carrying himself with such élan that it often has been said of him that he must surely descend from the giant black royalty of some Nubian empire," Deford remarked in the profile.

Baylor's knee forced him to sit out much of 1970–71 season. He retired nine games into the 1971–72 season at the age of 37; later that season Chamberlain led the Lakers to their first NBA title. In total, Baylor had played in 846 games and scored 23,149 points, averaging 27.4 points per game. After a stint as a color commentator for NBA games on the CBS network, Baylor went to work for the New Orleans Jazz as an assistant coach; two years later he was named head coach and spent three years in that role. He left after a dismal 1978–79 season for the Jazz.

In 1986 Baylor was hired by the Los Angeles Clippers, the city's second NBA team. The Clippers originated as the Buffalo Braves, then moved to San Diego with a new name in 1978; in 1984 they relocated a third and final time, to Los Angeles. Long considered the hapless, underfunded competitor to the mighty Lakers—the team that had the allegiance of most southern California's hardcore hoops fans—the Clippers struggled for decades. Baylor was hired as the general manager and was able to make some improvements in the roster, although the team's owner, Donald T. Sterling, was often derided for his unwillingness to pay for genuine talent. The Clippers managed to have their first winning season only in 1991–92, when they finished 45–37. Later in that decade Baylor made a savvy draft pick with Lamar Odom, who had graduated from high school as one of the country's top-ranked players.

Won Second NBA Honor

The Clippers finished the 2005–06 season with a 47-35 win-loss record. Baylor's ability to pick talent brought him the NBA's Executive of the Year award in 2006. Two years later it was announced that he and the Clippers had parted ways. The October of 2008 announcement came as a surprise, but he had put in one of the longest tenures in the history of NBA general managers, who tend to leave after five years, on average. A few months later Baylor filed a suit in Los Angeles Superior Court, claiming racial and age discrimination on the part of Sterling, team president Andy Roeser, and the NBA. "I want to make one thing clear: I did not retire," he said at a press conference, according to a Los Angeles *Daily News* report. "The way I was treated by the NBA and the Clippers was unfair and, in many ways, discriminatory."

As details of the suit unfolded, Baylor revealed that he had worked without a contract since 1993, that Sterling—who had been the target of other discrimination lawsuits as a real estate developer—made unsavory comments about African-American players, and that Roeser had made jokes about Baylor's age. He also said he was miffed when he learned that the new coach Mike Dunleavy had taken over his general-manager duties after 2006, and Baylor had been excluded from meetings and decision-making. Dunleavy had a four-year, $22 million contract, while Baylor was still making $350,000 a year. The suit also named the NBA because they knew about the disparity in his salary in contrast to other general managers in the league. "Given the shortage of blacks in the executive roles within the NBA, I felt obligated to hang in there and endure whatever came my way," the *Daily News* quoted him as saying. In March of 2011, a jury dismissed the claim of employment discrimination, tossing out the $2 million request for compensation.

The Lakers retired Baylor's No. 22 jersey in a 1983 ceremony. In 1996, for the NBA's 50th Anniversary celebrations, Baylor was selected to the All-Time Team of greatest players. When he left the Clippers in 2008, ESPN writer Bill Simmons wrote about the glory days of Baylor's career, citing him and Boston Celtics star Bill Russell as the ultimate game-changers. "Nobody played above the rim except Russell; nobody dunked, and everyone played the same way: Rebound, run the floor, get a quick shot," Simmons wrote, asserting that "Elgin would drive from the left side, take off with the basketball, elevate, hang in the air, hang in the air, then release the ball after everyone else was already back on the ground." You could point to his entrance into the league as the precise moment when basketball changed for the better. Along with Russell, Elgin turned a horizontal game into a vertical one."

Sources

Books

Thomas, Ron, *They Cleared the Lane: The NBA's Black Pioneers,* University of Nebraska Press, 2004, p. 67.

Periodicals

Daily News (Los Angeles), May 8, 2006, p. S10; February 13, 2009, p. C1.
Ebony, February 1965, pp. 35–38.

Investor's Business Daily, May 29, 2008, p. A3.

Jet, June 12, 2006, p. 50.

Los Angeles Magazine, January 2003, p. 42.

New York Times, March 28, 2009, p. D5.

Seattle Post-Intelligencer, March 19, 2008, p. C1.

Sports Illustrated, October 24, 1966, pp. 50–54.

Online

Simmons, Bill, "Elgin Took the Game to New Heights," ESPN.com, October 8, 2008, http://sports.espn.go.com/espn/page2/story?page=simmons/081008 (accessed July 29, 2011).

—Carol Brennan

Jacqueline A. Berrien

1961—

Chair of U.S. Equal Employment Opportunity Commission, civil rights lawyer

Berrien, Jacqueline A., photograph. AP Images/Charles Dharapak.

Jacqueline A. Berrien is the chair of the U.S. Equal Employment Opportunity Commission (EEOC), the government agency charged with enforcing laws that forbid workplace discrimination on the basis of race, color, religion, sex, pregnancy, nationality, age, disability, or genetic background. A career civil rights lawyer who worked in the nonprofit sector for more than 20 years, Berrien was nominated to the EEOC chair by President Barack Obama on July 16, 2009. She was sworn into office on April 7, 2010, and her term of service is scheduled to end on July 1, 2014.

Recognized Importance of Public Service

Berrien was born in Washington, DC, in 1961. Her parents, Clifford and Anna Berrien, who hailed, respectively, from Ohio and Kentucky, moved to Washington, DC, to pursue the educational opportunities uniquely available to African Americans there. Clifford Berrien studied pharmacy, and Anna Berrien studied nursing, at Freedman's Hospital, in degree programs affiliated with Howard University and later incorpo-

rated into that institution's College of Pharmacy, Nursing, and Allied Health Sciences. Berrien's father worked in the U.S. State Department to support himself while obtaining his education, and Berrien's mother was a longtime civil servant in the U.S. Public Health Service.

As a child Berrien spent a significant amount of time on the Howard University campus, and this early exposure to college as both a concept and a physical reality reinforced the notion that she herself would pursue a college education. Additionally, she became aware of the transformative role that Howard University, as a historically black institution, had played in the lives of African Americans and in the societal struggle for civil rights, from the time of slavery through the time of her own childhood.

Berrien's parents, furthermore, demonstrated the virtues of service in their careers as health professionals and in their private lives, volunteering at their church and in their daughter's schools, and Berrien was surrounded in Washington by people who worked in city and federal government. Before she reached an age when people normally decide on a career, then, Ber-

rien had developed an appreciation of the opportunity that education represented, of the fact that such opportunities were hers only because others had risked their own safety and comfort to create them, and of the need to continue creating such opportunities for others.

Chose Legal Career

After high school Berrien attended Oberlin College in Oberlin, Ohio, drawn by the school's long history of providing equal educational opportunities to African Americans and women as well as to its successful merging of the fine arts (it is home to a world-class conservatory of music) with the study of liberal arts. Although Berrien did not pursue a professional career in music, she had participated in the DC Youth Orchestra, and she continued her musical education at Oberlin. She has maintained a lifelong interest in music and the arts, and she credits her orchestral experiences with helping her to develop an understanding of group dynamics.

Berrien majored in government and English at Oberlin. She knew that she wanted to pursue a career in public

service, and she was the recipient of the Harry S. Truman Scholarship, a national award dedicated to aiding college juniors who have the potential to make significant leadership contributions in the nonprofit and advocacy sectors. She ultimately decided that she would be best able to fulfill her service goals through a career in law, mobilizing her talents with language, argument, and the creation of narratives in the service of civil rights.

Berrien graduated from Oberlin in 1983 with high honors in government and was accepted for admission to Harvard Law School. While at Harvard, she won an appointment to the position of general editor for the *Harvard Civil Rights-Civil Liberties Law Review*, which was founded during the civil rights movement and which has contributed meaningfully in the decades since to progressive legal scholarship. Berrien completed her law degree in 1986.

Won Distinction as Civil Rights Lawyer

After law school Berrien clerked for U.W. Clemon, the first African American to serve on the U.S. District Court in Birmingham, Alabama. After a year in Clemon's office she moved to a staff position with the American Civil Liberties Union (ACLU) in New York, where she worked in the National Legal Department and on the Women's Rights Project. Berrien left the ACLU in 1992 to work in Washington, DC, as an attorney with the Voting Rights Project of the Lawyers' Committee for Civil Rights a nonprofit organization established in 1963 to mobilize legal professionals in the fight against racial discrimination.

In 1994 Berrien took a leadership position within one of the nation's most important civil-rights advocacy groups, the Legal Defense and Education Fund (LDF) of the National Association for the Advancement of Colored People (NAACP). The LDF was established in 1940 by Thurgood Marshall, who later became the first African-American U.S. Supreme Court Justice; it was the legal arm of the civil rights movement during the 1940s, 1950s, and 1960s, and it continues to provide legal counsel in efforts to preserve and promote equality under the law. As assistant counsel with the LDF, Berrien managed the case load related to issues of voting rights and political representation, and she argued on behalf of individuals who brought such cases before state and federal courts and the U.S. Supreme Court.

After seven years of service to the LDF, Berrien took a top administrative position in the Ford Foundation's Peace and Social Justice Program, where she oversaw the funding of diverse initiatives meant to empower disenfranchised and marginalized peoples through the political process. She served in this capacity until 2004, when she returned to the LDF to work at the highest

levels of that organization's management. As associate director-counsel of the LDF, Berrien helmed the group's scholarship and national legal advocacy initiatives, and she worked directly with the LDF's director-counsel and president.

Confronted New Challenges at EEOC

This was the position Berrien occupied when President Barack Obama nominated her to serve as chair of the EEOC on July 16, 2009. The nomination languished, along with that of other Obama appointees, due to political opposition in the U.S. Senate, until March 27, 2010, when the president used his power to make recess appointments to install Berrien in the EEOC's top post. Recess appointments are those appointments of top federal officials made while the Senate is in recess and therefore unable to vote on them; a recess appointee must be confirmed by the Senate before the end of the subsequent session of Congress. Berrien was sworn in as EEOC Chair on April 7, 2010, and the Senate confirmed her appointment on December 22, 2010, to a term set to expire on July 1, 2014.

Berrien cites the nomination itself as the fulfillment of a career-long focus on defending and extending the civil rights of disempowered Americans. In a phone interview with *CBB*, she called the job a "blessing and a privilege" and "the pinnacle of my career." She cited the agency's 45-year history of transforming workplaces in America so as to foster economic opportunity for workers, and she expressed her sense of honor at being entrusted with the job of leading it and shaping its future.

Berrien took over the EEOC amid the worst economic recession since the Great Depression, with the unemployment rate hovering near 10 percent and workers feeling extremely vulnerable. At such a moment, the agency's work was more central to the lives of a greater number of Americans than at any time in recent memory. Likewise, changing national demographics promised to keep the agency at the forefront of public policy. For the first time in history, women made up almost exactly half of the American workforce, and the country's places of employment were characterized by

an unprecedented degree of racial, ethnic, linguistic, and religious diversity. Accordingly, Berrien felt a commitment to making the EEOC ever more effective at ensuring full and equal access to employment.

The EEOC was also adapting to technologies that were changing the workplace and the job-seeking environment, and these changes were among Berrien's top concerns in the early years of her appointment. The agency's mandate, which was to uphold laws protecting workers from discrimination on the basis of race, color, religion, sex, pregnancy, nationality, age, and disability, as well as from retaliation when reporting violations of such laws, had recently been extended to cover a worker or job seeker's genetic history. This expansion of jurisdiction came about due to the increasing centralization of medical records and the increasing ability of medical professionals to pinpoint genetic predispositions to disease or disability. It became explicitly illegal for employers to discriminate in hiring, benefits allocation, or termination based on a worker's genetic background, and this new realm of EEOC enforcement brought with it new policy and legal challenges.

Sources

Periodicals

Corporate Counsel, February 1, 2011.
Government Executive, July 24, 2009.
Miami Daily Business Review, December 17, 2010.
National Law Journal, January 18, 2010.
Washington Post, September 29, 2010.

Online

"Jacqueline A. Berrien, Chair," U.S. Equal Employment Opportunity Commission, http://www.eeoc.gov/eeoc/berrien.cfm (accessed July 25, 2011).

Other

Information for this profile was obtained in a phone interview with Jacqueline A. Berrien on June 14, 2011.

—Mark Lane

Daquan Chisholm

1994(?)—

Inventor

As the 21st century began, the city of Baltimore, Maryland, was frequently in the national spotlight. Thanks, in part, to HBO's widely acclaimed drama *The Wire* (2002–08), the city's struggles with drugs, poverty, urban decay, and underfunded public schools drew national attention. Amid the malaise, however, many Baltimoreans were as determined as ever to improve their lives and their community. Among them was Daquan Chisholm. A gifted student with a strong interest in mechanical engineering, Chisholm had designed an innovative helmet for police officers by the time he reached fifth grade.

Daquan James Chisholm was born in Baltimore in c. 1994. Raised by his mother and grandmother, he attended a public elementary school near his home. The quality of his work there deeply impressed his teachers, who identified him as gifted and facilitated his entrance into a summer program at a nearby facility called the Center for Talented Youth (CTY). Established and run by Johns Hopkins University (JHU), CTY has offered a broad range of programming to gifted pre-college students since its founding in 1972. As one of its staff members, Charles Beckman, noted in 2004 in the *JHU Gazette,* it has devoted considerable resources toward the recruitment of minority students, who often lack access to the advanced courses widely available to white students. As of 2004, more than 10 percent of the participants in its summer programs came from historically underrepresented groups. Many, like Chisholm, were lifelong residents of Baltimore, a predominately African-American community.

Chisholm began at CTY at the end of fourth grade, when he was just 10 years old. Asked by his instructors to design a solution to one of the world's pressing problems, he began by choosing a general issue: the dangers routinely faced by police officers and other safety personnel. He then narrowed the problem down by focusing on the moments when officers were particularly vulnerable. One of those moments, he realized, occurred whenever an officer had to remove his or her helmet to communicate. If a headpiece could be designed that incorporated a communications system, he reasoned, that vulnerability would be eliminated. He therefore began work on a helmet with a built-in walkie-talkie, using materials provided by CTY. He also took steps to make the whole apparatus bulletproof. The result so impressed his instructors that they arranged for him to meet Robert Cammarata, then the head of JHU's department of materials science and engineering.

Like most inventors, Chisholm was interested in obtaining a patent, typically the first step in bringing a device to market. The costs involved, however, were far beyond the reach of his family. He therefore put his design aside for the time being, resolving to focus instead on his broader education. At the end of junior high, he won entrance to Baltimore Polytechnic Institute (BPI), widely regarded as the most academically rigorous public high school in the city. Like most of his peers there, he focused on math, science, and engineering. A year before graduation, however, a family move brought him to Loch Raven High School, a

At a Glance . . .

Born Daquan James Chisholm in 1994(?), in Baltimore, MD.

Career: Independent inventor, 2005—.

Addresses: *Office*—c/o Next Generation Venture Fund, Center for Talented Youth, 5801 Smith Ave., Ste. 400, Baltimore, MD 21209.

Baltimore County institution several miles to the north. He was a senior there in 2011.

Throughout high school, Chisholm received support from the Next Generation Venture Fund (NGVF), a nonprofit institution dedicated, according to its website, to "build[ing] a pipeline for high potential students from diverse backgrounds that leads from middle school, to college, careers and key leadership roles—opportunities that might otherwise be missed." With support from a variety of donors, notably including the Goldman Sachs Foundation, the NGVF has provided internships and summer classes for hundreds of gifted students, Chisholm among them. It was under NGVF auspices, for example, that he traveled one summer to Rhode Island for a course in nuclear science at Roger Williams College. A highlight of that class, in his view, was its focus on neutrinos, a poorly understood particle with a range of unusual properties, including, potentially, the ability to move backward in time. "When I first heard that," Chisholm noted on the NGVF website, "I had to hear it again to actually believe that's what my instructor said."

As he prepared to enter college, Chisholm was contemplating a variety of career options. In an autobiographical video posted in January of 2011 in the online magazine *The Root,* he mentioned, in addition to engineering, a strong interest in fields as diverse as sports medicine and the natural sciences. Any one of these, he noted, would allow him to serve his community and satisfy his intellectual curiosity. "There's so much in science that's still unknown," he remarked in comments posted on the NGVF website. "I want to be the one who says something is not just possible. I want to be the one who says it's certain."

Sources

Periodicals

JHU Gazette, May 10, 2004.

Online

"About Us," Next Generation Venture Fund, http://ngvf.org/about.html (accessed July 25, 2011).

"Scholars," Next Generation Venture Fund, http://www.ngvf.org/scholars.html#p4 (accessed July 25, 2011).

Snyder, Deron, "The Young Futurists: Daquan Chisholm," *The Root,* January 27, 2011, http://www.theroot.com/content/daquan-chisholm (accessed July 25, 2011).

"Young Futurist Video: Daquan Chisholm," *The Root,* January 2011, http://www.theroot.com/multi med ia/young-futurist-video-daquan-chisholm (accessed June 20, 2011).

—R. Anthony Kugler

Kevin Clash

1960—

Puppeteer

Clash, Kevin, photograph. AP Images/Charles Sykes.

Puppeteer Kevin Clash is best known as the voice and inspiration behind Elmo, the ebullient red monster who has delighted generations of children on television's *Sesame Street.* Since Clash first gave life to the character in the 1980s, Elmo, with his distinctive squeaky falsetto and infectious laugh, has become one of the most popular creatures on the show, as well as a franchise in his own right, selling more than 5 million "Tickle Me Elmo" dolls in the late 1990s and spawning dozens of television specials, videos, books, and toys. Today, Clash—a big, broad-shouldered man with a deep baritone voice, most people are surprised to learn—is *Sesame Street*'s top puppeteer, with more than a dozen Emmy Awards to his credit. In 2006 Clash, who rarely is seen in public without Elmo, stepped out from behind his alter ego to publish an autobiography, *My Life as a Furry Red Monster,* and in 2011 he was the subject of the documentary *Being Elmo: A Puppeteer's Journey.*

Inspired by Sesame Street

Kevin Clash was born on September 17, 1960, in Baltimore, Maryland, and grew up with his three brothers and sisters in Turner Station, a predominantly black, working-class suburb located 30 minutes to the east. His father, George, worked as a welder at a local steel plant, while his mother ran a day care for neighborhood kids in their two-bedroom home. Though his family was often short on money, they were rich in creativity: his father liked to draw and paint and was a skilled carpenter, while his mother enjoyed sewing.

Clash was nine years old when *Sesame Street* debuted on PBS in 1969, and he was instantly transfixed by the "Muppets"—a combination of "marionette" and "puppet"—created by Jim Henson. He spent hours watching *Sesame Street* and other shows, such as *Kukla, Fran and Ollie, H.R. Pufnstuf,* and the *Banana Splits.* Clash began crafting his own puppets out of old stuffed animals, scraps of fabric, and clothes he found around the house, naming his first creation Bartee, after a school friend. Soon he was putting on shows for the children his mother cared for, charging 25 cents.

While his friends were playing sports and listening to music, Clash, a shy, serious boy, spent his time inside working on his puppets. Other children teased him

At a Glance . . .

Born on September 17, 1960, in Baltimore, MD; son of George (a welder) and Gladys (a day care operator) Clash; married Genia (divorced 2003); children: Shannon.

Career: WMAR, Baltimore, puppeteer, *Caboose,* 1977–79; CBS, puppeteer, *Captain Kangaroo,* 1979–84; Sunbow Productions, puppeteer and associate producer, *The Great Space Coaster,* 1980–84; Jim Henson Productions, puppeteer, Muppet captain for *Sesame Street,* 1985—.

Awards: Daytime Emmy Award, Outstanding Performer in a Children's Series, for *Sesame Street,* 1993, 2005, 2006, 2007, 2009, 2010; Outstanding Pre-School Children's Series, for *Sesame Street,* 2001, 2002, 2003, 2004, 2005, 2006, 2007, 2008, 2010; Daytime Emmy Award for Outstanding Directing in a Children's Series, for *Sesame Street,* 2007, 2009, 2010.

Addresses: *Production company*—Jim Henson Productions, Inc., 37–19 Northern Blvd., Ste. 400, Long Island City, NY 11101.

about his hobby: "Look at him, he's playing with dolls. He sews. He sleeps with puppets," they would taunt, Clash recalled in his autobiography, *My Life as a Furry Red Monster.* "Gladys, get that boy out of the house," his mother's friends urged. "He needs to play with the other kids." But Clash's parents recognized their son's talent and encouraged his creativity, often driving him to craft stores to get supplies and lending a hand by sewing or helping to construct sets for his puppet shows.

Became a Muppeteer in Training

Absorbed in puppetry, Clash was less enthusiastic about his schoolwork. But when his junior high social studies teacher assigned him to prepare a presentation on Russia, he decided to make a show of it, creating Russian puppets who spoke about their homeland, interviewed by Clash's partner, who was dressed as a reporter, a la Kermit the Frog. The report was a hit, and his teacher was so impressed that she asked him to perform for the entire school. The show made the "Young World" section of the Baltimore *News-American,* and before long Clash was invited to put on a weekly puppet show at Baltimore's harbor front. There he attracted the attention of Stu Kerr, a fixture on the local CBS affiliate, who invited Clash to perform

on a new children's television program that he was developing, called *Caboose.* With his parents' approval, Clash jumped at the chance, beginning his professional career while he was still in high school.

Kerr happened to be an old friend of Bob Keeshan, better known as Captain Kangaroo, and sent him a few episodes of *Caboose* that Clash had appeared in. Keeshan admired the young puppeteer's work—so much that he offered Clash a full-time job. After graduating from high school, Clash began commuting between Baltimore and New York, earning $3,000 per season working on *Captain Kangaroo* and an extra $1,200 for each puppet he created. The next year he was picked up by the syndicated program the *Great Space Coaster* and made his first appearances on *Sesame Street.*

In 1979, shortly after moving to New York, Clash visited the workshop of designer Kermit Love, the creator of *Sesame Street*'s Big Bird. Love arranged for Clash to work as an extra on the Sesame Street float in the Macy's Thanksgiving Day Parade. It was there that Clash first met his idol, Muppets creator Jim Henson.

A few years later, just as *Captain Kangaroo* and the *Great Space Coaster* were wrapping up production, Henson asked Clash to join the cast of *Sesame Street* full time. It was the fulfillment of a lifelong dream, and Clash took advantage of every opportunity to learn from his more experienced colleagues. At first the novice was relegated to playing "miscellaneous pigs and chickens," he recalled in a 1999 interview with the *New York Times.* That changed in 1985, when Richard Hunt, a veteran Muppeteer, walked into the green room (a backstage waiting room for actors) and tossed a furry red puppet at Clash. "He handed him to me like a piece of trash and said 'Here, come up with a voice,'" Clash told the *Times.*

Elmo Is Born

Elmo, a three-year-old furry red monster originally named simply "Little Monster," had been created years earlier to appeal to toddlers and preschool-age *Sesame Street* watchers. The character was originated by Muppeteer Brian Meehl, who left the show after playing Elmo only a few times. The monster passed to Hunt, who didn't care for the character and failed to come up with the right voice for him. He, in turn, challenged Clash to find a voice for Elmo, and almost immediately, Clash erupted in the high-pitched giggle that is now the monster's trademark.

Clash was inspired by the children he observed on a visit to his mother's day care, and he created Elmo as a curious, fun-loving, happy-go-lucky creature who spreads a message of love, peace, and happiness, chirping "Elmo loves you!" (Elmo always speaks of himself in the third person) while teaching children

important lessons. "To not only entertain but really connect with children, I must reach into my own heart to project love to every boy and girl in the audience," Clash explained in his autobiography. "My mother set a powerful example for me by loving all her daycare children as if they were her flesh and blood. . . . Like my mother, like Elmo, I strive to touch the heart of every child I come into contact with, because that connection is so vital."

Before long, Elmo became one of *Sesame Street*'s most popular characters, as famous as Kermit the Frog and Miss Piggy, and in 1990 Clash earned his first Emmy nomination for outstanding performer in a children's series, winning the award over Pee-Wee Herman and Mr. Rogers. After making an appearance on the *Rosie O'Donnell Show* in 1996, Elmo became a regular guest on that and other programs, including *Martha Stewart Living,* the *View, Emeril Live,* and the *West Wing.* In 1998 Elmo was given his own 15-minute segment at the end of each episode of Sesame Street, "Elmo's World," which lasted for eight seasons. Elmo starred in his first full-length motion picture, the *Adventures of Elmo in Grouchland,* in 1999, and in 2002 he became the first nonhuman ever to testify before the U.S. Congress, speaking on behalf of music education.

The Elmo character became a marketing juggernaut, spawning books, videos, toys, and games. Tyco's "Tickle Me Elmo" doll sold more than 5 million units leading up to Christmas of 1996, commanding prices as high as $1,000 from parents desperate to get the coveted toy. A subsequent model, Elmo TMX, was released in 2006. According to the stipulations that Henson set out before his death, Clash is the only person who is permitted be the voice of Elmo.

Stepped out from behind the Puppet

Clash serves as *Sesame Street*'s "Muppet captain," a title given to him by Henson, and as co-executive producer. Functioning as a sort of foreman, he oversees the show's staff of puppeteers and scouts for new talent. Over the course of his 25-plus years on the show, Clash has received more than 30 Emmy nominations, winning 18 awards as a performer and director.

Elmo is not the only character in Clash's puppet repertoire. He also has played Baby Natasha and Hoots the Owl on *Sesame Street,* Baby Sinclair on the ABC prime-time animated series *Dinosaurs,* and Clifford, who first appeared on the *Jim Henson Hour* in 1989 and later hosted *Muppets Tonight!* in 1996, in addition to scores of videos and television specials. On the big screen, Clash has appeared in puppet form in *Labyrinth* (1986), *Teenage Mutant Ninja Turtles I* and *II* (1990, 1991), *Muppet Treasure Island* (1996), and *Muppets from Space* (1999).

As a puppeteer, Clash's most important job is to remain unseen, and for that reason, he rarely appears in public without Elmo. In 2006 he appeared solo for the first time on an episode of the *Oprah Winfrey Show,* and that same year, he released his autobiography, *My Life as a Furry Red Monster: What Being Elmo Taught Me about Life, Love, and Laughing out Loud.* In 2011 Clash was the subject of the documentary *Being Elmo: A Puppeteer's Journey,* which premiered at the Sundance Film Festival, winning the Special Jury Prize.

Selected Works

Television

Caboose, WMAR (Baltimore), 1977–79.
Captain Kangaroo, CBS, 1979–84.
The Great Space Coaster, 1980–84.
Sesame Street, PBS, 1982—.
The Jim Henson Hour, NBC, 1989–92.
Dinosaurs, ABC, 1991–95.
Muppets Tonight!, ABC, 1996–98.

Films

Labyrinth, TriStar Pictures, 1986.
Teenage Mutant Ninja Turtles, New Line Cinema, 1990.
Teenage Mutant Ninja Turtles II: The Secret of the Ooze, New Line Cinema, 1991.
Muppet Treasure Island, Buena Vista Pictures, 1996.
The Adventures of Elmo in Grouchland, Columbia Pictures, 1999.
Muppets from Space, Columbia Pictures, 1999.
The Muppets, Mandeville Films, 2011.

Sources

Books

Clash, Kevin, with Gary Brozek, *My Life as a Furry Red Monster: What Being Elmo Has Taught Me about Life, Love, and Laughing out Loud,* Broadway Books, 2006.

Periodicals

Baltimore Sun, September 18, 1994.
Black Enterprise, February 1995, p. 95.
Chicago Sun-Times, February 17, 1997.
New York Amsterdam News, November 23–29, 2006.
New York Times, December 22, 1999; August 23, 2006.
Post-Tribune (Indiana), September 28, 2006.
Time, November 10, 2009.
Washington Post, May 15, 2005.

Online

Being Elmo: A Puppeteer's Journey, http://being elmo.com (accessed June 10, 2011).

"Sesame Street Turns 35: Kevin Clash and Elmo," *Tavis Smiley Show,* National Public Radio, April 7, 2004, http://www.npr.org/templates/story/story.php?storyId=1816191 (accessed June 10, 2011).

—Deborah A Ring

George Clinton

1941—

Musician

Clinton, George, photograph. AP Images/Krista Kennell.

George Clinton, recognizable by his rainbow-colored dreadlocks and outlandish sartorial choices, is considered the "godfather of funk," a musical pioneer whom the *New York Times* called "perhaps the most influential conceptualist in black popular music" in 1978. In the 1970s, Clinton was the mastermind behind the funk-rock groups Parliament and Funkadelic, known together as "P-Funk," a collective of dozens of artists who revolutionized popular music with their hybrid of funk and psychedelic rock, epitomized by songs such as "Give Up the Funk (Tear the Roof Off the Sucker") and "One Nation Under a Groove."

After P-Funk had run its course, Clinton continued his prolific output in the 1980s as a solo artist, turning out singles such as "Atomic Dog" and "Do Fries Go with That Shake?" In the 1990s, renewed attention to P-Funk's music helped make Clinton one of the most-sampled musicians of all time, his musical influence apparent among a new generation of rap, hip-hop, and funk-rock artists. Clinton's enormous contributions to music were recognized in 1997, when he and 15 members of Parliament/Funkadelic were inducted into the Rock and Roll Hall of Fame.

Started Career as Doo-Wop Singer

He was born George Edward Clinton on July 22, 1941, in Kannapolis, North Carolina; according to legend, his mother gave birth to him in an outhouse. When he was a teenager, he moved with his mother and eight siblings to Washington, DC, and then to Virginia before settling in Newark, New Jersey. At age 14, he joined with four friends to form a doo-wop vocal group called the Parliaments, inspired by Frankie Lyman and the Teenagers. The quintet practiced in the back room of the Uptown Tonsorial Parlor, a barbershop in nearby Plainfield where the boys styled hair when they were not in school (Clinton later owned the shop), and they performed at local hop and school dances and on street corners.

The Parliaments recorded for the first time in a record booth in Newark in 1956, singing "The Wind" and "Sunday Kind of Love." In May of 1958, they released their first two singles, "Poor Willie" and "Party Boys," on APT, and followed with another the next year, "Lonely Island" on Flipp, but none achieved any success.

At a Glance . . .

Born George Edward Clinton on July 22, 1941, in Kannapolis, NC; son of Julia Keaton.

Career: Uptown Tonsorial Parlor, Plainfield, NJ, hairdresser, 1955–67(?); The Parliaments, 1955–67; Parliament/Funkadelic, 1968—.

Awards: Rock and Roll Hall of Fame, 1997; Pioneer Award, Rhythm and Blues Foundation, 2003; Icon Award, BMI Urban Music Awards, 2009.

Addresses: *Booking Agent*—Monterey International, 200 West Superior, Ste. 202, Chicago, IL 60654. *Email*—brodie@montereyinternational.net. *Web*—http://www.georgeclinton.com/.

In 1962 Clinton took a job as a staff songwriter for Jobete Music, the New York branch of Motown's publishing company; when Jobete formed its own imprint as part of Motown, the label signed Clinton and the Parliaments, though nothing came of the arrangement. In 1964 Clinton moved to Detroit while the others stayed behind in New Jersey in the hope of signing the group directly with Motown. Again, however, he was disappointed. "By then I realized the Motown thing was sewn up," Clinton recalled in an interview with Dave Hoekstra of the *Chicago Sun-Times* in 1989. "I couldn't do nothing there. They had all the cool-looking groups. There wasn't nothing to do but change up."

After expanding their lineup to include guitarists Eddie Hazel and Lucius "Tawl" Ross, bassist Billy Nelson, organist Mickey Atkins, and drummer Ramon "Tiki" Fulwood, the Parliaments had a minor hit with the soulful "I Wanna Testify," released on Revilot in 1966; a year and a half later, the song made the top 20 on the pop charts and the top five on the R&B charts. They scored another hit in 1967 with "All Your Goodies Are Gone," which went to number 21 on the pop chart. Revilot soon went out of business, however, without paying the Parliaments any money, and the group temporarily lost the rights to their name.

Masterminded Parliament/ Funkadelic

By this time, Clinton saw that the sounds of doo-wop and Motown were on the wane, giving way to the psychedelic rock and hard blues of the late 1960s. He began to conceive a new kind of music, influenced by acid rockers such as Cream, Jimi Hendrix, and Sly and the Family Stone and garage bands such as MC5 and

the Stooges. One night in 1967, when the Parliaments were playing a show in upstate New York with Vanilla Fudge and the Box Tops, Clinton had a revelation. "We didn't have any equipment, so we had to use Vanilla Fudge's equipment and that stuff was powerful as all hell," he recounted to Hoekstra. "We heard what that sounded like, so we went out and got all the amps in the world." Clinton branded the sound "acid doo-wop."

No longer able call his group the Parliaments, Clinton brought the backing musicians to the front and pushed the singers to the back, renaming them Funkadelic, a name proposed by Billy Nelson. Funkadelic signed with Detroit's Westbound Records in 1969 and released their self-titled debut the next year. Meanwhile, after Clinton regained the rights to his group's old name, he dropped the "s" and created a second group called Parliament. He signed them to Invictus Records, and their debut, *Osmium*, came out in 1970.

The two groups had essentially the same lineup, but they developed distinct identities, recording different styles of music, usually on different labels. "Funkadelic was the rock and roll band, with guitars dominating, the crazy stream-of-consciousness lyrics," Clinton explained to *Rolling Stone* in 1990. "Parliament was going to be as close to structure as we could get," offering a more orchestrated sound with horns and complicated vocal arrangements. Together, Parliament and Funkadelic numbered more than two dozen musicians. By 1972 their roster included classically trained keyboardist Bernie Worrell and former James Brown bassist William "Bootsy" Collins. Both would be key architects of the P-Funk sounda mixture of rhythm and blues, soul, gospel, and psychedelic rock marked by a "communal energy rather than strictness of structure," as John Rockwell described it in the *New York Times* in 1979.

Rode the Mothership to Success

Between them, Parliament and Funkadelic released some 30 albums during the 1970s, three of which went platinum, spawning more than 40 R&B hit singles, including three that reached No. 1. Funkadelic released five albums between 1971 and 1974 that consistently made the top 20 on the R&B charts and broke into the lower reaches of the pop charts. Parliament, which had been silent since their debut, signed with the Casablanca label and returned in 1974 with *Up for the Down Stroke,* whose title track was Parliament's first chart hit. The album was more mainstream in its approach than any of Funkadelic's releases and featured lively horn arrangements that recalled James Brown.

By the mid-1970s, Parliament and Funkadelic were becoming known as a single entity, referred to collectively as "P-Funk." In April of 1976 Parliament released what is now considered their definitive work (and

their first platinum record), *Mothership Connection,* which produced a trio of funk classics—"P-Funk (Wants to Get Funked Up)," "Mothership Connection (Star Child)," and "Give Up the Funk (Tear the Roof Off the Sucker)." A concept album inspired by the Beatles' *Sgt. Pepper's Lonely Hearts Club Band* and the Who's rock opera *Tommy,* the tracks were bound by an outer-space theme and introduced a series of fictional characters—including Star Child, Dr. Funkenstein (Clinton's alter ego), and Sir Nose D'Voidoffunk—who would reappear on subsequent Parliament releases.

That same year, Funkadelic made its major-label debut on Warner Brothers with *Hardcore Jollies.* Bassist Bootsy Collins, who had begun to adopt a variety of personas on recordings and on stage, released *Stretchin' out in Bootsy's Rubber Band* with his spin-off group. Bootsy's Rubber Band was just one of several spin-offs of Parliament/Funkadelic, including Zapp, Brides of Funkenstein, Fred Wesley and the Horny Horns, Parlet, Sweat Band, and Godmoma.

In 1977 Parliament released *Funkentelechy vs. the Placebo Syndrome,* which produced the group's first number-one single, "Flash Light." The song topped the R&B charts for three weeks, followed by "Funkentelechy," which reached number 27. The album rose to number 13 on the pop charts and became Parliament's second platinum-selling record. Meanwhile, Funkadelic reached their peak with the 1978 album *One Nation Under a Groove,* whose anthemic title track spent six weeks in the top spot on the R&B chart that summer; it would be Funkadelic's first and only platinum record.

Parliament/Funkadelic became legendary in the mid-1970s for their live shows, which were extravagant productions lasting upwards of four hours. The centerpiece of the P-Funk show was the Mothership, an enormous spaceship that descended from a blue denim cap hanging above the stage, from which Clinton's band emerged. Adopting the glitter rock style popularized by David Bowie, Clinton often wore a silver spacesuit and star-shaped glasses, while other members appeared in a nun's habit, a bedsheet, or, in the case of guitarist Gary Shider, a diaper. Robert Palmer of the *New York Times* described a performance at Madison Square Garden in 1978: "At almost every moment, something besides music was taking place on the stage, whether it was a little pseudo-dramatic vignette, the appearance of a couple of silver-sprayed 'robot' dancers, or just musicians dancing and carrying on in outrageous costumes. With Mr. Clinton, spectacle is the thing, and the more complex and busy it is, the better."

Went Solo

By the late 1970s, Clinton was mired in legal and financial disputes with his various record companies and with other musicians. As the Parliament/ Funkadelic family had grown, Clinton had signed musicians to his own production company, Thang Incorporated, and then negotiated deals with record companies under the names of his different groups, without specifying any particular band members. The idea was that this arrangement freed the musicians from legal entanglements with record companies and allowed them to move back forth between groups as they wished. By the end of the decade, however, as Casablanca was acquired by Polygram Records, Clinton's system was a mess. For example, former Funkadelic members Fuzzy Haskins, Calvin Simon, and Grady Thomas claimed that they owned 42.9 percent of the name "Funkadelic" and released an album under that title (it later was renamed).

After Funkadelic released the album *Uncle Jam Wants You* and Parliament released *Gloryhallastoopid—Or Pin the Tail on the Funky,* both in 1979, Clinton moved to a country house west of Detroit and announced that he planned to retire from recording and touring so that he could concentrate on producing. In 1980 his label Uncle Jam Records produced albums for the Sweat Band and Philippe Wynne, and Clinton spearheaded Funkadelic's final release, the *Electric Spanking of War Babies,* which featured Sly Stone, in 1980.

In 1982 Clinton signed a recording contract with Capitol Records and put out his first solo album, the heavily electronic *Computer Games,* which spawned the now-familiar singles "Loopzilla" and "Atomic Dog." The next year he reconstituted the Parliament/ Funkadelic cast by creating the P-Funk All-Stars, who continued the P-Funk groove on *Urban Dancefloor Guerillas,* released by Uncle Jam. Clinton kept up his prolific output throughout the 1980s, releasing three more solo albums on Capitol—*You Shouldn't Nut Bit Fish* (1984), *Some of My Best Jokes Are Friends* (1985), and *R&B Skeletons in the Closet* (1986), the last of which featured the memorable single "Do Fries Go with That Shake?"

Clinton signed with Prince's Paisley Park label and released two albums, the *Cinderella Theory* (1988) and *Hey Man, Smell My Finger* (1993) before jumping to Sony. His first album on that label, 1996's *T.A.P.O.A.F.O.M.,* standing for "the awesome power of a fully operational mothership," reunited Clinton with several his P-Funk colleagues, while *Greatest Funkin' Hits* teamed Clinton with rappers Digital Underground, Ice Cube, and Q-Tip. He founded another record label, C Kunspruhzy, in 2005 and released the album *How Late Do U Have 2BB4UR Absent,* followed by *George Clinton and His Gangsters of Love* on Shanachie in 2008.

Influenced New Generation of Musicians

Clinton's musical influence reaches far and wide, inspir-

ing rap and hip-hop artists such as Dr. Dre, Digital Underground, Ice Cube, and Public Enemy as well as funk rockers such as Red Hot Chili Peppers (for whom Clinton produced the 1985 album *Freaky Styley*), Living Color, Faith No More, and Primus. In 1989 hip-hoppers De La Soul introduced a new generation of music fans to P-Funk when they sampled Funkadelic's "(Not Just) Knee Deep" for their hit single "My Myself and I," while rappers Digital Underground looped "Flash Light" and other P-Funk grooves on their debut album *Sex Packets* and then convinced Clinton to appear on their sophomore effort, *Sons of the P.*

Parliament/Funkedelic's prodigious output has made Clinton one of the most sampled artists of all time, second only to James Brown. He facilitated the sampling of his work by releasing *Sample Some of Disc-Sample Some of D.A.T.* (1993–95), a series of sample-ready tracks with accompanying permission request forms. To Clinton, sampling is a way of keeping funk alive and extending his music's longevity. "It's part of the plan to keep funk on top," he told *Jet* magazine. "Hip hop helped save funk. . . . Funk is the DNA for hip hop." By 1993 most of the P-Funk catalog had been reissued. Energized by the renewed attention to his music, Clinton reunited with the P-Funk All-Stars, performing with the Red Hot Chili Peppers at the 52nd Grammy Awards in 1993 and touring with the Lollapalooza festival the following year.

For more than a decade, Clinton was embroiled in a legal battle over the rights to Parliament/Funkadelic's recordings and the copyrights to their songs. In 1999 he filed suit against music publisher Bridgeport Music for an estimated $100 million in lost royalties on samples of his songs. Two years later a federal judge ruled against Clinton, finding that the musician had in fact signed away his rights to his music in a 1983 contract with Bridgeport and barring Clinton from profiting from his songs written between 1976 and 1983. In a separate case, however, a federal judge returned to Clinton ownership of four master recordings made by Funkadelic in the 1970s. The ruling gave Clinton the right to control licensing and distribution of the songs and to claim millions of dollars in past licensing fees.

In December of 2003 Clinton was arrested near his recording studio in Tallahassee, Florida, on charges of drug possession after he allegedly told a police officer that he had cocaine in his pocket. He pleaded no contest to two misdemeanor drug paraphernalia charges in August of the following year and was sentenced to 200 hours of community service and two years of probation.

On their third nomination, Clinton and 15 members of Parliament/Funkadelic were inducted into the Rock and Roll Hall of Fame in 1997. In 2002 *Spin* magazine named P-Funk sixth on its list of the "50 Greatest Bands of All Time," and in 2004, *Rolling Stone* ranked them at number 56 among the "100 Greatest Artists of All Time." Clinton was honored with a Pioneer Award from the Rhythm and Blues Foundation in 2003, and in 2009, he was given the Icon Award at the BMI Urban Music Awards. In 2011 Clinton donated a replica of the P-Funk Mothership to the National Museum of African American History and Culture.

Selected discography

With the Parliaments

"Poor Willie" / "Party Boys," APT, 1958.
"Lonely Island" / "(You Made Me Wanna) Cry," Flipp, 1959.
"Heart Trouble" / "(That Was) My Girl," Golden World, 1965.
"I Wanna Testify" / "I Can Feel the Ice Melting," Revilot, 1966.
"All Your Goodies Are Gone (Let Hurt Put You in the Loser's Seat)" / "Don't Be Sore at Me," Revilot, 1967.
"Little Man" / "The Goose (That Laid the Golden Egg)," Revilot, 1967.
"Look at What I Almost Missed" / "What You Been Growing," Revilot, 1967.
"A New Day Begins" / "I'll Wait," Revilot, 1968 (reissued by Atco in 1969).
"Good Old Music" / "Time," Revilot, 1968.

With Parliament

Osmium, Invictus, 1970.
Up for the Down Stroke, Casablanca, 1974.
Chocolate City, Casablanca, 1975.
Mothership Connection, Casablanca, 1976 (includes "P-Funk [Wants to Get Funked Up]," "Mothership Connection [Star Child]," and "Give Up the Funk [Tear the Roof Off the Sucker]."
The Clones of Dr. Funkenstein, Casablanca, 1977.
Live/P-Funk Earth Tour, Casablanca, 1977.
Funkentelechy vs. the Placebo System, Casablanca, 1977 (includes "Flash Light" and "Funkentelechy").
Motor-Booty Affair, Casablanca, 1978.
Gloryhallastoopid—Or Pin the Tail on the Funky, Casablanca, 1979.
Trombipulation, Casablanca, 1981.

With Funkadelic

Funkadelic, Westbound, 1970.
Free Your Mind . . . and Your Ass Will Follow, Westbound, 1971.
Maggot Brain, Westbound, 1971.
America Eats Its Young, Westbound, 1972.
Cosmic Slop, Westbound, 1973.
Standing on the Verge of Getting It On, Westbound, 1974.

Let's Take It to the Stage, Westbound, 1975.
Tales of Kidd Funkadelic, Westbound, 1976.
Hardcore Jollies, Warner Bros., 1976.
One Nation Under a Groove, Warner Bros., 1978.
Uncle Jam Wants You, Warner Bros., 1979.
The Electric Spanking of War Babies, Warner Bros., 1981.

Solo/P-Funk All-Stars

Computer Games (includes "Loopzilla" and "Atomic Dog"), Capitol, 1982.
Urban Dancefloor Guerillas, Uncle Jam, 1983.
You Shouldn't Nuf Bit Fish, Capitol, 1984.
Some of My Best Jokes Are Friends, Capitol, 1985.
R&B Skeletons in the Closet, Capitol, 1986 (includes "Do Fries Go with That Shake?").
The Cinderella Theory, Paisley Park, 1989.
Live at the Beverly Theater in Hollywood, Westbound, 1990.
Hey Man, Smell My Finger, Paisley Park, 1993.
T.A.P.O.A.F.O.M., Epic, 1996.
How Late Do U Have 2BB4UR Absent, C Kenspruhzy, 2005.
George Clinton and His Gangsters of Love, Shanachie, 2008.

Compilations and archival releases

The Mothership Connection Live from Houston, Capitol, 1987.
Dope Dog, One Nation, 1993.
Sample Some of Disc—Sample Some of D.A.T., AEM, 1993–1995.
Parliament & Funkadelic Live 1976–93, Essential (UK), 1994.

Greatest Funkin' Hits, Capitol, 1996.
Greatest Hits, Capitol, 2000.

Sources

Books

Gulla, Bob, *Icons of R&B and Soul,* Greenwood Press, 2008.
Thompson, Dave, *Funk,* Backbeat Books, 2001.

Periodicals

Chicago Sun-Times, October 22, 1989; June 30, 1995.
Jet, January 16, 2006.
New York Times, June 10, 1978; November 19, 1978; October 12, 1979; March 29, 1983; July 6, 1996; October 27, 1996; June 7, 2005.
Rolling Stone, September 20, 1990, pp. 75–78.

Online

Rock and Roll Hall of Fame, "Parliament-Funkadelic Biography," http://rockhall.com/inductees/parliament-funkadelic/ (accessed June 22, 2011).

Other

"Profile of George Clinton, the Master of Funk," *Weekend Edition,* National Public Radio, February 6, 1994.

—Deborah A. Ring

CoCo Brother

Radio and television personality

Coco Brother, photograph. AP Images/W.A. Harewood.

CoCo Brother, whose given name is Cory Condrey, rose to prominence as a hip-hop DJ in the late 1990s and the early years of the 21st century before recasting himself as gospel DJ with an on-air personality devoted to combining a Christian message and ministry with hip-hop culture. His syndicated gospel show "The Spirit Top 15 Countdown" (formerly known as "The Spirit of Hip-Hop") airs each weekend on urban and gospel radio stations nationwide, and his syndicated show "CoCo Brother Live," which mixes gospel music and news with inspirational segments and celebrity interviews, airs weekdays in major markets across the country. He is also the host of the gospel TV show "Lift Every Voice," which airs weekly on BET.

Born in Germany, Cory Condrey attended high school in Nashville, Tennessee. After graduating in 1995 he moved to Atlanta, Georgia, intent on becoming a radio personality. While working nights to support himself, he interned full-time for no pay at the radio station Hot 97.5, where he learned about the business side of radio and made connections with management that led to his first on-air job. In 1996 he was given a show on Hot 97.5, but the show did not attract a large audience, and he was fired in 1997.

After losing his job, Condrey struggled to find work, ultimately becoming homeless. After a year of homelessness he found a position as promotions coordinator for the Atlanta radio station V-103. He pursued his own show at the station, but management denied him a chance to work as a DJ, suggesting that he would never be an on-air personality. He settled for a DJ position with a smaller station, Foxy 107, in the nearby city of Macon, Georgia. Within a matter of months CoCo Brother's show was the top-rated program in the Macon market, and he had begun to develop a reputation as a vibrant and personable entertainer.

CoCo Brother's success at Foxy 107 led to a job with the Washington, DC, radio station WKYS in 2000, where his show went beyond music and commentary, often featuring segments intended to inspire and motivate the young people who comprised the majority of his audience. He returned to Georgia the following year to take a job with Hot 107.9 in Atlanta, where he developed one of the city's most popular hip-hop shows, featuring music and interviews with top artists

At a Glance . . .

Born Cory Condrey in Germany; married Joann Rosario on December 31, 2008; children: Arianna Christian-Elise Condrey.

Career: Hot 97.5 (Atlanta, GA), hip-hop radio DJ, 1996–97; Foxy 107 (Macon, GA), hip-hop radio DJ, 1999–2000(?); WKYS 93.9 (Washington, DC), hip-hop radio DJ, 2000–02; Hot 107.9 (Atlanta, GA), hip-hop radio DJ, 2001–05; host of nationally syndicated gospel/hip-hop radio shows "The Spirit of Hip-Hop," "The Spirit Top 15 Countdown," and "CoCo Brother Live," 2005; host of BET television show "Lift Every Voice," 2008.

Awards: Special Event CD of the Year, The Stellar Awards, 2011, for *Coco Brother Live Presents Stand 2010.*

Addresses: *Office*—PO Box 181, Winston, GA 30187. *Email*—itsme@cocobrotherlive.com. *Web*—http://www. thespiritofhiphop.com/.

including 50 Cent, Ludacris, and David Banner. CoCo Brother's fame grew beyond Atlanta during this time. He began making television appearances on BET, MTV, and UPN and print media appearances in outlets such as *Vibe* and *Source.*

In 2005, after helping to convince an on-air caller to his show not to commit suicide, CoCo Brother began to feel that God was telling him to take another approach to his radio career. He discontinued his hip-hop show in March of that year and was off the air for six weeks. He returned to radio as host of the weekend show "The Spirit of Hip-Hop," which featured Christian-themed hip-hop and urban music and interviews with prominent gospel and secular artists. "The Spirit of Hip-Hop," which was syndicated through the Radio One broadcast network, steadily grew beyond the precincts of Atlanta, reaching 40 American markets on a variety of gospel and urban stations.

In 2007 Condrey took his commitment to Christianity beyond the confines of the entertainment world, launching a ministry campaign called STAND. STAND involved a variety of efforts, including inspirational rallies featuring Condrey as well as guest preachers and gospel performers, and the youth outreach movement Exodus, which employed rappers and a hip-hop ambience to try to convert young people to Christianity. Although his attempt to spread Christianity via hip-hop

culture rankled some within religious circles, Condrey believed that God had called him to take the message of Christ's teachings to unlikely places. "There is a lot of ministering and preaching going on today, but nobody is going back into the streets," he told Hamil R. Harris of the *Washington Post.* "We have an opportunity to get into the streets, where people need hope." STAND launched a 10-city tour in 2010, with events ranging from a 500-person rally in a parking lot in the Washington, DC, metropolitan area to a rally in Atlanta's Georgia Dome that drew a crowd of 15,000.

In 2008 CoCo Brother extended his career in yet another direction, making the leap from radio to TV upon being chosen as the host of the new BET show "Lift Every Voice." The half-hour show aired every Sunday and consisted of interviews on the subject of faith with celebrities primarily drawn from the world of gospel music, as well as gospel performances. Also in 2008, Condrey met Joann Rosario, the Chicago-based gospel singer who would become his wife. Rosario's music had been played on "The Spirit of Hip-Hop," and she had been featured in an interview conducted by the show's producer. Condrey and Rosario did not actually make one another's acquaintance, however, until Rosario contacted him via email after seeing an interview he had conducted with a mutual friend. The two were married on December 31, 2008, and in 2010 their daughter, Arianna Christian-Elise Condrey, was born. After their marriage, the Condreys worked closely together on the STAND ministry campaign and other Christian causes.

In 2009 CoCo Brother extended the range of his radio personality considerably with the debut of "CoCo Brother Live," which was broadcast every weeknight. "CoCo Brother Live" included celebrity interviews, music, and news, as well as segments devoted to relationship advice, prayer, and other inspirational material. As of 2011, the show was among the highest-rated gospel radio programs, reaching audiences in 16 American markets.

Sources

Periodicals

Atlanta Journal-Constitution, October 31, 2008. *Washington Post*, December 11, 2010.

Online

Associated Press, "Rappers Spread Gospel, but Is It Hypocritical?" TODAY.com, http://today.msnbc. msn.com/id/24259102/ns/today-entertainment/t/ rappers-spread-gospel-it-hypocritical/ (accessed July 17, 2011).

CoCo Brother Live, http://www.thespiritofhiphop. com/ (accessed July 17, 2011).

"Cory 'CoCo Brother' Condrey," BET, http://www.

bet.com/topics/c/cory-condrey.html (accessed July 17, 2011).

—Mark Lane

De'Jaun Correia

1994—2011

Public speaker, human-rights activist

De'Jaun Correia, while still a high-school student, made a name for himself as a human-rights activist and public speaker. He has toured schools and traveled widely to address conventions and other gatherings as an advocate against the death penalty and for his uncle Troy Davis, a Georgia death-row inmate whose conviction for murder was based on what Correia and others regard as questionable evidence.

Antoné De'Jaun Correia (called by his first name in school and at home, and by his middle name in human-rights advocacy circles) was born in Savannah, Georgia, on June 22, 1994. An only child, Correia was raised by his mother, Martina Correia, who worked as a nurse until she was diagnosed with cancer. He excelled in school and was drawn particularly to math and the sciences. Although he grew up visiting his mother's brother, Troy Davis, in prison, he only gradually came to understand his uncle's situation.

Executed by lethal injection on September 22, 2011 for the 1989 murder of an off-duty police officer, Mark Macphail, Troy Davis had consistently maintained his innocence. No physical evidence had ever been presented linking him to the crime, and seven of the nine non-police prosecution witnesses have recanted their original testimony. One of the witnesses who has not recanted is, according to Davis's defense team, the likely perpetrator of the crime.

While Correia researched his uncle's case on his own during his early teens, he had no plans to become a public advocate. As a junior-high student, he discovered that he had significant rhetorical skills, but he did not

initially deploy them in the fight for his uncle's life. His first experience with public speaking came when a seventh-grade teacher recommended him for a school oratorical competition. He gave a speech about his mother's battle with breast cancer and how it informed his view of life. He placed first in the school and went on to win third prize in a county-wide oratorical competition.

Meanwhile, the Troy Davis case became renowned among human-rights advocates, and it generated increasing media attention. Davis twice came within hours of being executed in 2007 and 2008 before stays were issued to allow him to continue attempting to establish his innocence. Numerous activists and public figures, including Archbishop Desmond Tutu, Sister Helen Prejean, former President Jimmy Carter, Pope Benedict XVI, and Reverend Jesse Jackson, appealed to the courts and Georgia governor Sonny Perdue on Davis's behalf, arguing that he deserved a new trial. Correia's mother took a leading role in the fight to exonerate her brother, and local news reporters routinely visited the family's home to elicit comment from the family on developments in the courts. Correia himself began answering reporters' questions, and his ease in front of the camera led to a number of appearances on the local news. He went on to appear on national networks including CNN and BET.

The NAACP (National Association for the Advancement of Colored People), a staunch supporter of Davis's effort to procure a new trial, in 2009 invited Correia to deliver an introductory speech for the

group's president, Benjamin Todd Jealous, at the annual convention in New York City. Taking the stage in front of a live audience of 5,000 members, and with his speech being streamed live throughout the hotel to another 5,000 people, Correia initially felt nervous. He located his mother in the front row of the audience, however, and he delivered the entire speech looking directly at her, which allowed him to calm his nerves while also appearing to look at the audience.

Soon, Correia found himself being asked to participate in workshops and panels sponsored by Amnesty International and other groups interested in fighting the death penalty, and he began to give addresses regarding his uncle's case in schools. In November of 2009, he was invited to address a number of schools in England, and while there, he spoke to members of the British Parliament about his uncle's case and the death penalty. In March of 2011, Correia gave one of two keynote speeches at the Amnesty International Youth Summit at the University of California, Berkeley. Also in 2011, the online magazine *The Root* named Correia one of its 25 "Young Futurists," its selection of African Americans under age 21 who are making a difference in society. Correia was also selected to represent the Southern region on the NAACP Youth Council.

In March of 2011, Troy Davis's attempt to win a new trial appeared to have reached an unsuccessful conclusion. After ordering a district court to review the case in 2009, based in part on the clearly present risk of putting an innocent man to death, the U.S. Supreme Court denied Davis's requests to present new evidence. After several additional appeals were rejected an execution date of September 21, 2011 was set. Denied a last-minute appeal by the Supreme Court, Davis was executed by lethal injection on September 21, 2011.

Correia planned to continue his public-speaking and advocacy beyond high school, but he was also making other career plans. He was part of the International Baccalaureate Program at Sol C. Johnson High School in Savannah, Georgia, whereby advanced students were able to earn college credits while working toward high school diplomas. An enthusiast of robotics technologies both in and out of class, Correia planned to study robotics and biomedical research in college.

Sources

Periodicals

Atlanta Journal-Constitution, May 19, 2009.

Online

"15-Year-old Takes on the Death Penalty," Coastal Source, January 27, 2010, http://www.thecoastal source.com/content/news/crime/story/15-year-old-Takes-On-the-Death-Penalty/o2MdcZVfM02nz Nsc9u1csw.cspx (accessed July 20, 2011).

Denniston, Lyle, "Davis Innocence Plea Rejected," SCOTUSblog, March 28, 2011, http://www.scot usblog.com/2011/03/davis-innocence-plea-reject ed/ (accessed July 20, 2011).

"Mercer Student Is Tops at State Social Science Fair," Savannahnow.com, April 9, 2008, http://savanna hnow.com/west-chatham/2008-04-09/mercer-stu dent-tops-state-social-science-fair (accessed July 20, 2011).

"The Root's Young Futurists List of 25 Innovators," *The Root,* January 31, 2011, http://www.theroot. com/views/2011/young-futurists (accessed July 20, 2011).

Other

Additional information for this profile was obtained through a phone interview with De'Jaun Correia on June 2, 2011.

—Mark Lane

Donald Lee Cox

1936–2011

Political activist

Cox, Donald Lee, photograph. AP Images.

Although he was never as well known as some of his colleagues in the Black Panther Party (BPP), Donald Lee Cox played a major role in that radical organization. In the late 1960s and early 1970s, when it was at the peak of its influence, the BPP relied heavily on Cox's organizational abilities, particularly in the area of weapons procurement. His ideology shifted in later life, and in a 1992 interview with Safiya Bukhari he appeared to endorse a more moderate approach to African-American empowerment.

watched the beginnings of the civil rights movement closely. Although its goals were increasingly important to him, he disapproved of the nonviolent strategies adopted by the Rev. Dr. Martin Luther King Jr. and other mainstream leaders. "I had a little problem dealing with the philosophy of nonviolence," he told Bukhari. "I just at that time couldn't imagine myself being spit on or abused physically without doing anything." The most militant of the civil rights groups then operating in San Francisco, in his view, was the Congress of Racial Equality (CORE), and it was that organization that provided him with his first experience in grassroots activism.

Known to many as "DC," Cox was born on April 16, 1936, in Appleton, Missouri, a small community near the Kansas line. Like many of his peers, he spent much of his time hunting and fishing. He was also an avid reader, however, and a keen student of the natural world. In comments relayed by Bruce Weber in the *New York Times,* Cox recalled a particular interest in reptiles, noting that he had "read all the books in the library about snakes." Like virtually all African Americans at the time, he was well aware of racial injustice, but his political consciousness did not develop, by his own admission, until he moved to California at the age of 17. While living with relatives in San Francisco, he

Most of CORE's work in the late 1950s and early 1960s involved commercial boycotts; armed action of the sort later endorsed by the BPP was never part of the group's strategy. Although CORE's approach initially satisfied Cox's growing militancy, a series of violent incidents, chief among them the deadly bombing of an African-American church in Birmingham, Alabama, in 1963, convinced him that taking up arms was the only way to secure equal rights for African Americans. A pivotal point in Cox's development came around 1967, when he encountered the BPP for the

first time. Founded several months earlier in Oakland, California, the group was led by Huey P. Newton and Bobby Seale. Cox quickly became one of their chief lieutenants, and by 1969 he had been given the title of field marshal. In that role he took on a variety of responsibilities, including oversight of the group's regional affiliates. His chief task, however, involved firearms training and procurement. The group's military activities were never very effective, but its efforts to obtain weapons—efforts spearheaded by Cox—drew intense scrutiny from law enforcement, particularly the FBI. Its success in mobilizing public support, meanwhile, was mixed. While many citizens, both whites and African Americans, were horrified by the Panthers' violent rhetoric, others were entranced. Among the latter were a number of wealthy whites, including the composer Leonard Bernstein. In January of 1970 Bernstein and his wife held a successful fund-raiser at their apartment in support of several Panthers who were facing criminal charges.

Cox was a prominent figure at the Bernsteins' party, which was later regarded by many as the height of the BPP's power and influence. Its subsequent decline had a number of causes, including internal disputes and a series of criminal prosecutions that targeted most of the group's leaders, Cox included. In the spring of 1970 he was indicted for conspiracy in the murder of Eugene Anderson, a Panther who had been passing information to the authorities. Although he strenuously disputed the charges, he chose not to do so in court, arguing that the government's hostility toward the BPP precluded the possibility of a fair trial. He fled to Algeria, where he received strong support, including housing assistance and a job, from the government. By his own account, however, he never felt at home there, in part because of religious differences; while his hosts made clear their hope that he would convert to Islam, he resisted doing so. The tensions thus created exacerbated other cultural differences, and in April of 1977 he abandoned Algeria for France, settling in Camps-sur-l'Agly, a remote village in the southern region of Languedoc-Roussillon. He remained there for the rest of his life.

In contrast to his eventful years with the BPP, Cox led a quiet life in France, largely eschewing active involvement in national and international politics. He continued to read widely, particularly in history, and served as an informal mentor to Panthers worldwide, many of whom felt adrift after the group's dissolution in the 1970s. He spoke only rarely to the media, but he frequently discussed politics with friends and colleagues. The transcription of what is arguably the most important of those dialogues, the Bukhari interview, suggests that his views grew more moderate in exile. He showed there, for example, little inclination toward violence, arguing instead that today's activists needed to learn from "past mistakes." His concern for the downtrodden, however, appeared as robust as ever. "We have to start," he told Bukhari, "by coming up with something to deal with the economic problems of all those millions of people out there suffering from not having any shelter, not having means to eat, and no healthcare." The first step, he added, would be the creation of "a real true party . . . that represents the needs of the people."

On February 19, 2011, Cox died in Camps-sur-l'Agly. News of his passing reached the media primarily through his second wife, Barbara Cox Easley, who declined to give a cause of death. Other survivors included three children and a number of grandchildren and great-grandchildren. ItsAboutTimeBPP.com, a website for former members of the BPP, responded to his death by posting the Bukhari interview, offering it as a memorial to a man it called a "true warrior for the people."

Sources

Periodicals

New York Times, March 14, 2011, p. D11.
Time, March 28, 2011.

Online

Bukhari, Safiya, "An Interview with Donald Cox, Former Field Marshall, Black Panther Party," ItsAboutTimeBPP.com, March 31, 1992, http://www.itsabouttimebpp.com/Memorials/htm/In_Memory_Of_Exiled_Fallen_Black_Panther_Party_Field_Marshall_Donald_DC_Cox.htm (accessed June 3, 2011).

Del Signore, John, "Black Panther D. L. Cox Dies in Exile," Gothamist.com, March 14, 2011, http://gothamist.com/2011/03/14/black_panther_dl_cox_dies_in_exile.php (accessed June 3, 2011).

—R. Anthony Kugler

David Crosthwait

1892(?)–1976

Engineer

David Crosthwait was a mechanical engineer who designed and perfected climate-control systems for major building projects of the 1920s and '30s, including New York's Radio City Music Hall. A graduate of Purdue University, Crosthwait headed the research department at C.A. Dunham and Company of Marshalltown, Iowa, for decades, and was a prominent figure in his field at a time when African-American engineers in any field were a rarity. Crosthwait was granted more than 114 patents worldwide for various inventions and modifications related to steam-heat systems, which were the standard type of central heating during the first half of the 20th century.

Crosthwait came from a distinguished family in Tennessee. Many sources list his date of birth as 1898, but he is recorded as having earned his college degree from Purdue University in 1913, so an earlier birth date of 1892 is more likely; furthermore, a 1975 issue of *Jet* magazine gives his age as 82. Born in Nashville, he was named after his father, a physician who held degrees from Fisk University and Meharry Medical College. The elder Crosthwait's twin brother, Scott, also earned the same degrees, although in different classes. Crosthwait's aunt was one of the first black teachers hired by the Nashville school system, and Crosthwait's father went on to serve as principal of Nashville's Colored High School from 1881 to 1895. The family moved to Kansas City, Missouri, where his father taught chemistry and biology at Abraham Lincoln High School, the city's only college-preparatory school open to African-American students.

Crosthwait entered Purdue University's mechanical engineering program at the age of 17. The school, located in West Lafayette, Indiana, had admitted black students since the 1880s. He received his bachelor of science degree in 1913 and was hired by the C.A. Dunham Company that same year. The founder of the company, Clayton A. Dunham, had written to Purdue's mechanical engineering department to request the names of the top graduating students in order to offer them jobs. Dunham was apparently nonplussed to discover that the class of 1913's most promising new engineer was an African American; Crosthwait was said to have become the first black resident of Marshalltown when he started at C.A. Dunham. The town had been a leading center of furnace manufacturing for nearly 20 years by then, when a local entrepreneur named David Lennox developed the first riveted steel furnace. The company he created later became Lennox Industries.

Promoted to research engineer at the Dunham Company in 1919, Crosthwait earned a graduate degree from Purdue a year later and made a name for himself in the field by contributing articles to such industry journals as *Heating and Ventilation* and *Power and Industrial Management* that highlighted technical innovations he had developed. His first patent, for a thermostatic steam trap, was awarded in 1919 by the U.S. Patent Office. Crosthwait was particularly adept in devising new parts for boilers such as valves and other regulatory devices that were essential to the steam-heat systems of the era. He also spent a great deal of time in his lab working to improve the notoriously noisy steam

method, whose pipes and radiators tended to hiss and bang. In 1925 he was promoted to director of research at Dunham, and held the title of senior technical consultant and adviser after 1930.

Crosthwait was part of a team of talented engineers contracted by architect Edward Durell Stone for the construction of Radio City Music Hall at Rockefeller Center. When the venue opened in December of 1932, it boasted a state-of-the-art stage, screen, and acoustics, and was the largest movie theater in the world. Crosthwait also worked on heating and cooling systems for two massive residential complexes in New York City: Stuyvesant Town—Peter Cooper Village in Manhattan and Parkchester in the Bronx, both of which were built in the 1940s.

Crosthwait married E. Madolyne Towels in 1930, and they had a son, David Nelson III, who died before his sixth birthday. Crosthwait's wife passed away in August of 1939. Two years later he wed Blanche Ford, and the couple's 25th wedding anniversary celebration in 1966 was mentioned in *Jet*. He was active in community affairs in Michigan City, Indiana, and served as president of the Michigan City Redevelopment Commission. He remained a senior technical consultant and adviser at Dunham, which became Dunham-Bush in the 1950s, until his retirement in 1969. Following that, he returned to his alma mater to teach a course on steam heat theory and applications.

A National Technological Association Medalist of 1936, Crosthwait was a prominent figure in the American Society of Heating and Ventilation Engineers, and wrote or revised chapters in its official handbooks of 1939, 1959, and 1967. These guidebooks reflected major advances in climate-control technology, and even the name of the organization was modernized to include its merging with a sister organization to become the American Society of Heating, Refrigerating and Air Conditioning Engineers, or ASHRAE. Two years after he retired from Dunham, he became an ASHRAE fellow, the first African-American engineer to be accorded that honor. The professional accolade was noted in the February 18, 1971, issue of *Jet*. The magazine also ran a brief article in its July 17, 1975, issue, when Purdue University awarded him an honorary doctorate in technology. He died several months later on February 25, 1976, in Michigan City.

Sources

Books

"Crosthwait, David Nelson," *Who's Who of the Colored Race: A General Biographical Dictionary*, Volume 1, edited by Frank Lincoln Mather, self-published, 1915, pp. 81–82.

Periodicals

Engineered Systems, January 2006, p. 8.
Jet, February 18, 1971, p. 24; July 17, 1975, p. 29.

Online

"Black History Month, February 2008," State Library of Iowa, http://www.statelibraryofiowa.org/services/patents-trademark/blkinvetors (accessed July 26, 2011).

—Carol Brennan

John Dabiri

1980(?)—

Biophysicist, educator

Renowned biophysicist John Dabiri moves easily between the disciplines of aeronautics, engineering, and biology. The recipient of a 2010 MacArthur Fellowship, a $500,000 award widely known as a "genius grant," he is best known for his work with jellyfish. "Dabiri's research," noted the MacArthur Foundation on its website, "has profound implications not only for understanding the evolution and biophysics of locomotion in jellyfish and other aquatic animals, but also for a host of distantly related questions and applications in fluid dynamics, from blood flow in the human heart to the design of wind power generators."

The son of immigrants from Nigeria, Dabiri grew up in the industrial city of Toledo, Ohio. After high school he entered Princeton University, where he earned a bachelor's degree in mechanical and aerospace engineering in 2001. As an undergraduate, he had done summer research at the California Institute of Technology, and it was to that institution, known universally as Caltech, that he returned for graduate school. Working closely with his mentor, Morteza (Mory) Gharib, he earned a master's degree in aeronautics in 2003 and a doctorate in bioengineering and aeronautics two years later. In a sign of the esteem with which he was held by his Caltech peers, he was immediately offered a tenure-track post on the faculty. After serving from 2005 to 2009 as an assistant professor and from 2009 to 2010 as an associate professor, he was promoted again in the wake of his MacArthur prize, this time to a full professorship. As of June of 2011 he remained in that role, which included the directorship of the school's Biological Propulsion Laboratory.

Dabiri's rapid rise in the academic world reflected both the quality of his work and the excitement surrounding its implications for technology and for human life as a whole. At the most basic level, his efforts have involved the translation of observable phenomena—like moving jellyfish—into mathematical equations that can then be applied to a range of practical problems. It has long been noted, for example, that traditional, windmill-style wind generators are relatively inefficient, a characteristic that has limited their effectiveness in the fight against climate change. Eager to improve that situation, Dabiri and his team have constructed complex mathematical models of air flow, concentrating particularly on the swirling patterns known as vortices. Those efforts suggested, as of 2011, that a radically different design had the potential to deliver more energy at a lower cost. With the support of the Gordon and Betty Moore Foundation, Caltech established an experimental wind farm in 2010 to test Dabiri's design. Known as a vertical-axis wind turbine (VAWT), it was inspired by his observations of the ways schools of fish make use of water vortices as they move through the ocean. According to a university press release detailing the project, preliminary results suggested that VAWTs might increase a wind farm's efficiency by as much as a factor of 10.

Amid his wind-turbine investigations, Dabiri continued to work on other projects, many of them inspired by the jellyfish with which he began his career. These efforts included an ambitious plan to use models derived from the creatures' movement through the water to analyze the flow of blood in and around the human

At a Glance . . .

Born John O. Dabiri in 1980(?), probably in Toledo, OH; son of Nigerian immigrants. *Education*: Princeton University, BSE, mechanical and aerospace engineering, 2001; California Institute of Technology, MS, aeronautics, 2003, PhD, bioengineering and aeronautics, 2005. *Religion*: Evangelical Christian.

Career: California Institute of Technology, assistant professor of aeronautics and bioengineering, 2005–09, associate professor of aeronautics and bioengineering, 2009–10, professor of aeronautics and bioengineering, 2010.

Awards: Young Investigator Award, Office of Naval Research, 2008; Presidential Early Career Award for Scientists and Engineers, U.S. Government, 2009; inclusion in the "Power 100" list of the most influential black Americans, *Ebony*, 2010; fellowship, John D. and Catherine T. MacArthur Foundation, 2010.

Addresses: *Office*—Division of Engineering and Applied Science, Caltech, Mail Code 138-78, Pasadena, CA 91125. *Email*—jodabiri@caltech.edu. *Web*—http://dabiri.caltech.edu.

heart. That analysis, in turn, could help doctors diagnose several serious medical conditions, particularly congestive heart failure, which sends hundreds of thousands of Americans to the hospital every year.

Dabiri has won a host of honors over the years, including a Young Investigator Award from the U.S. Navy's Office of Naval Research in 2008; the Presidential Early Career Award for Scientists and Engineers (PECASE) in 2009; and inclusion in the "Power 100," *Ebony* magazine's list of the most influential black Americans, in 2010. The PECASE award was particularly notable; one of the U.S. government's most prominent prizes for scientific work, it earned him a trip to the White House and a visit with President Barack Obama. It was the MacArthur Fellowship, however, that brought him for the first time to the attention of the general public. First awarded in 1981, the fellowships have no application process; instead, an anonymous committee selects, in the words of the foundation's website, "talented individuals who have shown extraordinary originality and dedication in their creative pursuits and a marked capacity for self-direction." Because they have no involvement in the selection process, winners generally have no idea they have been chosen until they receive the foundation's con-

gratulatory phone call. The award, disbursed in quarterly allotments over a five-year span, is without strings, enabling recipients to spend it on anything they choose. Many use it to extend their research in new and unexpected directions, a option not often available with traditional sources of funding. As Dabiri explained to Beige Luciano-Adams in the *Pasadena Star-News*, "If your funding depends on the project being successful, you only bite off small bits. But because there are no strings attached with this, I can be very ambitious with the goals we set for our research." The youngest of the 23 recipients selected in 2010, Dabiri told Luciano-Adams that he intended to use some of the money for swimming lessons. "My students who do the measurements tell me [swimming with jellyfish and other aquatic creatures] is really a different experience from looking at them across the glass. So that's something I'd like to do, and now I don't really have an excuse anymore."

Dabiri has frequently mentioned his Christian faith as one of his most important motivations. "As a born-again Christian," he told Nava Friedman in the *Daily Princetonian*, "I feel that whatever work I do, I want it to have a positive aspect on society. So even though studying jellyfish just for the sake of understanding them I think would be a lot of fun, for me, it's important that I'm able to take what I learned and actually apply it to benefit society. I think that's what drives me to find these more practical applications, like diagnosing heart failure, like trying to come up with more effective technologies for clean energy."

Sources

Periodicals

Daily Princetonian, September 30, 2010.
PasadenaStar-News, September 28, 2010.

Online

"John O. Dabiri: Biography," California Institute of Technology, http://dabiri.caltech.edu/people/dabiri.html (accessed June 28, 2011).
"MacArthur Fellows Program," John D. and Catherine T. MacArthur Foundation, http://www.macfound.org/site/c.lkLXJ8MQKrH/b.959463/k.9D7D/Fellows_Program.htm (accessed June 29, 2011).
Tomlinson, Brett, "Tiger of the Week: John Dabiri '01," Princeton Alumni Weekly, September 29, 2010, http://blogs.princeton.edu/paw/2010/09/tiger_of_the_we_48.html (accessed June 28, 2011).
"2010 MacArthur Fellows: John Dabiri," John D. and Catherine T. MacArthur Foundation, 2010, http://www.macfound.org/site/c.lkLXJ8MQKrH/b.6241251/k.9162/John_Dabiri.htm (accessed June 28, 2011).
Weiner, Jon, "Schooling Fish Offer New Ideas for Wind Farming," California Institute of Technology, May

17, 2010, http://media.caltech.edu/press_releases
/13347 (accessed June 29, 2011).

—R. Anthony Kugler

Meri Nana-Ama Danquah

1967—

Writer, editor

Danquah, Meri Nana–Ama, photograph. Alexandra Wyman/Getty Images.

Meri Nana-Ama Danquah is a writer from Ghana who emigrated to the United States with her parents as a child. She is best known for her memoir *Willow Weep for Me: A Black Woman's Journey through Depression* (1998), which chronicles a battle with depression that was crucially tied to experiences of racism, sexual and physical abuse, single parenthood, and career difficulties. In linking depression with race and other social factors, Danquah brought attention to under-reported manifestations of a mental illness whose public perception remains associated largely with white culture. Danquah has also edited anthologies by immigrant women and black women and an anthology on the subject of the black body. She is a frequent contributor to periodicals and a sought-after public speaker on the subject of mental health.

Born in 1967 in Accra, the capital and largest city of Ghana, Meri Nana-Ama Danquah moved to the United States with her parents at the age of six. She spent most of her childhood in the Washington, DC, suburb of Takoma Park, Maryland. Although she would seem to have become fully Americanized as a result, she has written in Ghana's *Daily Graphic* that "the home I grew up in was so passionately insular it felt as though we were our own little territory, permanently tethered to Ghana." She attended public schools before attending the Foxcroft boarding school in Virginia and Montgomery Blair High School in Silver Spring, Maryland. She dropped out of the University of Maryland without obtaining a degree, relocating briefly to Richmond, Virginia, before moving to Los Angeles to embark on a career as a writer and actor.

Danquah's career goals were greatly complicated by events in her personal life, however. Two months after she gave birth to a daughter, Korama Afua, in 1991, her common-law spouse broke off their relationship and left Danquah to support herself and the infant on her own. She carved out a hand-to-mouth existence at a series of clerical and service jobs, and during this time a longstanding tendency toward melancholy became the full-blown clinical depression that became the subject of *Willow Weep for Me*.

Danquah's memoir in part details her gradual understanding of the ways in which childhood traumas associated with race and gender worked to undermine

her sense of self-worth. As one of a small number of black children in her Maryland school, she was mocked in racist terms implying that she was worthless, and when her father abandoned the family during these years, her feelings of worthlessness seemed to find confirmation. As a junior high student, she was raped by an older boy, and when she appealed to her stepfather for counsel, he, too, raped her. This familial sexual abuse continued in the years that followed.

These traumas led to periodic bouts of despair throughout her early years, but it was the sequence of events following the birth of her child in 1991 that triggered a mental health crisis that Danquah finally identified as severe depression requiring medical treatment. These events included postpartum depression, physical abuse and then desertion at the hands of her common-law partner, and the 1992 acquittal of the Los Angeles Police officers who had been videotaped beating Rodney King, an event whose message Danquah, like many others, took to be a statement about American society's view of black Americans. Danquah began to fear for her sanity and her ability to care for her daughter, and she began to pursue the medical treatment and self-understanding that led to her recovery and the writing of her memoir.

Danquah's ability to accept that she suffered from clinical depression was complicated, however, by normative ideas of black female identity. Black women, according to dominant American stereotypes that Danquah found hard to see beyond, were supposed to suffer stoically and silently and to take care of others. To illustrate this point, Danquah recounts an exchange she had with a white woman at a dinner party, to whom she confided that she was writing a book about black women and depression. "Black women and depression?" the woman joked. "Isn't that kinda redundant?" Stereotypes persisted within the African-American community as well, as Danquah tells it, in the form of

the notion that "If our people could make it through slavery, we could make it through anything." A crucial element in Danquah's journey toward overcoming depression thus involved confronting and dismissing such societal expectations.

Willow Weep for Me was reviewed favorably in the general press, and it was also embraced by mental-health professionals for its ability to speak to those, especially black women, who have long suffered from depression in silence due to societal expectations. After the book's publication, Danquah became a sought-after speaker and a spokesperson for the National Mental Health Association.

Danquah has also contributed to American literary culture as an anthology editor. *Becoming American: Personal Essays by First-Generation Immigrant Women*, published in 2000, featured contributions from prominent writers including Edwidge Danticat of Haiti, Lynn Freed of South Africa, Lucy Grealy of Ireland, and Judith Ortiz Cofer of Puerto Rico, among many others. *Shaking the Tree: A Collection of New Fiction and Memoir by Black Women* (2003) offered writing from the generation of black female writers who began to emerge in the 1990s, including Danzy Senna, Catherine E. McKinley, ZZ Packer, and Danticat. *The Black Body* (2009), meanwhile, used contributions from a wide array of writers, actors, artists, and others who identify variously as black, white, or multiracial to consider the subject of the black body's representation in American culture.

Danquah's essays and journalism have appeared widely in periodicals including *Allure*, *Essence*, the *Los Angeles Times*, the *Village Voice*, and the *Washington Post*, and she has contributed commentary to National Public Radio. She has also worked as a writing teacher at the University of Ghana, Otis College of Art and Science, and Antioch College, and as a ghostwriter, producing books and book proposals for celebrities and other public figures. In 2011 she returned to Accra with the intention of settling there for good. At work on a new book, she also began writing a weekly column for Ghana's *Daily Graphic* newspaper.

Sources

Periodicals

Booklist, February 15, 2000, p. 1056; August 2003, p. 1944.
Daily Graphic (Accra, Ghana), March 18, 2011.
Library Journal, January 2000, p. 138; September 1, 2003, p. 168.
MELUS, Fall 2006, pp. 67100.
Publishers Weekly, January 5, 1998, p. 53; January 10, 2000, p. 56.

Online

Mensah, Kent, "Ghana's Literary Icon: Nana-Ama

Danquah," AfricaNews, April 15, 2011, http://www.africanews.com/site/INTERVIEW_Unveiling_Ghanas_ghostwriter/list_messages/38161 (accessed July 17, 2011).

—Mark Lane

Jason Derülo

1989—

Vocalist, songwriter, actor

Vocalist Jason Derülo's smooth, warmly expressive voice has been a familiar one to radio listeners and R&B fans since the summer of 2009. A native of Florida and a nominee for Outstanding New Artist at the NAACP Image Awards in 2011, he had a successful career as a songwriter before taking the stage himself at the age of about 20.

Jason Joel Desrouleaux was born in the fall of 1989, probably in Miami; a few sources, however, point instead to the nearby suburb of Miramar, where he grew up in a solidly

Derülo, Jason, photograph. AP Images/Kristian Dowling/Picture Group.

middle-class household. Although his parents, natives of Haiti, were not inclined to the performing arts themselves, they strongly encouraged his interest in music. By the age of five, he was a frequent performer at family gatherings, and by the age of eight he had written his first song. A series of music classes and arts camps soon followed. These gave him a solid grounding in a variety of genres, including opera, musical theater, and ballet.

Derülo's first break came in junior high school, when a chance encounter on a basketball court brought him into contact with Frank Harris, who eventually became his manager. Impressed with Derülo's voice and song-

writing ability, Harris, then a law student, began contacting people he knew in the music business. Those efforts quickly paid off, and at the age of about 16 Derülo sold his first song. Over the next few years he wrote lyrics for a variety of R&B stars, including Lil Wayne and Pitbull. It was lucrative work, but he was not entirely happy. "It was killing me," he later recalled to Jason Lipshutz for Reuters. "I had a huge attachment to the songs I was writing, but I had to give them up to make a quick buck. Being in music, I was just hoping something would happen, that somebody would notice me."

In his efforts to move from songwriting into performance, Derülo auditioned successfully for the television program *Showtime at the Apollo,* which featured live musical performances by contestants. He proved an audience favorite, winning the grand prize at the end of the show's 2006 season. In the wake of that success, he met two of the industry's leading figures, Warner Brothers executive (and *American Idol* judge) Kara DioGuardi and producer J. R. Rotem. While both proved helpful, it was Rotem who sparked the next phase of his career. In an interview with Pete Lewis for BluesAndSoul.com, Derülo described his relationship

At a Glance . . .

Born Jason Joel Desrouleaux in 1989, probably in Miami, FL; son of Haitian immigrants.

Career: Songwriter, 2000—; performing vocal artist, 2000—; television performer and actor, 2006—.

Awards: NAACP Image Award nomination, for outstanding new artist, 2011.

Addresses: *Office*—c/o Frank Harris, The Harris Law Firm, LLC, 170 Prospect Ave., Ste. 3D, Hackensack, NJ 07601. *Web*—http://www.jasonderulo.com.

with the producer as "wonderful," noting that they recorded six songs at their first meeting. A record contract with Rotem's Beluga Heights label quickly followed.

As his recording career gained traction, Derülo continued to write songs. One of these, "Whatcha Say," was inspired by problems his brother was having in a romantic relationship. Rotem, known for his work with R&B stars Rihanna and Sean Kingston, found the lyrics compelling and helped Derülo construct a beat to go with them. The result, released as a single in the summer of 2009, raced up the charts, reaching number one on Billboard's influential Hot 100 list. It remained there for four consecutive weeks. Two follow-ups, "In My Head" and "Ridin' Solo," did nearly as well; all three sold several million copies. Buoyed by that reception, Derülo immediately began work on an album. Featuring six new songs in addition to the three singles, his self-titled debut, released in March of 2010, reached number 11 on Billboard's list of the nation's top albums. David Jeffries in AllMusic.com called it "well-crafted, futuristic R&B," adding, "If what you're looking for is R&B that sparkles and dazzles, there are nine quick fixes here, each one just dying to get stuck in your head." While many critics, perhaps the majority, echoed that praise, a few noted with dismay his use of Auto-Tune, a recording technology designed to correct errors in pitch. While many of the nation's top performers relied on it by 2011, its use remained controversial, with its detractors often claiming that it made music sound bland and generic.

Several months before the release of his first record, Derülo joined one of the most prominent concert tours of 2010. As an opening act for pop star Lady Gaga's "Monster Ball" tour, he performed at large arenas across North America. His appearances in these venues were designed, in part, to highlight his dancing abilities and engaging stage presence. Both qualities had already drawn the attention of MTV, which cast

him in a made-for-television movie called *Turn the Beat Around* (2010). Videos for his singles, meanwhile, remained extremely popular online. On YouTube.com alone, "Whatcha Say" had been viewed more than 100 million times by June of 2011. Derülo, for his part, has described his interest in acting as serious and abiding. "While music is very much at the forefront for me right now," he told Lewis for BluesAndSoul.com, "in the long-term [sic] I can see the acting becoming equally important in my career. To where I'll probably kind of end up juggling the two around."

Even as a teenager, Derülo was known for his perfectionism and attention to detail. Those qualities have persisted in his recording career. For his first album he recorded no less than 300 songs, then culled them relentlessly until he and Rotem had what they believed were the 9 best. According to his website, JasonDerulo.com, he has approached his second album the same way. Tentatively titled *Future History,* it had spawned one single, "Don't Wanna Go Home," by June of 2011. *Future History* was described in pre-release promotions as a genre-defying mix of R&B, electronica, and other styles. That eclecticism, visible also in the rock beats and hip-hop mannerisms that punctuated Derülo's debut, was fast becoming a trademark. "I'm not just an urban artist," he told Jo Piazza for CNN. "I just make music and I don't want to make music just for a niche audience. I want to make music for every single person. I want to expand. I want to make music for the world. I want to break musical barriers and not be pigeonholed by the color of my skin to do a certain kind of music."

Sources

Online

"History," jasonderulo.com, http://www.jasonderulo.com/bio/ (accessed June 24, 2011).

Jeffries, David, "*Jason Derülo:* Review," AllMusic.com, http://allmusic.com/album/jason-derlo-r1713 832/review (accessed June 25, 2011).

Lewis, Pete, "Jason Derulo: Watcha Think?," Blues AndSoul.com, http://www.bluesandsoul.com/feature/484/fix_up_look_sharp/ (accessed June 24, 2011).

Lipshutz, Jason, "Heartbreak Tale Pays Off for Singer Jason Derulo," Reuters, October 4, 2009, http://www.reuters.com/assets/print?aid=USTRE59 405N20091005 (accessed June 24, 2011).

Piazza, Jo, "Jason Derulo: The Man behind the Hit," CNN, December 23, 2009, http://edition.cnn.com/2009/SHOWBIZ/Music/12/23/jason.derulo.profile/ (accessed June 24, 2011).

Thurston, Jason, "Jason Derülo: Biography," AllMusic.com, http://allmusic.com/artist/jason-derlo-p10 08977/biography (accessed June 24, 2011).

—R. Anthony Kugler

Dave Duerson

1960–2011

Professional football player, business executive

Duerson, Dave, photograph. AP Images/NFL Photos.

Although Dave Duerson had a prominent career in professional football and business, he is probably best known for the tragedy that ended his life. A hard-hitting safety with more than a decade of experience in the National Football League (NFL), he began in later life to suffer from a range of medical problems, including memory loss and emotional distress, that researchers have linked to repeated head trauma. Known as chronic traumatic encephalopathy (CTE), the condition has been increasingly recognized as a major issue in football. Devastated by his deteriorating health, Duerson committed suicide in February of 2011.

David Russell Duerson was born on November 28, 1960, in Muncie, Indiana, a small city roughly 60 miles northeast of Indianapolis. By the time he entered Northside High School there, his athletic ability, particularly on the football field, was obvious. He was also a strong student, earning induction into the National Honor Society. Upon graduation he moved on to the University of Notre Dame (ND), matriculating there in the fall of 1979. Located several hours north of Muncie, ND has been a football powerhouse from the

sport's earliest days. By all accounts, Duerson adjusted quickly to the intensity of college play, earning All-American honors from several news organizations. A defensive specialist, he excelled at safety, an open-field position that gave him ample opportunity to use his speed and upper-body strength. It also placed him squarely in the path of offensive linemen, most of them much larger than he was. Although fearsome collisions occur everywhere in football, open-field hits—the primary business of safeties and linebackers—are known for being particularly violent. Like many of his peers, he suffered a number of concussions. These were not seen at the time as particularly dangerous; they have since been implicated, however, in the development of CTE.

By the end of his time at ND, Duerson had attracted interest from several NFL teams. Shortly before graduating with a bachelor's degree in economics, he was selected by the Chicago Bears in the third round of the league's 1983 draft. He remained with that franchise for the next seven seasons (1983–89), a period that included, in January of 1986, the Bears' first Super

At a Glance . . .

Born David Russell Duerson on November 28, 1960, in Muncie, IN; died on February 17, 2011, in Sunny Isles Beach, FL; married Alicia (divorced, 2007); children: four. *Education*: University of Notre Dame, BA, economics, 1983; Harvard University, MBA, 2001.

Career: Chicago Bears, safety, 1983–89; New York Giants, safety, 1990–91; Phoenix Cardinals, 1991–93; entrepreneur, 1993–2011; Brooks Sausage Company (later Fair Oaks Farms), president and CEO, 1995–2002; Duerson Foods, founder, president, and CEO, 2002–06(?).

Memberships: University of Notre Dame, board of trustees, 2001–05.

Awards: Pro Bowl selection, National Football League, 1985, 1986, 1987, and 1988; NFL Man of the Year Award, National Football League, 1987.

Bowl victory. Duerson played an integral role in the team's success, earning four consecutive trips (1985–88) to the Pro Bowl, an end-of-season event reserved for the league's best players. Following the last of his Pro Bowl appearances, he spent one more year in Chicago and then moved to the New York Giants for the 1990 season, which ended in a Super Bowl victory, his second. He finished his career with the Phoenix Cardinals (1991–93).

Unlike many of his colleagues, Duerson had clear goals for his retirement. Soon after leaving football, he moved into the restaurant field, buying several fast-food franchises in Kentucky. The experience he gained there quickly drew the attention of executives at Fair Oaks Farms. Then known as Brooks Sausage Company, Fair Oaks Farms was a major supplier of meat products to the restaurant industry. In a seven-year stint, from 1995 to 2002, as the company's president and CEO, Duerson oversaw a dramatic increase in sales, particularly abroad. He also found time to earn an MBA at Harvard University in 2001 and to serve on Notre Dame's board of trustees from 2001 to 2005. In 2002 he left Fair Oaks Farms to start his own sausage company, Duerson Foods.

It was at about that point, however, that his life began to go downhill. A series of financial setbacks doomed the new company, which went bankrupt in 2006; most of its assets were subsequently sold to satisfy debts. While the causes of the company's demise were complex, a significant factor, according to several of Duerson's associates, may have been a decline in his decision-making abilities. Such impairments are a hallmark of CTE. Even more troubling was an abrupt change in his personality. Known hitherto as a cheerful, gregarious person, he became much more aggressive, another change typical of CTE. One of the most ominous signs of that transformation came in February of 2005, when he was charged with two counts of battery and two counts of domestic battery, all misdemeanors. At the heart of the charges were allegations that he had pushed Alicia, his wife of many years, during an argument. In addition to placing an added strain on his marriage, which soon ended in divorce, the incident forced Duerson to resign his place on Notre Dame's board.

In the months that followed, his problems intensified. Amid the collapse of his business, he lost his house to foreclosure and was forced into personal bankruptcy. Although he remained in good health in most respects, he was increasingly concerned—as were those closest to him—about CTE. Doctors were of little help, however, in part because the condition was diagnosable only upon death; as of 2011 the physical examination of brain tissue remained the only way to confirm the long-term damage associated with the disorder. The NFL was also unable to provide help, either financially or socially. There were some indications at the time that the NFL's attitude was changing, but the organization remained resistant to the disability claims of former players. Duerson, ironically, had served for a time as a player representative on the league board that evaluated such requests. During his tenure, reported Rick Telander in the *Chicago Sun-Times*, he consistently voted to reject the claims under review. It should be noted, however, that CTE was virtually unknown at the time.

On February 17, 2011, Duerson committed suicide at his home in Sunny Isles Beach, Florida. In a note found near his body, he asked that his brain be sent to researchers. That request was honored, and in May of 2011 the leader of the postmortem investigation, Dr. Ann McKee of Boston University's Center for the Study of Traumatic Encephalopathy, announced that Duerson had indeed suffered from CTE. The news brought a renewed focus on the issue of head injuries in football, particularly in the NFL. In the spring of 2011 the league was actively evaluating a range of proposals to reduce the problem, including rule changes and new helmet designs. While the effectiveness of these initiatives remained to be seen, there seemed little doubt that future players would have cause to remember Duerson with sadness and gratitude. "There are now," wrote Telander in May of 2011, "two eras in modern football—before Dave Duerson and after Dave Duerson."

Sources

Periodicals

Associated Press, May 2, 2011.
Chicago Sun-Times, May 16, 2011.
Los Angeles Times, February 21, 2011.
New York Times, February 18, 2011, p. A21.

Online

"David Duerson Biography," TheHistoryMakers.com, http://www.thehistorymakers.com/biography/biography.asp?bioindex=517 (accessed May 28, 2011).

—R. Anthony Kugler

Percival Everett

1956—

Novelist, professor

Everett, Percival, photograph. Ulf Andersen/Getty Images.

Percival Everett is a prolific and critically acclaimed novelist known for his offbeat humor, his erudition, and his penchant for formal and conceptual experimentation. Although virtually all of his books have been well received by critics, he has neither pursued nor found mainstream success. His body of work boasts stories set in ancient Greece, the Old West, the post-apocalyptic future, and contemporary suburbs; among the protagonists are a slumping Major League Baseball player, the last fertile woman on Earth, an infant-philosopher with an IQ of 475, and a college professor who has his head severed in a car crash and then comes back to life.

Studied Philosophy and Began Writing

Born on December 22, 1956, in Fort Gordon, Georgia, Everett spent his childhood in Columbia, South Carolina. The son of a dentist and the grandson of a doctor, Everett grew up with relative freedom to determine his profession and to pursue an interest in the arts. He attended the University of Miami, where he studied philosophy and played jazz guitar in clubs at night, and then he worked briefly as a schoolteacher before enrolling in the graduate philosophy program at the University of Oregon. There Everett studied ordinary language philosophy, a school of thought associated with J. L. Austin and Ludwig Wittgenstein, among others, and which foregrounds the notion that philosophy is best approached as an attentiveness to the meanings of everyday language. He became disenchanted with scholastic philosophy, however, and in response he began writing fictional scenes in which characters discussed philosophical concepts.

While still at Oregon, Everett began applying to graduate writing programs, completing his first stories to include with his applications for admission. He was accepted into Brown University's prestigious graduate creative writing program, which was well known as an incubator for experimental and innovative approaches to literature. Everett wrote his first novel, *Suder* (1983), while still a student at Brown, and it was published soon after he earned his M.F.A.

Suder tells the story of its eponymous protagonist, a

At a Glance . . .

Born Percival Leonard Everett on December 22, 1956, in Fort Gordon, GA; son of Percival Leonard (a dentist) and Dorothy Everett; married Francesca Rochberg (divorced); married Danzy Senna; children: Henry, Miles. *Education*: University of Miami, AB, 1977; attended University of Oregon, 1978–80; Brown University, MFA, 1982.

Career: University of Kentucky, associate professor of English and director of graduate creative writing, 1985–89; University of Notre Dame, professor of English, 1989–92; University of California at Riverside, professor of creative writing and chair of creative writing program, 1992–99; University of Southern California, professor of English, 1999–2007, Distinguished Professor of English, 2007.

Memberships: Writers Guild of America, Modern Language Association.

Awards: D. H. Lawrence fellowship, University of New Mexico, 1984; Lila Wallace/*Reader's Digest* fellowship; New American Writing Award, 1990, for *Zulus;* South Carolina Governor's Award in the Arts, 1994; PEN/Oakland Josephine Miles Award for Excellence in Literature, 1997, for *Big Picture;* Zora Neale Hurston/Richard Wright Foundation Legacy Award, 2002, for *Erasure;* Academy Award for Literature, American Academy of Arts and Letters, 2003; Hillsdale Award; PEN/USA 2006 Literary Award, PEN American Center, for *Wounded; Believer* Book Award, *Believer* magazine, 2010, for *I Am Not Sidney Poitier.*

Addresses: *Office*—University Park Campus, English Department, University of Southern California, Los Angeles, CA 90089. *Email*—peverett@usc.edu. *Agent*—Alison Granucci, Blue Flower Arts, P.O. Box 1361, Millbrook, NY 12545.

its originality and humor, and it established Everett as an up-and-coming talent.

With his degree and the publication of his first book, Everett found a position teaching English and creative writing at the University of Kentucky. He has spent much of his subsequent career in academia, culminating with long stints at the University of California, Riverside, and the University of Southern California, where he has taught since 1999. Of his years in academia, Everett told the interviewer Robert Birnbaum of the online magazine Identity Theory, "I get paid fairly well to hang out with smart young people. That's hard to complain about."

Established Reputation for Adventurous Experimentation

Suder was followed by the novels *Walk Me to the Distance* (1985) and *Cutting Lisa* (1986) and the short story collection *The Weather and Women Treat Me Fair* (1987). Everett's fourth novel, *Zulus* (1989), considerably enhanced his standing among critics. Set in a post-apocalyptic world where city dwellers are zombies and all women are sterilized, *Zulus* tells the story of Alice Achitopel, an obese woman who has avoided sterilization, is impregnated by a rapist, and becomes a figure of hope to a band of rebels who want to preserve the future of the human race. Applauding Everett's skill in wedding the outlandish with the commonplace and his ability to make the fantastic and the phantasmagoric real to the reader, Clarence Major in the *Washington Post* opined that "what is most interesting about *Zulus* is its display of the author's interest in language and its relation to the activity of the imagination," comparing Everett to the pathbreaking modernists Ezra Pound and James Joyce.

Everett's embrace of a wide range of genres and cultural references continued with *For Her Dark Skin,* a refashioning of *Medea,* the ancient-Greek tragedy by Euripedes, and *God's Country* (1994), a send-up of the classic American Western. Everett's second volume of short fiction, *Big Picture,* appeared in 1996, as well as two novels, *Watershed* and *Frenzy.* Another take on the genre of the Western, *Watershed* tells the story of Robert Hawks, a hydrologist in the rural West who becomes embroiled in a dispute between the federal government and an Indian tribe; *Frenzy,* meanwhile, is set in ancient Greece and narrated by Vlepo, the assistant to the semi-divine Dionysus.

1999 saw the publication of *Glyph,* the novel that many readers, along with Everett himself, consider his best book. *Glyph* is narrated by a four-year-old genius, Ralph Townsend, who tells the story of his early infancy, when he began writing notes to his mother and devouring such texts as Wittgenstein's *Tractatus Logico-Philosophicus.* The book is, among other things, an irreverent investigation into language and

Major League Baseball player who, experiencing a hitting slump as well as domestic malaise, embarks on a road trip through the American Northwest. The novel's episodic, far-fetched plot calls to mind the tradition of the 18th-century picaresque novel, and in its pairing of serious inner dilemmas with fantastical external events, the book is characteristic of Everett's oeuvre as a whole. *Suder* was applauded by critics for

literature and a scathing send-up of the poststructuralist theory that long dominated academic English departments in American universities. Writing for *LA Weekly* in January 2000, Ben Ehrenreich observed that "if it doesn't quite stand up as literary theory, and if even as a novel it's got some holes in it, I suspect it will be some months before I have to stop saying that *Glyph* is the smartest and funniest novel I've read this century."

Satirized Racial Politics

2001's *Erasure*, meanwhile, turned a gimlet eye to the American publishing industry, and specifically to racial politics within the publishing industry. The book is narrated by an Everett-like novelist named Thelonious "Monk" Ellison who has failed to achieve breakthrough commercial success because mainstream publishers consider his work too experimental and not "black enough." In exasperated response to such criticisms, Ellison pens a sensational ghetto novel embodying all of the stereotypes about African Americans that, in his previous work, he has steadfastly avoided. Titled *My Pafology* and published under the pseudonym Stagg R. Leigh, the book becomes a runaway success applauded for its authenticity and insight into black culture.

A similarly sardonic take on the politics of race, *A History of the African-American People [Proposed] by Strom Thurmond, as Told to Percival Everett and James Kincaid* (2004), takes the form of an epistolary attempt by an aide to the segregationist South Carolina Senator Strom Thurmond to argue the merits of the absurd publishing project described by the novel's title. Also in 2004 Everett's *American Desert* was published; a Kafkaesque novel, it depicts college professor Theodore Street, who, en route to committing suicide by drowning, is hit by a truck and decapitated. His head is reconnected to his body for his funeral, and during the service Street sits up in his coffin. As he attempts to live an ordinary life after his resurrection, Street is abducted by a Christian cult whose leader determines that he is the devil. After being abducted by a government agency experimenting with technologies to overcome death, he decides to end his life a second time by undoing his stitches and removing his head from his body. Another volume of short stories, *Damned If I Do*, also appeared in 2004.

In 2005 Everett published *Wounded*, perhaps his most straightforwardly realistic novel. Addressing issues of race and gender with a solemnity that is comparatively rare in his work, *Wounded* is narrated by John Hunt, a horse trainer in Wyoming who happens to be African American. Living in self-imposed isolation on his ranch in the aftermath of his wife's death, Hunt finds himself unwillingly drawn into the confrontational politics resulting from the murder of a young gay man nearby, a hate-crime reminiscent of the real-life 1998 Wyoming murder of Matthew Shepard. Reviewing the British edition of the book for London's *Sunday Telegraph*, Matt Thorne wrote, "Although in some ways his most stylistically unadventurous book, this is my favorite of Everett's novels. . . . No doubt he'll be back in 12 months with something completely different, and equally good. His is a restless intellect."

Continued to Produce Thought-Provoking Work

Everett's next novel, *The Water Cure* (2007), was similarly topical. The book, which details the story of a romance novelist who imprisons and tortures the man he believes to have killed his daughter, was seen by many as a response to the authorization of torture as an intelligence-gathering tool by the administration of U.S. President George W. Bush. 2009's *I Am Not Sidney Poitier*, by contrast, marked a return to the antic and outlandish fictional scenarios that characterize much of Everett's oeuvre. The story of a man named Not Sidney Poitier who looks remarkably like the actor Sidney Poitier, the novel features a cast of supporting characters including the media baron Ted Turner, who adopts the novel's protagonist, and a novelist and professor named Percival Everett, who dispenses cryptic advice. Reviewing the book for the Minneapolis *Star Tribune*, Steve Weinberg declared that "a new Percival Everett novel is cause for celebration" and called Everett "one of the most talented contemporary novelists writing in English."

Selected works

Novels

Suder, Viking, 1983.
Walk Me to the Distance, Ticknor & Fields, 1985.
Cutting Lisa, Ticknor & Fields, 1986.
Zulus, Permanent Press, 1989.
For Her Dark Skin, Owl Creek Press, 1989.
God's Country, Faber, 1994.
The Body of Martin Aguilera, Owl Creek Press, 1994.
Watershed, Graywolf, 1996.
Frenzy, Graywolf, 1996.
Glyph, Graywolf, 1999.
Grand Canyon, Inc., Versus, 2001.
Erasure, UP of New England, 2001.
American Desert, Hyperion, 2004.
A History of the African-American People [Proposed] by Strom Thurmond, as Told to Percival Everett and James Kincaid, Akashic, 2004.
Wounded, Graywolf, 2005.
The Water Cure, Graywolf, 2007.
I Am Not Sidney Poitier, Graywolf, 2009.

Short stories

The Weather and Women Treat Me Fair, August House, 1987.
Big Picture, Graywolf, 1996.
Damned If I Do, Graywolf, 2004.

Sources

Periodicals

BOMB, Summer 2004.

Guardian (London), April 19, 2003; June 5, 2004; May 21, 2005; February 17, 2007; September 6, 2008.

LA Weekly, January 21, 2000; November 29, 2002.

Los Angeles Times, July 12, 2009.

New York Times, December 1, 1996; May 9, 2004.

San Francisco Chronicle, June 13, 2004.

Star Tribune (Minneapolis, MN), July 5, 2009.

Sunday Telegraph (London), February 25, 2007.

Washington Post, May 20, 1990.

Online

Birnbaum, Robert, "Interview: Percival Everett," Identity Theory, http://www.identitytheory.com/interviews/birnbaum105.php (accessed August 7, 2011).

—Mark Lane

Fabolous

1977—

Rap musician

Fabolous, photograph. AP Images/Fernando Leon/PictureGroup.

Brooklyn-born rapper Fabolous became an overnight sensation in 2001 with his breakout single "Can't Deny It" from his platinum-selling debut *Ghetto Fabolous,* establishing himself as an East Coast rapper with both street credentials and crossover appeal. He followed with another platinum album, *Street Dreams,* in 2003, and then two gold records, *Real Talk* in 2004 and *From Nothin' to Somethin'* in 2007, earning two Grammy nominations along the way. Amid his success, however, Fabolous also made headlines for his very public brushes with the law, most notably in 2006, when he was arrested on criminal weapons charges after being shot outside a Manhattan restaurant.

Born John David Jackson on November 18, 1977, in Brooklyn, New York, he grew up in the Brevoort housing projects, raised by his single mother. As a teenager, he was a fan of rap and hip-hop but never thought of making a career of music. That changed in 1998, when, as a senior in high school, he stumbled into an on-air audition on the popular *Monday Night Mixtape* radio show hosted by DJ Clue on New York's WQHT Hot 97. The performance showcased his natural talents, and soon DJ Clue began including the young rapper on his mixtape collections. Jackson adopted the moniker "Fabolous" after spelling out the name in a freestyle rap. "When I first started, I spelled my name in just about every song," he recalled in an interview with *Jet* magazine. "Now . . . [t]hat's my signature for people to know who I am."

Fabolous signed with DJ Clue's fledgling Desert Storm label, and in the summer of 1999, he joined Jay-Z, Method Man, Redman, and DMX on the "Hard Knock Life" tour. In 2001 he was featured on Lil' Mo's "Superwoman, Part II" remix, which reached No. 11 on the *Billboard* Hot 100. The video was a hit on MTV and BET, helping to make Fabolous a star almost overnight. That year, DJ Clue negotiated a production and distribution deal with Elektra Records for the rapper's debut.

In June, Fabolous released his first single, "Can't Deny It," featuring Nate Dogg. Produced by Rick Rock, the song sampled the infectious hook—"I can't deny it, I'm a f*ckin ridah"—from 2Pac's 1996 track "Ambitionz az a Ridah." "Can't Deny It" rose to No. 11 on the Hot Rap Tracks chart and No. 25 on the *Billboard* Hot

At a Glance . . .

Born John David Jackson on November 18, 1977, in Brooklyn, NY; son of Patricia Cain.

Career: Recording artist, 2001—.

Awards: ASCAP Rhythm and Soul Music Awards, Top Rap Song, for "Make Me Better," 2008; BET Hip Hop Awards, Viewer's Choice, for "Throw It in the Bag," 2009.

Addresses: *Record company*—Def Jam Recordings, 825 8th Ave., New York, NY 10019.

100. It also created buzz for his upcoming album, *Ghetto Fabolous,* which featured production work by the Neptunes, Timbaland, and Rockwilder, in addition to Rock, as well as guest appearances by Ja Rule, Lil' Mo, and Jagged Edge. Though *Ghetto Fabolous* was released on September 11, 2001, that did not dampen enthusiasm for the record: it shot to No. 4 on the *Billboard* 200 albums chart, selling 143,000 copies in the first week and eventually going platinum. The tragic events of that day made the video for "Can't Deny It" even more timely, with Fabolous rapping against a background of stars and stripes (a sheer coincidence, as the video had been shot weeks before).

Fabolous followed up with his sophomore effort, *Street Dreams,* in March of 2003. The album produced three hit singles—"Trade It All" (with Diddy and Jagged Edge), "Can't Let You Go" (featuring Lil' Mo and Mike Shorey), and "Into You" (featuring Tamia), with the last two songs breaking the top five on the *Billboard* Hot 100. Other guest appearances included Snoop Dogg, Missy Elliott, Ashanti, and Mary J. Blige. Though critics found the record less impressive than Fabolous's debut, it charted even higher, reaching No. 3 on both the *Billboard* 200 and Top R&B/Hip-Hop Albums. In November, Fabolous released his first mixtape, *More Street Dreams, Part 2: The Mixtape,* helping to bolster his street cred among underground rap and hip-hop fans.

That same year, Fabolous found himself in trouble with the law. In January he was arrested twice in two days in New York, first on a traffic violation and two counts of criminal possession of a weapon, and the next day for driving on a suspended license. The gun charges later were dropped, but Fabolous was arrested again in March after police found a loaded 9-millimeter handgun in a car in which he was riding. His bodyguard later showed proof of ownership of the weapon, clearing Fabolous, but the rapper threatened to sue the city of New York for $5 million for false arrest (the suit never was filed).

In 2004 Fabolous released his third studio album, *Real Talk,* on Atlantic Records. The record peaked at number six on the *Billboard* 200 and produced two minor hits—"Baby," featuring Mike Shorey, and "Breathe," produced by Just Blaze—but left many fans and critics disappointed. Fabolous received his first Grammy Award nomination in 2005 for "Dip It Low," a collaboration with Christina Milan.

The rapper's legal troubles continued in 2006, when he was the target of a shooting outside a Manhattan nightspot. Early in the morning on October 17, Fabolous was shot in the leg after leaving Justin's, a restaurant owned by Sean "Diddy" Combs, and then fled the scene with three other men. When the police arrived, they saw the rapper's vehicle run a red light and pulled it over. Officers found two semiautomatic pistols inside the car, one of which had the serial number removed. Fabolous had his wound treated at a local hospital and then was taken to the station house, where all four men in the car were charged with criminal possession of a weapon. A judge later dismissed the charges when prosecutors could not prove that Fabolous was the owner of either weapon.

After a three-year hiatus, Fabolous returned in 2007 with *From Nothin' to Somethin',* his first release on Def Jam Recordings. The record debuted at No. 1 on the Top R&B/Hip-Hop Albums chart and No. 2 on the *Billboard* 200, selling more than 150,000 copies in the first week. Heavy on guest stars, it featured Jay-Z, T-Pain, Akon, Ne-Yo, Young Jeezy, and Rihanna and spawned several successful singles, including "Make Me Better," which broke the top ten, "Baby Don't Go," and "Diamonds," in addition to the hometown anthem "Brooklyn." However, critics agreed that Fabolous offered nothing new on *From Nothin' to Somethin',* and even the clever rhymes that had become his trademark were not enough to sustain the album.

In 2009 Fabolous released *Loso's Way,* a conceptual album inspired by the 1993 film *Carlito's Way.* ("Loso" is one of the rapper's nicknames.) The lead single, "Throw It in the Bag" with The-Dream, reached No. 2 on *Billboard*'s Hot Rap Tracks and No. 14 on the Hot 100, and the video won Viewer's Choice honors at the BET Hip-Hop Awards. Other singles included the Grammy-nominated "Money Goes, Honey Stay" featuring Jay-Z, "Everything, Everyday, Everywhere" with Keri Hilson, and "My Time" featuring Jeremih. A deluxe edition of the album was released on the same day that included a bonus 30-minute movie dramatizing the rapper's 2006 shooting. A follow-up album, *Loso's Way 2: Rise to Power,* was scheduled for release in 2011.

Selected discography

Albums

Ghetto Fabolous, Elektra, 2001 (includes "Can't Deny It").

Street Dreams, Elektra, 2003 (includes "Trade It All," "Can't Let You Go," and "Into You").

Real Talk, Atlantic, 2004 (includes "Baby" and "Breathe").

From Nothin' to Somethin', Def Jam, 2007 (includes "Make Me Better," "Baby Don't Go," and "Diamonds").

Loso's Way, Def Jam, 2009 (includes "Throw It in the Bag," "Money Goes, Honey Stay," "Everything, Everyday, Everywhere," and "My Time").

Loso's Way 2: Rise to Power, Def Jam, 2011.

EPs

There Is No Competition 2: The Grieving Music EP, Def Jam, 2010.

Mixtapes

More Street Dreams, Part 2: The Mixtape, Atlantic, 2003.

Fabolous and the Street Family Presents: Loso's Way: Rise to Power, Street Family, 2006.

There Is No Competition, Def Jam, 2008.

There Is No Competition 2: The Funeral Service, Def Jam, 2010.

The S.O.U.L. Tape, Def Jam, 2011.

Sources

Periodicals

Billboard, May 12, 2007, p. 35.
Boston Herald, January 7, 2010.
Jet, June 16, 2003, p. 40.
New York Times, October 18, 2006; June 18, 2007.
Vibe, April 2003, p. 183.
Village Voice, February 5, 2008.

Online

Birchmeier, Jason, "Fabolous," All Music, http://www.allmusic.com/artist/fabolous-p483230 (accessed June 20, 2011).

Vineyard, Jennifer, "Fabolous Plans to Sue New York for False Arrest," MTV News, July 16, 2003, http://www.mtv.com/news/articles/1474060/fabolous-sue-new-york.jhtml (accessed June 20, 2011).

—Deborah A. Ring

Curt Flood

1938–1997

Professional baseball player

Flood, Curt, photograph. AP Images.

Although he amassed an impressive record as an outfielder and hitter while playing for the St. Louis Cardinals, Curt Flood is better known today for his precedent-setting challenge of major league baseball's reserve clause in 1970. Flood's suit against major league baseball over the rights of players to determine their own value on the open market opened the door to greater player rights in the decades that followed.

Overcame Racism and Excelled with Cardinals

Born in Houston, Texas, in 1938, Flood spent most of his childhood in Oakland, California, where he was a standout baseball player from an early age. He also developed, in junior high art classes, a deep attachment to drawing and painting that would remain with him through his life. As a baseball player for McClymonds High School in Oakland, Flood attracted the attention of scouts for the major league Cincinnati Reds organization. Upon graduation in 1956, he signed a contract with the team and reported to spring training in Tampa, Florida.

Although Jackie Robinson had officially breached the color line in major league baseball in 1946, integration had not, in the intervening years, proceeded uniformly among the league's various franchises, let alone in the minor leagues. Flood found himself, in Tampa and then while playing for Reds farm teams in North Carolina and Georgia during the Jim Crow era, faced with overt discrimination and denied numerous services and the basic dignity that his white teammates took for granted. "I used to break into tears as soon as I reached the safety of my room," he said of this era in *The Hard Road to Glory*. "I felt too young for that ordeal." Nevertheless, he posted impressive statistics and was called up to play stints with the Reds in both of his first two seasons.

After being traded to the St. Louis Cardinals after the 1958 season, Flood improved steadily to become one of the mainstays of the team. By 1964 he was considered by many to be one of the best center fielders in the major leagues. Armed with other outstanding players such as pitcher Bob Gibson and outfielder Lou Brock, the Cardinals won the National League pennant that

At a Glance . . .

Born Curtis Charles Flood, January 18, 1938, in Houston, TX; died January 20, 1997, in Los Angeles, CA; son of Herman (a hospital worker) and Laura (a hospital worker); married Beverly Collins, 1959 (divorced); married Judy Pace, 1978; children: Curt Flood Jr., Debbie Flood, Gary Flood, Shelly Flood, Scott Flood; stepchildren: Julia Flood, Shawn Flood.

Career: Minor league baseball player, Cincinnati Reds organization, 1956–58; Major League Baseball player, St. Louis Cardinals, 1959–69; Major League Baseball player, Washington Senators, 1971; portrait painter, 1960s–90s.

Awards: Set record for consecutive fielding chances without an error (568); received Rawlings Gold Glove Awards for fielding excellence, 1963–69; led National League in runs (112), 1963; led National League in hits (211), 1964; named to National League All-Star team three times.

year and defeated the New York Yankees in the World Series.

Peaked in the Late 1960s

The Cardinals were perpetual contenders during the 1960s, and Flood was a key ingredient in their success, generating especially impressive statistics as a fielder. During one stretch he set a major league record by playing 223 consecutive games without an error, for a total of 568 flawless fielding chances in a row. The Cardinals won the pennant again in 1967 and 1968, and they beat the Boston Red Sox in the 1967 World Series. During those seasons, Flood finished, respectively, fourth and fifth in batting in the league, with averages of .335 and .301. In 1968 he made the cover of *Sports Illustrated*, which declared him the best center fielder in the major leagues.

Having taken some art training in the late 1950s, Flood honed his painting talent into a marketable skill during his time in St. Louis. He painted three to four portraits every two weeks in the late 1960s, typically selling each for $250 to $350. His teammates called him "Rembrandt," and August Busch Jr., the Cardinals owner, commissioned a portrait from Flood and displayed it in his yacht. "Baseball and painting make a good balance," Flood told *Ebony*. "Baseball is virile. It's

rough and tough. Painting is sensitive, quiet. It's an outlet to overcome tension."

Despite his stellar performance during the 1968 season, Flood made a high-profile error in the World Series against Detroit that year. With the series tied at three games to three and the final game scoreless in the seventh inning, he misjudged a line drive and allowed what should have been a safe out to become a two-run triple. The Cardinals lost the game 4-1 and the series 4-3. Nevertheless, Flood refused the team's offer of a $77,500 salary for the following year, holding out for a contract worth $90,000, to which the club consented grudgingly.

By the standards he had set in preceding years, Flood posted sub-par statistics in 1969, batting only .285, and the Cardinals dropped to fourth place in the league. Still smarting from the salary dispute before the season, Cardinals owner Busch decided to trade Flood to Philadelphia. Flood had been with the team since 1958 and had a variety of business interests in the St. Louis area, and he did not want to be forced to leave. "There ain't no way I'm going to pack up and move twelve years of my life away from here," he told a friend, according to *Lords of the Realm*.

Challenged Baseball's Reserve Clause

The reserve clause that gave team owners total control over a player's professional life had been a sore point for years with players, and the Major League Players Association had already made attempts to change it. Flood and his lawyer, Allan H. Zerman, approached Marvin Miller, director of the Association, to see if the Association would support Flood's rejection of the clause. Flood's position was that the clause represented involuntary servitude and was therefore unconstitutional. Miller supported Flood but warned him that he was undertaking a thankless cause for which he would likely be denigrated by other players, management, and fans. But Flood believed himself to be fighting for his civil rights. In a letter to baseball commissioner Bowie Kuhn, he wrote, according to *USA Today*'s Sandy Grady, "After 12 years in the major leagues, I do not feel that I am a piece of property to be bought and sold irrespective of my wishes."

When Kuhn denied Flood's request to be allowed to determine his own future, Flood sued him, the presidents of the National and American Leagues, and all 24 major league clubs. The case came to trial in New York City in May of 1970, and Flood sat out the season as the trial progressed. His cause was indeed unpopular, as Miller had warned him it would be, and he was portrayed as a troublemaker motivated by simple greed. In August Flood's position was shot down by District Court Judge Irving Ben Cooper. Flood's legal

team then appealed the case to the Supreme Court, which ruled against him as well.

The pressure that Flood brought to bear on the league bore fruit outside of court, however, and strengthened solidarity among players. While arguing against Flood in court to uphold the reserve clause, the league opened up grievance hearings regarding the issue, which remained highly contested in subsequent years. In arbitration resulting from two different suits brought by players in 1975, the reserve clause was dismantled, completing the effort that Flood had begun and initiating the rise of free agency, whereby players became entitled to sell their skills to the highest bidders.

Died in Obscurity

Free agency went on to transform baseball into a sport characterized by player contracts running into the hundreds of millions and by the dominance of teams like the New York Yankees under owner George Steinbrenner, who were richer than other franchises and could thereby afford to assemble rosters of superstars. Many have bemoaned this state of affairs, and players, owners, and league management ostracized Flood in the later years of his life for having brought it about.

An attempt at a comeback with the Washington Senators in 1971 lasted only 13 games, and Flood was largely frozen out of Major League Baseball both professionally and socially in the years that followed. He became an alcoholic and had financial problems that compelled him to live for a time in Europe, before attempting to launch an alternative professional baseball league in the mid-1990s. That effort, designed to create a level playing field between players and owners, failed. Flood died of throat cancer on January 20, 1997, two days after turning 59. Although his illness was attributed to years of heavy drinking and smoking, his son Curt Flood Jr. wrote in *USA Today* in 2007, "[M]y old man died of a broken heart. And Major League Baseball broke it."

Despite having changed professional baseball arguably more than any other single individual in the twentieth century, Flood had not, as of 2011, been recognized officially by the league, the Cardinals organization, or players and fans in general. His name began to appear on Hall of Fame ballots, thanks to a handful of sportswriters who recognized the magnitude of his efforts, but the voting members of the Hall's Veterans Committee, made up of many of the players Flood had played against and alongside, as well as many others whose wealth would not have been possible without his ef-

forts, consistently failed to honor his legacy.

"He was a sacrificial lamb, and he knew it," Joe Torre, Flood's former Cardinals teammate and later a successful manager and league executive, told John Romano of the *St. Petersburg Times*. "He felt very strongly about what he was doing and, in spite of warnings that he may end his baseball career, he felt it was that important ... And it's very important for the players to be aware of that. They haven't always had this golden goose here."

Sources

Books

Ashe, Arthur Jr., *A Hard Road to Glory: A History of the African-American Athlete Since 1946*, Volume 3, Amistad, 1988, pp. 2022.

Flood, Curt, and Richard Carter, *The Way It Is*, Trident Press, 1970.

Helyar, John, *Lords of the Realm: The Real History of Baseball*, Villard, 1994, pp. 107–10, 246.

Schlossberg, Dan, *The Baseball Catalog*, Jonathan David Publishers, 1980, p. 301.

Snyder, Brad, *A Well-Paid Slave: Curt Flood's Fight for Free Agency in Professional Sports*, Viking, 2006.

Solomon, Abbot Neil, *Baseball Records Illustrated*, Chartwell Books, 1988, pp. 151–52.

Ward, Geoffrey C., and Ken Burns, *Baseball: An Illustrated History*, Knopf, 1994, pp. 339, 410.

Periodicals

Ebony, June 1968, pp. 143–45; July 1968, pp. 70–76; March 1970, pp. 110-11.

Encore, July 1973, pp. 62–63.

Jet, July 13, 1972, pp. 56–57; February 10, 1997, pp. 55–56.

Los Angeles Times, January 22, 1997.

New York Times, January 21, 1997, pp. B10, D23; October 26, 2006, p. D1; July 22, 2010, p. B12.

Sport, February 1988, p. 79; January 1994, p. 12; April 1995, p. 43.

Sporting News, January 15, 1990, pp. 37, 40; January 2, 1995, p. 32; February 3, 1997, p. 47.

Sports Illustrated, June 8, 1992, p. 68.

St. Petersburg Times, February 27, 2007, p. 1C.

USA Today, April 3, 2007, p. 15A; April 9, 2007, p. 11A.

Washington Post, January 22, 1997, p. D3.

—Ed Decker and Mark Lane

Thais Francis

1980—

Drama student

New York University drama student Thais Francis (her first name is pronounced tha-EES) has a lofty goal: to parlay the joy that she finds in acting to make the world a better and more understanding place. "The performing arts are among the most tangible forms of communication," she told The Root. "If they're used in a way to inspire, people can make a choice to change their lives." Already an accomplished actress, playwright, and essayist, she is putting that optimism into practice through her community service, teaching theater and dance to young people in New York schools. In 2010, Francis earned kudos for her award-winning essay on the Reverend Martin Luther King, "His Legacy Paves My Path."

A native of Trinidad and Tobago, Francis lived there until she was 10 years old, when her family relocated to the United States and settled in Bowie, Maryland, in the Washington, DC, area. As a student at Charles Herbert Flowers High School, she already was distinguishing herself for her thoughtful writing and speaking, winning a scholarship in the J. Franklyn Bourne Bar Association's annual Black History Month Oratorical Contest two years in a row. A standout student, she went on to enroll at New York University (NYU) in the Tisch School of the Arts, studying acting, singing, and dancing.

As a student, Francis performed in the theatrical orientation production NYU: The Reality Show created by director Elizabeth Swados and participated in Dance Theatre Etcetera's Summer Theatre Project as part of Maria Irene Fornes's What of the Night? In the

fall of 2010, she appeared Off Broadway at the Producers Club in the Veronica Page play Prayers for the Ghetto, in which a young Jewish girl and two African-American girls try to understand the crimes that have been perpetrated against their people.

For Francis, theater has a greater social purpose than just entertainment—she believes that it is a means of changing lives, and she views herself as an agent of that change. "I feel like acting is one of the most dynamic ways of conveying a message," she explained in a video on the website The Root. "And if someone sees a piece of art that I am a part of and it changes their life, I feel as if my purpose in terms of being an actress, a performer, a visionary, a revolutionary is fulfilled."

She went on to explain, "What I hope to do is use my art and my acting to inspire people. . . . I want to show people that theater is not only for a select few individuals, but everyone can relate to it because everyone can come to the theater and see things and they can hear things that pertain to their life. [I]f I create that theater and I'm a part of that, it is something bigger than me, it is bigger than me performing or being an actress or a dancer or a singer; it's me being a part of a change in someone's life for the better. And that's how I plan to change the world."

In January of 2010 Francis took first prize in a student essay contest at NYU, "Who Will Inspire You to Dream?" In her essay, titled "His Legacy Paves My Path," she wrote about the inspiration that she derives from Martin Luther King and elaborated her goals as an

At a Glance . . .

Born Thais Francis in 1980 in Trinidad and Tobago. *Education*: New York University, BFA, 2012.

Addresses: New York University, 70 Washington Square South, New York City, NY 10012.

actress: "When I read about Dr. King or watch films about his legacy, I am awed. Ambition spills out of my heart and determination crowds my mind. If I could summon the strength, endurance and philosophy of Dr. King I am sure that my hope for social justice through theater is within grasp. I aspire to act in, produce and write works that enlighten the world."

That same year, in April, Francis was one of 27 students from across the country chosen to present a paper at the Undergraduate Ethics Symposium at DePauw University. The symposium offered an opportunity for Francis and other undergraduates to take part in a dialog with leading scholars about the ethical issues facing us today. In her paper, Francis personified Africa as a young woman and explored the way in which we treat others. "It is important to think of how we treat others ethically, and consider the long-term consequences of our actions," she wrote. "Should we rethink the way we treat others in order to mend wounds, and prevent future hurt? Francis also represented NYU at the citywide Miss Caribbean New York Pageant, aimed at promoting awareness of Caribbean culture; as part of the competition, she performed Bob Marley's "Redemption Song."

Francis was selected by The Root in 2011 as one of 25 "Young Futurists," innovators under the age of 21 who are making extraordinary contributions to the world. She will graduate from New York University in the spring of 2012. She plans to pursue a career as an actress on Broadway and in film, with a particular emphasis on works with a message.

Sources

Online

New York University, Student Essay Contest, http://www.nyu.edu/life/events-traditions/mlk-week/student-essay.html (accessed June 30, 2011).

"Tisch Undergrad's Paper Chosen for Ethics Symposium at DePauw University," New York University, March 25, 2010, http://www.nyu.edu/about/news-publications/news/2010/03/25/tisch_undergrad_s_pa.html (accessed June 30, 2011).

"Veronica Page's 'Prayers for the Ghetto,'" Harlem World, December 19, 2010, https://harlemworldblog.wordpress.com/tag/thais-francis/ (accessed June 30, 2011).

Werner, Annie, "Thais Francis to Represent NYU in 1st Annual Miss Caribbean New York Pageant," April 2, 2010, http://nyulocal.com/on-campus/2010/04/02/thais-francis-to-represent-nyu-in-1st-annual-miss-caribbean-new-york-pageant/ (accessed June 30, 2011).

"Young Futurists: Thais Francis," January 31, 2011, http://www.theroot.com/content/thais-francis (accessed June 30, 2011).

—Deborah A. Ring

Michael Franti

1966—

Musician

Franti, Michael, photograph. AP Images/Vince Bucci/PictureGroup.

Michael Franti fronts the band Spearhead, one of the more enduring and innovative hip-hop acts in American music. The singer, songwriter, and political activist is often pegged on a line of musical heroes that includes Marvin Gaye, Gil Scott-Heron, and Chuck D of Public Enemy. In an interview with Elizabeth A. DiNovella in the *Progressive,* Franti reflected on the changes since he started his career as part of black punk-pioneers the Beatnigs in the late 1980s. "When hip-hop was really about Afro-centric ideals," he pointed out, "you weren't selling the numbers of units that you are today. That music was being bought by people who were concerned about those issues, mostly black people. But today you have songs about gang life that are a way for kids in the suburbs who don't live that type of life to live vicariously through the music. So those types of songs will sell a lot."

Cofounded the Beatnigs

Franti's surname comes from his adoptive parents, who were Finnish Americans. Charles Franti, an epidemiologist, and his wife, Carole, adopted their son out of the foster care system. Franti later learned his birth parents' names, and that his maternal grandparents had urged their daughter to put her biracial infant up for adoption shortly after his 1966 birth. Franti's formative years were spent in Davis, California, home to a large University of California campus, and he emerged as a talented basketball player in high school. He won an athletic scholarship to the University of San Francisco, where he found himself more drawn to the anti-apartheid movement on campus. He began writing poetry to express his creative urges and dropped out for a semester, taking a job in a commercial bakery. "I'd put these frozen cakes in these boxes and push the button, and the machine would go boom-chee-cha-chee," he recalled in the interview with DiNovella in the *Progressive.* "It had this rhythm to it. We started making rhymes to the rhythm of the machine."

After picking up a bass guitar in a pawn shop, Franti teamed with four other like-minded young adults in San Francisco and started a band. Calling themselves the Beatnigs, they played protest songs that were heavily influenced by the Bay Area's dynamic punk-rock and jazz scenes but with a heavy dose of industrial music, a subgenre whose artists deployed actual power tools to

At a Glance . . .

Born on April 21, 1966, in Oakland, CA; son of Charles Franti (an epidemiologist) and Carole Franti; married Tara Franti-Rye; children: (from a previous relationship) Cappy; (with Franti-Rye) Ade. *Education*: Attended the University of San Francisco, late 1980s.

Career: Musician. Founding member of the Beatnigs, 1986; band signed to Alternative Tentacles label; formed Disposable Heroes of Hiphoprisy with Rono Tse; released *Hypocrisy Is the Greatest Luxury,* 1992; opened for Arrested Development and U2 on concert tours, then disbanded; formed Spearhead, 1994; released *Home,* 1994; has also released spoken-word albums and produced-directed the documentary film *I Know I Am Not Alone,* 2005.

Addresses: *Record company*—Six Degrees Records, PO Box 411347, San Francisco, CA 94141-1347. *Web*— http://michaelfranti.com/.

create sound. The quintet was signed to Alternative Tentacles, a label founded by the punk-rock legend Jello Biafra, the onetime frontman for hardcore California punk pioneers the Dead Kennedys. The Beatnigs' self-titled debut was released in 1988 to modest critical acclaim, and *Spin* magazine profiled them in its February 1989 issue. The band chose the somewhat controversial name, Franti told music journalist Tony Fletcher, in part because "things in our society have not changed very much for a number of oppressed people since the time, in fact, of the beatniks," the literary rule-breakers of the late 1950s. "We use that word " as a reminder that we have to take it upon ourselves to promote change."

The Beatnigs eventually disbanded, and then Franti and one former bandmate, Rono Tse, started a new band they called the Disposable Heroes of Hiphoprisy. Once again, Franti's musical style defied easy categorization, with influences borrowed from hip-hop, jazz, and electronica, but his songs were still forcefully political in their lyrics. The Heroes released one intensely lauded album, *Hypocrisy Is the Greatest Luxury,* and received an enormous boost after being chosen to play opening slots on U2's mega-selling Zoo TV tour in 1992, but their album's biggest hit came with a reworking of a Beatnigs tune, "Television: The Drug of the Nation." The Heroes disbanded after working with the infamous Beatnik-era poet William S. Burroughs. "The truth is that Disposable Heroes wasn't even a record I would listen to at home," Franti said later in a *Rolling*

Stone interview with writer David Wild. "The big problem with Disposable Heroes was that it was a record people listened to because it was good for them—kind of like broccoli."

Broke with Major Label

In 1994 Franti put together a new band, Spearhead. Backed by a pair of vocalists, and featuring a shifting array of talented Bay Area musicians, the new outfit better showcased his own musical influences and the direction he wanted to explore in his music. With strains of soul, jazz, electronica, hip hop, reggae, and other world-music elements, Spearhead attracted major-label attention and was signed to Capitol Records, which released its debut LP, *Home,* in 1994.

The effort won major critical accolades. "Where Disposable Heroes spent its album issuing grim pronouncements," Ira Robbins wrote in the Trouser Press record guide, the new album "takes a subtler route, shining a megadose of deliriously warm sunlight to illuminate serious issues—poverty, HIV, police, suicide—as well as such cultural signifiers as food, basketball and nightlife." In *Vibe* Tricia Rose commended the Spearhead debut, which she judged to be "rich with the spirit of a young, adult black masculinity. . . . *Home* explores a range of ways to be a black man by going where vulnerability, fire, rage, and love hide out." One track, "Positive," about awaiting the result of an HIV test, received some college-radio airplay and was included on the 1994 benefit-compilation album *Stolen Moments: Red Hot + Cool.*

Franti put out one more record with Spearhead for the Capitol label, 1997's *Chocolate Supa Highway,* which failed to produce any hits. A new management team at Capitol suggested he team with Will Smith for a duet, which prompted Franti to hire a lawyer and spend the better part of a year extricating himself from the contract. He then launched his own label, Boo Boo Wax, with fellow Spearhead members and inked a distribution deal with Six Degrees, another independent label. The group's first effort dramatically showcased the new climate of artistic freedom: the 2001 album *Stay Human,* a conceptual work whose title is the name of a fictitious pirate radio station broadcasting the case of an innocent woman on death row. For years Franti had been one of the many vocal supporters of Mumia Abu-Jamal, a onetime Black Panther whose 1982 criminal trial for the killing of a Philadelphia police officer has been the source of debate and controversy for years. "I had really been wanting to write about the death penalty," Franti told *New York Times* journalist Ann Powers. "As I thought about it, I asked myself, How can I write about it in one song? It was too complex."

Visited Post-Invasion Baghdad

Franti and his Spearhead bandmates put out a 2003

record, *Everyone Deserves Music,* and he also issued a solo record—his first—titled *Songs from the Front Porch.* However, Franti was increasingly distressed by what he and other liberals viewed as an even more repressive political climate in United States than the Reagan-era 1980s, when Franti first found his voice as a protest songwriter. He decided to visit Iraq a year after the U.S.-led invasion, taking along a documentary film crew. They arrived in Baghdad in the spring of 2004, just days after a kidnapped American contractor was beheaded on video and the footage released to news sources. Franti and his adventurers found it was surprisingly easy to enter Iraq, which was technically a war zone, but that once outside the airport, "I felt every second that I was there like something would happen," he told Dorian Lynskey in the *Guardian* about the streets of Baghdad. "The only time I didn't feel afraid was when I was playing music, because suddenly everyone was happy. So I would play music as much as I could."

Franti served as producer and director of *I Know I Am Not Alone,* the documentary released in 2005 that showcased the trip to Iraq, Israel, and even the Gaza Territory. The next Spearhead effort, *Yell Fire!,* was released in 2006, and made a surprising appearance on the *Billboard* 200 album chart, peaking at No. 125. For his sixth Spearhead record, Franti traveled to Jamaica to work with noted reggae-production duo Sly & Robbie, who turned one of Franti's slower folk songs, "Say Hey (I Love You)," into an infectious dancehall-tinged stomp. It turned out to become the first genuine hit of Franti's career, but the timing of that feat became its own parable for fame: while playing tour dates with the Counting Crows in July of 2009, Franti began to suffer abdominal pains on stage. Rushed to the hospital after the show, Franti was told his appendix had burst and he would have to undergo surgery. Friends told him of the chart success as he was being wheeled to the operating room after doctors warned him his health crisis was approaching dire status. "I'm thinking, 'Great, I have a hit song after all these years and I'll never hear it on the radio,'" he told *Billboard*'s Gail Mitchell. However, Franti survived the surgery and recovered quickly enough to return to his scheduled tour with the Counting Crows.

Franti has spoken openly about the shift in his beliefs, toward a more humanist outlook, that he has gained via regular yoga practice, his trip to the Middle East, and even his ruptured appendix. His music has changed accordingly since his college-era punk-rock days in San Francisco, becoming bubblier as he realized that people, even Palestinians in the restricted territories of Gaza, were uninterested in the standard angry protest anthem. "Joy is a more powerful thing than any kind of political statement," he told Andrew Dansby in the *Houston Chronicle.* "That's what my mission has been now: not to make music that's politically inspired for this time but to make music to help people get through difficult times."

Selected discography

With The Beatnigs

The Beatnigs, Alternative Tentacles, 1988.

With Disposable Heroes of Hiphoprisy

Hypocrisy Is the Greatest Luxury (includes "Television: The Drug of the Nation"), 4th & Broadway, 1992.

With Spearhead

Home (includes "Positive"), Capitol, 1994.
Chocolate Supa Highway, Capitol, 1997.
Stay Human, Boo Boo Wax/Six Degrees Records, 2001.
Everyone Deserves Music, Boo Boo Wax/Parlophone, 2003.
Yell Fire!, Anti/Liberation, 2006.
All Rebel Rockers, Boo Boo Wax, 2008.
The Sound of Sunshine (includes "Say Hey [I Love You]"), Capitol/Boo Boo Wax, 2010.

Solo

Songs from the Front Porch, Boo Boo Wax/Six Degrees Records, 2003.
Live at the Baobab, Boo Boo Wax, 2007.

Sources

Periodicals

Billboard, September 12, 2009, p. 31.
Guardian (London), July 26, 2006.
Houston Chronicle, May 5, 2011, p. 14.
News Tribune (Tacoma, WA), March 26, 2010.
New York Times, June 27, 2001.
Progressive, February 2002, p. 39.
Rolling Stone, January 26, 1995.
Spin, February 1989, p. 20.
Vibe, November 1994; June 2002, p. 64.

Online

Robbins, Ira, "Spearhead," TrouserPress.com, http://www.trouserpress.com/entry.php?a=spearhead (accessed July 26, 2011).

—Carol Brennan

Doug E. Fresh

1966—

Musician

Doug E. Fresh pioneered beatboxing, or emulating the sounds of early drum machines, at the dawn of the hip-hop era in the early 1980s. Known as "the Human Beat Box," he was still in his teens when he appeared in the film *Beat Street* and had a string of hits with his Get Fresh Crew, which for a time included the rapper later known as Slick Rick. Fresh saw his career revived in 2010 when the rap act Cali Swag District paid homage to him in the single "Teach Me How to Dougie."

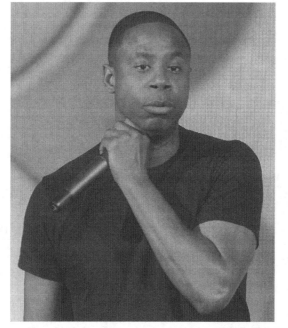

Fresh, Doug E., photograph. AP Images/Brad Barket/Picture-Group.

event where hip-hop legend Kurtis Blow was scheduled to perform. When the crew misplaced the turntables, Fresh was recruited to provide some of the backing sounds. That led to his first single, "Pass the Budda," done with Spoonie Gee and DJ Spivey, in 1983 for Spotlight Records, and he was signed as a solo artist to Enjoy Records, one of the first labels to put out hip-hop records in this era. The label was owned by longtime Harlem record store owner Bobby Robinson, and Fresh's label-mates included the aforementioned Gee plus Grandmaster Flash and the Furious Five as well as the Treacherous Three. His single "Just Having Fun" came out in 1984, and he turned up in the 1984 movie *Beat Street* during the stage performance of the Treacherous Three—Kool Moe Dee's original crew—and their song "Santa's Rap." He also cut another single, "Original Human Beatbox," for the Vinentertainment label that same year.

Fresh was born Douglas E. Davis on September 17, 1966, in the parish of Christ Church on the Caribbean island of Barbados. His family immigrated to New York City and settled in West Harlem, where Fresh discovered the poems of Langston Hughes and began writing his own verse. His beatboxing skills also developed at an early age, inspired by the noise of 1970s-era Harlem. "I started to mimic the different sounds," he told Michael Hewlett in the *Winston-Salem Journal.* "I would expand on it."

Gained Fame through Beatboxing

Fresh's first brush with fame came when he attended an

A mutual friend introduced Fresh to MC Ricky D, born Ricky Walters, who would later change his professional name to Slick Rick. Teaming with Barry Bee and Chill Will, they called themselves the Get Fresh Crew and began shopping for a label deal. Finally, Reality

At a Glance . . .

Born Douglas E. Davis on September 17, 1966, in Christ Church, Barbados; children: Solomon "Trips" Davis, Dayquan "Slim" Davis. *Religion*: Church of Scientology.

Career: New York beatboxing performer, early 1980s; recorded single "Pass the Budda" with Spoonie Gee and DJ Spivey for Spotlight Records, 1983; signed to Enjoy Records and released "Just Having Fun," 1984; appeared in the film *Beat Street*, 1984; signed to Reality Records and released first full-length LP with the Get Fresh Crew, *Oh, My God!*, 1986; signed to MC Hammer's Bust It Records, early 1990s; signed to Gee Street/Island Records, 1993; recorded with the E-Z Rollers and performed with Square Off; opened Doug E's, a Harlem restaurant, 2010.

Addresses: *Office*—c/o Doug E.'s, 2245 Adam Clayton Powell Jr. Blvd., New York, NY 10027.

Records signed them and assigned producer Dennis Bell to work with them in the studio. In 1985 their first single, "The Show" became a massive hit, as did its B-side, "La Di Da Di." The 12-inch was just the fourth rap record to achieve gold status as certified by the Recording Industry Association of America (RIAA) and fared equally well in Britain, even making it into the Top Five; for a time it held the spot as the top-selling rap single in European chart history. "The record is a perverse phenomenon," wrote John Leland in *Spin* a few months later. "People who don't like rap like it; people who like rap love it. In its own sly way, it mocks the whole conceit of macho posturing that is at the core of hip hop."

Both tracks appeared on the 1986 full-length release from Fresh and the Get Fresh Crew, *Oh, My God!* For a time Fresh had a spirited rivalry with another beatboxer, Darren Robinson of the Fat Boys, one of rap's first successfully mainstream acts. Ricky D left the Get Fresh Crew after that album and did not appear on the next LP, *The World's Greatest Entertainer*, released on Reality Records in 1988. Its lead single, "Keep Risin' to the Top," borrowed from a classic bass riff pulled out of a 1981 song by Chicago soul singer Keni Burke (of "O-o-h Child" fame) titled "Risin' to the Top." In the summer of 1988 Fresh and his crew played tour dates with Tony! Toni! Toné!. Reporting in the *New York Times* about a performance at New York City's Palladium nightclub, music journalist Peter Watrous wrote, "The audience, knowing its cues, set up the chant 'Go Dougie! Go Dougie!' . . . At the end of the

first number, he looked around as if he and the audience had just pulled off something astonishing."

Ricky D, meanwhile, turned up on Def Jam Records as Slick Rick, his new name, and issued one of that year's best-selling rap albums, *The Great Adventures of Slick Rick*. However, the divergent lifestyles of the two—both of Caribbean heritage—was thought to be the root of their split, with Fresh favoring tracks like the quasi-religious "All the Way to Heaven" and rejecting Slick Rick's "Treat Her Like a Prostitute," which appeared on his Def Jam debut. In 1990 Rick was involved in a shooting incident and spent the better part of the decade incarcerated on Rikers Island.

Originated "The Dougie" Dance Sensation

Fresh's own corporate home, Reality Records, was part of the Fantasy label empire run by Saul Zaentz, who made a small fortune from the rock band Creedence Clearwater Revival in the late 1960s and then engaged in a fractious legal battle with the band's singer-songwriter John Fogerty, which dragged on for years. Fresh eventually signed with MC Hammer's new label, Bust It Records, and released *Doin' What I Gotta Do* in 1992. The album's biggest hit was "Bustin' Out (on Funk)," which paid homage to a Rick James track from 1979, but failed to capture the success of Fresh's two earlier albums. He then signed with a British label called Gee Street—part of Island Records at the time—and put out one epic 1993 single that contained three songs: "Freaks," "I-ight (Alright)," and "Bounce." He re-teamed with Slick Rick for a track on his 1995 release for Gee Street called *Play*, but his career faltered after that, and there was a seven-year hiatus between singles from 1997's "Superstition" to 2004, when he and Nas guested on the Ludacris track "Virgo."

By 2007 Fresh was performing with his sons' act, Square Off, and was invited to make an appearance on the finale of *American Idol*'s sixth season. He joined finalist Blake Lewis on stage to reprise "The Show," the first hip-hop track ever performed on the hit series. Later that year, Fresh's signature dance move—a swipe of the hand past the ear that was informally known as "The Dougie"—was brought back to life by Dallas rapper Lil' Wil. "My Dougie" appeared on the 2007 LP *Dolla$, TX*. Lil' Wil was not even born when "The Show/La Di Da Di" was released, but his mother had been a fan. Another rap act, Cali Swag District from Inglewood, California, further revived interest in vintage Fresh with the song "Teach Me How to Dougie" in 2010. Fresh even performed with them in June of 2010 at a pre-BET Awards concert event. The following spring, First Lady Michelle Obama showed off several dance moves, including a smooth "Dougie," during an impromptu dance off at a District of Columbia middle school. Mrs. Obama was in attendance as

part of her "Let's Move" campaign to eradicate childhood obesity when she stepped forward to join the kids dancing to Beyoncé's "Move Your Body" track; the video footage gained popularity online for several days, and the First Lady even cracked jokes with Health and Human Services Secretary Kathleen Sebelius a few weeks later over the correct pronunciation of the "Dougie."

Fresh is a member of the Church of Scientology, whose celebrity adherents include Tom Cruise and John Travolta. His name has occasionally surfaced in the news over back taxes owed to the Internal Revenue Service. In 2010 he opened a soul food and Caribbean restaurant in New York City called Doug E.'s at the corner of West 132nd Street and Adam Clayton Powell Jr. Boulevard. "Thank you for the love and support over the years and for those who are just meeting me now, get ready for some new music and a lot more fun," he said in a live chat on ESPN's SportsNation Web portal. "And if you're ever in Harlem, come by Doug E.'s restaurant and tell them I sent you. If you tell them I sent you and you do the Dougie, I'll give you a waffle for free."

Selected works

Albums

(With the Get Fresh Crew) *Oh, My God!,* Reality/Danya Records, 1986.
(With the Get Fresh Crew) *The World's Greatest Entertainer* (includes "Keep Risin' to the Top"), Reality/Danya Records, 1988.
(With New Get Fresh Crew) *Doin' What I Gotta Do* (includes "Bustin' Out [On Funk]"), Bust It Records, 1992.
Play, Gee Street/Island Records, 1995.
Alright, Gee Street/Island Records, 1996.

Singles

(With Spoonie Gee and DJ Spivey) "Pass the Budda,"
Spotlight, 1983.
"Just Having Fun," Enjoy, 1984.
"Original Human Beatbox," Vinentertainment, 1984.
"The Show"/"La Di Da Di," Reality/Danya Records, 1985.
"Freaks"/"I-ight (Alright)"/"Bounce," Gee Street/Island Records, 1993.
"Superstition," Hollywood Records, 1997.
(Featured performer with Nas), Ludacris, "Virgo," Disturbing Tha Peace/Def Jam, 2004.

Books

Hipkidhop (with audio CD), illustrated by Joseph Buckingham, Scholastic Inc., 2002.

Sources

Periodicals

Atlanta Journal-Constitution, November 8, 2010, p. D2.
New York Times, July 21, 1988.
San Jose Mercury News, January 4, 2007.
Spin, May 1986.
Winston-Salem Journal, March 12, 2009.

Online

"Chat with Doug E. Fresh," SportsNation, ESPN, December 10, 2010, http://espn.go.com/sports nation/chat/_/id/35972/rapper-doug-e-fresh (accessed July 26, 2011).
"Doug E. Fresh," MTV.com, http://www.mtv.com/music/artist/doug_e_fresh/artist.jhtml#biographyEnd (accessed July 26, 2011).
Sietsema, Robert, "Doug E. Fresh Finally Gets It Together (Badah Badah Badha) at Harlem Restaurant," Village Voice, December 6, 2010, http://blogs.villagevoice.com/forkintheroad/2010/12/doug_e_fresh_fi.php (accessed July 26, 2011).

—Carol Brennan

Roscoe C. Giles

1890–1970

Physician

Giles, Roscoe C., photograph. Charles E. Steinheimer/Time & Life Pictures/Getty Images.

Roscoe C. Giles was the first African-American graduate of Cornell University College of Medicine and the first African American to be certified by the American Board of Surgery. A prominent physician and community figure in Chicago, Illinois, from 1915 until his death in 1970, Giles was recognized as one of the top surgeons in the city, serving on the staff at several major hospitals and publishing a number of professional papers over the course of his career. He consistently advanced the cause of equality in the medical field. In addition to leading by example through his pioneering roles at Cornell and the American Board of Surgery, he fought for institutional change within the American Medical Association (AMA) and the U.S. military.

Born in Albany, New York, on May 6, 1890, Roscoe Conkling Giles was the son of Francis F. Giles, a minister who became a prominent attorney, and Laura C. Giles. The family lived in Brooklyn, New York, where Giles attended Boys' High School. While at Boys', he won an oratory award and a scholarship to Cornell University, in Ithaca, New York, worth $600. He entered Cornell in 1907, studying literature, win-

ning a spot on the school's rowing team, and joining the fraternity Alpha Phi Alpha. Upon taking his bachelor's degree in 1911, he was admitted to the Cornell University College of Medicine in New York City.

The first African American admitted to the medical school, Giles immediately encountered obstacles meant to preserve the discriminatory status quo. The secretary of the faculty asked Giles to leave the school, according to a *Chicago Defender* article published in 1917, and he received death threats for daring to break the institution's color line. He persevered with his studies, however, graduating with honors in 1915. That same year, Giles began an internship at Chicago's Provident Hospital, the first black-owned hospital in the United States, after being denied a place at New York's Bellevue Hospital because of his race. The following year, Giles scored highest among all candidates for junior physician positions in Chicago, but he was again denied the post he was seeking at the city's Municipal Tuberculosis Sanitarium on account of his race.

In January of 1917 Giles married Frances Reeder, a nurse trained at Provident and employed by the Chi-

At a Glance . . .

Born Roscoe Conkling Giles on May 6, 1890, in Albany, NY; died on February 19, 1970, in Chicago, IL; son of Francis Fenard Giles (a minister and attorney) and Laura Caldwell Giles; married Frances Reeder on January 9, 1917; children: Roscoe I (died in infancy), Oscar, Roscoe II. *Education*: Cornell University, AB, 1911; Cornell College of Medicine, MD, 1915; University of Vienna, Julius Rosenwald fellow in surgery, 1930–31. *Military service*: U.S. Army Medical Corps, achieved rank of lieutenant colonel during World War II; Officers' Reserve Corps. *Religion*: Christian.

Career: Physician in private practice (Chicago, IL), 1915–60s; Provident Hospital, Cook County Hospital, West Side Veterans Hospital, staff surgeon and teaching surgeon; author of numerous professional papers published in medical journals.

Memberships: Alpha Phi Alpha Fraternity, American Board of Surgery, American Medical Association, Chicago Medical Society, Free and Accepted Masons, International College of Surgeons, John A. Andrews Clinical Society (Tuskegee, AL), National Medical Association.

Awards: Named one of the "100 Outstanding Citizens of Chicago," 1957.

cago public school system. The couple had three children, the first of whom, named after his father, died in infancy. The Gileses later had twin sons, one of whom was again named for his father and the other of whom was named after Oscar DePriest, a Chicago alderman who had helped Giles with his career. Frances Giles became, with her husband, a prominent figure among Chicago's black elite, assuming a leading role in numerous civic and social organizations.

Giles ultimately made a spot for himself at Municipal Tuberculosis Sanitarium as well as at the South Side Tuberculosis Dispensary, and he launched a private practice in 1917. He also began teaching at Provident Hospital, helping to establish what would become one of the most important U.S. institutions for the training of black postgraduate medical students. In the following years Giles added to his reputation as a top physician by publishing numerous papers in the *Journal of the National Medical Association*. The National Medical Association (NMA), an African-American counterpart to the mainstream AMA, extended Giles an offer of membership in 1926. Over the following decades Giles continued writing on a variety of subjects for medical journals, including tuberculosis, appendicitis, intestinal problems, bone disorders, and gall stones.

The Giles family lived in Vienna, Austria, in 1930 and 1931, so that Giles could do postgraduate surgical study at the University of Vienna. Granted fellowships from the University of Chicago and the Julius Rosenwald fund to pursue the training, Giles described his experience to the *Chicago Defender* thus: "One finds himself surrounded everywhere by mementos of the men who have made an intelligible impression upon the medical thought of the world. . . . Every door is open and nowhere can one find any limitations because of color or creed." While in Europe, Frances Giles studied languages, the Giles children were enrolled in a private school, and the family toured Austria, Italy, and France.

In 1935 Giles was elected president of the NMA, a confirmation of the high regard in which he was held among black physicians in Chicago and beyond. During and after his tenure as president, Giles worked with the organization to lobby for increased equality for African Americans within the medical field. Giles played a leading role in NMA appeals to the AMA for a relaxing of discriminatory professional practices, including the failure, in many parts of the United States, of local AMA chapters to recognize black physicians, which made it difficult for these physicians to practice their profession effectively. Giles also led a committee within the NMA to lobby for the removal of the abbreviation "col." (signifying "colored") that had accompanied the names of African-American doctors listed in the organization's national directory; and a committee to further the rights of black physicians within the U.S. military, urging that they be appointed to positions of authority.

In 1938 Giles's status at the top of his field was further recognized when he became the first African American to gain admission to the American Board of Surgery. Open to those who had demonstrated particular distinction in surgical matters, who had undergone specialized postgraduate training, who had published professionally about matters of import to their peers, and who could pass a thorough examination, membership in the group was considered among the highest honors for a practicing surgeon.

Following the attack on Pearl Harbor and the U.S. entry into World War II, Giles served in the Army Medical Corps, which posted him to Fort Huachuca, Arizona, where he was named chief surgeon of a military hospital and promoted in 1943 to the rank of lieutenant colonel. Upon the war's end, he served in the Officers' Reserve Corps and was a consultant to the Secretary of War.

In 1945 Giles became a founding member of the International College of Surgeons, and he was admitted to another top professional organization, the American College of Surgeons, which had for the previous 20 years admitted no African Americans. In 1947 he joined the staff of Cook County Hospital, Chicago's largest and one of the nation's most prominent medical facilities. During the latter years of his career he worked as a surgeon there and at Westside Veterans Hospital, and he remained active in private practice into the 1960s.

Giles died after a prolonged illness on February 19, 1970, in Chicago. He is remembered as a pioneer in black medicine and one of the most highly regarded surgeons of his time.

Sources

Books

Organ, Claude H., and Margaret Kosiba, eds., *A Century of Black Surgeons: The U.S.A. Experience*, Volume 1., Transcript Press, 1987.

Periodicals

Chicago Defender, June 16, 1917, p. 5; August 3, 1918, p. 16; September 17, 1927, p. 5; December 21, 1929, p. 5; December 19, 1931, p. 6; April 16, 1932, p. 13; August 24, 1935, p. 3; October 1, 1938, p. 3; November 19, 1938, p. 2; December 22, 1945, p. 3; August 16, 1947, p. 2; February 21, 1970, p. 1.
Journal of Negro Education, Vol. 12 (3), Summer 1943, pp. 335–44.

—Mark Lane

Peter J. Gomes

1942–2011

Scholar, theologian

As Harvard University's Plummer Professor of Christian Morals and minister of the Memorial Church located on storied Harvard Yard, Peter J. Gomes was one of the school's most visible and beloved faculty members for more than 40 years before his sudden demise in 2011. Gomes's famously mellifluous baritone was often the first official voice to greet incoming freshman at Harvard and one of the final speakers at their commencement ceremonies as he delivered the closing prayer over the newly minted grads. His profile rose considerably in the early 1990s when he took a strong stance against homophobia and admitted he was a gay man as well as a minister, a Baptist, an African American, and a registered Republican. A minor furor erupted, but Gomes remained on the job and went on to write a well-received 1996 book that served as a counter to the Christian fundamentalist movement. "Those who speak for the religious right do not speak for all American Christians," he wrote in a *New York Times* op-ed piece, "and the Bible is not theirs alone to interpret."

Hailed from African, Virginian Roots

Peter John Gomes was born on May 22, 1942, in Boston, an only child. His father, Peter Lobo Gomes, was born in the Cape Verde Islands in 1908. The elder Gomes immigrated to the United States in the 1920s and settled in Plymouth, Massachusetts. He found work in the cranberry bogs around the area, eventually rising to the position of superintendent at one of them.

Gomes's mother, Orissa Josephine White, was born on Boston's wealthy Beacon Hill in 1901. One of nine children, she was the daughter of Jacob Merrit Pedford White, a well-to-do Baptist minister originally from Virginia, and graduated from the New England Conservatory of Music. She was the first African-American woman to work in the Massachusetts State House, where she was a clerk.

In his public-school student years in Plymouth, Gomes demonstrated an early precocity for academics, classical music, and the ministry. Raised in the Baptist faith, he first preached his own sermon when he was only 12 years old and authored the entry on Plymouth, Massachusetts, for the 1960 edition of the *Americana Encyclopedia* while still in high school. One of his first jobs was at the Plymouth Public Library, where he had charge of the research and genealogy department. Gomes graduated as president of his class from Plymouth High School in 1961, and he enrolled at Bates College in Lewiston, Maine, that fall. He paid his way through school with work as the organist and choirmaster of the First Congregational Church in Lewiston and by working summers at the Pilgrim Hall museum in Plymouth. He also held the Theodore Presser Scholarship in music during all of his four years at Bates.

Devoted to Historical Scholarship

A history major, Gomes was not yet convinced that the clergy was his calling. "I thought religion was for nice but weak-minded people and believed I had to give it up

At a Glance . . .

Born Peter John Gomes (rhymes with "homes") on May 22, 1942, in Boston, MA; died of a brain aneurysm and heart attack on February 28, 2011, in Boston; son of Peter Lobo (a cranberry bog worker) and Orissa Josephine (a government employee; maiden name, White) Gomes. *Education*: Bates College, BA, 1965; Harvard University, BD, 1968; New England College, DD, 1974. *Politics*: Democrat. *Religion*: Baptist.

Career: Ordained minister in the American Baptist Church, 1968; Tuskegee Institute, history instructor and director of Freshman Experimental Program, 1968–70; Harvard University, Memorial Church, assistant minister, 1970–74, Pusey minister, 1974–2011; Harvard University, Plummer Professor of Morals, 1974–2011; W.E.B. DuBois Institute for Afro-American History, acting director, 1989–91; Nannerl Keohane Distinguished Visiting Professor at University of North Carolina—Chapel Hill and Duke Divinity School, 2008.

Memberships: Phi Beta Kappa (trustee); International Defense Fund and Aid in South Africa; American Baptist Historical Society; National Association of University Chaplains; Massachusetts Historical Society; Colonial Society of Massachusetts; North Baptist Educational Society (director after 1973); Royal Society of Chorale Music; Handel and Haydn Society (governor, 1991–93); New England Conservatory of Music (member, Board of Overseers, 1991–94); Pilgrim Society (trustee, after 1972, and president, 1989–92); trustee of the Roxbury Latin School, after 1982, of Wellesley College, 1985–97, of the Boston Foundation, 1985–90, of Bates College, 1989–95 and again after 2001, and of the Public Broadcasting Service, 1992–96.

Awards: Rockefeller fellow, 1967–68; Pilgrim Society award for history, 1970; honorary chair, North American Friends of Emmanuel College (Cambridge University), 1986; fellow, Emmanuel College, Cambridge University, 1996; Earle B. Pleasant Clergy of the Year Award, Religion in America, 1998; Benjamin Elijah Mays Award, Bates College, 1998; Harvard University Phi Beta Kappa Teaching Award, 2001; Spirituality & Health Award for "one of the best spiritual books of 2002, for *The Good Life: Truths That Last in Times of Need*; Preston N. Williams Award, Harvard Divinity School, 2006; awarded several dozen honorary degrees.

if I wanted to be a real intellectual," he told Robert S. Boynton, who profiled him for the *New Yorker* in 1996. By his senior year he planned to become the first curator of American Decorative Arts at the Boston Museum of Fine Arts. Upon graduation in 1965, he was persuaded to spend a trial year at the Harvard Divinity School. One year stretched into three, and Gomes earned his Bachelor of Divinity in 1968. While there, he won the Harvard preaching prize, served as proctor of Divinity Hall, and chaired both the Worship and Publications committees.

After graduation Gomes was offered a position teaching history at the Tuskegee Institute in Alabama. He taught humanities courses there from 1968 to 1970. The embodiment of a Yankee blue blood, Gomes experienced some culture shock in Alabama. "I saw more black people in my first half hour at Tuskegee than I had ever seen in my entire life," he commented in the *New Yorker* interview. During his two years at Tuskegee, Gomes directed the Freshman Experimental Program, which he has described as "an innovative seminar-based experiment in the reorganization of the freshman year."

Gomes also served as choirmaster at St. Andrew's Episcopal Church in Tuskegee and assisted at the Institute Chapel. Although he expressed to Boynton that he would have been content to spend the rest of his life at Tuskegee, fate intervened. In 1970 Gomes was appointed assistant minister of Harvard's Memorial Church. His rise was rapid. In 1972 he was acting minister, and by 1974 he held the dual positions of minister to the Memorial Church and Plummer Professor of Christian Morals.

Emerged from Ivy League Closet

Gomes was named one of America's seven "star preachers" by *Time* in 1979, and he pronounced the benediction at the second inauguration of U.S. President Ronald Reagan in 1985. Six years later he acquired enhanced celebrity stature when he declared himself "a Christian who happens as well to be gay" before a cheering crowd of students in Harvard Yard. Gomes and other faculty members had been asked to comment at a protest against a student publication devoted to denouncing homosexuality. His admission rocked the campus and the entire Ivy League—and there were a few outraged calls for his resignation—but the administration backed him. Harvard's president, Neil Rudenstine, stated in *Time* that it was not up to the school to "apply a doctrinal test concerning issues that may be controversial" but rather to apply the test to issues "that are part of current theological debate, where reasonable people of different religious persuasions hold different views."

Gomes often stated that he never regretted his declaration. He told the *Washington Post* in 1992, "I now

have an unambiguous vocation—a mission—to address the religious causes and roots of homophobia. . . . I will devote the rest of my life to addressing the 'religious case' against gays." In 1996 Gomes's book *The Good Book: Reading the Bible with Mind and Heart* was published. The book, which *Time* called an "entertaining bid to grab serious Bible study back from the religious right," received largely favorable reviews and even became a *New York Times* bestseller. A *Library Journal* review called the book "honest, down-to-earth, personal, and thoughtful," and *Booklist* suggested it would be "a source of endless discussion, both internal and external."

The Good Book takes a close look at what the Bible actually says about many controversial subjects. Gomes examines the Bible's literal words on these subjects and then offers thoughtful reinterpretations of the scripture, based on original language translations and contexts, both cultural and historical. Although, as *Time* noted, "fundamentalists will have little use for this book," Gomes stressed the need for interpretive commentary as an additional resource for understanding the Bible. "The Bible alone is the most dangerous thing I can think of," he commented in the *Los Angeles Times*. "You need an ongoing context and a community of interpretation to keep the Bible current and to keep yourself honest. Forget the thought that the Bible is an absolute pronouncement."

Remained Popular Campus Idealist

Gomes's Sunday sermons at Memorial Church were well attended, even as religious-worship habits in America changed dramatically over the decades of his tenure. His eloquence was collected into several Harvard-issued volumes as well as mainstream tomes, such as *Sermons: Biblical Wisdom for Daily Living, The Good Life: Truths That Last in Times of Need,* and *Strength for the Journey: Biblical Wisdom for Daily Living—A New Collection of Sermons.* Upon publication of *The Scandalous Gospel of Jesus: What's So Good about the Good News?* in 2007, Gomes was interviewed by *Library Journal*'s Graham Christian and asked about a recent spate of atheist literature. "I have a theory, part of which is that the [atheists] of this world long ago expected religions to shrivel up and blow away," he reflected. "Yet not only do religions persist, but they are gaining adherents. You would think they'd remember we already had this argument over the course of the 19th century. They expected a secular universe by now, and they are quite surprised to find believers."

An ardent Republican for many years who delivered a sermon at the National Cathedral for the inauguration of President George Bush in 1992, Gomes famously switched parties in 2006 to endorse Democrat Deval Patrick a former student of his in the Massachusetts

gubernatorial race. Gomes had stated that he planned to retire in 2012 or 2013. In December of 2010 he was felled by a stroke, and died on February 28, 2011, at the age of 68. Dr. Henry Louis Gates Jr.—one of Harvard's most eminent professors and a leading scholar of African-American history, literature, and race relations in America—issued a statement for the *Harvard Crimson*'s tribute to the iconic minister and voice of tolerance on Harvard Yard. "No one epitomizes all that is good about Harvard," said Gates, "more than Peter J. Gomes." Deval Patrick, who won that 2006 election and became the first African American to serve as Massachusetts governor, hailed his former professor as "a unique individual and beloved friend," according to the *Crimson*. "He taught so many that faith is not just what you say you believe, but how you live."

Selected writings

Books

(With Lawrence D. Geller) *The Books of the Pilgrims,* Garland, 1972.

(With Howard Clark Lee) *Proclamation Series C: Pentecost,* Augsburg Fortress, 1980.

(And editor) *History of Harvard Divinity School,* Harvard University, 1992.

Proclamation Series 6, Series A, Lent: Interpreting the Lessons of the Church Year, Augsburg Fortress, 1995.

Sundays at Harvard: Sermons for an Academic Year, Harvard Printing and Publication Services, 1996.

The Good Book: Reading the Bible with Mind and Heart, William Morrow, 1996.

Yet More Sundays at Harvard, Harvard Printing and Publication Services, 1997.

Sermons: Biblical Wisdom for Daily Living, William Morrow, 1998.

Preaching at Harvard: Sermons for an Academic Year, Harvard Printing and Publication Services, 1998.

When You Feel Abandoned, Judson Press, 1999.

Thomas Hollis of London: Piety, Philanthropy, and Harvard at Two Hundred Seventy-five Years, Thomas Jefferson Press, 1999.

Plymouth in My Time: A Memoir of a Curious Boy, Memorial Press Group, 1999.

Life before Death and Other Sermons at Harvard, Harvard Printing and Publication Services, 1999.

There Is a Plan! and Other Sermons Preached at Harvard, Harvard Printing and Publication Services, 2000.

You Can Do This! and Other Sermons Preached at Harvard, Harvard Printing and Publication Services, 2001.

Growing Up and Other Sermons Preached at Harvard, Harvard Printing and Publication Services, 2002.

The Good Life: Truths That Last in Times of Need,

HarperCollins, 2002.

Strength for the Journey: Biblical Wisdom for Daily Living—A New Collection of Sermons, Harper, 2003.

What We Forgot to Tell You: Sermons Given by The Reverend Professor Peter J. Gomes from 2002 to 2003, Harvard Printing and Publication Services, 2004.

Doing What You Can: Sermons Given by The Reverend Professor Peter J. Gomes from 2003 to 2004, Harvard Printing and Publication Services, 2005.

The Scandalous Gospel of Jesus: What's So Good about the Good News?, HarperOne, 2007.

A Word to the Wise: Sermons Given by The Reverend Professor Peter J. Gomes from 2004 to 2008, Harvard Printing and Publication Services, 2009.

Never Give Up! Sermons Given by The Reverend Professor Peter J. Gomes from 2008–2010, Harvard Printing and Publication Services, 2011.

Sources

Books

Gomes, Peter J., *The Good Book: Reading the Bible with Mind and Heart,* William Morrow & Co., 1996.

Periodicals

Booklist, October 1, 1996.
Chicago Tribune, December 13, 1996.
Christianity Today, April 7, 1997.
Chronicle of Higher Education, January 10, 1997.
Library Journal, December 1996; October 1, 2007, p. 54.
Los Angeles Times, December 8, 1996.
Los Angeles Times Book Review, January 5, 1997.
New York Times, August 17, 1992; March 2, 2011, p. A23.
New Yorker, November 11, 1996.
People, March 3, 1997.
Sojourners, January-February 2003, p. 20.
Time, December 31, 1979; March 16, 1992; January 27, 1997.
U.S. News & World Report, December 23, 1996.
Washington Post, April 15, 1992.

Online

Worland, Justin C., "Remembering Reverend Peter Gomes, Beloved Harvard Spiritual Leader," *Harvard Crimson,* March 2, 2011, http://www.thecrimson.com/article/2011/3/2/gomes-harvard-university-cox/ (accessed June 13, 2011).

—Ellen Dennis French and Carol Brennan

Edward O. Gourdin

1897–1966

Attorney, judge, military officer, athlete

Few people accomplish as much as Edward O. Gourdin did. An Olympic medalist who once held the world record in the broad jump, he was also a distinguished military commander and a leading jurist. The first African American to be appointed to the Massachusetts Superior Court, he served as a role model for many younger jurists, among them Thurgood Marshall, who later became the first African American on the U.S. Supreme Court. In 1958, when Gourdin took his seat for the first time on the Massachusetts Superior Court bench, Marshall wrote, as quoted by Jacksonville.com's Gene Frenette, "This swearing-in is doubly important. First, because it is the first of its kind in New England, and, secondly, because it represents another step along the road of justice rendered without regard for race or color."

One of nine children, Edward Orval Gourdin was born on August 10, 1897, in Jacksonville, Florida. His father, meat cutter Walter Holmes Gourdin, was of mixed African-American and Seminole ancestry, and his mother, Felicia Garvin Gourdin, was an African American. A strong student, the young Gourdin was valedictorian of his class at Stanton High School, a

Gourdin, Edward O., photograph. Hulton Archive/Getty Images.

segregated institution. Following his graduation there in 1916, he moved to Massachusetts for a year of supplementary course work at a high school in the city of Cambridge. He then entered Harvard University, also in Cambridge, earning a bachelor's degree there in 1921 and a law degree three years later.

It was during college and law school that Gourdin had his finest moments as an athlete. The National Amateur Athletic Union's junior 100-yard-dash champion in 1920 and its pentathlon champion in 1921 and 1922, he broke the broad-jump record as a Harvard senior. The first man ever to jump more than 25 feet in sanctioned competition, he was heavily favored to win the event again at the Paris Olympics in the summer of 1924. Distracted, perhaps, by the law exams he had just taken, he came in second, earning a silver medal behind fellow American William Hubbard. As it happened, he beat Hubbard's jump by more than a foot several days later. He did so, however, at an unofficial meet, so he was not given credit for what was, essentially, another world record.

On his return to Massachusetts, Gourdin prepared for a legal career, passing the state bar in 1925 and the

At a Glance . . .

Born Edward Orval Gourdin (pronounced "gor-DEEN") on August 10, 1897, in Jacksonville, FL; died on July 22, 1966, in Quincy, MA; son of Walter Holmes (a meat cutter) and Felicia Garvin Gourdin; married Amalia Ponce, 1923; children: four. *Education*: Harvard University, BA, 1921, LLB, 1924. *Military service*: Massachusetts National Guard, 1925–41 and 1947–59, became brigadier general; U.S. Army, 1941–47, became colonel.

Career: Worked as a postal clerk; attorney, 1925–66; Massachusetts National Guard, achieved rank of brigadier general, 1925–41 and 1947–59; U.S. Department of Justice, assistant U.S. attorney, 1936–41 and 1947–51; U.S. Army, achieved rank of colonel, 1941–47; Commonwealth of Massachusetts, special justice for Roxbury District Court, 1951–58, Superior Court judge, 1958–66; papers housed in Special Collections Department, Mugar Memorial Library, Boston University.

Awards: Silver medal, Olympic Games, 1924, for broad jump; portrait installed in his honor, Old Suffolk County Courthouse (Boston, MA), 1997; General E. O. Gourdin Veterans Memorial Park (Roxbury, MA) established in his honor, 2005(?).

federal bar four years later. Because of the color of his skin, he was unable to find a job at an established firm. While in law school, however, he had served part time as a postal clerk, and it was that occupation that sustained him as he worked to build his own law practice. He began to take an interest in state politics, a field that brought him into contact with a number of powerful jurists, many of them fellow Harvard alumni. In 1936 one of these mentors, federal prosecutor Francis Ford, asked President Franklin Delano Roosevelt to make Gourdin an assistant U.S. attorney. The request was granted, and Gourdin remained in that post, with a break for military service, until 1951. Many of the prosecutions he managed, particularly in the second half of his tenure, involved murder, bank robbery, racketeering, and other serious offenses.

Alongside his career in the courtroom, Gourdin had a flourishing military career. By the time the United States entered the Second World War in 1941, he already had more than a decade of experience as an officer, having joined the National Guard in 1925. With the nation's entry into the war, he moved to the U.S. Army, where he served as commander of the 372nd Infantry Regiment, a segregated unit that saw extensive duty in the Pacific, particularly in Hawaii. By the time Gourdin left the army in 1947, he held the rank of colonel. He then returned to the National Guard, where he rose to the rank of brigadier general. The first African American to reach that post in Massachusetts, he retired from military service in 1959.

His legal career, meanwhile, was progressing rapidly. After nearly ten years as an assistant U.S. attorney (from 1936 to 1941 and from 1947 to 1951), he was appointed in 1951 to the bench of Roxbury (Massachusetts) District Court. He served there as special justice until his appointment to the Massachusetts Superior Court seven years later. Known as a careful and scrupulously impartial judge, he presided over a number of important cases, including murder trials at the Massachusetts Superior Court and a variety of civil rights cases. His impact was particularly evident in Roxbury, a Boston neighborhood often regarded as the center of African-American life in Massachusetts. Gourdin served at Roxbury District Court at a time when the area's African-American population was exploding, primarily as a result of migration from the rural South. By mediating disputes and encouraging nonviolent solutions to conflict, Gourdin helped smooth the newcomers' transition to urban life. Widely revered for his efforts, he did much to legitimize state government in the eyes of Boston's African-American residents, many of whom had been unfairly treated in the past by the Massachusetts court system and other public institutions.

Gourdin's health declined sharply in his later years. He died on July 22, 1966, in Quincy, a Boston suburb, and was buried several days later in the town of Cotuit on Cape Cod, where he had a home. Surviving him were his wife, the former Amalia Ponce, and four children. In the years since his death, he has received a number of honors. One of the most prominent of these came in 1997, when his portrait was installed in Boston's Old Suffolk County Courthouse, the heart of the city's legal establishment. Roughly eight years later, the General E. O. Gourdin Veterans Memorial Park was established at the corner of Malcolm X Boulevard and Washington Street in Roxbury. Built with funds from the Boston Redevelopment Authority and local veterans, the park hosts annual Memorial Day ceremonies and provides needed green space to the residents of a heavily urbanized area.

As of 2011 Gourdin's papers were housed in the Special Collections Department of Boston University's Mugar Memorial Library. Established in 1963, the department focuses, according to Amy Dean in *B.U. Bridge*, on the "accomplishments and passions of the century's great thinkers, politicians, and personalities."

Sources

Periodicals

Bay State Banner, May 19, 2011.
B.U. Bridge, February 15, 2002.
Harvard Magazine, November 1997.

Online

Frenette, Gene, "Athletes of the Century: Discover Jacksonville's Hidden Treasure," Jacksonville.com, http://jacksonville.com/special/athletes_of_century/stories/gourdin.shtml (accessed June 25, 2011).

—R. Anthony Kugler

Tanya Hamilton

1968—

Filmmaker

Hamilton, Tanya, photograph. AP Images/Brian Zak.

Filmmaker Tanya Hamilton made her feature debut in 2010 with the drama *Night Catches Us,* a portrait of two former members of the Black Panther Party who are forced to confront their radical past and the legacy of the Black Power movement. More than a decade in the making, the film, which Hamilton wrote and directed, featured a cast of critically acclaimed actors, including Anthony Mackie, Kerry Washington, Wendell Pierce, and Jamie Hector. *Night Catches Us* premiered at the Sundance Film Festival as a nominee for the Special Jury Prize and went on to earning a host of honors on the film festival circuit. Critics hailed Hamilton as one of the most promising new filmmakers.

Tanya Hamilton was born in 1968 in Spanish Town, Jamaica. As a girl, she knew little of her father, a policeman, and when she was seven years old, her mother immigrated to the United States and settled in Silver Springs, Maryland; a year later, in 1976, she and her brother joined her there.

She attended the Duke Ellington School of the Arts in Washington, DC, where she studied painting and draw-

ing, and made the leap to filmmaking as a student at the Cooper Union in New York. "[My paintings] were all completely narrative," Hamilton explained to Alaina Lewis in an interview for BeSoulFullyUnique.com. "There was always a story to them. . . . I loved doing portraits, but the stuff I did in college was where I started bringing in other characters instead of just painting a portrait of one person. While I was there, I would sneak up to the fifth floor [where the film department was located], and somehow I started making narrative movies with my friends." As a graduate student at Columbia University's film school, she learned the art and craft of screenwriting.

Hamilton's first project was a short film titled the *Killers,* released in 1995. Shot in Jamaica, it tells the story of Jamaican children whose mother leaves them behind on the island to find work in the United States, only to disappear. The *Killers* was named best short film at the Berlin International Film Festival in 1996 and won the New Line Cinema Award in 1997; in the latter year, Hamilton was chosen as best female director by the Directors Guild of America.

At a Glance . . .

Born in 1968 in Spanish Town, Jamaica; married to Michael W. Pollock (a fiction writer). *Education*: Cooper Union, BFA, 1990; Columbia University, School of the Arts, MFA, 2000.

Career: Independent filmmaker, 1995—.

Awards: Best Short Film, Berlin International Film Festival, 1996, for the *Killers*; New Line Cinema Award, 1997; Best Female Director, Directors Guild of America, 1997; Screenplay Competition Award, Urbanworld Film Festival, 1999, for *Stringbean & Marcus*; Gordon Parks Award for Best Screenplay, Independent Feature Project, 1999, for *Stringbean & Marcus*; Audience Award, New Orleans Film Festival, 2010, for *Night Catches Us*; Best American Film, Seattle Film Festival, 2010, for *Night Catches Us*; Black Reel Award, Best Screenplay, Original or Adapted, 2011, for *Night Catches Us*.

Addresses: *Management*—Southfield Village Entertainment, 8228 Sunset Blvd., Ste. 109, Los Angeles, CA 90046.

In 1999 Hamilton began developing the script that would become *Night Catches Us,* originally titled *Stringbean & Marcus,* at the Sundance Institute's Filmmaking and Writing Lab, winning the Independent Film Project's Gordon Parks Award for her initial draft. She continued working on the script for more than a decade, changing the focus of the story and fine-tuning the characters while she secured financing and distribution for the film.

In 2001 Hamilton received a pre-production grant from the Minnesota Film Fund; additional funding came from a $50,000 grant from the Pew Center for Arts and Heritage—Hamilton is the only filmmaker to receive the award—and a $10,000 fellowship from the Maryland Film Office. After more than a decade, *Night Catches Us* finally went into production in Philadelphia in the summer of 2009, with shooting completed in just 18 days. The film premiered at the Sundance Film Festival in January of 2010 and was released in theaters in the United States in December.

Night Catches Us is set in the summer of 1976 in Philadelphia, where a chapter of the radical Black Panther Party once operated and racial tensions between African Americans and the police ran high; now the neighborhood seems to be filled only with broken dreams. The film tells the story of Marcus Washington, a former Panther who has returned home after a mysterious four-year absence to attend his father's funeral. Before he left, one of his fellow Panthers, Neil, was killed in a police shootout; Marcus is suspected of having told the cops where to find him. Upon his return, Marcus meets Patricia, Neil's widow, who is now a civil rights attorney raising a daughter on her own.

The film traces the ways in which Marcus and Patricia try to make sense of their own radical pasts and the uncertain legacy of the Black Power movement. "I often . . . say that there's something both tragic and very romantic in that period, during the civil rights [movement] and the transition into black power," Hamilton told National Public Radio. "I felt like the film not only needed to talk about the waning days [of the Black Panthers], but also what ultimately destroyed the Panthers and the complexity of that destruction." The film's title, *Night Catches Us,* comes from a common expression in Jamaica, "Don't let night catch you." "That simply means come back at a decent hour," she explained. "I felt like the film is about these people who are all running various directions. And it spoke . . . of their history and how it was going to catch up with them, and they were going to have to contend with it."

The inspiration behind *Night Catches Us* came from a friend of Hamilton's mother, Carol Lawson-Green. In 1965 Lawson-Green helped organize a sit-in at the White House to protest racial violence in Selma, Alabama. When she refused to leave, she was arrested and sentenced to one year in jail for an offense that normally would warrant only a $50 fine; she later went on to become a civil rights lawyer, like Patricia in the film. "That tiny moment reverberated far and wide in Carol's life. I was fascinated," she told the *Washington Post*. After Lawson-Green's death, Hamilton inherited a trove of her old letters and photographs, and those prompted her to think about how one moment could shape a person's life forever.

Night Catches Us was acclaimed on the film festival circuit, earning a nomination for the Special Jury Prize for Drama at Sundance—where she was the only black female filmmaker represented—and winning the Audience Award at the New Orleans Film Festival and Best American Film honors at the Seattle Film Festival. The film also was nominated for an Independent Spirit Award for best feature film and a Gotham Award.

Critics praised Hamilton's sensitive, yet honest, portrayal of the personal stories of the Black Power movement and her gentle directorial touch. Reviewing the film in the *New York Times,* A. O. Scott noted that "Ms. Hamilton tells a modest, complex story with admirable clarity and nuance. That her film is so quiet, so evidently invested in contemplation rather than confrontation, give it power as well as insight." Likewise, Peter Travers of *Rolling Stone* wrote, "She lets her mesmerizing movie sneak up on you and seep in until you feel it in your bones. . . . Hamilton manifests

her vision of what politics can do to individual thinking with subtlety and sophistication."

Sources

Periodicals

Los Angeles Times, January 26, 2010.
New York Times, December 2, 2010.
Rolling Stone, December 2, 2010.
Washington Post, December 25, 2010.

Online

Balfour, Brad, "Chronicling Black Panthers, Award-Winning Director Knows Where Night Catches Us," Huffington Post, February 11, 2011, http://www.huffingtonpost.com/brad-balfour/exclusive-chronicling-bla_b_821948.html (accessed June 26, 2011).
Burton, Nsenga, "Tanya Hamilton on 'Night Catches Us,'" The Root, December 14, 2010, http://www.theroot.com/views/root-interview-director-tanya-hamilton-night-catches-us (accessed June 26, 2011).
"Filmmaker Hamilton 'Catches' Up with Ex-Panthers," *Fresh Air,* National Public Radio, December 7, 2010, http://www.npr.org/2010/12/07/131788451/filmmaker-hamilton-catches-up-with-ex-panthers (accessed June 26, 2011).
Lewis, Alaina L., "Night Catches Us: The Tanya Hamilton Interview," March 7, 2011, http://besoulfullyunique.com/ARTICLES/2011/03/night-catches-us-the-tanya-hamilton-interview/ (accessed June 26, 2011).
O'Hehir, Andrew, "'Night Catches Us': A 'Casablanca' for the Black Power Era, Salon.com, http://www.salon.com/entertainment/movies/andrew_ohehir/2010/12/02/night_catches (accessed June 26, 2011).

—Deborah A. Ring

Tony Hansberry II

1994—

Inventor

Tony Hansberry II was just 14 years old when he became a minor media sensation for developing a new surgical technique. A student at Darnell-Cookman Middle/High School of the Medical Arts—a magnet school in Jacksonville, Florida, that is the first of its kind in the United States—Hansberry spent the summer of 2008 working at the Center for Simulation Education and Safety Research (CSESaR), which is run by the University of Florida inside Shands Jacksonville Medical Center. While there Hansberry devised a new method for the suturing that follows hysterectomies. "The potential of what Hansberry and his young colleagues can bring to the professional medical table," asserted Brentin Mock in TheGriot, "is evidence of what's possible with the right outreach and investments."

Hansberry and his twin brother, Tyler, were born on June 29, 1994. Their father is a pastor of Greater Grant Memorial, an African Methodist Episcopal church in Jacksonville, and Hansberry's mother is a registered nurse. Naturally drawn to science and medicine, Hansberry chose Darnell-Cookman and was disappointed when his eighth-grade science fair project failed to earn any merit citations. Later that year, in the summer of 2008, he began the internship at CSESaR, a program run by the University of Florida College of Medicine—Jacksonville at a local hospital. There, medical students from the University of Florida practice techniques on high-tech medical mannequins, and Hansberry was part of a select group from Darnell-Cookman chosen to participate in the program.

At the Shands Jacksonville Medical Center, Hansberry met two important new mentors: urogynecologist Dr. Brent Siebel and Bruce Nappi, the CSESaR administrative director. Hansberry and other students practiced simulations of laparoscopic surgeries, a relatively modern advancement in medicine that permits surgeons to see inside the body with the help of a small camera inserted through an incision. Such techniques have been particularly helpful in hysterectomies, one of the most commonly performed surgical procedures in the United States. Hysterectomy refers to the removal of a woman's uterus, and sometimes the ovaries, fallopian tubes, and cervix. For decades surgeons made a major abdominal incision in order to remove the organs, but improvements via laparoscopic techniques vastly reduced post-operative complications.

A specialist in obstetrics and gynecology (OB-GYN) spoke to Hansberry's group and showed them an Endo Stitch device, a suturing tool commonly used in gastric lap band surgery and other types of procedures where stitches to close up soft internal tissues are necessary. It has clamps on both ends, and a special needle is used that lets the surgeon make quick sutures. In hysterectomies the internal tissues are usually closed up with a different type of suturing device, the needle driver. The OB-GYN asked the students to investigate why the Endo Stitch was not used in hysterectomies. "The problem was that the [E]ndo [S]titch couldn't clamp down properly to close the tube where the patient's uterus had been," explained Jeremy Cox in the *Jacksonville News*. "Tony figured that by suturing the tube

At a Glance . . .

Born on June 29, 1994, in Jacksonville, FL; son of Tony (a minister) and Kathi Sloan (a registered nurse) Hansberry. *Religion*: African Methodist Episcopal.

Career: University of Florida College of Medicine—Jacksonville, Center for Simulation Education and Safety Research (CSESaR), Shands Jacksonville Medical Center, intern, 2008.

Memberships: Boy Scouts of America.

Addresses: *Home*—Jacksonville, FL. *Office*—c/o Greater Grant Memorial AME Church, 5533 Gilchrist Rd., Jacksonville, FL 32219-2607.

vertically instead of horizontally, it could be done. And he was right."

Hansberry demonstrated the procedure to Nappi and Dr. Siebel, and he then turned the idea into his ninth-grade science fair entry. "The project I did was, basically, the comparison of novel laparoscopic instruments in doing a hysterectomy repair," he told Jackie Jones in an article that appeared on BlackAmericaWeb. His vertical Endo Stitch closures were indeed three times faster than needle-driver sutures, which meant patients spent less time under anesthesia. The Endo Stitch technique also portended a reduced risk for post-operative infections. This time, Hansberry's science fair entry won a place in the regional science fair in February of 2009, and he took second place in the medical category. That led to an offer to present a paper on his findings at a medical education conference hosted by the University of Florida in April of 2009, when he was still two months shy of his fifteenth birthday. His achievement was promoted by duly impressed University of Florida professors and his teachers at Darnell-Cookman, and it was widely covered by the local media; he even appeared on NBC's *Today Show*. "I would put him up against a first-year med student," one of his teachers, Angela TenBroeck, told Cox in the *Jacksonville News*. "He's an outstanding

young man, and I'm proud to have him representing us."

Not surprisingly, Hansberry is planning on a pre-med undergraduate major once he graduates from Darnell-Cookman in 2012, and then medical school, specializing either in neuroscience or trauma care. During his junior year he was one of nine Boy Scouts chosen to deliver the "Boy Scouts of America Report to the Nation to President Barack Obama." Hansberry represented Troop 175 in Jacksonville and is working toward the Eagle Scout rank. "Push yourself and have persistence," he offered fellow students as advice in an interview with the newsletter *Healthcare Pathways*. "If you have a passion for it—it's probably for you."

Sources

Periodicals

Boys' Life, January 2011, p. 14.
Florida Times-Union, January 25, 2011, p. B1.
Jacksonville News, April 22, 2009.

Online

Jones, Jackie, "Black Youth Invents Surgical Techniqueat 14," BlackAmericaWeb, June 16, 2009, http://www.blackamericaweb.com/?q=articles/news/the_black_diaspora_news/10190 (accessed June 17, 2011).

Mock, Brentin, "TheGrio's 100: Tony Hansberry, Whiz-kid Considered 'the Next Charles Drew,'" TheGriot, February 3, 2010, http://2010.thegrio.com/black-history/thegrios-100/thegrios-100-tony-hansberry.php (accessed June 17, 2011).

"Our Pastor," Greater Grant Memorial AME Church, http://www.wix.com/hatchers1/greater-grant#!__page-5 (accessed June 17, 2011).

"Tony Hansberry II," The Root, January 31, 2011, http://www.theroot.com/views/2011/young-futurists (accessed June 16, 2011).

"Tony Hansberry II: Medical Inventor," *Healthcare Pathways*, California Office of Statewide Healthcare Planning and Development, November 2009, pp. 12, http://www.oshpd.ca.gov/HWDD/pdfs/HP_November_2009_WEB.pdf (accessed June 16, 2011).

—Carol Brennan

Elvin Hayes

1945—

Basketball player

Hayes, Elvin, photograph. AP Images.

Elvin Hayes, a power forward famed for his turnaround jump shot, was one of the top professional basketball players of his era and remains among the all-time National Basketball Association (NBA) leaders in scoring, rebounding, and games and minutes played. After a storied college career with the University of Houston Cougars, he spent 16 years in the NBA, 9 of them with the Baltimore/Washington Bullets franchise. There, he and center Wes Unseld constituted one of basketball's premier front-court duos, leading the team to three NBA Finals appearances and taking the league title in 1978. Hayes made the NBA All-Star Team every year for his first 12 seasons and was an All-NBA first team selection three times. In 1990 he was inducted into the Naismith Memorial Basketball Hall of Fame, and in 1996, as part of the league's 50th anniversary, he was named one of the 50 Greatest Players in NBA History.

Overcame Poverty and Racism

Born in rural Rayville, Louisiana, in 1945, Hayes was the son of cotton-mill workers Christopher and Savannah Hayes. Racially segregated and impoverished, Rayville offered little in the way of opportunity for most of its African-American inhabitants, and Hayes's parents, who managed to send all six of their children to college, struggled to make ends meet. "I used to wake up at night with rats in my bed at home," Hayes later told Jerry Wizig in the *Houston Chronicle.* "I used to eat two-for-a-penny cookies for my supper." Hayes did not own shoes until the tenth grade, going barefoot in winter and summer except when, on occasion, he was able to borrow shoes from a cousin. "When I first started playing basketball," he said, according to Chris Broussard in the *New York Times,* "I wore two left-footed tennis shoes I pulled out of the trash and taped to my feet."

By practicing 11 hours a day during the summer on a dirt-floored outdoor basketball court, Hayes as a high schooler developed the turnaround jump shot that would make him an almost unstoppable scorer in college and at the professional level. To shoot a turnaround jumper, a player facing away from the basket pivots in the direction of the hoop and shoots simultaneously. Even defenders who are taller than the shooter can do little to defend against the shot. Hayes

At a Glance . . .

Born Elvin Ernest Hayes on November 17, 1945, in Rayville, LA; son of Christopher (a cotton mill worker) and Savannah (a cotton mill worker) Hayes; married Erna Beth Livingston, 1967(?); children: Elvin Jr., Elisse, Erica, Ethan. *Education*: University of Houston, BA, speech and recreation, 1986.

Career: Basketball player for University of Houston, 1965–68, San Diego Rockets, 1968–71, Houston Rockets, 1971–72, Baltimore Bullets, 1972–74, Capital Bullets, 1973–74, Washington Bullets, 1974–81, and Houston Rockets, 1981–84; owner of car dealerships; worked as a rancher, a deputy sheriff, and a sports analyst.

Memberships: Iota Phi Theta fraternity.

Awards: Division I Consensus First-Team All-American, National Collegiate Athletics Association (NCAA), 1967 and 1968; Division I Consensus Player of the Year, 1968; All-Rookie Team, National Basketball Association (NBA), 1969; 12-time NBA All-Star, 1969–80; Second-Team All-NBA, 1973, 1974, and 1976; First-Team All-NBA, 1975, 1977, and 1979; elected to Naismith Memorial Basketball Hall of Fame, 1990; named one of 50 Greatest Players in NBA History, 1996.

Addresses: *Agent*—PB Talent, 6300 West Loop South, Ste. 350, Houston, TX 77401.

led Eula Britton High School to 54 consecutive wins and averaged 35 points per game in his senior year. He scored 45 points and over 20 rebounds in the state championship game and was voted tournament MVP.

In 1965 Hayes entered the University of Houston as part of the first group of black athletes in school history. Hayes's basketball teammate Don Chaney and the football player Warren McVea, both of whom, like Hayes, went on to professional careers, were the other two African Americans to play sports that year for the Cougars. Integration of the student body at large had barely begun, and Hayes, having never associated on friendly terms with white people in the small town of Rayville, had trouble adapting to life as one of only 100 blacks in a student body numbering 20,000.

His alienation carried over to his relations with white teammates and coaches until head coach Guy Lewis, who had risked his career by recruiting Hayes and Chaney, confronted Hayes before the start of his

sophomore season. As Hayes later told the *Houston Chronicle*, "He asked me, 'Why do you hate me? I put my job on the line. I try to do everything I can for you.' I sat there and I realized there was no reason for my dislike. That totally changed my life. All the anger I'd held in left me."

Excelled but Encountered Difficulties

Lewis became a father figure for Hayes, whose own father had recently died, and Hayes led Houston to two final-four National Collegiate Athletic Association (NCAA) tournament appearances. A Houston sportswriter began calling him "The Big E," and the name stuck with Hayes through the rest of his playing days. He earned first-team All-America honors in both 1967 and 1968 and was named the NCAA's consensus player of the year in 1968.

One game in particular stands out among Hayes's many college triumphs: a regular-season game on January 20, 1968, against Lew Alcindor (who later changed his name to Kareem Abdul-Jabbar) and the top-ranked UCLA Bruins. Often referred to since as "the Game of the Century," the contest was the first nationally televised college basketball game in history, and Hayes made the most of the exposure. He scored 39 points and posted 15 rebounds, including the two free throws that gave the second-ranked Cougars the win in the game's final seconds.

Hayes was the first pick in the 1968 NBA draft, and his professional career started as promisingly as his college career had ended. Joining the San Diego Rockets—a previously dismal expansion franchise—he led the league in scoring and was fourth in rebounding from 1968 to 1969, averaging 28.4 points per game and 17.1 rebounds, and the team made the playoffs. Hayes continued, in the two seasons that followed, to deliver scoring and rebounding numbers that placed him among the league's top few players in both categories, but the Rockets failed to make the playoffs.

Since Hayes was the team's marquee player, sportswriters blamed him for the team's travails, and he began to develop a reputation as a difficult and self-centered star who could not be counted on in the clutch. When the Rockets franchise moved to Houston for Hayes's fourth season, he was happy to return to the city where he had made his name, but his playing style conflicted with the offense that the team's new coach tried to implement that year. He still averaged 25.2 points per game, 10th in the NBA, but the Rockets again failed to make the playoffs.

Anchored Excellent Bullets Teams, 1972–80

At the end of the 1971–72 season, Hayes was traded

to the Baltimore Bullets. He had been playing center with the Rockets, but the Bullets already had an All-Star center, Wes Unseld. This allowed Hayes to move to the power-forward position, which was a more natural fit for his abilities. Together Hayes and Unseld established the Bullets, who moved to Washington, DC, in the 1973–74 season, as a perpetual contender.

Through the end of the decade Hayes averaged between 19 and 24 points per game and remained among the NBA's top rebounders. The Bullets were consistently among the league's best teams during these years, but they were repeatedly stymied in the postseason. In Hayes's first two seasons with the team, the Bullets won the NBA's Central Division during the regular season, before losing in the first round of the playoffs, both times to the New York Knicks. In 1974–75 the Bullets tied the Boston Celtics for the league's best regular-season record, and they beat the Buffalo Braves and the Celtics on the way to the NBA finals. Heavy favorites in the finals, they were swept 40 by the Golden State Warriors.

The next two seasons followed the same basic pattern: the Bullets played well all season long, only to perform disappointingly in the playoffs. By this time Hayes was often characterized as an enormously talented player who did not have the leadership skills or the postseason nerves to deliver a team championship.

The 1977–78 season, however, reversed the narrative of the previous years, as the Bullets had one of their worst regular seasons in recent history, only to become unstoppable in the playoffs. They beat the Atlanta Hawks, the San Antonio Spurs, and the Philadelphia 76ers, and then they overcame the Seattle Supersonics in the 7th game of the NBA finals to take home the championship.

Although Hayes had seemingly disproved the notion that he did not have the character of a champion, some observers suggested that the Bullets' title was the result of luck more than excellence, as other, better teams collapsed or were plagued by injuries in the playoffs. When the Bullets failed to repeat their championship season, meeting the Supersonics in the NBA finals again in 1978–79 only to lose, and then getting knocked out of the playoffs in the first round in 1979–80, Hayes's critics found new evidence for their case against him.

As John Papanek observed in a *Sports Illustrated* profile of Hayes following the championship season of 1977–78, however, the case against Hayes had always been based more on his difficult personality than on statistics. Pegged as a regular-season powerhouse who routinely folded in the postseason, Hayes had in fact, over time, delivered better statistics in the postseason than in the regular season.

Ended Career as All-Time Great

In 1980–81 the Bullets failed to make the playoffs for the first time in the Hayes–Unseld years, and Hayes was traded back to the Houston Rockets. He ended his career in the city where he had first made his name. He was past his prime and one of the oldest players in the league, but the 1981–82 season saw him average over 16 points and 9 rebounds per game. In his final two years he played more sparingly, and he retired in 1984, at the end of his sixteenth NBA season.

Over his 16 years in the league, Hayes accumulated statistics that placed him among the greatest players in NBA history. He was the third-leading scorer (27,313 points), rebounder (16,279), and shot-blocker (1,743) in league history, and he was an all-time leader in categories measuring endurance, ranking first in minutes played (50,000) and third in games played (1,303). A handful of players have since superseded him in each of these categories, but his career statistics remain remarkable by any standard. In 1990 he was inducted into the Naismith Memorial Basketball Hall of Fame, and in 1996 he was named one of the NBA's 50 Greatest Players of All Time.

After his retirement Hayes returned to the University of Houston to finish the credits he still lacked for his diploma. He earned a bachelor's degree in speech and recreation in 1986. In the years since he has been a successful owner of Houston-area car dealerships, a rancher, a deputy sheriff, and a sports analyst.

Selected works

Hayes, Elvin, and Bill Gilbert, *They Call Me "The Big E,"* Prentice Hall, 1978.

Sources

Books

Hayes, Elvin, and Bill Gilbert, *They Call Me "The Big E,"* Prentice Hall, 1978.

Periodicals

Houston Chronicle, December 18, 1993; February 17, 2006.
New York Times, November 30, 1985, February 1, 2004, p. SP2.
Sports Illustrated, October 16, 1978; June 9, 1997, p. 7.
Washington Post, September 27, 1981, p. D1; May 13, 1990, p. D1.

Online

"Elvin E. Hayes," The Naismith Memorial Basketball

Hall of Fame, http://www.hoophall.com/hall-of-famers/tag/elvin-e-hayes (accessed August 3, 2011).

"Elvin Hayes Bio," NBA.com, http://www.nba.com/history/players/hayes_bio.html (accessed August 3, 2011).

—Mark Lane

Derek Jeter

1974—

Baseball player

Jeter, Derek, photograph. AP Images/Carlos Osorio.

The New York Yankees' all-time hit leader and a five-time World Series champion, shortstop Derek Jeter established himself as one of the greatest baseball players of the 1990s and first decade of the 21st century. Jeter is the face of a baseball dynasty responsible for 11 division titles and 14 playoff appearances in his 15 years in the majors. Despite the rather low opinion fans of other franchises have of the Yankees' free-spending ways, throughout his career Jeter has been one of the most respected players in baseball due to his quiet leadership style and general aversion to publicity.

never let me win anything," Jeter told Tom Verducci of *Sports Illustrated*. Every day before afternoon kindergarten, he watched the *Price Is Right* with his father, and the two would play along with the game show. "Now, I'm five years old," Jeter told Ed Bradley of *60 Minutes*. "And he used to beat me at the Showcase Showdown and send me to school." For his part, Charles Jeter told Bradley he was tough on his son to "Just teach him to be competitive, and nobody's going to let you win anything. It's not going to be fair all the time."

Drafted by the New York Yankees

Derek Sanderson Jeter was born on June 26, 1974, in Pequannok, New Jersey, to Charles and Dorothy Jeter. The Jeter family moved to Kalamazoo, Michigan, when he was four years old so that Jeter's father could pursue a PhD in psychology. Despite growing up in Michigan, Jeter was Yankee fan, a fact he attributed to the influence of his maternal grandmother in New Jersey. His competitive nature he attributed to his father. "He

Although Jeter played different sports as a youth, baseball occupied a special place in his family's dynamic. Jeter's high school baseball coach told Ian O'Connor of *USA Today* that he would often see Jeter out with his parents and his sister, Sharlee—a talented softball player—running baseball drills after practice. "Some people go to the movies for fun," Sharlee told O'Connor. "We went to the field. It was part of being close." The result of all this hard work was that even in his teens, Jeter had tremendous confidence in himself. "[H]e had a quiet arrogance," Charles Jeter told O'Connor. "Even in basketball, he always wanted the

At a Glance . . .

Born Derek Sanderson Jeter on June 26, 1974, in Pequannok, NJ; son of Charles (a psychologist) and Dorothy Jeter (an accountant). *Education*: University of Michigan.

Career: New York Yankees, 1995—.

Awards: American League Rookie of the Year, 1996; member of World Series champion team, 1996, 1998–2000, 2009; American League All-Star Team, 1998–02, 2004, 2006–10; World Series MVP, 2000; Babe Ruth award, 2000; All-Star Game MVP, 2000; Gold Glove award, 2004–06, 2009–10; Silver Slugger award, 2006–09; American League Hank Aaron award, 2006, 2009; Roberto Clemente Award, 2009; *Sports Illustrated* Sportsman of the Year, 2009.

Addresses: *Office*—The New York Yankees, Yankee Stadium, 1 East 161st St., Bronx, NY 10451 *Agent*—Casey Close, Excel Sports Management, 1156 Avenue of the Americas, Ste. 400, New York, NY 10036. *Web*—http://mlb.mlb.com/players/jeter_derek/index.jsp.

last shot. He usually didn't make them, but he was never afraid to fail."

Following an impressive high school career at Kalamazoo Central, Jeter was selected by the Yankees as the sixth overall pick in the June of 1992 amateur draft. Things did not go smoothly for Jeter right off the bat: in his first season in the minor leagues, he struggled to break a .200 batting average. The next season his hitting improved, but his defense was embarrassing— the young shortstop committed 56 errors in the low minors. For the arrogant high school star, the experience was humbling. According to Anthony McCarron of the *New York Daily News*, he told his high school coach that he thought the Yankees had wasted the $800,000 signing bonus they gave him out of high school. After bad games, his parents came to expect a late-night phone call from their homesick son.

Things turned around in 1994. Jeter tore the cover off the ball at three different minor league levels. Overall, he hit .344 with 50 stolen bases. He also cut his errors by more than half. After the season, *Baseball America* declared Jeter the fourth-best prospect in baseball. In 1995 Jeter was hitting .354 at the Yankees' AAA affiliate when the team's major league shortstop, Tony Fernandez, was injured in late May. Jeter became the first Yankees first-round pick to reach the majors in 11 years. His first major league experience was just two weeks long—he was sent back down to the majors as soon as the injured shortstop was eligible to come off the disabled list—but the 20-year-old impressed his teammates with his maturity and composure.

Became a Rookie Sensation

The following season, Jeter was in line to be the team's starting shortstop, with Fernandez moving to second base. However, after a lackluster performance in spring training—Jeter made 6 errors in 23 exhibition games—some in the organization had their doubts about the youngster. Rumors spread that the team was willing to trade a young pitcher, Mariano Rivera, for a veteran shortstop in order to give Jeter more time in the minors. Others speculated that the organization— which was notorious for being impatient with rookies— would turn to Fernandez at shortstop if the youngster stumbled out of the gate. Luckily for Jeter, the trade talk dissipated and Fernandez was injured shortly before the start of the season.

On Opening Day 1996 the young shortstop hit the ground running, hitting a solo home run and making several sharp plays in the Yankees 7-1 victory in Cleveland. He never looked back. In the second half of the season Jeter was a key player as the Yankees made a run for the playoffs, hitting .350 after the All-Star break. The Yankees held on to win their division despite a late charge by the Baltimore Orioles. At season's end, Jeter had batted .314 with 183 hits, 78 RBI, and 10 home runs in his inaugural campaign. He would eventually be the unanimous selection for the American League's Rookie of the Year. However, before he could collect those accolades, Jeter would have to prove himself once again in the playoffs.

Jeter's hot hitting continued through the month of October, as the Yankees vied for the franchise's first World Series title since 1978. Sometimes, though, luck plays as large a role as skill in building a legend. In the first game of the American League Championship Series (ALCS) against the Baltimore Orioles, the Yankees trailed by one run going into the eighth inning. Jeter hit a fly ball down the right field line, which a 12-year-old fan reached over the outfield fence and caught. In one of the most controversial decisions in playoff history, the umpire ruled the ball a home run despite the fan's interference, and the Yankees went on to win the game in extra innings and the series in five games. In the World Series, Jeter and the Yankees staged a dramatic comeback after losing their first two games at home against the Atlanta Braves, recording four straight wins against the National League's juggernaut. Jeter scored the decisive run in the final game of the Series. Overall, he hit .364 with 12 runs scored in 15 playoff games. Although he was just barely old enough to drink, Jeter was a star.

New York's Favorite Son

Jeter proved that his rookie season wasn't a fluke with a solid, if unspectacular, sophomore campaign. The

Yankees made it to the playoffs once again, but this time they lost in the first round to the Cleveland Indians. It was Jeter's first taste of failure at the major league level, and he came back in 1998 determined not to repeat the experience. The 1998 season proved to be a banner year for Jeter and the Yankees. Jeter led the league in runs scored and batted .324 with 19 home runs, 84 RBI, and 30 stolen bases. He finished third in voting for the league's Most Valuable Player (MVP) Award and was selected to his first All-Star Game. His team was dominant, winning 114 games and sweeping the San Diego Padres to secure Jeter's second World Series title.

Still in his early twenties, Jeter was the star of the most successful team in baseball, featured as prominently in the New York tabloids for his relationships with starlets such as Mariah Carey as for his exploits on the baseball diamond. Still, success did not go to his head. Instead, Jeter stepped up his performance for the 1999 season. The shortstop closed out the final season of the 20th century in grand fashion, breaking most of his personal records. He had career-highs in home runs (24), runs scored (134), triples (nine), and RBIs (102). Jeter's .349 batting average—another career-high—was second-best in the American League, only 8 points shy of the league leader. His continued success did not go unnoticed. Jeter was selected to his second All-Star roster. More importantly, the Yankees once again dominated the league, winning 98 games and going 11-1 in the playoffs en route to another World Series victory.

Although Jeter put up sterling numbers the following year—.339 batting average, 15 home runs, 73 RBI, 119 runs scored, and 201 hits—his team did not enjoy the same level of dominance they had in 1998 and 1999. The Yankees took advantage of a weak year in the American League East to reach the playoffs with just 87 wins. After a few scares in the early rounds of the playoffs, the Yankees once again reached the World Series, this time facing the team's cross-town rivals, the New York Mets, in a "Subway Series." The Yankees savaged the Mets, winning the series in five games. Jeter, who batted .409 with two homers and scored six runs, was the World Series MVP.

Signed 10-Year Contract

In the aftermath of the Subway Series, the Yankees had to consider Jeter's next contract. In December Jeter's close friend and fellow shortstop Alex Rodriguez had signed a historic 10-year, $252 million free agent contract. Although Jeter was not yet eligible for free agency, it was clear that the four-time world champion would be looking for a comparable payday. In February of 2001 Jeter signed a 10-year, $189 million contract, then the second-richest salary package in sports history. Throughout the negotiations, Jeter insisted that he had never really been tempted to test the open market. "I never intended to play elsewhere," Jeter told the Associated Press, "and to be honest with you, I never intended to look elsewhere."

Although Jeter's 2001 performance represented a step back from his 1999-2000 peak, the playoffs showcased his knack for big-game performance. With the Yankees on the verge of elimination in the third game of the Division Series against Oakland, Jeter made a spectacular defensive play. In the seventh inning with a one-run lead, Jeter ranged from his position all the way to the foul territory past the first base line to intercept an errant throw from the outfield just in time to flip the ball to the catcher and cut off the tying run at the plate. The Yankees won the game, 1-0, and reached the World Series for the fifth time in six seasons. This, however, would be the first time the Yankees' star would be on the losing end of a World Series match-up, as the Arizona Diamondbacks beat the Yankees in a dramatic seven-game series.

The 2001 World Series was in many ways a turning point for Jeter's Yankees. Many of the players who had starred along with Jeter in the championship seasons were older and now on the downslope of their careers. To stay on top, the Yankees had to sign veteran free agents to augment the core of players who had come up with Jeter through the Yankees' minor league system. Over the next seven seasons, the Yankees' payroll ballooned from $125 million to more than $205 million. The results were, by Jeter's standards, disappointing: six division titles, but only one World Series appearance and no championships.

During this period, Jeter attained a number of individual achievements. In June of 2003, he was named the Yankees' captain, becoming one of only 11 players to officially hold that honor. After the 2004 season, Jeter received his first American League Gold Glove award for fielding excellence at shortstop. The award was controversial, as for years many baseball analysts had been critical of Jeter's defense, citing statistics that indicated that not only was the Yankee shortstop not one of the best defenders at his position, he was actually one of the worst. In spite of those statistics, Jeter would go on to win the award again in 2005, 2006, 2009, and 2010. In May of 2006, he earned his 2,000th major-league hit, in a season that saw the resurgent Yankee captain hit .343, steal a career-best 34 bases, and finish a close second in the American League MVP voting. These accolades were a bitter consolation to Jeter in the face of his team's postseason futility. Finally, in 2008, the Yankees failed to make it to the playoffs for the first time in Jeter's career.

Collected 3000th Hit

The 2009 season saw a number of changes for Jeter: a new work address, as the team opened a new ballpark built across the street from the original Yankee

Stadium, and new teammates with the free-agent signings of first baseman Mark Teixeira and starting pitchers C. C. Sabathia and A. J. Burnett. It also featured a return to championship form for the Yankee captain. Jeter hit .334 and finished third in the MVP voting, and the team won its first World Series since 2000. Along the way Jeter became the franchise's all-time leader in career hits, surpassing Lou Gehrig; he was named one of the 10 best active players by the *Sporting News*; he received the Henry Aaron Award as the best batter in the American League and the Roberto Clemente Award for his community involvement; and he was named *Sports Illustrated*'s Sportsman of the Year, the first Yankee ever granted that honor.

After the championship season, Jeter finally began to show his age in 2010. He set career lows in batting average (.270), on-base percentage (.340), and slugging percentage (.370). The worst performance of his career came at an unfortunate time, as Jeter was in the final season of his 10-year contract. After losing to the Texas Rangers in the ALCS, Jeter would face a bitter negotiation for his next contract. Unlike the previous negotiations, these were conducted in full light of the media, with the Yankees openly disparaging their captain's contract demands and at times all but daring him to explore the free agent market. In the end, the contract Jeter signed was a compromise for both parties: at three years, it was shorter than Jeter wanted, and at $51 million, it featured a higher annual salary than the Yankees wanted to pay.

In the early going of the 2011 season, the contract looked like a poor investment. Through early July, Jeter was hitting .257 with no power—just two home runs for the entire season. However, on July 9, 2011, Jeter showed his penchant for the big moment one more time. Sitting 2 hits shy of the 3,000 mark, Jeter rained 5 hits on the Tampa Bay Rays, his first 5-hit performance since 2006. For the historic 3,000th hit, Jeter left no doubt, blasting a home run deep into the left field bleachers off All-Star David Price. "It was one of those special days," Jeter told *USA Today*. "Coming in, I've been lying to (the press) for a long time saying I wasn't nervous and there was no pressure. I felt a lot of pressure to do it here while we're at home."

As the 28th person to collect 3,000 career hits, and only the 4th to do it while primarily playing shortstop, Jeter seemed assured a place in history. It was all but guaranteed that some day he would be inducted into baseball's Hall of Fame, have a bronze plaque in Yankee Stadium's Monument Park, and be officially recognized as one of the all-time greats of the game. However, Jeter's near future was less certain. Despite his dazzling performance that one day in July, Derek Jeter was still a 37-year-old man playing one of the most demanding positions in front of some of the most demanding fans in baseball.

Sources

Periodicals

Detroit Free Press, October 26, pp. 1D, 6D.
Jet, March 8, 1999, p. 46.
New York Daily News, September 6, 2009.
New York Times, June 4, 2003; November 3, 2004; December 8, 2010, B19; July 9, 2011.
Sports Illustrated, November 6, 2000; November 30, 2009.
USA Today, October 26, 1999; July 11, 2011.

Online

ESPN.com, July 6, 2008, http://sports.espn.go.com/mlb/allstar08/news/story?id=3475435 (accessed August 7, 2011).
Milwaukee Journal Sentinel, May 20, 2009, http://www.jsonline.com/sports/45556307.html (accessed August 7, 2011).
"Derek Jeter: Biography," MLB.com, http://mlb.mlb.com/players/jeter_derek/about/bio.jsp (accessed August 7, 2011).
"Derek Jeter: The Captain," *60 Minutes*, CBSNews.com, September 22, 2005, http://www.cbsnews.com/stories/2005/09/22/60minutes/main880059_page2.shtml (accessed August 7, 2011).
SI.com, July 14, 2004, http://sportsillustrated.cnn.com/2004/baseball/mlb/specials/all_star/2004/07/14/bc.bbo.all.star.jeter.ap/index.html; November 2, 2004, http://sportsillustrated.cnn.com/2004/baseball/mlb/11/02/bc.bba.algoldgloves.ap/index.html; November 1, 2005, http://sportsillustrated.cnn.com/2005/baseball/mlb/wires/11/01/2010.ap.bba.al.gold.gloves.2nd.ld.writethru.0456/inde.html; November 3, 2006, http://sportsillustrated.cnn.com/2006/baseball/mlb/wires/11/03/2014.ap.bbo.2006.gold.gloves.winners.0136/index.html; July 8, 2007, http://sportsillustrated.cnn.com/2007/baseball/mlb/specials/all_star/2007/07/06/al.nlrosters/index.html (accessed August 7, 2011) .

—John Horn and Derek Jacques

Lonnie G. Johnson

1949—

Engineer, inventor

Johnson, Lonnie G., photograph. Thomas S. England/Time & Life Pictures/Getty Images.

Lonnie G. Johnson's name sometimes appears on lists of influential African-American inventors and scientists through the ages. Although he is not accorded the fame bestowed on George Washington Carver or Benjamin Banneker, Johnson quietly earned a small fortune for his Super Soaker water gun, one of the best-selling water toys ever manufactured. The Alabama native and former National Aeronautics and Space Administration (NASA) scientist then plowed much of those earnings into his real passion: developing a revolutionary new power-generation technology using hydrogen fuel cells.

Launched Career as a Rocket Scientist

Lonnie George Johnson was born on October 6, 1949, the third of six children. He grew up in Mobile, Alabama, where his father, David, was employed as a civilian driver at the local Air Force base. His mother, Arline, was primarily a homemaker, with occasional stints as a laundry worker or nurse's aid. Their son's knack for science and mechanics was apparent early

on: Johnson and his brothers spent hours fashioning go-carts powered by lawn mower engines (one of which he once tested on a stretch of Interstate-10 that was then under construction) and weapons that shot projectiles from pressurized chambers. Johnson made his biggest bang, literally, cooking up a batch of rocket fuel in the family kitchen. The homemade fuel recipe eventually came out right, resulting in the launch of a miniature rocket Johnson built for a school project.

Johnson's breakthrough invention was a remote-controlled robot he built during his senior year at L.B. Williamson High School, one of the city's formerly all-black high schools. He called the robot Linex, and it had been inspired by the Robinson family's bubble-headed companion on the 1960s television series *Lost in Space*. Linex ambled about thanks to a combination of junkyard pickings, walkie-talkie innards, and a reel-to-reel tape recorder belonging to Johnson's sister, and earned Johnson first prize in a statewide science fair in 1968. The Junior Engineering Technical Society Exposition event was hosted by the University of Alabama, and Williamson High was the sole black school

At a Glance . . .

Born Lonnie George Johnson on October 6, 1949, in Mobile, AL; son of David Johnson (a U.S. Air Force civilian employee) and Arline Johnson (a domestic worker and nurse's aide); married Linda Moore; four children. *Military service:* Served in the U.S. Air Force; reached rank of captain. *Education:* Tuskegee University, BS, mechanical engineering, 1973, MS, nuclear engineering, 1976.

Career: U.S. Air Force Weapons Laboratory, acting chief of Space Nuclear Power Safety section, 1978–79; Jet Propulsion Laboratory, senior systems engineer, Galileo Project, 1979–82, engineer on Mariner Mark II Spacecraft series for Comet Rendezvous and Saturn Orbiter Probe missions, 1987–91; U.S. Air Force, Advanced Space Systems Requirements manager for nonnuclear strategic weapons technology, 1982–85, Strategic Air Command, chief of data management branch, 1985–87; Johnson Research and Development Co., Inc., founder and president, 1991—; also the founder of Johnson Electro-Mechanical Systems and Excellatron Solid State LLC.

Memberships: Georgia Alliance for Children (chair).

Awards: First place, University of Alabama Junior Engineering Technical Society Exposition, for "Linex the Robot," 1968; elected to Pi Tau Sigma National Engineering Honor Society, 1973; Air Force Commendation Medal, 1979, 1986; Air Force Achievement Medal, 1984; inducted into Hasbro Inventor's Hall of Fame, 2000, for the Super Soaker water gun; Golden Torch Award, National Society of Black Engineers, 2001; honorary PhD, Tuskegee University.

Addresses: *Home*—Atlanta, GA. *Office*—Johnson Research and Development Co., Inc., 263 Decatur St., Atlanta, GA 30312. *Web*—http://www.johnsonrd.com.

permitted to enter. Johnson's Linex won first prize, which came with a $250 check. The college campus had been the site of a notorious desegregation battle just five years earlier. "The only thing anybody from the university said to us during the entire competition," Johnson told a writer for the *Atlantic*, Logan Ward, "was 'Goodbye, and y'all drive safe, now.'"

After graduating from high school, Johnson entered Tuskegee University on an Air Force Reserve Officers' Training Corps (ROTC) scholarship. He earned a bachelor's degree in mechanical engineering in 1973, followed by a master's degree in nuclear engineering three years later. After completing a master of science degree, Johnson joined the Air Force, serving during the late 1970s as acting chief of the Space Nuclear Power Safety Section at the Air Force Weapons Laboratory near Albuquerque, New Mexico, where he worked on methods for using atomic energy in space. He earned his first patent in 1979 for a digital distance measuring instrument.

That same year, Johnson moved to the Jet Propulsion Laboratory in Pasadena, California, a renowned center for research and experimentation on aerospace technology. There he worked as a senior systems engineer on the Galileo mission, helping to develop nuclear power systems for the $1.6 billion spacecraft designed to study Jupiter and its 16 moons. After three years there, Johnson returned to the Air Force, and was assigned to Strategic Air Command in Omaha, Nebraska, where he worked on nonnuclear strategic weapons technology, followed by a three-year stint on the B-2 Stealth bomber program at Edwards Air Force Base in California. Over the course of his Air Force career, Johnson received numerous honors, including two commendation medals and the Air Force Achievement Medal. He was also nominated for NASA astronaut training in 1985.

Invented Popular Super Soaker Water Toy

Johnson left the military in 1987 and returned to the Jet Propulsion Lab, where he worked on the Mars Observer project and the Cassini-Huygens mission to Saturn. Meanwhile, Johnson had dabbled with various inventions in his spare time throughout his career in both the military and civilian aerospace industries. The idea for the invention that eventually made him famous popped into his head in 1982, while he was fiddling in his home workshop with a model of a heat pump that used water instead of Freon, a gas known to harm the Earth's ozone layer. Hooking the pump up to the bathroom sink, Johnson was amazed to witness a powerful stream of water shoot across the room. It immediately occurred to him that the same idea could be used for an intense squirt gun. The concept for the Super Soaker, first called the Power Drencher, was born.

Johnson built a prototype of his pneumatic water gun out of PVC pipe, a plastic soft-drink bottle, and Plexiglas. He set his six-year-old daughter, Aneka, loose in the neighborhood armed with the new device, and it instantly received rave reviews from the other children. The revolutionary thing about Johnson's squirt gun was that it allowed the shooter to build up a huge amount of pressure by pumping air into a chamber with repeated

pump strokes before shooting, as opposed to conventional water weaponry, which fired only with the pressure of a single trigger pull. He applied for a patent on October 14, 1983, eventually receiving U.S. patent number 4,591,071 on May 27, 1986, for a "toy squirt gun that shoots a continuous, high velocity stream of water."

While Johnson had the idea and the patent, he did not have the resources to bring the Super Soaker to the public on his own. He spent most of the 1980s trying to find a company willing to manufacture and market his toy. Finally, Johnson caught the attention of a representative of Larami Corporation at a New York toy fair in 1989. He arranged a meeting at Larami's Philadelphia headquarters. Larami executives were immediately impressed by the prototype, and quickly agreed to take on the Super Soaker. They had access to the major manufacturing resources that could bring the toy to market, which also required a hefty investment of capital to get the production model made, packaged, and shipped out. There was little money left over for marketing or promotion. "We put them in the stores," Johnson said when interviewed for the CNBC television series *How I Made My Millions* in 2011, "and they just blew out, right away."

Johnson had licensed the design to Larami in exchange for a percentage of sales. The first royalty check was shocking, he recalled in the CNBC interview, but then the national television ads rolled out and the next royalty figure floored him. In 1992 the Super Soaker surpassed Nintendo as the number-one selling toy in America. By then Johnson left the Jet Propulsion Lab to strike out on his own, forming Johnson Research and Development Company, Inc., with his Super Soaker profits.

Sought to Develop Alternative-Energy Source

In 1993 Johnson Research was awarded a contract by NASA to develop the Johnson Tube, a water-based cooling system that is 25 percent more efficient than conventional heat pumps and air conditioners. Johnson spent much of the 1990s devising gadgets for serious scientists and kids alike, including an advanced dart gun he licensed to toymaker Hasbro—which became Larami's parent company—in 1998. In the first years of the new millennium he began devoting more time to his idea for an alternative-fuel engine. His NASA connections helped him gain entry to top military research-and-development officials, and in 2003 he was given a grant to develop a new kind of fuel cell with a ceramic membrane that could withstand temperatures as high as 400 degrees Celsius.

Johnson called his project JTEC, or the Johnson Thermo-electrochemical Converter system. JTEC can harness solar energy and channel that into two closed hydrogen cells; the power moves through the membrane, and heat forces the ions apart in a method that generates power. The closed-cell design makes the JTEC self-charging, and there are no moving parts nor by-products. The energy produced can be converted into other uses, like electricity. Highly esteemed scientists—among them National Science Foundation program director Paul Werbos—believe Johnson's prototype has revolutionary potential. It produces no carbon footprint and could double the efficiency rate of thermal-power plants, helping them reach a much lower cost-per-kilowatt hour, which is about 25 cents. The JTEC system could halve that energy cost, making solar energy as cheap a source of fuel as coal. "There's a lot of debate in Washington about carbon emissions and energy—about coal, nuclear power, and oil, what I call the three horsemen of the apocalypse," Werbos told Ward in the *Atlantic* article. "If we can cut the cost of solar energy in half, it becomes possible to escape from the three horsemen. The importance of this is just unbelievable."

Johnson's JTEC system was honored by *Popular Mechanics* magazine as one of the Breakthrough inventions of 2008. He teamed with the legendary subsidiary of Xerox, called the Palo Alto Research Center (known as PARC), though he remained at work in Atlanta, where he had renovated old industrial spaces on Decatur Street to serve as corporate headquarters. The CNBC *How I Made My Millions* story estimated that he may have earned as much as $20 million in royalties by 2011 in the 20 years since the Super Soaker first appeared in stores. While not divulging details, Johnson said he has invested a significant share of his toy earnings into his research and development companies, telling CNBC, "I literally pay to come to work."

Sources

Periodicals

Atlanta Journal-Constitution, October 27, 2008.
Black Enterprise, November 1993, p. 71.
Chicago Tribune, August 14, 2001.
Newsweek, June 22, 1992, p. 58.
New York Times, July 31, 2001.
Time, December 4, 2000, p. 108.

Online

"Johnson Thermo-Electrochemical Converter System," *Popular Mechanics,* http://www.popularmechan ics.com/technology/gadgets/news/ 4286850-10 (accessed July 25, 2011).
Ward, Logan, "Shooting for the Sun," *The Atlantic,* November 2010, http://www.theatlantic.com/ magazine/archive/2010/11/shooting-for-the-sun/ 8268/1/ (accessed July 25, 2011).

Other

Episode 4, *How I Made My Millions,* CNBC, March 7, 2011, http://video.cnbc.com/gallery/?video=3000 008999 (accessed July 25, 2011).

—Robert R. Jacobson and Carol Brennan

Talib Kweli

1975—

Rapper

Kweli, Talib, photograph. AP Images/Jean-Christophe Bott.

Talib Kweli, a socially conscious rapper lauded for his intelligent and imaginative lyrics, enjoyed critical acclaim for a series of collaborations and solo albums beginning in the late 1990s. Kweli first attracted attention as part of Black Star, his collaboration with Mos Def and the producer Hi-Tek. Though Black Star made only one album, Kweli and Hi-Tek continued to collaborate as the group Reflection Eternal, and Kweli's solo career began in earnest with 2002's *Quality*. *Beautiful Struggle* (2004) flirted with mainstream success, and subsequent albums have performed respectably amid slumping industry-wide sales, but true popular success has eluded Kweli. He remains an admired figure in the world of hip-hop.

Gravitated to Hip-Hop

Born in Brooklyn, New York, in 1975, Talib Kweli was raised in an educated and socially conscious household, the elder of two sons born to Perry and Brenda Greene. The Greenes, shaped by the civil rights movement and knowledgeable about their African heritage, gave their son a name that combines the Arabic word for seeker or student ("Talib") with a word from a Ghanaian language meaning knowledge or truth ("Kweli"). Kweli spent his early years in the Brooklyn neighborhood of Park Slope, which was highly diverse, before the family relocated to a predominantly West Indian neighborhood, Flatbush.

During his junior high years, Kweli was already actively writing poetry and plays, and when his verbal talents were recognized by a self-styled rapper in the neighborhood, he began to develop the idea that he could write rhymes himself. Kweli attended the elite Connecticut boarding school Cheshire Academy during his high school years, where he began to act in plays while continuing to write them. After high school he studied experimental theater at New York University's Tisch School of the Arts, but he did not take his academic life seriously.

Kweli's main goal during this time was to be in New York for social and cultural reasons. His roommate at NYU was John Forte, who became part of the hip-hop group the Fugees. The two collaborated on rhymes during this time, and Forte produced Kweli's first demo. Kweli began to make a name for himself as an MC in the hip-hop underground in the mid-1990s, first with

At a Glance . . .

Born Talib Kweli Greene, on October 3, 1975, in Brooklyn, NY; son of Dr. Perry Greene (a professor and academic administrator) and Dr. Brenda H. Greene (a professor); married DJ Eque in 2009; children: Amani Fela Greene (son), Diyani Eshe Greene (daughter). *Education*: Attended New York University's Tisch School for the Arts.

Career: Rapper with the group Reflection Eternal, 1997–2000; rapper with the group Black Star, 1998; solo rapper, 2002—.

Addresses: *Record label*—Blacksmith, 45 Rockefeller Plaza at 630 Fifth Ave., 20th Fl., New York, NY 10020. *Email*—info@blacksmithnyc.com. *Web*—http://www.yearoftheblacksmith.com/.

contributions to *Doom*, a 1995 album by the Cincinnati-based group Mood, and then through collaborations with Mood's producer, DJ Hi-Tek.

Won Critical Acclaim with Black Star

Kweli and Hi-Tek called themselves Reflection Eternal, and some of their early songs appeared on compilations released by the independent label Rawkus. During this time Kweli reconnected with a longtime Brooklyn acquaintance, Dante Smith, who had begun performing as Mos Def and who was also associated with Rawkus. Kweli began regularly joining Mos Def on stage in New York clubs, and although both had plans for their own projects, Kweli for a Reflection Eternal album and Mos Def for a solo album, the two decided to join forces under the name Black Star, with Hi-Tek in charge of most of the production.

The result, 1998's *Mos Def and Talib Kweli Are Black Star*, appeared at a time when hip-hop was increasingly identified with gangster rap and the culture that surrounded it. The recent shooting deaths of Tupac Shakur and The Notorious B.I.G. had shaken the hip-hop world, and Black Star responded by offering more affirmative material and a socially informed style that recalled "old-school" rappers like KRS-One and Public Enemy. A nod to Marcus Garvey—the early 20th century leader of the Back-to-Africa movement who incorporated the Black Star shipping line with the goal of helping African Americans resettle on the continent of their ancestors—*Mos Def and Talib Kweli Are Black Star* mined the symbolism of that earlier era to craft an up-to-date vision of black empowerment.

In addition to critiques of the violence that was plaguing hip-hop culture, the album included a song that put forward positive images of blackness, a song inspired by the Toni Morrison novel the *Bluest Eye*, and a song about respecting and valuing women. The album was an underground hit that never broke through to mainstream success, but it was instantly embraced by critics and other rappers, and as a stylish counter-example to the gangster posture, it went on to have a powerful influence on other artists. It is now widely considered to be one of the best rap albums of the 1990s.

Mos Def released his first solo album, *Black on Both Sides*, the following year, and Kweli and DJ Hi-Tek, recording as Reflection Eternal, continued the partnership that had predated their collaboration with Mos Def, releasing *Train of Thought* in 2000. *Train of Thought* was well received, and it demonstrated that Kweli and Hi-Tek were capable of generating a high-caliber product on their own. Between Black Star, Reflection Eternal, and Mos Def's solo work, the Rawkus label was poised to become a major force in hip-hop.

Launched Solo Career

As it happened, Mos Def focused on his acting career, and both Kweli and Hi-Tek turned to solo careers. Kweli did not utilize Hi-Tek's production on his first solo album, 2002's *Quality*, working instead with an assortment of producers including DJ Quik and Kanye West, who was then little known. One of the tracks that West produced, "Get By," became Kweli's most popular single to that date, breaking into the Billboard Hot 100 with help from Jay–Z and Busta Rhymes, who made appearances on a remixed version that was picked up on radio stations. Although the song reached only No. 77 on the Hot 100, *Billboard*'s Rashaun Hall named it the single of the year for 2003, noting the applicability of its message in a world still adjusting to the anxieties provoked by the September 11 terrorist attacks of two years before. *Quality* thus bolstered Kweli's already formidable critical reputation, without putting him over the top in mainstream terms.

A further endorsement by Jay–Z, who combined critical acclaim with sales success, suggested, however, that Kweli might yet reach a wider audience. On "Moment of Clarity," a song on the *Black Album* (2003), Jay–Z ranked Kweli's lyrical prowess above his own, rapping, "If skills sold, truth be told / I'd probably be lyrically Talib Kweli." Kweli's second solo album, *Beautiful Struggle* (2004), which again featured the production stylings of Kanye West, whose profile was rapidly growing at this time, as well as guest artists Mary J. Blige, Faith Evans, and Anthony Hamilton, appeared to some critics to be an attempt to capitalize on his growing reputation. Kweli himself maintained, according to Mark Anthony Neal of *PopMatters*, "This album I tried to let the music decide what I was gonna write, instead of vice versa." The album indeed connected

with a wider audience than Kweli's previous efforts, reaching No. 3 on the R&B charts and No. 14 on the Billboard 200.

A 2005 Kweli release, *Right about Now*, occupied a middle ground between a mixtape and an album proper, with some critics embracing it as a significant outing and others seeing it as an attempt to keep the public's attention while work was ongoing on an actual album. Kweli's next album, *Eardrum*, appeared the following year on his own label, Blacksmith, which he launched in a partnership with Warner Brothers. Kweli again called on a number of guest artists, including Justin Timberlake, Norah Jones, UGK, and Strong Arm Steady, and his production partners included West, Hi-Tek, and will.i.am, among others. *Eardrum* reached number No. 2 on the Billboard 200 as well as the R&B charts, and it won a warmer critical reception than *Beautiful Struggle*.

In 2008 Blacksmith became truly independent, splitting with Warner Brothers. Blacksmith continued to release albums, but Kweli himself planned a digital-only release, via a Blacksmith imprint, of his next full-length recording, *Gutter Rainbows*. After he debuted the album online, however, the independent label Duck Down stepped in to release the album on CD in 2011. *Gutter Rainbows* sold well by Kweli's standards, reaching No. 7 on the R&B charts, and though it met with a generally warm reception among his fans, it did not win the kinds of raves some of his earlier albums had.

Kweli's fans were interested in another project rumored to be on the horizon: a Black Star reunion. Kweli and Mos Def, who had appeared on one another's albums over the years, suggested that a new collaboration was in the works. Well established as a top-flight lyricist and solo artist, Kweli continued to be best known for his ground-breaking 1998 collaboration with Mos Def.

Selected Discography

(As Black Star) *Mos Def and Talib Kweli Are Black Star*, Rawkus, 1998.
(As Reflection Eternal) *Train of Thought*, Rawkus, 2000.
Quality, MCA (includes "Get By"), 2002.
The Beautiful Struggle, Rawkus, 2004.
Right about Now, Koch, 2005.
Eardrum, Blacksmith, 2007.
Gutter Rainbows, Duck Down, 2011.

Sources

Periodicals

Billboard, September 30, 2000, p. 28; December 27, 2003, p. 47; January 14, 2006, pp. 52–53; February 12, 2011, p. 42.
Callaloo 29.3, 2006, pp. 993–1011.
Chicago Tribune, February 4, 2011.
People, October 25, 2004.
Progressive, October 2005, pp. 42–44.
Rolling Stone, January 23, 2003; December 15, 2005, p. 155.

Online

Neal, Mark Anthony, "Talib Kweli's Beautiful Struggle," PopMatters, http://www.popmatters.com/pm/feature/041112-talibkweli/ (accessed August 7, 2011).
Paine, Jake, "Talib Kweli: Say Something," AllHip Hop.com, http://allhiphop.com/stories/features/archive/2007/08/21/18452878.aspx (accessed August 7, 2011).
"Talib Kweli," AllMusic, http://allmusic.com/artist/talib-kweli-p311367 (accessed August 7, 2011).

—Mark Lane

LaChanze

1961—

Actress

Actress and singer LaChanze earned acclaim for her performance in the 2005 Broadway musical *The Color Purple,* adapted from the Pulitzer Prize–winning novel by Alice Walker. Playing the lead role of Celie, a woman who overcomes life's hardships to find happiness, seemed a natural fit for LaChanze, who had suffered through her own burdens, losing her husband in the September 11, 2001, terrorist attacks when she was eight months pregnant with their second child. The actress, a veteran of the stage who has appeared in Broadway productions of *Once on This Island, Company,* and *Ragtime,* found solace from her grief in a familiar place—the theater—emerging as triumphant as the character she portrayed in *The Color Purple.*

LaChanze, photograph. Thos Robinson/Getty Images.

She was born Rhonda LaChanze Sapp on December 16, 1961, in St. Augustine, Florida, the oldest of eight children of Walter Sapp, a former officer in the U.S. Coast Guard, and Rosalie Hamm Sapp (now Hines). Her middle name, LaChanze (pronounced la-SHANSE), meaning "one who is charmed" in Creole, comes from her grandmother; the actress now uses that single name professionally.

As a young girl, she had a passion for performing, always wanting to "burst out into song and . . . poetic recitations," she told the *Crisis* in 2005. Her mother first enrolled her in dance lessons at age six. Later, when the family relocated to Bridgeport, Connecticut, after her parents' divorce, she continued her dance studies at the Bowen Peters Cultural Arts Center in New Haven. There, her mentor and teacher, Angela Bowen Peters, impressed on LaChanze's mother that she had a very gifted daughter whose talent was worth nurturing. LaChanze made her dramatic debut in a high school production of *Damn Yankees.*

Debuted on Broadway

After high school, LaChanze attended Morgan State University in Baltimore for two years before transferring to the University of the Arts in Philadelphia, where she studied theater, dance, voice, and acting. She left school in 1986 when she landed her first professional job as a tap dancer in the musical revue *Uptown . . . It's Hot* at the Tropicana Hotel in Atlantic City, which transferred to Broadway for a short run later that year. "It was on Broadway for about 35 seconds," the actress

At a Glance . . .

Born Rhonda LaChanze Sapp on December 16, 1961, in St. Augustine, FL; daughter of Walter Sapp (a retired U.S. Coast Guard officer) and Rosalie Hines; married Calvin J. Gooding in 1998 (died 2001); married Derek Fordjour in 2005; children: Celia, Zaya, Langston (stepson). *Education*: Morgan State University; University of the Arts, Philadelphia.

Career: Actress, 1987—.

Awards: Theatre World Award, for *Once on This Island,* 1991; OBIE Award, for *Dessa Rose,* 2005; Tony Award, Best Leading Actress in a Musical, for *The Color Purple,* 2006.

Addresses: *Agent*—Innovative Artists, 235 Park Ave., 10th Fl., New York, NY 10003. *Web*—http://www.lachanze.com/.

remembered in an interview with Ira Weitzman of Lincoln Center Theater, "but in that time I got my Equity card [membership in the Actors Equity Association, the union of professional performers], and I became a legitimate professional actor and dancer . . . in New York."

The next year LaChanze was cast in the first international tour of the rhythm-and-blues musical *Dreamgirls,* which ended with a five-month Broadway run. The actress landed her breakout role in 1990, when she played Ti Mourne in *Once on This Island,* a musical adaptation of Trinidadian author Rosa Guy's novel *My Love, My Love,* at the Booth Theatre on Broadway. She earned Tony and Drama Desk award nominations for her performance and won a Theatre World Award in 1991. The show also marked the beginning of LaChanze's long collaboration with composers Lynn Ahrens and Stephen Flaherty, whose niche was turning historical narratives into musicals.

After a string of regional theater productions, including *Jesus Christ Superstar* (1991) at the Walnut Street Theatre in Philadelphia, *From the Mississippi Delta* (1991) at the Cincinnati Playhouse in the Park, and *Spunk* (1995) at Hartford Stage in Connecticut, LaChanze returned to the Great White Way in 1995 in the first Broadway revival of the musical *Company.* Three years later, she reunited with Ahrens and Flaherty, starring in their best-known musical, *Ragtime,* based on the novel by E. L. Doctorow, at the Ford Center for the Performing Arts. She received an Ovation Award nomination for her portrayal of Sarah,

a role that she took over from veteran actress Audra McDonald.

Found Solace from Grief on Stage

By 2001 life was treating LaChanze well: she had a successful acting career, a loving husband—Calvin Gooding, whom she had married in 1998—a beautiful daughter, Celia, and another child on the way. All of that changed on the morning of September 11, when her husband, a bond trader at Cantor Fitzgerald, lost his life in the terrorist attacks on the World Trade Center. At the time, LaChanze was eight months pregnant; she gave birth to a daughter, Zaya, in October.

In the aftermath of the tragedy, as she tried to find the strength to care for her two small children, LaChanze alternated between rage and despair. "After I had the baby, I didn't want to be angry, because I was nursing. But there were times I was so sad that my 2-year-old would crawl over to me and say, 'Mommy, what's the matter?' But I couldn't stop crying," she told Meryl Gordon in *New York Magazine* a year after the attacks. "There are days when I want to take a sledgehammer and crack every window on Fifth Avenue."

The actress found solace in a familiar place—the stage. In December of 2001, she returned to the theater in a production of Eve Ensler's *The Vagina Monologues.* Although she was apprehensive about going back to work, the experience proved to be therapeutic. "I got to be funny and happy and loved for an hour and a half. It was the best thing for me," she told Gordon. In November of 2002 she made her solo debut at Lincoln Center, giving an emotional vocal performance of "Song for LaChanze," a poem written by Ahrens and put to music by Flaherty; the composers had written the ballad as a memorial to Gooding. "She began to sing and was so triumphant," Joseph Langworth, a close friend of the actress, told *People* magazine. "I saw a survivor who chose to continue living."

Renewed Personal and Professional Life

In November of 2003 LaChanze's life took yet another unexpected turn. Wishing to give a gift of thanks to the law firm that had provided pro bono legal representation for her family after Gooding's death, she decided to commission a work of art. She contacted Derek Fordjour, a painter who was then best known for his work *An Experiment in Brotherhood,* which commemorated the founding of the African-American fraternity Alpha Phi Alpha. The two spent hours on the telephone discussing the work, and by the time they met in person, "It was like I had known him all my life," LaChanze explained in *People.* A year and a half later, Fordjour proposed marriage, and the couple wed in July of 2005.

By this time, LaChanze's career was back in full swing. In the summer of 2004, she landed the lead role in a new musical adaptation of *The Color Purple,* featuring lyrics and music by Brenda Russell, Allee Willis, and Stephen Bray and book by playwright Marsha Norman. Based on the Pulitzer Prize–winning novel by Alice Walker, the production opened in September at the Alliance Theatre in Atlanta, with LaChanze playing Celie, the role made famous by Whoopi Goldberg in the 1985 Steven Spielberg film. Spanning four decades, the play chronicles Celie's development from a frightened 14-year-old slave girl who is raped by her father, has her children taken away from her, and then is sold into an abusive marriage to become a self-assured, empowered woman who has overcome life's hardships.

The role was a perfect match for LaChanze, who felt a deep connection to Celie that was informed by her own experience of loss. "The focus and faith that Celie has—I understood," she explained in the *Crisis,* "the vulnerability and resilience to have faith as the world is falling down around her, pulling at her. That Celie's able to stay focused and trust her faith . . . is just astounding. That she's able to have this raw faith that says, 'This is not it. This is not all there is for me.' I understood that immediately."

Audiences and critics responded enthusiastically to *The Color Purple* and to LaChanze's performance. In the *Atlanta Journal-Constitution,* theater critic Wendell Brock wrote, "*Color Purple* is a visually mesmerizing, vocally soaring gospel-jazz-and-blues pastiche," calling LaChanze's performance "eloquent." The show's nearly six-week run produced the highest box office gross in the theater's history, selling out 30 of 46 performances.

Gave Tony-Winning Performance

In 2005 LaChanze appeared Off-Broadway in the Ahrens and Flaherty musical *Dessa Rose,* for which she won an OBIE Award, and in the television movie *Lucy.* The Color Purple transferred to Broadway the following year, backed by the star power of investor Oprah Winfrey, who had been nominated for an Academy Award for her role as Sofia in the Spielberg film. Opening in December, the show once again was a hit. Ben Brantley of the *New York Times* described the production as "a bright, shiny and muscular storytelling machine" and praised LaChanze's "considerable natural light," while David Rooney of *Variety* singled out the actress's "honest, giving performance." *The Color Purple* earned 11 Tony Award nominations in 2006, with the award for best leading actress in a musical going to LaChanze over Patti Lupone and Chita Rivera.

LaChanze left the cast of *The Color Purple* in November of 2006 and published her first children's book, *The Little Diva,* in 2008. In 2009 she starred alongside pop singer Ashanti in the musical *The Wiz* at Lincoln Center and performed in the Off-Broadway premiere of Kristina Anderson's play *Inked Baby* at Playwrights Horizons. That same year, she appeared in the production *Handel's Messiah Rocks,* featuring rock renditions of George Frideric Handel's classical oratorios, with the Boston Pops; the performance was filmed at Emerson College in Massachusetts and broadcast nationally on PBS.

In addition to her many stage roles, LaChanze also has made guest appearances on television in *The Cosby Show, Law & Order SVU, Sex and the City, New York Undercover,* and *The Gregory Hines Show.* Her film credits include *Leap of Faith* (1993), the animated feature *Hercules* (1997), *Breaking Upwards* (2009), and *The Help* (2011).

Selected works

Theater

Uptown . . . It's Hot!, Tropicana Hotel, Atlantic City, NJ, Lunt-Fontanne Theatre, New York, 1986.
Dreamgirls, Ambassador Theatre, New York, 1987.
Once on This Island, Playwrights Horizons, Booth Theatre, New York, 1990–91.
From the Mississippi Delta, Cincinnati Playhouse in the Park, Cincinnati, OH, 1991.
Jesus Christ Superstar, Walnut Street Theatre, Philadelphia, 1991.
Company, Criterion Center Stage Right, New York, 1995.
Out of This World, City Center Theatre, New York, 1995.
Spunk, Hartford Stage, Hartford, CT, 1995.
Ragtime, Ford Center for the Performing Arts, New York, 1998–2000.
The Bubbly Black Girl Sheds Her Chameleon Skin, Playwrights Horizons, New York, 2000.
The Vagina Monologues, Westside Theatre, New York, 2001–02.
Baby, Papermill Playhouse, Millburn, NJ, 2004.
The Color Purple, Alliance Theatre, Atlanta, GA, 2004; Broadway Theatre, New York, 2005–06.
Dessa Rose, Mitzi E. Newhouse Theatre, New York, 2005.
Inked Baby, Peter Jay Sharp Theater, New York, 2009.
The Wiz, Lincoln Center, New York, 2009.

Films

Leap of Faith, Paramount Pictures, 1992.
My New Gun, IRS Media, 1992.
For Love or Money, Paramount Pictures, 1993.
David Searching, Backpain Productions, 1997.
Hercules (voice), Buena Vista Pictures, 1997.
Heartbreak Hospital, Bergman Lustig, 2002.

Breaking Upwards, IFC Films, 2009.
The Help, Walt Disney, 2011.

Television

Hercules (voice), ABC, 1998.
Lucy (television movie), CBS, 2003.

Books

(With Brian Pinckney) *The Little Diva,* Feiwel & Friends, 2010.

Sources

Periodicals

Atlanta Journal-Constitution, September 18, 2004; October 23, 2004.
Crisis, November 2005, p. 43.

New York Magazine, September 11, 2002.
New York Times, November 19, 2002; December 2, 2005.
People, December 12, 2005.
St. Augustine Record, February 5, 2006.

Online

"LaChanze and Celie: Tough Times in Common," National Public Radio, December 15, 2006, http://www.npr.org/templates/story/story.php?storyId=5056574 (accessed August 4, 2011).

LaChanze Official Website, http://www.lachanze.com/ (accessed August 4, 2011).

Weitzman, Ira, "LaChanze and Rachel York, the Leading Cast Members of *Dessa Rose,*" Lincoln Center Theater, http://www.lct.org/showMain.htm?id=157 (accessed August 4, 2011).

—Deborah A. Ring

Lunsford Lane

1803–(?)

Slave, entrepreneur, author, lecturer

Lunsford Lane, born a slave near Raleigh, North Carolina, discovered an entrepreneurial streak during his youth and began raising money in an attempt to improve his lot. His success as a tobacconist and businessman allowed him to marry, have children, and buy his own freedom. As he was working to buy the freedom of his wife and children, he was forced by unsympathetic whites to flee Raleigh for the North. In New York and Boston, Lane told his story to abolitionists and was able to raise the money to purchase his family's freedom. He completed the purchase, but not without complication, and he brought his family north.

Encouraged to document the story that had so affected the sympathetic Northerners he encountered, he wrote a narrative of his experiences negotiating the difficulties of slavery and freedom. That short document, *The Narrative of Lunsford Lane, Formerly of Raleigh, N.C.: Embracing an Account of His Early Life, the Redemption by Purchase of Himself and Family from Slavery, and His Banishment from the Place of His Birth for the Crime of Wearing a Colored Skin* (1842), is an important social and historical text and the source of most of the information known about him today.

Discovered Talent for Business

Lunsford Lane was born on May 30, 1803, on the plantation of Sherwood Haywood, a planter and banker with property in and outside of the state capital of Raleigh, North Carolina. Lane's mother, Clarissa

Haywood, was one of Haywood's favored house servants, and his father, Edward Lane, belonged to the owner of a neighboring plantation. As the son of a house servant, Lane grew up in close proximity not only to the children of the other house servants but to the children of his owners. As he wrote in his *Narrative*, "I knew no difference between myself and the white children nor did they seem to know any in turn. Sometimes my master would come out and give a biscuit to me, and another to one of his own white boys but I did not perceive the difference between us."

When Lane was old enough to work, however, the difference between his own station and that of his master's children became clear. His former playmates began issuing commands to him, and he saw that they were encouraged to read while he and other slaves were not permitted access to books. He also became acquainted with the knowledge that, at any time, his master might break up families and friendships by selling him or those he cared about, which he called the "worst (to us) of all calamities."

It was while brooding on the nature of his predicament that Lane discovered the power of money. His father gave him a basket of peaches, and he sold it for 30 cents. Later he sold some marbles for 60 cents. To his store of money was added several sums given him by visiting friends of his master, and soon he became possessed by the notion that he might one day be able to obtain enough money to buy his freedom. He began working in secret, at night, after the end of a long day of unpaid toil on his master's behalf, cutting wood and

selling it the next morning. Technically such autonomous pursuit of capital was illegal, and any money Lane made could have been seized by his owners. The Haywoods were comparatively lenient masters, however. Before long Lane had accumulated $100, and the idea of purchasing his own freedom was no longer a mere fantasy.

The breakthrough in Lane's entrepreneurial efforts came from his father, who had discovered a method for treating tobacco that "had the double advantage of giving the tobacco a peculiarly pleasant flavor, and of enabling me to manufacture a good article out of a very indifferent material." Lane also began manufacturing pipes out of reeds and clay. He sold his special brand of tobacco and the pipes he made outside of the Raleigh capitol building, primarily to members of the state congressional delegation, and soon he had a reputation as a tobacconist and the tacit consent of the white community to continue operating in this capacity. He saved enough money that he felt emboldened to seek a wife, and he successfully proposed to Martha Curtis, a slave on a nearby plantation. Her master, Mr. Boylan, authorized the union.

Purchased His Own Freedom

The Lanes soon had a growing family, but a few years into their marriage, Martha was sold to a new owner, Mr. Benjamin B. Smith, who did not provide adequate food and clothing for his slaves. Lane, forced to work not only for his own master but also as a tobacconist to pay for his family's basic necessities on another plantation, soon exhausted the capital he had been accumulating over the years. On the point of despair, his life was transformed by a sudden event: the death of his master, Sherwood Haywood.

Haywood's widow, named executrix of the estate, found that her husband owed the bank that employed him tens of thousands of dollars. To raise the money needed to pay the debt, she sold some of her slaves and

hired out others. Lane convinced her to allow him to hire himself out, working as a tobacconist full-time and then paying her the amount of money she would have received for a day's worth of his labor. He acquired a store and was able to manufacture pipes and tobacco on a much larger scale than previously, with sales representatives carrying his wares beyond Raleigh to other towns across the state. Thus, he was able to pay his owner the amount due to her for his time, pay for the support of his family on Smith's plantation, and also accumulate money toward the goal of purchasing his own and then his family's freedom.

When, after six or eight years, Lane had accumulated $1,000, he arranged with his wife's master to purchase his freedom for him, since he was not legally allowed to transact such business on his own behalf. Complications with local law required Lane to go with Smith to New York, where he was officially manumitted on September 9, 1835. He returned to Raleigh a free man by law, and he continued to work as a tobacconist as well as in the office of the North Carolina Governor Edward B. Dudley, accumulating money toward the purchase of his wife and children, who now numbered six.

Experienced Traumatic Setbacks

The owner of Lane's wife and children, Benjamin Smith, set the price for the seven Lanes at $3,000, even though he had purchased Martha and the youngest two Lane children for a mere $560 several years earlier, and even though he had since enjoyed the benefit of their labor as well as that of the subsequent children born into the family. Lane persuaded Smith to lower the price to $2,500, and the two men entered into a contract involving a schedule of five yearly payments of $500 apiece, beginning in 1840, two years from the date of the sales agreement.

Smith allowed the Lane family to live together as Lane saved the money for the first payment, which he made in January of 1840. In September of that year, however, amid rising local aggression toward free blacks, Lane was notified that, because he had been freed by a Northern state, New York, he was not legally authorized to reside in North Carolina. He was ordered to leave the state in 20 days or face a potential return to slavery. Although powerful friends in the legislature and the plantations on which he and his family had worked attempted to intercede on his behalf, they were only able to achieve a delay in the proceedings, enabling him to stay in the area and conduct business for a matter of months.

Lane was forced to flee to the North on May 18, 1841, leaving his family behind except for one daughter, whose purchase price he had already paid in full. In

New York and Boston he made the acquaintance of abolitionists, and through telling the story of his enslavement, his purchase of his freedom, and his family's predicament, he was able to raise the $1,380 he still needed to free his family. He corresponded with Smith to ensure that he would be allowed, upon his return to Raleigh, to complete the purchase. Although Smith was unable to procure definite legal assurances, he was able to pass along the convictions of both Governor Dudley and a Raleigh lawyer that Lane need not fear for his safety.

Nevertheless Lane, back in Raleigh, was accused of associating with abolitionists and suspected of trying to spread the abolitionist message among local slaves. He was apprehended and questioned in an informal courtroom by members of the city's white elite, who released him when he told them the story of how he raised his money in accordance with the agreement he had made with Mr. Smith. Outside of the building, a mob had gathered, and Lane's white friends believed that he would be killed if the mob were to seize him. They placed him in jail for his own safety. When he was released from jail after nightfall to make his way home, however, the mob was waiting for him. Lane had no doubt that he was going to be killed, but in the end, after telling his story, he was tarred and feathered instead.

Escaped the South with Family Intact

The next day, with help from some of his white friends, Lane concluded the business of purchasing his family and selling his property in Raleigh, and he left for New York. As the family was preparing to leave, Lane's former owner Mrs. Haywood allowed Lane's mother, Clarissa, to go with the family, rather than forcing a separation of mother and son. Mrs. Haywood suggested that Lane might someday pay her $200 for his mother if he became able to afford it in the future, but if not, she would not seek to reclaim her right to ownership.

Lane, his wife, his mother, and his seven children lived in various places after leaving the South, including Philadelphia, New York, Boston, and Oberlin, Ohio, before settling in Worcester, Massachusetts. Lane's father, Edward, won his freedom and joined the extended family, as well. The publication of Lane's *Narrative* in 1842 appears to have made him a public figure of some renown, and he supported his family at least partly through speaking engagements and lectures.

The only known sources of biographical information dating from Lane's lifetime are his own book and an 1863 biography (based largely on the *Narrative*) written by an abolitionist minister, William G. Hawkins. Lane's last known whereabouts were a Worcester hospital, where, according to Hawkins, he was working as head steward in 1862, as the Civil War raged. What became of Lane after this date is unknown.

Selected works

The Narrative of Lunsford Lane, Formerly of Raleigh, N.C.: Embracing an Account of His Early Life, the Redemption by Purchase of Himself and Family from Slavery, and His Banishment from the Place of His Birth for the Crime of Wearing a Colored Skin, J.G. Torrey, 1842.

Sources

Books

Andrews, William L., *North Carolina Roots of African American Literature: An Anthology*, UNC Press, 2006.

Bassett, John Spencer, *Anti-Slavery Leaders of North Carolina*, Volume 16, Johns Hopkins Press, 1898.

Franklin, John Hope, *The Free Negro in North Carolina, 1790–1860*, UNC Press Books, 1943.

Hawkins, William G. *Lunsford Lane: Another Helper from North Carolina*, Crosby & Nichols, 1863.

McCarthy, B. Eugene, and Thomas L. Doughton, eds., *From Bondage to Belonging: The Worcester Slave Narratives*, University of Massachusetts Press, 2007.

—Mark Lane

Ollie Matson

1930–2011

Professional football player, coach, scout, sports administrator

Matson, Ollie, photograph. AP Images/NFL Photos.

Hall of Famer Ollie Matson's athletic talent was extraordinary. Widely regarded as one of the finest and most versatile running backs in the history of the National Football League (NFL), he was also the winner of two Olympic medals in track and field. Amid the racism that once pervaded American sports, he conducted himself with quiet professionalism. Although he later went on to success as a coach, scout, and sports administrator, he is best remembered for his speed, agility, and leadership on the gridiron.

feated season, scoring no less than 19 touchdowns in the process. He then transferred to the University of San Francisco (USF), where he earned a bachelor's degree in history in 1952.

Matson's football career at USF was legendary. The squad as a whole was unusually talented, with no less than eight players going on to the NFL; two (Gino Marchetti and Bob St. Clair) later joined Matson in the Pro Football Hall of Fame. The team was also notable, however, for its relative diversity. At a time when many colleges refused to take the field if African Americans were on the opposing side, the presence of Matson and teammate Burl Toler isolated the USF squad and damaged its chances for national recognition. The most notorious incident in this regard came in 1951, when the organizers of many of the nation's leading bowl games refused an invitation to USF, even though the team had a sterling record of 9-0. When it was made known that an invitation might be forthcoming if Matson and Toler remained home, the duo's teammates, to their credit, refused. "After we said no and removed ourselves from consideration," Marchetti later recalled to the *New York Times,* "nobody ever had a second thought about it."

The son of a railroad worker and a schoolteacher, Ollie Genoa Matson II was born May 1, 1930, in Trinity, Texas, a small community in the east-central region of the state. His parents divorced when he was young, and he spent several years with his mother and twin sister in Houston before moving with them to California. At George Washington High School in San Francisco, he anchored both the football team and the track squad. Although he played a variety of positions in football, he was best known as a halfback, and it was that role that brought him several all-city honors. Upon graduation in 1948, he entered San Francisco City College and quickly led its football team to an unde-

At a Glance . . .

Born Ollie Genoa Matson II on May 1, 1930, in Trinity, TX; died on February 19, 2011, in Los Angeles, CA; son of Ollie (a train worker) and Gertrude (a schoolteacher) Matson; married Mary, 1954; children: four. *Education*: University of San Francisco, BA, history, 1952. *Military service*: U.S. Army, 1953–54.

Career: Chicago Cardinals, halfback, 1952, 1954–59; Los Angeles Rams, halfback, 1959–62; Detroit Lions, halfback, 1963; Philadelphia Eagles, halfback, 1964–66; Philadelphia Eagles and other organizations, coach and scout, 1960s-late 1970s; Los Angeles Memorial Coliseum, special-events supervisor, late 1970s–1989.

Awards: Rookie of the Year (co-winner), National Football League, 1952; Pro Football Hall of Fame, 1972; College Football Hall of Fame, 1976.

Buoyed by the support of his colleagues, Matson prepared to enter the NFL. Scouts throughout the league were dazzled by his performance at USF; the nation's leading collegiate rusher in 1951, he was also recognized for his defensive play, earning All-American honors at least once in the latter role. Although it seemed all but certain that he would thrive as a professional, many NFL teams worried that drafting an African American would alienate their white fans. The Chicago Cardinals, however, were in desperate need of Matson's talents, and in the spring of 1952 they selected him in the first round of the league's annual draft. In the midst of his preparations for the fall season, he found time to compete with the U.S. track and field team at the Olympic Games in Helsinki, Finland. After winning a bronze medal in the 400-meter dash and a silver in the 4x400-meter relay, he began his NFL career in earnest. Adjusting easily to professional play, he quickly became indispensable to the Cardinals. His performance in 1952 was so strong, in fact, that he was named one of two Rookies of the Year. He lost the following season, however, to military service. On his return from the U.S. Army in 1954, he solidified his growing reputation as one of the league's best rushers. The Cardinals as a whole generally struggled in this period, but Matson excelled, earning several invitations to the Pro Bowl, an end-of-season event for the league's best players; he would earn a total of six such invitations before the end of his career. Arguably the clearest sign of his stature, however, came

in 1959, when, in one of the most lopsided exchanges in league history, he was traded to the Los Angeles Rams for eight players and a draft choice.

Matson spent four seasons (1959–62) with the Rams, a franchise that relied on him as heavily as the Cardinals had done. He then moved on to the Detroit Lions, with whom he spent the 1963 season, before ending his career with the Philadelphia Eagles (1964–66). He left the field with nearly 13,000 total yards, a performance that virtually guaranteed him a spot in the Pro Football Hall of Fame. He was formally inducted there in 1972, the first year he was eligible for the honor. He later became a member of the College Football Hall of Fame as well. Amid these tributes, he found time for a varied career in sports administration. In addition to serving as a high-school and college coach, he spent several years scouting for the Eagles. He later went to work for Los Angeles Memorial Coliseum, one of the most prominent sports venues in the country. His duties there included the coordination of special events like the Olympics. He retired permanently in 1989.

Doctors have increasingly recognized the toll that years of football can inflict on players' bodies. Because they are tackled so often, running backs are particularly at risk for long-term injury. Unlike many of his peers, however, Matson remained in apparent good health for years. That changed around 2007, when he began to suffer several serious problems, among them a form of dementia. His condition slowly deteriorated, and on February 19, 2011, he died of respiratory failure in Los Angeles. Surviving him were four children, numerous grandchildren and great-grandchildren, and his twin sister. Their grief at his passing was shared by football fans around the nation, many of whom paused to remember the man coach Joe Kuharich once called, in comments relayed by John Crumpacker of the *San Francisco Chronicle,* "the best all-around football player I've ever seen."

Sources

Periodicals

Associated Press, February 20, 2011.
New York Times, February 21, 2011, p. B7.
San Francisco Chronicle, February 20, 2011.

Online

"Ollie Matson," Pro Football Hall of Fame, http://www.profootballhof.com/hof/member.aspx?PlayerId=143 (accessed June 5, 2011).

—R. Anthony Kugler

Benjamin Matthews

1933–2006

Opera singer, opera company founder

Remembered as one of the foremost interpreters of the African-American musical tradition, opera singer Benjamin Matthews dedicated his career to preserving the black spirituals, folk songs, and work songs of the 19th and 20th centuries and championing the work of little-known black composers. In 1973 he co-founded Opera Ebony to provide performance opportunities for black artists; it would become the longest-surviving African-American opera company in the United States, offering all-black productions of classic operas and commissioning new works by minority and women composers. On the stage, Matthews was renowned for his expressive bass-baritone voice, earning acclaim for such roles as Porgy in George Gershwin's *Porgy and Bess,* Mephistopheles in Charles Gounod's opera *Faust,* and Prince Itelo in Leon Kirchner's *Lily.*

Matthews was born on June 20, 1933, in Mobile, Alabama, one of nine children of Willie Matthews and Estella Johnson. As a boy, he grew up hearing traditional spirituals and work songs. "I heard them sung in the cornfields and the cottonfields. My neighbors sang them as they washed and they sang them as they worked," he recalled in an interview on the website NewSun.com. That music left a tremendous impression on the future singer. "We used to sit on our front porch at night and that was our entertainment. We would sing almost every day and every night. I learned those spirituals at my mother's feet and my grandmother's feet."

As a teenager, Matthews moved to Chicago to attend high school and then enlisted in the U.S. Army. While he was stationed in Germany, he took first place in an army singing contest. He had never had any formal training in music, but upon his discharge from the army, he enrolled at the Chicago Conservatory to study voice and followed with operatic training under Russian impresario Boris Goldovsky. At the time, most African-American singers were primarily recitalists, as there were few dramatic roles available to them. "Classical music being a European art form, one did not think of blacks . . . singing opera," Matthews explained in a 1991 interview with the *Lexington Herald-Leader.* Nevertheless, Matthews persisted in pursuing a career as an opera singer. "My teachers encouraged me, and I realized I could go wherever music would take me."

In 1973 Matthews joined with two African-American musicians—pianist Wayne Sanders and conductor Margaret Harris—and a white nun named Sister Mary Elise to found Opera Ebony, a company dedicated to providing a professional platform for black artists to practice their craft and opportunities for them to perform. Initially, Opera Ebony divided its time between Philadelphia and New York, forming guilds in both cities to drum up financial support and audience interest. In 1976 the company mounted its first production, performing Giuseppe Verdi's opera *Aida* at the Academy of Music in Philadelphia with an all-black cast. Opera Ebony debuted in New York the following year with *Highway 1 U.S.A.,* by African-American composer William Still Grant, and in 1980 had its first full-scale production in Harlem, performing Wolfgang Amadeus Mozart's *Marriage of Figaro* at the Metropolitan A.M.E. Church.

At a Glance . . .

Born Benjamin Matthews on June 20, 1933, in Mobile, AL; died on February 14, 2006, in New York, NY; son of Willie Matthews and Estella Johnson. *Education*: Chicago Conservatory. *Military service*: U.S. Army.

Career: Opera and concert singer, 1973–2006; Opera Ebony, founder and artistic director, 1973–2006.

Opera Ebony became known for its innovative productions of works from the classical repertoire as well as rarely performed works by minority and woman composers. In 1985 the company commissioned its first opera, Dorothy Rudd Moore's *Frederick Douglass,* based on the life of the famous black orator of the 19th century. Other original works produced by the company include *Sojourner Truth* (1986) by Valerie Capers; *The Outcasts* (1990) by Noah Ain; *Oh Freedom!* (1990), written by Matthews and Lena McLin; and *Journin'* (1991), also by Matthews. As of 2011, Opera Ebony was the longest-surviving African-American opera company in the United States.

Meanwhile, Matthews distinguished himself as a commanding performer in his own right, earning a reputation for his fine bass-baritone voice (higher than a bass, the lowest vocal range for men, but lower than a baritone), making his Metropolitan Opera debut in 1973 as the Compere in Virgil Thompson's *Four Saints in Three Acts* opposite African-American soprano Betty Allen. In April of 1977 Matthews appeared in a production of Felix Mendelssohn's *Elijah* at Avery Fisher Hall in New York and, the same month, made his New York City Opera debut in Leon Kirchner's *Lily,* originating the role of Prince Itelo.

In 1983 Matthews earned praise for his portrayal of Mephistopheles in Opera Ebony's all-black production of Charles Gounod's *Faust,* with Edward Rothstein of the *New York Times* calling his performance "authoritative." The following year, he performed the role of Porgy in George Gershwin's operatic musical *Porgy and Bess*—a part to which he would return repeatedly in his career—with the Collegiate Chorale at Carnegie Hall. The singer gave his first solo recital at Carnegie Hall in 1986, performing works by George Fredric Handel, Franz Joseph Haydn, and Mozart as well as African-American spirituals and work songs, accompanied by Opera Ebony co-founder Wayne Sanders. The *New York Amsterdam News* commented, "Matthews is a born performer. He has that rare ability to get to

the musical and dramatic core of each piece of music."

A prolific collector of African-American music, Matthews assembled a large library of religious and folk music, work songs, field calls, and Creole tunes, as well as manuscripts of concert arrangements, and he was a frequent lecturer on the traditional singing style of this repertoire. "Spirituals have a style and a tradition," he told NewSun.com, "and unless it's preserved, it's gonna be completely lost. They are to be studied just as one would study the German, French or Italian style of repertoire." Matthews's collection often served as a source of material for his recitals and master classes, and he drew from these works for the 1995 Opera Ebony recording *Done Crossed Every River: Freedom's Journey,* on which he provided a solo rendition of the spiritual "If He Change Mah Name."

Over his 40-year career, Matthews assembled an impressive resume of operatic credits, performing with companies across the United States and abroad, including the New York City Opera, the Philadelphia Grand Opera, the Detroit and Milwaukee Symphonies, the Graz Opera in Austria, Sinfonica Municipal of São Paulo and Rio de Janeiro in Brazil, Santa Cecilia Orchestra of Rome, and L'Orchestre Symphonique in Quebec. In 2000 he recorded *A Spiritual Journey,* an album of spirituals and hymns, and a companion record, *A Balm in Gilead,* both released on the Ebony Classic label.

Matthews died of complications of a stroke at a hospital in Manhattan on February 14, 2006, at the age of 72.

Sources

Periodicals

Lexington (KY) Herald-Ledger, April 21, 1991.
New York Amsterdam News, May 3, 1986.
New York Times, June 30, 1981; June 30, 1985; March 3, 2006.

Online

"Freedom's Journey" (review of Done Crossed Every River), http://www.newsun.com/Freedom.html (accessed July 1, 2011).
Opera Ebony, http://www.operaebony.org/ (accessed July 1, 2011).

Other

Additional information for this profile was provided by Wayne Sanders of Opera Ebony, July 1, 2011.

—Deborah A. Ring

Jan Matzeliger

1852–1889

Inventor, entrepreneur

For centuries, new shoes were out of many people's reach. Those unable to afford them either went barefoot or made do with hand-me-downs. Inventor Jan Matzeliger changed that situation almost single-handedly. After years of solitary work, he perfected in 1883 the world's first lasting machine, a device that automated the most difficult step in the manufacture of footwear. His invention reduced prices and fueled a rapid expansion of the industry, particularly in the United States. By his death in 1889, his adopted home of Lynn, Massachusetts, was known as the shoe capital of the world.

Jan Ernst Matzeliger was born in 1852 in Paramaribo, the capital of Dutch Guiana, a colony on the northern coast of South America. It later became the independent nation of Suriname. At the time of his birth, Dutch Guiana's population was a mixture of native peoples, European settlers, and slaves; the latter were primarily of African ancestry. As the son of a Dutch engineer and a slave woman, Matzeliger personified the region's ethnic diversity. Raised largely by an aunt and known-even as a youth for his skill with machinery, he received the bulk of his education through a series of formal and informal apprenticeships in the rudimentary factories that were beginning to spring up in and around the capital. He was also interested, however, in seeing the world, and at the age of 19 he joined the crew of a merchant ship. Long voyages occupied him until 1873, when, having reached Philadelphia, he decided to settle in the United States. Supporting himself with odd jobs, he remained in Pennsylvania until 1876, when he moved to Massachusetts. By the end of the following

year, he was living in Lynn, where he remained for the rest of his life.

As a worker in one of Lynn's many footwear factories, Matzeliger was able to study the shoe-making process from start to finish. By the second half of the 1800s, many of its steps had been automated. One crucial task, however, continued to require the skills of highly trained cobblers. In this step the leather upper was fitted over a foot-shaped tool called a last and nailed to the sole. Because lasting, as it was known, was more labor intensive and time consuming than the other steps in the process, it contributed disproportionately to the final price of shoes. Manufacturers, meanwhile, were unhappy because much of their equipment had to sit idle while the cobblers finished each pair by hand. While many attempts had been made before Matzeliger to remedy the situation, all had failed, and it was widely believed that lasting was simply too complex for machinery to handle.

It was amid those dispiriting circumstances that Matzeliger began constructing his own machine. Working at night with whatever tools and materials were at hand, he built a series of increasingly complex prototypes. His coworkers initially offered little encouragement. By about 1880, however, it was undeniable that he was making progress. When his employer offered him $50 for the latest model, he declined, returning to his workroom to make further refinements. Only when he was satisfied that all the technical issues had been solved did he seek out the funding he needed to obtain a patent. In return for a two-thirds interest in his

machine, he obtained from two investors the sum of $1,500, which he used to build a final prototype and to complete the blueprints required by the U.S. Patent Office. Those drawings were so complex that patent officials took the unusual step of dispatching an employee to see the prototype in person. The machine passed inspection, and in March of 1883 Matzeliger received his patent.

Commercial exploitation of the device now began. After obtaining additional capital from two more investors, the partners laid plans for a new corporation, the Consolidated Lasting Machine Company (CLMC). It was at that point, however, that Matzeliger sold out, receiving a large share of CLMC stock in return for his remaining interest. The company prospered, and by the end of the century its machines were running in nearly every shoe factory in the country. With an output as high as 700 pairs per day, Matzeliger's invention could produce roughly 14 times as many shoes as a highly skilled cobbler. Prices quickly fell, bringing major benefits to consumers, particularly those with limited incomes. The industry as a whole benefited as well, for the drop in prices was more than offset by a dramatic increase in sales. Nowhere was that growth more evident than in Lynn. Because the city's manufacturers recognized the strengths of Matzeliger's machine long before their competitors elsewhere, they enjoyed a dramatic advantage that persisted for many years.

The success of CLMC enabled Matzeliger to leave the drudgery of factory work behind. In other respects, however, his life remained much as it had been. An inveterate tinkerer, he continued to design new machines for industrial use. His health, however, was no longer good, a situation contemporaries attributed to his habit of working long hours without food or rest. Diagnosed with tuberculosis just months after the founding of CLMC, Matzeliger deteriorated steadily, and on August 24, 1889, he died in Lynn. A bachelor, he left most of his considerable estate to a local church that had welcomed him after several other congregations, upset by his race, had declined to do so.

In the decades following Matzeliger's death, his name was largely forgotten. Contributing to his obscurity were rapid changes in Lynn's footwear industry. By about 1950 its factories were losing orders to companies overseas, where both labor and materials were significantly cheaper. As its plants closed, few remembered Matzeliger's brilliance and the other advantages the city had once enjoyed. The civil rights era, however, did much to restore his place in industrial history. As interest in the contributions of non-whites grew, researchers and educators took care to highlight Matzeliger's career. Those efforts bore fruit in 1984, when the city of Lynn named a bridge after him. Seven years later the U.S. Postal Service issued a stamp in his honor as part of its Black Heritage series.

Sources

Online

"Jan Ernst Matzeliger," Inventions.org, http://www. inventions.org/culture/african/matzeliger.html (accessed June 9, 2011).

"Jan Matzeliger," BlackInventor.com, http://www. blackinventor.com/pages/jan-matzeliger.html (accessed June 9, 2011).

"Jan Matzeliger: Shoe Lasting Machine," Massachusetts Institute of Technology, August 2002, http:// web.mit.edu/invent/iow/matzeliger.html (accessed June 9, 2011).

Lienhard, John H., "No. 522: Jan Matzeliger," University of Houston, http://www.uh.edu/engines/epi 522.htm (accessed June 9, 2011).

—R. Anthony Kugler

George McJunkin

1851–1922

Ranch worker, self-taught naturalist

Without any formal training, George McJunkin made an archaeological discovery that dramatically changed scientific understanding of human history in the Western Hemisphere. A cowhand by trade, he found in New Mexico what proved to be the remains of animals slaughtered by hunters more than 10,000 years ago. Scientists had previously dated the arrival of humans in North America to roughly 1,000 BC—an error of more than 7,000 years.

McJunkin was born into slavery in 1851 on a ranch in Midway, Texas, a small community between Dallas and Houston. Like many slaves, he was known only by his first name. He later assumed the surname of one of his masters. His father, a blacksmith, passed many specialized skills on to him, and by the start of his teens McJunkin was adept at handling horses and cattle. He had no formal education, however, and it was only through his own initiative as a young adult that he became literate. He did so, according to several sources, primarily through barter, offering ranch lore to would-be cowhands in exchange for reading lessons.

After obtaining his freedom at the end of the Civil War, McJunkin, then a young teenager, continued to work on the Midway ranch. About 1868, however, he joined a series of cattle drives that took him to eastern New Mexico, where he settled permanently. Over the next half century, he developed a reputation as one of the region's best cowhands. A voracious reader, he combined his work with an intense interest in science and natural history, often carrying a telescope in one of his saddle bags. His intellectual curiosity was well known in the area, and it was not uncommon for leading members of the white community to seek his advice on an array of subjects. On the range, meanwhile, he grew steadily in authority, and by 1908 he was serving as foreman of Crowfoot Ranch, an enormous property near the town of Folsom. It was in that role that he made his famous discovery.

In August of 1908, a flash flood devastated Folsom, killing more than a dozen people and destroying fencing and other ranch infrastructure. On a ride the following month to assess the damage, McJunkin noticed that the raging waters had cut a deep gash at the bottom of an arroyo, or dry river bed. As he peered into the hole, which was well over 10 feet deep, he noticed some large bones protruding from the soil. Climbing down, he dug several out and carried them home. From his reading, he knew that they were too large and too heavy to be the bones of any modern animal. Realizing he had found something prehistoric, he alerted several white men he knew were interested in natural history. The site was a remote one, however, and his contacts were unwilling to undertake a visit to it with him. It remained unexcavated for two decades.

By that point, however, McJunkin was no longer alive. His final years had been difficult; deeply frustrated by the indifferent response to his discovery, he suffered a further blow when his cabin burned down, destroying many of the artifacts he had collected since his youth. With the support of friends, many of whom had been his protégés on the range, he moved into a hotel in downtown Folsom. Weakened by illness and alcohol,

At a Glance . . .

Born in 1851 in Midway, TX; died on January 21, 1922, in Folsom, NM; son of a blacksmith.

Career: Ranch worker, participated in cattle drive from Texas to New Mexico, c. 1868; foreman of Crowfoot Ranch, Folsom, NM, early 1900s.

he died there on January 21, 1922. A bachelor, he had no known survivors.

In the years that followed, interest in his discovery gradually increased, thanks in part to the growing availability of cars, which made visiting the site much less arduous. In 1926 two of McJunkin's contacts, Fred Howarth and Carl Schwachheim, took some remains they had gathered from the pit to Jesse D. Figgins, the director of the Colorado Museum of Natural History. Figgins quickly identified the bones as those of an extinct species of prehistoric bison. While rare, such bones were found throughout the West with some regularity. More intriguing was the size of the find, because it suggested that many animals had died in one place. If so, Figgins realized, the site was very likely a "kill pit"—a place where hunters had trapped, killed, and butchered a number of animals at once. Found throughout North America, kill pits were used frequently by Native American peoples. Never before, however, had one been discovered with bones so old. The implication was clear: hunters, it seemed, had been active in North America much earlier than previously thought.

Sources

Periodicals

Natural History, February 1997.

Online

"No. 2010: George McJunkin and AleA! Hrdlicka," University of Houston, http://www.uh.edu/engines/epi2010.htm (accessed July 26, 2011).

Peterson, Heather, "McJunkin, George (1851—1922)," BlackPast.org, http://www.blackpast.org/?q=aaw/mcjunkin-george-1851-1922 (accessed July 26, 2011).

Wilkinson, Brenda, "George McJunkin: A Chapter in New Mexico History," U.S. Bureau of Land Management, http://www.blm.gov/nm/st/en/prog/more/cultural_resources/george_mcjunkin_feature/george_mcjunkin_feature.print.html (accessed July 26, 2011).

—R. Anthony Kugler

Tracy McMillan

1964—

Screenwriter, memoirist

Tracy McMillan is a television writer and memoirist. Raised in foster homes in Minneapolis, Minnesota, she overcame enormous obstacles to make a career in broadcast journalism, writing for TV news for 15 years, beginning in 1990. In 2005 she pursued a screenwriting career and subsequently found work on shows including NBC's *Journeyman,* ABC's *Life on Mars,* Showtime's *United States of Tara,* AMC's *Mad Men,* NBC's *Chase,* and USA's *Necessary Roughness.* In 2010 McMillan published a best-selling memoir, *I Love You and I'm Leaving You Anyway,* which, with its humorous treatment of her difficult childhood and its lasting effects on her adult relationships, found a receptive audience and established her as an author of note.

McMillan was born on September 12, 1964, in Minneapolis to an African-American father and a white mother; both were involved in criminal enterprises. She has described her father (whom she calls Freddie in *I Love You and I'm Leaving You Anyway*) as a pimp and her mother (whom she calls Linda) as a drug addict. Although McMillan's father was frequently in trouble with the law, he maintained contact with her during her youth, and their complex relationship has informed, for better and for worse, her adult romantic relationships. Her mother, meanwhile, has been largely absent from her life.

McMillan spent her childhood primarily in foster homes in Minneapolis. Like many children of her generation, she was immersed in television from an early age, soaking up programming irrespective of genre. Hired to deliver newspapers at the age of 11, she developed the habit of reading the paper every morning prior to leaving on her route. In an interview with *Contemporary Black Biography,* she said, "Looking back, it seems obvious I would pursue a career in media. But of course, I grew up in foster care, so at the time, it seemed highly unlikely that I would become successful in a career of any kind!"

McMillan navigated the risks and difficulties of life as a foster child and attended college, studying broadcast journalism and mass communications at the University of Utah. After taking her B.A. in 1989, she moved to Portland, Oregon, and found a job as an associate producer on the local NBC TV affiliate's four o'clock newscast. She relocated to New York City in the early 1990s and worked as a freelance writer for local news broadcasts and eventually for *NBC Nightly News.*

While freelancing for newsrooms, McMillan began trying to build a career in feature film and documentary writing. She co-wrote *A,B,C . . . Manhattan,* a 1997 feature that went to the Cannes and Sundance film festivals, and with the idea of furthering her career as a screenwriter, she moved to Los Angeles. Soon after the move, however, she gave birth to a son, and in the ensuing years, although she continued to write for newscasts on a freelance basis, she was unable to find time for her creative efforts.

In 2005 McMillan decided to make a concerted effort to establish herself as a screenwriter. She wrote three feature film scripts that year, two of which she consid-

At a Glance . . .

Born on September 12, 1964, in Minneapolis, MN; married three times; children: one. *Education*: University of Utah, BA, 1989.

Career: Writer for local and national television news broadcasts, 1990–2005; screenwriter, 2006—; memoirist, 2010—.

Memberships: Writers Guild of America.

Addresses: *Publisher*—HarperCollins Publishers, 10 East 53rd St., New York, NY 10022. *Web*—http://www.tracymcmillan.com/.

ered failures. Pleased with the third screenplay, she passed it along to a friend who was in the entertainment business, and the friend shared it with her agent. After eight months, the agent got back to McMillan with an offer of representation, and she was soon interviewing for jobs writing for TV and the movies. A little more than a year after she had committed herself to her screenwriting gambit, she was hired as a staff writer for the NBC science fiction series *Journeyman*. The series, which focuses on the exploits of a time-traveling San Francisco reporter, premiered in the fall of 2007, but its run was interrupted by a Writers Guild of America strike, and the network discontinued it.

McMillan had long intended to tell the story of her own life someday, so while waiting for the strike to be resolved, she decided to devote her time to crafting a proposal for a projected memoir. Her agent began shopping the proposal to publishers in March of 2009 and sold the book idea in two days. McMillan set to work on the memoir, originally writing a sober, emotionally wrenching account of her troubled childhood and her three failed marriages, before rewriting the story in a more comic vein. "The first version was a Mike Figgis film," she told the *San Francisco Chronicle*. "The second one is a James L. Brooks film." 2010's *I Love You and I'm Leaving You Anyway* traces the ways in which her relationship with her loving but deeply flawed father led to her propensity for involving herself with the wrong men. According to Edward Lovett in *SMITH* magazine, "These things aren't 'issues' that her experience illuminates for the benefit of society. This isn't an eat-your-vegetables book. They're just her 'extreme-sports version,' as she winningly puts it, of every woman's quest for sustainable love and how this quest is complicated by old pain, doubts, and fears about Daddy." The book became a *New York Times* bestseller and established McMillan as a marketable author.

Meanwhile, with the resolution of the writer's strike, McMillan continued to build her screenwriting career. In the 2008-09 television season she wrote for the ABC series *Life on Mars,* which mixed the genres of science fiction and police procedural and received significant critical praise but failed to catch on with audiences. In the 2009-10 season McMillan wrote numerous episodes of the award-winning Showtime series *United States of Tara,* which focuses on a suburban housewife with multiple personalities. In 2010 she penned an episode of the acclaimed AMC series *Mad Men* as well as two episodes of the NBC police drama *Chase*.

In February of 2011 McMillan wrote an essay for the online news and entertainment site the *Huffington Post* called "Why You're Not Married," which uses irreverent humor to argue that unmarried 30-something women should look to themselves, rather than to society or to men, to locate the reasons for their inability to find a spouse. With its provocative title and bold argument, the essay polarized audiences and spread virally across the Internet, becoming the *Huffington Post*'s second most-popular article ever. McMillan sold a book proposal based on the essay later that year, and a publication date was set for 2012.

In addition to her work on the memoir, McMillan was working, as of 2011, as a writer on the USA Network series *Necessary Roughness,* about a single mother working as a therapist for a professional football team. The series debuted in June of that year and was slated to run for 12 episodes.

Sources

Periodicals

San Francisco Chronicle, April 22, 2010, p. G26.

Online

Lovett, Edward, "Interview: Tracy McMillan, Author of *I Love You and I'm Leaving You Anyway,*" SMITH, http://www.smithmag.net/memoirville/2010/04/13/interview-tracy-mcmillan-author-of-i-love-you-and-im-leaving-you-anyway/ (accessed June 28, 2011).
Malmberg, Mel, "Love, Leave, Laugh (Repeat): Tracy McMillan," Hometown Pasadena, http://hometown-pasadena.com/creative-types/love-leave-laugh-repeat-tracy-mcmillan/ (accessed June 28, 2011).

Other

Additional information for this profile was obtained through an email interview with Tracy McMillan on June 21, 2011.

—Mark Lane

Omar Benson Miller

1978—

Film and television actor

Miller, Omar Benson, photograph. AP Images/Matt Sayles.

Character actor Omar Benson Miller is best known for his supporting roles in such major motion pictures as *8 Mile, Get Rich or Die Tryin', Miracle of St. Anna, The Express,* and *The Sorcerer's Apprentice.* Since making his big screen debut in 2002 in the Disney film *Sorority Boys*—not even out of film school yet—Miller quickly has built a Hollywood career working with some of the biggest names in the business, including Richard Gere, Halle Berry, Nicolas Cage, and Spike Lee. In addition, he has distinguished himself by the diversity of his roles, appearing at ease in drama, comedy, sci-fi, and even animated films. In 2009 Miller landed his first major television role, joining the cast of the popular CBS television series *CSI: Miami* as art theft specialist Walter Simmons.

Miller was born on October 7, 1978, in Los Angeles, California, the youngest of seven children. When he was a boy, his family relocated to Orange County, where they were the only black family on their block. In high school he was active in sports, playing baseball and basketball, but acting was not yet on his radar. When he got to college at San Jose State University, he planned to continue playing baseball, but as he became more interested in the opposite sex, he lost his focus on sports and stumbled into theater. A theater professor took Miller under his wing and became his mentor, while another instructor introduced the young actor to his first agent. His natural talent already was apparent.

In 2002, before he even had finished school, Miller landed his first film gig in the Disney college comedy *Sorority Boys*. That year, he was named the best male actor in his graduating class, and soon after graduation he was cast in his breakout role as Sol George in the biopic *8 Mile,* alongside Eminem, Brittany Murphy, Mekhi Phifer, and Kim Basinger. The feature ignited Miller's career, and the following year he appeared in the HBO movie *Undefeated*—cast against type in a "bad guy" role as a crooked boxing promoter—written and directed by John Leguizamo. He originally was slated to play the title role in the 2003 film *Fat Albert,* because at 6 feet, 6 inches, and 300 pounds, he seemed a natural choice for the part; however, he later pulled out of the project, and the role went to *Saturday Night Live*'s Kenan Thompson.

At a Glance . . .

Born on October 7, 1978, in Los Angeles, CA; son of Gloria Miller. *Education*: San Jose State University, BA, radio, film, and television, 2001.

Career: Film and television actor, 2002; owner of Big Easy Productions; founder of the Omar Miller Foundation.

Awards: Canada Lee Award, Pan American Film Festival, 2009, for *Miracle at St. Anna*.

Addresses: *Agent*—Pinnacle Public Relations, 8265 Sunset Blvd., Los Angeles, CA 90046.

Miller showed his lighter side in 2004 when he joined Richard Gere, Jennifer Lopez, and Susan Sarandon in the romantic comedy *Shall We Dance?* The next year he appeared in the independent film *Man of God*, followed by director Jim Sheridan's drama *Get Rich or Die Tryin'* starring 50 Cent and Terence Howard.

The year 2007 proved to be a busy one for Miller, who appeared in four feature films, including the Michael Bay science fiction blockbuster *Transformers* and the drama *Things We Lost in the Fire*, with stars Halle Berry and Benicio del Toro. Miller also made his directorial debut with *Gordon Glass*, a small-budget film that he wrote while he was recovering from knee surgery. The film tells the story of an aspiring actor, played by Miller, who moves to Los Angeles after making a promise to his grandmother on her deathbed. He finds work as a security guard at a Hollywood studio, experiencing the highs and lows of the road to stardom. The production was a family affair for Miller, who enlisted the help of several of his family members, including his oldest brother Anthony, who handled security, and his mother, who fed the cast and crew. The film was produced by Miller's own company, Big Easy Productions, in partnership with Crescent Hollywood Films.

In 2008 Miller starred in back-to-back historical films that brought attention to African-American heroes. The first, Spike Lee's *Miracle of St. Anna*, based on the book by James McBride, tells the story of four soldiers from the all-black 92nd Division of the U.S. Army—known as "Buffalo Soldiers"—who are stranded in an Italian village behind enemy lines during World War II. Under mortar fire, Miller's character, Private Sam Train, risks his life to save an injured Italian boy, who brands him the "chocolate giant." To prepare for the role, the actor followed a strict diet, losing 50 pounds in 9 weeks. Karen Durbin in the *New York Times* praised Miller's performance, writing, "He plays

Train stolid and straight-faced, with a touch of old-fashioned comedy," with "his eyes saying it all."

Just a week after *Miracle at St. Anna* opened, Miller appeared in another high-profile film, Gary Fleder's *The Express*, an inspirational movie about Ernie Davis, the first black football player to win the Heisman Trophy who then had his pro career cut short by leukemia. Miller played the role of Jack Buckley, Davis's black friend on the team who advises the star of the odds against him. *Variety* called his portrayal of Buckley "terrific" and "funny," while Roger Ebert of the *Chicago Sun-Times* called Miller's the "key supporting performance" of the film.

As he was building his résumé on the big screen, Miller also found roles on television, appearing on episodes of *The West Wing, Law & Order: Special Victims Unit,* and *Eleventh Hour.* In 2005 he played Coop on the short-lived UPN drama *Sex, Love & Secrets,* and in 2009 he joined the cast of the highly rated CBS series *CSI: Miami,* playing art theft specialist Walter Simmons, a role created for him by producer Jerry Bruckheimer.

Miller returned to historical drama in 2010 with *Blood Done Sign My Name,* based on the true story of a black Vietnam veteran who allegedly is murdered by a local white businessman. The same year, he appeared in the Disney hit *The Sorcerer's Apprentice,* starring Nicolas Cage. In 2011 he had his first animated role, performing the voice of Horace in *The Lion of Judah.*

In 2010 Miller established the Omar Miller Foundation to alleviate hunger in the Los Angeles community. The organization donates food left over from television and film sets and distributes it to local soup kitchens, food pantries, and homeless shelters.

Sources

Periodicals

Chicago Sun-Times, October 10, 2008.
New York Times, September 7, 2008; September 26, 2008.
Variety, September 29, 2008.

Online

Gordon Glass, http://www.gordonglassthemovie.com/ (accessed June 25, 2011).
Truitt, Brian, "Omar Miller Makes His Presence Felt on TV, in Films," *USA Weekend* Who's News Blog, February 19, 2010, http://whosnews.usaweekend.com/2010/02/omar-miller-makes-his-presence-felt-on-tv-in-films/ (accessed June 25, 2011).
Williams, Kam, "Interview: Omar Benson Miller, *Black Star News,* October 13, 2008, http://www.black

starnews.com/news/132/ARTICLE/4995/2008-
10-13.html (accessed June 25, 2008).

—Deborah A. Ring

Frederick A. Morton Jr.

1967(?)—

Media executive, lawyer, entrepreneur

Morton, Frederick A., Jr., photograph. MTV/Getty Images.

Although the number of cable networks in the United States has exploded since the 1980s, other regions of the world have embraced the medium much more slowly. Until 2005, for example, the Caribbean basin, home to well over 20 million people, lacked a channel of its own. Frederick A. Morton Jr. changed that. A native of the region and a lawyer by training, he is the founder of Tempo Networks, a broadcaster often described as the Caribbean's MTV. The network's eclectic mix of music videos, news, and original programming reached, as of 2010, as many as three million people.

Morton was born in 1967 or 1968 in Christiansted, a historic town on St. Croix, the largest of the U.S. Virgin Islands. His parents were natives of Nevis, a nearby island populated primarily by people of African descent. Educated in local schools, Morton left the region in the 1980s to enter Rutgers University in New Jersey. Upon receipt of his bachelor's degree, probably about 1990, he completed law school at the same institution. That degree, in turn, was followed by a stint at Columbia University, where he earned a master's degree in public administration. He then began what quickly became a distinguished career in corporate law.

His first major employer in that field was Simpson Thacher & Bartlett, a well-known firm in New York City. After serving there as a staff attorney, he moved on to pharmaceutical giant Johnson & Johnson, where he held the post of corporate counsel. He then entered the cable business, joining media conglomerate Viacom as its chief litigation counsel. Among Viacom's most important divisions at the time was MTV Networks (MTVN), a constellation of cable channels that had sprung up around MTV, one of the most recognized media properties in the world. As Morton's cable expertise grew, it became clear that he had much to offer Viacom beyond litigation. In an internal transfer, he moved to MTVN, where he became deputy general counsel for business and legal affairs.

Morton's MTVN appointment gave him the opportunity to propose a Caribbean network, a venture he had been thinking about for some time. "He had this passion for it; it just became a personal crusade," Tom Freston, then MTV's chief executive, recalled to Peter Applebome in the *New York Times*. "The whole idea inspired him. He had this fire in his *eyes*." Moved by Morton's enthusiasm, Freston and the other members

At a Glance . . .

Born in 1967(?) in Christiansted, St. Croix, U.S. Virgin Islands. *Education*: Rutgers University, bachelor's degree, 1990(?), JD, 1990s; Columbia University, MA, public administration, 1990s.

Career: Simpson Thacher & Bartlett, staff attorney, 1990s; Johnson & Johnson, corporate counsel, late 1990s(?); Viacom, chief litigation counsel, early 2000s(?); MTV Networks, deputy general counsel for business and legal affairs, early 2000s(?)–05; Tempo Networks, founder, 2005, senior vice president and general manager, 2005–07, and chairman, CEO, and co-owner, 2007—.

Addresses: *Office*—Tempo Networks, LLC, 58 Park Place, 3rd Fl., Newark, NJ 07102.

of MTV's board approved the project. Work then began on the host of financial, technical, and regulatory issues involved in the establishment of an international network. In November of 2005 the last of these issues was resolved, and Tempo debuted across the Caribbean.

Like its predecessor MTV, Tempo relied heavily, particularly in its first years, on music videos. The two networks differed sharply, however, in their approach. While MTV rarely ventured beyond the standard genres of rock, rap, and pop, Tempo embraced the rich diversity of Caribbean music. In addition to reggae and calypso, arguably the region's most familiar sounds, the network emphasized soca, an offshoot of calypso; dancehall reggae, rougher and faster than the traditional version; and punta rock, a style closely associated with the nation of Belize. Tempo's broadcast of videos, together with its sponsorship of concerts across the Caribbean, gave a major boost to many of the region's artists, including soca stars Alison Hinds and Machel Montano, gospel vocalist Landlord, and dancehall master Elephant Man.

Morton was the founder and driving force behind Tempo, but he was not its chief executive initially. Instead, he served as senior vice president and general manager. While these roles gave him ample opportunity to set the network's tone, he also saw advantages in greater independence. In 2007, therefore, he led a group of investors in purchasing the network from MTVN; in the process he became Tempo's chairman and CEO. Terms of the transaction were not disclosed.

By the end of its fifth year in operation, Tempo had established a reputation as one of the most socially engaged networks on television, thanks in large part to an emphasis on public-service programming. Arguably the best known of its initiatives in this area was, as of 2011, an ongoing antiviolence campaign called "Badness Outta Style." In a 2007 interview with *Core* magazine, Morton noted that the campaign began after he witnessed fistfights at a network event on the island of Trinidad. "I took it as a message from God, saying that I needed to focus on this issue," he recalled, adding, "Our message is that disagreements can be resolved in nonviolent ways."

To Tempo's music shows and public-service spots, Morton gradually added news, documentaries, and original programming on topics like food, spirituality, and household finance. In all of these, he attempted to balance the diversity of Caribbean culture with the need to standardize certain aspects of the viewing experience, particularly language. Although a variety of languages and dialects are spoken throughout the region, English is the *lingua franca*. Well aware of that fact, Morton has emphasized the use of English from the network's earliest days.

Tempo's growth has not been without occasional obstacles. One of the most challenging of these involved ongoing efforts to penetrate the United States, home to millions of Caribbean immigrants and expatriates. The U.S. cable market is arguably the most lucrative and competitive in the world, with hundreds of channels vying for viewers, advertisers, and bandwidth. As he worked to complete the complex licensing deals needed to enter the field, Morton took care to ensure that a selection of Tempo programming was available online to Americans and others beyond the reach of its broadcasts.

By the end of 2010 Morton was busy planning Tempo's future growth, telling Applebome in the *New York Times* that he envisioned a number of subsidiary networks of the sort MTV had spawned. A Tempo amusement park was also mentioned. "Maybe it's a little dreamy. I don't know," Morton said of his ambitious designs. "I do have people around me that bring me back to reality every now and then, but I like to dream."

Sources

Periodicals

Broadcasting & Cable, December 7, 2007.
Core, July-August 2007.
New York Times, November 28, 2010.

Online

"Biography," Tempo Networks, http://www.got tempo.com/about_us.php (accessed June 21, 2011).
"How He Built It: Frederick A. Morton, Founder of

Caribbean Media Company Tempo Networks," At-
lantaPost.com, February 26, 2011, http://atlanta
post.com/2011/02/26/how-he-built-it-founder-of-
caribbean-media-company-tempo-networks/
(accessed June 21, 2011).

—R. Anthony Kugler

Abdias do Nascimento

1914–2011

Activist, artist, scholar, politician

Abdias do Nascimento was arguably the most important black Brazilian intellectual of the 20th and early 21st centuries. As an activist, scholar, actor, playwright, artist, and politician, he tirelessly battled entrenched racism in his home country and sought to increase understanding and appreciation of African cultural values. Among his diverse accomplishments were the founding of the Black Experimental Theater (Teatro Experimental do Negro, or TEN) in Rio de Janeiro, a performing group and political organization committed to creating theatrical and other opportunities for black Brazilians; the development of successful careers as a visual artist and a scholar; and his election as a congressman and senator in the Legislature of Brazil. As Ollie Johnson, a Wayne State University professor of Africana Studies, told the *New York Times*, "There was no more important Brazilian than Nascimento since the abolition of slavery in 1888.... For Americans to understand him and his contribution, you'd have to say he was a little bit of Marcus Garvey, a little bit of W. E. B. Du Bois, a little bit of Langston Hughes and a little bit of Adam Clayton Powell."

Fought Racism as Young Adult

Nascimento was born on March 14, 1914, in the city of Franca, Brazil, in the state of São Paulo. Slavery was central to the Brazilian economy from the 16th through the 19th centuries, and its aftereffects influenced the shape of Nascimento's life profoundly. Brazil, as a Portuguese colony, was the destination for nearly a third of all enslaved black Africans, and the institution was not abolished there until 1888. Nascimento's grandparents had been born into slavery, and his parents were of modest means. His father worked as a cobbler, his mother as a street vendor of candies she made at home.

Racism in 20th-century Brazil was not exhaustively systematized by law as in the southern United States or South Africa, but Brazilians of African descent had dramatically limited opportunities for economic and social advancement, and numerous forms of discrimination persisted. From an early age Nascimento devoted himself to addressing the unacknowledged forms of racism that governed life for black Brazilians. When he moved to the city of São Paulo in the early 1930s, he became active in the civil rights movement led by the Brazilian Black Front (Frente Negra Brasileira), and he campaigned to end racial discrimination by the city's shopkeepers. During this time he also served in the army, taking part in the successive revolutions of 1930 and 1932 that brought about changes in the country's political leadership.

Nascimento relocated to Rio de Janeiro in 1936 to study economics at the University of Rio de Janeiro (now the Federal University of Rio de Janeiro), taking a bachelor's degree in 1938. After moving to the city, Nascimento helped organize black militants to discuss and take action against racial discrimination, and in 1940 he traveled extensively in South America with a group of like-minded poets.

Founded Black Experimental Theater

While in Lima, Peru, Nascimento attended a performance of Eugene O'Neill's 1920 play *The Emperor Jones*, whose lead character, Brutus Jones, is an African-American man. Although the black actors Charles Sidney Gilpin and Paul Robeson had played Jones in its most prominent early productions, the star of the Lima production was a white man wearing blackface. Nascimento found this fact troubling, both for the obvious racism inherent in such a casting choice but also because he realized that, even though blacks in the United States were subject to harsh institutional racism, they nevertheless had opportunities for theatrical expression that had so far been denied Brazilians of African descent. While appearances of minor black characters marked as comic, criminal, or submissive types were relatively common in Brazilian theater, no complex or heroic roles, such as that of Brutus Jones, were open to black actors.

With a view toward remedying this situation, Nascimento began planning a theater group consisting of black actors, but upon his return to Brazil in 1941, he was jailed, having been convicted in absentia for his political activities during the 1930s. He organized a theater company in prison, and then upon his release in 1943 he resumed planning the creation of what would emerge, the following year, as the Black Experimental Theater (Teatro Experimental do Negro, or TEN) of Rio de Janeiro.

Nascimento later described TEN in the following way, as quoted in a Phyllis Peres translation of an essay on the group by the scholar Leda Martins, which appeared in the journal *Callaloo*: "It was fundamentally conceived of as an instrument of redemption and revindication of black African values.... Our theater would be a laboratory of cultural and artistic experimentation whose work, action and production explicitly and clearly confronted the elitist and Aryan supremacy of the dominant classes. TEN existed as a systematic unmasking of the racial hypocrisy that permeated the nation."

TEN staged its first play, *The Emperor Jones*, on May 8, 1945, the day Allied forces officially declared victory in Europe in World War II. Over the next twenty-three years, TEN was to have a substantial impact on Brazilian theater and culture, staging all-black productions of plays written specifically for the company as well as other O'Neill plays and works by Augusto Boal and Albert Camus, among others. In addition to his role as leader and organizer of the group, Nascimento acted in productions, including Vinicius de Moraes's *Orfeu de Conceição*, the play upon which the classic 1959 movie *Black Orpheus* was based, and he wrote a play, *Sortilege: A Black Mystery*, which TEN staged in 1957. TEN also organized wide-ranging cultural and political activities, including conferences, debates,

seminars, publishing outlets, and literacy and acting classes, all of which were united by their commitment to improving conditions for black Brazilians.

Remained Active in Exile

After a 1964 coup brought a new, right-wing government to power in Brazil, Nascimento was targeted by numerous police investigations, and he was forced into exile in 1968. He went to the United States, where from 1968 to 1970 he lectured, taught drama at Yale University, and participated in a series of talks at Wesleyan University with leading intellectuals including Buckminster Fuller, John Cage, and Norman Mailer. In 1970 Nascimento took a position with the State University of New York in Buffalo, serving as an associate professor and the first chair of the African Cultures in the New World program, part of the school's Center for Puerto Rican Studies. He remained at SUNY Buffalo until 1981.

Nascimento remained politically active while in exile, participating in numerous conferences and organizations devoted to international black political and artistic issues. He traveled frequently to speak and lecture in Africa, Europe, and the Americas, and he spent the 1976–77 academic year at the University of Ife (now Obafemi Awolowo University), in Ile-Ife, Nigeria, as a visiting professor of African Languages and Literatures. He also remained deeply involved with Brazilian politics during these years, participating in efforts to create a viable opposition to the ongoing military dictatorship. In the late 1970s he helped found the leftist Democratic Labor Party of Brazil (Partido Democrático Trabalhista, or PDT), pushing for the inclusion, in the party platform, of an anti-discrimination agenda. In 1981 Nascimento also founded the Afro-Brazilian Studies and Research Institute (Instituto de Pesquisas e Estudos Afro-Brasileiros, or IPEAFRO), based in Rio de Janeiro.

Also while in exile, Nascimento began a career as a painter. Utilizing a vibrant palette of colors, geometrical arrangements of shapes, and images drawn from African cultures and religions, his style drew on folk art traditions while demonstrating a thorough consciousness of the Western art canon. During his stay in the United States, Nascimento's work was exhibited in galleries and museums in New York City, Boston, Philadelphia, Los Angeles, New Orleans, and Washington, DC, among other cities.

Held Political Office in Brazil

Upon his return from exile and the decline of the right-wing military government, Nascimento was elected to Congress as a member of the PDT. He held this office from 1983 to 1986, and he continued to promote African cultural values at home and abroad through a wide variety of efforts.

Nascimento was a visiting professor of African-American Studies at Temple University in Philadelphia, Pennsylvania, for the 1990–91 academic year. Upon his return to Brazil in 1991, he was appointed secretary of state for defense and promotion of Afro-Brazilian populations in the Rio de Janeiro state government. Later that year, he was elected to Brazil's Senate. After leaving office in 1992, he resumed his secretary of state post with the Rio de Janeiro government, and then he returned to the Senate in 1996, serving until 1999.

Whether in or out of government service, Nascimento was an outspoken advocate for Afro-Brazilian civil rights. He received numerous awards and honors in his later years and was among the most renowned figures in worldwide movements to expand civil and human rights. In addition to his play *Sortilege*, a number of his political and scholarly writings have appeared in English translation. These include *Africans in Brazil: a Pan-African Perspective* (1987) and *Brazil, Mixture or Massacre?: Essays in the Genocide of a Black People* (1989). Nascimento died from complications related to diabetes at the age of 97, in May of 2011.

Selected writings

Sortilege: Black Mystery, Third World Press, 1978.
Africans in Brazil: A Pan-African Perspective, Africa World Press, 1987.
Brazil, Mixture or Massacre?: Essays in the Genocide of a Black People, Majority Press, 1989.

Sources

Periodicals

Callaloo, Autumn 1995, pp. 863–70.
Educational Theatre Journal, March 1977, pp. 5–17.
New York Times, May 30, 2011.
Theatre Journal, December 2005, pp. 600–603.

Online

Abdias Nascimento, http://www.abdias.com.br/index.htm (accessed June 30, 2011).

—Mark Lane

Sophia A. Nelson

1967—

Political commentator, author

A rare black female Republican, Sophia A. Nelson writes op-ed pieces and appears regularly on major new outlets to discuss issues relevant to African Americans. The former attorney, political appointee, and policy analyst has forged a successful career as a media pundit and contributor to *Essence,* the *Washington Post,* and The Root, and while she disagrees with some of President Barack Obama's initiatives, she has written extensively on the First Lady as a role model. Nelson's first book, *Black Woman Redefined: Dispelling Myths and Discovering Fulfillment in the Age of Michelle Obama,* was published in the spring of 2011.

Nelson was born in 1967 in Munich, Germany, where her father was stationed with the U.S. Army, but her family eventually settled in the south New Jersey community of Somerdale, near Camden. Her parents were committed Democrats and had deep ties to local community leaders—Nelson's cousin, in fact, became Camden's first black mayor in 1981. Another Camden Democrat was Jim Florio, who served in the U.S. House of Representatives from 1975 to 1990 and then became New Jersey's first governor of Italian-American heritage. Nelson was 14 years old when she met Florio. "He said to me, 'This is something you can do one day,'" she told Brett Pulley in the *New York Times.* "From that moment on, I've never stopped talking about going to Congress."

After earning a degree in political science from San Diego State University in 1990, Nelson began law school at Washington and Lee University but later transferred to American University in Washington, DC. By that point she had already become a registered Republican, which shocked many in her family. She was initially drawn to the party, she wrote in a *Washington Post* column, during the 1988 presidential campaign season, when she found herself "attracted by George H. W. Bush's message of a 'kinder, gentler' America and Jack Kemp's mantra of economic development and urban enterprise zones, which seemed a natural fit for the black community."

Nelson's first exposure to politics in earnest came when she landed an internship with Pete Wilson, the Republican governor of California from 1991 to 1999. She later worked as a policy analyst in Trenton, New Jersey's state capital; recruited African-American voters for Bush's 1992 reelection campaign; and was hired by New Jersey's first female governor, Christine Todd Whitman, as a special assistant in the Business Ombudsman's office. In 1996 Nelson made a bid for Florio's former Congressional seat. She gained a modest amount of media attention for being a young black Republican candidate and was the first African-American woman ever to secure the backing of the state's GOP organization in her quest for elected office. She won the Republican primary but then dropped out of the race due to a health crisis. She went on to work in two prestigious posts in Washington, DC: as investigative counsel to the House Government Reform Committee's investigation into campaign finance, and then director of Congressional & Public Affairs for the U.S. Chamber of Commerce. For a time, she ran her

At a Glance . . .

Born Sophia Angeli Nelson on January 5, 1967, in Munich, Germany; daughter of a former U.S. Army sergeant and Sandria Nelson (a licensed practical nurse). *Education*: San Diego State University, BA, 1990; post-graduate work at Washington and Lee University, 1991–92; American University, JD, 1994. *Politics*: Republican.

Career: Intern in the office of California Governor Pete Wilson, early 1990s; New Jersey Legislature, legislative policy analyst; special assistant to the Business Ombudsman in New Jersey Governor Christine Todd Whitman's administration in 1994; attorney with Horn, Goldberg, Gorny, Daniels, Plackier & Weiss, mid-1990s; became first African-American New Jersey woman to win Republican nomination for a seat in Congress, 1996; House Government Reform Committee, Campaign Finance Investigation, investigative counsel, 1996–97; U.S. Chamber of Commerce, director of Congressional & Public Affairs, 1998–99; ALN Consulting, Inc., president and chief executive officer, and counsel to Dutko Worldwide; Holland & Knight, senior counsel in its Public Policy and Regulation Group until 2008; political commentator and policy analyst for national news organizations; regular contributor to the *Washington Post*'s op-ed section; Political Intersection (a think tank), founder and editor in chief of its blog.

Memberships: Alpha Kappa Alpha; iask, Inc. (I Am My Sister's Keeper), founder and president, 2004—.

Addresses: *Home*—Virginia. *Web*—http://www.sophia anelson.com/.

own consulting firm that guided minority firms through the government contract bidding process.

Nelson's career as a political pundit blossomed after she left Holland & Knight, a Washington law firm where she had served as senior counsel in its Public Policy and Regulation Group, but she had been writing occasional pieces for the Outlook section of the *Washington Post* since 2001. She founded a think tank, Political Intersection, and served as editor in chief of its blog. Already a culture commentator for *Essence* and *Jet,* she began appearing regularly as a political commentator and policy analyst for Fox News, CNN, C-SPAN, National Public Radio, and BET. Her articles have appeared in the *New York Times, Wall Street Journal, Politico,* and The Root. In addition, she began working on her first book, which was an outgrowth of a mentoring organization she founded for African-American professional women called iask, Inc. (I Am My Sister's Keeper).

Nelson wrote extensively on Barack Obama's 2008 campaign and historic victory. "What the American people showed in this election is that they're looking for a more thoughtful and soulful politics," she wrote 19 days after Obama's election in a piece for the *Washington Post*. "The Republican Party has to find its soul again. Only then will it be ready to lead and govern in a way that attracts a broad spectrum of people to it and makes them want to stay with it for generations to come." In the months that followed she was often asked to comment on the Tea Party movement, a grass-roots coalition of disaffected conservative voters; at some events Tea Party supporters displayed objectionable signs or made remarks about black politicians, and the NAACP strongly condemned its tactics. In a controversial article she wrote for The Root in July of 2010 titled "Should Black Folks Give the Tea Party a Second Look?," Nelson asserted that "the biggest challenge with the Tea Party movement, like the Republican Party, is that it is 99 percent white." She pointed out that the core beliefs found among Tea Partiers were legitimate. "Does anyone among us really believe that government knows what is best for our lives? Does anyone among us really believe that paying more taxes will solve what is wrong with the poorest and least among us?" she asked. "Perhaps the African-American community needs to consider what we can do to secure our own economic wealth and our own individual liberties."

Nelson's first book grew in part out of a column she wrote for the *Washington Post* on Michelle Obama in the summer of 2008 that ran under the headline "Black. Female. Accomplished. Attacked." Her book, *Black Woman Redefined: Dispelling Myths and Discovering Fulfillment in the Age of Michelle Obama,* was published on May 31, 2011, and was one of the featured cover blurbs for the June issue of *Essence;* bestseller status loomed, with Amazon pre-publication orders prompting the publisher to order a second printing two weeks before it even appeared in stores. Part of Nelson's book includes in-depth analysis of a survey she commissioned querying 1,000 African-American professionals, both men and women. Financial pressures were at the forefront of most modern black women's concerns, second to building a successful romantic partnership. Negative images of African-American females in popular culture were also paramount. While Nelson has remarked that she wrote the book for women of her own "Gen X" generation, she also hoped to reach daughters and other relatives, like her own two young nieces. "I don't want them to have this conversation 20 years from now," she told Jackie Jones, a writer for the website Black America Web. "I want us to stop being wounded (as portrayed in

Ntozake Shange's play) 'For Colored Girls.' We are more than that. We can be more."

Sources

Books

Nelson, Sophia A., *Black Woman Redefined: Dispelling Myths and Discovering Fulfillment in the Age of Michelle Obama,* BenBella Books, 2011.

Periodicals

New York Times, April 21, 1996.
Washington Post, October 23, 2005; July 20, 2008; November 23, 2008; July 18, 2010, p. B2.

Online

Jones, Jackie, "'Black Woman Redefined' Explores Sisters' Issues," BlackAmericaWeb.com, May 16, 2011, http://www.blackamericaweb.com/?q=print/news/the_black_diaspora_news/28492 (accessed May 31, 2011).
Nelson, Sophia, "The Age of Michelle Obama," May 20, 2011, http://www.sophiaanelson.com/ (ac-

cessed May 25, 2011).
Nelson, Sophia, "Clair Huxtable & Me," The Root, September 20, 2009, http://www.theroot.com/blogs/cosby-show/clair-huxtable-me (accessed May 25, 2011).
Nelson, Sophia, "Crazy Love," The Root, August 27, 2009, http://www.theroot.com/blogs/north-carolina/crazy-love (accessed May 25, 2011).
Nelson, Sophia, "Should Black Folks Give the Tea Party a Second Look?," The Root, July 14, 2010, http://www.theroot.com/print/42628 (accessed May 30, 2011).
"Sophia Nelson," Essence.com, http://www.essence.com/microsites/summit/speakers-sophianelson.html (accessed May 25, 2011).
"Sophia A. Nelson," Huffington Post, http://www.huffingtonpost.com/sophia-a-nelson (accessed May 25, 2011).

Other

"Sherrod Case: Focus Shifts to Cheryl Cook," *American Morning,* CNN, July 23, 2010, http://transcripts.cnn.com/TRANSCRIPTS/1007/23/ltm.02.html (accessed August 7, 2011).

—Carol Brennan

Eleanor Holmes Norton

1937—

Politician, legal scholar

Eleanor Holmes Norton has served as the District of Columbia's delegate to Congress since 1991. A longtime civil rights activist, law professor, and the first woman to head the U.S. Equal Employment Opportunity Commission, the DC native has spent the better part of her career working to ensure that her constituents are represented fairly in Congress despite peculiar laws that limit their political participation. In 2010 Norton won her 11th term as a nonvoting member of the U.S. House of Representatives. "Racial justice has been Eleanor's anchor," wrote civil rights icon Coretta Scott King in the foreword to Norton's 2003 authorized biography *Fire in My Soul,* "but she has used her experience as a black woman in America to set sail to many other shores of injustice as well."

Norton, Eleanor Holmes, photograph. AP Images/Lauren Victoria Burke.

12 years old, Norton watched a protest outside of Hecht's department store. Activist Mary Church Terrell was picketing the store because black shoppers were allowed to make purchases there but not allowed to use Hecht's bathrooms. Norton held on to that memory of protest when she left Washington in 1955 to attend Antioch College in Ohio, from which she received her undergraduate degree. She then attended Yale University, where in 1963 she received a master's degree in American studies and in 1964 she earned a law degree. During these years she was active in the Student Nonviolent Coordinating Committee (SNCC) and took part in scores of protests to end segregation, some of which resulted in her arrest and detention in the heated, often violent civil rights clashes in Southern states.

Graduated from Yale Law School

A fourth-generation Washingtonian, Norton was born on June 13, 1937. Her father was a government worker in the District's bureaucracy, and her mother taught school. She has said that an event she experienced while growing up in Washington helped shape her beliefs about human justice. In 1949, when she was

Following an assignment in Philadelphia as clerk to the federal court judge A. Leon Higginbotham Jr.—a prominent African-American jurist of the mid-20th century—Norton was appointed the assistant legal director of the American Civil Liberties Union (ACLU) in 1965. Three years later she won the first case she argued before the U.S. Supreme Court. In that proceeding, Norton—an unswerving advocate of free

At a Glance . . .

Born Eleanor Katherine Holmes on June 13, 1937, in Washington, DC; daughter of Coleman Holmes (a civil servant) and Vela Lynch Holmes (a schoolteacher); married Edward Norton, 1965 (divorced, 1993); children: Katherine Felicia Norton, John Holmes Norton. *Education*: Antioch College, BA, 1960; Yale University, MA, 1963, LLB, 1964. *Politics*: Democrat.

Career: U.S. District Court for the Eastern District of Pennsylvania, law clerk to A. Leon Higginbotham Jr., 1964–65; American Civil Liberties Union, assistant legal director, 1965–70; NYC Commission on Human Rights, chair, 1970–77; executive assistant to mayor of New York City, 1971–74; U.S. Equal Employment Opportunity Commission, chair, 1977–81; Urban Institute, senior fellow, 1981–82; Georgetown University, professor of law, 1982–90; at-large delegate from the District of Columbia to United States Congress, 1991—.

Memberships: D.C. Bar Association (member of board of governors), Rockefeller Foundation (board member).

Awards: Young Woman of the Year Award, Junior Chamber of Commerce, 1965; Louise Waterman Wise Award, American Jewish Congress, 1971; named Outstanding Alumna of Yale Law School, 1980; Wilbur Cross Medal, Yale Graduate School, 1990; holds honorary degrees from more than 60 colleges and universities.

Addresses: *Office*—1415 Longworth House Office Building, Washington, DC 20515. *Web*—http://www.norton.house.gov/.

speech—argued on behalf of a white supremacist group that had been barred from holding a rally in Maryland. During these turbulent years, Norton rose to national prominence for her civil rights work. In 1970 New York City Mayor John Lindsay appointed her as new head of the city's Human Rights Commission.

In her first political post, Norton began a remarkable string of achievements, tenaciously battling prejudice and injustice in America's largest and most diverse city. Combating housing discrimination, intervening to reverse a state ruling that denied a polio victim a teaching certificate, and suing a real estate broker who would not rent to black tenants were just a few of the actions Norton undertook as human rights commissioner. In doing so, she made enemies. Conservatives fretted

about her activism, while some members of the black community criticized her for placing too much emphasis on women's issues at the expense of stamping out racial prejudice. "It's a shame that this criticism exists," *McCall's* magazine quoted her as saying, "because black people and women are going to have to get together if we're going to create some change in this country. I don't for a moment believe that women have suffered the same kind of injustices that blacks have—women have never been enslaved. But still, many of the psychological and economic problems are the same. This country would go bankrupt in a day if the Supreme Court suddenly ordered the powers–that–be to pay back wages to children of slaves and to the women who've worked all their lives for half wages or no pay."

Elected as Congressional Delegate

After her impressive performance in New York City, Norton was appointed by President Jimmy Carter to serve as chairperson of the Equal Employment Opportunity Commission (EEOC), a post she held from 1977 to 1981. Following her government service, she focused on teaching law and became a tenured professor at Georgetown University. A staunch supporter of affirmative action legislation, Norton told *Essence* magazine that "affirmative action is the most important antidiscrimination technique ever instituted in the United States. It is the one tool that has had a demonstrable effect on discrimination. . . . Affirmative action, by all statistical measures, has been the central ingredient to the creation of the Black middle class."

During his 1988 bid for the presidency, Reverend Jesse Jackson named Norton his representative at the convention during debate over the Democratic Party platform. The party "outsider," Jackson was thought to have chosen Norton partly because she was so well respected among Democrats. Soon *Ebony* was calling her a "national Democratic Party power broker." When Walter Fauntroy, the man who had represented the District in Congress for 20 years, announced he would be stepping down in 1990 to run (unsuccessfully) for mayor, Norton entered the race to replace him.

In the days preceding the September primary, Norton was hit with a stunning setback. According to the *Washington Post*, reporters had received an anonymous tip that Norton and her husband had failed to pay District income taxes between 1982 and 1989. At a hastily called news conference, Norton tearfully explained that her husband, Edward, not she, was responsible for the family finances. The Nortons eventually paid $88,000 in back taxes and penalties. "But many voters were skeptical of the explanation, and what had been expected to be a lopsided victory turned into a closer race," the *Washington Post* reported. Norton won the primary with 40 percent of the vote, compared to 33 percent for the second-place finisher.

In November, she gathered 62 percent of the vote against Republican candidate Harry Singleton.

While Norton's political career survived the tax scandal, her marriage did not. The couple legally separated just days after the 1990 election; the *Washington Post* quoted her friends as saying the Nortons' split resulted directly from the tax controversy. The two were divorced in 1993. The Nortons have two children, including a daughter, Katherine, who has Down syndrome. The Congresswoman spoke of Katherine in *Fire in My Soul* and revealed that years earlier, concerned friends and family thought that perhaps her school-aged daughter needed to be in a more permanent care facility for the developmentally disabled. "God made these children," she told Joan Steinau Lester, her authorized biographer. "He knew we would take care of them because they're so easy. Katherine is easy!"

Advocated for DC Statehood

Once in Congress Norton quickly began to distinguish herself from previous District delegates, working tirelessly to listen to residents and fulfill her duties as the District's at-large representative. At-large delegates are not permitted a vote on House legislation, but can hold committee assignments and may participate in floor debates. Elected representatives from Puerto Rico and the U.S. Virgin Islands share similar constrictions—a status Norton has long campaigned to change. Nevertheless, in her first term she secured $300 million in new federal money for the District. She was also a frequent critic of then-President George H. W. Bush, becoming the first elected leader to urge Bush to do something positive in the wake of the rioting that erupted in Los Angeles after the Rodney King/police brutality verdict.

At the 1992 Democratic convention, Norton made a pitch for DC statehood, which President Bush opposed. The *Washington Post* quoted her as telling the convention, "Give us a president who is not afraid to support at home the democracy he demands abroad. . . . Give us full-service democracy, not lip-service paternalism." During her second two-year term, Norton—a respected constitutional scholar—successfully devised a legal strategy to grant her and other at-large delegates the right to vote on House legislation. Norton noted that the full House meets in what parliamentarians call a "committee of the whole." Since delegates can vote in committee, she reasoned that the committee of the whole—which is how Congress gathers to debate and vote on substantive issues—is in fact yet another committee of Congress. Delegates are still barred from final congressional votes, but by the time legislation reaches that stage most legislation has already been reshaped and the issues decided. "As far as I'm concerned it's added immeasurably to my ability to get things done in the House," she told the *Washington Post.* "This

shows that the House has done everything for the District it can, short of granting statehood. And that means something."

As for statehood, Norton and other District politicians have always complained that Congress micromanages the city's affairs. Appropriations committees in Congress can overrule sections of the city's budget, and Congress has a significant influence in how the city operates. In 1992 Norton's statehood bill died in committee when it became apparent that President Bush would veto the measure no matter what Congress did. Her bill would create the state of New Columbia with the federal government controlling only the White House, Capitol, and Supreme Court, as well as federal monuments and some other governmental buildings. Republicans consistently oppose the measure since statehood would almost certainly guarantee that the heavily Democratic District of Columbia would send two new Democrats to the Senate.

Allied with Barack Obama

Reelected by wide margins every two years, Norton spent much of the 1990s campaigning for increased home rule in the District of Columbia. She lost a significant battle in 1995 when Congress enacted the District of Columbia Financial Responsibility and Management Assistance Authority, taking control of the city's finances after allegations of mismanagement and corruption surfaced. The DC Financial Control Board oversaw budget and bond issues for the next six years. In 2003 Norton introduced the No Taxation without Representation Act, which stalled in committee. Four years later she sponsored the District of Columbia House Voting Rights Act of 2007, which passed in the house but stalled in the Senate due to a filibuster tactic by Republican senators. Barack Obama, at the time the U.S. Senator from Illinois, was a co-sponsor of the bill.

Norton tried again in 2009 with the District of Columbia House Voting Rights Act, onto which Nevada senator John Ensign attached an amendment removing the power of DC authorities to limit guns and weapons in the city. Had it passed, this would have abrogated several important safety laws, including one that required gun owners to register their weapons. The provision had potentially dramatic ramifications for homeland security issues in the nation's capital. Once again, Norton's bill stalled and died with the adjournment of the 111th Congress.

The 112th Congress, which returned the House to Republican majority control in 2011, immediately moved to rescind some of the hard-won rights Norton had secured over the years. One was the ability for at-large delegates to vote on amendments. There was also renewed battle over control of the budget, and Norton was arrested in April of 2011 along with DC Mayor Vincent Gray and members of the City Council

during a protest against some of the renewed restrictions on local spending of federal appropriations for the coming fiscal year 2011–12. These included a controversial move to reinstitute a school voucher program and a ban on government-funded abortions in DC women's health clinics. With 601,000 residents, the District of Columbia and its businesses contribute about $5 billion in tax revenue to the U.S. Treasury, and Holmes continues to lead the crusade to permit Washingtonians more say in how their tax dollars are used, even at the local level. "The first strategy is resistance," she told she told journalist Ben Pershing in the *Washington Post*. "I don't expect Republicans to see the light by themselves any more than I expected Southern racists to see the light. . . . If there hadn't been resistance, there would not be change."

Selected writings

(With Barbara Allen Babcock) *Sex Discrimination and the Law: Causes and Remedies,* Little, Brown, 1975.
(With Joan Steinau Lester) *Fire in My Soul: Joan Steinau Lester in Conversation with Eleanor Holmes Norton,* foreword by Coretta Scott King, Atria Books, 2003.

Sources

Books

Holmes, Eleanor Norton, and Joan Steinau Lester, *Fire in My Soul: Joan Steinau Lester in Conversation with Eleanor Holmes Norton,* Atria Books, 2003.

Periodicals

Black Issues Book Review, March–April 2003, p. 55.
Christian Science Monitor, March 31, 1992, p. 14.
Ebony, January 1991, p. 105.
Emerge, March 1993, p. 32.
Essence, May 1990, p. 66.
McCall's, October 1971, p. 51.
New York Times, April 10, 2011.
Publishers Weekly, November 11, 2002.
Washington Post, March 5, 1991, p. B1; January 12, 1992, p. B1; May 3, 1992, p. B1; July 15, 1992, p. A23; October 28, 1992, p. 24; December 8, 1992, p. C1; August 2, 1993, p. D1; June 8, 2011.
Washington Post Magazine, July 4, 1993, p. 21.

Online

Madden, Mike, "House Republicans: No Vote for You!," Washington City Paper, December 22, 2010, http://www.washingtoncitypaper.com/blogs/loose lips/2010/12/22/house-republicans-no-vote-for-you (accessed July 29, 2011).
Martin, Michel, "Congresswoman Probes Solutions to Black Male Unemployment," Tell Me More, National Public Radio, August 10, 2010, http://ic.galegroup. com/ic/bic1/AudioDetailsPage/AudioDetailsWin dow?displayGroupName=Audio&disableHighlight ing=false&prodId=BIC2&action=e&windowstate= normal&catId=&documentId= GALE%7CA234084213&mode=view&userGroup Name=itsbtrial&jsid=521ff754bf02d1b79238e79 52cb857ed (accessed July 29, 2011).

—John LoDico and Carol Brennan

Stephanie Rawlings-Blake

1970—

Politician

Stephanie Rawlings-Blake stepped into the role of Baltimore mayor in 2010 when her predecessor, Sheila Dixon, was forced to resign in the wake of a financial scandal. Rawlings-Blake is the second woman to lead the Maryland city of 620,000 people and the fourth black mayor of a city with a rich African-American history and demonstrated preference for electing Democratic candidates. She spent several years on the Baltimore City Council while working in the county public defender's office. "I was often surprised when one of my clients had finished high school because most hadn't," she told Eric Siegel in the *Baltimore Sun* about her former career as a public defender. "The majority of my clients were dependent on illegal drugs; very few of them had steady employment. That basically sums the significant problems of the city."

Rawlings-Blake was born in Baltimore in 1970 and grew up in the Northwestern district, which was evolving from a largely Jewish enclave to an African-American residential area during her youth. Her mother, Nina, was one of the first black woman to earn a degree from the medical school of the University of Maryland and had a thriving pediatric practice by the

Rawlings-Blake, Stephanie, photograph. AP Images/Rob Carr.

time Rawlings-Blake was born; the family included Lisa, Rawlings-Blake's older sister, and Wendall, a younger brother. Their father was Howard "Pete" Rawlings, a well-known figure in Baltimore politics who in 1979 was elected to the Maryland House of Delegates and remained in office until his death 24 years later from cancer. Her father would eventually chair the appropriations committee in the state legislature and served as a mentor to an up-and-coming generation of younger African-American political leaders, including former schoolteacher Sheila Dixon.

Rawlings-Blake graduated from Western High School, a single-sex public school in Baltimore, and entered Oberlin College in Ohio, from which she earned a political science degree in 1992. Future mayor of Washington, DC, Adrian M. Fenty, was one of her classmates at Oberlin. Rawlings-Blake went on to law school at the University of Maryland, graduating in 1995. That same year, she stood for and won a seat on the Baltimore City Council from District 5 in the Northwestern district, becoming the youngest person ever elected to the municipal body in the city's history. She practiced law at the same time, working first for

At a Glance . . .

Born Stephanie Cole Rawlings on March 17, 1970, in Baltimore, MD; daughter of Howard "Pete" (a politician) and Nina (a pediatrician; maiden name, Cole) Rawlings; married Kent Blake (a hospital employee); children: Sophia. *Education*: Oberlin College, BA, 1992; University of Maryland Law School, JD, 1995. *Politics*: Democrat.

Career: Young Democrats of Maryland, lobbyist, 1993; Legal Aid Bureau, administrative law attorney, 1997–98; Maryland Office of Public Defender, staff attorney, 1998–2006; elected to Baltimore City Council from District 5, 1995, 1999, and from District 6, 2004, 2008; became city council vice president, 1999, and city council president, 2007; became mayor of Baltimore, 2010.

Memberships: Alpha Kappa Alpha; Federal Bar Association; Maryland State Bar Association; National Conference of Mayors (advisory board member, 2010); Baltimore City Democratic State Central Committee; Living Classrooms Foundation (board member).

Addresses: *Home*—Baltimore, MD. *Office*—City Hall, Rm. 250, 100 N. Holliday St., Baltimore, MD 21202.

the Legal Aid Bureau and then in the Baltimore Office of the Public Defender representing indigent clients in court. In 1999 her colleagues on the council elected her to serve as vice president.

Until 2003 Baltimore voters chose their city council representatives from six districts, each of which was served by three members. The districts were redrawn in 2004, the electoral-reform package reduced the number of council members, and the districts became single-member precincts. Rawlings-Blake faced a tougher challenge to secure her third four-year term, facing off against a black Muslim Republican who claimed Rawlings-Blake had spent the past eight years ineffectually. Rawlings-Blake countered by noting the Home Depot store and drug treatment center she had brought to District 5, and a new "stop receipt" measure she championed, which compelled Baltimore police to issue a receipt to any person stopped, which would help the city and state compile racial profiling statistics to avoid potential Department of Justice scrutiny. Rawlings-Blake beat her challenger, attorney Melvin Bilal, in the 2004 race for the redrawn District 6, her new home base. "I'm a workhorse, not a show horse," she told Christina Royster-Hemby in the *Baltimore*

City Paper as election day neared, and she discounted Bilal's attacks that she had coasted to office on her father's name. "He was always steadfast in his determination to use his skills to do his best to work for his constituents—whether it got headlines or not, and whether or not people gave him credit," she said of her famous, recently deceased father. "And that's the lesson he taught me, and that's what I'm doing."

Rawlings-Blake was said to have been instrumental in securing her father's endorsement of Martin O'Malley, a council colleague who entered the 1999 mayoral race. The white Democrat succeeded Kurt Schmoke, Baltimore's first black mayor, in that contest, and then went on to win the Maryland gubernatorial election in 2006. Because O'Malley still held the mayor's office, council president Sheila Dixon succeeded O'Malley as mayor upon his resignation in January of 2007. At that point Rawlings-Blake succeeded Dixon as the new council president. Dixon ran for mayor in November of 2007 and won, while Rawlings-Blake campaigned for citywide office for the first time in her bid to remain city council president, which she also won.

Married and the mother of a young daughter, Rawlings-Blake left her job in the public defender's office in late 2006 in advance of succeeding Dixon as council president. Few foresaw Dixon's downfall, which came a little over a year after she became the first woman ever elected by Baltimore voters to serve as mayor. Dixon was accused of using gift cards ostensibly donated by retail chains to help the city's poorest, and she also faced perjury and misconduct charges tied to the scandal. She agreed to resign as part of a plea agreement, thus avoiding a trial and the loss of her city pension.

As city council president, Rawlings-Blake once again succeeded Dixon on the job. She was sworn in as the 49th mayor of Baltimore on February 4, 2010. Initially, there were rumblings that Governor O'Malley might appoint a new mayor, even a Republican, but to reject the rules of the Baltimore City Charter would have incited a contentious political conflagration. "Ironically, all of this anxiety about the racial complexion of the city's leadership has deflected attention from what is perhaps the more interesting and certainly historic feature of Baltimore politics," wrote Sherrilyn A. Ifill in The Root in late 2009. "It is the only major city in the U.S. in which all of the major citywide elected positions—mayor, city council president, district attorney and comptroller—are held by black women."

In her first week in office Rawlings-Blake faced two significant snowstorms which brought the Southern seaport city to a standstill. In her first year in office she negotiated a tricky budget battle to resolve a $121 million deficit. While her father had passed away in 2003, Rawlings-Blake's retired physician mother remained a part of her daily life, helping care for the young daughter born just after the city council primary

races that year. "I could not do what I do as mayor without my mom," she told Julie Scharper in the *Baltimore Sun.* "She taught me by example how to be a strong person without apologizing for living your own life."

Sources

Periodicals

Baltimore Sun, January 21, 2007; December 3, 2009; May 8, 2010; January 25, 2011.

Online

Ifill, Sherrilyn A., "Baltimore's (Political) Race Men," The Root, October 19, 2009, http://www.theroot.com/views/baltimores-political-race-men (accessed June 7, 2011).

Royster-Hemby, Christina, "The Contender," *Baltimore City Paper,* September 8, 2004, http://www2.citypaper.com/news/story.asp?id=8765 (accessed June 8, 2011).

—Carol Brennan

Dana Redd

1968—

Politician

Redd, Dana, photograph. AP Images/Mel Evans.

Camden mayor Dana Redd presides over one of the most financially imperiled and derelict cities in the United States. New Jersey's 12th-largest municipality, which sits just across the Delaware River from Philadelphia, has a population of more than 77,000, but one of the lowest average per-capita incomes in the nation, at $12,000. Camden's long history of municipal troubles include endemic corruption and graft, but Redd, a Democrat, was elected in 2009 on a promise to reform and revitalize the city.

Redd is a native of Camden. Born in 1968, she grew up with a brother and endured a tragedy of unimaginable heartbreak when she was eight years old. In July of 1976 her parents checked into the Laurel Notch Motor Lodge in the South Jersey community of Bordentown on the way back from a vacation in Canada. Just a few weeks earlier, her father, Ronald, had voluntarily committed himself to psychiatric hospital; reportedly he was under stress because of his job as president of the 1,800-member-strong Local 80 of the Amalgamated Meat Cutters and Butcher Workmen of North America at the Campbell Soup Company plant, which was Camden's biggest employer. Redd's mother, Brenda,

was a medical technician and worked at another major employer in the city, Cooper Hospital. The police report detailing the crime scene at Laurel Notch Motor Lodge claimed that Ronald Redd shot his wife, then turned the rifle on himself, using his toe to pull the trigger.

Redd and her brother were raised by both sets of grandparents. Just a few weeks after her parents' funerals the eight-year-old student at the parochial school attached to the Roman Catholic church Sacred Heart was chosen by parish leaders to present flowers to one of the world's most famous living nuns, Mother Teresa, on her visit to Camden. The humanitarian hugged Redd, and offered her a special blessing. Although Redd is not Roman Catholic, she has often cited that moment as a source of enormous spiritual strength to her, both during that summer of grief and over the course of her adult life.

After earning her high school diploma from another Catholic school Redd worked full time to support herself, her brother, and help out her grandparents while taking evening classes at the Rutgers University's School of Business in Camden. She earned a bachelor of science degree in business in 1996 and later took

At a Glance . . .

Born on March 7, 1968, in Camden, NJ; daughter of Ronald Redd (a union official) and Brenda Redd (a medical technician). *Education*: Rutgers University—Camden, BS, 1996; attended Edward J. Bloustein School of Planning and Public Policy of Rutgers University. *Politics*: Democrat. *Religion*: Baptist.

Career: Worked in the office of Camden County Freeholder Aletha Wright, early 1990s; chief of staff and aide to Camden County Freeholder Riletta L. Cream, 1994–99; Camden County Board of Social Services, member; worked in the finance department of Camden Parking Authority; Camden Department of Buildings and Operations, director of operations after 1999; elected to Camden City Council, 2001, and served as vice chair after 2001; reelected, 2005; Camden Housing Authority, chair, 2004–06; appointed to fill a vacancy in the 5th legislative district, New Jersey Senate, 2008 (resigned seat, 2010); elected mayor of Camden, 2009.

Memberships: Democratic National Committee, New Jersey Democratic State Committee, vice chair, 2006—.

Addresses: *Home*—Camden, NJ. *Office*—Mayor's Office, 520 Market St., Camden City Hall, 4th Fl., Camden, NJ 08101-5120.

courses at the Edward J. Bloustein School of Planning and Public Policy at the main campus of Rutgers in New Brunswick.

Redd's father had been active in Camden politics, and she was drawn to local Democratic circles as a young adult. She went to work as an aide in the office of Aletha Wright, a Camden County official, and later worked for another freeholder, as the members of the county legislatures in New Jersey are called, before taking a finance job with the Camden Parking Authority. As the 1990s drew to a close, Redd began to contemplate a run for office.

Redd won a seat on the Camden City Council in 2001 on the Democratic Party ticket. She became its vice chair, and she also had supervisory oversight of the city's Housing Authority from 2004 to 2006. Active in the South New Jersey Democratic Party organization and a Democratic National Convention delegate, in 2007 she was appointed to fill the remaining term of Wayne Bryant, a state senator from Camden who was indicted on corruption charges. She represented the 5th legislative district in the New Jersey Senate from January 8, 2008, to January 5, 2010.

Corruption charges are a hallmark of politics in both Camden proper and Camden County dating back several decades. One mayor was indicted for attempts to bribe undercover agents posing as Arab sheikhs in the infamous Abscam sting operation run by the Federal Bureau of Investigation (FBI) in the late 1970s. Another was removed from office in 2000 after receiving a federal prison sentence for laundering drug money, among other charges. Camden's financial mismanagement had grown so dire that in 2002 lawmakers in Trenton, the state capital, agreed to hand over $175 million in bailout funds only if the city relinquished control to a chief operating officer. The official chosen to hold that post was a former mayor and City Council member, Melvin Primas. The deal required the current mayor, Gwendolyn Faison, to give up much of her executive authority. The five-year deal was eventually extended until 2012.

Many in Camden resented the state takeover. The strategy had failed to remedy any of the city's major fissures—although its waterfront aquarium did get a gleaming new $40 million renovation. Campaigning on a pledge to end state oversight, Redd entered the 2009 mayoral race and won the June Democratic primary with 86 percent of the vote. She won the general election on November 3, 2009, and was sworn into office on January 1, 2010.

Redd had a solid ally in her bid to regain control of the city's decision-making authority in the form of New Jersey's new Republican governor, Chris Christie. A few short weeks into their new terms, a deal was cut to end state oversight in Camden—but Trenton lawmakers also cut off the financial pipeline that the city had relied upon to meet its basic operating expenses for the past few years. Under these conditions, the already struggling city—with a 17 percent unemployment rate and 36 percent of its residents living at or below the poverty line—faced a frightening future. The city even teetered on the brink of becoming the first mid-sized American city to shut all its library branches; Camden's once-magnificent main branch had been closed for years and was one of its more infamous derelict properties, with a large tree growing inside.

Crime, abandoned houses, vermin, and scattershot city services were among the most worrisome issues that Redd faced as mayor, but the coming budget shortfall would mean drastic layoffs for city hall workers and even public safety workers. Camden consistently appeared on "worst cities" lists; it lost its title as America's most dangerous city, in statistics compiled by Congressional Quarterly Press, to St. Louis, Missouri, during Redd's first year in office. Her plan to excise a significant number of jobs from the payroll prompted widespread outrage, but Trenton provided an emergency loan to permit her to hire back some of the laid off police and firefighters who lost their jobs in early 2011.

One of Redd's biggest boosters is the Roman Catholic priest who now serves as monsignor of Sacred Heart

Church, where just weeks after the loss of her parents, Redd had met with Mother Teresa. "People who have wings fly out of Camden, and those who have broken wings come back to it," Rev. Michael Doyle told journalist Matt Katz in the *Philadelphia Inquirer*. "Dana grew wondrous wings but she's choosing to take on her city, the city of her childhood, the city of her parents, the city of her grandparents, taking it on when she could have a life easier than that."

Sources

Books

"Dana Redd," *State Directory,* Carroll Publishing, 2009.

Periodicals

New York Times, November 12, 2010.
Philadelphia Daily News, February 17, 2009.
Philadelphia Inquirer, January 1, 2010; January 22, 2011.
Philadelphia Tribune, February 20, 2011.

Online

Heininger, Claire, "Camden Mayor Dana Redd Takes Oath of Office, Says Goal Is to Return Local Authority," NJ.com, January 5, 2010, http://www.nj.com/news/index.ssf/2010/01/camden_mayor_dana_redd_takes_o.html (accessed July 31, 2011).

—Carol Brennan

Cedric Richmond

1973—

Politician, lawyer

Richmond, Cedric, photograph. AP Images/Alex Brandon.

Cedric Richmond first stepped into the national spotlight in November of 2010, when he was elected to Congress as the representative for Louisiana's Second District, which includes most of the city of New Orleans. A Democrat, he is known for his staunch support of small businesses.

Cedric Levon Richmond was born on September 13, 1973, in New Orleans. Raised by his mother, a schoolteacher and business owner, and his stepfather, he spent many hours on sports teams sponsored by the city's recreation department, and he has frequently cited the coaches in these programs as some of his most influential role models. After graduating from Benjamin Franklin High School on the city's east side, he entered Atlanta's Morehouse College, where he earned a bachelor's degree in about 1995. He then returned to New Orleans for law school at Tulane University. After receiving his degree there, he passed the state bar exam and began laying the groundwork for a career in public service, setting his sights on the state legislature. Aided by an endorsement from U.S. Representative William Jefferson, then the Second District incumbent, he easily won election to the Louisiana House in the fall of 1999. He remained there for more than a decade, winning reelection twice (in 2003 and 2007).

Enjoying strong support from his constituents in New Orleans, Richmond developed significant influence in the state capitol of Baton Rouge. His rise was particularly apparent in the context of the powerful Judiciary Committee, which he chaired for a time. He was also known for his work to secure financial aid for small businesses damaged by Hurricanes Katrina and Rita in 2005. One of the highlights of that effort was the New Markets Tax Credit (NMTC) program, which he championed. According to his personal website, CedricRichmond.com, NMTC sparked more than a quarter of a billion dollars in new investment in the areas most damaged by the storms.

Richmond's career as a state legislator was not without controversy. In 2008 the Louisiana Supreme Court suspended his law license for two months in response to charges that he had made false statements in election documents. The affair began in 2005, when he announced his intention to run for a seat on the New Orleans City Council. During the campaign, opponents alleged that he was unqualified to run, on the grounds that he was not a resident of the area, though he did

At a Glance . . .

Born Cedric Levon Richmond on September 13, 1973, in New Orleans, LA.; son of a schoolteacher and business owner. *Education*: Morehouse College, bachelor's degree, 1995(?); Tulane University, JD, 1998(?). *Politics*: Democrat.

Career: State of Louisiana, state representative, 2000–11; U.S. House of Representatives, representative, 2011.

Memberships: Congressional Black Caucus; New Democrat Coalition.

Addresses: *Office*—2021 Lakeshore Dr., Ste. 309, New Orleans, LA 70122. *Web*—http://www.CedricRichmond.com.

own a home there. The Supreme Court responded at the time by simply taking his name off the ballot; the suspension of his license was later imposed as a penalty. Richmond, for his part, apologized, declaring in a written statement quoted on the news site NOLA.com, "I accept full responsibility for my conduct in this matter and will move forward with my legal career, and my commitment to public service."

Richmond's reelection in 2007 came at a time when the political fortunes of Jefferson, his former mentor, were declining rapidly. Jefferson was dogged by serious corruption charges, and his hold on the Second District appeared to be weakening. No fewer than six Democrats, Richmond among them, quickly seized the opportunity to run for the seat themselves. In a party primary in October of 2008, he came in third, trailing Jefferson and fellow challenger Helena Moreno; the seat was eventually taken by Anh "Joseph" Cao, a Republican.

In the wake of his 2008 defeat, Richmond returned to Baton Rouge. His interest in a career in Washington remained strong, however, in part because Cao, as a Republican newcomer in a Democratic stronghold, was considered vulnerable. In 2010 he tried again, this time with the endorsement of U.S. President Barack Obama, who appeared in a television spot for the candidate. It was the only advertisement the president recorded for a congressional candidate in the 2010 elections. Cao responded aggressively, highlighting in particular what he portrayed as a series of ethical lapses by Richmond. These included the 2005 election incident, a 2007 summons for disturbing the peace, and alleged financial wrongdoing. According to Cao, Richmond had steered nearly $600,000 in state funds to a

nonprofit, New Orleans Community Enhancement (NOCE), directed by a woman with whom he was romantically involved. He also alleged that Richmond had paid for an expensive watch with the organization's credit card. While a 2004 police inquiry and subsequent investigations did uncover a substantial misuse of funds at NOCE, nothing surfaced that directly implicated Richmond, who vehemently denied wrongdoing, showing reporters a jeweler's receipt that appeared to vindicate him in the matter of the watch. The ethics of the $600,000 appropriation, meanwhile, remained a matter of opinion.

Even by the standards of New Orleans, a city known for political infighting, the 2010 race for the Second District was a bitter one. While Richmond enjoyed support from Obama, Cao was largely on his own. He was widely viewed as a moderate, and his willingness to join the Democrats on certain issues was vexing to Republican leaders, many of whom gave him only tepid support. Richmond, meanwhile, seemed to gain confidence daily. On Election Day (November 2, 2010) he won a decisive victory, taking nearly two-thirds of the vote. He was sworn into office the following January.

According to Richmond's website, once in Congress he focused in particular on issues of national security and economic development. A member of the Congressional Black Caucus and the New Democrat Coalition, he served on the Small Business and Homeland Security Committees. A highlight of his first months in office came in April of 2011, when he joined a bipartisan congressional delegation to Europe and Afghanistan. Over the course of the week-long trip, he visited American troops and attended meetings to discuss ongoing counterterrorism efforts. "Gaining greater insight from our folks on the ground," he said in a press release, "is critically important as we deliberate our next steps."

Sources

Online

"Cedric Richmond Jewelry Purchase Allegations Not Backed up by Credit Card Records," NOLA.com, October 8, 2010, http://blog.nola.com/politics/print.html?entry=/2010/10/cedric_richmond_jewelry-purcha.html (accessed June 23, 2011).

"Congressional Delegation Mission to Europe and Afghanistan," Office for Congressman Cedric Richmond, http://richmond.house.gov/congressional-delegation-mission-europe-and-afghanistan (accessed June 24, 2011).

Donze, Frank, "President's Endorsement Goes a Long Way for Cedric Richmond in Bid for 2nd District House Seat," NOLA.com, October 20, 2010, http://blog.nola.com/politics/print.html?entry=/2010/10/presidents_endorsement_goes_a.html (accessed June 23, 2011).

"State Rep. Cedric Richmond's Law License Sus-

pended," NOLA.com, September 28, 2009, http://www.nola.com/news/index.ssf/2008/12/state_rep_cedric_richmonds_law.html (accessed June 23, 2011).

"Full Biography," Office for Congressman Cedric Richmond, http://richmond.house.gov/about-me/full-biography (accessed June 23, 2011).

"Meet Cedric Richmond," CedricRichmond.com, http://cedricrichmond.com/about-cedric (accessed June 23, 2011).

—R. Anthony Kugler

Cecilia Rouse

1963—

Economist

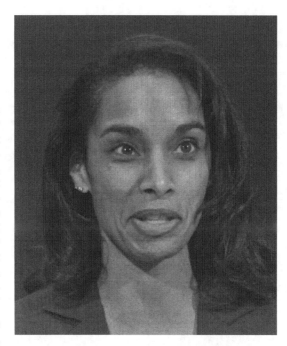

Rouse, Cecilia, photograph. Jay Mallin/Bloomberg via Getty Images.

Economist Cecilia Rouse spent two years as deputy chair of President Barack Obama's Council of Economic Advisers (CEA). Tasked with informing the president on matters of labor and education, she helped advise the White House on the Student Aid and Fiscal Responsibility Act of 2009, which President Obama signed into law in 2010. Rouse left the CEA post in 2011 to return to her job at Princeton University, where she is a professor of economics at the Woodrow Wilson School of Public and International Affairs.

Born in 1963, Rouse grew up in the Pacific oceanfront community of Del Mar, California, near San Diego. Her father, Carl A. Rouse, was originally from Youngstown, Ohio, where his father ran an auto-repair business; other relatives, who had left South Carolina, worked in the steel mills of the area. Rouse's father went on to become a noted atomic scientist at the Lawrence Livermore National Laboratory in California. Her mother, Lorraine, was working for the Girl Scouts in Pasadena, California, when she met Carl Rouse, a student at Cal Tech at the time. Rouse was one of their three bright and uniformly accomplished children.

Rouse entered Harvard University with the intention of studying engineering but was unexpectedly fascinated by an economics class. She declared that as her major, and also took French and Farsi language courses while playing flute and piano in two campus orchestras. Few who knew her were surprised when she graduated with magna cum laude distinction in 1986. She spent the next six years working on her PhD in economics, which Harvard awarded her in 1992. That same year, she joined the faculty of Princeton University as an assistant professor of economics and public affairs.

Rouse's involvement in classical music led to her first major research paper: she and a Harvard economist, Claudia Goldin, examined hiring data at major symphonies and orchestras and reported their findings in "Orchestrating Impartiality: The Impact of Blind Auditions on Female Musicians," published as a working paper in 1997 and in the September of 2000 issue of the *American Economic Review*. Organizations that conducted "blind" orchestra auditions—in which the hiring committee cannot see the applicant, only judge their playing abilities—resulted in significant gains for women musicians, their study showed. A second widely

cited paper was "Private School Vouchers and Student Achievement: An Evaluation of the Milwaukee Parental Choice Program," which Rouse completed for the National Bureau of Economic Research. It was published in Harvard's *Quarterly Journal of Economics* in 1998.

At Princeton Rouse received tenure and rose to become director of the University's Industrial Relations Section (IRS), which compiles vital research data on labor, management, and income in the U.S. workforce. She also joined the National Bureau of Economic Research as a faculty research fellow. Known by its acronym, NBER, the Bureau charts U.S. gross domestic product figures and also serves as the primary forecaster for recession start and end dates.

In 2002 Rouse became the founding director of the Princeton Educational Research Section at the Woodrow Wilson School of Public and International Affairs. Five years later she was named the Theodore A. Wells '29 Professor of Economics and Public Affairs at Princeton, the same year she co-edited her first book, *The Price of Independence: The Economics of Early Adulthood*. Its contents assessed trends in the late 20th and early 21st centuries that pointed to what sociologists termed a delayed progression from adolescence into adulthood for a large swath of young Americans, using one significant marker: full-time,

long-term employment. "People are getting married later, they're having children later, and they're buying houses later," Rouse told writer Steven Greenhouse in the *New York Times* a few months before *The Price of Independence* was published. "There's been a lengthening of the transition to adulthood, and it is very possible that what has happened in the economy is leading to some of these changes."

Rouse's work at Princeton continued to focus on education issues in the U.S. economy, examining rising rates of student loan debt, the long-term benefits of a college degree, and the impact of community colleges. Her name was mentioned as a possible head of the White House Council of Economic Advisers (CEA) shortly after Barack Obama was elected, but University of Chicago professor Austan Goolsbee was named chair of the body, with Rouse and Christina Romer of the University of California—Berkeley as deputy chairs. Rouse took leave from Princeton and, after Senate confirmation, began her new job on March 11, 2009.

Among her new duties, Rouse advised the White House on the Student Aid and Fiscal Responsibility Act of 2009, or SAFRA. This expanded the Pell Grant program, which provides financial aid packages to income-qualified students, among other changes, and directed more funding into community colleges. Another part of her job was discussing vital economic-relief packages, such as the federal emergency extension to the temporary unemployment insurance program. She left the White House job in February of 2011, and a few months later was named to an endowed chair at Princeton, the Lawrence and Shirley Katzman and Lewis and Anna Ernst Professor in the Economics of Education. Her replacement as deputy chair at the CEA was Carl Shapiro, a Department of Justice attorney specializing in antitrust cases. "Working with the Council of Economic Advisers was very focused on dealing with the issue or the crisis of the moment," she told Jason Jung in the *Daily Princetonian* about the transition back to campus. "Being a professor was thinking about the long-term, planning research projects and letting the long-term ideas germinate."

Rouse is the mother of two children. Her sister, Carolyn Rouse, also teaches at Princeton and is the author of *Engaged Surrender: African American Women and Islam*, and her brother Forest Rouse is a physicist. Shortly after leaving her White House job, Rouse was asked to comment about new data that showed the U.S. student loan debt nearing the trillion-dollar mark in 2010, surpassing even consumer credit-card debt for the first time in U.S. history. "College is still a really good deal," she told Tamar Lewin in the *New York Times* about the return on the investment. "Even if you don't land a plum job, you're still going to earn more over your lifetime, and the vast majority of graduates can expect to cover their debts." She did voice concern "about this cohort of young people, because their

unemployment rates are much higher and early job changing is how you get those increases over their lifetime," she reflected. "In this economy, it's a lot harder to go from job to job. We know that there's some scarring to cohorts who graduate in bad economies, and this is the mother of bad economies."

Sources

Periodicals

New York Times, September 4, 2006; April 11, 2011.

Online

"Cecilia Rouse Chosen to Serve on President Obama's Council of Economic Advisers," Woodrow Wilson School of Public and International Affairs, Princeton University, http://wws.princeton.edu/news/CC%20RouseObama/ (accessed July 31, 2011).

"Cecilia Rouse," WhoRunsGov, http://www.whorunsgov.com/Profiles/Cecilia_Rouse (accessed July 31, 2011).

Guan, Amy, "Cecilia Rouse," *Harvard Crimson,* May 25, 2011, http://www.thecrimson.com/article/2011/5/25/rouse-obama-economics-social/ (accessed July 31, 2011).

Jung, Jason, "Economic Adviser Rouse to Return to U. in March," *Daily Princetonian,* February 17, 2011, http://www.dailyprincetonian.com/2011/02/17/27633/ (accessed July 31, 2011).

—Carol Brennan

Danzy Senna

1970—

Novelist and short story writer

Senna, Danzy, photograph. Ulf Andersen/Getty Images.

Danzy Senna is a novelist, short-story writer, and memoirist known for frank and complex assessments of the situation of biracial women in contemporary America. The daughter of a white mother and a black father, Senna identifies as an African American even though her appearance leads many to assume that she is white. The central characters in her novels *Caucasia* and *Symptomatic*, and in the stories collected in *You Are Free*, similarly occupy both sides of the American racial divide, and the narratives Senna constructs around them pose necessary if at times uncomfortable questions about the ongoing roles that race plays in private and public life. In *Where Did You Sleep Last Night? A Personal History*, Senna approaches the subject of her heritage from another angle, investigating her father's Southern roots as a means of understanding his later personal and professional failures.

Occupied Both Sides of Racial Divide

Senna was born on September 13, 1970, in Boston, Massachusetts, the daughter of Carl Senna, a poet and editor, and Fanny Howe, a poet and novelist. Senna's father was of mixed African-American and Mexican heritage, and her mother came from a well-heeled white Boston family that could trace its roots to the Mayflower. Her parents were politically progressive and deeply involved in the civil rights movement, and they consciously chose a black identity for their two daughters and their son, even though, of the three, only Senna's older sister appeared to be black. This was partly a function of the way race functioned in 1970s Boston, where to be multiracial was to be considered black, but it was also a political choice. "I feel really lucky because I was raised in a household where my parents were very politically conscious," Senna said. "To say I'm black is to take a political stance, I think, and to say that this is something worth choosing—that there's so much value in that culture and that identity."

Outside of the family, however, Senna often found herself in situations where whites, not suspecting that she was black, spoke insultingly about African Americans. She also found herself frequently met with suspicion in groups of African Americans until she revealed that she was black. This predicament of being caught

At a Glance . . .

Born Danzy Senna on September 13, 1970, in Boston, MA; daughter of Carl Senna (a writer) and Fanny Howe (a writer); married Percival Everett; children: Henry, Miles. *Education*: Stanford University, BA, 1992; University of California, Irvine, MFA, 1996. *Politics*: Democrat.

Career: *Newsweek*, researcher and reporter, 1992–94; novelist, 1998—.

Awards: Stephen Crane Award for First Fiction, Book-of-the-Month Club, for *Caucasia*; Alex Award, American Library Association, 1999, for *Caucasia*; Whiting Writers' Award, 2002; Fellow, New York Public Library's Cullman Center for Scholars and Writers, 2004.

Addresses: *Agent*—Sarah Chalfant, The Wylie Agency, 250 West 57th St., Ste. 2114, New York, NY 10107. *Web*—http://danzysenna.com/.

between the white and black worlds, her true identity invisible to both groups unless she asserted it, became one of her central concerns as a writer.

Senna attended Stanford University, taking a BA with honors in 1992. Among her scholarly interests was a research project focusing on two canonical novels about the biracial experience, James Weldon Johnson's *The Autobiography of an Ex-Colored Man* and Nella Larsen's *Passing*. Critical responses to Senna's work have since frequently invoked Larsen as a key forerunner. Another aspect of Senna's college experience that would find its way into her work was her involvement in student activism and her acquaintance with political radicals. She would later identify the political radicals in her novel *Caucasia* as modeled on the lovable but unhinged people she met in the political circles she frequented while at Stanford.

Won Acclaim for Caucasia

After college, Senna worked at *Newsweek* magazine in New York before entering the graduate program in creative writing at the University of California, Irvine. While at Irvine, she wrote *Caucasia*, her first novel. She returned to New York in 1996 with an MFA, the manuscript, and $700. Within a matter of months, she had found an agent to represent the book. It was sold that winter and published in 1998.

Caucasia tells the story of the Lees, a mixed-race family that resembles Senna's in several important

respects. Deck Lee, a black man whose single mother came north alone from Louisiana, is married to Sandra, a blue-blooded Bostonian. One of the two Lee daughters, Cole, appears African-American, whereas the book's narrator, Birdie, looks white. Although the Lees are united in their commitment to radical politics, their marriage is falling apart, and when Sandra's political activity forces the whole family to go into hiding, they split up according to appearance, with Cole and her father fleeing to Brazil to live among black people and Birdie and her mother settling in New Hampshire and posing as the family of a deceased Jewish professor.

Caucasia won an extraordinary amount of critical praise and remains Senna's most acclaimed book. As Margo Jefferson wrote in the *New York Times*, "What Ms. Senna gets so painfully well is how the standard-issue cruelties of adolescence (like being the new kid trying to win acceptance) are revitalized when they encounter race. With its tone of passionate irony and dispassionate melancholy, [*Caucasia*] left nothing unexamined and made nothing easy." Jake Lamar of the *Washington Post* similarly applauded the book for its ability to illuminate difficult social and personal terrain: "Birdie Lee does not allow people the comforts of silence. In no uncertain terms, she eventually speaks her mind, telling painful truths about white and black America alike. Attention must be paid."

Continued to Produce Accomplished Work

Symptomatic, which appeared in 2004, likewise explores the phenomenon of occupying the fraught middle ground between the worlds of white and black America. The novel's unnamed heroine, working at a New York magazine, is biracial but looks white. She becomes romantically involved with a white man, but after witnessing a conversation in which he and his friends speak disparagingly about black people, she leaves him. She takes up with a biracial coworker, an older woman with whom she has nothing else in common, only to discover, too late, that the woman is psychologically disturbed. *Symptomatic* was greeted with mixed reviews, its heroine generally failing to win readers over to the degree that *Caucasia*'s Birdie Lee had, but most critics continued to point to the powerful nature of Senna's subject matter.

Senna followed *Symptomatic* with a memoir, *Where Did You Sleep Last Night? A Personal History*, which is structured as an investigation into her father's origins and family life. Her father, once an up-and-coming writer on the Boston literary scene, had over time become an abusive husband and an out-of-work alcoholic, and Senna wanted to discover what role his race and his impoverished background might have played in this sad transition. Traveling through the Deep South with him to try and locate evidence of the stories he had been told about his past, Senna fails to fix all the details of his identity but succeeds at depicting his character,

illuminating the fraught weave of personal history and social forces that make him who he is. The book was on the whole warmly received, but as with *Symptomatic*, it fell short of the extremely receptive readership that *Caucasia* had found.

In 2011 Senna published her first volume of short stories. Titled (with palpable irony) *You Are Free*, the book consists of eight stories, each of which is narrated in the first person by a woman of mixed race. As in her other work, Senna explores the ways in which being black without looking black complicates one's life, and despite the election of president Barack Obama, who is referred to in the book as "blackish," she seems intent on pushing back against notions that America has solved its race problem. One story features a protagonist who can look black or white depending on whether she wears her hair straight or curly; her boyfriend's attentions to her vary accordingly. In another story, the light-skinned female protagonist is irritated that others see her marriage as that of a black man to a white woman, when really they are both biracial. "Though Senna's stories address race, class and gender, they never devolve into simple case studies," Polly Rozenwaike wrote in the *New York Times*. "Rather, her collection offers nuanced portraits of characters confronting anxieties and prejudices that leave them not as free as they would like to be."

Senna lives in the Los Angeles area with her husband, the novelist Percival Everett, and their two sons.

Selected Writings

Novels

Caucasia, Riverhead, 1998.
Symptomatic, Riverhead, 2000.

Memoir

Where Did You Sleep Last Night? A Personal History, Farrar, Straus & Giroux, 2009.

Short stories

You Are Free, Riverhead, 2011.

Sources

Periodicals

Booklist, April 15, 2009; May 15, 2011.
Chattanooga Times Free Press (TN), June 12, 2011.
Library Journal, April 1, 2011.
Los Angeles Times, June 21, 2009.
New York Times, May 4, 1998; August 9, 2009; May 6, 2011.
Plain Dealer (Cleveland, OH), July 6, 1999.
Village Voice, June 22, 2004.
Washington Post, March 8, 1998.

—Mark Lane

Terri Sewell

1965—

Politician, lawyer

Sewell, Terri, photograph. AP Images/Dave Martin.

Democrat Terri Sewell made history in November of 2010 when she became the first African-American woman to represent Alabama in Congress. As the representative for that state's Seventh Congressional District, one of the poorest areas of the country, she has proved a staunch advocate for education and economic development. A lawyer by training, she gave up a lucrative career in private practice to enterpublic service.

Born on January 1, 1965, in Huntsville, Alabama, Terrycina Andrea Sewell grew up in the small town of Selma, several hours to the south. Within weeks of Sewell's birth, Selma drew international attention as the starting point for the March to Montgomery, one of the most pivotal moments of the civil rights era. According to Sewell's website (SewellforCongress.com), her extended family helped feed and house a number of marchers who had arrived from out of town to express their support for voting rights and equality under the law. Despite the violent and intimidating tactics of the Alabama state troopers arrayed against them, the activists succeeded in walking roughly 50 miles to the state capitol of Montgomery. Their achievement galvanized the civil rights movement and led directly to the passage of the Voting Rights Act of 1965.

Growing up in the wake of these tumultuous events, Sewell drew inspiration from her maternal grandfather, a farmer and Baptist minister. His farm, like the town of Selma, was in the heart of the so-called "Black Belt," a swath of central Alabama "named," according to E. R. Shipp in The Root, "not so much for its demography as for the richness of the soil." Sewell has frequently said that the chores her grandfather gave her instilled in her a love of the land and a deep respect for the resources of the area, much of which remained, as of 2011, rural and agricultural. A strong student, she was also influenced by her parents' focus on education and public service. Both worked in the local school system, her father, Andrew A. Sewell, as a coach and her mother, Nancy Gardner Sewell, as a librarian. Nancy Sewell also had a political career, serving for several years on the Selma City Council. She was the first African-American woman to do so.

Valedictorian of her class at Selma High School, Sewell headed north for college, entering Princeton University in New Jersey. Upon receipt of her bachelor's degree

At a Glance . . .

Born Terrycina Andrea Sewell on January 1, 1965, in Huntsville, AL; daughter of Andrew A. (a coach) and Nancy Gardner (a librarian and city council member) Sewell. *Education*: Princeton University, BA, 1986; Oxford University, MA, politics, 1988; Harvard University, JD, 1992. *Politics*: Democrat.

Career: Office of U.S. Representative Richard Shelby, intern, 1980s; office of U.S. Senator Howell Heflin, intern, 1980s; office of Honorable Chief Judge U. W. Clemon (U.S. District Court, Northern District of Alabama), judicial law clerk, 1992–94; Davis Polk & Wardwell, staff attorney, 1994–2004(?); Maynard Cooper & Gale, partner, 2004(?); U.S. House of Representatives, member, 2011—.

Memberships: Congressional Black Caucus; New Democrat Coalition.

Addresses: *Office*—1133 Longworth House Office Building, Washington, DC 20515. *Web*—http://www.SewellForCongress.com.

in 1986, she studied politics at Oxford University, earning a master's degree there in 1988. On her return to the United States, she entered law school at Harvard University, where she helped edit a civil rights journal. After receiving her degree there in 1992, she began her legal career as a clerk for U. W. Clemon, a federal judge in Alabama. The experience she gained as Clemon's assistant soon drew the attention of Davis Polk & Wardwell, one of the largest and most prominent law firms in the country. Hired by its New York City branch in 1994, she served as one of its leading specialists in securities law, a complex field of vital importance to banks and to the economy as a whole. After roughly a decade in that role, she moved back to Alabama to become a partner in the firm of Maynard Cooper & Gale, where she focused on public finance. In the course of that work, she helped dozens of schools and other institutions throughout the state obtain desperately needed financing.

Sewell's interest in a political career, meanwhile, was growing steadily. While at Princeton, she had served as an intern for U.S. Representative Richard Shelby and U.S. Senator Howell Heflin, both of Alabama. That experience proved helpful to her in 2009, when she spotted an opportunity to enter the House herself. The Seventh District incumbent at the time, fellow Democrat Artur Davis, was rapidly losing support from his constituents, among them the residents of Selma.

When Davis, confident that he would do better at the statewide level, announced his decision to run for governor, Sewell stepped into the breach, announcing her candidacy for the House. Her chief opponent was Don Chamberlain, a Republican businessman.

As in other districts, the 2010 campaign was a difficult one in Selma and its environs. Although both major candidates agreed that reducing the area's unemployment rate, among the highest in the country, was the top priority, they differed sharply on the best way to go about it. Chamberlain, adhering closely to the Republican platform, argued that reducing government expenditures would help small businesses create jobs. Sewell, for her part, stressed the importance of vocational training, education, and infrastructure development. As she noted to Lauren Seifert for CBS News shortly after her election, "There are parts of this district that you just can't access. You can't freely move your good[s] and services and we're not going to be able to attract industry until we get better infrastructure." In keeping with this theme, her campaign materials stressed the many public works projects she had helped finance while in private practice.

In the weeks before the election, Sewell was heavily favored to win, largely because of the Seventh District's reputation as a Democratic stronghold. Those predictions were borne out on election day, November 2, 2010, when she coasted to victory with well over 70 percent of the vote. She was sworn into office in Washington the following January. As of June of 2011 it was far too early to assess the impact of her arrival on Capitol Hill. It was clear, however, that she had already faced a number of challenges, many of them stemming from leadership changes within Congress. Because the same election that brought her to Washington gave the Republicans control of the House, she and other incoming Democrats were at a disadvantage in the allocation of committee posts. She nevertheless managed to secure spots on two key panels, the Agriculture Committee and the Science, Space & Technology Committee. She was also an active member of the Congressional Black Caucus and the New Democrat Coalition; the latter is a Congressional organization of centrist Democrats, many of whom share Sewell's focus on economic development and job growth.

Sources

Online

"About Terri," SewellForCongress.com,http://www.sewellforcongress.com/about_terri (accessed June 26, 2011).

Cosby, Frederick, "Black Lawmakers Break New Ground, Suffer Losses," BlackAmericaWeb.com, November 4, 2010, http://www.blackamericaweb.com /?q=articles/news/moving_america_news/23242 (accessed June 26, 2011).

"Full Biography," Office of Congresswoman Terri A. Sewell, http://sewell.house.gov/about-me/full-bio graphy (accessed June 26, 2011).

Seifert, Lauren, "Terri Sewell on Making Alabama History," CBS News, November 10, 2010, http://www.cbsnews.com/2102-503544_162-200224 10.html?tag=contentMain;contentBody (accessed June 26, 2011).

Shipp, E. R., "Terri Sewell: From the Black Belt to the House," The Root, November 4, 2010, http://www.theroot.com/print/47859 (accessed June 26, 2011).

—R.Anthony Kugler

Slick Rick

1965—

Rapper

Slick Rick, photograph. AP Images/Evan Agostini.

Slick Rick, a British-American rapper, is one of the most influential hip-hop artists in history. His reputation rests primarily on his first solo album, 1988's *The Great Adventures of Slick Rick,* which demonstrated his unparalleled storytelling gifts, his sense of humor, and his subtle, stylish delivery, while also including overtly misogynistic sentiments that continue to cloud his legacy. Soon after the much-heralded release of his debut, Slick Rick was convicted of attempted murder, and he spent what should have been the peak of his career in prison. Two albums recorded amid the turmoil of these years are generally considered lesser outing. A fourth effort, 1999's *The Art of Storytelling,* marked a belated return to form and suggested what might have been. Slick Rick continued to perform in the following decade, but his place in the hip-hop pantheon was cemented not so much by his newer work as by the samples of his classic songs and the obvious signs of his influence appearing in the work of some of the most acclaimed rappers of the generation that followed him.

Emigrated from England, Embraced Rap

Slick Rick was born Richard (Ricky) Walters in suburban London on January 14, 1965, the son of Jamaican parents. A childhood accident cost him the sight in one eye, and he began wearing the eye patch that would later become one of his signature accessories as a performer. His family immigrated to the United States when he was 12 years old. They settled in the Bronx, the hard-scrabble borough of New York City where rap was beginning to emerge as a distinct art form.

Walters was a strong student with a particular aptitude for English. "So when rap came about," he told Elena Oumano for *Billboard,* "I transferred my love of stories into rap form." He attended the La Guardia Arts High School, the prestigious specialized public school in New York designed to nurture students with artistic talent. There he befriended Dana McLeese, also an aspiring rapper who would go on to perform as Dana Dane, and the two formed the hip-hop group the Kangol Crew.

At a Glance . . .

Born Richard Walters on January 14, 1965, in South Wimbledon, England; married Mandy Aragones, 1997; children: Latisha, Ricky.

Career: Performed with Kangol Crew; Doug E. Fresh & the Get Fresh Crew, rapper, 1985–87, released singles "The Show" and "La Di Da Di"; solo performer and recording artist, 1988—.

Addresses: *Record label*—The Island Def Jam Group, Worldwide Plaza, 825 8th Ave., 28th Fl., New York, NY 10019. *Web*—http://www.ricktheruler.net/.

As a duo, the Kangol Crew began appearing at hip-hop parties and clubs; one such event brought Walters into contact with the emerging rapper and beat-boxer Doug E. Fresh. Fresh invited Walters to perform with his group the Get Fresh Crew, and in 1985, as MC Ricky D, he rapped on two songs, "The Show" and "La Di Da Di," that would go on to become milestones in the history of rap. "The Show," a humorous conversational track supposed to represent pre-performance chatter, was named *Spin*'s top rap single of the year, and it became only the fourth rap single in history to be certified gold by the Recording Industry Association of America (RIAA). "La Di Da Di," appearing on the b-side of "The Show," was even more influential. It became a consensus rap classic, sampled by top artists including the Notorious B.I.G., De La Soul, Mary J. Blige, and Snoop Dogg, among many others.

Made History with Solo Album

On the heels of his success with Doug E. Fresh, Walters signed with Russell Simmons's Def Jam Records as a solo act. His first album under the stage name Slick Rick, *The Great Adventures of Slick Rick,* appeared in 1988 and won him a place in the hip-hop pantheon. Consisting of tracks that became immensely popular for admirable as well as troubling reasons, the album showcases Slick Rick's sense of humor and his story-telling chops. He voices songs from the points of view of alter egos Slick Rick the Ruler and MC Ricky D (of Doug E. Fresh fame), and his smoothly rhythmic, British-accented delivery stood out among hip-hop artists of the day.

The album's biggest hit, "Children's Story," a cautionary tale about the rise and fall of a stick-up artist, is also its most enduring single. It has been sampled frequently, and the renowned duo Black Star (made up of Mos Def and Talib Kweli) recorded a prominent remake in 1998. Other frequently sampled tracks include

"Mona Lisa," "Hey Young World," and "The Ruler's Back." In addition to its many charms, however, the album has a troubling side that reflects the reality not only of Slick Rick's career and persona but of hip-hop more generally. The opening track, "Treat Her Like a Prostitute," which found an enthusiastic audience on the streets even as DJs refused to play it on the radio, offers an unapologetically degrading view of women, and "Indian Girl," an apparently unselfconscious tale of explicit sex and venereal disease, has likewise been faulted for its misogynistic outlook.

The Great Adventures of Slick Rick climbed to number one on the R&B charts and reached number 31 on the Billboard 200, before being certified platinum by the RIAA. Slick Rick, with his outsized stage persona involving copious gold chains and a diamond-encrusted eye patch, became one of the definitive personalities of hip-hop's so-called golden age.

Served Time in Prison

Slick Rick's reign among rap royalty did not last long. In July of 1990 he opened fire on his cousin Mark Plummer, injuring him and a bystander before fleeing police. He claimed that he was acting in self-defense—that Plummer had threatened his life along with that of his mother—but he was tried and convicted of attempted second-degree murder.

After his arrest but before he began his five-and-a-half-year prison sentence, Slick Rick recorded his vocals for a number of tracks that would constitute his next album. Featuring beats cobbled together without his participation, *The Ruler's Back* appeared in 1991, after he had begun to serve his prison time. The album was generally considered an artistic flop compared with his debut, and it fared poorly commercially.

In June of 1993 Slick Rick was allowed to live at home through a prison work-release program, and he began working on his next album. His work-release privileges were revoked in 1994, however, when the U.S. Immigration and Naturalization Service (INS) began preparing to deport him. Federal law allowed for the deportation of noncitizens convicted of a felony, and Slick Rick, having entered the United States as a child, had never become a naturalized citizen, even though all of his family and his business interests were in the country.

Once again, Slick Rick was unable to complete the tracks for the album he was preparing before he had to report to prison, and the final product, 1994's *Behind Bars,* suffered as a result. Def Jam head Russell Simmons acknowledged to J. R. Reynolds in *Billboard* that the album was an attempt to pacify Slick Rick's fan base with a product that was not what it would have been had the artist been free to make an album under ordinary circumstances. For his part, Slick Rick later

looked back at both his second and third albums as failures that likely lost him fans. "Those albums were put together like puzzles," he told Jim Farber in the *Daily News*. "I did the lyrics and they put the beats on four months later, so there was no chemistry. And the tracks were too fast. They sped them up. I guess they figured they'd be bouncier."

Lived Quietly after Prison Term

Upon his release from prison in 1996, Slick Rick appeared more mature and thoughtful than he had been at the beginning of his sentence. He claimed to have become able to value the small things in life, and he participated in family life with renewed devotion. Even though he had changed, his next album showed him still able to summon up the entertainer's charisma that had won him breakthrough acclaim in the 1980s.

Titled *The Art of Storytelling* and released in 1999, the album is widely considered a return to form, far surpassing his previous two albums and standing as a worthy successor, if not quite the equal, of his seminal debut. Although rap fashions had changed dramatically during the time of his imprisonment, the album was a demonstration of the influence that Slick Rick had exerted on the art form's evolution. Many of the hip-hop artists who had honed their styles listening to Doug E. Fresh and *The Great Adventures of Slick Rick* made guest appearances on *The Art of Story-telling*. The roster of guest artists included Snoop Dogg, Nas, Outkast's Big Boy, Wu-Tang Clan's Raekwon, A Tribe Called Quest's Q-Tip, and the Fugees' Wyclef Jean, among others. Talented as these lyricists were, David Wall Rice in the *Washington Post* maintained that "the album shines brightest when Rick is on his own" and applauded "his uncanny ability to use the simplest vocal inflections to help illustrate his stories."

Slick Rick performed over the course of the next decade, but he did not release another album. Meanwhile, his immigration troubles continued. The INS had not ceased in its attempts to deport him, and in 2003, amid a Homeland Security led effort to crack down on immigrants who had been convicted of felonies, Slick Rick received notice that he would soon be forced to return to the United Kingdom.

After a prolonged fight with immigration officials, he won the right to remain with his family in the United States in 2008, when New York governor David Paterson granted him a pardon for his attempted-murder conviction, citing his exemplary behavior since his arrest. By all accounts, Slick Rick had by this time settled into a quiet life in the Bronx with his wife and two children. Whatever his future musical plans, he remained one of the most admired artists of rap's golden age, and his status as a hip-hop pioneer was uncontested.

Selected discography

The Great Adventures of Slick Rick (includes "Children's Story," "Mona Lisa," "Hey Young World," "The Ruler's Back," "Treat Her Like a Prostitute," and "Indian Girl"), Def Jam, 1988.
The Ruler's Back, Def Jam, 1991.
Behind Bars, Def Jam, 1994.
The Art of Storytelling, Def Jam, 1999.

Sources

Periodicals

Billboard, December 17, 1994, p. 14; May 29, 1999, p. 26; August 9, 2003, p. 10.
Daily News (New York), May 23, 1999, p. 12.
Dallas Morning News, December 13, 2006, p. 1G.
New York Amsterdam News, May 29, 2008, p. 4.
New York Times, January 28, 2004, p. E7; May 24, 2008, p. 1B.
Rolling Stone, January 23, 2003, p. 16.
Spin, April 1999, p. 60.
USA Today, December 21, 1994, p. 6D.
Washington Post, May 26, 1999, p. C05.

Online

"Slick Rick," AllMusic.com, http://allmusic.com/artist/slick-rick-p97 (accessed August 5, 2011).

—Mark Lane

Wole Soyinka

1934—

Writer

Wole Soyinka, a Nigerian who writes in English, came to prominence as a playwright but has also won recognition as a poet, novelist, memoirist, essayist, theatrical producer, actor, and activist. In 1986 he became the first African to be awarded the Nobel Prize in literature. The Swedish Academy's presentation of the award recognized Soyinka's artistic commitment to render the full complexity of his African culture—a culture that Soyinka and other African intellectuals feel has often been reduced in the West to a flat symbol of primitiveness. Soyinka celebrates African life without romanticizing it; as a writer and a public figure, he is as willing to charge Nigerian politicians and bureaucrats with barbarity and corruption as he is to condemn the greed and materialism of the West.

Soyinka, Wole, photograph. AP Images/Sunday Alamba.

Influenced by Tribal and Western Cultures

Soyinka was born July 13, 1934, in Abeokuta, a village near the city of Ibadan in western Nigeria. Born into the tribe of the Yoruba, who inhabit southwestern Nigeria and the nearby country of Benin, Soyinka's youth was marked by a balance of tribal traditions with European, modernizing tendencies. Soyinka's mother became a Christian convert so devout that he nicknamed her "Wild Christian," and his father was the scholarly, agnostic headmaster of a Christian primary school established in their village by the British. Meanwhile, Soyinka's paternal grandfather and the village tribal elders saw to it that young Wole was also steeped in Yoruba mythology.

Soyinka attended the University College at Ibadan, in keeping with his father's wishes. Among his classmates there was Chinua Achebe, who later also earned an international reputation as a novelist. Soyinka studied literature, with an emphasis on drama, from 1952 to 1954. In his studies he explored Yoruba and Greek mythology, laying the groundwork for the imaginative synthesis of tribal and western sources that characterized his theatrical output. While at Ibadan Soyinka published several poems and short stories in the literary magazine *Black Orpheus*.

Soyinka left Africa to study drama at Leeds University in England under the influential British critic and professor G. Wilson Knight. After concluding his studies,

At a Glance . . .

Name pronounced "*Woh*-le Shaw-*yin*-ka"; born Akinwande Oluwole Soyinka, July 13, 1934, in Abeokuta, Nigeria; son of Soditan Akinyode (nicknamed "Essay"; a school headmaster) and Eniola Soyinka. *Education*: Attended University College in Ibadan, Nigeria, 1952–54; University of Leeds, England, BA (with honors), 1958. *Religion*: "Human liberty."

Career: Royal Court Theater (London), dramaturgist, 1958–59; University of Ibadan, Nigeria, Rockefeller research fellow in drama, 1960, chairman of department of theater arts, beginning in 1967; University of Ife, Nigeria, lecturer in English literature, 1961–63; Lagos University, Nigeria, senior lecturer in English, 1965–67; political prisoner at Kaduna Prison, 1967–69; Cambridge University, Cambridge, England, fellow of Churchill College, 1972–73; editor of African cultural magazine *Transition,* 1973–75; University of Ife (name changed to Obafemi Awolowo University in 1987), professor of comparative literature and chairman of department of dramatic arts, beginning in 1975; reassumed editorial post at *Transition,* 1991; director of Nigerian theater groups the 1960 Masks and the Orisun Repertory; Cornell University, professor of African Studies and Theatre Arts, 1988–91; Emory University, Professor of the Arts; University of Nevada, Las Vegas, professor of literature; Loyola Marymount University (Los Angeles), President's Marymount Professor in Residence.

Awards: Rockefeller Foundation grant, 1960; John Whiting Drama Prize, 1966; Dakar Negro Arts Festival award, 1966; Jock Campbell Award, 1968; D.Litt., Yale University, University of Leeds, 1973, University of Montpellier, France, and University of Lagos; Nobel Prize in literature from the Swedish Academy, 1986; named Commander of the Federal Republic of Nigeria by General Ibrahim Babangida, 1986; named Commander of the French Legion of Honor, 1989; named Commander of Order of the Italian Republic, 1990; Prisoner of Conscience Prize, Amnesty International.

he worked as a dramaturgist at London's Royal Court Theater, where his first play, the *Invention*, was staged in 1957. The *Invention* revolves around a fantastic plot element: the disappearance of skin pigment among South African's black population, which renders the apartheid government unable to distinguish between the races and enforce their laws. Horrified at this circumstance, the government assigns the nation's scientists to the task of restoring the visible difference on which apartheid is based.

Returned to Nigeria

In 1960 Soyinka triumphantly returned to the University of Ibadan as a Rockefeller research fellow in drama, and he commenced serious study of Nigerian folklore. His arrival was marked with productions at the Arts Theater in Ibadan of two of his early plays, the *Swamp Dwellers*, which had been given a student production in London in 1958, and the *Lion and the Jewel*. The former is a verse tragedy depicting the manipulation of a community of poor, superstitious swamp farmers by greedy religious leaders, the latter a comedy that warns against reckless modernization and strives to demonstrate that some of the old values ought not to be thoughtlessly abandoned. These two productions established Soyinka as a literary figure of serious consequence in Nigeria.

It was at this time that Soyinka founded an influential amateur theater group, called the 1960 Masks, dedicated to forging a new Nigerian drama. This drama was to be written in English while drawing its inspiration from the ceremonial performance traditions of Africa—religious festivals, pantomime, and traditional music among them. The Masks' first major production was Soyinka's *Dance of the Forests*, which had been commissioned for the Nigerian independence celebrations in October of 1960. In the play, the tribes assemble for a great festival during which ancestral spirits are ritually summoned. The people expect their ancestral spirits to be as heroic and noble as they are in legend, only to discover in their ancestors a capacity for petty meanness that rivals their own bickering.

In 1964 Soyinka disbanded the Masks to assemble a professional theater troupe, which he called the Orisun Repertory. The following year he returned to England for the Commonwealth Festival production of what some have called his most beautiful tragedy, the *Road*, inspired by the Yoruba god Ogun. Soyinka's grandfather consecrated him to Ogun in childhood, and as an adult Soyinka declared the god his muse. In modern Nigeria, Ogun—god of iron and the forge, of creation and destruction—has become the god of electricity and the guardian of highways. In the *Road*, car accidents symbolize Ogun's destructive power over the careless traveler. Ogun's high priest is the Professor, a madman who deliberately rearranges crucial road signs, hoping to discover the meaning of life amid the carnage he helps to create.

Soyinka's first novel, the *Interpreters*, appeared in 1965. The narrative, whose formal experimentation is

reminiscent of the work of William Faulkner and James Joyce, follows a group of young Nigerian intellectuals who gather periodically to discuss their country's tribal past and its westernized future. Each of them has been away to study in England or America and has returned hoping to help shape the new Nigeria. It becomes apparent that the young intellectuals are also searching for clues to their own identities.

Imprisoned for Political Activities

In 1965 Soyinka was also arrested by the Nigerian government, accused of forcing a radio announcer at gunpoint to broadcast incorrect election results. His arrest sparked a protest campaign by PEN, the international writers' organization. Such influential American authors as Norman Mailer and William Styron called for his release. No evidence was ever produced by the police to prove the allegation, and Soyinka was released after three months.

In 1967 Soyinka became the chairman of the Department of Theater Arts at the University of Ibadan, but in August of that same year he was once again arrested—this time during Nigeria's civil war, to which he was implacably opposed. He had been organizing Nigerian intellectuals to push for a ban on arms sales to both the Nigerian government and the Ibo tribe with which the state was at war. Though he was never formally charged, a faked confession released by the government indicated that he was being accused of assisting the Ibo people in their attempt to overthrow the government.

Soyinka spent two years as a political prisoner at the Kaduna Prison facility, mainly in solitary confinement, where he was denied medical treatment and access to reading and writing materials. He manufactured his own ink and began keeping a prison diary and writing poetry on cigarette packages and toilet paper. Every time a letter or poem was miraculously smuggled from prison, the international press seized upon it both as an important literary event and as welcome evidence that he was still alive. Soyinka was released in 1969.

International Reputation Grew in Exile

Many critics have remarked on a distinct darkening of tone in Soyinka's writing after his second imprisonment. The play *Madmen and Specialists* (first produced in 1970), for example, focuses on a young doctor who returns from war freshly trained in techniques of torture; he practices his new skills on his seemingly mad old father. Soyinka's second novel, *Season of Anomy* (1973) is also notable for its darkness of tone and subject matter. Some critics found the book horrifying in its explicit descriptions of torture and

murder but compelling in its message that those who hope for peace must first confront such sickening realities.

Soyinka's prison diary was published in 1972 as *The Man Died: Prison Notes of Wole Soyinka*. It is a fragmented account of his experience, disorderly and wildly various in tone, ranging from political commentary to detailed observations of daily life in prison, a document of one man's struggle to maintain his human dignity in extremely adverse conditions. Two poems smuggled from Soyinka's cell had been published in 1969 in a pamphlet entitled *Poems from Prison*; an expanded version of the collection, *A Shuttle in the Crypt*, appeared in 1972.

The tenuous political situation in early-1970s Nigeria led Soyinka to fear for his safety yet again, and he undertook a period of voluntary exile that ended in 1975 when he accepted a post as professor of comparative literature at the University of Ife. The year 1976 saw the production of *Death and the King's Horseman*, which uses the situation of a ritual suicide to explore the beauty of Yoruba traditions; the publication of the book-length poem *Ogun Abibiman*; and the publication of the essay collection *Myth, Literature, and the African World*. A light opera based on John Gay's *Beggar's Opera* and Bertolt Brecht's *Threepenny Opera*, *Opera Wonyosi*, followed in 1977. The lovingly detailed memoir *Ake: The Years of Childhood* appeared in 1981, along with the essay collection *The Critic and Society* (1981).

Soyinka went into voluntary exile again in 1983 after learning that he was in danger of being killed, yet again, for his political beliefs. Among other literary and political activities in the mid-1980s, Soyinka wrote *A Play of Giants* (first produced in 1984), a scathing vision of African politics featuring characters who were thinly veiled versions of four contemporary heads of state.

Awarded Nobel Prize

Soyinka's status as an international literary figure of the first rank was confirmed when he was awarded the Nobel Prize for Literature in 1986, the first African to win the award. He devoted his acceptance speech to honoring South African anti-apartheid activist Nelson Mandela, who was imprisoned at that time, and to delivering a scathing critique of the politics of apartheid. Reflecting on Soyinka's many run-ins with government authorities in Nigeria, the American scholar Henry Louis Gates Jr., a friend of the Nobel laureate, told the *New York Times*, "It's a miracle that Soyinka's alive to get this prize."

Soyinka's safety remained under threat despite the fame and prestige that the Nobel brought him. He lived

in exile through most of the 1990s, following the 1993 nullification of democratic elections in Nigeria and a resulting charge of treason filed against him in absentia (the penalty for which was death). When a new government took power in 1998, Soyinka returned to Nigeria, but he continued to oppose corruption and power, and in 2004, he was tear-gassed, arrested, and briefly imprisoned. No matter what government was in power, Soyinka's international political influence made him a figure to be reckoned with, and even in his 70s, he was unwilling to bend to the wishes of any government whose exercise of power fell short of his democratic ideals.

Selected poems

Poetry

Idanre and Other Poems, Methuen, 1967.
Poems from Prison, Rex Collings, 1969, expanded version published as *A Shuttle in the Crypt,* Hill & Wang, 1972.
Ogun Abibiman, Rex Collings, 1976.
Mandela's Earth and Other Poems, Random House, 1989.
Early Poems, Oxford University Press, 1997.
Samarkand and Other Markets I Have Known, Methuen, 2003.

Novels

The Interpreters, Deutsch, 1965.
Season of Anomy, Rex Collings, 1973.

Plays

The Invention, first produced in England at the Royal Court Theater, 1957.
A Dance of the Forests, Oxford University Press, 1962.
The Lion and the Jewel, Oxford University Press, 1962.
Five Plays (includes *The Lion and the Jewel, The Swamp Dwellers, The Trials of Brother Jero, The Strong Breed,* and *A Dance of the Forests*), Oxford University Press, 1964.
The Road, Oxford University Press, 1965.
Kongi's Harvest, Oxford University Press, 1966, screen adaptation produced by Calpenny-Nigerian Films, 1970.
Three Short Plays, Oxford University Press, 1969.
The Trials of Brother Jero, Oxford University Press, 1969.
Madmen and Specialists, Methuen, 1971.
Before the Blackout, Orisun Acting Editions, 1971.
The Jero Plays, Methuen, 1973.
Camwood on the Leaves, Methuen, 1973.
The Bacchae of Euripides: A Communion Rite, Methuen, 1973.
Collected Plays, Oxford University Press, volume 1,

1973, and volume 2, 1974.
Death and the King's Horseman, Norton, 1975.
Opera Wonyosi, Indiana University Press, 1981.
A Play of Giants, Methuen, 1984.
Six Plays, Methuen, 1984.
Requiem for a Futurologist, Rex Collings, 1985.
The Beatification of Area Boy, first produced in Leeds, England, 1996.
King Baabu, produced in Lagos, Nigeria, 2001.

Other

The Man Died: Prison Notes of Wole Soyinka, Harper, 1972.
Myth, Literature, and the African World (essays), Cambridge University Press, 1976.
Ake: The Years of Childhood (autobiography), Random House, 1981.
Isara: A Voyage around Essay, Random House, 1988.
Ibadan: The Penkelemes Years: A Memoir, Random House, 1989.
Art, Dialogue, and Outrage: Essays on Literature and Culture, New Horn Press, 1990.
Isara: A Voyage around "Essay," Spectrum Books (Ibadan), 1994.
The Open Sore of a Continent: A Personal Narrative of the Nigerian Crisis, Oxford University Press, 1996.
The Burden of Memory, the Muse of Forgiveness, Oxford University Press, 1998.
Arms and the Arts—A Continent's Unequal Dialogue, University of Cape Town (Cape Town, South Africa), 1999.

Sources

Books

Gibbs, James, editor, *Critical Perspectives on Wole Soyinka,* Three Continents, 1980.
Jeyifo, Biodun, editor, *Conversations with Wole Soyinka*, University Press of Mississippi, 2001.
Jones, Eldred, *Wole Soyinka,* Twayne, 1973.
Katrak, Ketu, *Wole Soyinka and Modern Tragedy: A Study of Dramatic Theory and Practice,* Greenwood Press, 1986.
King, Bruce, editor, *Introduction to Nigerian Literature,* Africana Publishing, 1972.
Larson, Charles R., *The Emergence of African Fiction,* revised edition, Indiana University Press, 1972.
Laurence, Margaret, *Long Drums and Cannons: Nigerian Dramatists and Novelists,* Praeger, 1968.
Moore, Gerald, *Wole Soyinka,* Africana Publishing, 1971.
Omotoso, Kole, *Achebe or Soyinka? A Re-Interpretation and a Study in Contrasts,* K.G. Saur, 1992.
Pieterse, Cosmo, and Dennis Dueren, editors, *African Writers Talking: A Collection of Radio Interviews,*

Africana Publishing, 1972.

Rajeshwar, M., *The Novels of Wole Soyinka,* Advent, NY, 1990.

Roscoe, Adrian A., *Mother Is Gold: A Study in West African Literature,* Cambridge University Press, 1971.

Periodicals

Africa News, December 22, 2008; July 23, 2009; October 18, 2010.

Black American Literature Forum, Fall 1988.

Book Forum, Volume 3, Number 1, 1977.

Booklist, March 15, 2006.

Denver Post, May 21, 2006.

Drama, Winter 1975.

Economist, September 2, 2006.

Guardian (London), May 17, 2004; April 8, 2009.

Hudson Review, Autumn 1990.

Jet, July 28, 1997; November 2, 1998.

Library Journal, March 15, 1992.

London Magazine, April/May 1974.

New Republic, October 12, 1974; May 9, 1983.

Newsweek, November 1, 1982.

New Yorker, May 16, 1977.

New York Review of Books, July 31, 1969; October 21, 1982.

New York Times, October 17, 1986; October 15, 1998; May 18, 2004; August 5, 2004.

New York Times Book Review, July 29, 1973; October 10, 1982; April 23, 2006.

New York Times Magazine, September 18, 1983.

Philadelphia Inquirer, October 17, 1998.

Progressive, August 1997.

Time, October 27, 1986.

Times (London), May 30, 2009.

Time International, June 26, 2006.

Tri-Quarterly, Fall 1966.

Variety, April 20, 2009.

Wilson Quarterly, Spring 1990; Spring 2006.

World, February 13, 1973.

—Susan M. Marren and Mark Lane

Tom Stith

1939–2010

Athlete

Tom Stith is considered a hero in the small town of Olean in western New York State, the home of St. Bonaventure University. Stith, together with his older brother Sam, helped bring the school's basketball program to national prominence in the early 1960s, leading the team to two National Invitation Tournament (NIT) berths, their first-ever appearance at the tournament, and a number-three national ranking. During his three seasons at St. Bonaventure, from 1958 to 1961, Stith set a scoring record of 2,052 points, one of the best players in school history, second only to the future National Basketball Association (NBA) star Bob Lanier. Stith was the school's first consensus All-American in 1960, earning the honor two years in a row. After college, Stith was drafted by the New York Knicks, but his professional career was cut short when he contracted tuberculosis just before the beginning of his first season. He played only a single season before his health forced him to retire.

Teamed with Brother to Dominate Opponents

Thomas Alvin Stith was born on January 21, 1939, in Emporia, Virginia, and grew up in Harlem, New York, where his family moved when he was a boy. Both Tom and his brother Sam received scholarships to attend St. Francis Preparatory School in Brooklyn, where they were standouts on the basketball team. The Stith brothers led St. Francis to the Catholic High Schools Athletic Association championships in the mid-1950s, and Tom was considered one of the top 10 high school players in New York City.

Stith followed his brother to St. Bonaventure University in 1957 to play for Coach Eddie Donovan. In his first year, Stith was relegated to the freshman squad, but already his natural talent and shooting skills were evident. Even before he played his first varsity game, the local *Olean Times Herald* was boasting that "Tom Stith should be Bona's 'best big man' in history."

When Stith joined the Bonnies varsity squad for 1958–59 season, he did not disappoint. He quickly distinguished himself as an unstoppable shooter with a strong left-handed hook shot, showing a confidence and composure on the court that belied his youth. "It's natural for him to score 'em by the bucketful," the *Times Herald* reported. "But the real mark of his ability is not in the scoring column. It's in his ability to command respect of teammate and foe alike." The Bonnies earned a berth in the NIT, losing in the quarterfinal round to St. John's University.

In his junior season, the 6-foot- 5-inch Stith, nicknamed the "Big T," averaged 31.5 points per game. He and his brother—combined for 52 points per game—again led St. Bonaventure to the NIT, where the Bonnies scored victories over Holy Cross and St. John's before falling to Bradley University in the semifinals. Stith's performance attracted national attention, and he was selected as St. Bonaventure's first consensus All-American in 1960.

Led Bonnies to NCAA Tournament

The next season Stith scored an all-time record of 830 points. In one memorable game against Ohio State

University at Madison Square Garden, he put up 35 points despite being triple-teamed, and in another against Villanova University, he scored 42 points using mostly his hook shot. In one of Stith's few losses during his college career, the Bonnies went down 87–77 to Niagara University, ending a 13-year, 99-game home-court winning streak.

Stith drove the team to an impressive 21–3 regular-season record. Going into the National Collegiate Athletic Association (NCAA) Tournament, St. Bonaventure, a first-time participant, ranked third in the country. Stith scored 29 points in three consecutive games, as the Bonnies defeated the University of Rhode Island, then lost to Wake Forest University in the second round, and won against Princeton University in the consolation game.

Taking place in segregated Charlotte, North Carolina, the NCAA tournament exposed Stith to a racism that he had never experienced during the regular season, as St. Bonaventure played mainly Eastern teams that were integrated. During their semifinal game against Wake Forest, the players were booed, and the opposing coach held onto the ball when it went out of bounds so that the black Bonnies could not inbound. At the hotel where the team stayed, "[T]he four of us [Stith, Fred Crawford, Ronald 'Whitey' Martin, and Orrie Jirele] weren't able to eat in the same room as everyone else," he recalled in a 1998 interview with the *Bona Ventura* student newspaper. "The four of us were told that we had to go and eat in the back room." When Stith and the three other black players walked to the back room, their white teammates and coaches joined them. "We were a team," Stith said. "We couldn't eat in the main room, so no one did."

Stith was chosen as an All-American again in 1961. Over his college career, St. Bonaventure posted a 65–12 record and earned three post-season tournament berths. Averaging 27 points per game, Stith scored 2,052 points over three years, a school record that held until Lanier exceeded that mark by 15 points in 1970. Five decades later Stith remained the fourth-leading scorer in St. Bonaventure history. He ranks 11th in career rebounding, with 691, and averaged a double-double (double-digit numbers in points and rebounds) over his first two years.

Retired from Basketball after Illness, Injury

In the spring of 1961 Stith was chosen in the NBA draft as the number two pick overall by the New York Knicks, signing a three-year contract. During his senior year he had lost 15 pounds, and when he failed to regain the weight after the season, his doctor ordered a thorough physical. Stith was diagnosed with pulmonary tuberculosis, a contagious bacterial infection that affects the lungs. At the time tuberculosis patients often were confined for long periods of time; in Stith's case, he spent six months recuperating at a sanitarium in upstate New York, forcing him to miss his first pro season.

Stith made the 1962–63 Knicks squad, which was coached by Eddie Donovan, the former coach at St. Bonaventure. When Stith made his debut on November 13 in a game against the Boston Celtics, the crowd at Madison Square Garden gave him a standing ovation. However, the former college star played in only 25 games that year, averaging just 3.1 points per game, and he was released at the beginning of the next season. He played for three seasons in the Eastern Professional Basketball League with the Wilkes-Barre Barons and the Allentown Jets, but a serious automobile accident in 1966 forced him to retire from the game.

In retirement, Stith partnered with his brother in operating a restaurant in Queens, New York, and later worked as a sales executive for Shell Oil and Cablevision. He was inducted into the St. Bonaventure Athletics Hall of Fame as part of its inaugural class in 1969, and his number 42 jersey was retired. He was named to the Greater Buffalo Sports Hall of Fame in 1999 and to the Bob Douglas Hall of Fame, honoring African-American athletes, in 2000.

After a long battle with cancer and kidney ailments, Stith died at a hospital in Melville, New York, on June 13, 2010, at the age of 71.

Sources

Periodicals

Bona Ventura, February 20, 1998; September 10, 2010.

Buffalo News, June 16, 2010.
New York Post, June 15, 2010.
New York Times, February 26, 1961; May 2, 1961;
  November 13, 1962; June 16, 2010.
Olean (NY) Times Herald, June 17, 2010.

—Deborah A. Ring

David E. Talbert

1966(?)—

Writer

David E. Talbert crafts plays that resonate with African-American audiences and have helped him build a mini entertainment empire that approaches the success of Tyler Perry, with whom he is often compared. Like Perry, Talbert has transitioned to film with the 2008 comedy *First Sunday*. Black creative professionals like himself and Tyler, he told Fern Gillespie in the *Crisis* in 2008, "have a sense of ownership of their art. We don't let anyone give us filters on what we feel the audience wants."

Began Playwriting Career in San Francisco

Talbert, born in the mid-1960s, grew up on Kentucky Avenue S.E. in the District of Columbia. He attended a Pentecostal church in Washington's Capitol Hill neighborhood, and later studied marketing at Morgan State University. He began writing poetry while working as a disc jockey in Ohio after a failed romance, and those early efforts segued into short stories which he abandoned after a time.

A few years later, after losing his disc-jockey job at San Francisco's KSOL-FM in a reorganization, Talbert received free tickets to a performance of Shelly Garrett's hit play *Beauty Shop*. "I sat there in the theatre and had a surreal moment watching the audience," Talbert told Talley in *Back Stage West*. "They were having such a good ol' time. I remember saying to myself, I bet I could give them something that was not only comedic but thought-provoking, spiritually grounded without the politically correct and over-the-top slapstick feel."

Talbert began writing for the stage that very night, and his first play, *Tellin' It Like It Tiz,* premiered at the Black Repertory Group Theater in Berkeley, California, in August of 1991. The story and its focus on relationships among a group of African-American men and women was set in a women's clothing store and a barbershop. As befitting the title, it featured mature content that proved a hit with Bay Area audiences, and then took to the road for dates in Baltimore, Washington, Philadelphia, and Chicago. Talbert wrote two more plays, *Lawd Ha' Mercy* and *What Goes around Comes Around,* before enrolling at New York University's graduate film school in 1995.

Crossed Genres into Musicals, Film

Talbert returned to writing for the stage with *He Say She Say ... But What Does God Say?* The 1996 musical drew audiences with the help of its leading man, the gospel star Kirk Franklin, who played the pastor of a debt-ridden church enmeshed in a turf war with a local crime boss turned real-estate mogul. The production also featured some 1970s television personalities: BernNadette Stanis, who played Thelma on the 1970s sitcom *Good Times,* appeared, and Ernest Thomas, who played Raj on another hit show of the era, *What's Happening!!* Talbert's play was such a hit that it served as the basis for the UPN sitcom *Good News* in 1997.

Talbert's next work, *A Fool and His Money,* was a characteristically comic Talbert tale with a social mes-

At a Glance . . .

Born c. 1966, in Washington, DC; married Lyn E. Talbert (an actor), 1998. *Education*: Morgan State University, BA, marketing, 1989; attended New York University's Graduate Film Program, mid-1990s.

Career: Playwright, theatrical producer, and director. Radio announcer in Baltimore, MD, and Washington, DC; KSOL–FM, disc jockey, late 1980s; first play, *Tellin' It like It Tiz*, produced in 1991; made feature–film directorial debut with *A Woman Like That*, 1997 (unreleased); second feature film, *First Sunday*, released in 2008; Urban Broadway Series, artistic director and executive producer, 2001—.

Awards: Best Dramatic Feature, Urbanworld Film Festival, for *A Woman Like That*, 1997; NAACP Image Awards, including Best Playwright for *The Fabric of a Man*, 2001, and Trailblazer Award, 2008.

Addresses: *Agent*—United Talent Agency, 9560 Wilshire Blvd., Beverly Hills, CA 90212. *Web*—http://www.davidetalbert.com/.

sage. It portrayed the economic travails of the Jordan family: James Sr. loses his job while his son James Jr. becomes enmeshed in the illegal drug trade. Junior's "boss," a crime figure, starts dating the Jordans' daughter, Tabitha. Then James Sr. comes into a small fortune after winning a contest. Act II showed the Jordans freely spending their new money, but moral consciousness arrives via the voice of Mother Jordan, matriarch of the family, and the reappearance of a long-lost sibling, Skeeter.

Armed with some film experience from his graduate classes, Talbert directed his first feature film, *A Woman Like That*. It starred Tyra Banks and Malik Yoba and was shown at the Urbanworld Film Festival, but failed to win a distribution deal. Returning to live stage plays once again, Talbert recruited another television actor, *Welcome Back, Kotter*'s Lawrence Hilton-Jacobs, to play a suave romantic lead in his next play, *Mr. Right Now*, in 1998. The plot centered on Angel, the single mother of a teenaged son, who was on solid ground professionally and financially, but longed for a "Mr. Right" with whom she could share her life. She made bad choices, ignoring the plumber she must call occasionally who harbored a crush on her, and headed toward disaster when she met Hilton-Jacobs's character. "The moral of the story is crystal-clear, but it's delivered with a degree of panache," wrote critic Don Shirley in the *Los Angeles Times*.

Mr. Right Now was the first of Talbert's plays to be released on DVD, a format that proved a terrific source of revenue. His plays were consistent earners, sometimes grossing as much as $500,000 in one week. They were costly to stage but were not in the same price range as a typical touring production of a Broadway show. Because of this, ticket prices were reasonable, and Talbert's works were commended for winning over a new generation of first-time theater-goers.

Addressed Contemporary Concerns in His Works

Talbert had another hit in 2000 with *His Woman, His Wife*, which starred Tommy Ford as Stuart, an attorney who lived with his girlfriend, Denise, but was wary of marriage. The plot was complicated by the machinations of two other women: Denise's mother, who wanted to see their union made legal, and Stuart's ex-girlfriend, who hoped to win him back. "The script follows the usual rhythmic pattern, with brash sitcom exchanges evolving into preachy, feel-good moments," noted Shirley in a *Los Angeles Times* review.

Talbert's ninth stage work, *The Fabric of a Man*, was produced in a 30-city tour. The story focused on the romantic travails of an increasingly successful clothing designer. Cheryl "Pepsii" Riley, a veteran of other Talbert plays, was cast in the lead. Her boyfriend, played by *Roc*'s Clifton Powell, was an Ivy League graduate who resented her busy life and inattention to his needs. Actor Shemar Moore, best known for his heartthrob role on the daytime drama *The Young & the Restless*, played a third element of the romantic triangle. Again, the work was a hit with audiences in several cities and was nominated for 13 NAACP Image Awards. It was later turned into a television movie for BET.

Talbert shied away from any attempt to classify his work. "What I try to put onstage is the truth about black people's experiences and what we are going through," he told Denise Barnes in the *Washington Times*. "I give it a comedic spin, a dramatic spin, and a spiritual resolve. All of my plays have moral messages and characters that go thorough redemptive processes."

Teamed with Babyface, Foxx, Snoop Dogg

In 2002 Talbert launched his Urban Broadway Series with *Love Makes Things Happen*. The work featured songs written by record producer and hitmaker Kenneth "Babyface" Edmonds, and starred his brother Kevon Edmonds in the male lead as a postal clerk in love with a recently divorced computer-industry executive, played by En Vogue's Dawn Robinson. Their friends and families all doomed the romance, noting that their income differences were simply too great to surmount. The four-city tour included a stop at New York's Beacon Theater.

Talbert's plays continued to set theater attendance records at many venues, particularly in cities like Miami and Houston. These included 2004's *Love on Lay-a-Way*, *Love in the Nick of Tyme* in 2007, and *What My Husband Doesn't Know*, which premiered in 2011. In the meantime, Talbert wrote two novels—*Baggage Claim* and *Love on the Dotted Line* for Simon & Schuster's Atria imprint, and co-authored *Love Don't Live Here No More: Book One of Doggy Tales* with rapper/actor Snoop Dogg. He also wrote and produced a 2006 NBC special, *Jamie Foxx: Unpredictable*, and began reworking some of his stories into television movies for BET, including *The Fabric of a Man*, which snagged high ratings when it aired on the cable network in January of 2008.

First Sunday was technically Talbert's second feature film, but this time fared better in Hollywood circles thanks to an all-star cast that included Ice Cube, Katt Williams, and Tracy Morgan. "Talbert's first feature starts off as straight ghetto capering, then evolves into an inner-city morality play," wrote *Village Voice* critic Nick Pinkerton. The story, which is set in Baltimore, centers around Ice Cube's character, who is desperate to keep his children in his life. His hapless best friend (Morgan) concocts a scheme to burgle a church, while Williams provides comic fodder as a high-strung choir director. The movie was saddled with a January release date—considered the traditional Hollywood dumping ground for films that studios want to get out but are unenthusiastic about promoting—but on its opening weekend in January of 2008 grossed $17 million, coming in second only to *The Bucket List*, a Jack Nicholson-Morgan Freeman comedy. Most of the mainstream media reviews were less than kind, but *Chicago Tribune* writer Jessica Reaves found that "Talbert has done something unexpected and very unusual: he's made a nearly violence-free, pointedly hopeful movie that actually touches on a few of the big issues (joblessness, crime, community) facing American cities."

Selected writings

Plays

Tellin' It Like It Tiz, 1991.
Lawd Ha' Mercy, 1993.
What Goes around Comes Around, 1994.
He Say She Say ... But What Does God Say?, 1996.
A Fool and His Money, 1997.
Mr. Right Now, 1998.
Talk Show Live, 1998.
His Woman, His Wife, 2000.
The Fabric of a Man, 2001.

Love Makes Things Happen, 2002.
Love on Lay-a-Way, 2004.
Love in the Nick of Tyme, 2007.
What My Husband Doesn't Know, 2011.

Television

(And co-producer) *Jamie Foxx: Unpredictable*, NBC, 2006.
David E. Talbert Presents: StageBlack, TV One, 2007.
The Fabric of a Man (television movie), BET, 2008.

Films

(And director) *A Woman Like That*, 1997.
(And director) *First Sunday*, Screen Gems, 2008.

Books

Baggage Claim, Simon & Schuster, 2005.
Love on the Dotted Line, Simon & Schuster, 2005.
(With Snoop Dogg) *Love Don't Live Here No More: Book One of Doggy Tales*, Atria/Simon & Schuster, 2006.

Sources

Periodicals

Back Stage West, May 17, 2001, p. 3.
Chicago Tribune, January 9, 2008.
Crisis, Summer 2008, pp. 40—41.
Dallas Morning News, April 18, 1997, p. 3.
Detroit News, March 5, 2002, p. 3.
Essence, June, 2000, p. 66.
Jet, February 4, 2008.
Los Angeles Times, April 16, 1999, p. 6; May 4, 2000, p. F61.
San Francisco Chronicle, September 19, 1996, p. E1; July 23, 2001, p. D2.
Variety, February 19, 2007.
Washington Times, March 8, 1996, p. 10; May 1, 1997, p. 11; May 8, 2001, p. 4.

Online

"Interview: David E. Talbert," ClaytonPerry.com, September 30, 2010, http://claytonperry.com/2010/09/30/interview-david-e-talbert-playwright-director-and-producer/ (accessed July 31, 2011).
Pinkerton, Nick, "First Sunday," Village Voice, January 3, 2008, http://www.villagevoice.com/2008-01-01/film/first-sunday/ (accessed July 31, 2011).

—Carol Brennan

Mike Tyson

1966—

Athlete

Tyson, Mike, photograph. AP Images/Jeff Christensen.

Mike Tyson proved himself to be one of the greatest boxers ever to enter the ring. For a time during the late 1980s, he was not only the youngest heavyweight champion in the history of the sport, but the first to hold all three belts—from bouts sanctioned by the World Boxing Council (WBC), the World Boxing Association (WBA), and the International Boxing Federation (IBF)—at the same time. His career statistics are astonishing: out of a total of 58 fights, he won 50 of them, 44 by knockout. "He is the purest of fighters," declared Pat Putnam in *Sports Illustrated* in 1986. "He hits people, and they fall down." Yet Tyson's reputation for brute strength unfortunately extended into his personal life, and he spent three years in prison for rape, a charge he has always denied. "I think I was insane for a great period of my life," he told Daphne Merkin in a *New York Times Magazine* profile that appeared in 2011. "It was just too quick. I didn't understand the dynamics then. I just knew how to get on top, I didn't know what to do once I got there."

Michael Gerard Tyson was born in Brooklyn, New York, on June 30, 1966, to Lorna Tyson and Jimmy Kirkpatrick. Kirkpatrick left the family when his son was two years old. Lorna drank heavily and could be violent, and was said to have once tossed a pot of scalding water at a male friend. "We knew to stay away from her," Tyson's longtime friend, David Malone, told Merkin in *New York Times Magazine*. The family lived in the rough area of Bedford-Stuyvestant before moving to Amboy Street in Brownsville, an even worse part of the borough. In middle school Tyson fell in with a group of other tough kids and soon came to the attention of law-enforcement authorities.

Became a Teen Boxing Prodigy

After an arrest for armed robbery he was sent to the Tryon School for Boys in 1978, a juvenile correctional center in upstate New York. It was there that his life changed direction. The school's physical education teacher saw potential in the young man and introduced him to legendary boxing trainer Cus D'Amato, who lived near the facility at the time. Tyson thrived under the new structure and discipline in his life, and D'Amato pledged to turn him into a world-class champion.

At a Glance . . .

Born Michael Gerard Tyson on June 30, 1966, in Brooklyn, NY; son of Jimmy Kirkpatrick and Lorna Smith Tyson; married Robin Givens, February 7, 1988 (divorced, February 1989); married Monica Turner (a pediatrician), April 1997 (divorced, January 2003); married Lakiha "Kiki" Spicer, June 6, 2009; children: (with Kimberly Scarborough) Michael Lorna "Mickey" Tyson; (with Natalie Joiyce Fears) D'Amato Kilraine Tyson; (with Turner) Rayna, Amir; (with Sol Xochitl) Miguel, Exodus (deceased, 2009); (with Spicer) daughter Milan, son Morocco.

Career: Amateur boxer on the junior circuit, early 1980s; professional boxer, 1985–2005; won World Boxing Council (WBC) heavyweight championship title, 1986; won World Boxing Association (WBA) title, 1987; won International Boxing Federation (IBF) title, 1987; regained WBC championship, 1996.

Awards: Inducted into the International Boxing Hall of Fame, 2010.

Addresses: *Home*—Henderson, NV. *Office*—c/o Jeff Wald Entertainment, Professional Boxer, 2121 Avenue of the Stars, Ste. 2630, Los Angeles, CA 90067-5050. *Agent*—CWH Promotions, Nelson House, Ravenscliffe Rd., Kidsgrove, Stoke-on-Trent, ST7 4HZ, England. *Web*—http://officialtyson.com/.

Once released from Tryon, Tyson spent his teen years living and training at D'Amato's compound. He made stunning progress as an amateur but failed to earn a spot on the U.S. boxing team for the 1984 Olympics. On March 6, 1985, Tyson stepped into the ring for his first professional fight in Albany, New York, and knocked out Hector Mercedes in the first round. That first year, he compiled a 15-0 record. However, it was also a period marked by loss: D'Amato died in November of 1985, and a few years later Tyson would lose Jimmy Jacobs, his co-manager. Both men had served as a substitute family for Tyson during his formative years.

On November 22, 1986, Tyson became the youngest heavyweight champion ever when he gained the WBC championship belt after a second-round knockout of Trevor Berbick. In March of 1987 Tyson united the heavyweight championship, defeating James "Bonecrusher" Smith for the WBA belt in March and Tony Tucker for the IBF belt in August. By that point he was a household name, known as "Iron Mike" Tyson and hyped as one of the most feared boxers of all time.

Retired Michael Spinks with a Punch

In the ring Tyson was at the absolute pinnacle of his power, defeating former IBF champ Michael Spinks in 91 seconds in June of 1988 in what was the first-ever loss of Spinks's career. Outside the ring Tyson's life was spinning out of control. He had agreed to let Don King, boxing's most notorious promoter, manage him, but that decision would prove disastrous: King's organization did little to quell the savagery that Tyson could erupt into at times, and indeed even seemed to encourage it. The boxer broke his hand in a street fight with former opponent Mitch "Blood" Green, crashed his BMW into a tree on D'Amato's former estate, and had a troubled marriage to television actress Robin Givens, whom he had married after just two weeks of dating.

In September of 1988 Tyson and Givens sat down for an interview with Barbara Walters for ABC's *20/20*. Tyson appeared drugged as Givens characterized life with him as "pure hell" and told Walters her husband suffered from manic depression that brought on episodes of rage and physical violence. A few months later, the couple divorced.

The exit of Givens left Don King firmly in control of Tyson. For five years Tyson had destroyed opponent after opponent, but that would soon change. On February 11, 1990, Tyson fought James "Buster" Douglas, a 42–1 underdog. From the very beginning of the fight, there was a different atmosphere. Tyson was sluggish—some claim from anti-depressant medication—and his journeyman opponent seemed to be different also, as if he were not afraid of the man so many others had feared to fight. Tyson knocked down Douglas, but the challenger recovered and ended up knocking out the champion in the 10th round. It marked the first official loss of Tyson's boxing career.

Convicted of Sexual Assault

Tyson recovered from his loss to win two more bouts in 1990. The next year he defeated Donovan "Razor" Ruddock twice. His next fight was for the heavyweight championship against Evander Holyfield, but that scheduled bout never happened. In July of 1991 Tyson—by then an infamous womanizer and known for crudely misogynist public remarks—attended the Miss Black America Pageant in Indianapolis. He met 18-year-old Rhode Island contestant Desiree Washington, who accepted a late-night invitation from the boxer to attend a party. She filed sexual assault charges more than 24 hours later, and Tyson was arrested. The trial and appeal was a low point in Tyson's life, with his high-paid defense attorneys describing the encounter

as consensual while national debate raged about the politics of sexual assault, what happens when African-American women file rape charges, and the potentially biased judicial system in America. Contrasting it with the Palm Beach County, Florida, rape trial of William Kennedy Smith, a scion of the political dynasty who was acquitted in 1991, *New Republic* writer Robert Wright theorized why public opinion had turned so strongly against Tyson despite the weak evidence against him. Wright described Smith as "a polite and innocuous-looking white guy. Tyson, by contrast, comes off as middle America's nightmare: a crude, violent, sexually aggressive black male.

In March of 1992, Tyson was sentenced to six years in prison. He spent three years of his six-year sentence at the Plainfield Correctional Facility in Indiana. Word leaked that he was reading political tracts and had even converted to Islam. The 28-year-old Tyson was released from prison on March 25, 1995, and returned to the ring for his comeback match on August 19 in Las Vegas. Tyson knocked down Boston boxer Peter Mc-Neely twice, and then McNeely's manager threw in the towel after 89 seconds of the first round.

Over the next year Tyson beat up on lesser fighters and won easy victories, collecting prize purses totaling some $65 million. One of his wins gave Tyson the WBA championship and a legitimate claim to fighting Evander Holyfield, whom he had been waiting to fight since 1991. Holyfield was seen as a washed-up fighter, in danger even of being killed in the ring by Tyson, but was the first man whom Tyson faced since he was released from prison who would fight back. The much-anticipated fight took place on November 9, 1996. In the sixth round of the contest, Holyfield opened a cut over Tyson's left eye with a head butt and then dropped Tyson with a left hook. It was only the second time Tyson was knocked down in his whole career. At that point Holyfield said that he knew he had beaten Tyson and for the rest of the fight, he jabbed Tyson and stayed out of his rival's reach. Tyson lost, but the fight grossed $100 million and a rematch was assured.

Bit Off Piece of Holyfield's Ear

Anticipation for the Tyson-Holyfield rematch on June 28, 1997, was so great that the MGM Grand Garden Arena in Las Vegas sold out its 16,000 tickets on the first day. The spectators and the millions watching on pay-per-view television expected to be part of another unforgettable moment in Tyson's career. They were not disappointed. The opening round seemed to pick up where the first match left off. Holyfield was the aggressor, sometimes leading with his head. In the second round, Holyfield head-butted Tyson and cut him above his right eye. The fight became more brutal, with both fighters seeming to abandon the rules.

Then, in the third round, Tyson and Holyfield clinched in the middle of the ring. Tyson seemed to search for

his opponent's ear, find it, and then purposely chomped down on it. Holyfield propelled himself into the air, and Tyson spit out his mouthpiece and a piece of Holyfield's ear. Tyson then followed Holyfield back to his corner and pushed him with both hands. There was a two-minute delay, after which it was decided the fight could continue. The two clinched in the center of the ring, and Tyson reached over and bit Holyfield's other ear. The ring immediately filled with people and chaos ensued. As Tyson left the arena spectators threw objects at him, and his handlers quickly marshaled forces around him to keep him from charging at the crowd.

The ear incident portended the possible end of Tyson's boxing career. The Nevada State Commission withheld Tyson's paycheck and suspended his license. Tyson appeared before the press on the Monday after the fight and apologized for his behavior, but the public was outraged—perhaps more so than when he was convicted for rape. "He realized he couldn't whup me, and he got frustrated," Holyfield explained to Richard Lacayo in *Time* magazine. In the end Tyson was banned from boxing for one year and fined $3 million.

Set Pay-Television Record versus Lewis

Tyson's controversial defeat at the hands of the aging Holyfield led many to believe that his career was finished. However, enduring financial troubles, including $13 million in debt from back taxes, lured Tyson back into the ring through the late 1990s and early 2000s. Tyson took steps to bring more discipline to his fighting and his life. He parted ways with Don King in a flurry of lawsuits. He married again, this time to a pediatrician. His training regimen became steadier, and he returned to the ring, once again earning a small fortune by beating opponents who offered little opposition throughout 2000 and 2001.

Despite these positive steps, Tyson's public behavior continued to spiral out of control, In March of 1999 he spent a short time in jail after pleading no contest to two misdemeanor assault charges stemming from a road rage incident. He made bizarre remarks following a 2000 match in which he defeated Lou Savarese in 38 seconds, claiming he was looking forward to his next bout, this one against heavyweight champion Lennox Lewis. In a clip that lasted longer than the actual Savarese fight, Tyson proclaimed his faith in Islam to Showtime correspondent Jim Gray, then declared, "There is no one who can match me. My style is impetuous, my defense is impregnable, and I'm just ferocious. I want his heart! I want to eat his children! Praise be to Allah!"

Upon hearing of Tyson's comments, Lewis remarked that "Mike Tyson is a train wreck waiting to happen." His prediction came true in January of 2002, when a

press conference announcing a match between Tyson and Lewis became a fierce brawl between the entourages surrounding the two fighters, ending with Tyson biting Lewis on the leg. Boxing commentator Dr. Ferdie Pacheco told the *Sporting News* that "someone needs to put Tyson in a hospital for a year. He has no self-control and is filled with self-loathing."

The Tyson-Lewis fight, scheduled for June of 2002 in Memphis, Tennessee, was one of the most anticipated sporting events of the year. It set a new pay-per-view record of $103 million but hardly met expectations. Lewis took command early and appeared to toy with an overmatched Tyson for the early rounds. Then, in the eighth round, he leveled Tyson with a hard right to the head. The defeated Tyson was oddly tender after the fight. He hugged Lewis and then, noticing that he had left blood on the champion's cheek, reached up and gently wiped his face. Tyson proclaimed that Lewis "was splendid, a masterful boxer, and I take my hat off to him." Asked about a rematch, Tyson said, "I'd be crazy to ask for a rematch. He's too big and too strong. I mean, for the right price, I'll fight a lion. But I don't think I can beat that guy."

Retired from the Ring

Although the Lewis match clearly showed Tyson to be past his prime, his reputation and ability to draw fans continued to tempt fight promoters looking to cash in on the spectacle of a Tyson match. His finances remained in disarray, and despite earning approximately $20 million from the Lewis fight, Tyson filed for bankruptcy in August of 2003. That same year, his always-imposing physical form was further enhanced with a large Maori-design tattoo over his face. By that point he had split from his second wife, Monica Turner, whose brother Michael Steele would later go on to fame as chair of the Republican National Committee. The couple had two children together, joining two children both born in 1990 to different mothers—daughter Mickey and son D'Amato—and Tyson went on to father two more with Sol Xochitl, a Phoenix, Arizona, woman, in a relationship that followed his second divorce.

Tyson's stunning career thudded to a halt over several months between 2004 and 2005. He lost to Danny Williams in July of 2004 and 11 months later went up against a fighter named Kevin McBride, but gave up after six rounds, asserting he was officially retired. His income came from a series of exhibition matches in 2006, and he lived near Phoenix with Xochitl and their two children—a son, Miguel, and a daughter they named Exodus. Late in 2006 Tyson was arrested after nearly hitting a police car after leaving a Scottsdale bar, and was charged with driving under the influence and cocaine possession. He spent much of 2007 in a substance-abuse treatment facility in California.

A newly sober Tyson reunited with a woman he had known since her teens. Lakiha "Kiki" Spencer was the daughter of a boxing promoter, and the pair had had an on-again, off-again relationship for years. She became pregnant by Tyson, and their daughter Milan was born in late 2008. A turning point in Tyson's life came in May of 2009, when his four-year-old daughter Exodus died in Phoenix after becoming entangled in a cord on a treadmill; her brother Miguel discovered her. Devastated, Tyson blamed himself, although the incident had happened while he was living in the Las Vegas area with Spicer. He and Spicer wed a few days later, and he retreated into a house he had bought from basketball star Jalen Rose in Henderson, Nevada. Committed to remaining a sober father and faithful husband, he removed all destructive influences from his life. "If you make a lot of money, you end up being around people you don't want to be around," he told Merkin in the *New York Times Magazine* profile. "Guys on allowance. It takes years to gather the audacity to get rid of them."

Tyson even adopted a vegan diet, which he asserted helps him manage his mood swings. The couple had a son, Morocco, born in early 2011, just as Tyson was preparing to star in his own six-episode series for Animal Planet, *Taking on Tyson*. Some of the show was devoted to his homing pigeons, which he had raised since his Brooklyn childhood. "The first thing I ever loved in my life was a pigeon," he confessed to Merkin. "It's a constant with my sanity in a weird way." With his finances still imperiled, he hoped to support his family via a second career in movies. He appeared in both *Hangover* movies and was a contestant on the Italian television franchise of *Dancing with the Stars*.

Having missed out on much of a formal education, Tyson reads avidly and even discussed nineteenth-century German philosopher Friedrich Nietzsche with *Sports Illustrated* writer Pablo S. Torre. Referring to Nietzsche's controversial idea of the Aoebermensch—translated as "Overman" or "Superman"—he noted the figure was linked indelibly "with Nazism. But the Overman is a superior being only because he's supposed to endure everything a society has to give to him, and still he stands tall and absorbs it and he's a decent man and still hasn't hurt anybody." He declared that his former self—the terrifying giant with gold teeth and a bulletproof Lamborghini originally built for the king of Saudi Arabia, the celebrity athlete who appeared on the cover of *Sports Illustrated* 15 times—was gone. "My life is empty being that guy," he told Torre. "I want to count for something. Not in the name of God or any religion, but in the name of just self-dignity. I just want to do nice things so my kids can respect me."

Sources

Books

Berger, Mike, *Blood Season: Mike Tyson and the World of Boxing*, Four Walls Eight Windows, 1995.
Heller, Peter, *Bad Intentions: The Mike Tyson Story*,

New American Library, 1989.

Hoffer, Richard, *A Savage Business: The Comeback and Comedown of Mike Tyson,* Simon and Schuster, 1998.

Iron Mike: A Mike Tyson Reader, edited by Daniel O'Connor, foreword by George Plimpton, Da Capo Press, 2002.

Layden, Joe, *The Last Great Fight: The Extraordinary Tale of Two Men and How One Fight Changed Their Lives Forever,* Macmillan, 2008.

Periodicals

Esquire, March 1994, p. 98.
Jet, October 29, 2001, p. 51.

New Republic, April 17, 1995, p. 4.
New York Times Magazine, March 15, 2011.
Sporting News, March 4, 2002, p. 64.
Sports Illustrated, September 16, 1986; January 18, 1999; June 17, 2002; August 2, 2010.
Time, July 14, 1997.

Online

"Mike Tyson," *ESPN*, July 8, 2011, http://espn.go.com/sports/boxing/topics/_/page/mike-tyson (accessed July 21, 2011).

—Michael J. Watkins; Tom Pendergast and
Carol Brennan

Denzel Washington

1954—

Actor, director

Washington, Denzel, photograph. AP Images/Jacquelyn Martin.

Since the late 1980s actor Denzel Washington has dominated the silver screen as one of the great African-American icons of his generation. The first black man to win an Academy Award for Best Actor since Sidney Poitier's historic civil-rights era first back in 1964, Washington can be expected to deliver cool, controlled performances in standard Hollywood action fare or gritty dramas. The classically trained stage veteran was also the obvious choice for the title role in one of the landmarks of American cinema, Spike Lee's 1992 biopic *Malcolm X*. He won the Best Actor Oscar for 2001's *Training Day*, playing a corrupt Los Angeles cop in a performance hailed by critics as one of the most riveting of the year. "Washington, perhaps the most effortlessly charismatic American film actor since Paul Newman, is, like Newman, best when his magnetism is dented by failure or tarnished by meanness or sleaze," asserted *New York Times* film critic A. O. Scott.

Discovered Theater Interest in College

Denzel Washington was born late in 1954, the son of a Pentecostal minister and a gospel singer mother who went on to own a chain of hair salons. He grew up on the edge of the Bronx, in the middle-class neighborhood of Mt. Vernon, New York. "My father was down on the movies, and his idea of something worthwhile would be *The King of Kings, The Ten Commandments* and *101 Dalmatians*," the actor told the *Chicago Tribune*. "And I knew no actors. It's a wonder I ever went into acting." Washington was a good student as a youth, and he drew his friends from a diverse mix of ethnicities common to the Bronx and other outer boroughs.

When Washington was 14 years old, his parents divorced, and he and his brother and sister remained with their mother. "I went through a phase where I got into a lot of fights," he told the *Washington Post*. A guidance counselor at his high school suggested that Washington apply to a private boarding school in upstate New York, Oakland Academy, and he was accepted with a full scholarship. Washington graduated from Oakland Academy in 1972 and entered Fordham University in the Bronx. He eventually switched his major from pre-med to journalism, with a minor in drama.

At a Glance . . .

Born Denzel Hayes Washington Jr. on December 28, 1954, in Mt. Vernon, NY; son of Denzel Sr. (a minister) and Lennis Washington (a hairdresser); married Pauletta Pearson (an actor), June 25, 1983; children: John David, Katia, Malcolm, and Olivia. *Education*: Fordham University, BA, 1977; attended the American Conservatory Theater, c. 1977–78.

Career: YMCA summer camp counselor in Connecticut, mid-1970s; appeared in summer stock productions in St. Mary's City, MD, 1976; made television debut in *Wilma* (movie), 1977; first appeared on the New York stage in *Coriolanus* with the New York Public Theater, 1979; made film debut in *Carbon Copy*, 1981; directed first movie, *Antwone Fisher*, 2002.

Awards: Obie Award for Distinguished Ensemble Performance, *Village Voice*, 1982, for *A Soldier's Play*; Academy Award for Best Supporting Actor, Academy of Motion Picture Arts and Sciences, 1989, for *Glory*, and Academy Award for Best Actor, 2001, for *Training Day*; Golden Globe Award for Best Supporting Actor in a Motion Picture, Hollywood Foreign Press Association, 1989, for *Glory*, and Best Actor in a Motion Picture (Drama), 1999, for *The Hurricane*; Antoinette Perry Award (Tony Award) for Excellence in Theatre for Best Performance by a Leading Actor in a Play, 2010, for *Fences*.

Addresses: *Home*—Beverly Hills, CA. *Agent*—William Morris Endeavor, 9601 Wilshire Blvd., Beverly Hills, CA 90210.

A talented athlete who grew up shooting hoops in local playgrounds and at YMCA facilities, Washington worked summers as a YMCA counselor at the Connecticut camp he had attended as a kid. On one summer break from Fordham, he organized a staff talent show. "Someone told me, 'You seem real natural on the stage; did you ever think of becoming an actor?'" he recalled in a *Chicago Tribune* interview. "That's all it took." When he returned to Fordham in the fall, he auditioned for the university's production of Eugene O'Neill's *The Emperor Jones*, and won the part over a number of theater majors. He went on to star in several more dramas at Fordham, including Shakespeare's *Othello*.

Received Career Advice from Poitier

Robinson Stone, a retired actor, was Washington's drama instructor at Fordham. Remembering his gifted student, Stone told the *Chicago Tribune* that the novice "was thrilling even then. . . . He was easily the best Othello I had ever seen, and I had seen Paul Robeson play it. I remember José Ferrer came to look at it. He and I agreed that Denzel had a brilliant career ahead of him. He played Othello with so much majesty and beauty but also rage and hate that I dragged agents to come and see it."

Even before Washington graduated from Fordham in 1977 he was offered a small role in a television drama, *Wilma*, based on the life of Olympic athlete Wilma Rudolph. After he earned his degree, Washington headed to San Francisco to enroll at the graduate school of the American Conservatory Theater, then returned to the New York area when he won a small part in a well-received New York Public Theater production of Shakespeare's *Coriolanus*, with Morgan Freeman in the title role. Washington soon landed a part in a television miniseries titled *Flesh & Blood*, and then his first film role. He made his big-screen debut in what would be one of the rare comedies of his entire career: the 1981 movie was called *Carbon Copy* and co-starred George Segal as a successful, white executive whose life is disrupted by the appearance of the now-grown son—played by Washington—he never knew he had. "Washington's performance was unpolished, but his lucid intelligence and physical grace were already apparent," noted *New York* magazine writer Phoebe Hoban.

It was a difficult era for an ambitious black actor who hoped to forge a career as a serious actor, but Washington looked to the career of Poitier to guide him, and even managed to meet his hero. "I get this script that I like to call 'The [__] That Wouldn't Die,'" he recalled in an interview with Allison Samuels in *Newsweek*. "I don't remember the exact name—tried to forget it—but it was about a black man who raped and killed a white woman in the '40s. They tried to execute him but he wouldn't die, and then they tried to hang him but he wouldn't die. So he became a celebrity." The subject matter was distasteful, but the part also came with an enormous paycheck. He asked Poitier for advice, and the veteran told him, "Son, your first three or four films will dictate how you are viewed your entire career. Choose wisely, follow your gut and wait it out if you can."

Won Off-Broadway Acclaim

Washington waited it out and was offered a leading part in a new off-Broadway drama, *A Soldier's Play*, at the

Negro Ensemble Company that was one of the surprise hits of the 1981–82 theater season and won its author, Charles Fuller, the 1982 Pulitzer Prize for drama. Washington shared an Obie Award for his performance and was invited to reprise the part of a lowly U.S. Army private on a segregated U.S. Army base in Louisiana during World War II in the film adaptation, which was retitled *A Soldier's Story* for its 1984 release. At the time, Washington was gaining wider recognition for his role in the ensemble cast of the acclaimed NBC medical series *St. Elsewhere.* He played Dr. Phillip Chandler, an Ivy League—educated physician at a fictional Boston hospital.

International attention amplified Washington's career with *Cry Freedom* from British director Richard Attenborough. Released in 1987, the drama brought the story of South African antiapartheid activist Stephen Biko to a wider audience. Biko had died in police custody 10 years earlier, and Attenborough's film was made at a time when future South African president Nelson Mandela was still imprisoned. Washington gave a stirring performance as Biko and was nominated for an Academy Award for Best Supporting Actor, as much of the plot centers on the work of a white newspaper editor, played by Kevin Kline, to force the apartheid regime to answer for the crime. "Washington is particularly good in the courtroom scenes that provide his character with an excellent forum," wrote Janet Maslin in the *New York Times,* adding that while the movie had some flaws, "it can be appreciated for what it tries to communicate about heroism, loyalty and leadership, about the horrors of apartheid, about the martyrdom of a rare man."

Washington won his first Academy Award for the 1989 film *Glory,* the period drama recounting the travails of the first black regiment to fight in the Civil War. Washington was cast as Trip, a runaway slave, and he read slave narratives to prepare for the role. One line, he told Samuels in the *Newsweek* interview, galled him. "'The master threw the dog a bone, but I got there first.' That line just hit me hard," and he drew upon that empathy to craft Trip's persona. He became only the second black actor to win an Oscar for a supporting role, after Louis Gossett Jr. eight years earlier for *An Officer and a Gentleman.*

Cast as Malcolm X

Washington was the natural choice for one of the ultimate roles of the century for a black actor: that of slain civil rights leader Malcolm X. He had already worked with writer-director Spike Lee on Lee's paean to jazz musicians, *Mo' Better Blues,* and had played Malcolm on the New York stage in the early 1980s in *When the Chickens Came Home to Roost.* Lee's 1992 tour de force was hailed as a turning point for the director's career and that of Hollywood, which seemed to suddenly realize that African-American filmgoers

were eager to see their history on screen. "Much of the film's strength lay in the performance of Denzel Washington, who enabled us to see Malcolm think, making his conversion and straight-arrow drive altogether convincing and heroic," wrote Donald Bogle in *Toms, Coons, Mulattoes, Mammies, and Bucks: An Interpretive History of Blacks in American Films.* Washington was widely favored to win the Oscar for Best Actor for *Malcolm X* at the 65th Academy Awards, but lost to Al Pacino, who won for his role in *Scent of a Woman.*

Washington went on to appear with Tom Hanks in *Philadelphia,* Jonathan Demme's 1993 courtroom drama, and *The Pelican Brief,* a John Grisham thriller, that same year. His co-star in the latter, Julia Roberts, called him "the best actor of this generation, hands down," according to *Newsweek.* "I cannot absorb living in a world where I have an Oscar for best actress and Denzel doesn't have one for best actor," Samuels quoted her as saying. Washington returned to work with Lee again in 1998 for the basketball drama *He Got Game* and a year later was widely favored to win the Best Actor Academy Award once again for his portrayal of controversial boxing great Rubin "Hurricane" Carter in *The Hurricane,* but lost to Kevin Spacey for *American Beauty.*

Washington finally won the Best Actor Oscar for 2001's *Training Day.* He played a corrupt Los Angeles narcotics cop who introduces his rookie partner, played by Ethan Hawke, to all the sizzle and grime of the job. As Detective Alonzo Harris, "he's his usual direct, charming, handsome self," wrote *Village Voice* film critic Amy Taubin about Washington's performance, "except that he also has a sadistic streak that, as it gradually surfaces, turns him . . . into a complete monster." When Washington won the Oscar, he thanked Poitier for the career advice years ago. The older actor was in the audience, having received an honorary achievement Academy Award that night. There had been a 38-year gap from Poitier's historic win in April of 1964 as the first black actor to take home the Oscar for a lead performance—for the 1963 film *The Lilies of the Field*—and Washington's victory on March 24, 2002. *Training Day* had been a departure from his usual choices, Washington admitted to writer Josh Rottenberg in *Entertainment Weekly.* "My son talked me into doing that movie. He was like, 'Dad, you've never done anything like this.' I just hadn't been asked before. The only film that was sort of dark that I'd turned down was *Seven.* They offered me the Brad Pitt part, but I was like, 'This is so dark and evil.' Then when I saw the movie, I was like, 'Oh, shoot.'"

Made Directorial Debut

The year 2001 also marked another turning point for Washington when he made his directorial debut with *Antwone Fisher,* in which he also co-starred. The true

story of a security guard at Sony Pictures who managed to get his self-penned autobiographical script into the right hands, the drama was several years in the making, with Washington working with Fisher to finesse the story and bring it to the screen. Washington played a Navy psychiatrist who helps Fisher (played by Derek Luke) come to terms with his troubled past. "The first day of shooting was the most frightening thing I've ever done in my life," Washington confessed to *New York Times* writer Sean Mitchell.

In 2004 Washington starred in the long-awaited remake of *The Manchurian Candidate,* a political thriller. A year later, he returned to the New York stage in a revival of Shakespeare's *Julius Caesar* at the Belasco Theatre. In 2006 he appeared in another Spike Lee movie, *Inside Man,* then took on a new project as director, 2007's *The Great Debaters.* That same year he also performed in director Ridley Scott's epic *American Gangster,* based on the true story of Harlem crime boss Frank Lucas who managed to wrest control of the illicit heroin trade in New York City from the Mafia by the early 1970s. The rise of Lucas, wrote *New Yorker* film critic David Denby, "is presented simply—not with irony, or as a mini-tragedy, or as a cruel joke on his own community, but as a long-delayed victory of black capitalism. . . . The Mafia, in effect, works for Frank, who winds up again and again impressing people not disposed to be impressed by a black man."

Washington turned out heroic leading-man performances in *The Taking of Pelham 123* (2009), as the rail engineer of a doomed freight train in *Unstoppable* (2010), and as a warrior in a post-apocalyptic world in *The Book of Eli* (2010). In June of 2010 he won his first Tony Award for a revival of August Wilson's *Fences* on Broadway. His co-star, Viola Davis, also won a Tony, as did the production itself as Best Revival of a Play for the 2009–10 Broadway season. He had two more action movies on his schedule for 2012: *Safe House* and *Flight,* and he was also booked for *Matarese,* the first film adaptation of another Robert Ludlum international-espionage series that was predicted to follow the success of the gripping *Bourne Identity* franchise.

Selected works

Plays

Coriolanus, 1979.
A Soldier's Play, 1981.
When the Chickens Came Home to Roost, 1981.
Checkmates, 1988.
Richard III, 1991.
Julius Caesar, 2005.
Fences (revival), 2010.

Films

Carbon Copy, Avco-Embassy Pictures, 1981.
A Soldier's Story, Columbia, 1984.
Power, Twentieth Century-Fox, 1986.
Cry Freedom, Universal, 1987.
For Queen & Country, Atlantic Releasing, 1988.
Glory, TriStar, 1989.
Heart Condition, New Line Cinema, 1990.
The Mighty Quinn, Metro-Goldwyn-Mayer, 1990.
Mo' Better Blues, Universal, 1990.
Malcolm X, Warner Bros., 1992.
Mississippi Masala, Paramount, 1992.
The Pelican Brief, Warner Bros., 1993.
Philadelphia, TriStar, 1993.
Crimson Tide, Buena Vista, 1995.
Devil in a Blue Dress, TriStar, 1995.
Courage under Fire, Twentieth Century-Fox, 1996.
The Preacher's Wife, Buena Vista, 1996.
Fallen, Warner Bros., 1997.
He Got Game, Buena Vista, 1998.
The Siege, Twentieth Century-Fox, 1998.
The Bone Collector, Universal, 1999.
The Hurricane, Universal, 1999.
Remember the Titans, Buena Vista, 2000.
John Q, New Line Cinema, 2001.
Training Day, Warner Bros., 2001.
(And director) *Antwone Fisher,* Fox Searchlight Pictures, 2002.
Out of Time, Metro-Goldwyn-Mayer, 2003.
The Manchurian Candidate, Paramount, 2004.
Man on Fire, Twentieth Century-Fox, 2004.
Deja Vu, Buena Vista, 2006.
Inside Man, Universal, 2006.
American Gangster, Universal, 2007.
(And director) *The Great Debaters,* Metro-Goldwyn-Mayer, 2007.
The Taking of Pelham 123, Columbia, 2009.
The Book of Eli, Warner Brothers, 2010.
Unstoppable, 20th-Century Fox, 2010.
Flight, Paramount, 2012.
Matarese, United Artists, 2012.
Safe House, Intrepid Pictures, 2012.

Television

Wilma (television movie), NBC, 1977.
Flesh & Blood (miniseries), CBS, 1979.
St. Elsewhere, NBC, 1982–88.

Sources

Books

Bogle, Donald, *Toms, Coons, Mulattoes, Mammies, and Bucks: An Interpretive History of Blacks in American Films,* Continuum International, fourth edition, 2006.

Periodicals

Boston Globe, February 1, 1990.
Chicago Tribune, March 15, 1986; December 30, 1987; August 5, 1990.
Daily Variety, May 2, 2011, p. A1.
Ebony, April 2000, p. 154.
Entertainment Weekly, July 19, 1996; January 8, 2010.
Esquire, May 1998, p. 66.
Essence, December, 1996.
International Motion Picture Almanac, 1997.
Newsweek, February 25, 2002, p. 54.
New Yorker, November 5, 2007, p. 84.
New York Times, November 6, 1987; November 3, 2002; June 12, 2009, p. C1.
Washington Post, September 18, 1985; August 25, 1989.

Online

Taubin, Amy, "Temples of the Familiar," Village Voice, October 2, 2001, http://www.villagevoice.com/2001-10-02/film/temples-of-the-familiar/1/250/ (accessed August 1, 2011).

—Mark Kram and Carol Brennan

Kanye West

1977—

Musician, record producer

West, Kanye, photograph. AP Images/Paul Beaty.

Kanye West emerged as one of the 21st century's most daring—and successful—figures in urban music, quickly ascending to platinum-star status along with cohorts like Jay-Z and 50 Cent. A multiple-award winning producer and songwriter whose debut LP, 2004's *The College Dropout,* won him the first of three Grammy Awards for Best Rap Album of the Year, West has gone on to issue an evolving string of musical classics, with his records usually landing on lists of the year's most critically acclaimed works. West has also become the focal point of controversy for what some consider his deft publicity-generating stunts, including a live-television rebuke of President George W. Bush and interrupting pop star Taylor Swift at an awards ceremony. "Not since Tupac Shakur has a rapper been so compelling, so ridiculously brash, so irresistibly entertaining," asserted *Rolling Stone* writer Lola Ogunnaike for a cover story in which West appeared—again, in an infamously, potentially imprudent decision—as a Christ-like figure wearing a crown of thorns.

Born on June 8, 1977, in Atlanta, Georgia, Kanye Omari West was raised on Chicago's South Side. His father, Ray West, was a former Black Panther who earned two master's degrees, becoming an award-winning photojournalist and later a counselor. His mother, Donda West, raised him while holding down a job as an English professor at Chicago State University, but after his parents' divorce West would spend summers with his father in Maryland. In a memoir his mother wrote that was published shortly before her untimely death in 2007, Donda West described her only child as a headstrong and confident youngster from an early age—traits she encouraged, while also making sure he had a strong belief system.

"I didn't sit down and tell him, 'You have to be the best,'" West's mother wrote in *Raising Kanye: Life Lessons from the Mother of a Hip-Hop Superstar.* "I just always thought he would be. He was always extremely competitive by nature. I saw it in him at seven months old. He was determined even then to get out of his crib and be free, even if he split his head in the process—and he did. He has fought ever since to do exactly what he wanted to do—no matter what."

At a Glance . . .

Born Kanye Omari West on June 8, 1977, in Atlanta, GA; son of Ray West (a photojournalist) and Donda West (a college professor). *Education*: Attended the American Academy of Art, Chicago, and Chicago State University.

Career: Record producer, Chicago, IL, beginning in 1996; worked on Jermaine Dupri's album *Life in 1472*, 1998; produced five tracks on Jay-Z's album *The Blueprint*, 2001; produced number-one hits "Stand Up" by Ludacris and "You Don't Know My Name" by Alicia Keys, 2004; released solo albums, *The College Dropout*, 2004, *Late Registration*, 2005, *Graduation*, 2007, *808s & Heartbreak*, 2008, and *My Beautiful Dark Twisted Fantasy*, 2010; collaborated with Jay-Z on the album *Watch the Throne*, 2011.

Awards: Winner of 14 Grammy Awards, National Academy of Recording Arts & Sciences, including three in 2005, for Best Rap Album (*The College Dropout*), Best Rap Song ("Jesus Walks"), and Best R&B Song (co-songwriter with Alicia Keys for "You Don't Know My Name"); won three Grammy Awards in 2006 for Best Rap Solo Performance ("Gold Digger"), Best Rap Song ("Diamonds from Sierra Leone"), and Best Rap Album (*Late Registration*); won four Grammy Awards in 2008 for Best Rap Solo Performance ("Stronger"), Best Rap Performance by a Duo or Group ("Southside," with Common), Best Rap Song ("Good Life"), and Best Rap Album (*Graduation*); won three Grammy Awards in 2009, including Best Rap/Sung Collaboration ("American Boy," with Estelle) and Best Rap Performance by a Duo or Group ("Swagga Like Us," with Jay-Z, Lil Wayne, and T.I.); won two Grammy Awards in 2010 for Best Rap/Sung Collaboration and Best Rap Song (both for "Run This Town," with Jay-Z and Rihanna); MTV Video Music Award for Best Male Video, 2005, for "Jesus Walks"; six BET/Hip-Hop Awards; American Music Awards, 2008, for Favorite Rap/Hip-Hop Male Artist and Favorite Rap/Hip-Hop Album, for *Graduation*.

Addresses: *Home*—Los Angeles, CA, and New York, NY. *Agent*—Jeff Frasco, Creative Artists Agency (CAA), 9830 Wilshire Blvd., Beverly Hills, CA 90212.

Started Music Career as a Producer

When West was 10, his mother landed a one-year teaching job in Nanjing, China, and West became proficient enough in the Chinese language to be an interpreter for his mother in restaurants. "I think that got me ready to be a celeb because, at that time, a lot of Chinese had never seen a black person," he told Chris Campion in England's *Daily Telegraph*. West became fascinated by hip-hop music at a young age, badgered his mother into buying him a sophisticated electronic keyboard, and wrote his first raps by the time he was 10. His abilities first became apparent at school talent shows back in Chicago.

By the time he was 13 years old, West was already dreaming of major stardom, looking for a record deal that would make him the next Kriss Kross, the tween rap stars of the early 1990s. After graduating from Chicago's Polaris High School, he won a scholarship to the American Academy of Art. He then transferred to Chicago State, where his mother taught, but was an admittedly indifferent student and was still determined to land a major record deal. Columbia showed some interest, and sent a limousine to ferry him to a meeting. However, West committed a massive faux pas in front of Columbia executive Michael Mauldin, bragging that he would be bigger than superstar Michael Jackson or Atlanta producer and rapper Jermaine Dupri—not knowing at the time that Mauldin was Dupri's father.

West dropped out of Chicago State, which alarmed his parents. Initially, it was his production skills that helped him break into the music business. In 1997 he co-produced some cuts on rapper Mase's album *Harlem World*, then his profile spiked sharply upward after he began working with rapper Jay-Z, one of the top hip-hop hitmakers of the day. He produced Jay-Z's "This Can't Be Life" and composed such Jay-Z cuts as "Izzo H.O.V.A.," "Encore," and "'03 Bonnie and Clyde." Soon West found himself in demand as a producer, working with the rappers Twista and Ludacris and with the R&B chanteuse and pianist Alicia Keys ("You Don't Know My Name").

West's production style was distinctive, and he succeeded in transferring it to his own music after being signed to entrepreneur Damon Dash's Roc-a-Fella label in 2002. He favored samples from classic soul and R&B pieces, with the vocals often sped up so that they turned into rhythmic high-pitched squeaks but were not distorted to a point where they were totally unrecognizable. One night in October of 2002, West was driving home from a late-night studio session in Los Angeles and fell asleep at the wheel of his rented Lexus. He would later say that he remembered almost nothing of the accident, save for the intense pain and the sensation of the steering wheel hitting his face. His jaw was broken in three places, he underwent reconstructive surgery, and his jaw was wired shut for a time to facilitate the recovery process.

Won Best Rap Album Grammy

During his rehabilitation, West continued working on the album that became *The College Dropout*—not just thinking about it, but actually rapping through his wired jaw about his own predicament on "Through the Wire," a piece that cleverly samples a song by the R&B vocal diva Chaka Khan called "Through the Fire." The record was released in early 2004 and won intense praise.

Its 21 tracks diverged sharply from the gangster stereotypes current in hip-hop music and, in its hit single "Jesus Walks," merged hip-hop and gospel musical languages in an entirely new way. Religiously oriented hip-hop had been attempted almost since the genre's beginnings, but "Jesus Walks," with its serious marching-band rhythms and rhythmically complex gospel vocal-group backing, sounded completely new. The song referred to police abuse and included a long passage in which West listed "hustlers, killers, murderers, drug dealers, even the strippers" and had his backing vocal group affirm that "Jesus walks for them." In *Ebony* Kimberly Davis praised West for his "amalgamation of the street hustler's credo and the Black Protestant ethos." West, clad in white, performed "Jesus Walks" at the 47th Grammy Awards ceremony in February of 2005. His debut album was nominated for a eight awards, winning Best Rap Album and collecting another for Best Rap Song for "Jesus Walks."

West's eagerly anticipated follow-up, *Late Registration,* was released in August of 2005 and debuted in the No. 1 spot on the *Billboard* 200 chart. This time, West had teamed with music producer Jon Brion to create several hits and win him a second Grammy for Best Rap Album. Its standout track was "Gold Digger," which tallied more than three million downloads and featured actor/comedian Jamie Foxx channeling the voice of Ray Charles, whom Foxx had portrayed in the biopic *Ray.* "With its layered arrangements and meticulous attention to songwriting, it's evident," wrote Noah Callahan-Bever in *Vibe,* "that West and Brion are crafting some of the most sophisticated, baroque hip hop ever."

Rebuked President Bush over Katrina Response

West's name appeared in headlines across the United States on September 3, 2005, the day after he appeared on a special NBC telethon for victims of Hurricane Katrina in New Orleans. Standing next to comedian Mike Myers, West went off-script and ignored the words he was supposed to read from the teleprompter. "I hate the way they portray us in the media," he started off. "You see a black family, it says they're looting. If you see a white family, it says they're looking for food." He went on for nearly 90 seconds,

stammering and visibly moved by the catastrophe, while Myers looked on, aghast, waiting for a pause to step in. West claimed U.S. military personnel were "given permission to go down and shoot us," then Myers managed to get in a few words of his own before West blurted out, "George Bush doesn't care about black people." At that point, producers of the live event cut the microphones and cameras on Myers and West and switched over to another studio, where a surprised Chris Tucker was standing by and suddenly found himself live.

West's statements generated intense media coverage, and NBC was forced to issue a formal statement. "Tonight's telecast was a live television event wrought with emotion," the network asserted, as reported in the *Washington Post,* and claimed that West's "opinions in no way represent the views of the networks. It would be most unfortunate if the efforts of the artists who participated tonight and the generosity of millions of Americans who are helping those in need are overshadowed by one person's opinion." West's words made him a hero to many, however, for he echoed sentiments expressed others, including African-American leaders like Rev. Al Sharpton and NAACP president Bruce S. Gordon, who compared the federal response to Katrina to that marshaled by federal, state, and local officials on 9/11 and found it lacking. A few months later, West appeared on the cover of *Rolling Stone,* posing with a crown of thorns under the headline, "The Passion of Kanye West," which generated further controversy.

West's third album, *Graduation,* was released in September of 2007, again debuting in the No. 1 spot and selling near one million copies in its first week. T-Pain, Mos Def, and Lil' Wayne made guest appearances, and it went on to win him a third Grammy Award for Best Rap Album. In *Spin* Charles Aaron described it as "mesmerizing and alienating, like all the purest forms of pop culture. Its music is a rush of designer adrenaline, its personality insatiable self-justification."

Honored His Mother's Memory in Performances

The intervening months, however, were marked by a heart-wrenching personal tragedy for West: his beloved mother died of a heart attack on November 10, 2007, in Los Angeles following a pair of surgeries, one of them an abdominoplasty, otherwise known as a "tummy tuck" and the other for breast augmentation. Donda West apparently had a heart condition that made elective surgery risky, and one surgeon she consulted had been reluctant to operate. She found another, and the operation took twice as long as expected. The coroner's inquiry eventually resulted in California's "Donda West Law," which requires patients to submit full medical clearance before undergoing elective cosmetic surgery procedures.

West returned to his tour commitments just 12 days after his mother's death, and dedicated songs to her at every show. At the 50th annual Grammy Awards in February of 2008, West performed a tribute to his mother, "Hey Mama," a track from *Late Registration,* which earned a standing ovation. In addition to the Grammy for Best Rap Album, he won awards for Best Rap Solo Performance ("Stronger") and Best Rap Song ("Good Life").

West spent much of 2008 on tour but made a stop in Denver for a performance at the Democratic National Convention. He recorded his fourth album, *808s & Heartbreak,* in just two months that fall, and it was released on November 24, 2008. Fans and critics were taken aback by it, for he sang all the songs, not rapped, with the help of Auto-Tune. Once again, it debut in the No. 1 spot, and the singles "Heartless" and "Love Lockdown" proved its biggest hits. "His new sound is a bold departure from his previous efforts, but also a challenge to the parameters of what many listeners would consider hip-hop," declared Matthew Newton in *Spin.* This time, however, the album did not receive any Grammy nominations, though one track, "Amazing," was nominated but failed to win.

Created Controversy at MTV Awards

Pop-culture critics theorized that West was overlooked at the Grammys because of another reckless outburst, this one at the 2009 MTV Music Awards on September 13, 2009. When 19-year-old pop singer Taylor Swift took the stage to accept the award for Best Female Video, West suddenly barged up on stage beside her, took the microphone, and said, "Yo, Taylor, I'm really happy for you and I'mma let you finish, but Beyoncé had one of the best videos of all time. One of the best videos of all time!" The audience booed, and even Beyoncé, sitting in the audience, looked shocked. She went on to win Video of the Year for the song, "Single Ladies (Put a Ring on It)," and West's "I'mma let you finish" quickly entered the vernacular. West apologized several times over, but even President Barack Obama was secretly heard criticizing him when some leaked audio from an interview suddenly turned up on the gossip site TMZ. "The young lady seems like a perfectly nice person, she's getting her award and what's he doing up there? He's a jackass," the president was heard to remark in a segment not meant for broadcast, according to People.com.

West's fifth album helped him earn a spot on the *Forbes* list of the top-earning celebrities of 2010. *My Beautiful Dark Twisted Fantasy,* released in November of 2010, featured guest artists and producers Jay-Z, Rick Ross, Kid Cudi, RZA, Nicki Minaj, even Chris Rock. *Pitchfork* magazine gave it a 10.0 rating, a first for a review in that publication in nearly a decade. "The record comes off like a culmination and an instant greatest hits, the ultimate realization of his strongest talents and divisive public persona," asserted reviewer Ryan Dombal. Logan Hill, writing in *New York* magazine, also gave it robust accolades. "It is in many ways pop's event of the year, a stunning comeback for an artist whom many people had started to think of as more of a clown," Hill wrote. "It reveals West in all his complicated splendor: the bully, the innovator, the polymath genius, the diamond-studded blowhard. Most of all, it showcases the undeniable singularity of his talent, which has gotten lost in months of extraordinarily bizarre behavior."

West's next record was also eagerly awaited: what started out as a simple five-song EP turned into a full-length record with another superstar, Jay-Z. *Watch the Throne* was set for release in August of 2011 and was predicted to become the hottest release of the summer; reportedly Beyoncé—Jay-Z's wife—would even make an appearance on one track. "Both rappers have already reached legend status as artists in a way that almost none of their peers could even aspire to, and almost nobody in the business has more clout," the music Web site Idolator said of the hotly anticipated collaboration. "But they also have very different strengths and styles to their music—is there room for all that ego on one tiny album? Can they share the throne?"

Selected discography

The College Dropout (includes "Through the Wire" and "Jesus Walks"), Roc-A-Fella/Def Jam, 2004.
Late Registration (includes "Gold Digger" and "Hey Mama"), Roc-A-Fella/Def Jam, 2005.
Graduation (includes "Stronger" and "Good Life"), Roc-A-Fella/Def Jam, 2007.
808s & Heartbreak (includes "Heartless" and "Love Lockdown"), Roc-A-Fella/Def Jam, 2008.
My Beautiful Dark Twisted Fantasy, Roc-A-Fella/Def Jam, 2010.
(With Jay-Z) *Watch the Throne,* Roc-A-Fella/Def Jam, 2011.

Sources

Books

West, Donda, with Karen Hunter, *Raising Kanye: Life Lessons from the Mother of a Hip-Hop Superstar,* Simon & Schuster, 2007.

Periodicals

Daily Telegraph (London, England), September 11, 2004, Arts section, p. 8.
Ebony, June 2004, p. 90; April 2005, p. 156.
Jet, January 31, 2005, p. 54; February 25, 2008, pp. 60–61.
New York, November 29, 2010.

Rolling Stone, September 8, 2005, pp. 109–10; February 9, 2006.
Spin, December 2008, p. 32.
Vibe, July 2005, p. 88.
Washington Post, September 3, 2005.

Online

Aaron, Charles, "Kanye West: 'Graduation,'" *Spin,* November 6, 2007, http://www.spin.com/reviews/kanye-west-graduation-roc-fella (accessed July 25, 2011).

"Audio: President Obama Calls Kanye West a 'Jackass,'" People, September 15, 2009, http://www.people.com/people/package/article/0,,20302940_20304704,00.html (accessed July 25, 2011).

Dombal, Ryan, "Kanye West: *My Beautiful Dark Twisted Fantasy* (review)," *Pitchfork,* November 22, 2010, http://pitchfork.com/reviews/albums/14880-my-beautiful-dark-twisted-fantasy/ (accessed July 25, 2011).

"Kanye West & Jay-Z's 'Watch The Throne,'" Idolator, June 15, 2011, http://idolator.com/5902052/kanye-west-jay-z-watch-the-throne-summer-preview (accessed July 25, 2011).

Other

"Rising Career of Kanye West," *Day to Day,* National Public Radio (transcript), December 7, 2004.

—James M. Manheim and Carol Brennan

Cumulative Nationality Index

Volume numbers appear in **bold**

American

Aaliyah **30**
Aaron, Hank **5**
Aaron, Quinton **82**
Abbott, Robert Sengstacke **27**
Abdul-Jabbar, Kareem **8**
Abdur-Rahim, Shareef **28**
Abele, Julian **55**
Abernathy, Ralph David **1**
Aberra, Amsale **67**
Abu-Jamal, Mumia **15**
Ace, Johnny **36**
Adams, Eula L. **39**
Adams, Floyd, Jr. **12**
Adams, Jenoyne **60**
Adams, Johnny **39**
Adams, Leslie **39**
Adams, Oleta **18**
Adams, Osceola Macarthy **31**
Adams, Sheila J. **25**
Adams, Yolanda **17, 67**
Adams-Campbell, Lucille L. **60**
Adams Earley, Charity **13, 34**
Adams-Ender, Clara **40**
Adderley, Julian "Cannonball" **30**
Adderley, Nat **29**
Adebimpe, Tunde **75**
Adkins, Rod **41**
Adkins, Rutherford H. **21**
Adu, Freddy **67**
Agyeman, Jaramogi Abebe **10, 63**
Ailey, Alvin **8**
Akil, Mara Brock **60, 82**
Akon **68**
Al-Amin, Jamil Abdullah **6**
Albright, Gerald **23**
Alcorn, George Edward, Jr. **59**
Alert, Kool DJ Red **33**
Alexander, Archie Alphonso **14**
Alexander, Clifford **26**
Alexander, Elizabeth **75**
Alexander, Joyce London **18**
Alexander, Khandi **43**
Alexander, Margaret Walker **22**
Alexander, Sadie Tanner Mossell **22**
Alexander, Shaun **58**
Ali, Hana Yasmeen **52**
Ali, Laila **27, 63**
Ali, Muhammad **2, 16, 52**
Ali, Rashied **79**
Ali, Russlynn H. **92**
Ali, Tatyana **73**
Allain, Stephanie **49**

Allen, Betty **83**
Allen, Byron **3, 24**
Allen, Claude **68**
Allen, Debbie **13, 42**
Allen, Dick **85**
Allen, Ethel D. **13**
Allen, Eugene **79**
Allen, Geri **92**
Allen, Lucy **85**
Allen, Marcus **20**
Allen, Ray **82**
Allen, Robert L. **38**
Allen, Samuel W. **38**
Allen, Tina **22, 75**
Allen, Will **74**
Allen-Buillard, Melba **55**
Alonso, Laz **87**
Alston, Charles **33**
Amaker, Norman **63**
Amaker, Tommy **62**
Amaki, Amalia **76**
Amerie **52**
Ames, Wilmer **27**
Ammons, James H. **81**
Amos, Emma **63**
Amos, John **8, 62**
Amos, Wally **9**
Anderson, Anthony **51, 77**
Anderson, Carl **48**
Anderson, Charles Edward **37**
Anderson, Eddie "Rochester" **30**
Anderson, Elmer **25**
Anderson, Fred **87**
Anderson, Jamal **22**
Anderson, Lauren **72**
Anderson, Marian **2, 33**
Anderson, Michael P. **40**
Anderson, Mike **63**
Anderson, Norman B. **45**
Anderson, Reuben V. **81**
Anderson, William G(ilchrist) **57**
Andrews, Benny **22, 59**
Andrews, Bert **13**
Andrews, Raymond **4**
Andrews, Tina **74**
Angelou, Maya **1, 15**
Ansa, Tina McElroy **14**
Anthony, Carmelo **46**
Anthony, Wendell **25**
apl.de.ap **84**
Appiah, Kwame Anthony **67**
Archer, Dennis **7, 36**
Archer, Lee, Jr. **79**
Archibald, Tiny **90**

Archie-Hudson, Marguerite **44**
Ardoin, Alphonse **65**
Arenas, Gilbert **84**
Arkadie, Kevin **17**
Armstrong, Govind **81**
Armstrong, Louis **2**
Armstrong, Robb **15**
Armstrong, Vanessa Bell **24**
Arnez J **53**
Arnold, Tichina **63**
Arnwine, Barbara **28**
Arrington, Richard **24**
Arroyo, Martina **30**
Artest, Ron **52**
Asante, Molefi Kete **3**
Ashanti **37**
Ashe, Arthur **1, 18**
Ashford, Calvin, Jr. **74**
Ashford, Emmett **22**
Ashford, Evelyn **63**
Ashford, Nickolas **21**
Ashley-Ward, Amelia **23**
Ashong, Derrick **86**
Asim, Jabari **71**
Atkins, Cholly **40**
Atkins, Erica **34**
Atkins, Juan **50**
Atkins, Russell **45**
Atkins, Tina **34**
Aubert, Alvin **41**
Auguste, Donna **29**
Austin, Gloria **63**
Austin, Jim **63**
Austin, Junius C. **44**
Austin, Lovie **40**
Austin, Patti **24**
Autrey, Wesley **68**
Avant, Clarence **19, 86**
Avant, Nicole A. **90**
Avery, Byllye Y. **66**
Ayers, Roy **16**
Babatunde, Obba **35**
Babyface **10, 31, 82**
Bacon-Bercey, June **38**
Badu, Erykah **22**
Bahati, Wambui **60**
Bailey, Buster **38**
Bailey, Chauncey **68**
Bailey, Clyde **45**
Bailey, DeFord **33**
Bailey, Philip **63**
Bailey, Radcliffe **19**
Bailey, Xenobia **11**
Baines, Harold **32**

Baiocchi, Regina Harris **41**
Baisden, Michael **25, 66**
Baker, Anita **21, 48**
Baker, Augusta **38**
Baker, Dusty **8, 43, 72**
Baker, Ella **5**
Baker, Gwendolyn Calvert **9**
Baker, Houston A., Jr. **6**
Baker, Josephine **3**
Baker, LaVern **26**
Baker, Matt **76**
Baker, Maxine B. **28**
Baker, Thurbert **22**
Baker, Vernon Joseph **65, 87**
Baldwin, Cynthia A. **74**
Baldwin, James **1**
Ballance, Frank W. **41**
Ballard, Allen Butler, Jr. **40**
Ballard, Hank **41**
Baltimore, Richard Lewis, III **71**
Bambaataa, Afrika **34**
Bambara, Toni Cade **10**
Bandele, Asha **36**
Banks, Ernie **33**
Banks, Jeffrey **17**
Banks, Michelle **59**
Banks, Paula A. **68**
Banks, Tyra **11, 50**
Banks, William **11**
Banneker, Benjamin **93**
Banner, David **55**
Bannister, Edward Mitchell **88**
Baquet, Dean **63**
Baraka, Amiri **1, 38**
Barbee, Lloyd Augustus **71**
Barber, Ronde **41**
Barber, Tiki **57**
Barboza, Anthony **10**
Barclay, Paris **37**
Barden, Donald H. **9, 20, 89**
Barker, Danny **32**
Barkley, Charles **5, 66**
Barlow, Roosevelt **49**
Barnes, Ernie **16, 78**
Barnes, Melody **75**
Barnes, Roosevelt "Booba" **33**
Barnes, Steven **54**
Barnett, Amy Du Bois **46**
Barnett, Etta Moten **56**
Barnett, Marguerite **46**
Barney, Lem **26**
Barnhill, David **30**
Barrax, Gerald William **45**
Barrett, Andrew C. **12**

175

Barrett, Jacquelyn **28**
Barrino, Fantasia **53**
Barrow, Willie T. **85**
Barry, Marion S(hepilov, Jr.) **7, 44**
Barthé, Earl **78**
Barthe, Richmond **15**
Basie, Count **23**
Basquiat, Jean-Michel **5**
Bass, Charlotta Spears **40**
Bass, Karen **70**
Bassett, Angela **6, 23, 62**
Baszile, Jennifer **79**
Bates, Daisy **13**
Bates, Karen Grigsby **40**
Bates, Peg Leg **14**
Bath, Patricia E. **37**
Batiste, Alvin **66**
Battle, Kathleen **70**
Baugh, David **23**
Baylor, Don **6**
Baylor, Elgin **93**
Baylor, Helen **36**
Beach, Michael **26**
Beal, Bernard B. **46**
Beals, Jennifer **12**
Beals, Melba Patillo **15**
Bearden, Romare **2, 50**
Beasley, Jamar **29**
Beasley, Phoebe **34**
Beatty, Talley **35**
Bechet, Sidney **18**
Beckford, Tyson **11, 68**
Beckham, Barry **41**
Belafonte, Harry **4, 65**
Belgrave, Cynthia **75**
Belgrave, Marcus **77**
Bell, Darrin **77**
Bell, Derrick **6**
Bell, James "Cool Papa" **36**
Bell, James A. **50**
Bell, James Madison **40**
Bell, Michael **40**
Bell, Robert Mack **22**
Bellamy, Bill **12**
Bellamy, Terry **58**
Belle, Albert **10**
Belle, Regina **1, 51**
Belton, Sharon Sayles **9, 16**
Benberry, Cuesta **65**
Benét, Eric **28, 77**
Benham, Robert **78**
Ben-Israel, Ben Ami **11**
Benjamin, Andre **45**
Benjamin, Regina **20, 75**
Benjamin, Tritobia Hayes **53**
Bennett, Estelle **77**
Bennett, George Harold "Hal" **45**
Bennett, Gwendolyn B. **59**
Bennett, Lerone, Jr. **5, 84**
Benson, Angela **34**
Bentley, Lamont **53**
Berrien, Jacqueline A. **93**
Berry, Edwin C. **81**
Berry, Halle **4, 19, 57, 91**
Berry, Bertice **8, 55**
Berry, Chuck **29**
Berry, Fred "Rerun" **48**
Berry, Mary Frances **7**
Berry, Moses **84**
Berry, Theodore **31**
Berrysmith, Don Reginald **49**
Bethune, Mary McLeod **4**
Betsch, MaVynee **28**

Bettis, Jerome **64**
Betts, Keter **85**
Betts, R. Dwayne **86**
Bevel, James L. **75**
Beverly, Frankie **25**
Beyoncé **39, 70**
Bibb, Eric **49**
Bibb, Henry and Mary **54**
Bickerstaff, Bernie **21**
Big Daddy Kane **79**
Biggers, John **20, 33**
Biggers, Sanford **62**
Billops, Camille **82**
bin Wahad, Dhoruba **85**
Bing, Dave **3, 59, 78**
Birch, Adolpho A., Jr. **85**
Birch, Glynn R. **61**
Bishop, Sanford D., Jr. **24**
Bivins, Michael **72**
Black, Albert **51**
Black, Barry C. **47**
Black, Joe **75**
Black, Keith Lanier **18, 84**
Black Thought **63**
Blackburn, Robert **28**
Blackman, Toni **86**
Blackmon, Brenda **58**
Blackshear, Leonard **52**
Blackwell, David **79**
Blackwell, Kenneth, Sr. **61**
Blackwell, Robert D., Sr. **52**
Blackwell, Unita **17**
Blacque, Taurean **58**
Blade, Brian **88**
Blair, Jayson **50**
Blair, Paul **36**
Blake, Asha **26**
Blake, Charles E. **82**
Blake, Eubie **29**
Blake, James **43**
Blakely, Edward J. **88**
Blakey, Art **37**
Blanchard, Terence **43**
Bland, Bobby "Blue" **36**
Bland, Eleanor Taylor **39**
Blanks, Billy **22**
Blanks, Deborah K. **69**
Blanton, Dain **29**
Blassingame, John Wesley **40**
Blaylock, Ronald **86**
Blayton, Jesse B., Sr. **55**
Bleu, Corbin **65**
Blige, Mary J. **20, 34, 60**
Blockson, Charles L. **42**
Bloomer, George **86**
Blow, Charles M. **73**
Blow, Kurtis **31**
Bluford, Guy **2, 35**
Bluitt, Juliann S. **14**
B.o.B. **91**
Bobb, Robert C. **83**
Bobo, Lawrence **60**
Bogle, Donald **34**
Bogues, Tyrone "Muggsy" **56**
Bolden, Buddy **39**
Bolden, Charles Frank, Jr. **7, 78**
Bolden, Frank E. **44**
Bolden, Tonya **32**
Bolin, Jane **22, 59**
Bolton, Terrell D. **25**
Bolton-Holifield, Ruthie **28**
Bond, Beverly **53**
Bond, J. Max, Jr. **76**

Bond, Julian **2, 35**
Bonds, Barry **6, 34, 63**
Bonds, Bobby **43**
Bonds, Margaret **39**
Bonet, Lisa **58**
Bontemps, Arna **8**
Booker, Cory Anthony **68**
Booker, Simeon **23**
Borders, James **9**
Bosh, Chris **85**
Bosley, Freeman, Jr. **7**
Boston, Kelvin E. **25**
Boston, Lloyd **24**
Bow Wow **35**
Bowe, Riddick **6**
Bowen, John W. E., Sr. **89**
Bowen, Ruth **83**
Bowman, Bertie **71**
Bowser, Yvette Lee **17**
Boyd, Edward **70**
Boyd, Gerald M. **32, 59**
Boyd, Gwendolyn **49**
Boyd, John W., Jr. **20, 72**
Boyd, Melba Joyce **86**
Boyd, T. B., III **6**
Boykin, Keith **14**
Boykin, Otis **92**
Boyz II Men **82**
Bradford, Mark **89**
Bradley, David Henry, Jr. **39**
Bradley, Ed **2, 59**
Bradley, J. Robert **65**
Bradley, Jennette B. **40**
Bradley, Thomas **2, 20**
Brady, Wayne **32, 71**
Brae, C. Michael **61**
Braithwaite, William Stanley **52**
Bramlett, Joseph **91**
Branch, William Blackwell **39**
Brand, Elton **31**
Brandon, Barbara **3**
Brandon, Terrell **16**
Brandy **14, 34, 72**
Branham, George, III **50**
Branson, Herman **87**
Brashear, Carl **29**
Brashear, Donald **39**
Braugher, Andre **13, 58, 91**
Braun, Carol Moseley **4, 42**
Brawley, Benjamin **44**
Braxton, Brad **77**
Braxton, Toni **15, 61, 91**
Brazile, Donna **25, 70**
Bridges, Ruby **77**
Bridges, Sheila **36**
Bridges, Todd **37**
Bridgewater, Dee Dee **32, 92**
Bridgforth, Glinda **36**
Briggs, Curtis **84**
Brimmer, Andrew F. **2, 48**
Briscoe, Connie **15**
Briscoe, Marlin **37**
Britt, Donna **28**
Broadbent, Hydeia **36**
Brock, Lou **18**
Brock, Roslyn McCallister **86**
Bromery, Randolph Wilson **85**
Bronner, Nathaniel H., Sr. **32**
Brooke, Edward W. **8, 88**
Brooks, Aaron **33**
Brooks, Avery **9**
Brooks, Derrick **43**
Brooks, Golden **62**

Brooks, Gwendolyn **1, 28**
Brooks, Hadda **40**
Brooks, Mehcad **62**
Brooks, Tyrone **59**
Broonzy, Big Bill **82**
Brower, William **49**
Brown, Angela M. **54**
Brown, Anne **76**
Brown, Anthony G. **72**
Brown, Antron **85**
Brown, Bobby **58**
Brown, Byrd **49**
Brown, Byron W. **72**
Brown, Cecil M. **46**
Brown, Charles **23**
Brown, Chris **74**
Brown, Chuck **78**
Brown, Clarence Gatemouth **59**
Brown, Claude **38**
Brown, Clifford **86**
Brown, Cora **33**
Brown, Corrine **24, 90**
Brown, Cupcake **63**
Brown, Donald **19**
Brown, Eddie C. **35**
Brown, Elaine **8**
Brown, Ernest **80**
Brown, Erroll M. **23**
Brown, Foxy **25**
Brown, George Leslie **62**
Brown, Homer S. **47**
Brown, James **15, 60**
Brown, James **22**
Brown, Jamie Foster **91**
Brown, Janice Rogers **43**
Brown, Jesse **6, 41**
Brown, Jesse Leroy **31**
Brown, Jim **11**
Brown, Joe **29**
Brown, Joyce F. **25**
Brown, Kwame R. **91**
Brown, Lee Patrick **1, 24**
Brown, Les **5**
Brown, Lloyd Louis **42**
Brown, Marie Dutton **12**
Brown, Mike **77**
Brown, Nappy **73**
Brown, Oscar, Jr. **53**
Brown, Patrick "Sleepy" **50**
Brown, Robert **65**
Brown, Ron **5**
Brown, Ronald K. **91**
Brown, Ruth **90**
Brown, Sterling Allen **10, 64**
Brown, Tony **3**
Brown, Uzee **42**
Brown, Vivian **27**
Brown, Warren **61**
Brown, Wesley **23**
Brown, Willa **40**
Brown, Willard **36**
Brown, Willie **7, 85**
Brown, Zora Kramer **12**
Browne, Roscoe Lee **66**
Brownlee, Lawrence **88**
Broyard, Anatole **68**
Broyard, Bliss **68**
Bruce, Blanche Kelso **33**
Bruce, Bruce **56**
Bruce, Isaac **26**
Brunson, Dorothy **1, 87**
Bryan, Ashley F. **41**
Bryant, Cullen **81**

Bryant, John **26**
Bryant, John R. **45**
Bryant, Kobe **15, 31, 71**
Bryant, Wayne R. **6**
Bryant, William Benson **61**
Buchanan, Ray **32**
Buckley, Gail Lumet **39**
Buckley, Victoria (Vikki) **24**
Bullard, Eugene **12**
Bullins, Ed **25**
Bullock, Steve **22**
Bully-Cummings, Ella **48**
Bumbry, Grace **5**
Bunch, Lonnie G., III **91**
Bunche, Ralph J. **5**
Bunkley, Anita Richmond **39**
Burgess, John **46**
Burgess, Marjorie L. **55**
Burke, Selma **16**
Burke, Solomon **31, 86**
Burke, Yvonne Brathwaite **42**
Burks, Mary Fair **40**
Burleigh, Henry Thacker **56**
Burnett, Charles **16, 68**
Burnim, Mickey L. **48**
Burns, Eddie **44**
Burns, Ursula **60**
Burnside, R. L. **56**
Burrell, Tom **21, 51**
Burris, Chuck **21**
Burris, Roland W. **25, 75**
Burroughs, Margaret Taylor **9**
Burrows, Stephen **31**
Burrus, William Henry "Bill" **45**
Burt-Murray, Angela **59**
Burton, LeVar **8**
Burwell, Bryan **83**
Busby, Jheryl **3, 74**
Bush, Gordon **82**
Bush, Reggie **59, 88**
Butler, George, Jr. **70**
Butler, Jerry **26**
Butler, Leroy, III **17**
Butler, Louis **70**
Butler, Octavia **8, 43, 58**
Butler, Paul D. **17**
Butts, Calvin O., III **9, 90**
Butts, Cassandra **78**
Bynoe, Peter C. B. **40**
Bynum, Juanita **31, 71**
Byrd, Donald **10**
Byrd, Eugene **64**
Byrd, Michelle **19**
Byrd, Robert **11**
Cadoria, Sherian Grace **14**
Caesar, Shirley **19**
Cage, Byron **53**
Cain, Herman **15, 92**
Calabrese, Karyn **89**
Caldwell, Benjamin **46**
Caldwell, Earl **60**
Caldwell, Jim **81**
Caldwell, Kirbyjon **55**
Calhoun, Lillian Scott **87**
Callender, Clive O. **3**
Calloway, Cab **14**
Cameron, James **80**
Camp, Kimberly **19**
Campanella, Roy **25**
Campbell, Bebe Moore **6, 24, 59**
Campbell, Bill **9, 76**
Campbell, Donald J. **66**
Campbell, E. Simms **13**

Campbell, Mary Schmidt **43**
Campbell-Martin, Tisha **8, 42**
Canada, Geoffrey **23**
Canady, Alexa **28**
Cannon, Katie **10**
Cannon, Nick **47, 73**
Cannon, Reuben **50**
Cara, Irene **77**
Carr, Johnnie **69**
Carr, Keela **74**
Cardozo, Francis L. **33**
Carew, Rod **20**
Carey, Mariah **32, 53, 69**
Cargill, Victoria A. **43**
Carr, Kurt **56**
Carr, Leroy **49**
Carroll, Diahann **9**
Carroll, L. Natalie **44**
Carroll, Rocky **74**
Carruthers, George R. **40**
Carson, André **69**
Carson, Benjamin **1, 35, 76**
Carson, Johnnie **85**
Carson, Julia **23, 69**
Carson, Lisa Nicole **21**
Carter, Anson **24**
Carter, Benny **46**
Carter, Betty **19**
Carter, Butch **27**
Carter, Cris **21**
Carter, Joe **30**
Carter, Joye Maureen **41**
Carter, Kenneth **53**
Carter, Majora **77**
Carter, Mandy **11**
Carter, Nell **39**
Carter, Pamela Lynn **67**
Carter, Regina **23**
Carter, Robert L. **51**
Carter, Rubin **26**
Carter, Stephen L. **4**
Carter, Vince **26**
Carter, Warrick L. **27**
Cartey, Wilfred **47**
Cartiér, Xam Wilson **41**
Carver, George Washington **4**
Cary, Lorene **3**
Cary, Mary Ann Shadd **30**
Cash, Rosalind **28**
Cash, Swin **59**
Cashin, Sheryll **63**
CasSelle, Malcolm **11**
Catchings, Tamika **43**
Catlett, Elizabeth **2**
Catto, Octavius V. **83**
Cayton, Horace **26**
Cedric the Entertainer **29, 60**
Cee-Lo **70**
Chadiha, Jeffri **57**
Chamberlain, Wilt **18, 47**
Chambers, Julius **3**
Chamillionaire **82**
Chaney, John **67**
Chanticleer, Raven **91**
Chapman, Nathan A., Jr. **21**
Chapman, Tracy **26**
Chappell, Emma **18**
Chappelle, Dave **50**
Charles, Ray **16, 48**
Charleston, Oscar **39**
Chase, Debra Martin **49**
Chase, Leah **57**
Chase-Riboud, Barbara **20, 46**

Chatard, Peter **44**
Chavis, Benjamin **6**
Cheadle, Don **19, 52**
Checker, Chubby **28**
Cheeks, Maurice **47**
Chenault, John **40**
Chenault, Kenneth I. **4, 36**
Cherry, Deron **40**
Chesnutt, Charles **29**
Chestnut, J. L., Jr. **73**
Chestnut, Morris **31**
Chideya, Farai **14, 61**
Childress, Alice **15**
Chineworth, Mary Alice **79**
Chinn, May Edward **26**
Chisholm, Daquan **93**
Chisholm, Samuel **32**
Chisholm, Shirley **2, 50**
Christian, Barbara T. **44**
Christian, Spencer **15**
Christian-Green, Donna M. **17**
Christie, Angella **36**
Christie, Ron **83**
Chuck D **9**
Churchwell, Robert, Sr. **76**
Ciara **56**
Ciara, Barbara **69**
Clack, Zoanne **73**
Claiborne, Loretta **34**
Clark, Celeste **15**
Clark, Joe **1**
Clark, Kenneth B. **5, 52**
Clark, Mamie Phipps **79**
Clark, Mattie Moss **61**
Clark, Patrick **14**
Clark, Septima **7**
Clark-Cole, Dorinda **66**
Clarke, Cheryl **32**
Clarke, Hope **14**
Clarke, John Henrik **20**
Clarke, Kenny **27**
Clarke, Yvette **92**
Clark-Sheard, Karen **22**
Clash, Kevin **14, 93**
Clay, Bryan **57, 74**
Clay, William Lacy **8**
Clayton, Constance **1**
Clayton, Eva M. **20**
Clayton, Mayme Agnew **62**
Clayton, Xernona **3, 45**
Claytor, Helen **14, 52**
Cleage, Pearl **17, 64**
Cleaver, Eldridge **5**
Cleaver, Emanuel **4, 45, 68**
Cleaver, Kathleen **29**
Clemente, Rosa **74**
Clements, George **2**
Clemmons, Reginal G. **41**
Clemons, Clarence **41**
Clemons, Michael "Pinball" **64**
Clendenon, Donn **26, 56**
Cleveland, James **19**
Cliff, Michelle **42**
Clifton, Lucille **14, 64, 91**
Clifton, Nathaniel "Sweetwater" **47**
Clinton, George **9, 93**
Clyburn, James E. **21, 71**
Clyburn, Mignon **78**
Coachman, Alice **18**
Coates, Ta-Nehisi **76**
Cobb, Jewel Plummer **42**
Cobb, W. Montague **39**
Cobb, William Jelani **59**

Cobbs, Price M. **9**
Cochran, Johnnie **11, 39, 52**
Cockrel, Kenneth V., Jr. **79**
Cockrel, Kenneth Vern, Sr. **79**
CoCo Brother **93**
Cohen, Anthony **15**
Cohen, Cathy J. **88**
Colbert, Virgis William **17**
Cole, Johnnetta B. **5, 43**
Cole, Keyshia **63**
Cole, Lorraine **48**
Cole, Nat "King" **17**
Cole, Natalie **17, 60, 84**
Cole, Rebecca **38**
Coleman, Bessie **9**
Coleman, Donald **24, 62**
Coleman, Gary **35, 86**
Coleman, James E., Jr. **79**
Coleman, Ken **57**
Coleman, Leonard S., Jr. **12**
Coleman, Mary **46**
Coleman, Michael B. **28, 79**
Coleman, Ornette **39, 69**
Coleman, Wanda **48**
Coleman, William F., III **61**
Coleman, William T. **76**
Colemon, Johnnie **11**
Coles, Alice **80**
Colescott, Robert **69**
Collins, Albert **12**
Collins, Barbara-Rose **7, 87**
Collins, Bootsy **31**
Collins, Cardiss **10, 80**
Collins, Janet **33, 64**
Collins, Lyn **53**
Collins, Marva **3, 71**
Collins, Patricia Hill **67**
Collins, Paul **61**
Colston, Hal **72**
Colter, Cyrus J. **36**
Coltrane, Alice **70**
Coltrane, John **19**
Coltrane, Ravi **71**
Combs, Sean **17, 43, 92**
Comer, James P. **6**
Common **31, 63**
Compton-Rock, Malaak **86**
Cone, James H. **3, 82**
Coney, PonJola **48**
Connerly, Ward **14**
Conrad, Barbara Smith **90**
Contee, Cheryl **88**
Conyers, John, Jr. **4**
Conyers, Monica **85**
Conyers, Nathan G. **24, 45**
Cook, Charles "Doc" **44**
Cook, (Will) Mercer **40**
Cook, Samuel DuBois **14**
Cook, Suzan D. Johnson **22**
Cook, Toni **23**
Cook, Will Marion **40**
Cooke, Marcia **60**
Cooke, Marvel **31**
Cooper, Andrew W. **36**
Cooper, Andy "Lefty" **63**
Cooper, Anna Julia **20**
Cooper, Barry **33**
Cooper, Charles "Chuck" **47**
Cooper, Chuck **75**
Cooper, Edward S. **6**
Cooper, Evern **40**
Cooper, Helene **74**
Cooper, J. California **12, 85**

Cooper, Lisa 73
Cooper, Margaret J. 46
Cooper, Michael 31
Cooper Cafritz, Peggy 43
Cooper-Dyke, Cynthia 17, 89
Copeland, Michael 47
Coppola, Imani Francesca 82
Corbi, Lana 42
Corley, Tony 62
Cornelius, Don 4
Cornish, Sam 50
Cornwell, Edward E., III 70
Correia, De'Jaun 93
Cortez, Jayne 43
Corthron, Kia 43
Cortor, Eldzier 42
Cosby, Bill 7, 26, 59
Cosby, Camille 14, 80
Cose, Ellis 5, 50
Cotter, Joseph Seamon, Sr. 40
Cottrell, Comer 11
Counter, S. Allen 74
Cowans, Adger W. 20
Cowboy Troy 54
Cox, Bryan 83
Cox, Donald Lee 93
Cox, Ida 42
Cox, Joseph Mason Andrew 51
Cox, Renée 67
Cox, William E. 68
Craig, Carl 31, 71
Craig-Jones, Ellen Walker 44
Crawford, Carl 90
Crawford, Hank 77
Crawford, Randy 19
Cray, Robert 30
Creagh, Milton 27
Crennel, Romeo 54
Crenshaw, Kimberlé Williams 88
Crew, Rudolph F. 16
Crew, Spencer R. 55
Crichlow, Ernest 75
Crite, Alan Rohan 29
Croal, N'Gai 76
Crocker, Frankie 29
Crockett, George W., Jr. 10, 64
Croom, Sylvester 50
Cross, Dolores E. 23
Crosthwait, David 93
Crothers, Scatman 19
Crouch, Andraé 27
Crouch, Stanley 11, 87
Crowder, Henry 16
Crumpler, Rebecca Lee 89
Cruse, Harold 54
Crutchfield, James N. 55
Cullen, Countee 8
Cullers, Vincent T. 49
Culpepper, Daunte 32, 85
Cummings, Elijah E. 24
Cuney, William Waring 44
Cunningham, Evelyn 23, 85
Cunningham, Randall 23
Currie, Betty 21
Currie, Ulysses 73
Curry, George E. 23
Curry, Mark 17
Curry, Michael 85
Curtis, Christopher Paul 26
Curtis-Hall, Vondie 17
Da Don, Polow 86
Dabiri, John 93
Daemyon, Jerald 64

Dailey, Ulysses Grant 87
Daly, Marie Maynard 37
Dandridge, Dorothy 3
Dandridge, Ray 36
Dandridge, Raymond Garfield 45
D'Angelo 27
Daniels, Lee 36, 76
Daniels-Carter, Valerie 23
Danner, Margaret Esse 49
Danquah, Meri Nana Ama 93
Dantley, Adrian 72
Dara, Olu 35
Darden, Calvin 38
Darden, Christopher 13
Dash, Damon 31
Dash, Julie 4
Dash, Leon 47
Datcher, Michael 60
David, Keith 27
Davidson, Jaye 5
Davidson, Tommy 21
Davis, Allison 12
Davis, Altovise 76
Davis, Angela 5
Davis, Angela J. 88
Davis, Anthony 11
Davis, Arthur Paul 41
Davis, Artur 41
Davis, Belva 61
Davis, Benjamin O., Jr. 2, 43
Davis, Benjamin O., Sr. 4
Davis, Bing 84
Davis, Charles T. 48
Davis, Chuck 33
Davis, Danny K. 24, 79
Davis, Ed 24
Davis, Eisa 68
Davis, Ernie 48
Davis, Erroll B., Jr. 57
Davis, Frank Marshall 47
Davis, Gary 41
Davis, George 36
Davis, Gordon J. 76
Davis, Guy 36
Davis, James E. 50
Davis, Mike 41
Davis, Miles 4
Davis, Milt 74
Davis, Nolan 45
Davis, Ossie 5, 50
Davis, Piper 19
Davis, Ruth 37
Davis, Shani 58, 84
Davis, Terrell 20
Davis, Thulani 61
Davis, Tyrone 54
Davis, Viola 34, 76
Dawes, Dominique 11
Dawkins, Wayne 20
Dawn, Marpessa 75
Dawson, Andre 85
Dawson, Matel "Mat," Jr. 39
Dawson, Michael C. 63
Dawson, Rosario 72
Dawson, William Levi 39
Day, Leon 39
Days, Drew S., III 10
De' Alexander, Quinton 57
de Lavallade, Carmen 78
de Passe, Suzanne 25
De Priest, Oscar Stanton 80
De Shields, André 72
De Veaux, Alexis 44

Dean, Mark E. 35
Deas, Gerald 85
DeBaptiste, George 32
DeBarge, El 89
DeCarava, Roy 42, 81
Deconge-Watson, Lovenia 55
Dee, Merri 55
Dee, Ruby 8, 50, 68
Deezer D 53
DeFrantz, Anita 37
Deggans, Eric 71
DeJongh, John, Jr. 85
Delaney, Beauford 19
Delaney, Joe 76
Delaney, Joseph 30
Delany, Bessie 12
Delany, Martin R. 27
Delany, Sadie 12
Delany, Samuel R., Jr. 9
Delco, Wilhemina 33
DeLille, Henriette 30
Dellums, Ronald 2, 81
DeLoach, Nora 30
Delsarte, Louis 34
Demby, William 51
Dennard, Brazeal 37
Dennis, Gary C. 91
Dent, Thomas C. 50
DePreist, James 37
Derülo, Jason 93
DeVard, Jerri 61
DeVaughn, Raheem 91
Devers, Gail 7, 87
Devine, Loretta 24
Dickens, Helen Octavia 14, 64
Dickenson, Vic 38
Dickerson, Debra J. 60
Dickerson, Eric 27
Dickerson, Ernest R. 6, 17
Dickey, Eric Jerome 21, 56
Diddley, Bo 39, 72
Diesel, Vin 29
Diggs, Charles C. 21
Diggs, Taye 25, 63
Diggs-Taylor, Anna 20
Dillard, Godfrey J. 45
Dinkins, David 4
Divine, Father 7
Dixon, Bill 87
Dixon, Dean 68
Dixon, Ivan 69
Dixon, Julian C. 24
Dixon, Margaret 14
Dixon, Sharon Pratt 1
Dixon, Sheila 68
Dixon, Willie 4
DMX 28, 64
Dobbs, John Wesley 89
Dobbs, Mattiwilda 34
Doby, Lawrence Eugene, Sr. 16, 41
Dodson, Howard, Jr. 7, 52
Dodson, Owen Vincent 38
Dogan, Matthew Winifred 91
Doley, Harold, Jr. 26
Domino, Fats 20
Donald, Arnold Wayne 36
Donaldson, Jeff 46
Donegan, Dorothy 19
Dorrell, Karl 52
Dorsey, Lee 65
Dorsey, Thomas Andrew 15
Dorsey, Thomas J. 90
Dortch, Thomas W., Jr. 45

Dougherty, Mary Pearl 47
Douglas, Aaron 7
Douglas, Derek 88
Douglas, Emory 89
Douglass, Frederick 87
Dourdan, Gary 37
Dove, Rita 6, 78
Dove, Ulysses 5
Downing, George T. 91
Downing, Will 19
Draper, Sharon Mills 16, 43
Dre, Dr. 10, 14, 30
Drew, Alvin, Jr. 67
Drew, Charles Richard 7
Drexler, Clyde 4, 61
Driskell, David C. 7
Driver, David E. 11
Drummond, William J. 40
Du Bois, David Graham 45
Du Bois, W. E. B. 3
du Cille, Michel 74
DuBois, Joshua 88
DuBois, Shirley Graham 21
Ducksworth, Marilyn 12
Dudley, Edward R. 58
Due, Tananarive 30
Duerson, Dave 93
Duggins, George 64
Duke, Bill 3
Duke, George 21
Dukes, Hazel Nell 56
Dumars, Joe 16, 65
Dumas, Henry 41
Dunbar, Paul Laurence 8
Dunbar-Nelson, Alice Ruth Moore 44
Duncan, Michael Clarke 26
Duncan, Tim 20, 91
Duncan, Todd 76
Dungey, Merrin 62
Dungy, Camille 86
Dungy, Tony 17, 42, 59
Dunham, Katherine 4, 59
Dunlap, Ericka 55
Dunn, Jerry 27
Dunn, Warrick 90
Dunner, Leslie B. 45
Dunnigan, Alice Allison 41
Dunston, Georgia Mae 48
Duplechan, Larry 55
Dupri, Jermaine 13, 46
Durant, Kevin 76
Durham, Bobby 73
Durham, James 90
Dutton, Charles S. 4, 22
Dworkin, Aaron P. 52
Dwight, Edward 65
Dye, Jermaine 58
Dyson, Michael Eric 11, 40
Eagleson, William Lewis 90
Early, Gerald 15
Earthquake 55
Easley, Annie J. 61
Easton, Hosea 91
Ebanks, Michelle 60
Eckstine, Billy 28
Edelin, Ramona Hoage 19
Edelman, Marian Wright 5, 42
Edley, Christopher 2, 48
Edley, Christopher F., Jr. 48
Edmonds, Terry 17
Edmonds, Tracey 16, 64
Edmunds, Gladys 48

Edwards, Donna 77
Edwards, Esther Gordy 43
Edwards, Harry 2
Edwards, Herman 51
Edwards, Lena Frances 76
Edwards, Melvin 22
Edwards, Teresa 14
Edwards, Willarda V. 59
El Wilson, Barbara 35
Elder, Larry 25
Elder, Lee 6
Elder, Lonne, III 38
Elders, Joycelyn 6
Eldridge, Roy 37
Elise, Kimberly 32
Ellerbe, Brian 22
Ellington, Duke 5
Ellington, E. David 11
Ellington, Mercedes 34
Elliott, Missy 31, 90
Elliott, Sean 26
Ellis, Charles H., III 79
Ellis, Clarence A. 38
Ellis, Dock 78
Ellis, Jimmy 44
Ellis-Lamkins, Phaedra 88
Ellison, Keith 59
Ellison, Ralph 7
Elmore, Ronn 21
Emanuel, James A. 46
Emeagwali, Dale 31
Ephriam, Mablean 29
Epperson, Sharon 54
Epps, Archie C., III 45
Epps, Mike 60
Epps, Omar 23, 59
Ericsson-Jackson, Aprille 28
Ervin, Anthony 66
Ervin, Clark Kent 82
Erving, Julius 18, 47
Escobar, Damien 56
Escobar, Tourie 56
Esposito, Giancarlo 9
Espy, Mike 6
Estes, Rufus 29
Estes, Simon 28
Estes, Sleepy John 33
Eubanks, Kevin 15
Eugene-Richard, Margie 63
Europe, James Reese 10
Evans, Darryl 22
Evans, Etu 55
Evans, Faith 22
Evans, Harry 25
Evans, Mari 26
Evans, Melvin H. 88
Evans, Warren C. 76
Eve 29
Everett, Francine 23
Everett, Percival 93
Evers, Medgar 3
Evers, Myrlie 8
Ewing, Patrick 17, 73
Fabio, Sarah Webster 48
Fabolous 93
Fabre, Shelton 71
Fair, Ronald L. 47
Faison, Donald 50
Faison, Frankie 55
Faison, George 16
Falana, Lola 42
Falconer, Etta Zuber 59
Fales-Hill, Susan 88

Fargas, Antonio 50
Farley, Christopher John 54
Farmer, Art 38
Farmer, Forest J. 1
Farmer, James 2, 64
Farmer-Paellmann, Deadria 43
Farr, Mel 24
Farrakhan, Louis 2, 15
Farrell, Herman D., Jr. 81
Farris, Isaac Newton, Jr. 63
Fattah, Chaka 11, 70
Faulk, Marshall 35
Fauntroy, Walter E. 11
Fauset, Jessie 7
Favors, Steve 23
Fax, Elton 48
Feelings, Muriel 44
Feelings, Tom 11, 47
Felix, Allyson 48
Felix, Larry R. 64
Feemster, Herbert 72
Fennoy, Ilene 72
Fenty, Adrian 60, 88
Ferguson, Roger W. 25
Ferguson, Ronald F. 75
Ferrell, Rachelle 29
Fetchit, Stepin 32
Fiasco, Lupe 64
Fielder, Cecil 2
Fielder, Prince Semien 68
Fields, C. Virginia 25
Fields, Cleo 13
Fields, Evelyn J. 27
Fields, Felicia P. 60
Fields, Julia 45
Fields, Kim 36
50 Cent 46, 83
Files, Lolita 35
Fils-Aimé, Reggie 74
Fine, Sam 60
Finner-Williams, Paris Michele 62
Fishburne, Laurence 4, 22, 70
Fisher, Ada Lois Sipuel 76
Fisher, Ada M. 76
Fisher, Antwone 40
Fisher, Gail 85
Fisher, Miles Mark 91
Fitzgerald, Ella 1, 18
Flack, Roberta 19
Flanagan, Tommy 69
Flavor Flav 67
Fleming, Erik R. 75
Fleming, Raymond 48
Fletcher, Arthur A. 63
Fletcher, Benjamin 90
Fletcher, Bill, Jr. 41
Fletcher, Geoffrey 85
Flo Rida 78
Flood, Curt 10, 93
Flowers, Sylester 50
Flowers, Vonetta 35
Floyd, Elson S. 41
Forbes, Calvin 46
Forbes, James A., Jr. 71
Ford, Barney 90
Ford, Cheryl 45
Ford, Clyde W. 40
Ford, Harold E(ugene) 42
Ford, Harold E(ugene), Jr. 16, 70
Ford, Jack 39
Ford, Johnny 70
Ford, Nick Aaron 44
Ford, T-Model 91

Ford, Wallace 58
Forman, James 7, 51
Forman, James, Jr. 89
Forrest, Leon 44
Forrest, Vernon 40, 79
Forté, John 74
Forte, Linda Diane 54
Fortune, James 92
Foster, Andrew 79
Foster, Ezola 28
Foster, George "Pops" 40
Foster, Henry W., Jr. 26
Foster, Jylla Moore 45
Foster, Marie 48
Foster, William P. 88
Fowler, Reggie 51
Fox, Vivica A. 15, 53
Foxx, Anthony 81
Foxx, Jamie 15, 48
Foxx, Redd 2
Francis, Norman (C.) 60
Francis, Thais 93
Franklin, Aretha 11, 44
Franklin, C. L. 68
Franklin, Hardy R. 9, 87
Franklin, J. E. 44
Franklin, John Hope 5, 77
Franklin, Kirk 15, 49
Franklin, Shirley 34, 80
Franti, Michael 93
Frazer, Jendayi 68
Frazier, E. Franklin 10
Frazier, Joe 19
Frazier, Kevin 58
Frazier, Oscar 58
Frazier, Ryan 89
Frazier, Walt 91
Frazier-Lyde, Jacqui 31
Freelon, Nnenna 32
Freeman, Aaron 52
Freeman, Al, Jr. 11
Freeman, Charles 19
Freeman, Harold P. 23
Freeman, Leonard 27
Freeman, Marianna 23
Freeman, Morgan 2, 20, 62
Freeman, Paul 39
Freeman, Yvette 27
French, Albert 18
Fresh, Doug E. 93
Friday, Jeff 24
Fryer, Roland G. 56
Fudge, Ann (Marie) 11, 55
Fudge, Marcia L. 76
Fulani, Lenora 11
Fuller, A. Oveta 43
Fuller, Arthur 27
Fuller, Blind Boy 86
Fuller, Charles 8
Fuller, Howard L. 37
Fuller, Hoyt 44
Fuller, Meta Vaux Warrick 27
Fuller, S. B. 13
Fuller, Solomon Carter, Jr. 15
Fuller, Thomas O. 90
Fuller, Vivian 33
Funderburg, I. Owen 38
Funnye, Capers C., Jr. 73
Fuqua, Antoine 35
Fuqua, Harvey 90
Futch, Eddie 33
Gaines, Brenda 41
Gaines, Clarence E., Sr. 55

Gaines, Ernest J. 7
Gaines, Grady 38
Gaines, Lloyd 79
Gaiter, Dorothy J. 80
Gaither, Alonzo Smith (Jake) 14
Gaither, Israel L. 65
Gamble, Kenny 85
Gans, Joe 91
Gantt, Harvey 1
Gardere, Jeffrey 76
Gardner, Chris 65
Gardner, Edward G. 45
Garner, Erroll 76
Garnett, Kevin 14, 70
Garrett, James F. 78
Garrett, Joyce Finley 59
Garrison, Zina 2
Garvin, Gerry 78
Gary, Willie E. 12
Gaskins, Eric 64
Gaskins, Rudy 74
Gaspard, Patrick 84
Gaston, Arthur George 3, 38, 59
Gaston, Cito 71
Gaston, Marilyn Hughes 60
Gates, Henry Louis, Jr. 3, 38, 67
Gates, Sylvester James, Jr. 15
Gaye, Marvin 2
Gaye, Nona 56
Gayle, Addison, Jr. 41
Gayle, Helene D. 3, 46
Gaynor, Gloria 36
Gentry, Alvin 23
George, Eddie 80
George, Nelson 12
George, Zelma Watson 42
Gervin, George 80
Ghostface Killah 90
Gibbs, Marla 86
Gibson, Althea 8, 43
Gibson, Bob 33
Gibson, Donald Bernard 40
Gibson, John Trusty 87
Gibson, Johnnie Mae 23
Gibson, Josh 22
Gibson, Kenneth Allen 6
Gibson, Ted 66
Gibson, Truman K., Jr. 60
Gibson, Tyrese 27, 62
Gibson, William F. 6
Giddings, Paula 11
Gidron, Richard D. 68
Gilbert, Christopher 50
Gilbert, John Wesley 91
Giles, Roscoe C. 93
Gill, Gerald 69
Gill, Johnny 51
Gill, Turner 83
Gilles, Ralph 61
Gillespie, Dizzy 1
Gilliam, Frank 23
Gilliam, Joe 31
Gilliam, Sam 16
Gilliard, Steve 69
Gilmore, Marshall 46
Gilpin, Charles Sidney 81
Ginuwine 35
Giovanni, Nikki 9, 39, 85
Gist, Carole 1
Givens, Adele 62
Givens, Robin 4, 25, 58
Givhan, Robin Deneen 72
Glanville, Douglas Metunwa 82

Gloster, Hugh Morris, Sr. **90**
Glover, Corey **34**
Glover, Danny **1, 24**
Glover, Donald **85**
Glover, Keith **79**
Glover, Nathaniel, Jr. **12**
Glover, Savion **14**
Goapele **55**
Goines, Donald **19**
Goings, Russell **59**
Goldberg, Whoopi **4, 33, 69**
Golden, Marita **19**
Golden, Thelma **10, 55**
Goldsberry, Ronald **18**
Golson, Benny **37**
Golston, Allan C. **55**
Gomes, Peter J. **15, 93**
Gomez, Jewelle **30**
Gomez-Preston, Cheryl **9**
Gomillion, Charles **90**
Goode, Mal **13**
Goode, W. Wilson **4**
Gooden, Dwight **20**
Gooding, Cuba, Jr. **16, 62**
Goodlett, Carlton B. **91**
Goodman, Al **87**
Goodnight, Paul **32**
Gorden, W. C. **71**
Gordon, Bruce S. **41, 53, 82**
Gordon, Carl **87**
Gordon, Dexter **25**
Gordon, Ed **10, 53**
Gordone, Charles **15**
Gordon-Reed, Annette **74**
Gordy, Berry, Jr. **1**
Goss, Carol A. **55**
Goss, Tom **23**
Gossett, Louis, Jr. **7**
Gotti, Irv **39**
Gourdin, Edward O. **93**
Gourdine, Meredith **33**
Gourdine, Simon **11**
Grace, George H. **48**
Graham, Lawrence Otis **12**
Graham, Lorenz **48**
Graham, Stedman **13**
Graham, Trevor **84**
Granderson, Curtis **66**
Granger, Lester B. **75**
Grant, Augustus O. **71**
Grant, Bernie **57**
Grant, Gwendolyn Goldsby **28**
Granville, Evelyn Boyd **36**
Gravely, Samuel L., Jr. **5, 49**
Graves, Butch **77**
Graves, Denyce Antoinette **19, 57**
Graves, Earl G. **1, 35**
Gray, Darius **69**
Gray, F. Gary **14, 49**
Gray, Farrah **59**
Gray, Fred **37**
Gray, Ida **41**
Gray, Macy **29**
Gray, Vincent C. **88**
Gray, William H., III **3**
Gray, Willie **46**
Gray, Yeshimbra "Shimmy" **55**
Greaves, William **38**
Greely, M. Gasby **27**
Green, A. C. **32**
Green, Al **13, 47, 74**
Green, Darrell **39, 74**
Green, Dennis **5, 45**

Green, Grant **56**
Green, Isaac H. **79**
Green, Jonathan **54**
Greene, Jimmy **74**
Greene, Joe **10**
Greene, Maurice **27, 77**
Greene, Petey **65**
Greene, Richard Thaddeus, Sr. **67**
Greenfield, Eloise **9**
Greenhouse, Bunnatine "Bunny" **57**
Greenlee, Sam **48**
Greenwood, Monique **38**
Greer, Hal **92**
Gregory, Ann **63**
Gregory, Dick **1, 54**
Gregory, Frederick **8, 51**
Gregory, Wilton **37**
Grier, David Alan **28**
Grier, Eliza Ann **90**
Grier, Mike **43**
Grier, Pam **9, 31, 86**
Grier, Roosevelt **13**
Griffey, Dick **89**
Griffey, Ken, Jr. **12, 73**
Griffin, Anthony **71**
Griffin, Bessie Blout **43**
Griffin, Johnny **71**
Griffin, LaShell **51**
Griffith, Mark Winston **8**
Griffith, Yolanda **25**
Griffith-Joyner, Florence **28**
Grimké, Archibald H. **9**
Grist, Reri **84**
Grooms, Henry R(andall) **50**
Guillaume, Robert **3, 48**
Guinier, Lani **7, 30**
Gumbel, Bryant **14, 80**
Gumbel, Greg **8**
Gunn, Moses **10**
Gurira, Danai **73**
Guru **84**
Guy, George "Buddy" **31**
Guy, Jasmine **2**
Guy, Rosa **5**
Guy-Sheftall, Beverly **13, 92**
Guyton, Tyree **9**
Gwynn, Tony **18, 83**
Haddon, Dietrick **55**
Hageman, Hans **36**
Hageman, Ivan **36**
Hailey, JoJo **22**
Hailey, K-Ci **22**
Hairston, Jester **88**
Hairston, Sam **88**
Hale, Clara **16**
Hale, Lorraine **8**
Haley, Alex **4**
Haley, George Williford Boyce **21**
Hall, Aaron **57**
Hall, Alvin D. **86**
Hall, Arsenio **58**
Hall, Arthur **39**
Hall, Elliott S. **24**
Hall, Juanita **62**
Hall, Kevan **61**
Hall, Lloyd A. **8**
Halliburton, Warren J. **49**
Ham, Cynthia Parker **58**
Hamblin, Ken **10**
Hamburg, Beatrix **84**
Hamburg, Margaret **78**
Hamer, Fannie Lou **6**
Hamilton, Anthony **61**

Hamilton, Samuel C. **47**
Hamilton, Lisa Gay **71**
Hamilton, Virginia **10**
Hamlin, Larry Leon **49, 62**
Hammond, Fred **23**
Hammonds, Evelynn **69**
Hammons, David **69**
Hampton, Fred **18**
Hampton, Henry **6**
Hampton, Lionel **17, 41**
Hancock, Herbie **20, 67**
Handy, W. C. **8**
Haney, Lee **77**
Hannah, Marc **10**
Hansberry, Lorraine **6**
Hansberry, Tony, II **93**
Hansberry, William Leo **11**
Hansen, Austin **88**
Hardaway, Anfernee (Penny) **13**
Hardaway, Tim **35**
Hardin Armstrong, Lil **39**
Harding, Vincent **67**
Hardison, Bethann **12**
Hardison, Kadeem **22**
Hare, Nathan **44**
Harkless, Necia Desiree **19**
Harmon, Clarence **26**
Harold, Erika **54**
Harper, Ben **34, 62**
Harper, Frances Ellen Watkins **11**
Harper, Hill **32, 65**
Harper, Michael S. **34**
Harper, Rachel M. **92**
Harrell, Andre **9, 30**
Harrington, Oliver W. **9**
Harris, Alice **7**
Harris, Barbara **12**
Harris, Barry **68**
Harris, Bernard A. **90**
Harris, Bill **72**
Harris, Carla A. **67**
Harris, Corey **39, 73**
Harris, E. Lynn **12, 33**
Harris, Eddy L. **18**
Harris, Gary L. **87**
Harris, James **79**
Harris, Jay T. **19**
Harris, Jessica B. **91**
Harris, Kamala D. **64**
Harris, Leslie **6**
Harris, Lyle Ashton **83**
Harris, Marcelite Jordon **16**
Harris, Mary Styles **31**
Harris, Maya Lakshmi **88**
Harris, Monica **18**
Harris, Patricia Roberts **2**
Harris, Richard E. **61**
Harris, Robin **7**
Harris, Sylvia **70**
Harris, Wesley L. **92**
Harris-Lacewell, Melissa **81**
Harrison, Alvin **28**
Harrison, Calvin **28**
Harrison, Charles **72**
Harris-Stewart, Lusia **90**
Harsh, Vivian Gordon **14**
Hart, Alvin Youngblood **61**
Harvard, Beverly **11**
Harvey, Steve **18, 58**
Harvey, William R. **42**
Haskins, Clem **23**
Haskins, James **36, 54**
Hassell, Leroy Rountree, Sr. **41**

Hastie, William H. **8**
Hastings, Alcee L. **16**
Hatcher, Andrew T. **90**
Hatcher, Richard G. **55**
Hatchett, Glenda **32**
Hathaway, Donny **18**
Hathaway, Isaac Scott **33**
Hathaway, Lalah **57, 88**
Hawkins, Augustus F. **68**
Hawkins, Coleman **9**
Hawkins, Connie **91**
Hawkins, Erskine **14**
Hawkins, La-Van **17, 54**
Hawkins, Screamin' Jay **30**
Hawkins, Steven **14**
Hawkins, Tramaine **16**
Hawkins, Walter **87**
Hayden, Carla D. **47**
Hayden, Palmer **13**
Hayden, Robert **12**
Hayes, Bob **77**
Hayes, Cecil N. **46**
Hayes, Dennis **54**
Hayes, Elvin **93**
Hayes, Isaac **20, 58, 73**
Hayes, James C. **10**
Hayes, Roland **4**
Hayes, Teddy **40**
Haygood, Wil **83**
Haynes, George Edmund **8**
Haynes, Marques **22**
Haynes, Roy **87**
Haynes, Trudy **44**
Haysbert, Dennis **42**
Haysbert, Raymond V., Sr. **87**
Haywood, Gar Anthony **43**
Haywood, Jimmy **58**
Haywood, Margaret A. **24**
Hazel, Darryl B. **50**
Healy, James Augustine **30**
Healy, Michael **90**
Heard, Gar **25**
Heard, Nathan C. **45**
Hearns, Thomas **29**
Hedgeman, Anna Arnold **22**
Height, Dorothy I. **2, 23, 78**
Hemphill, Essex **10**
Hemphill, Jessie Mae **33, 59**
Hemsley, Sherman **19**
Henderson, Cornelius Langston **26**
Henderson, David **53**
Henderson, Fletcher **32**
Henderson, Gordon **5**
Henderson, Henry Fairfax, Jr. **89**
Henderson, Jeff **72**
Henderson, Rickey **28, 78**
Henderson, Stephen E. **45**
Henderson, Thelton E. **68**
Henderson, Wade J. **14**
Henderson, Zelma **71**
Hendrix, Jimi **10**
Hendryx, Nona **56**
Hendy, Francis **47**
Henries, A. Doris Banks **44**
Henry, Aaron **19**
Henry, Clarence "Frogman" **46**
Henry, Troy **85**
Henson, Darrin **33**
Henson, Josiah **90**
Henson, Matthew **2**
Henson, Taraji P. **58, 77**
Herbert, Bob **63**
Hercules, Frank **44**

Herenton, Willie W. **24, 81**
Herman, Alexis M. **15**
Hernandez, Aileen Clarke **13**
Herndon, Alonzo Franklin **89**
Herndon, Angelo **90**
Hernton, Calvin C. **51**
Hickman, Fred **11**
Higginbotham, A. Leon, Jr. **13, 25**
Higginbotham, Jay C. **37**
Higginsen, Vy **65**
Hightower, Dennis F. **13**
Hill, Andrew **66**
Hill, Anita **5, 65**
Hill, Bonnie Guiton **20**
Hill, Calvin **19**
Hill, Donna **32**
Hill, Dulé **29**
Hill, Grant **13**
Hill, Hugh Morgan **83**
Hill, Janet **19**
Hill, Jesse, Jr. **13**
Hill, Lauryn **20, 53**
Hill, Leslie Pinckney **44**
Hill, Marc Lamont **80**
Hill, Oliver W. **24, 63**
Hill, Peter **92**
Hillard, Terry **25**
Hillary, Barbara **65**
Hilliard, Asa Grant, III **66**
Hilliard, David **7**
Hilliard, Earl F. **24**
Hilliard, Wendy **53**
Hilson, Keri **84**
Himes, Chester **8**
Hinderas, Natalie **5**
Hine, Darlene Clark **24**
Hines, Earl "Fatha" **39**
Hines, Garrett **35**
Hines, Gregory **1, 42**
Hinton, Milt **30**
Hinton, William Augustus **8**
Hoagland, Everett H. **45**
Hobson, Julius W. **44**
Hobson, Mellody **40**
Hogan, Beverly Wade **50**
Holder, Eric H., Jr. **9, 76**
Holder, Laurence **34**
Holdsclaw, Chamique **24**
Holiday, Billie **1**
Holland, Endesha Ida Mae **3, 57**
Holland, Kimberly N. **62**
Holland, Robert, Jr. **11**
Holland-Dozier-Holland **36**
Holloway, Brenda **65**
Hollowell, Donald L. **57**
Holmes, Amy **69**
Holmes, Clint **57**
Holmes, Hamilton E. **82**
Holmes, Larry **20, 68**
Holmes, Santonio **87**
Holmes, Shannon **70**
Holsey, Lucius Henry **92**
Holstein, Casper **89**
Holt, Lester **66**
Holt, Nora **38**
Holt Baker, Arlene **73**
Holton, Hugh, Jr. **39**
Holyfield, Evander **6**
Honeywood, Varnette P. **54, 88**
Honoré, Russel L. **64**
Hood, James Walker **91**
Hooker, John Lee **30**
hooks, bell **5, 90**

Hooks, Benjamin L. **2, 85**
Hooks, Robert **76**
Hope, John **8**
Hope, Lugenia Burns **89**
Hopkins, Bernard **35, 69**
Hopkins, Donald R. **89**
Hopkins, Lightnin' **83**
Horn, Shirley **32, 56**
Horne, Frank **44**
Horne, Lena **5, 86**
Horsford, Steven **88**
Horton, Andre **33**
Horton, Gladys **92**
Horton, James Oliver **58**
Horton, Suki **33**
Houghton, Israel **92**
House, Son **8**
Houston, Charles Hamilton **4**
Houston, Cissy **20, 83**
Houston, Whitney **7, 28, 83**
Howard, Ayanna **65**
Howard, Desmond **16, 58**
Howard, Juwan **15**
Howard, M. William, Jr. **26**
Howard, Michelle **28**
Howard, Ryan **65**
Howard, Sherri **36**
Howard, Terrence Dashon **59**
Howell, Ayinde **91**
Howlin' Wolf **9**
Howroyd, Janice Bryant **42**
Hoyte, Lenon **50**
Hrabowski, Freeman A., III **22**
Hubbard, Arnette Rhinehart **38**
Hubbard, Freddie **75**
Hudlin, Reginald **9, 86**
Hudlin, Warrington **9**
Hudson, Cheryl **15**
Hudson, Ernie **72**
Hudson, Jennifer **63, 83**
Hudson, Wade **15**
Huff, Leon **86**
Huggins, Edie **71**
Huggins, Larry **21**
Huggins, Nathan Irvin **52**
Hughes, Albert **7**
Hughes, Allen **7**
Hughes, Cathy **27**
Hughes, Dora **88**
Hughes, Ebony **57**
Hughes, Langston **4**
Hughley, D. L. **23, 76**
Hull, Akasha Gloria **45**
Humphrey, Bobbi **20**
Humphries, Frederick **20**
Hunt, Darnell **92**
Hunt, Richard **6**
Hunter, Alberta **42**
Hunter, Clementine **45**
Hunter, Torii **43**
Hunter-Gault, Charlayne **6, 31**
Hurston, Zora Neale **3**
Hurt, Byron **61**
Hurt, Mississippi John **84**
Hurtt, Harold **46**
Hutch, Willie **62**
Hutcherson, Hilda Yvonne **54**
Hutchinson, Earl Ofari **24**
Hutson, Jean Blackwell **16**
Hyde, Cowan F. "Bubba" **47**
Hyman, Earle **25, 79**
Hyman, Phyllis **19**
Ice Cube **8, 30, 60**

Iceberg Slim **11**
Ice-T **6, 31**
Iman, Chanel **66**
Ifill, Gwen **28**
Imes, Elmer Samuel **39**
India.Arie **34**
Ingram, James **84**
Ingram, Rex **5**
Innis, Roy **5**
Irvin, Michael **64**
Irvin, Monford Merrill **31**
Irvin, Vernon **65**
Irving, Larry, Jr. **12**
Irvis, K. Leroy **67**
Isaacs, John **76**
Isley, Marvin **87**
Isley, Ronald **25, 56**
Iverson, Allen **24, 46**
Ivey, Phil **72**
Ja Rule **35, 91**
Jackson, Alexine Clement **22**
Jackson, Alphonso R. **48**
Jackson, Brenda **87**
Jackson, Earl **31**
Jackson, Edison O. **67**
Jackson, Frank G. **76**
Jackson, Fred James **25**
Jackson, George **14**
Jackson, George **19**
Jackson, Hal **41**
Jackson, Isaiah **3**
Jackson, Jamea **64**
Jackson, James A. **90**
Jackson, Janet **6, 30, 68**
Jackson, Jermaine **79**
Jackson, Jesse **1, 27, 72**
Jackson, Jesse, Jr. **14, 45, 81**
Jackson, Joe **78**
Jackson, John **36**
Jackson, Judith D. **57**
Jackson, Lisa **77**
Jackson, Mae **57**
Jackson, Mahalia **5**
Jackson, Mannie **14**
Jackson, Mary **73**
Jackson, Maynard **2, 41**
Jackson, Michael **19, 53, 76**
Jackson, Millie **25**
Jackson, Milt **26**
Jackson, Rampage **83**
Jackson, Randy **40**
Jackson, Reggie **15**
Jackson, Rickey **88**
Jackson, Samuel **8, 63**
Jackson, Sheneska **18**
Jackson, Shirley Ann **12**
Jackson, Tito **81**
Jackson, Tom **70**
Jackson, Vera **40**
Jackson Lee, Sheila **20**
Jacob, John E. **2**
Jacobs, Regina **38**
Jacquet, Illinois **49**
Jaheim **58**
Jakes, Thomas "T. D." **17, 43**
Jamal, Ahmad **69**
Jamerson, James **59**
James, Charles H., III **62**
James, Daniel, Jr. **16**
James, Donna A. **51**
James, Etta **13, 52**
James, G. Larry **74**
James, Juanita **13**

James, LeBron **46, 78**
James, Rick **19**
James, Sharpe **23, 69**
James, Skip **38**
Jamison, Judith **7, 67**
Jarreau, Al **21, 65**
Jarrett, Valerie **73**
Jarrett, Vernon D. **42**
Jarvis, Charlene Drew **21**
Jarvis, Erich **67**
Jarvis, Kristen **85**
Jasper, John J. **91**
Jasper, Kenji **39**
Jay-Z **27, 69**
Jazzy Jeff **32**
Jealous, Benjamin **70**
Jefferson, Blind Lemon **81**
Jefferson, Denise **87**
Jefferson, Mildred Fay **89**
Jefferson, William J. **25, 72**
Jeffries, Leonard **8**
Jemison, Mae C. **1, 35**
Jemison, Major L. **48**
Jenifer, Franklyn G. **2**
Jenkins, Beverly **14**
Jenkins, Ella **15**
Jenkins, Ray **77**
Jennings, Lyfe **56, 69**
Jerkins, Rodney **31**
Jeter, Claude **75**
Jeter, Derek **27, 93**
Jimmy Jam **13**
Joe, Yolanda **21**
John, Daymond **23**
Johns, Vernon **38**
Johnson, Angela **52**
Johnson, Anthony M. **92**
Johnson, Avery **62**
Johnson, Beverly **2**
Johnson, Buddy **36**
Johnson, Charles **1, 82**
Johnson, Charles S. **12**
Johnson, Chris **92**
Johnson, Clifford "Connie" **52**
Johnson, Dennis **89**
Johnson, Earvin "Magic" **3, 39**
Johnson, Eddie Bernice **8, 90**
Johnson, Eunice W. **83**
Johnson, Fenton **91**
Johnson, George E. **29**
Johnson, Georgia Douglas **41**
Johnson, Gus **92**
Johnson, Hall **90**
Johnson, Hank, Jr. **80**
Johnson, Harry E. **57**
Johnson, Harvey, Jr. **24, 82**
Johnson, J. J. **37**
Johnson, Jack **8**
Johnson, James Weldon **5**
Johnson, Je'Caryous **63**
Johnson, Jeh C. **76**
Johnson, Jeh Vincent **44**
Johnson, John H. **3, 54**
Johnson, Johnnie **56**
Johnson, Katherine (Coleman Goble) **61**
Johnson, Kevin **70**
Johnson, Keyshawn **91**
Johnson, Larry **28**
Johnson, Leroy R. **89**
Johnson, Levi **48**
Johnson, Lonnie **85**
Johnson, Lonnie G. **32, 93**

Johnson, Mamie "Peanut" 40
Johnson, Mat 31
Johnson, Michael 13
Johnson, Mordecai Wyatt 79
Johnson, Norma L. Holloway 17
Johnson, R. M. 36
Johnson, Rafer 33
Johnson, Robert 2
Johnson, Robert L. 3, 39
Johnson, Robert T. 17
Johnson, Rodney Van 28
Johnson, Sheila Crump 48
Johnson, Shoshana 47
Johnson, Virginia 9
Johnson, William 91
Johnson, William Henry 3
Johnson-George, Tamara 79
Jolley, Willie 28
Jones, Absalom 52
Jones, Alex 64
Jones, Bill T. 1, 46, 80
Jones, Bobby 20
Jones, Booker T. 84
Jones, Carl 7
Jones, Caroline 29
Jones, Clara Stanton 51
Jones, Cobi N'Gai 18
Jones, Cullen 73
Jones, Deacon 92
Jones, Donell 29
Jones, Doris W. 62
Jones, E. Edward, Sr. 45
Jones, Ed "Too Tall" 46
Jones, Edith Mae Irby 65
Jones, Edward P. 43, 67
Jones, Elaine R. 7, 45
Jones, Elvin 14, 68
Jones, Emil, Jr. 74
Jones, Etta 35
Jones, Eugene Kinckle 79
Jones, Frederick McKinley 68
Jones, Gayl 37
Jones, Hank 57, 86
Jones, Ingrid Saunders 18
Jones, James Earl 3, 49, 79
Jones, John 89
Jones, Jonah 39
Jones, K. C. 83
Jones, Lois Mailou 13
Jones, Lou 64
Jones, Marion 21, 66
Jones, Merlakia 34
Jones, Orlando 30
Jones, Paul R. 76
Jones, Quincy 8, 30
Jones, Randy 35
Jones, Robert Elijah 90
Jones, Robert G. 81
Jones, Sam 85
Jones, Sarah 39
Jones, Sharon 86
Jones, Thad 68
Jones, Thomas W. 41
Jones, Van 70
Jones, Wayne 53
Jones, William A., Jr. 61
Joplin, Scott 6
Jordan, Barbara 4, 78
Jordan, Eddie 82
Jordan, Eddie 83
Jordan, June 7, 35
Jordan, Michael 6, 21
Jordan, Montell 23

Jordan, Vernon E. 3, 35
Joseph, Kathie-Ann 56
Josey, E. J. 10
Joyce, Dru 81
Joyner, Marjorie Stewart 26
Joyner, Matilda Sissieretta 15
Joyner, Tom 19, 90
Joyner-Kersee, Jackie 5
Julian, Hubert 90
Julian, Percy Lavon 6
July, William 27
Just, Ernest Everett 3
Justice, David 18
Kaigler, Denise 63
Kaiser, Cecil 42
Kandi 83
Kani, Karl 10
Karenga, Maulana 10, 71
Karim, Benjamin 61
Kaufman, Monica 66
Kay, Ulysses 37
Kearney, Janis 54
Kearse, Amalya Lyle 12
Keckley, Elizabeth 90
Kee, John P. 43
Keene, John 73
Keflezighi, Meb 49
Keith, Damon J. 16, 74
Keith, Floyd A. 61
Kelis 58
Kelley, Cliff 75
Kelley, Elijah 65
Kelley, Malcolm David 59
Kellogg, Clark 64
Kelly, Patrick 3
Kelly, R. 18, 44, 71
Kem 47
Kendrick, Erika 57
Kendricks, Eddie 22
Kennedy, Adrienne 11
Kennedy, Florynce 12, 33
Kennedy, Randall 40
Kennedy-Overton, Jayne Harris 46
Kenney, John A., Jr. 48
Kenoly, Ron 45
Kenyatta, Robin 54
Kerry, Leon G. 46
Keyes, Alan L. 11
Keys, Alicia 32, 68
Khan, Chaka 12, 50
Khanga, Yelena 6
Kid Cudi 83
Kidd, Jason 86
Kidd, Mae Street 39
Killens, John O. 54
Killings, Debra 57
Killingsworth, Cleve, Jr. 54
Kilpatrick, Carolyn Cheeks 16
Kilpatrick, Kwame 34, 71
Kimbro, Dennis 10
Kimbro, Henry A. 25
Kimbro, Warren 76
Kincaid, Bernard 28
Kincaid, Jamaica 4
King, Alonzo 38
King, B. B. 7
King, Barbara 22
King, Bernice 4, 81
King, Colbert I. 69
King, Coretta Scott 3, 57
King, Dexter 10
King, Don 14
King, Freddie 92

King, Gayle 19
King, Martin Luther, III 20
King, Martin Luther, Jr. 1
King, Martin Luther, Sr. 89
King, Preston 28
King, Reatha Clark 65
King, Regina 22, 45
King, Robert Arthur 58
King, Robert Hillary 84
King, Teresa 80
King, Woodie, Jr. 27
King, Yolanda 6
King Curtis 92
Kirby, George 14
Kirk, Ron 11, 75
Kitt, Eartha 16, 75
Kitt, Sandra 23
Kittles, Rick 51
Kitwana, Bakari 86
Klugh, Earl 59
Knight, Etheridge 37
Knight, Gladys 16, 66
Knight, Marie 80
Knight, Suge 11, 30
Knowles, Tina 61
Knowling, Robert E., Jr. 38
Knox, Simmie 49
Knuckles, Frankie 42
Komunyakaa, Yusef 9
Kong, B. Waine 50
Kool Moe Dee 37
Kotto, Yaphet 7
Kountz, Samuel L. 10
Kravitz, Lenny 10, 34
KRS-One 34
K-Swift 73
Kunjufu, Jawanza 3, 50
Kweli, Talib 93
La Salle, Eriq 12
LaBelle, Patti 13, 30
LaChanze 93
Lacy, Sam 30, 46
Ladd, Ernie 64
Ladner, Joyce A. 42
Lafontant, Jewel Stradford 3, 51
Lampkin, Daisy 19
Lampley, Oni Faida 43, 71
Lane, Charles 3
Lane, Dick 92
Lane, Lunsford 93
Lane, Vincent 5
Lane, William Henry 90
Langford, Larry P. 74
Langhart Cohen, Janet 19, 60
Lanier, Bob 47
Lanier, Willie 33
Lankford, Ray 23
Larkin, Barry 24
Larrieux, Amel 63
Lars, Byron 32
Larsen, Nella 10
Laryea, Thomas Davies, III 67
Lashley, Bobby 63
Lassiter, Roy 24
Lateef, Yusef 91
Lathan, Sanaa 27
Latimer, Lewis H. 4
Lattany, Kristin Hunter 88
Lattimore, Kenny 35
LaVette, Bettye 85
Lavizzo-Mourey, Risa 48
Lawless, Theodore K. 8
Lawrence, Jacob 4, 28

Lawrence, Martin 6, 27
Lawrence, Robert H., Jr. 16
Lawrence-Lightfoot, Sara 10
Laws, Hubert 90
Lawson, James M., Jr. 90
Lawson, Jennifer 1, 50
Layton, William 87
Leadbelly 82
Leary, Kathryn D. 10
Leavell, Dorothy R. 17
Ledisi 73
Lee, Annie Frances 22
Lee, Barbara 25
Lee, Bertram M., Sr. 46
Lee, Canada 8
Lee, Consuela 84
Lee, Debra L. 62
Lee, Eric P. 79
Lee, Joe A. 45
Lee, Joie 1
Lee, Leslie 85
Lee, Malcolm D. 75
Lee, Raphael C. 87
Lee, Spike 5, 19, 86
Lee-Smith, Hughie 5, 22
Leevy, Carrol M. 42
Leffall, Lasalle, Jr. 3, 64
Legend, John 67
Leggs, Kingsley 62
Leland, Mickey 2
Lemmons, Kasi 20
Lennox, Betty 31
LeNoire, Rosetta 37
Lenox, Adriane 59
Leon, Kenny 10
Leonard, Buck 67
Leonard, Sugar Ray 15
Leslie, Lisa 16, 73
Lester, Bill 42, 85
Lester, Julius 9
Lesure, James 64
LeTang, Henry 66
Letson, Al 39
Levert, Eddie 70
Levert, Gerald 22, 59
Lewis, Ananda 28
Lewis, Aylwin B. 51, 88
Lewis, Butch 71
Lewis, Byron E. 13
Lewis, Carl 4
Lewis, David Levering 9
Lewis, Delano 7
Lewis, Edmonia 10
Lewis, Edward T. 21
Lewis, Emmanuel 36
Lewis, Henry 38
Lewis, John 2, 46, 83
Lewis, Marvin 51, 87
Lewis, Norman 39
Lewis, Oliver 56
Lewis, Ramsey 35, 70
Lewis, Ray 33
Lewis, Reginald F. 6
Lewis, Samella 25
Lewis, Shirley A. R. 14
Lewis, Terry 13
Lewis, Thomas 19
Lewis, William Henry 89
Lewis, William M., Jr. 40
Lewis-Thornton, Rae 32
Ligging, Alfred, III 43
Ligon, Glenn 82
Lil' Kim 28

Lil Wayne 66, 84
Liles, Kevin 42
Lincoln, Abbey 3, 88
Lincoln, C. Eric 38
Lindsey, Tommie 51
Lipscomb, Mance 49
LisaRaye 27
Lister, Marquita 65
Liston, Sonny 33
Little, Benilde 21
Little, Floyd 86
Little, Larry 90
Little, Robert L. 2
Little Milton 36, 54
Little Richard 15
Little Walter 36
Littlepage, Craig 35
LL Cool J 16, 49
Llewellyn, J. Bruce 13, 85
Lloyd, Earl 26
Lloyd, John Henry "Pop" 30
Lloyd, Reginald 64
Locke, Alain 10
Locke, Attica 85
Locke, Eddie 44
Lofton, James 42
Lofton, Kenny 12
Logan, Onnie Lee 14
Logan, Rayford W. 40
Loguen, J. W. 91
Lomax, Louis E. 90
Lomax, Michael L. 58
Long, Eddie L. 29, 89
Long, Huey 79
Long, Loretta 58
Long, Nia 17
Long, Richard Alexander 65
Lopes, Davey 92
Lopes, Lisa "Left Eye" 36
Lorde, Audre 6
Lott, Ronnie 9
Loueke, Lionel 88
Louis, Errol T. 8
Louis, Joe 5
Loury, Glenn 36
Love, Darlene 23, 92
Love, Ed 58
Love, Laura 50
Love, Nat 9
Love, Reggie 77
Lovell, Whitfield 74
Lover, Ed 10
Loving, Alvin, Jr. 35, 53
Loving, Mildred 69
Lowe, Herbert 57
Lowe, Sidney 64
Lowery, Joseph 2
Lowery, Myron 80
Lowry, A. Leon 60
Lucas, John 7
Lucie, Lawrence 80
Lucien, Jon 66
Luckett, Letoya 61
Lucy, William 50
Lucy Foster, Autherine 35
Ludacris 37, 60
Luke, Derek 61
Lumbly, Carl 47
Lumet, Jenny 80
Luna, Donyale 88
Lyles, Lester Lawrence 31
Lymon, Frankie 22
Lynch, Shola 61

Lyons, Henry 12
Lyttle, Hulda Margaret 14
Mabley, Moms 15
Mabrey, Vicki 26
Mabry, Marcus 70
Mac, Bernie 29, 61, 72
Mackey, Biz 82
Mackey, Nathaniel 75
Madhubuti, Haki 7, 85
Madison, Joseph E. 17
Madison, Paula 37
Madison, Romell 45
Madlib 88
Mahal, Taj 39
Mahorn, Rick 60
Maitreya, Sananda 85
Majette, Denise 41
Major, Clarence 9
Majors, Jeff 41
Malco, Romany 71
Mallett, Conrad, Jr. 16
Mallory, Mark 62
Malone, Annie 13
Malone, Karl 18, 51, 90
Malone, Maurice 32
Malone, Moses 79
Malone Jones, Vivian 59
Malveaux, Floyd 54
Malveaux, Julianne 32, 70
Malveaux, Suzanne 88
Mane, Gucci 91
Manigault, Earl "The Goat" 15
Manigault-Stallworth, Omarosa 69
Manley, Audrey Forbes 16
Mann, Tamela 92
Manning, Frankie 78
Marable, Manning 10
March, William Carrington 56
Mariner, Jonathan 41
Marino, Eugene Antonio 30
Mario 71
Marrow, Queen Esther 24
Marsalis, Branford 34
Marsalis, Delfeayo 41
Marsalis, Ellis 90
Marsalis, Wynton 16, 90
Marsh, Henry, III 32
Marshall, Bella 22
Marshall, Kerry James 59
Marshall, Paule 7, 77
Marshall, Thurgood 1, 44
Martin, Darnell 43, 78
Martin, Helen 31
Martin, Jesse L. 31
Martin, Louis E. 16
Martin, Roberta 58
Martin, Roland S. 49, 84
Martin, Ruby Grant 49
Martin, Sara 38
Mase 24
Mason, Biddy 89
Mason, Felicia 31
Mason, Herman, Jr. 83
Mason, Ronald 27
Massaquoi, Hans J. 30
Massenburg, Kedar 23
Massey, Brandon 40
Massey, Walter E. 5, 45
Massie, Samuel Proctor, Jr. 29
Master P 21
Matejka, Adrian 87
Mathis, Greg 26
Mathis, Johnny 20

Matson, Ollie 93
Matthews, Benjamin 93
Matthews, Mark 59
Matthews Shatteen, Westina 51
Matzeliger, Jan 93
Maupin, John E., Jr. 92
Maxey, Randall 46
Maxis, Theresa 62
Maxwell 20, 81
May, Derrick 41
Mayfield, Curtis 2, 43
Mayhew, Martin R. 76
Mayhew, Richard 39
Maynard, Nancy Hicks 73
Maynard, Robert C. 7
Maynor, Dorothy 19
Mayo, Whitman 32
Mays, Benjamin E. 7
Mays, Leslie A. 41
Mays, William G. 34
Mays, Willie 3
Mayweather, Floyd, Jr. 57
MC Breed 75
M.C. Hammer 20, 80
MC Lyte 34
McAdoo, Bob 75
McAnulty, William E., Jr. 66
McBay, Henry C. 91
McBride, Bryant 18
McBride, Chi 73
McBride, James 35, 87
McCabe, Jewell Jackson 10
McCall, H. Carl 27
McCall, Nathan 8
McCann, Renetta 44
McCarthy, Sandy 64
McCarty, Osceola 16
McCauley, Gina 76
McClellan, George Marion 91
McClendon, Lisa 61
McClinton, Marion Isaac 77
McClurkin, Donnie 25
McCoo, Marilyn 53
McCoy, Elijah 8
McCrary Anthony, Crystal 70
McCray, Nikki 18
McCullough, Geraldine 58, 79
McDaniel, Hattie 5
McDaniel, Randall Cornell 81
McDaniels, Ralph 79
McDonald, Audra 20, 62
McDonald, Erroll 1
McDonald, Gabrielle Kirk 20
McDougall, Gay J. 11, 43
McDuffie, Dwayne 62
McEwen, Mark 5
McFadden, Bernice L. 39
McFarlan, Tyron 60
McFarland, Roland 49
McFerrin, Bobby 68
McGee, Charles 10
McGee, James D. 74
McGee, James Madison 46
McGill, Anthony 76
McGlowan, Angela 64, 86
McGrady, Tracy 80
McGriff, Fred 24
McGriff, Jimmy 72
McGruder, Aaron 28, 56
McGruder, Robert 22, 35
McGuire, Raymond J. 57
McHenry, Donald F. 83
McJunkin, George 93

McKay, Claude 6
McKay, Nellie Yvonne 17, 57
McKee, Lonette 12
McKenzie, Vashti M. 29
McKinney, Cynthia 11, 52, 74
McKinney, Nina Mae 40
McKinney-Whetstone, Diane 27
McKinnon, Isaiah 9
McKissack, Leatrice 80
McKissick, Floyd B. 3
McKnight, Brian 18, 34
McLean, Jackie 78
McLendon, John B., Jr. 89
McLeod, Gus 27
McMillan, Rosalynn A. 36
McMillan, Terry 4, 17, 53
McMillan, Tracy 93
McMurray, Georgia L. 36
McNabb, Donovan 29
McNair, Ronald 3, 58
McNair, Steve 22, 47, 79
McNeil, Lori 1
McPhail, Sharon 2
McPherson, David 32
McPherson, James Alan 70
McQueen, Butterfly 6, 54
McRae, Carmen 77
McRae, Hal 84
McTell, Blind Willie 89
McWhorter, John 35
McWorter, Free Frank 91
Meadows, Tim 30
Meek, Carrie 6, 36
Meek, Kendrick 41, 89
Meeks, Gregory 25
Meeks, James T. 92
Mehretu, Julie 85
Mell, Patricia 49
Melton, Frank 81
Melton, Harold D. 79
Memphis Minnie 33
Menard, John Willis 90
Mengestu, Dinaw 66
Mercado-Valdes, Frank 43
Meredith, James H. 11
Merkerson, S. Epatha 47, 83
Metcalfe, Ralph 26
Method Man 81
Mfume, Kweisi 6, 41
Michaux, Solomon Lightfoot 91
Micheaux, Oscar 7
Michele, Michael 31
Mickelbury, Penny 28
Miles, Buddy 69
Millender-McDonald, Juanita 21, 61
Miller, Bebe 3
Miller, Cheryl 10, 74
Miller, Dorie 29
Miller, Larry G. 72
Miller, Marcus 84
Miller, Omar Benson 93
Miller, Reggie 33
Miller, Warren F., Jr. 53
Miller, Wentworth 75
Miller-Travis, Vernice 64
Millines Dziko, Trish 28
Millner, Denene 76
Mills, Florence 22
Mills, Joseph C. 51
Mills, Sam 33
Mills, Stephanie 36
Mills, Steve 47
Milner, Ron 39

Milton, DeLisha 31
Minaj, Nicki 86
Mingo, Frank 32
Mingus, Charles 15
Minoso, Minnie 89
Minor, DeWayne 32
Mitchell, Arthur 2, 47
Mitchell, Arthur Wergs 91
Mitchell, Brian Stokes 21
Mitchell, Clarence M., Jr. 88
Mitchell, Corinne 8
Mitchell, Elvis 67
Mitchell, Kel 66
Mitchell, Leona 42
Mitchell, Loften 31
Mitchell, Nicole 66
Mitchell, Parren J. 42, 66
Mitchell, Russ 21, 73
Mitchell, Sam 82
Mitchell, Shireen 89
Mitchell, Stephanie 36
Mo', Keb' 36
Mohammed, Nazr 64
Mohammed, W. Deen 27
Mokae, Zakes 80
Monáe, Janelle 86
Monica 21
Mo'Nique 35, 84
Monk, Art 38, 73
Monk, Thelonious 1
Monroe, Bryan 71
Monroe, Earl 89
Monroe, Mary 35
Montgomery, Isaiah T. 91
Montgomery, Tim 41
Montgomery, Wes 88
Moody, James 83
Moody-Adams, Michele 76
Moon, Warren 8, 66
Mooney, Paul 37
Moore, Barbara C. 49
Moore, Chante 26
Moore, Dorothy Rudd 46
Moore, Gwendolynne S. 55
Moore, Harry T. 29
Moore, Jessica Care 30
Moore, Johnny B. 38
Moore, Juanita 83
Moore, LeRoi 72
Moore, Melba 21
Moore, Minyon 45
Moore, Shemar 21
Moore, Undine Smith 28
Moore, Wes 86
Moorer, Michael 19
Moose, Charles 40
Moran, Jason 89
Morgan, Garrett 1
Morgan, Gertrude 63
Morgan, Irene 65
Morgan, Joe Leonard 9
Morgan, Rose 11
Morgan, Tracy 61
Morial, Ernest "Dutch" 26
Morial, Marc H. 20, 51
Morón, Alonzo G. 91
Morris, Garrett 31
Morris, Greg 28
Morris, Raheem 77
Morrison, Sam 50
Morrison, Toni 2, 15, 86
Morrison, Vanessa 84
Morton, Azie Taylor 48

Morton, Ferdinand Q. 90
Morton, Frederick A., Jr. 93
Morton, Jelly Roll 29
Morton, Joe 18
Mos Def 30
Moses, Edwin 8
Moses, Gilbert 12
Moses, Robert Parris 11
Mosley, Shane 32
Mosley, Walter 5, 25, 68
Moss, Carlton 17
Moss, J. 64
Moss, Otis, Jr. 72
Moss, Otis, III 72
Moss, Preacher 63
Moss, Randy 23, 90
Mossell, Gertrude Bustill 40
Mossell, Nathan Francis 91
Moten, Etta 18
Motley, Archibald, Jr. 30
Motley, Constance Baker 10, 55
Motley, Marion 26
Moton, Robert Russa 83
Mourning, Alonzo 17, 44
Moutoussamy-Ashe, Jeanne 7
Mowry, Jess 7
Mowry, Tamera 79
Mowry, Tia 78
Moyo, Karega Kofi 36
Moyo, Yvette Jackson 36
Muhammad, Ava 31
Muhammad, Elijah 4
Muhammad, Jabir Herbert 72
Muhammad, Khallid Abdul 10, 31
Mullen, Harryette 34
Mullen, Nicole C. 45
Murphy, Eddie 4, 20, 61
Murphy, John H. 42
Murphy, Laura M. 43
Murray, Albert L. 33
Murray, Cecil 12, 47
Murray, Eddie 12
Murray, Lenda 10
Murray, Pauli 38
Murray, Tai 47
Murrell, Sylvia Marilyn 49
Muse, Clarence Edouard 21
Musiq 37, 84
Mya 35
Myers, Walter Dean 8, 70
Myles, Kim 69
Nabrit, Samuel Milton 47
Nagin, Ray 42, 57, 88
Nail, John E. 92
Nance, Cynthia 71
Nanula, Richard D. 20
Napoleon, Benny N. 23
Nas 33
Nash, Diane 72
Nash, Joe 55
Nash, Johnny 40
Nash, Niecy 66
Nash, Shannon King 84
Nate Dogg 92
Naylor, Gloria 10, 42
Ndegeocello, Meshell 15, 83
Neal, Elise 29
Neal, Larry 38
Neal, Mark Anthony 74
Neal, Raful 44
Neals, Otto 73
Nelly 32, 90
Nelson, Jill 6, 54

Nelson, Sophia A. 93
Nelson, Stanley 92
Nelson Meigs, Andrea 48
Neville, Aaron 21
Neville, Arthel 53
Newcombe, Don 24
Newkirk, Pamela 69
Newman, David 76
Newman, Lester C. 51
Newsome, Ozzie 26
Newton, Huey 2
Ne-Yo 65
Ngaujah, Sahr 86
Nicholas, Denise 82
Nicholas, Fayard 20, 57
Nicholas, Harold 20
Nichols, Nichelle 11
Nissel, Angela 42
Nix, Robert N. C., Jr. 51
N'Namdi, George R. 17
Noble, Gil 76
Noble, Ronald 46
Norman, Christina 47
Norman, Jessye 5
Norman, Maidie 20
Norman, Pat 10
Norris, Michele 83
Norton, Eleanor Holmes 7, 93
Norton, Meredith 72
Notorious B.I.G. 20
Nottage, Lynn 66
Nugent, Richard Bruce 39
Nunn, Annetta 43
Nutter, Michael 69
Obadele, Imari 84
Obama, Barack 49, 74, 91
Obama, Michelle 61, 90
O'Brien, Soledad 88
Odetta 37, 74
Odom, Lamar 81
Oglesby, Zena 12
Ogletree, Charles, Jr. 12, 47
O'Grady, Lorraine 73
Ojikutu, Bayo 66
Ojikutu, Bisola 65
Ol' Dirty Bastard 52
Olden, Georg(e) 44
O'Leary, Hazel 6
Oliver, Jerry 37
Oliver, Joe "King" 42
Oliver, John J., Jr. 48
Oliver, Kimberly 60
Oliver, Pam 54
O'Neal, Rodney 88
O'Neal, Ron 46
O'Neal, Shaquille 8, 30
O'Neal, Stanley 38, 67
O'Neil, Buck 19, 59
Onyewu, Oguchi 60
Orange, James 74
Orlandersmith, Dael 42
Orman, Roscoe 55
Ormes, Jackie 73
Osborne, Jeffrey 26
Osborne, Na'taki 54
Otis, Clarence, Jr. 55
Otis, Clyde 67
Ouattara, Morou 74
Owens, Helen 48
Owens, Jack 38
Owens, Jesse 2
Owens, Major 6
Owens, Terrell 53

Pace, Betty 59
Pace, Orlando 21
Packer, Daniel 56
Packer, Will 71
Packer, Z. Z. 64
Page, Alan 7
Page, Clarence 4
Page, Greg 78
Page, Inman 82
Paige, Rod 29
Paige, Satchel 7
Painter, Nell Irvin 24, 88
Palmer, Keke 68
Palmer, Rissi 65
Palmer, Violet 59
Parham, Marjorie B. 71
Parish, Robert 43
Parker, Barrington D. 92
Parker, Candace 74
Parker, Charlie 20
Parker, Jim 64
Parker, Kellis E. 30
Parker, Maceo 72
Parker, Nicole Ari 52
Parker, Pat 19
Parker, Ray, Jr. 85
Parker, Star 70
Parks, Bernard C. 17
Parks, Gordon 1, 35, 58
Parks, Henry Green, Jr. 89
Parks, Rosa 1, 35, 56
Parks, Suzan-Lori 34, 85
Parr, Russ 51
Parsons, James 14
Parsons, Richard Dean 11, 33
Paterson, Basil A. 69
Paterson, David A. 59
Patrick, Deval 12, 61
Patterson, Floyd 19, 58
Patterson, Frederick Douglass 12
Patterson, Gilbert Earl 41
Patterson, J. O., Jr. 80
Patterson, Louise 25
Patterson, Mary Jane 54
Patton, Antwan 45
Patton, Paula 62
Paul, Chris 84
Payne, Allen 13
Payne, Donald M. 2, 57
Payne, Ethel L. 28
Payne, Freda 58
Payne, Les 89
Payne, Ulice 42
Payne, William D. 60
Payton, Benjamin F. 23
Payton, John 48
Payton, Philip A., Jr. 88
Payton, Walter 11, 25
Peck, Carolyn 23
Peete, Calvin 11
Peete, Holly Robinson 20
Peete, Rodney 60
Pena, Paul 58
Pendergrass, Teddy 22, 83
Peoples, Dottie 22
Perez, Anna 1
Perkins, Edward 5
Perkins, James, Jr. 55
Perkins, Marion 38
Perkins, Pinetop 70
Perkins, Tony 24
Perren, Freddie 60
Perrineau, Harold, Jr. 51

Perrot, Kim 23
Perry, Herman 89
Perry, James 83
Perry, Laval 64
Perry, Lowell 30
Perry, Tyler 40, 54
Perry, Warren 56
Person, Waverly 9, 51
Peters, Margaret 43
Peters, Matilda 43
Petersen, Frank E. 31
Peterson, James 38
Peterson, James 81
Peterson, Jesse Lee 81
Peterson, Karen Carter 90
Peterson, Marvin "Hannibal" 27
Petry, Ann 19
Phifer, Mekhi 25
Phillips, Charles E., Jr. 57
Phillips, Helen L. 63
Phillips, Joseph C. 73
Phillips, Teresa L. 42
Phipps, Wintley 59
Pickens, James, Jr. 59
Pickett, Bill 11
Pickett, Cecil 39
Pierce, Elijah 84
Pierce, Harold 75
Pierce, Paul 71
Pierce, Wendell 90
Pierre, Percy Anthony 46
Pincham, R. Eugene, Sr. 69
Pinchback, P. B. S. 9
Pinckney, Bill 42
Pinckney, Sandra 56
Pindell, Howardena 55
Pinder, Jefferson 77
Pinderhughes, John 47
Pinkett, Randal 61
Pinkett Smith, Jada 10, 41
Pinkney, Fayette 80
Pinkney, Jerry 15
Pinkston, W. Randall 24
Pinn, Vivian Winona 49
Piper, Adrian 71
Pippen, Scottie 15, 89
Pippin, Horace 9
Pitts, Byron 71
Pitts, Derrick 77
Pitts, Robb 84
Pitts, Leonard, Jr. 54, 85
Player, Willa B. 43
Pleasant, Mary Ellen 9
Pleasure P 84
Plessy, Homer Adolph 31
P.M. Dawn 54
Poindexter, Hildrus A. 87
Poitier, Sidney 11, 36
Poitier, Sydney Tamiia 65
Polite, Carlene Hatcher 82
Pollard, Fritz 53
Pollard, William L. 91
Pope.L, William 72
Porter, James A. 11
Porter, Terry 75
Potter, Myrtle 40
Pough, Terrell 58
Pounder, CCH 72
Poussaint, Alvin F. 5, 67
Poussaint, Renee 78
Powell, Adam Clayton, Jr. 3
Powell, Benny 87
Powell, Bud 24

Powell, Colin 1, 28, 75
Powell, Debra A. 23
Powell, Kevin 31, 74
Powell, Maxine 8
Powell, Michael 32
Powell, Mike 7
Powell, Renee 34
Powell, William J. 82
Power, Will 83
Pratt, Awadagin 31
Pratt, Geronimo 18
Pratt, Kyla 57
Preer, Evelyn 82
Premice, Josephine 41
Pressley, Condace L. 41
Preston, Billy 39, 59
Price, Florence 37
Price, Frederick K. C. 21
Price, Glenda 22
Price, Hugh B. 9, 54
Price, Kelly 23
Price, Leontyne 1
Price, Richard 51
Pride, Charley 26
Primus, Pearl 6
Prince 18, 65
Prince, Richard E. 71
Prince, Ron 64
Prince, Tayshaun 68
Prince-Bythewood, Gina 31, 77
Pritchard, Robert Starling 21
Procope, Ernesta 23
Procope, John Levy 56
Prophet, Nancy Elizabeth 42
Prothrow-Stith, Deborah 10
Pryce, Trevor 89
Pryor, Rain 65
Pryor, Richard 3, 24, 56
Puckett, Kirby 4, 58
Pugh, Charles 81
Purdie, Bernard 77
Purnell, Silas 59
Puryear, Martin 42
Putney, Martha S. 75
Quarles, Benjamin Arthur 18
Quarles, Norma 25
Quarterman, Lloyd Albert 4
Queen Latifah 1, 16, 58
?uestlove 74
Quigless, Helen G. 49
Quince, Peggy A. 69
Quivers, Robin 61
Rabb, Maurice F., Jr. 58
Radcliffe, Ted 74
Ragin, Derek Lee 84
Rahman, Aishah 37
Raines, Franklin Delano 14
Rainey, Ma 33
Ralph, Sheryl Lee 18
Ramsey, Charles H. 21, 69
Rand, A. Barry 6
Randall, Alice 38
Randall, Dudley 8, 55
Randle, John 87
Randle, Theresa 16
Randolph, A. Philip 3
Randolph, Linda A. 52
Randolph, Willie 53
Rangel, Charles B. 3, 52, 85
Ransome, James E. 88
Raoul, Kwame 55
Rapier, James T. 82
Rashad, Ahmad 18

Rashad, Phylicia 21
Raspberry, William 2
Raven 44
Rawlings-Blake, Stephanie 93
Rawlinson, Johnnie B. 79
Rawls, Lou 17, 57
Ray, Charlotte E. 60
Ray, Gene Anthony 47
Ray J 86
Razaf, Andy 19
Reagon, Bernice Johnson 7
Reagon, Toshi 76
Reason, J. Paul 19
Record, Eugene 60
Redd, Dana 93
Reddick, Lance 52
Reddick, Lawrence Dunbar 20
Redding, Ann Holmes 77
Redding, J. Saunders 26
Redding, Louis L. 26
Redding, Otis 16
Redman 81
Redman, Joshua 30
Redmond, Eugene 23
Redwood, John Henry 78
Reed, A. C. 36
Reed, Ishmael 8
Reed, Jimmy 38
Reed, Kasim 82
Reed, Willis, Jr. 86
Reed Hall, Alaina 83
Reems, Ernestine Cleveland 27
Reese, Della 6, 20
Reese, Milous J., Jr. 51
Reese, Pokey 28
Reese, Tracy 54
Reeves, Dianne 32
Reeves, Gregory 49
Reeves, Martha 85
Reeves, Rachel J. 23
Reeves, Triette Lipsey 27
Reid, Antonio "L.A." 28
Reid, Irvin D. 20
Reid, Senghor 55
Reid, Tim 56
Reid, Vernon 34
Reverend Ike 79
Reynolds, Harold 77
Reynolds, Star Jones 10, 27, 61
Rhames, Ving 14, 50
Rhimes, Shonda Lynn 67
Rhoden, Dwight 40
Rhoden, William C. 67
Rhodes, Jewell Parker 84
Rhodes, Ray 14
Rhone, Sylvia 2
Rhymes, Busta 31
Ribbs, Willy T. 2
Ribeau, Sidney 70
Ribeiro, Alfonso 17
Rice, Condoleezza 3, 28, 72
Rice, Constance LaMay 60
Rice, Jerry 5, 55, 89
Rice, Jim 75
Rice, Linda Johnson 9, 41
Rice, Louise Allen 54
Rice, Norm 8
Rice, Susan E. 74
Richard, Dawn 92
Richard, J. R. 87
Richards, Beah 30
Richards, Hilda 49
Richards, Sanya 66

Richardson, Desmond 39
Richardson, Donna 39
Richardson, Julieanna 81
Richardson, LaTanya 71
Richardson, Laura 81
Richardson, Nolan 9
Richardson, Rupert 67
Richardson, Salli 68
Richie, Leroy C. 18
Richie, Lionel 27, 65
Richmond, Cedric 93
Richmond, Mitch 19
Rideau, Iris 46
Ridley, John 69
Riggs, Marlon 5, 44
Riles, Wilson C. 79
Riley, Boots 89
Riley, Helen Caldwell Day 13
Riley, Rochelle 50
Rillieux, Norbert 92
Ringgold, Faith 4, 81
Riperton, Minnie 32
Rivers, Doc 25, 81
Rivers, Eugene F., III 81
Roach, Max 21, 63
Roberts, Darryl 70
Roberts, Deborah 35
Roberts, Kimberly Rivers 72
Roberts, Lillian 83
Roberts, Marcus 19
Roberts, Mike 57
Roberts, Robin 16, 54
Roberts, Roy S. 14
Robertson, Gil L., IV 85
Robertson, Oscar 26
Robeson, Eslanda Goode 13
Robeson, Paul 2
Robinson, Aminah 50
Robinson, Bill "Bojangles" 11
Robinson, Bishop L. 66
Robinson, Cleo Parker 38
Robinson, David 24, 90
Robinson, Eddie G. 10
Robinson, Eugene 77
Robinson, Fatima 34
Robinson, Fenton 38
Robinson, Frank 9, 87
Robinson, Jackie 6
Robinson, LaVaughn 69
Robinson, Malcolm S. 44
Robinson, Matt 69
Robinson, Max 3
Robinson, Patrick 19, 71
Robinson, Rachel 16
Robinson, Randall 7, 46
Robinson, Reginald R. 53
Robinson, Sharon 22
Robinson, Shaun 36
Robinson, Smokey 3, 49
Robinson, Spottswood W., III 22
Robinson, Sugar Ray 18
Robinson, Sylvia 79
Robinson, Will 51, 69
Roble, Abdi 71
Roby, Kimberla Lawson 86
Roche, Joyce M. 17
Rochon, Lela 16
Rochon, Stephen W. 78
Rock, Chris 3, 22, 66
Rock, The 29, 66
Rodgers, Johnathan 6, 51
Rodgers, Rod 36
Rodman, Dennis 12, 44

Rodriguez, Jimmy 47
Rodriguez, Cheryl 64
Rogers, Alan G. 72
Rogers, Desirée 88
Rogers, Jimmy 38
Rogers, Joe 27
Rogers, Joel Augustus 30
Rogers, John W., Jr. 5, 52
Roker, Al 12, 49
Roker, Roxie 68
Rolle, Esther 13, 21
Rollins, Charlemae Hill 27
Rollins, Howard E., Jr. 16
Rollins, Jimmy 70
Rollins, Sonny 37
Rose, Anika Noni 70
Rose, Derrick 82
Ross, Charles 27
Ross, Diana 8, 27
Ross, Don 27
Ross, Isaiah "Doc" 40
Ross, Rick 79
Ross, Tracee Ellis 35
Ross-Lee, Barbara 67
Roundtree, Dovey 80
Roundtree, Richard 27
Rouse, Cecilia 93
Rowan, Carl T. 1, 30
Rowell, Victoria 13, 68
Roxanne Shante 33
Roy, Kenny 51
Rubin, Chanda 37
Rucker, Darius 34, 74
Rudolph, Maya 46
Rudolph, Wilma 4
Ruffin, Josephine St. Pierre 75
Ruffins, Kermit 85
Ruley, Ellis 38
Run 31, 73, 75
RuPaul 17, 91
Rush, Bobby 26, 76
Rush, Bobby 78
Rush, Otis 38
Rushen, Patrice 12
Rushing, Jimmy 37
Russell, Bill 8
Russell, Brenda 52
Russell, Herman Jerome 17
Russell, Nipsey 66
Russell-McCloud, Patricia A. 17
Rust, Art, Jr. 83
Rustin, Bayard 4
RZA 80
Saar, Alison 16
Saar, Betye 80
Sabathia, CC 74
St. Jacques, Raymond 8
Saint James, Synthia 12
St. John, Kristoff 25
St. Julien, Marlon 29
St. Patrick, Mathew 48
Saldana, Zoe 72
Sallee, Charles 38
Salter, Nikkole 73
Salters, Lisa 71
Samara, Noah 15
Sample, Joe 51
Sampson, Charles 13
Sanchez, Sonia 17, 51
Sanders, Angelia 86
Sanders, Barry 1, 53
Sanders, Bob 72
Sanders, Deion 4, 31

Sanders, Joseph R., Jr. 11
Sanders, Malika 48
Sanders, Pharoah 64
Sanders, Satch 77
Sands, Diana 87
Sanford, Isabel 53
Santamaria, Mongo 81
Santiago-Hudson, Ruben 85
Sapp, Marvin 74
Sapp, Warren 38
Sapphire 14
Satcher, David 7, 57
Savage, Augusta 12
Sawyer, Eugene 81
Sayers, Gale 28
Sayles Belton, Sharon 9, 16
Sbraga, Kevin 88
Scantlebury-White, Velma 64
Schmoke, Kurt 1, 48
Schuyler, George Samuel 40
Schuyler, Philippa 50
Scott, C(ornelius) A(dolphus) 29
Scott, David 41
Scott, George 55
Scott, Harold Russell, Jr. 61
Scott, Hazel 66
Scott, Jill 29, 83
Scott, John T. 65
Scott, "Little" Jimmy 48
Scott, Milton 51
Scott, Robert C. 23
Scott, Stuart 34
Scott, Tim 87
Scott, Wendell Oliver, Sr. 19
Scurry, Briana 27
Seals, Son 56
Sears, Leah Ward 5, 79
Sears, Stephanie 53
Sebree, Charles 40
Seele, Pernessa 46
Sengstacke, John 18
Senna, Danzy 93
Sermon, Erick 81
Serrano, Andres 3
Sewell, Terri 93
Shabazz, Attallah 6
Shabazz, Betty 7, 26
Shabazz, Ilyasah 36
Shadd, Abraham D. 81
Shakur, Afeni 67
Shakur, Assata 6
Shakur, Tupac 14
Shakur, Yusef 85
Shange, Ntozake 8, 89
Shank, Suzanne F. 77
Shannon, Randy 82
Sharper, Darren 32
Sharpton, Al 21
Shavers, Cheryl 31
Shaw, Bernard 2, 28
Shaw, William J. 30
Sheard, Kierra "Kiki 61
Sheffield, Gary 16
Shell, Art 1, 66
Shelton, Paula Young 86
Shepherd, Sherri 55
Sherrod, Clayton 17
Sherrod, Shirley 87
Shider, Garry 87
Shinhoster, Earl 32
Shipp, E. R. 15
Shippen, John 43
Shirley, George 33

Shockley, Ann Allen 84
Short, Bobby 52
Short, Columbus 79
Shorter, Wayne 75
Showers, Reggie 30
Shropshire, Thomas B. 49
Shuttlesworth, Fred 47
Sidibe, Gabourey 84
Sifford, Charlie 4, 49
Sigur, Wanda 44
Silas, Paul 24
Silver, Horace 26
Simmons, Bob 29
Simmons, E. Denise 79
Simmons, Gary 58
Simmons, Henry 55
Simmons, Jamal 72
Simmons, Kimora Lee 51, 83
Simmons, Russell 1, 30
Simmons, Ruth J. 13, 38
Simone, Nina 15, 41
Simpson, Carole 6, 30
Simpson, Lorna 4, 36
Simpson, O. J. 15
Simpson, Valerie 21
Simpson-Hoffman, N'kenge 52
Sims, Howard "Sandman" 48
Sims, Lowery Stokes 27
Sims, Naomi 29, 79
Sinbad 1, 16
Singletary, Mike 4, 76
Singleton, John 2, 30
Sinkford, Jeanne C. 13
Sir Mix-A-Lot 82
Sisqo 30
Sissle, Noble 29
Sister Souljah 11
Sizemore, Barbara A. 26
Skinner, Kiron K. 65
Sklarek, Norma Merrick 25
Slater, Rodney E. 15
Slaughter, John Brooks 53
Sledge, Percy 39
Sleet, Moneta, Jr. 5
Slice, Kimbo 73
Slick Rick 93
Slim Thug 86
Slocumb, Jonathan 52
Slyde, Jimmy 70
Smalls, Robert 82
Smaltz, Audrey 12
Smiley, Rickey 59
Smiley, Tavis 20, 68
Smith, Anna Deavere 6, 44
Smith, B(arbara) 11
Smith, Barbara 28
Smith, Bessie 3
Smith, Bruce 80
Smith, Bruce W. 53
Smith, Cladys "Jabbo" 32
Smith, Clarence O. 21
Smith, Damu 54
Smith, Danyel 40
Smith, DeMaurice 92
Smith, Dr. Lonnie 49
Smith, Emmitt 7, 87
Smith, Greg 28
Smith, Hilton 29
Smith, Ian 62
Smith, Jaden 82
Smith, Jane E. 24
Smith, Jessie Carney 35
Smith, John L. 22

Smith, Joshua 10
Smith, Kemba 70
Smith, Lonnie Liston 49
Smith, Lovie 66
Smith, Malcolm A. 75
Smith, Mamie 32
Smith, Marie F. 70
Smith, Marvin 46
Smith, Mary Carter 26
Smith, Morgan 46
Smith, Myrna 92
Smith, Nate 49
Smith, Ozzie 77
Smith, Princella 86
Smith, Randy 81
Smith, Rick 72
Smith, Roger Guenveur 12
Smith, Stephen A. 69
Smith, Stuff 37
Smith, Tasha 73
Smith, Trixie 34
Smith, Tubby 18, 83
Smith, Vincent D. 48
Smith, Will 8, 18, 53
Smith, Willi 8
Smith, Willow 92
Smyre, Calvin 90
Smythe Haith, Mabel 61
Sneed, Paula A. 18
Snipes, Wesley 3, 24, 67
Snoop Dogg 35, 84
Snow, Samuel 71
Snowden, Frank M., Jr. 67
Solomon, Jimmie Lee 38
Somi 85
Sommore 61
Songz, Trey 88
Southern, Eileen 56
Southgate, Martha 58
Sowell, Thomas 2
Sparks, Jordin 66
Spaulding, Charles Clinton 9
Spearman, Leonard H. O., Sr. 81
Spears, Warren 52
Spector, Ronnie 77
Speech 82
Spencer, Anne 27
Spencer, Michael G. 87
Spigner, Archie 81
Spikes, Dolores 18
Spiller, Bill 64
Sprewell, Latrell 23
Spriggs, William 67
Stackhouse, Jerry 30
Staley, Dawn 57
Stallings, George A., Jr. 6
Stampley, Micah 54
Stanford, John 20
Stanford, Olivia Lee Dilworth 49
Stanton, Alysa 78
Stanton, Robert 20
Staples, Brent 8
Staples, Mavis 50, 88
Staples, "Pops" 32
Stargell, Willie 29
Staton, Candi 27
Staton, Dakota 62
Staupers, Mabel K. 7
Stearnes, Norman "Turkey" 31
Steave-Dickerson, Kia 57
Steele, Claude Mason 13
Steele, Lawrence 28
Steele, Michael 38, 73, 91

Steele, Shelby **13, 82**
Steinberg, Martha Jean "The Queen" **28**
Stephens, Charlotte Andrews **14**
Stew **69**
Steward, David L. **36**
Steward, Emanuel **18**
Stewart, Alison **13**
Stewart, Ella **39**
Stewart, James "Bubba," Jr. **60**
Stewart, Kordell **21**
Stewart, Maria W. Miller **19**
Stewart, Nzingha **89**
Stewart, Paul Wilbur **12**
Stewart, Tonea Harris **78**
Sticky Fingaz **86**
Still, William Grant **37**
Stingley, Darryl **69**
Stinson, Denise L. **59**
Stith, Charles R. **73**
Stith, Tom **93**
Stokes, Carl **10, 73**
Stokes, Louis **3**
Stone, Angie **31**
Stone, Chuck **9**
Stone, Sly **85**
Stone, Toni **15**
Stoney, Michael **50**
Stoudemire, Amaré **59**
Stout, Juanita Kidd **24**
Stout, Renee **63**
Stoute, Steve **38**
Strahan, Michael **35, 81**
Strautmanis, Michael **87**
Strawberry, Darryl **22**
Strayhorn, Billy **31**
Street, John F. **24**
Streeter, Sarah **45**
Stringer, C. Vivian **13, 66**
Stringer, Korey **35**
Stringer, Vickie **58**
Strong, Barrett **89**
Studdard, Ruben **46**
Sudarkasa, Niara **4**
Sudduth, Jimmy Lee **65**
Sugarhill Gang, The **79**
Sullivan, Jazmine **81**
Sullivan, Leon H. **3, 30**
Sullivan, Louis **8**
Sullivan, Maxine **37**
Summer, Donna **25**
Sun Ra **60**
Sundiata, Sekou **66**
Sutphen, Mona **77**
Sutton, Percy E. **42, 82**
Swann, Lynn **28**
Sweat, Keith **19**
Sweet, Ossian **68**
Swoopes, Sheryl **12, 56**
Swygert, H. Patrick **22**
Sykes, Roosevelt **20**
Sykes, Wanda **48, 81**
Syler, Rene **53**
Tademy, Lalita **36**
Tait, Michael **57**
Talbert, David E. **34, 93**
Talbert, Mary B. **77**
Talley, André Leon **56**
Tamar-kali **63**
Tamia **24, 55**
Tampa Red **63**
Tancil, Gladys Quander **59**
Tanksley, Ann **37**

Tanner, Henry Ossawa **1**
Tate, Eleanora E. **20, 55**
Tate, Larenz **15**
Tatum, Art **28**
Tatum, Beverly Daniel **42, 84**
Tatum, Elinor R. **78**
Tatum, Jack **87**
Tatum, Wilbert **76**
Taulbert, Clifton Lemoure **19**
Taylor, Billy **23, 92**
Taylor, Bo **72**
Taylor, Cecil **70**
Taylor, Charles **20**
Taylor, Ephren W., II **61**
Taylor, Gardner C. **76**
Taylor, Helen (Lavon Hollingshed) **30**
Taylor, Jason **70**
Taylor, Jermain **60**
Taylor, Koko **40, 80**
Taylor, Kristin Clark **8**
Taylor, Lawrence **25**
Taylor, Marshall Walter "Major" **62**
Taylor, Meshach **4**
Taylor, Mildred D. **26**
Taylor, Natalie **47**
Taylor, Recy **92**
Taylor, Regina **9, 46**
Taylor, Robert Robinson **80**
Taylor, Ron **35**
Taylor, Susan C. **62**
Taylor, Susan L. **10, 86**
Taylor, Susie King **13**
Teasley, Lisa **92**
Teer, Barbara Ann **81**
Terrell, Dorothy A. **24**
Terrell, Mary Church **9**
Terrell, Tammi **32**
Terrell-Kearney, Kim **83**
Terry, Clark **39**
Terry, Sonny **88**
Tharpe, Rosetta **65**
The-Dream **74**
Thigpen, Lynne **17, 41**
Thomas, Alma **14**
Thomas, Arthur Ray **52**
Thomas, Clarence **2, 39, 65**
Thomas, Claudia Lynn **64**
Thomas, Debi **26**
Thomas, Derrick **25**
Thomas, Emmitt **71**
Thomas, Frank **12, 51**
Thomas, Franklin A. **5, 49**
Thomas, Irma **29**
Thomas, Isiah **7, 26, 65**
Thomas, Jefferson **88**
Thomas, Michael **69**
Thomas, Mickalene **61**
Thomas, Rozonda **34, 78**
Thomas, Rufus **20**
Thomas, Sean Patrick **35**
Thomas, Thurman **75**
Thomas, Trisha R. **65**
Thomas, Vivien **9**
Thomas-Graham, Pamela **29**
Thompson, Bennie G. **26**
Thompson, Cynthia Bramlett **50**
Thompson, Don **56**
Thompson, John Douglas **81**
Thompson, John W. **26**
Thompson, Kenan **52**
Thompson, Larry D. **39**
Thompson, Tazewell **13**

Thompson, Tina **25, 75**
Thompson, William C. **35**
Thoms, Tracie **61**
Thornton, Big Mama **33**
Thornton, Yvonne S. **69**
Thrash, Dox **35**
Thrower, Willie **35**
Thurman, Howard **3**
Thurman, Wallace **16**
Thurmond, Nate **88**
Thurston, Baratunde **79**
Thurston, Stephen J. **49**
Till, Emmett **7**
Tillard, Conrad **47**
Tillis, Frederick **40**
Tillman, Dorothy **76**
Tillman, George, Jr. **20**
Timbaland **32**
Tinsley, Boyd **50**
Tirico, Mike **68**
Tisdale, Wayman **50**
Tobias, Channing H. **79**
Tobin, Patricia **75**
Todman, Terence A. **55**
Tolbert, Terence **74**
Toler, Burl **80**
Tolliver, Mose **60**
Tolliver, William **9**
Tolson, Melvin **37**
Tolton, Augustine **62**
Tomlinson, LaDainian **65**
Tonex **54**
Toney, James **89**
Tooks, Lance **62**
Toomer, Jean **6**
Toote, Gloria E. A. **64**
Torres, Gina **52**
Torry, Guy **31**
Touré, Askia (Muhammad Abu Bakr el) **47**
Touré, Faya Ora Rose **56**
Toussaint, Allen **60**
Towns, Edolphus **19, 75**
Townsend, Robert **4, 23**
T-Pain **73**
Tresvant, Ralph **57**
Tribbett, Tye **81**
Tribble, Israel, Jr. **8**
Trotter, Donne E. **28**
Trotter, Lloyd G. **56**
Trotter, Monroe **9**
Troupe, Quincy **83**
Trouppe, Quincy Thomas, Sr. **84**
True, Rachel **82**
Trueheart, William E. **49**
Tubbs Jones, Stephanie **24, 72**
Tubman, Harriet **9**
Tucker, C. Delores **12, 56**
Tucker, Chris **13, 23, 62**
Tucker, Cynthia **15, 61**
Tucker, Rosina **14**
Tuckson, Reed V. **71**
Tunie, Tamara **63**
Tunnell, Emlen **54**
Turnbull, Charles Wesley **62**
Turnbull, Walter **13, 60**
Turner, Big Joe **92**
Turner, Henry McNeal **5**
Turner, Ike **68**
Turner, Tina **6, 27**
Tyler, Aisha N. **36**
Tyner, McCoy **92**
Tyree, Omar Rashad **21**

Tyson, Andre **40**
Tyson, Asha **39**
Tyson, Cicely **7, 51**
Tyson, Mike **28, 44, 93**
Tyson, Neil deGrasse **15, 65**
Uggams, Leslie **23**
Ulmer, James **79**
Underwood, Blair **7, 27, 76**
Union, Gabrielle **31, 92**
Unseld, Wes **23**
Upshaw, Gene **18, 47, 72**
Usher **23, 56**
Usry, James L. **23**
Ussery, Terdema, II **29**
Utendahl, John **23**
Valentino, Bobby **62**
Van Lierop, Robert **53**
Van Peebles, Mario **2, 51**
Van Peebles, Melvin **7**
Vance, Courtney B. **15, 60**
VanDerZee, James **6**
Vandross, Luther **13, 48, 59**
Vanzant, Iyanla **17, 47**
Vaughan, Sarah **13**
Vaughn, Countess **53**
Vaughn, Gladys Gary **47**
Vaughn, Mo **16**
Vaughn, Viola **70**
Vaughns, Cleopatra **46**
Vega, Marta Moreno **61**
Velez-Rodriguez, Argelia **56**
Verdelle, A. J. **26**
Vereen, Ben **4**
Verrett, Shirley **66, 91**
Vick, Michael **39, 65**
Villarosa, Clara **85**
Vincent, Marjorie Judith **2**
Vincent, Troy **91**
Von Lipsey, Roderick K. **11**
Waddles, Charleszetta "Mother" **10, 49**
Wade, Dwyane **61**
Wade-Gayles, Gloria Jean **41**
Wagner, Albert **78**
Wagner, Annice **22**
Wainwright, Joscelyn **46**
Wale **92**
Walker, Albertina **10, 58, 89**
Walker, A'lelia **14**
Walker, Alice **1, 43**
Walker, Arthur, II **87**
Walker, Bernita Ruth **53**
Walker, Cedric "Ricky" **19**
Walker, Cora T. **68**
Walker, Dianne **57**
Walker, George **37**
Walker, Herschel **1, 69**
Walker, Hezekiah **34**
Walker, John T. **50**
Walker, Kara **16, 80**
Walker, Lucius, Jr. **88**
Walker, Madame C. J. **7**
Walker, Maggie Lena **17**
Walker, Margaret **29**
Walker, Rebecca **50**
Walker, T. J. **7**
Walker, Wyatt Tee **80**
Wall, Orindatus S. B. **92**
Wallace, Ben **54**
Wallace, Joaquin **49**
Wallace, Michele Faith **13**
Wallace, Perry E. **47**
Wallace, Phyllis A. **9**

Wallace, Rasheed **56**
Wallace, Sippie **1**
Wallace, William **75**
Waller, Fats **29**
Walters, Ronald **83**
Ward, Andre **62**
Ward, Benjamin **68**
Ward, Douglas Turner **42**
Ward, Hines **84**
Ward, Lloyd **21, 46**
Ware, Andre **37**
Ware, Carl H. **30**
Ware, DeMarcus **92**
Warfield, Marsha **2**
Warner, Malcolm-Jamal **22, 36**
Warren, Michael **27**
Warwick, Dionne **18**
Washington, Alonzo **29**
Washington, Booker T. **4**
Washington, Denzel **1, 16, 93**
Washington, Dinah **22**
Washington, Ebonya **79**
Washington, Elsie B. **78**
Washington, Fredi **10**
Washington, Gene **63**
Washington, Grover, Jr. **17, 44**
Washington, Harold **6**
Washington, Harriet A. **69**
Washington, Hayma **86**
Washington, Isaiah **62**
Washington, James, Jr. **38**
Washington, James Melvin **50**
Washington, Kenny **50**
Washington, Kerry **46**
Washington, Laura S. **18**
Washington, MaliVai **8**
Washington, Mary T. **57**
Washington, Patrice Clarke **12**
Washington, Pauletta Pearson **86**
Washington, Regynald G. **44**
Washington, Val **12**
Washington, Walter **45**
Wasow, Omar **15**
Waters, Benny **26**
Waters, Ethel **7**
Waters, Maxine **3, 67**
Waters, Muddy **34**
Watkins, Donald **35**
Watkins, Joe **86**
Watkins, Levi, Jr. **9**
Watkins, Perry **12**
Watkins, Shirley R. **17**
Watkins, Tionne "T-Boz" **34**
Watkins, Walter C. **24**
Watley, Jody **54**
Watson, Bob **25**
Watson, Carlos **50**
Watson, Diane **41**
Watson, Johnny "Guitar" **18**
Watt, Melvin **26**
Wattleton, Faye **9**
Watts, J. C., Jr. **14, 38**
Watts, Reggie **52**
Watts, Rolonda **9**
Wayans, Damien **78**
Wayans, Damon **8, 41**
Wayans, Keenen Ivory **18**
Wayans, Kim **80**
Wayans, Marlon **29, 82**
Wayans, Shawn **29**
Weathers, Carl **10**
Weaver, Afaa Michael **37**
Weaver, Robert C. **8, 46**

Webb, Veronica **10**
Webb, Wellington **3, 81**
Webber, Chris **15, 30, 59**
Webster, Katie **29**
Wedgeworth, Robert W. **42**
Weeks, Thomas, III **70**
Weems, Carrie Mae **63**
Weems, Renita J. **44**
Wein, Joyce **62**
Welburn, Edward T. **50**
Welch, Elisabeth **52**
Wells, Henrietta Bell **69**
Wells, James Lesesne **10**
Wells, Mary **28**
Wells, Vernon **91**
Wells-Barnett, Ida B. **8**
Welsing, Frances Cress **5**
Wesley, Dorothy Porter **19**
Wesley, Richard **73**
Wesley, Valerie Wilson **18**
West, Allen **89**
West, Cornel **5, 33, 80**
West, Dorothy **12, 54**
West, James E. **87**
West, Kanye **52, 93**
West, Togo D., Jr. **16**
Westbrook, Kelvin **50**
Westbrook, Peter **20**
Westbrooks, Bobby **51**
Whack, Rita Coburn **36**
Whalum, Kirk **37, 64**
Wharton, Clifton R., Jr. **7**
Wharton, Clifton Reginald, Sr. **36**
Wheat, Alan **14**
Whitaker, Forest **2, 49, 67**
Whitaker, Mark **21, 47**
Whitaker, Pernell **10, 89**
White, Armond **80**
White, Barry **13, 41**
White, Bill **1, 48**
White, Charles **39**
White, Dondi **34**
White, Jesse **22, 75**
White, Jessica **83**
White, John H. **27**
White, Josh **86**
White, Josh, Jr. **52**
White, Linda M. **45**
White, Lois Jean **20**
White, Maurice **29**
White, Michael Jai **71**
White, Michael R. **5**
White, Reggie **6, 50**
White, Terri **82**
White, Walter F. **4**
White, Willye **67**
White-Hammond, Gloria **61**
Whitehead, Colson **77**
Whitfield, Fred **23**
Whitfield, LeRoy **84**
Whitfield, Lynn **18**
Whitfield, Mal **60**
Whitfield, Norman **73**
Whitfield, Van **34**
Whitlock, Jason **78**
Wideman, John Edgar **5, 87**
Wilbekin, Emil **63**
Wilbon, Michael **68**
Wilder, L. Douglas **3, 48**
Wiley, Kehinde **62**
Wiley, Ralph **8, 78**
Wilkens, J. Ernest, Jr. **43**
Wilkens, Lenny **11, 88**

Wilkerson, Isabel **71**
Wilkins, David **77**
Wilkins, Dominique **74**
Wilkins, Ray **47**
Wilkins, Roger **2, 84**
Wilkins, Roy **4**
Wilkins, Thomas Alphonso **71**
will.i.am **64**
Williams, Ann Claire **82**
Williams, Anthony **21**
Williams, Armstrong **29**
Williams, Bert **18**
Williams, Billy **86**
Williams, Billy Dee **8**
Williams, Clarence **33**
Williams, Clarence **70**
Williams, Clarence, III **26**
Williams, Claude **80**
Williams, Daniel Hale **2**
Williams, David Rudyard **50**
Williams, Deniece **36**
Williams, Deron **92**
Williams, Doug **22**
Williams, Dudley **60**
Williams, Eddie N. **44**
Williams, Evelyn **10**
Williams, Fannie Barrier **27**
Williams, Frederick (B.) **63**
Williams, George Washington **18**
Williams, Gregory **11**
Williams, Hosea Lorenzo **15, 31**
Williams, J. Mayo **83**
Williams, Joe **5, 25**
Williams, John A. **27**
Williams, Juan **35, 80**
Williams, Ken **68**
Williams, Lauryn **58**
Williams, Lindsey **75**
Williams, Maggie **7, 71**
Williams, Malinda **57**
Williams, Marco **53**
Williams, Mary Lou **15**
Williams, Michael L. **86**
Williams, Michelle **73**
Williams, Montel **4, 57**
Williams, Nat D. **91**
Williams, Natalie **31**
Williams, O. S. **13**
Williams, Patricia **11, 54**
Williams, Paul R. **9**
Williams, Pharrell **47, 82**
Williams, Preston Warren, II **64**
Williams, Rhonda Y. **86**
Williams, Ricky **85**
Williams, Robert F. **11**
Williams, Ronald A. **57**
Williams, Russell, II **70**
Williams, Samm-Art **21**
Williams, Saul **31**
Williams, Serena **20, 41, 73**
Williams, Sherley Anne **25**
Williams, Stanley "Tookie" **29, 57**
Williams, Stevie **71**
Williams, Ted **91**
Williams, Terrie M. **35**
Williams, Tony **67**
Williams, Vanessa A. **32, 66**
Williams, Vanessa L. **4, 17**
Williams, Venus **17, 34, 62**
Williams, Walter E. **4**
Williams, Wendy **62**
Williams, William T. **11**
Williams, Willie L. **4**

Williamson, Fred **67**
Williamson, Mykelti **22**
Williamson, Sonny Boy **84**
Willie, Louis, Jr. **68**
Willingham, Tyrone **43**
Willis, Bill **68**
Willis, Deborah **85**
Willis, Dontrelle **55**
Wills, Harry **80**
Wills, Maury **73**
Wilson, August **7, 33, 55**
Wilson, Cassandra **16**
Wilson, Chandra **57**
Wilson, Charlie **31, 77**
Wilson, Debra **38**
Wilson, Donald E. **88**
Wilson, Dorien **55**
Wilson, Ellis **39**
Wilson, Flip **21**
Wilson, Frederica **92**
Wilson, Gerald **49**
Wilson, Jackie **60**
Wilson, Jimmy **45**
Wilson, Margaret Bush **79**
Wilson, Mary **28**
Wilson, Nancy **10**
Wilson, Natalie **38**
Wilson, Phill **9**
Wilson, Stephanie **72**
Wilson, Sunnie **7, 55**
Wilson, Tracey Scott **777**
Wilson, William Julius **20**
Winans, Angie **36**
Winans, BeBe **14**
Winans, CeCe **14, 43**
Winans, David **77**
Winans, Debbie **36**
Winans, Marvin L. **17**
Winans, Ronald **54**
Winans, Vickie **24**
Winfield, Dave **5, 91**
Winfield, Paul **2, 45**
Winfrey, Oprah **2, 15, 61**
Winkfield, Jimmy **42**
Winslow, Kellen **83**
Wisdom, Kimberlydawn **57**
Withers, Bill **61**
Withers, Ernest C. **68, 88**
Withers-Mendes, Elisabeth **64**
Witherspoon, John **38**
Witt, Edwin T. **26**
Wolfe, Ann **82**
Wolfe, George C. **6, 43**
Womack, Bobby **60, 92**
Wonder, Stevie **11, 53**
Woodard, Alfre **9**
Woodard, Lynette **67**
Woodruff, Hale **9**
Woodruff, John **68**
Woods, Abraham, Jr. **74**
Woods, Georgie **57**
Woods, Granville T. **5**
Woods, Jacqueline **52**
Woods, Mattiebelle **63**
Woods, Scott **55**
Woods, Sylvia **34**
Woods, Teri **69**
Woods, Tiger **14, 31, 81**
Woodson, Ali Ollie **89**
Woodson, Carter G. **2**
Woodson, Mike **78**
Woodson, Robert L. **10**
Woodson, Rod **79**

Worrill, Conrad 12
Worthy, James 49
Worthy, Kym 84
Wright, Antoinette 60
Wright, Bruce McMarion 3, 52
Wright, Charles H. 35
Wright, Deborah C. 25
Wright, Jeffrey 54
Wright, Jeremiah A., Jr. 45, 69
Wright, Lewin 43
Wright, Louis Tompkins 4
Wright, Nathan, Jr. 56
Wright, Rayfield 70
Wright, Richard 5
Wright, Timothy 74
Wyatt, Addie L. 56
Wynn, Albert R. 25, 77
X, Malcolm 1
X, Marvin 45
Xuma, Madie Hall 59
Xzibit 78
Yancy, Dorothy Cowser 42
Yarbrough, Camille 40
Yarbrough, Cedric 51
Yette, Samuel F. 63
Yoba, Malik 11
York, Dwight D. 71
York, Vincent 40
Young, Al 82
Young, Andrew 3, 48
Young, Charles 77
Young, Coleman 1, 20
Young, Donald, Jr. 57
Young, Jean Childs 14
Young, Jimmy 54
Young, Lee 72
Young, Lester 37
Young, Roger Arliner 29
Young, Whitney M., Jr. 4
Young Jeezy 63
Youngblood, Johnny Ray 8
Youngblood, Shay 32
Zane 71
Zollar, Alfred 40
Zollar, Jawole Willa Jo 28
Zook, Kristal Brent 62

Angolan
Bonga, Kuenda 13
dos Santos, José Eduardo 43
Neto, António Agostinho 43
Roberto, Holden 65
Savimbi, Jonas 2, 34

Antiguan
McGuire, George Alexander 80
Spencer, Winston Baldwin 68
Williams, Denise 40

Aruban
Williams, David Rudyard 50

Australian
Freeman, Cathy 29
Mundine, Anthony 56
Rose, Lionel 56

Austrian
Kodjoe, Boris 34, 89

Bahamian
Christie, Perry Gladstone 53
Ferguson, Amos 81
Ingraham, Hubert A. 19
Pindling, Lynden 81

Barbadian
Adams, Grantley 82
Arthur, Owen 33
Brathwaite, Kamau 36
Clarke, Austin C. 32
Foster, Cecil 32
Fresh, Doug E. 93
Grandmaster Flash 33, 60
Kamau, Kwadwo Agymah 28
Lamming, George 35
Rihanna 65

Belizean
Barrow, Dean 69
Jones, Marion 21, 66

Beninese
Gantin, Bernardin 70
Hounsou, Djimon 19, 45
Joachim, Paulin 34
Kerekou, Ahmed (Mathieu) 1
Kidjo, Angelique 50
Loueke, Lionel 88
Soglo, Nicéphore 15
Yayi, Boni T. 84

Bermudian
Cameron, Earl 44
Gordon, Pamela 17
Smith, Jennifer 21

Bissau-Guinean
Sanhá Malam Bacai 84
Vieira, João Bernardo 14, 84

Botswanan
Masire, Quett 5
Mogae, Festus Gontebanye 19, 79

Brazilian
Brown, Carlinhos 81
Caymmi, Dorival 72
da Silva, Benedita 5
dos Santos, Manuel Francisco 65
Gil, Gilberto 53
Jorge, Seu 73
Machado de Assis 74
Mello, Breno 73
Moura, Paulo 87
Nascimento, Abdias do 93
Nascimento, Milton 2, 64
Pelé 7
Pitta, Celso 17
Querino, Manuel Raimundo 84
Ronaldinho 69
Silva, Marina 80

British
Abbott, Diane 9
Adjaye, David 38, 78
Akinnuoye-Agbaje, Adewale 56
Akomfrah, John 37
Amos, Valerie 41
Anderson, Ho Che 54
Anthony, Trey 63
Appiah, Kwame Anthony 67
Armah, Esther 87
Armatrading, Joan 32
Bailey Rae, Corinne 83
Barnes, John 53
Bassey, Shirley 25
Berry, James 41
Blackwood, Maureen 37

Boateng, Ozwald 35
Boateng, Paul Yaw 56
Breeze, Jean "Binta" 37
Brown, Melanie 73
Campbell, Naomi 1, 31
Carby, Hazel 27
Christie, Linford 8
Coleridge-Taylor, Samuel 75
Crooks, Garth 53
D'Aguiar, Fred 50
Danjah, Terror 91
David, Craig 31, 53
Davidson, Jaye 5
DeGale, James 74
Edwards, Trevor 54
Ejiofor, Chiwetel 67
Elba, Idris 49, 89
Emmanuel, Alphonsia 38
Equiano, Olaudah 78
Estelle 75
Evans, Diana 72
Fenton, Kevin 87
Ferdinand, Rio 82
Garrett, Sean 57
Gladwell, Malcolm 62
Griffin, Angela 80
Hall, Stuart 78
Hamilton, Lewis 66
Harewood, David 52
Harris, Naomie 55
Haye, David 82
Henriques, Julian 37
Henry, Lenny 9, 52
Holmes, Kelly 47
Ibrahim, Mo 67
Ince, Paul 83
Jamelia 51
James, David 84
Jean-Baptiste, Marianne 17, 46
Jordan, Ronny 26
Julien, Isaac 3
Kay, Jackie 37
King, Oona 27
Kwei-Armah, Kwame 84
Lester, Adrian 46
Lewis, Denise 33
Lewis, Lennox 27
Lewis, Leona 75
Lindo, Delroy 18, 45
Markham, E. A. 37
Mbatha-Raw, Gugu 89
McGrath, Pat 72
McKinney Hammond, Michelle 51
McQueen, Steve 84
Miller, Wentworth 75
Morris, William "Bill" 51
Newton, Thandie 26
Okonedo, Sophie 67
Oyelowo, David 82
Pitt, David Thomas 10
Rascal, Dizzee 82
Regis, Cyrille 51
Sade 15, 92
Scantlebury, Janna 47
Seacole, Mary 54
Seal 14, 75
Siji 56
Slash 75
Slick Rick 93
Smith, Anjela Lauren 44
Smith, Richard 51
Smith, Zadie 51
Stoutt, H. Lavity 83

Stuart, Moira 82
Taylor, John (David Beckett) 16
Thomason, Marsha 47
Walker, Eamonn 37
Williams, Roy 89

Burkinabé
Compaore, Blaise 87
Somé, Malidoma Patrice 10

Burundian
Ndadaye, Melchior 7
Nkurunziza, Pierre 78
Ntaryamira, Cyprien 8

Cameroonian
Ahidjo, Ahmadou 81
Bebey, Francis 45
Beti, Mongo 36
Biya, Chantal 89
Biya, Paul 28
Eto'o, Samuel 73
Kotto, Yaphet 7
Milla, Roger 2
Njawe, Pius 87
Oyono, Ferdinand 38

Canadian
Auguste, Arnold A. 47
Augustine, Jean 53
Bannister, Edward Mitchell 88
Bell, Ralph S. 5
Best, Carrie 80
Boyd, Suzanne 52
Brand, Dionne 32
Brathwaite, Fred 35
Brown, Rosemary 62
Brown, Sean 52
Carnegie, Herbert 25
Chanté, Keshia 50
Chong, Rae Dawn 62
Clarke, Austin 32
Clarke, George 32
Cools, Anne 64
Cooper, Afua 53
Cox, Deborah 28
Croal, N'Gai 76
Curling, Alvin 34
Dixon, George 52
Doig, Jason 45
Drake 86
Elliot, Lorris 37
Fiona, Melanie 84
Foster, Cecil 32
Fox, Rick 27
Fuhr, Grant 1, 49
Grand-Pierre, Jean-Luc 46
Hammond, Lenn 34
Harris, Claire 34
Iginla, Jarome 35
Isaac, Julius 34
James, Vanessa 84
Jean, Michaëlle; 70
Jenkins, Fergie 46
Johnson, Ben 1
K'naan 76
Laraque, Georges 48
Lewis, Daurene 72
Mayers, Jamal 39
McKegney, Tony 3
Mollel, Tololwa 38
Neale, Haydain 52
O'Ree, Willie 5
Peterson, Oscar 52

Philip, Marlene Nourbese 32
Reuben, Gloria 15
Richards, Lloyd 2
Rodrigues, Percy 68
Sadlier, Rosemary 62
Salvador, Bryce 51
Scarlett, Millicent 49
Senior, Olive 37
Sparks, Corinne Etta 53
Vanity 67
Verna, Gelsy 70
Weekes, Kevin 67
Williams, Denise 40

Cape Verdean
Evora, Cesaria 12
Pereira, Aristides 30

Caymanian
Ebanks, Selita 67

Chadian
Déby, Idriss 30
Habré, Hissène 6

Colombian
Pomare, Eleo 72

Congolese
Kabila, Joseph 30
Kintaudi, Leon 62
Kolosoy, Wendo 73
Lumumba, Patrice 33
Mudimbe, V. Y. 61
Nkunda, Laurent 75

Costa Rican
McDonald, Erroll 1

Cuban
Ferrer, Ibrahim 41
Güines, Tata 69
León, Tania 13
Maceo, Antonio 82
Minoso, Minnie 89
Portuondo, Omara 53
Quirot, Ana 13
Rodríguez, Arsenio 87
Santamaria, Mongo 81
Valdés, Chucho 89
Velez-Rodriguez, Argelia 56

Dominican (from Dominica)
Charles, Mary Eugenia 10, 55
Charles, Pierre 52
Skerrit, Roosevelt 72

Dominican (from Dominican Republic)
Martinez, Pedro 81
Ortiz, David 52, 82
Sosa, Sammy 21, 44
Virgil, Ozzie 48

Dutch
Ali, Ayaan Hirsi 58, 92
Liberia-Peters, Maria Philomena 12

Eritrean
Keflezighi, Meb 49

Ethiopian
Aberra, Amsale 67
Afro, Teddy 78
Astatke, Mulatu 81
Bekele, Kenenisa 75

Dibaba, Tirunesh 73
Gabre-Medhin, Tsegaye 64
Gebrselassie, Haile 70
Gerima, Haile 38, 80
Haile Selassie 7
Kebede, Liya 59
Meles Zenawi 3
Mengistu, Haile Mariam 65
Samuelsson, Marcus 53

Filipino
apl.de.ap 84

French
Baker, Josephine 3
Baldwin, James 1
Baugé, Grégory 86
Bebey, Francis 45
Bonaly, Surya 7
Chase-Riboud, Barbara 20, 46
Dieudonné 67
Fanon, Frantz 44
Henry, Thierry 66
James, Vanessa 84
Kanouté, Fred 68
Noah, Yannick 4, 60
Parker, Tony 75
Tanner, Henry Ossawa 1

Gabonese
Bongo, Ali Ben 80
Bongo, Omar 1, 79

Gambian
Jammeh, Yahya 23
Peters, Lenrie 43

German
Massaquoi, Hans J. 30
Watts, Andre 42

Ghanaian
Adu, Freddy 67
Aidoo, Ama Ata 38
Ali, Mohammed Naseehu 60
Annan, Kofi Atta 15, 48
Appiah, Kwame Anthony 67
Armah, Ayi Kwei 49
Atta Mills, John 75
Awoonor, Kofi 37
Bartels, Peggielene 80
Danquah, Meri Nana Ama 93
DuBois, Shirley Graham 21
Gyan, Asamoah 87
Jawara, Dawda Kairaba 11
Kufuor, John Agyekum 54, 82
Mensah, John 87
Mensah, Thomas 48
Nkrumah, Kwame 3
Rawlings, Jerry 9
Rawlings, Nana Konadu Agyeman 13
Yeboah, Emmanuel Ofosu 53

Grenadian
Bishop, Maurice 39
Gairy, Eric Matthew 83
Isaac, Julius 34
Mitchell, Keith 82

Guinean
Camara, Moussa Dadis 76
Conté, Lansana 7, 76
Diallo, Amadou 27
Niane, Katoucha 70

Touré, Sekou 6

Guyanese
Amos, Valerie 41
Beaton, Norman 14
Burnham, Forbes 66
Carter, Martin 49
Dabydeen, David 48
D'Aguiar, Fred 50
Damas, Léon-Gontran 46
Dathorne, O. R. 52
Griffith, Patrick A. 64
Jagan, Cheddi 16
Lefel, Edith 41
van Sertima, Ivan 25

Haitian
Aristide, Jean-Bertrand 6, 45
Auguste, Rose-Anne 13
Beauvais, Garcelle 29
Beauvoir, Max 74
Charlemagne, Manno 11
Christophe, Henri 9
Danticat, Edwidge 15, 68
Delice, Ronald 48
Delice, Rony 48
Jean, Wyclef 20, 86
Jean-Juste, Gérard 78
Jean-Louis, Jimmy 76
Laferriere, Dany 33
Laraque, Paul 67
Laroche, Joseph Philippe Lemercier 85
Magloire, Paul Eugène 68
Manigat, Mirlande 90
Martelly, Michel 90
Pascal-Trouillot, Ertha 3
Peck, Raoul 32
Pierre, Andre 17
Pierre-Louis, Michèle 75
Préval, René 87
Siméus, Dumas M. 25
Verna, Gelsy 70

Irish
Adebari, Rotimi 83
Mumba, Samantha 29

Italian
Esposito, Giancarlo 9

Ivorian
Bedie, Henri Konan 21
Blondy, Alpha 30
Dadié, Bernard 34
De Bankolé, Isaach 78
Drogba, Didier 78
Gbagbo, Laurent 43, 90
Guéï, Robert 66
Houphouët-Boigny, Félix 4, 64
Ouattara 43
Ouattara, Alassane 90
Ouattara, Morou 74

Jamaican
Ashley, Maurice 15, 47
Banton, Buju 93
Barnes, John 53
Barnes, Lloyd 77
Barrett, Lindsay 43
Beenie Man 32
Belafonte, Harry 4
Bennett, Louise 69
Berry, James 41
Bolt, Usain 73

Burning Spear 79
Channer, Colin 36
Cliff, Jimmy 28, 92
Cliff, Michelle 42
Cooper, Afua 53
Cox, Renée 67
Curling, Alvin 34
Dunbar, Sly 34
Ellis, Alton 74
Ewing, Patrick 17, 73
Fagan, Garth 18
Fenton, Kevin 87
Figueroa, John J. 40
Ford, Vincent 75
Garvey, Marcus 1
Golding, Bruce 78
Goodison, Lorna 71
Graham, Trevor 84
Griffiths, Marcia 29
Hamilton, Tanya 93
Hammond, Lenn 34
Hearne, John Edgar Caulwell 45
Heavy D 58
Isaacs, Gregory 89
James, Marlon 85
Johnson, Ben 1
Johnson, Linton Kwesi 37
Joseph, Kathie-Ann 56
Kong, B. Waine 50
Manley, Edna 26
Manley, Ruth 34
Marley, Bob 5
Marley, Rita 32, 70
Marley, Ziggy 41
McKay, Claude 6
McKenzie, Jaunel 73
Minott, Sugar 86
Moody, Ronald 30
Morrison, Keith 13
Mowatt, Judy 38
Palmer, Everard 37
Patterson, Orlando 4
Patterson, P. J. 6, 20
Perry, Ruth 19
Ranglin, Ernest 78
Reece, E. Albert 63
Rhoden, Wayne 70
Rhone, Trevor 80
Rogers, Joel Augustus 30
Senior, Olive 37
Shaggy 31
Shakespeare, Robbie 34
Simpson-Miller, Portia 62
Sinclair, Madge 78
Steely 80
Taylor, Karin 34
Tosh, Peter 9
White, Willard 53
Yabby You 83

Kenyan
Cheruiyot, Robert 69
Juma, Calestous 57
Kariuki, J. M. 67
Kenyatta, Jomo 5
Kibaki, Mwai 60
Kobia, Samuel 43
Loroupe, Tegla 59
Maathai, Wangari 43
Mazrui, Ali A. 12
Moi, Daniel Arap 1, 35

Mutu, Wangechi **44**
Mwangi, Meja **40**
Ngilu, Charity **58**
Ngugi wa Thiong'o **29, 61**
Odinga, Raila **67**
Otunga, Maurice Michael **55**
Tergat, Paul **59**
Wambugu, Florence **42**

Korean
Ward, Hines **84**

Lesothoian
Mofolo, Thomas **37**

Liberian
Conneh, Sekou Damate, Jr. **51**
Cooper, Lisa **73**
Fuller, Solomon Carter, Jr. **15**
Gbowee, Leymah **76**
Keith, Rachel Boone **63**
Perry, Ruth **15**
Sawyer, Amos **2**
Sirleaf, Ellen Johnson **71**
Taylor, Charles **20**
Weah, George **58**

Malawian
Banda, Hastings Kamuzu **6, 54**
Kayira, Legson **40**
Muluzi, Bakili **14, 76**

Malian
Keita, Salif **83**
Souleymane, Mahamane **78**
Touré, Amadou Toumani **18**

Martinican
Césaire, Aimé **48, 69**

Mozambican
Chissano, Joaquim **7, 55, 67**
Couto, Mia **45**
Diogo, Luisa Dias **63**
Guebuza, Armando **81**
Machel, Graca Simbine **16**
Machel, Samora Moises **8**
Mutola, Maria **12**

Namibian
Mbuende, Kaire **12**
Nujoma, Samuel **10**

Nigerian
Abacha, Sani **11, 70**
Abani, Chris **77**
Abiola, Moshood **70**
Abubakar, Abdulsalami **66**
Achebe, Chinua **6**
Ade, King Sunny **41**
Adichie, Chimamanda Ngozi **64**
Ake, Claude **30**
Akinola, Peter Jasper **65**
Akpan, Uwem **70**
Akunyili, Dora Nkem **58**
Amadi, Elechi **40**
Arinze, Francis **19**
Azikiwe, Nnamdi **13**
Babangida, Ibrahim **4**
Bandele, Biyi **68**
Clark-Bekedermo, J. P. **44**
Darego, Agbani **52**
Ekwensi, Cyprian **37**
Emeagwali, Philip **30**
Emecheta, Buchi **30**

Fela **1, 42**
Jonathan, Goodluck **83**
Kuti, Femi **47**
Lawal, Kase L. **45**
Obasanjo, Olusegun **5, 22**
Obasanjo, Stella **32, 56**
Ogunlesi, Adebayo O. **37**
Okara, Gabriel **37**
Okosuns, Sonny **71**
Olajuwon, Hakeem **2, 72**
Olatunji, Babatunde **36**
Olojede, Dele **59**
Olopade, Olufunmilayo Falusi **58**
Onwueme, Tess Osonye **23**
Onwurah, Ngozi **38**
Rotimi, Ola **1**
Sade **15, 92**
Saro-Wiwa, Kenule **39**
Siji **56**
Sowande, Fela **39**
Soyinka, Wole **4, 93**
Tutuola, Amos **30**
Ukpabio, Helen **86**
Wiwa, Ken **67**
Yar'Adua, Umaru **69, 89**

Nigerien
Tandja, Mamadou **33, 78**

Norwegian
Brown, Anne **76**

Panamanian
Bailey, Preston **64**
Williams, Juan **35, 80**

Peruvian
Baca, Susana **80**

Polish
Bridgetower, George **78**

Puerto Rican
Schomburg, Arthur Alfonso **9**

Rhodesian
Brutus, Dennis **38**

Russian
Khanga, Yelena **6**

Rwandan
Bizimungu, Pasteur **19**
Habyarimana, Juvenal **8**
Ilibagiza, Immaculée **66**
Kagame, Paul **54**
Mushikiwabo, Louise **88**
Rusesabagina, Paul **60**

St. Kitts and Nevis
Douglas, Denzil Llewellyn **53**

Saint Lucian
Compton, John **65**

Saudi
Amoudi, Mohammed al- **88**
Kalbani, Adil **77**

Senegalese
Acogny, Germaine **55**
Akon **68**
Ba, Mariama **30**
Boye, Madior **30**
Diop, Birago **53**
Diop, Cheikh Anta **4**
Diouf, Abdou **3**

Maal, Baaba **66**
Mbaye, Mariétou **31**
Mboup, Souleymane **10**
Ndiaye, Iba **74**
N'Dour, Youssou **1, 53, 79**
Sané, Pierre Gabriel **21**
Sembène, Ousmane **13, 62**
Senghor, Augustin Diamancoune **66**
Senghor, Léopold Sédar **12, 66**
Sy, Oumou **65**
Wade, Abdoulaye **66**

Sierra Leonean
Beah, Ishmael **69**
Cheney-Coker, Syl **43**
Jones, Monty **66**
Kabbah, Ahmad Tejan **23**
Koroma, Ernest Bai **84**
Sankoh, Foday **74**

Somali
Ahmed, Sharif **80**
Ali, Ayaan Hirsi **58, 92**
Ali Mahdi Mohamed **5**
Dirie, Waris **56**
Farah, Nuruddin **27**
Iman **4, 33, 87**
K'naan **76**
Roble, Abdi **71**

South African
Abrahams, Peter **39**
Adams, Paul **50**
Biko, Steven **4**
Brutus, Dennis **38**
Buthelezi, Mangosuthu Gatsha **9**
Butler, Jonathan **28**
Chweneyagae, Presley **63**
Dandala, Mvume **77**
Dube, Lucky **77**
Grae, Jean **51**
Hani, Chris **6**
Head, Bessie **28**
Ka Dinizulu, Mcwayizeni **29**
Kente, Gibson **52**
Khumalo, Leleti **51**
Kuzwayo, Ellen **68**
LaGuma, Alex **30**
Luthuli, Albert **13**
Mabuza, Lindiwe **18**
Mabuza-Suttle, Felicia **43**
Mahlasela, Vusi **65**
Makeba, Miriam **2, 50, 74**
Mandela, Nelson **1, 14, 77**
Mandela, Winnie **2, 35**
Masekela, Barbara **18**
Masekela, Hugh **1**
Mathabane, Mark **5**
Mbeki, Govan A. **80**
Mbeki, Thabo **14, 73**
Mhlaba, Raymond **55**
Mokae, Zakes **80**
Motlanthe, Kgalema **74**
Mphalele, Es'kia (Ezekiel) **40**
Naki, Hamilton **63**
Ngubane, Ben **33**
Nkoli, Simon **60**
Nkosi, Lewis **46**
Ntshona, Winston **52**
Nyanda, Siphiwe **21**
Nzo, Alfred **15**
Plaatje, Sol. T. **80**
Ramaphosa, Cyril **3**

Ramphele, Mamphela **29**
Sisulu, Albertina **57**
Sisulu, Sheila Violet Makate **24**
Sisulu, Walter **47**
Sono, Jomo **86**
Thugwane, Josia **21**
Tutu, Desmond (Mpilo) **6, 44**
Tutu, Nontombi Naomi **57**
Zuma, Jacob **33, 75**
Zuma, Nkosazana Dlamini **34**

Spanish
Eto'o, Samuel **73**

Sudanese
Bashir, Halima **73**
Bashir, Omar al- **77**
Bol, Manute **1**
Cham, Adongo Agada Akway **77**
Hussein, Lubna **80**
Kiir, Salva **85**
Nour, Nawal M. **56**
Salih, Al-Tayyib **37**
Wek, Alek **18, 63**

Swazi
Mswati III **56**

Swedish
Hendricks, Barbara **3, 67**
Valdés, Bebo **75**

Tanzanian
Kikwete, Jakaya Mrisho **73**
Mkapa, Benjamin W. **16, 77**
Mollel, Tololwa **38**
Mongella, Gertrude **11**
Mwinyi, Ali Hassan **1, 77**
Nyerere, Julius **5**
Ongala, Remmy **9, 91**
Rugambwa, Laurean **20**

Togolese
Eyadéma, Gnassingbé **7, 52**
Gnassingbé, Faure **67**
Soglo, Nicéphore **15**

Trinidadian
Anthony, Michael **29**
Auguste, Arnold A. **47**
Brand, Dionne **32**
Carmichael, Stokely **5, 26**
Cartey, Wilfred **47**
Dymally, Mervyn **42**
Francis, Thais **93**
Guy, Rosa **5**
Harris, Claire **34**
Hendy, Francis **47**
Hercules, Frank **44**
Hill, Errol **40**
Holder, Geoffrey **78**
Julian, Hubert **90**
Lushington, Augustus Nathaniel **56**
Nakhid, David **25**
Nunez, Elizabeth **62**
Primus, Pearl **6**
Rudder, David **79**
Shorty, Ras, I **47**
Toussaint, Lorraine **32**
Williams, Eric Eustace **65**

Tunisian
Memmi, Albert **37**

Ugandan
Amin, Idi **42**
Arac de Nyeko, Monica **66**
Atim, Julian **66**
Atyam, Angelina **55**
Museveni, Yoweri **4**
Mutebi, Ronald **25**
Obote, Milton **63**
Okaalet, Peter **58**
Sentamu, John **58**

Upper Voltan
Sankara, Thomas **17**

West Indian
Césaire, Aimé **48, 69**
Coombs, Orde M. **44**
Innis, Roy **5**
Kincaid, Jamaica **4**
Knight, Gwendolyn **63**
Rojas, Don **33**
Staupers, Mabel K. **7**
Pitt, David Thomas **10**
Taylor, Susan L. **10, 86**

Walcott, Derek **5**

Zairean
Kabila, Laurent **20**
Mobutu Sese Seko **1, 56**
Mutombo, Dikembe **7**

Zambian
Chiluba, Frederick **56, 80**
Kaunda, Kenneth **2**
Moyo, Dambisa **76**
Mwanawasa, Levy **72**

Zulu, Princess Kasune **54**

Zimbabwean
Chideya, Farai **14**
Marechera, Dambudzo **39**
Moyo, Lovemore **76**
Mugabe, Robert **10, 71**
Mukoko, Jestina **75**
Muzorewa, Abel **85**
Nkomo, Joshua **4, 65**
Tsvangirai, Morgan **26, 72**
Vera, Yvonne **32**

Cumulative Occupation Index

*Volume numbers appear in **bold***

Art and design

Abele, Julian **55**
Aberra, Amsale **67**
Adjaye, David **38, 78**
Allen, Tina **22, 75**
Alston, Charles **33**
Amaki, Amalia **76**
Amos, Emma **63**
Anderson, Ho Che **54**
Andrews, Benny **22, 59**
Andrews, Bert **13**
Armstrong, Robb **15**
Ashford, Calvin, Jr. **74**
Bailey, Preston **64**
Bailey, Radcliffe **19**
Bailey, Xenobia **11**
Baker, Matt **76**
Bannister, Edward Mitchell **88**
Barboza, Anthony **10**
Barnes, Ernie **16, 78**
Barthé, Earl **78**
Barthe, Richmond **15**
Basquiat, Jean-Michel **5**
Bearden, Romare **2, 50**
Beasley, Phoebe **34**
Bell, Darrin **77**
Benberry, Cuesta **65**
Benjamin, Tritobia Hayes **53**
Biggers, John **20, 33**
Biggers, Sanford **62**
Billops, Camille **82**
Blackburn, Robert **28**
Bond, J. Max, Jr. **76**
Bradford, Mark **89**
Brandon, Barbara **3**
Brown, Donald **19**
Brown, Robert **65**
Burke, Selma **16**
Burroughs, Margaret Taylor **9**
Camp, Kimberly **19**
Campbell, E. Simms **13**
Campbell, Mary Schmidt **43**
Catlett, Elizabeth **2**
Chanticleer, Raven **91**
Chase-Riboud, Barbara **20, 46**
Colescott, Robert **69**
Collins, Paul **61**
Cortor, Eldzier **42**
Cowans, Adger W. **20**
Cox, Renée **67**
Crichlow, Ernest **75**
Crite, Alan Rohan **29**
Davis, Bing **84**

De Veaux, Alexis **44**
DeCarava, Roy **42, 81**
Delaney, Beauford **19**
Delaney, Joseph **30**
Delsarte, Louis **34**
Donaldson, Jeff **46**
Douglas, Aaron **7**
Douglas, Emory **89**
Driskell, David C. **7**
Dwight, Edward **65**
Edwards, Melvin **22**
El Wilson, Barbara **35**
Ewing, Patrick **17, 73**
Fax, Elton **48**
Feelings, Tom **11, 47**
Ferguson, Amos **81**
Fine, Sam **60**
Freeman, Leonard **27**
Fuller, Meta Vaux Warrick **27**
Gantt, Harvey **1**
Garvin, Gerry **78**
Gilles, Ralph **61**
Gilliam, Sam **16**
Golden, Thelma **10, 55**
Goodnight, Paul **32**
Green, Jonathan **54**
Guyton, Tyree **9**
Hammons, David **69**
Hansen, Austin **88**
Harkless, Necia Desiree **19**
Harrington, Oliver W. **9**
Harris, Lyle Ashton **83**
Harrison, Charles **72**
Hathaway, Isaac Scott **33**
Hayden, Palmer **13**
Hayes, Cecil N. **46**
Holder, Geoffrey **78**
Honeywood, Varnette P. **54, 88**
Hope, John **8**
Hudson, Cheryl **15**
Hudson, Wade **15**
Hunt, Richard **6**
Hunter, Clementine **45**
Hutson, Jean Blackwell **16**
Jackson, Earl **31**
Jackson, Mary **73**
Jackson, Vera **40**
John, Daymond **23**
Johnson, Jeh Vincent **44**
Johnson, William Henry **3**
Jones, Lois Mailou **13**
Jones, Paul R. **76**
King, Robert Arthur **58**

Kitt, Sandra **23**
Knight, Gwendolyn **63**
Knox, Simmie **49**
Lawrence, Jacob **4, 28**
Lee, Annie Frances **22**
Lee-Smith, Hughie **5, 22**
Lewis, Edmonia **10**
Lewis, Norman **39**
Lewis, Samella **25**
Ligon, Glenn **82**
Lovell, Whitfield **74**
Loving, Alvin, Jr. **35, 53**
Manley, Edna **26**
Marshall, Kerry James **59**
Mayhew, Richard **39**
McCullough, Geraldine **58, 79**
McDuffie, Dwayne **62**
McGee, Charles **10**
McGruder, Aaron **28, 56**
McQueen, Steve **84**
Mehretu, Julie **85**
Mitchell, Corinne **8**
Moody, Ronald **30**
Morrison, Keith **13**
Motley, Archibald, Jr. **30**
Moutoussamy-Ashe, Jeanne **7**
Mutu, Wangechi **44**
Myles, Kim **69**
Nascimento, Abdias do **93**
Ndiaye, Iba **74**
Neals, Otto **73**
N'Namdi, George R. **17**
Nugent, Richard Bruce **39**
O'Grady, Lorraine **73**
Olden, Georg(e) **44**
Ormes, Jackie **73**
Ouattara **43**
Perkins, Marion **38**
Pierce, Elijah **84**
Pierre, Andre **17**
Pindell, Howardena **55**
Pinder, Jefferson **77**
Pinderhughes, John **47**
Pinkney, Jerry **15**
Piper, Adrian **71**
Pippin, Horace **9**
Pope.L, William **72**
Porter, James A. **11**
Prophet, Nancy Elizabeth **42**
Puryear, Martin **42**
Querino, Manuel Raimundo **84**
Ransome, James E. **88**
Reid, Senghor **55**
Ringgold, Faith **4, 81**

Roble, Abdi **71**
Ruley, Ellis **38**
Saar, Alison **16**
Saar, Betye **80**
Saint James, Synthia **12**
Sallee, Charles **38**
Sanders, Joseph R., Jr. **11**
Savage, Augusta **12**
Scott, John T. **65**
Sebree, Charles **40**
Serrano, Andres **3**
Shabazz, Attallah **6**
Shonibare, Yinka **58**
Simmons, Gary **58**
Simpson, Lorna **4, 36**
Sims, Lowery Stokes **27**
Sklarek, Norma Merrick **25**
Sleet, Moneta, Jr. **5**
Smith, Bruce W. **53**
Smith, Marvin **46**
Smith, Morgan **46**
Smith, Vincent D. **48**
Steave-Dickerson, Kia **57**
Stout, Renee **63**
Sudduth, Jimmy Lee **65**
Tanksley, Ann **37**
Tanner, Henry Ossawa **1**
Taylor, Robert Robinson **80**
Thomas, Alma **14**
Thrash, Dox **35**
Tolliver, Mose **60**
Tolliver, William **9**
Tooks, Lance **62**
VanDerZee, James **6**
Verna, Gelsy **70**
Wagner, Albert **78**
Wainwright, Joscelyn **46**
Walker, A'lelia **14**
Walker, Kara **16, 80**
Washington, Alonzo **29**
Washington, James, Jr. **38**
Weems, Carrie Mae **63**
Wells, James Lesesne **10**
White, Charles **39**
White, Dondi **34**
White, John H. **27**
Wiley, Kehinde **62**
Williams, Billy Dee **8**
Williams, Clarence **70**
Williams, O. S. **13**
Williams, Paul R. **9**
Williams, William T. **11**
Willis, Deborah **85**
Wilson, Ellis **39**

Withers, Ernest C. **68, 88**
Woodruff, Hale **9**

Business

Abbott, Robert Sengstacke **27**
Abiola, Moshood **70**
Adams, Eula L. **39**
Adams, Jenoyne **60**
Adkins, Rod **41**
Akil, Mara Brock **60, 82**
Al-Amin, Jamil Abdullah **6**
Alexander, Archie Alphonso **14**
Allen, Byron **24**
Allen-Buillard, Melba **55**
Ames, Wilmer **27**
Amos, Wally **9**
Amoudi, Mohammed al- **88**
Archer, Lee, Jr. **79**
Armstrong, Govind **81**
Auguste, Donna **29**
Austin, Gloria **63**
Austin, Jim **63**
Avant, Clarence **19, 86**
Avant, Nicole A. **90**
Baker, Dusty **8, 43, 72**
Baker, Ella **5**
Baker, Gwendolyn Calvert **9**
Baker, Maxine **28**
Banks, Jeffrey **17**
Banks, Paula A. **68**
Banks, William **11**
Barden, Donald H. **9, 20, 89**
Barrett, Andrew C. **12**
Beal, Bernard B. **46**
Beamon, Bob **30**
Beasley, Phoebe **34**
Bell, James A. **50**
Bing, Dave **3, 59, 78**
Blackshear, Leonard **52**
Blackwell, Robert D., Sr. **52**
Blaylock, Ronald **86**
Blayton, Jesse B., Sr. **55**
Bolden, Frank E. **44**
Borders, James **9**
Boston, Kelvin E. **25**
Boston, Lloyd **24**
Bowen, Ruth **83**
Boyd, Edward **70**
Boyd, Gwendolyn **49**
Boyd, John W., Jr. **20, 72**
Boyd, T. B., III **6**
Bradley, Jennette B. **40**
Brae, C. Michael **61**
Bridges, Shelia **36**
Bridgforth, Glinda **36**
Briggs, Curtis **84**
Brimmer, Andrew F. **2, 48**
Bronner, Nathaniel H., Sr. **32**
Brown, Eddie C. **35**
Brown, Jamie Foster **91**
Brown, Les **5**
Brown, Marie Dutton **12**
Brunson, Dorothy **1, 87**
Bryant, John **26**
Burgess, Marjorie L. **55**
Burns, Ursula **60**
Burrell, Tom **21, 51**
Burroughs, Margaret Taylor **9**
Burrus, William Henry **45**
Burt-Murray, Angela **59**
Butler, George, Jr. **70**
Cain, Herman **15, 92**
Calabrese, Karyn **89**

Caldwell, Earl **60**
Cameron, James **80**
Carter, Pamela Lynn **67**
CasSelle, Malcolm **11**
Chamberlain, Wilt **18, 47**
Chapman, Nathan A., Jr. **21**
Chappell, Emma **18**
Chase, Debra Martin **49**
Chase, Leah **57**
Chenault, Kenneth I. **4, 36**
Cherry, Deron **40**
Chisholm, Samuel J. **32**
Clark, Celeste **15**
Clark, Patrick **14**
Clay, William Lacy **8**
Clayton, Xernona **3, 45**
Clyburn, Mignon **78**
Cobbs, Price M. **9**
Colbert, Virgis William **17**
Coleman, Donald **24, 62**
Coleman, Ken **57**
Compton-Rock, Malaak **86**
Connerly, Ward **14**
Conyers, Nathan G. **24**
Cooper, Barry **33**
Cooper, Evern **40**
Corbi, Lana **42**
Cornelius, Don **4**
Cosby, Camille **14, 80**
Cottrell, Comer **11**
Cox, William E. **68**
Creagh, Milton **27**
Cullers, Vincent T. **49**
Daniels-Carter, Valerie **23**
Darden, Calvin **38**
Dash, Darien **29**
Davis, Belva **61**
Davis, Ed **24**
Davis, Erroll B., Jr. **57**
Dawson, Matel, Jr. **39**
de Passe, Suzanne **25**
Dean, Mark **35**
Dee, Merri **55**
Delany, Bessie **12**
Delany, Martin R. **27**
Delany, Sadie **12**
DeVard, Jerri **61**
Diallo, Amadou **27**
Doley, Harold, Jr. **26**
Donald, Arnold Wayne **36**
Dorsey, Thomas J. **90**
Downing, George T. **91**
Dre, Dr. **10, 14, 30**
Driver, David E. **11**
Ducksworth, Marilyn **12**
Duerson, Dave **93**
Easley, Annie J. **61**
Ebanks, Michelle **60**
Edelin, Ramona Hoage **19**
Edmonds, Tracey **16, 64**
Edmunds, Gladys **48**
Edwards, Trevor **54**
El Wilson, Barbara **35**
Elder, Lee **6**
Ellington, E. David **11**
Evans, Darryl **22**
Evers, Myrlie **8**
Farmer, Forest J. **1**
Farr, Mel **24**
Farrakhan, Louis **15**
Fauntroy, Walter E. **11**
Ferdinand, Rio **82**
50 Cent **46, 83**

Fils-Aimé, Reggie **74**
Fletcher, Alphonse, Jr. **16**
Flowers, Sylester **50**
Ford, Barney **90**
Ford, Harold E(ugene), Jr. **16, 70**
Forte, Linda Diane **54**
Foster, Jylla Moore **45**
Fowler, Reggie **51**
Franklin, Hardy R. **9**
Friday, Jeff **24**
Fryer, Roland G. **56**
Fudge, Ann **11, 55**
Fuller, S. B. **13**
Funderburg, I. Owen **38**
Gaines, Brenda **41**
Gardner, Chris **65**
Gardner, Edward G. **45**
Garrett, James F. **78**
Gaskins, Rudy **74**
Gaston, Arthur George **3, 38, 59**
Gibson, John Trusty **87**
Gibson, Kenneth Allen **6**
Gibson, Ted **66**
Gidron, Richard D. **68**
Gilles, Ralph **61**
Goings, Russell **59**
Goldsberry, Ronald **18**
Golston, Allan C. **55**
Gordon, Bruce S. **41, 53, 82**
Gordon, Pamela **17**
Gordy, Berry, Jr. **1**
Goss, Carol A. **55**
Goss, Tom **23**
Grace, George H. **48**
Graham, Stedman **13**
Graves, Butch **77**
Graves, Earl G. **1, 35**
Gray, Farrah **59**
Greely, M. Gasby **27**
Green, Isaac H. **79**
Greene, Richard Thaddeus, Sr. **67**
Greenwood, Monique **38**
Griffith, Mark Winston **8**
Grooms, Henry R(andall) **50**
Hale, Lorraine **8**
Hall, Alvin D. **86**
Ham, Cynthia Parker **58**
Hamer, Fannie Lou **6**
Hamilton, Samuel C. **47**
Handy, W. C. **8**
Hannah, Marc **10**
Hardison, Bethann **12**
Harrell, Andre **9, 30**
Harris, Alice **7**
Harris, Carla A. **67**
Harris, E. Lynn **12, 33**
Harris, Monica **18**
Harris, Richard E. **61**
Harvey, Steve **18, 58**
Harvey, William R. **42**
Hawkins, La-Van **17, 54**
Hayden, Carla D. **47**
Haysbert, Raymond V., Sr. **87**
Hazel, Darryl B. **50**
Henderson, Gordon **5**
Henderson, Henry Fairfax, Jr. **89**
Henry, Lenny **9, 52**
Henry, Troy **85**
Herndon, Alonzo Franklin **89**
Hightower, Dennis F. **13**
Hill, Bonnie Guiton **20**
Hill, Calvin **19**
Hill, Janet **19**

Hill, Jesse, Jr. **13**
Hill, Peter **92**
Hobson, Mellody **40**
Holland, Kimberly N. **62**
Holland, Robert, Jr. **11**
Holmes, Larry **20, 68**
Holstein, Casper **89**
Howell, Ayinde **91**
Howroyd, Janice Bryant **42**
Hudlin, Warrington **9**
Hudson, Cheryl **15**
Hudson, Wade **15**
Huggins, Larry **21**
Hughes, Cathy **27**
Ibrahim, Mo **67**
Ice Cube **8, 30, 60**
Irvin, Vernon **65**
Jackson, George **19**
Jackson, Joe **78**
Jackson, Mannie **14**
Jackson, Michael **19, 53, 76**
Jakes, Thomas "T. D." **17, 43**
James, Charles H., III **62**
James, Donna A. **51**
James, Juanita **13**
Jenkins, Ray **77**
John, Daymond **23**
Johnson, Earvin "Magic" **3, 39**
Johnson, Eunice W. **83**
Johnson, George E. **29**
Johnson, John H. **3, 54**
Johnson, Kevin **70**
Johnson, Robert L. **3, 39**
Johnson, Sheila Crump **48**
Johnson, William **91**
Jolley, Willie **28**
Jones, Bobby **20**
Jones, Carl **7**
Jones, Caroline **29**
Jones, Ingrid Saunders **18**
Jones, John **89**
Jones, Thomas W. **41**
Jones, Wayne **53**
Jordan, Michael **6, 21**
Jordan, Montell **23**
Joyner, Marjorie Stewart **26**
Julian, Percy Lavon **6**
Kaigler, Denise **63**
Keith, Floyd A. **61**
Kelly, Patrick **3**
Kendrick, Erika **57**
Kidd, Mae Street **39**
Killingsworth, Cleve, Jr. **54**
Kimbro, Dennis **10**
King, Dexter **10**
King, Don **14**
Knight, Suge **11, 30**
Knowles, Tina **61**
Knowling, Robert E., Jr. **38**
Lane, Vincent **5**
Langhart Cohen, Janet **19, 60**
Lanier, Willie **33**
Laryea, Thomas Davies, III **67**
Lawal, Kase L. **45**
Lawless, Theodore K. **8**
Lawson, Jennifer **1, 50**
Leary, Kathryn D. **10**
Leavell, Dorothy R. **17**
Lee, Annie Frances **22**
Lee, Bertram M., Sr. **46**
Lee, Debra L. **62**
Leonard, Sugar Ray **15**
Lewis, Aylwin B. **51, 88**

Lewis, Byron E. 13
Lewis, Delano 7
Lewis, Edward T. 21
Lewis, Reginald F. 6
Lewis, William M., Jr. 40
Ligging, Alfred, III 43
Llewellyn, J. Bruce 13, 85
Long, Eddie L. 29, 89
Louis, Errol T. 8
Lucas, John 7
Lucy, William 50
Madison, Paula 37
Malone, Annie 13
March, William Carrington 56
Marshall, Bella 22
Massenburg, Kedar 23
Master P 21
Matthews Shatteen, Westina 51
Matzeliger, Jan 93
Maynard, Robert C. 7
Mays, Leslie A. 41
Mays, William G. 34
McCabe, Jewell Jackson 10
McCann, Renetta 44
McCoy, Elijah 8
McDonald, Erroll 1
McGee, James Madison 46
McGuire, Raymond J. 57
McKissack, Leatrice 80
McLeod, Gus 27
McPherson, David 32
McWorter, Free Frank 91
Miller, Larry G. 72
Millines Dziko, Trish 28
Mills, Steve 47
Mingo, Frank 32
Mitchell, Shireen 89
Monk, Art 38, 73
Monroe, Bryan 71
Montgomery, Isaiah T. 91
Moore, Wes 86
Morgan, Garrett 1
Morgan, Joe Leonard 9
Morgan, Rose 11
Morris, William 51
Moyo, Karega Kofi 36
Moyo, Yvette Jackson 36
Muhammad, Jabir Herbert 72
Nagin, Ray 42, 57, 88
Nail, John E. 92
Nanula, Richard D. 20
Nash, Diane 72
Nelson Meigs, Andrea 48
Nichols, Nichelle 11
Norman, Christina 47
Ogunlesi, Adebayo O. 37
Olojede, Dele 59
O'Neal, Rodney 88
O'Neal, Stanley 38, 67
Otis, Clarence, Jr. 55
Ouattara, Morou 74
Packer, Daniel 56
Parham, Marjorie B. 71
Parks, Henry Green, Jr. 89
Parsons, Richard Dean 11, 33
Payton, Philip A., Jr. 88
Peck, Carolyn 23
Perez, Anna 1
Perkins, James, Jr. 55
Perry, Laval 64
Perry, Lowell 30
Phillips, Charles E., Jr. 57
Pierce, Harold 75

Pinckney, Bill 42
Pinkett, Randal 61
Pleasant, Mary Ellen 9
Potter, Myrtle 40
Powell, Maxine 8
Price, Frederick K. C. 21
Price, Hugh B. 9, 54
Procope, Ernesta 23
Procope, John Levy 56
Queen Latifah 1, 16, 58
Quivers, Robin 61
Rand, A. Barry 6
Reeves, Rachel J. 23
Reid, Antonio "L.A." 28
Rhone, Sylvia 2
Rice, Linda Johnson 9, 41
Rice, Norm 8
Richardson, Donna 39
Richie, Leroy C. 18
Rideau, Iris 46
Roberts, Mike 57
Roberts, Roy S. 14
Robertson, Oscar 26
Robeson, Eslanda Goode 13
Robinson, Jackie 6
Robinson, Rachel 16
Robinson, Randall 7, 46
Roche, Joyce M. 17
Rodgers, Johnathan 6, 51
Rodriguez, Jimmy 47
Rogers, Desirée 88
Rogers, John W., Jr. 5, 52
Rojas, Don 33
Ross, Charles 27
Ross, Diana 8, 27
Russell, Bill 8
Russell, Herman Jerome 17
Russell-McCloud, Patricia 17
Saint James, Synthia 12
Samara, Noah 15
Samuelsson, Marcus 53
Sanders, Angelia 86
Sanders, Dori 8
Sbraga, Kevin 88
Scott, C. A. 29
Scott, Milton 51
Scott, Tim 87
Sengstacke, John 18
Shakur, Afeni 67
Shank, Suzanne F. 77
Shropshire, Thomas B. 49
Siméus, Dumas M. 25
Simmons, Kimora Lee 51, 83
Simmons, Russell 1, 30
Sims, Naomi 29, 79
Sinbad 1, 16
Smith, B(arbara) 11
Smith, Clarence O. 21
Smith, Jane E. 24
Smith, Joshua 10
Smith, Willi 8
Sneed, Paula A. 18
Spaulding, Charles Clinton 9
Staley, Dawn 57
Stanford, Olivia Lee Dilworth 49
Steinberg, Martha Jean "The Queen" 28
Steward, David L. 36
Stewart, Ella 39
Stewart, Paul Wilbur 12
Stinson, Denise L. 59
Stringer, Vickie 58
Sullivan, Leon H. 3, 30

Sutton, Percy E. 42, 82
Taylor, Ephren W., II 61
Taylor, Karin 34
Taylor, Kristin Clark 8
Taylor, Natalie 47
Taylor, Susan L. 10, 86
Terrell, Dorothy A. 24
Thomas, Franklin A. 5, 49
Thomas, Jefferson 88
Thomas-Graham, Pamela 29
Thompson, Cynthia Bramlett 50
Thompson, Don 56
Thompson, John W. 26
Tobin, Patricia 75
Tribble, Israel, Jr. 8
Trotter, Lloyd G. 56
Trotter, Monroe 9
Tuckson, Reed V. 71
Tyson, Asha 39
Ussery, Terdema, II 29
Utendahl, John 23
VanDerZee, James 6
Vaughn, Gladys Gary 47
Vaughns, Cleopatra 46
Villarosa, Clara 85
Walker, A'lelia 14
Walker, Cedric 19
Walker, Madame C. J. 7
Walker, Maggie Lena 17
Walker, T. J. 7
Ward, Lloyd 21, 46
Ware, Carl H. 30
Washington, Alonzo 29
Washington, Mary T. 57
Washington, Regynald G. 44
Washington, Val 12
Wasow, Omar 15
Watkins, Donald 35
Watkins, Walter C., Jr. 24
Wattleton, Faye 9
Wein, Joyce 62
Wek, Alek 18, 63
Welburn, Edward T. 50
Wells-Barnett, Ida B. 8
Westbrook, Kelvin 50
Wharton, Clifton R., Jr. 7
White, Linda M. 45
White, Walter F. 4
Wilkins, Ray 47
Williams, Armstrong 29
Williams, Lindsey 75
Williams, O. S. 13
Williams, Paul R. 9
Williams, Ronald A. 57
Williams, Terrie 35
Williams, Walter E. 4
Williams, Wendy 62
Willie, Louis, Jr. 68
Wilson, Phill 9
Wilson, Sunnie 7, 55
Winfrey, Oprah 2, 15, 61
Woods, Jacqueline 52
Woods, Sylvia 34
Woodson, Robert L. 10
Wright, Antoinette 60
Wright, Charles H. 35
Wright, Deborah C. 25
Wright, Rayfield 70
Yoba, Malik 11
Zollar, Alfred 40

Dance
Acogny, Germaine 55
Adams, Jenoyne 60
Ailey, Alvin 8
Allen, Debbie 13, 42
Anderson, Lauren 72
Atkins, Cholly 40
Babatunde, Obba 35
Baker, Josephine 3
Bates, Peg Leg 14
Beatty, Talley 35
Brown, Ernest 80
Brown, Ronald K. 91
Byrd, Donald 10
Chanticleer, Raven 91
Clarke, Hope 14
Collins, Janet 33, 64
Davis, Chuck 33
de Lavallade, Carmen 78
Dove, Ulysses 5
Dunham, Katherine 4, 59
Ellington, Mercedes 34
Fagan, Garth 18
Falana, Lola 42
Glover, Savion 14
Hall, Arthur 39
Henson, Darrin 33
Hines, Gregory 1, 42
Jamison, Judith 7, 67
Jefferson, Denise 87
Johnson, Virginia 9
Jones, Bill T. 1, 46, 80
Jones, Doris W. 62
King, Alonzo 38
Lane, William Henry 90
LeTang, Henry 66
Manning, Frankie 78
Miller, Bebe 3
Mills, Florence 22
Mitchell, Arthur 2, 47
Moten, Etta 18
Muse, Clarence Edouard 21
Nash, Joe 55
Nicholas, Fayard 20, 57
Nicholas, Harold 20
Nichols, Nichelle 11
Polite, Carlene Hatcher 82
Pomare, Eleo 72
Powell, Maxine 8
Premice, Josephine 41
Primus, Pearl 6
Ray, Gene Anthony 47
Rhoden, Dwight 40
Ribeiro, Alfonso 17
Richardson, Desmond 39
Robinson, Bill "Bojangles" 11
Robinson, Cleo Parker 38
Robinson, Fatima 34
Robinson, LaVaughn 69
Rodgers, Rod 36
Sims, Howard "Sandman" 48
Slyde, Jimmy 70
Spears, Warren 52
Tyson, Andre 40
Vereen, Ben 4
Walker, Dianne 57
Washington, Fredi 10
Williams, Dudley 60
Zollar, Jawole Willa Jo 28

Education
Abani, Chris 77
Achebe, Chinua 6

Adams, Leslie 39
Adams-Ender, Clara 40
Adkins, Rutherford H. 21
Aidoo, Ama Ata 38
Ake, Claude 30
Alexander, Margaret Walker 22
Allen, Robert L. 38
Allen, Samuel W. 38
Allen-Buillard, Melba 55
Alston, Charles 33
Amadi, Elechi 40
Ammons, James H. 81
Anderson, Charles Edward 37
Appiah, Kwame Anthony 67
Archer, Dennis 7
Archie-Hudson, Marguerite 44
Aristide, Jean-Bertrand 6, 45
Asante, Molefi Kete 3
Aubert, Alvin 41
Awoonor, Kofi 37
Bacon-Bercey, June 38
Bahati, Wambui 60
Baiocchi, Regina Harris 41
Baker, Augusta 38
Baker, Gwendolyn Calvert 9
Baker, Houston A., Jr. 6
Baldwin, Cynthia A. 74
Ballard, Allen Butler, Jr. 40
Bambara, Toni Cade 10
Baraka, Amiri 1, 38
Barbee, Lloyd Augustus 71
Barboza, Anthony 10
Barnett, Marguerite 46
Barthé, Earl 78
Bath, Patricia E. 37
Batiste, Alvin 66
Beckham, Barry 41
Belgrave, Marcus 77
Bell, Derrick 6
Benberry, Cuesta 65
Benjamin, Tritobia Hayes 53
Berry, Bertice 8, 55
Berry, Mary Frances 7
Bethune, Mary McLeod 4
Biggers, John 20, 33
Black, Albert 51
Blackwell, David 79
Blakely, Edward J. 88
Blassingame, John Wesley 40
Blockson, Charles L. 42
Bluitt, Juliann S. 14
Bobo, Lawrence 60
Bogle, Donald 34
Bolden, Tonya 32
Bosley, Freeman, Jr. 7
Boyd, Melba Joyce 86
Boyd, T. B., III 6
Bradley, David Henry, Jr. 39
Branch, William Blackwell 39
Brathwaite, Kamau 36
Braun, Carol Moseley 4, 42
Briscoe, Marlin 37
Bromery, Randolph Wilson 85
Brooks, Avery 9
Brown, Claude 38
Brown, Joyce F. 25
Brown, Sterling Allen 10, 64
Brown, Uzee 42
Brown, Wesley 23
Brown, Willa 40
Bruce, Blanche Kelso 33
Brutus, Dennis 38
Bryan, Ashley F. 41

Bunch, Lonnie G., III 91
Burke, Selma 16
Burke, Yvonne Brathwaite 42
Burks, Mary Fair 40
Burnim, Mickey L. 48
Burroughs, Margaret Taylor 9
Burton, LeVar 8
Butler, Paul D. 17
Butts, Calvin O., III 9, 90
Callender, Clive O. 3
Campbell, Bebe Moore 6, 24, 59
Campbell, Mary Schmidt 43
Cannon, Katie 10
Carby, Hazel 27
Cardozo, Francis L. 33
Carnegie, Herbert 25
Carruthers, George R. 40
Carter, Joye Maureen 41
Carter, Kenneth 53
Carter, Warrick L. 27
Cartey, Wilfred 47
Carver, George Washington 4
Cary, Lorene 3
Cary, Mary Ann Shadd 30
Catlett, Elizabeth 2
Cayton, Horace 26
Chaney, John 67
Cheney-Coker, Syl 43
Clark, Joe 1
Clark, Kenneth B. 5, 52
Clark, Septima 7
Clarke, Cheryl 32
Clarke, George 32
Clarke, John Henrik 20
Clayton, Constance 1
Cleaver, Kathleen Neal 29
Clements, George 2
Clemmons, Reginal G. 41
Cobb, Jewel Plummer 42
Cobb, W. Montague 39
Cobb, William Jelani 59
Cobbs, Price M. 9
Cohen, Anthony 15
Cohen, Cathy J. 88
Cole, Johnnetta B. 5, 43
Coleman, William F., III 61
Colescott, Robert 69
Collins, Janet 33, 64
Collins, Marva 3, 71
Collins, Patricia Hill 67
Comer, James P. 6
Coney, PonJola 48
Cook, Mercer 40
Cook, Samuel DuBois 14
Cook, Toni 23
Cooper, Afua 53
Cooper, Anna Julia 20
Cooper, Edward S. 6
Cooper Cafritz, Peggy 43
Copeland, Michael 47
Cortez, Jayne 43
Cosby, Bill 7, 26, 59
Cotter, Joseph Seamon, Sr. 40
Cottrell, Comer 11
Counter, S. Allen 74
Cox, Joseph Mason Andrew 51
Cox, William E. 68
Creagh, Milton 27
Crenshaw, Kimberlé Williams 88
Crew, Rudolph F. 16
Crew, Spencer R. 55
Cross, Dolores E. 23
Cruse, Harold 54

Cullen, Countee 8
Daly, Marie Maynard 37
Dathorne, O. R. 52
Davis, Allison 12
Davis, Angela 5
Davis, Angela J. 88
Davis, Arthur P. 41
Davis, Charles T. 48
Davis, Erroll B., Jr. 57
Davis, George 36
Davis, Milt 74
Dawson, William Levi 39
Days, Drew S., III 10
Deconge-Watson, Lovenia 55
Delany, Sadie 12
Delany, Samuel R., Jr. 9
Delco, Wilhemina R. 33
Delsarte, Louis 34
Dennard, Brazeal 37
Dickens, Helen Octavia 14, 64
Diop, Cheikh Anta 4
Dixon, Margaret 14
Dodson, Howard, Jr. 7, 52
Dodson, Owen Vincent 38
Dogan, Matthew Winifred 91
Donaldson, Jeff 46
Douglas, Aaron 7
Dove, Rita 6, 78
Dove, Ulysses 5
Draper, Sharon Mills 16, 43
Driskell, David C. 7
Drummond, William J. 40
Du Bois, David Graham 45
Dumas, Henry 41
Dunbar-Nelson, Alice Ruth Moore 44
Dunnigan, Alice Allison 41
Dunston, Georgia Mae 48
Dymally, Mervyn 42
Dyson, Michael Eric 11, 40
Early, Gerald 15
Edelin, Ramona Hoage 19
Edelman, Marian Wright 5, 42
Edley, Christopher 2, 48
Edley, Christopher F., Jr. 48
Edwards, Harry 2
Elders, Joycelyn 6
Elliot, Lorris 37
Ellis, Clarence A. 38
Ellison, Ralph 7
Epps, Archie C., III 45
Evans, Mari 26
Everett, Percival 93
Falconer, Etta Zuber 59
Fauset, Jessie 7
Favors, Steve 23
Feelings, Muriel 44
Ferguson, Ronald F. 75
Figueroa, John J. 40
Fleming, Raymond 48
Fletcher, Bill, Jr. 41
Floyd, Elson S. 41
Ford, Jack 39
Forman, James, Jr. 89
Foster, Ezola 28
Foster, Henry W., Jr. 26
Foster, William P. 88
Francis, Norman (C.) 60
Franklin, Hardy R. 9, 87
Franklin, John Hope 5, 77
Franklin, Robert M. 13
Frazier, E. Franklin 10
Freeman, Al, Jr. 11

Fryer, Roland G. 56
Fuller, A. Oveta 43
Fuller, Arthur 27
Fuller, Howard L. 37
Fuller, Solomon Carter, Jr. 15
Futrell, Mary Hatwood 33
Gaines, Ernest J. 7
Gates, Henry Louis, Jr. 3, 38, 67
Gates, Sylvester James, Jr. 15
Gayle, Addison, Jr. 41
George, Zelma Watson 42
Gerima, Haile 38, 80
Gibson, Donald Bernard 40
Giddings, Paula 11
Gilbert, John Wesley 91
Gill, Gerald 69
Gloster, Hugh Morris, Sr. 90
Golden, Marita 19
Gomes, Peter J. 15, 93
Gomez, Jewelle 30
Gomillion, Charles 90
Goodison, Lorna 71
Granville, Evelyn Boyd 36
Greenfield, Eloise 9
Guinier, Lani 7, 30
Guy-Sheftall, Beverly 13, 92
Hageman, Hans and Ivan 36
Hale, Lorraine 8
Hall, Stuart 78
Halliburton, Warren J. 49
Hamburg, Beatrix 84
Hammonds, Evelynn 69
Handy, W. C. 8
Hansberry, William Leo 11
Harding, Vincent 67
Harkless, Necia Desiree 19
Harper, Michael S. 34
Harris, Alice 7
Harris, Barry 68
Harris, Bill 72
Harris, Gary L. 87
Harris, Jay T. 19
Harris, Jessica B. 91
Harris, Patricia Roberts 2
Harris-Lacewell, Melissa 81
Harsh, Vivian Gordon 14
Harvey, William R. 42
Haskins, James 36, 54
Hathaway, Isaac Scott 33
Hayden, Carla D. 47
Hayden, Robert 12
Haynes, George Edmund 8
Henderson, Stephen E. 45
Henries, A. Doris Banks 44
Herenton, Willie W. 24, 81
Hill, Andrew 66
Hill, Anita 5, 65
Hill, Bonnie Guiton 20
Hill, Errol 40
Hill, Leslie Pinckney 44
Hill, Marc Lamont 80
Hilliard, Asa Grant, III 66
Hine, Darlene Clark 24
Hinton, William Augustus 8
Hoagland, Everett H. 45
Hogan, Beverly Wade 50
Holland, Endesha Ida Mae 3, 57
Holt, Nora 38
Hope, John 8
Horton, James Oliver 58
Houston, Charles Hamilton 4
Hoyte, Lenon 50
Hrabowski, Freeman A., III 22

Huggins, Nathan Irvin 52
Hughes, Ebony 57
Hull, Akasha Gloria 45
Humphries, Frederick 20
Hunt, Darnell 92
Hunt, Richard 6
Hutcherson, Hilda Yvonne 54
Hutson, Jean Blackwell 16
Imes, Elmer Samuel 39
Jackson, Edison O. 67
Jackson, Fred James 25
Jackson, Vera 40
Jarrett, Vernon D. 42
Jarvis, Charlene Drew 21
Jarvis, Erich 67
Jefferson, Denise 87
Jeffries, Leonard 8
Jenifer, Franklyn G. 2
Jenkins, Ella 15
Johns, Vernon 38
Johnson, Anthony M. 92
Johnson, Hazel 22
Johnson, James Weldon 5
Johnson, Katherine 61
Johnson, Mordecai Wyatt 79
Jones, Bobby 20
Jones, Clara Stanton 51
Jones, Edward P. 43, 67
Jones, Gayl 37
Jones, Ingrid Saunders 18
Jones, Lois Mailou 13
Joplin, Scott 6
Jordan, June 7, 35
Josey, E. J. 10
Just, Ernest Everett 3
Karenga, Maulana 10, 71
Kay, Ulysses 37
Keith, Damon J. 16, 74
Kennedy, Florynce 12, 33
Kennedy, Randall 40
Kilpatrick, Carolyn Cheeks 16
Kimbro, Dennis 10
King, Preston 28
King, Reatha Clark 65
Kittles, Rick 51
Komunyakaa, Yusef 9
Kunjufu, Jawanza 3, 50
Ladner, Joyce A. 42
Lawrence, Jacob 4, 28
Lawrence-Lightfoot, Sara 10
Lee, Annie Frances 22
Lee, Joe A. 45
Leevy, Carrol M. 42
Leffall, Lasalle 3, 64
Lester, Julius 9
Lewis, David Levering 9
Lewis, Norman 39
Lewis, Samella 25
Lewis, Shirley A. R. 14
Lewis, Thomas 19
Liberia-Peters, Maria Philomena 12
Lincoln, C. Eric 38
Lindsey, Tommie 51
Locke, Alain 10
Logan, Rayford W. 40
Lomax, Michael L. 58
Long, Loretta 58
Long, Richard Alexander 65
Lorde, Audre 6
Loury, Glenn 36
Loving, Alvin, Jr. 35, 53
Lowry, A. Leon 60
Lucy Foster, Autherine 35

Lyttle, Hulda Margaret 14
Mackey, Nathaniel 75
Major, Clarence 9
Malveaux, Floyd 54
Manley, Audrey Forbes 16
Marable, Manning 10
Markham, E. A. 37
Marsalis, Ellis 90
Marshall, Paule 7, 77
Masekela, Barbara 18
Mason, Herman, Jr. 83
Mason, Ronald 27
Massey, Walter E. 5, 45
Massie, Samuel P., Jr. 29
Matejka, Adrian 87
Maupin, John E., Jr. 92
Mayhew, Richard 39
Maynard, Robert C. 7
Maynor, Dorothy 19
Mayo, Whitman 32
Mays, Benjamin E. 7
McBay, Henry C. 91
McCarty, Osceola 16
McCullough, Geraldine 58, 79
McDaniel, Randall Cornell 81
McKay, Nellie Yvonne 17, 57
McLendon, John B., Jr. 89
McMillan, Terry 4, 17, 53
McMurray, Georgia L. 36
McPherson, James Alan 70
McWhorter, John 35
Mell, Patricia 48
Memmi, Albert 37
Meredith, James H. 11
Millender-McDonald, Juanita 21, 61
Mitchell, Corinne 8
Mitchell, Nicole 66
Mitchell, Sharon 36
Mofolo, Thomas Mokopu 37
Mollel, Tololwa 38
Mongella, Gertrude 11
Moody-Adams, Michele 76
Mooney, Paul 37
Moore, Barbara C. 49
Moore, Harry T. 29
Moore, Melba 21
Morón, Alonzo G. 91
Morrison, Keith 13
Morrison, Sam 50
Morrison, Toni 2, 15, 86
Moses, Robert Parris 11
Moton, Robert Russa 83
Mphalele, Es'kia (Ezekiel) 40
Mudimbe, V. Y. 61
Mullen, Harryette 34
Murray, Pauli 38
Nabrit, Samuel Milton 47
Nance, Cynthia 71
Naylor, Gloria 10, 42
Neal, Larry 38
Neal, Mark Anthony 74
Newkirk, Pamela 69
Newman, Lester C. 51
N'Namdi, George R. 17
Norman, Maidie 20
Nour, Nawal M. 56
Obadele, Imari 84
Ogletree, Charles, Jr. 12, 47
Ojikutu, Bisola 65
Oliver, Kimberly 60
Onwueme, Tess Osonye 23
Onwurah, Ngozi 38
Owens, Helen 48

Page, Alan 7
Page, Inman 82
Paige, Rod 29
Painter, Nell Irvin 24, 88
Palmer, Everard 37
Parker, Kellis E. 30
Patterson, Frederick Douglass 12
Patterson, Mary Jane 54
Patterson, Orlando 4
Payton, Benjamin F. 23
Perry, Warren 56
Peters, Margaret 43
Peters, Matilda 43
Peterson, James 81
Pickett, Cecil 39
Pinckney, Bill 42
Pindell, Howardena 55
Piper, Adrian 71
Player, Willa B. 43
Pollard, William L. 91
Porter, James A. 11
Poussaint, Alvin F. 5, 67
Powell, Benny 87
Price, Florence 37
Price, Glenda 22
Price, Richard 51
Primus, Pearl 6
Prophet, Nancy Elizabeth 42
Purnell, Silas 59
Puryear, Martin 42
Putney, Martha S. 75
Quarles, Benjamin Arthur 18
Querino, Manuel Raimundo 84
Quigless, Helen G. 49
Rahman, Aishah 37
Ramphele, Mamphela 29
Reagon, Bernice Johnson 7
Reddick, Lawrence Dunbar 20
Redding, J. Saunders 26
Redmond, Eugene 23
Reid, Irvin D. 20
Rhodes, Jewell Parker 84
Ribeau, Sidney 70
Rice, Condoleezza 3, 28, 72
Rice, Louise Allen 54
Richards, Hilda 49
Riles, Wilson C. 79
Robinson, Sharon 22
Robinson, Spottswood W., III 22
Rodriguez, Cheryl 64
Rogers, Joel Augustus 30
Rollins, Charlemae Hill 27
Ross-Lee, Barbara 67
Rouse, Cecilia 93
Russell-McCloud, Patricia 17
Salih, Al-Tayyib 37
Sallee, Charles Louis, Jr. 38
Satcher, David 7, 57
Schomburg, Arthur Alfonso 9
Sears, Stephanie 53
Senior, Olive 37
Shabazz, Betty 7, 26
Shange, Ntozake 8, 89
Shelton, Paula Young 86
Shipp, E. R. 15
Shirley, George 33
Shockley, Ann Allen 84
Simmons, Ruth J. 13, 38
Sinkford, Jeanne C. 13
Sisulu, Sheila Violet Makate 24
Sizemore, Barbara A. 26
Smith, Anna Deavere 6
Smith, Barbara 28

Smith, Jessie Carney 35
Smith, John L. 22
Smith, Mary Carter 26
Smith, Tubby 18, 83
Snowden, Frank M., Jr. 67
Southern, Eileen 56
Sowande, Fela 39
Spearman, Leonard H. O., Sr. 81
Spears, Warren 52
Spikes, Dolores 18
Spriggs, William 67
Stanford, John 20
Steele, Claude Mason 13
Steele, Shelby 13, 82
Stephens, Charlotte Andrews 14
Stewart, Maria W. Miller 19
Stewart, Tonea Harris 78
Stone, Chuck 9
Sudarkasa, Niara 4
Sullivan, Louis 8
Swygert, H. Patrick 22
Talbert, Mary B. 77
Tancil, Gladys Quander 59
Tanksley, Ann 37
Tatum, Beverly Daniel 42, 84
Taylor, Helen (Lavon Hollingshed) 30
Taylor, Susie King 13
Terrell, Mary Church 9
Thomas, Alma 14
Thomas, Michael 69
Thurman, Howard 3
Tillis, Frederick 40
Tobias, Channing H. 79
Toler, Burl 80
Tolson, Melvin 37
Tribble, Israel, Jr. 8
Trueheart, William E. 49
Tucker, Rosina 14
Turnbull, Charles Wesley 62
Turnbull, Walter 13, 60
Tutu, Desmond 6
Tutu, Nontombi Naomi 57
Tutuola, Amos 30
Tyson, Andre 40
Tyson, Asha 39
Tyson, Neil deGrasse 15, 65
Usry, James L. 23
van Sertima, Ivan 25
Vaughn, Viola 70
Vega, Marta Moreno 61
Velez-Rodriguez, Argelia 56
Verna, Gelsy 70
Wade-Gayles, Gloria Jean 41
Walcott, Derek 5
Walker, George 37
Wallace, Michele Faith 13
Wallace, Perry E. 47
Wallace, Phyllis A. 9
Walters, Ronald 83
Washington, Booker T. 4
Watkins, Shirley R. 17
Wattleton, Faye 9
Weaver, Afaa Michael 37
Wedgeworth, Robert W. 42
Wells, Henrietta Bell 69
Wells, James Lesesne 10
Wells-Barnett, Ida B. 8
Welsing, Frances Cress 5
Wesley, Dorothy Porter 19
Wesley, Richard 73
West, Cornel 5, 33, 80
Wharton, Clifton R., Jr. 7

White, Charles 39
White, Lois Jean 20
Wilkens, J. Ernest, Jr. 43
Wilkins, Roger 2, 84
Williams, David Rudyard 50
Williams, Fannie Barrier 27
Williams, Gregory 11
Williams, Patricia 11, 54
Williams, Rhonda Y. 86
Williams, Sherley Anne 25
Williams, Walter E. 4
Wilson, Donald E. 88
Wilson, William Julius 22
Woodruff, Hale 9
Woodson, Carter G. 2
Worrill, Conrad 12
Wright, Antoinette 60
Xuma, Madie Hall 59
Yancy, Dorothy Cowser 42
Young, Jean Childs 14
Zook, Kristal Brent 62

Fashion

Aberra, Amsale 67
Bailey, Xenobia 11
Banks, Jeffrey 17
Banks, Tyra 11, 50
Barboza, Anthony 10
Beals, Jennifer 12
Beckford, Tyson 11, 68
Boateng, Ozwald 35
Bond, Beverly 53
Boyd, Suzanne 52
Bridges, Sheila 36
Brown, Joyce F. 25
Burrows, Stephen 31
Campbell, Naomi 1, 31
Chanticleer, Raven 91
Common 31, 63
Darego, Agbani 52
Dash, Damon 31
Davidson, Jaye 5
De' Alexander, Quinton 57
Delice, Ronald 48
Delice, Rony 48
Dirie, Waris 56
Ebanks, Selita 67
Evans, Etu 55
Gaskins, Eric 64
Gibson, Ted 66
Givhan, Robin Deneen 72
Hall, Kevan 61
Harold, Erika 54
Henderson, Gordon 5
Hendy, Francis 47
Iman 4, 33, 87
Iman, Chanel 66
John, Daymond 23
Johnson, Beverly 2
Johnson, Eunice W. 83
Jones, Carl 7
Kani, Karl 10
Kebede, Liya 59
Keckley, Elizabeth 90
Kelly, Patrick 3
Kodjoe, Boris 34, 89
Lars, Byron 32
Luna, Donyale 88
Malone, Maurice 32
McGrath, Pat 72
McKenzie, Jaunel 73
Michele, Michael 31
Niane, Katoucha 70

Onwurah, Ngozi 38
Powell, Maxine 8
Reese, Tracy 54
Rhymes, Busta 31
Robinson, Patrick 19, 71
Rochon, Lela 16
Rowell, Victoria 13, 68
Simmons, Kimora Lee 51, 83
Sims, Naomi 29, 79
Smaltz, Audrey 12
Smith, B(arbara) 11
Smith, Willi 8
Smythe Haith, Mabel 61
Steele, Lawrence 28
Stoney, Michael 50
Sy, Oumou 65
Talley, André Leon 56
Taylor, Karin 34
Walker, T. J. 7
Webb, Veronica 10
Wek, Alek 18, 63
White, Jessica 83
Williams, Serena 20, 41, 73

Film

Aaliyah 30
Aaron, Quinton 82
Adebimpe, Tunde 75
Akinnuoye-Agbaje, Adewale 56
Akomfrah, John 37
Ali, Tatyana 73
Allain, Stephanie 49
Allen, Debbie 13, 42
Alonso, Laz 87
Amos, John 8, 62
Anderson, Anthony 51, 77
Anderson, Eddie "Rochester" 30
Andrews, Tina 74
Armah, Esther 87
Awoonor, Kofi 37
Babatunde, Obba 35
Babyface 10, 31, 82
Baker, Josephine 3
Banks, Michelle 59
Banks, Tyra 11, 50
Barclay, Paris 37
Barnett, Etta Moten 56
Bassett, Angela 6, 23, 62
Beach, Michael 26
Beals, Jennifer 12
Beckford, Tyson 11, 68
Belafonte, Harry 4, 65
Bellamy, Bill 12
Bennett, Louise 69
Bentley, Lamont 53
Berry, Fred "Rerun" 48
Berry, Halle 4, 19, 57, 91
Beyoncé 39, 70
Billops, Camille 82
Bivins, Michael 72
Blackwood, Maureen 37
Bleu, Corbin 65
Bogle, Donald 34
Bonet, Lisa 58
Brady, Wayne 32, 71
Brandy 14, 34, 72
Breeze, Jean "Binta" 37
Brooks, Golden 62
Brooks, Hadda 40
Brown, Chris 74
Brown, Jim 11
Brown, Tony 3
Browne, Roscoe Lee 66

Burnett, Charles 16, 68
Byrd, Michelle 19
Byrd, Robert 11
Calloway, Cab 14
Campbell, Naomi 1, 31
Campbell-Martin, Tisha 8, 42
Cannon, Nick 47, 73
Cannon, Reuben 50
Cara, Irene 77
Carroll, Diahann 9
Carroll, Rocky 74
Carson, Lisa Nicole 21
Cash, Rosalind 28
Cedric the Entertainer 29, 60
Chase, Debra Martin 49
Cheadle, Don 19, 52
Chestnut, Morris 31
Chong, Rae Dawn 62
Chweneyagae, Presley 63
Cortez, Jayne 43
Crothers, Scatman 19
Curtis-Hall, Vondie 17
Dandridge, Dorothy 3
Daniels, Lee 36, 76
Dash, Julie 4
David, Keith 27
Davidson, Jaye 5
Davidson, Tommy 21
Davis, Eisa 68
Davis, Guy 36
Davis, Ossie 5, 50
Davis, Sammy, Jr. 18
Davis, Viola 34, 76
Dawn, Marpessa 75
Dawson, Rosario 72
De Bankolé, Isaach 78
de Passe, Suzanne 25
De Shields, André 72
Dee, Ruby 8, 50, 68
Devine, Loretta 24
Dickerson, Ernest 6, 17
Diesel, Vin 29
Dieudonné 67
Diggs, Taye 25, 63
Dixon, Ivan 69
DMX 28, 64
Driskell, David C. 7
Duke, Bill 3
Duncan, Michael Clarke 26
Dunham, Katherine 4, 59
Dutton, Charles S. 4, 22
Earthquake 55
Ejiofor, Chiwetel 67
Elba, Idris 49, 89
Elder, Lonne, III 38
Elise, Kimberly 32
Emmanuel, Alphonsia 38
Epps, Omar 23, 59
Esposito, Giancarlo 9
Evans, Darryl 22
Everett, Francine 23
Faison, Donald 50
Faison, Frankie 55
Fetchit, Stepin 32
Fishburne, Laurence 4, 22, 70
Fisher, Antwone 40
Fisher, Gail 85
Fletcher, Geoffrey 85
Fox, Rick 27
Fox, Vivica A. 15, 53
Foxx, Jamie 15, 48
Franklin, Carl 11
Freeman, Al, Jr. 11

Freeman, Morgan 2, 20, 62
Freeman, Yvette 27
Friday, Jeff 24
Fuller, Charles 8
Fuqua, Antoine 35
Gaye, Nona 56
George, Nelson 12
Gerima, Haile 38, 80
Gibbs, Marla 86
Gibson, Tyrese 27, 62
Givens, Adele 62
Givens, Robin 4, 25, 58
Glover, Danny 1, 24
Glover, Donald 85
Glover, Savion 14
Goldberg, Whoopi 4, 33, 69
Gooding, Cuba, Jr. 16, 62
Gordon, Dexter 25
Gossett, Louis, Jr. 7
Gray, F. Gary 14, 49
Greaves, William 38
Grier, David Alan 28
Grier, Pam 9, 31, 86
Guillaume, Robert 3, 48
Gunn, Moses 10
Gurira, Danai 73
Hairston, Jester 88
Hall, Arsenio 58
Hall, Juanita 62
Hamilton, Lisa Gay 71
Hamilton, Tanya 93
Hampton, Henry 6
Hardison, Kadeem 22
Harewood, David 52
Harper, Hill 32, 65
Harris, Leslie 6
Harris, Naomie 55
Harris, Robin 7
Hawkins, Screamin' Jay 30
Hayes, Isaac 20, 58, 73
Hayes, Teddy 40
Hemsley, Sherman 19
Henriques, Julian 37
Henry, Lenny 9, 52
Henson, Darrin 33
Henson, Taraji P. 58, 77
Hill, Lauryn 20, 53
Hines, Gregory 1, 42
Hooks, Robert 76
Horne, Lena 5, 86
Hounsou, Djimon 19, 45
Houston, Whitney 7, 28, 83
Howard, Sherri 36
Howard, Terrence 59
Howell, Ayinde 91
Hudlin, Reginald 9, 86
Hudlin, Warrington 9
Hudson, Ernie 72
Hudson, Jennifer 63, 83
Hughes, Albert 7
Hughes, Allen 7
Hughley, D. L. 23, 76
Hurt, Byron 61
Ice Cube 8, 30, 60
Ice-T 6, 31
Ingram, Rex 5
Jackson, George 19
Jackson, Janet 6, 30, 68
Jackson, Rampage 83
Jackson, Samuel 8, 19, 63
Jean, Michaëlle; 70
Jean-Baptiste, Marianne 17, 46
Jean-Louis, Jimmy 76

Johnson, Beverly 2
Jones, James Earl 3, 49, 79
Jones, Orlando 30
Jones, Quincy 8, 30
Jorge, Seu 73
Julian, Hubert 90
Julien, Isaac 3
Kelley, Elijah 65
Keys, Alicia 32, 68
Khumalo, Leleti 51
King, Regina 22, 45
King, Woodie, Jr. 27
Kirby, George 14
Kitt, Eartha 16, 75
Kodjoe, Boris 34, 89
Kool Moe Dee 37
Kotto, Yaphet 7
Kunjufu, Jawanza 3, 50
Lane, Charles 3
Lathan, Sanaa 27
Lawrence, Martin 6, 27, 60
Lee, Joie 1
Lee, Malcolm D. 75
Lee, Spike 5, 19, 86
Lemmons, Kasi 20
LeNoire, Rosetta 37
Lester, Adrian 46
Lewis, Samella 25
Lil' Kim 28
Lincoln, Abbey 3, 88
Lindo, Delroy 18, 45
LisaRaye 27
LL Cool J 16, 49
Long, Nia 17
Lover, Ed 10
Luke, Derek 61
Lumet, Jenny 80
Luna, Donyale 88
Lynch, Shola 61
Mac, Bernie 29, 61, 72
Malco, Romany 71
Mann, Tamela 92
Marsalis, Branford 34
Martin, Darnell 43, 78
Martin, Helen 31
Master P 21
Mbatha-Raw, Gugu 89
McBride, Chi 73
McDaniel, Hattie 5
McKee, Lonette 12
McKinney, Nina Mae 40
McQueen, Butterfly 6, 54
McQueen, Steve 84
Meadows, Tim 30
Mello, Breno 73
Merkerson, S. Epatha 47, 83
Micheaux, Oscar 7
Miller, Omar Benson 93
Miller, Wentworth 75
Mitchell, Kel 66
Mokae, Zakes 80
Mo'Nique 35, 84
Mooney, Paul 37
Moore, Chante 26
Moore, Juanita 83
Moore, Melba 21
Moore, Shemar 21
Morris, Garrett 31
Morrison, Vanessa 84
Morton, Joe 18
Mos Def 30
Moses, Gilbert 12
Moss, Carlton 17

Murphy, Eddie 4, 20, 61
Muse, Clarence Edouard 21
Nas 33
Nash, Johnny 40
Nash, Niecy 66
Neal, Elise 29
Nelson, Stanley 92
Newton, Thandie 26
Nicholas, Fayard 20, 57
Nicholas, Harold 20
Nichols, Nichelle 11
Norman, Maidie 20
Okonedo, Sophie 67
O'Neal, Ron 46
Onwurah, Ngozi 38
Oyelowo, David 82
Packer, Will 71
Palmer, Keke 68
Parker, Nicole Ari 52
Parks, Gordon 1, 35, 58
Patton, Paula 62
Payne, Allen 13
Peck, Raoul 32
Perrineau, Harold, Jr. 51
Perry, Tyler 54
Phifer, Mekhi 25
Pierce, Wendell 90
Pinkett Smith, Jada 10, 41
Poitier, Sidney 11, 36
Poitier, Sydney Tamiia 65
Pounder, CCH 72
Pratt, Kyla 57
Preer, Evelyn 82
Prince 18, 65
Prince-Bythewood, Gina 31, 77
Pryor, Richard 3, 24, 56
Queen Latifah 1, 16, 58
Ralph, Sheryl Lee 18
Randle, Theresa 16
Reddick, Lance 52
Reuben, Gloria 15
Rhames, Ving 14, 50
Rhimes, Shonda Lynn 67
Rhymes, Busta 31
Richards, Beah 30
Richardson, LaTanya 71
Richardson, Salli 68
Ridley, John 69
Riggs, Marlon 5, 44
Roberts, Darryl 70
Roberts, Kimberly Rivers 72
Robinson, Matt 69
Robinson, Shaun 36
Rochon, Lela 16
Rock, Chris 3, 22, 66
Rock, The 29, 66
Rodrigues, Percy 68
Rolle, Esther 13, 21
Rollins, Howard E., Jr. 16
Rose, Anika Noni 70
Ross, Diana 8, 27
Roundtree, Richard 27
Rowell, Victoria 13, 68
St. Jacques, Raymond 8
St. John, Kristoff 25
Saldana, Zoe 72
Salter, Nikkole 73
Sands, Diana 87
Schultz, Michael A. 6
Scott, Hazel 66
Scott, Jill 29, 83
Sembène, Ousmane 13, 62
Shakur, Tupac 14

Shepherd, Sherri 55
Short, Columbus 79
Sidibe, Gabourey 84
Simpson, O. J. 15
Sinbad 1, 16
Sinclair, Madge 78
Singleton, John 2, 30
Sisqo 30
Smith, Anjela Lauren 44
Smith, Anna Deavere 6, 44
Smith, Jaden 82
Smith, Roger Guenveur 12
Smith, Tasha 73
Smith, Will 8, 18, 53
Smith, Willow 92
Snipes, Wesley 3, 24, 67
Souleymane, Mahamane 78
Sullivan, Maxine 37
Sykes, Wanda 48, 81
Tate, Larenz 15
Taylor, Meshach 4
Taylor, Regina 9, 46
Thigpen, Lynne 17, 41
Thomas, Sean Patrick 35
Thompson, Kenan 52
Thurman, Wallace 16
Tillman, George, Jr. 20
Torres, Gina 52
Torry, Guy 31
Toussaint, Lorraine 32
Townsend, Robert 4, 23
True, Rachel 82
Tucker, Chris 13, 23, 62
Tunie, Tamara 63
Turner, Tina 6, 27
Tyler, Aisha N. 36
Tyson, Cicely 7, 51
Uggams, Leslie 23
Underwood, Blair 7, 27, 76
Union, Gabrielle 31, 92
Usher 23, 56
Van Lierop, Robert 53
Van Peebles, Mario 2, 51
Van Peebles, Melvin 7
Vance, Courtney B. 15, 60
Vanity 67
Vereen, Ben 4
Walker, Eamonn 37
Wallace, William 75
Ward, Douglas Turner 42
Warfield, Marsha 2
Warner, Malcolm-Jamal 22, 36
Warren, Michael 27
Warwick, Dionne 18
Washington, Denzel 1, 16, 93
Washington, Fredi 10
Washington, Kerry 46
Waters, Ethel 7
Wayans, Damien 78
Wayans, Damon 8, 41
Wayans, Keenen Ivory 18
Wayans, Kim 80
Wayans, Marlon 29, 82
Wayans, Shawn 29
Weathers, Carl 10
Webb, Veronica 10
Wesley, Richard 73
Whitaker, Forest 2, 49, 67
White, Armond 80
White, Michael Jai 71
Whitfield, Lynn 18
Williams, Billy Dee 8
Williams, Clarence, III 26

Williams, Marco 53
Williams, Russell, II 70
Williams, Samm-Art 21
Williams, Saul 31
Williams, Vanessa A. 32, 66
Williams, Vanessa L. 4, 17
Williamson, Fred 67
Williamson, Mykelti 22
Wilson, Debra 38
Wilson, Dorien 55
Winfield, Paul 2, 45
Winfrey, Oprah 2, 15, 61
Witherspoon, John 38
Woodard, Alfre 9
Wright, Jeffrey 54
Yarbrough, Cedric 51
Yoba, Malik 11

**Government and politics--
international**
Abacha, Sani 11, 70
Abbott, Diane 9
Abiola, Moshood 70
Abubakar, Abdulsalami 66
Achebe, Chinua 6
Adebari, Rotimi 83
Ahidjo, Ahmadou 81
Akunyili, Dora Nkem 58
Ali Mahdi Mohamed 5
Amadi, Elechi 40
Amin, Idi 42
Amos, Valerie 41
Annan, Kofi Atta 15, 48
Aristide, Jean-Bertrand 6, 45
Arthur, Owen 33
Atta Mills, John 75
Augustine, Jean 53
Avant, Nicole A. 90
Awoonor, Kofi 37
Azikiwe, Nnamdi 13
Babangida, Ibrahim 4
Baker, Gwendolyn Calvert 9
Banda, Hastings Kamuzu 6, 54
Barnes, Melody 75
Barrow, Dean 69
Bartels, Peggielene 80
Bashir, Omar al- 77
Bedie, Henri Konan 21
Berry, Mary Frances 7
Biko, Steven 4
Bishop, Maurice 39
Biya, Chantal 89
Biya, Paul 28
Bizimungu, Pasteur 19
Boateng, Paul Yaw 56
Bongo, Ali Ben 80
Bongo, Omar 1, 79
Boye, Madior 30
Brown, Rosemary 62
Bunche, Ralph J. 5
Burnham, Forbes 66
Buthelezi, Mangosuthu Gatsha 9
Camara, Moussa Dadis 76
Césaire, Aimé 48, 69
Cham, Adongo Agada Akway 77
Charlemagne, Manno 11
Charles, Mary Eugenia 10, 55
Charles, Pierre 52
Chiluba, Frederick 56, 80
Chissano, Joaquim 7, 55, 67
Christie, Perry Gladstone 53
Christophe, Henri 9
Compaore, Blaise 87

Compton, John **65**
Conneh, Sekou Damate, Jr. **51**
Conté, Lansana **7, 76**
Cools, Anne **64**
Curling, Alvin **34**
da Silva, Benedita **5**
Dadié, Bernard **34**
Dandala, Mvume **77**
Davis, Ruth **37**
Déby, Idriss **30**
Diogo, Luisa Dias **63**
Diop, Cheikh Anta **4**
Diouf, Abdou **3**
dos Santos, José Eduardo **43**
Douglas, Denzil Llewellyn **53**
Ekwensi, Cyprian **37**
Eyadéma, Gnassingbé **7, 52**
Fela **1, 42**
Frazer, Jendayi **68**
Gairy, Eric Matthew **83**
Gbagbo, Laurent **43, 90**
Gnassingbé, Faure **67**
Golding, Bruce **78**
Gordon, Pamela **17**
Grant, Bernie **57**
Guebuza, Armando **81**
Habré, Hissène **6**
Habyarimana, Juvenal **8**
Haile Selassie **7**
Haley, George Williford Boyce **21**
Hani, Chris **6**
Houphouët-Boigny, Félix **4, 64**
Hussein, Lubna **80**
Ifill, Gwen **28**
Ingraham, Hubert A. **19**
Isaac, Julius **34**
Jagan, Cheddi **16**
Jammeh, Yahya **23**
Jawara, Dawda Kairaba **11**
Jean, Michaëlle; **70**
Jean, Wyclef **20, 86**
Jonathan, Goodluck **83**
Ka Dinizulu, Mcwayizeni **29**
Kabbah, Ahmad Tejan **23**
Kabila, Joseph **30**
Kabila, Laurent **20**
Kabunda, Kenneth **2**
Kagame, Paul **54**
Kariuki, J. M. **67**
Kenyatta, Jomo **5**
Kerekou, Ahmed (Mathieu) **1**
Kibaki, Mwai **60**
Kiir, Salva **85**
Kikwete, Jakaya Mrisho **73**
King, Oona **27**
Koroma, Ernest Bai **84**
Kufuor, John Agyekum **54, 82**
Laraque, Paul **67**
Lewis, Daurene **72**
Liberia-Peters, Maria Philomena **12**
Lumumba, Patrice **33**
Luthuli, Albert **13**
Maathai, Wangari **43**
Mabuza, Lindiwe **18**
Machel, Samora Moises **8**
Magloire, Paul Eugène **68**
Mandela, Nelson **1, 14, 77**
Mandela, Winnie **2, 35**
Manigat, Mirlande **90**
Martelly, Michel **90**
Masekela, Barbara **18**
Masire, Quett **5**
Mbeki, Govan A. **80**

Mbeki, Thabo **14, 73**
Mbuende, Kaire **12**
Meles Zenawi **3**
Mengistu, Haile Mariam **65**
Mhlaba, Raymond **55**
Mitchell, Keith **82**
Mkapa, Benjamin W. **16, 77**
Mobutu Sese Seko **1, 56**
Mogae, Festus Gontebanye **19, 79**
Moi, Daniel Arap **1, 35**
Mongella, Gertrude **11**
Motlanthe, Kgalema **74**
Moyo, Dambisa **76**
Moyo, Lovemore **76**
Mswati III **56**
Mugabe, Robert **10, 71**
Mukoko, Jestina **75**
Muluzi, Bakili **14, 76**
Museveni, Yoweri **4**
Mushikiwabo, Louise **88**
Mutebi, Ronald **25**
Muzorewa, Abel **85**
Mwanawasa, Levy **72**
Mwinyi, Ali Hassan **1, 77**
Nascimento, Abdias do **93**
Ndadaye, Melchior **7**
Nelson, Sophia A. **93**
Neto, António Agostinho **43**
Ngilu, Charity **58**
Ngubane, Ben **33**
Nkoli, Simon **60**
Nkomo, Joshua **4, 65**
Nkrumah, Kwame **3**
Nkurunziza, Pierre **78**
Ntaryamira, Cyprien **8**
Nujoma, Samuel **10**
Nyanda, Siphiwe **21**
Nyerere, Julius **5**
Nzo, Alfred **15**
Obasanjo, Olusegun **5, 22**
Obasanjo, Stella **32, 56**
Obote, Milton **63**
Odinga, Raila **67**
Okara, Gabriel **37**
Ouattara, Alassane **90**
Oyono, Ferdinand **38**
Pascal-Trouillot, Ertha **3**
Patterson, P. J. **6, 20**
Pereira, Aristides **30**
Perkins, Edward **5**
Perry, Ruth **15**
Pierre-Louis, Michèle **75**
Pindling, Lynden **81**
Pitt, David Thomas **10**
Pitta, Celso **17**
Préval, René **87**
Ramaphosa, Cyril **3**
Rawlings, Jerry **9**
Rawlings, Nana Konadu Agyeman **13**
Roberto, Holden **65**
Robinson, Randall **7, 46**
Sampson, Edith S. **4**
Sanhá Malam Bacai **84**
Sankara, Thomas **17**
Sankoh, Foday **74**
Savimbi, Jonas **2, 34**
Sawyer, Amos **2**
Senghor, Augustin Diamacoune **66**
Senghor, Léopold Sédar **12, 66**
Silva, Marina **80**
Simpson-Miller, Portia **62**
Sirleaf, Ellen Johnson **71**

Sisulu, Walter **47**
Skerrit, Roosevelt **72**
Skinner, Kiron K. **65**
Smith, Jennifer **21**
Soglo, Nicephore **15**
Spencer, Winston Baldwin **68**
Tandja, Mamadou **33, 78**
Taylor, Charles **20**
Taylor, John (David Beckett) **16**
Todman, Terence A. **55**
Touré, Amadou Toumani **18**
Touré, Sekou **6**
Tsvangirai, Morgan **26, 72**
Tutu, Desmond (Mpilo) **6, 44**
Van Lierop, Robert **53**
Vieira, João Bernardo **14, 84**
Wade, Abdoulaye **66**
Weah, George **58**
Wharton, Clifton R., Jr. **7**
Wharton, Clifton Reginald, Sr. **36**
Williams, Eric Eustace **65**
Wiwa, Ken **67**
Yar'Adua, Umaru **69, 89**
Yayi, Boni T. **84**
Zuma, Jacob G. **33, 75**
Zuma, Nkosazana Dlamini **34**

Government and politics--U.S.
Adams, Floyd, Jr. **12**
Adams, Grantley **82**
Ahmed, Sharif **80**
Alexander, Archie Alphonso **14**
Alexander, Clifford **26**
Allen, Claude **68**
Allen, Ethel D. **13**
Allen, Eugene **79**
Archer, Dennis **7, 36**
Arrington, Richard **24**
Avant, Clarence **19, 86**
Baker, Thurbert **22**
Ballance, Frank W. **41**
Baltimore, Richard Lewis, III **71**
Barbee, Lloyd Augustus **71**
Barrett, Andrew C. **12**
Barrett, Jacqueline **28**
Barry, Marion S. **7, 44**
Bass, Karen **70**
Bell, Michael **40**
Bellamy, Terry **58**
Belton, Sharon Sayles **9, 16**
Berrien, Jacqueline A. **93**
Berry, Edwin C. **81**
Berry, Mary Frances **7**
Berry, Theodore M. **31**
Bethune, Mary McLeod **4**
Bing, Dave **3, 59, 78**
Blackwell, Kenneth, Sr. **61**
Blackwell, Unita **17**
Bobb, Robert C. **83**
Bond, Julian **2, 35**
Booker, Cory Anthony **68**
Bosley, Freeman, Jr. **7**
Bowman, Bertie **71**
Boykin, Keith **14**
Bradley, Jennette B. **40**
Bradley, Thomas **2**
Braun, Carol Moseley **4, 42**
Brazile, Donna **25, 70**
Brimmer, Andrew F. **2, 48**
Brooke, Edward W. **8, 88**
Brooks, Tyrone **59**
Brown, Anthony G. **72**
Brown, Byrd **49**

Brown, Byron W. **72**
Brown, Cora **33**
Brown, Corrine **24, 90**
Brown, Elaine **8**
Brown, George Leslie **62**
Brown, Jesse **6, 41**
Brown, Kwame R. **91**
Brown, Lee Patrick **24**
Brown, Les **5**
Brown, Ron **5**
Brown, Willie **7, 85**
Bruce, Blanche K. **33**
Bryant, Wayne R. **6**
Buckley, Victoria (Vicki) **24**
Bunche, Ralph J. **5**
Burke, Yvonne Brathwaite **42**
Burris, Chuck **21**
Burris, Roland W. **25, 75**
Bush, Gordon **82**
Butler, Jerry **26**
Butts, Cassandra **78**
Caesar, Shirley **19**
Campbell, Bill **9, 76**
Cardozo, Francis L. **33**
Carson, André **69**
Carson, Johnnie **85**
Carson, Julia **23, 69**
Carter, Pamela Lynn **67**
Carter, Robert L. **51**
Chavis, Benjamin **6**
Chisholm, Shirley **2, 50**
Christian-Green, Donna M. **17**
Christie, Ron **83**
Clarke, Yvette **92**
Clay, William Lacy **8**
Clayton, Eva M. **20**
Cleaver, Eldridge **5**
Cleaver, Emanuel **4, 45, 68**
Clemente, Rosa **74**
Clyburn, James E. **21, 71**
Clyburn, Mignon **78**
Cockrel, Kenneth V., Jr. **79**
Cockrel, Kenneth Vern, Sr. **79**
Coleman, Mary **46**
Coleman, Michael B. **28, 79**
Coleman, William T. **76**
Collins, Barbara-Rose **7, 87**
Collins, Cardiss **10, 80**
Colter, Cyrus J. **36**
Connerly, Ward **14**
Conyers, John, Jr. **4, 45**
Conyers, Monica **85**
Cook, Mercer **40**
Cose, Ellis **5, 50**
Craig-Jones, Ellen Walker **44**
Crockett, George W., Jr. **10, 64**
Cummings, Elijah E. **24**
Cunningham, Evelyn **23, 85**
Currie, Betty **21**
Currie, Ulysses **73**
Davis, Angela **5**
Davis, Artur **41**
Davis, Benjamin O., Jr. **2, 43**
Davis, Benjamin O., Sr. **4**
Davis, Danny K. **24, 79**
Davis, Gordon J. **76**
Davis, James E. **50**
Days, Drew S., III **10**
De Priest, Oscar Stanton **80**
DeJongh, John, Jr. **85**
Delany, Martin R. **27**
Delco, Wilhemina R. **33**
Dellums, Ronald **2, 81**

Diggs, Charles R. 21
Dinkins, David 4
Dixon, Julian C. 24
Dixon, Sharon Pratt 1
Dixon, Sheila 68
Dougherty, Mary Pearl 47
Douglas, Derek 88
Du Bois, W. E. B. 3
Dudley, Edward R. 58
Dukes, Hazel Nell 56
Dunbar-Nelson, Alice Ruth Moore 44
Dymally, Mervyn 42
Easley, Annie J. 61
Edmonds, Terry 17
Edwards, Donna 77
Elders, Joycelyn 6
Ellison, Keith 59
Ervin, Clark Kent 82
Espy, Mike 6
Evans, Melvin H. 88
Farmer, James 2, 64
Farrakhan, Louis 2
Farrell, Herman D., Jr. 81
Fattah, Chaka 11, 70
Fauntroy, Walter E. 11
Felix, Larry R. 64
Fenty, Adrian 60, 88
Ferguson, Roger W. 25
Fields, C. Virginia 25
Fields, Cleo 13
Fisher, Ada M. 76
Flake, Floyd H. 18
Fleming, Erik R. 75
Fletcher, Arthur A. 63
Flipper, Henry O. 3
Ford, Harold E(ugene) 42
Ford, Harold E(ugene), Jr. 16, 70
Ford, Jack 39
Ford, Johnny 70
Fortune, T. Thomas 6
Foster, Ezola 28
Foxx, Anthony 81
Franklin, Shirley 34, 80
Franks, Gary 2
Frazer, Jendayi 68
Frazier, Ryan 89
Fudge, Marcia L. 76
Fulani, Lenora 11
Fuller, Thomas O. 90
Gantt, Harvey 1
Garrett, Joyce Finley 59
Garvey, Marcus 1
Gaspard, Patrick 84
Gibson, Johnnie Mae 23
Gibson, Kenneth Allen 6
Gibson, William F. 6
Goode, W. Wilson 4
Gravely, Samuel L., Jr. 5, 49
Gray, Vincent C. 88
Gray, William H., III 3
Grimké, Archibald H. 9
Guinier, Lani 7, 30
Haley, George Williford Boyce 21
Hamer, Fannie Lou 6
Harmon, Clarence 26
Harris, Alice 7
Harris, Patricia Roberts 2
Harvard, Beverly 11
Hastie, William H. 8
Hastings, Alcee L. 16
Hatcher, Andrew T. 90
Hatcher, Richard G. 55

Hawkins, Augustus F. 68
Hayes, James C. 10
Henderson, Thelton E. 68
Henry, Aaron 19
Herenton, Willie W. 24, 81
Herman, Alexis M. 15
Hernandez, Aileen Clarke 13
Hill, Bonnie Guiton 20
Hilliard, Earl F. 24
Hobson, Julius W. 44
Holder, Eric H., Jr. 9, 76
Holmes, Amy 69
Holt Baker, Arlene 73
Horsford, Steven 88
Hughes, Dora 88
Ifill, Gwen 28
Irving, Larry, Jr. 12
Irvis, K. Leroy 67
Jackson, Alphonso R. 48
Jackson, Frank G. 76
Jackson, George 14
Jackson, Jesse 1, 27, 72
Jackson, Jesse, Jr. 14, 45, 81
Jackson, Lisa 77
Jackson, Mae 57
Jackson, Maynard 2, 41
Jackson, Shirley Ann 12
Jackson Lee, Sheila 20
Jacob, John E. 2
James, Sharpe 23, 69
Jarrett, Valerie 73
Jarvis, Charlene Drew 21
Jarvis, Kristen 85
Jefferson, William J. 25, 72
Johnson, Eddie Bernice 8, 90
Johnson, Hank, Jr. 80
Johnson, Harvey, Jr. 24, 82
Johnson, James Weldon 5
Johnson, Jeh C. 76
Johnson, Katherine (Coleman Goble) 61
Johnson, Kevin 70
Johnson, Leroy R. 89
Johnson, Norma L. Holloway 17
Johnson, Robert T. 17
Jones, Elaine R. 7, 45
Jones, Emil, Jr. 74
Jones, John 89
Jordan, Barbara 4, 78
Jordan, Vernon 3, 35
Kelley, Cliff 75
Kennard, William Earl 18
Keyes, Alan L. 11
Kidd, Mae Street 39
Kilpatrick, Carolyn Cheeks 16
Kilpatrick, Kwame 34, 71
Kincaid, Bernard 28
King, Martin Luther, III 20
Kirk, Ron 11, 75
Lafontant, Jewel Stradford 3, 51
Langford, Larry P. 74
Layton, William 87
Lee, Barbara 25
Leland, Mickey 2
Lewis, Delano 7
Lewis, John 2, 46, 83
Lewis, William Henry 89
Love, Reggie 77
Lowery, Myron 80
Majette, Denise 41
Mallett, Conrad, Jr. 16
Mallory, Mark 62
Marsh, Henry, III 32

Marshall, Bella 22
Marshall, Thurgood 1, 44
Martin, Louis E. 16
Martin, Ruby Grant 49
McCall, H. Carl 27
McGee, James D. 74
McGee, James Madison 46
McGlowan, Angela 64, 86
McHenry, Donald F. 83
McKinney, Cynthia 11, 52, 74
McKissick, Floyd B. 3
Meek, Carrie 6, 36
Meek, Kendrick 41, 89
Meeks, Gregory 25
Meeks, James T. 92
Melton, Frank 81
Menard, John Willis 90
Meredith, James H. 11
Metcalfe, Ralph 26
Mfume, Kweisi 6, 41
Millender-McDonald, Juanita 21, 61
Mitchell, Arthur Wergs 91
Mitchell, Parren J. 42, 66
Moore, Gwendolynne S. 55
Moore, Minyon 45
Morial, Ernest "Dutch" 26
Morial, Marc H. 20, 51
Morton, Azie Taylor 48
Morton, Ferdinand Q. 90
Moses, Robert Parris 11
Murrell, Sylvia Marilyn 49
Nagin, Ray 42, 57, 88
Nix, Robert N. C., Jr. 51
Norton, Eleanor Holmes 7, 93
Nutter, Michael 69
Obama, Barack 49, 74, 91
Obama, Michelle 61, 90
O'Leary, Hazel 6
Owens, Major 6
Page, Alan 7
Paige, Rod 29
Paterson, Basil A. 69
Paterson, David A. 59
Patrick, Deval 12, 61
Patterson, J. O., Jr. 80
Patterson, Louise 25
Payne, Donald M. 2, 57
Payne, William D. 60
Perez, Anna 1
Perkins, Edward 5
Perkins, James, Jr. 55
Perry, James 83
Perry, Lowell 30
Peterson, Karen Carter 90
Pinchback, P. B. S. 9
Pitts, Robb 84
Powell, Adam Clayton, Jr. 3
Powell, Colin 1, 28, 75
Powell, Debra A. 23
Powell, Michael 32
Pugh, Charles 81
Raines, Franklin Delano 14
Randolph, A. Philip 3
Rangel, Charles B. 3, 52, 85
Raoul, Kwame 55
Rapier, James T. 82
Rawlings-Blake, Stephanie 93
Redd, Dana 93
Reed, Kasim 82
Reeves, Gregory 49
Reeves, Martha 85
Reeves, Triette Lipsey 27
Rice, Condoleezza 3, 28, 72

Rice, Norm 8
Rice, Susan E. 74
Richardson, Laura 81
Richardson, Rupert 67
Richmond, Cedric 93
Riles, Wilson C. 79
Roberts, Lillian 83
Robinson, Bishop L. 66
Robinson, Randall 7, 46
Rochon, Stephen W. 78
Rogers, Desirée 88
Rogers, Joe 27
Ross, Don 27
Rouse, Cecilia 93
Rush, Bobby 26, 76
Rustin, Bayard 4
Sampson, Edith S. 4
Sanders, Malika 48
Satcher, David 7, 57
Sawyer, Eugene 81
Sayles Belton, Sharon 9
Schmoke, Kurt 1, 48
Scott, David 41
Scott, Robert C. 23
Scott, Tim 87
Sewell, Terri 93
Shakur, Assata 6
Shavers, Cheryl 31
Shelton, Paula Young 86
Sherrod, Shirley 87
Simmons, E. Denise 79
Simmons, Jamal 72
Simpson, Carole 6, 30
Sisulu, Sheila Violet Makate 24
Slater, Rodney E. 15
Smith, Malcolm A. 75
Smith, Nate 49
Smith, Princella 86
Smyre, Calvin 90
Smythe Haith, Mabel 61
Spearman, Leonard H. O., Sr. 81
Spigner, Archie 81
Stanton, Robert 20
Staupers, Mabel K. 7
Steele, Michael 38, 73, 91
Stewart, Nzingha 89
Stokes, Carl 10, 73
Stokes, Louis 3
Stone, Chuck 9
Stoutt, H. Lavity 83
Strautmanis, Michael 87
Street, John F. 24
Sullivan, Louis 8
Sutphen, Mona 77
Sutton, Percy E. 42, 82
Terry, Clark 39
Thomas, Clarence 2, 39, 65
Thompson, Bennie G. 26
Thompson, Larry D. 39
Thompson, William C. 35
Tillman, Dorothy 76
Todman, Terence A. 55
Tolbert, Terence 74
Toote, Gloria E.A. 64
Towns, Edolphus 19, 75
Tribble, Israel, Jr. 8
Trotter, Donne E. 28
Tubbs Jones, Stephanie 24, 72
Tucker, C. Delores 12, 56
Turnbull, Charles Wesley 62
Turner, Henry McNeal 5
Usry, James L. 23
Vaughn, Gladys Gary 47

Von Lipsey, Roderick K. 11
Wallace, Phyllis A. 9
Washington, Harold 6
Washington, Val 12
Washington, Walter 45
Waters, Maxine 3, 67
Watkins, Joe 86
Watkins, Shirley R. 17
Watson, Diane 41
Watt, Melvin 26
Watts, J. C., Jr. 14, 38
Weaver, Robert C. 8, 46
Webb, Wellington 3, 81
West, Allen 89
Wharton, Clifton R., Jr. 7
Wharton, Clifton Reginald, Sr. 36
Wheat, Alan 14
White, Jesse 22, 75
White, Michael R. 5
Wilder, L. Douglas 3, 48
Williams, Anthony 21
Williams, Eddie N. 44
Williams, George Washington 18
Williams, Hosea Lorenzo 15, 31
Williams, Maggie 7, 71
Williams, Michael L. 86
Wilson, Frederica 92
Wilson, Margaret Bush 79
Wilson, Sunnie 7, 55
Woods, Abraham, Jr. 74
Wynn, Albert 25, 77
Young, Andrew 3, 48

Law
Alexander, Clifford 26
Alexander, Joyce London 18
Alexander, Sadie Tanner Mossell 22
Ali, Russlynn H. 92
Allen, Samuel W. 38
Amaker, Norman 63
Anderson, Reuben V. 81
Archer, Dennis 7, 36
Arnwine, Barbara 28
Bailey, Clyde 45
Baldwin, Cynthia A. 74
Banks, William 11
Barbee, Lloyd Augustus 71
Barrett, Andrew C. 12
Barrett, Jacqueline 28
Baugh, David 23
Bell, Derrick 6
Benham, Robert 78
Berrien, Jacqueline A. 93
Berry, Mary Frances 7
Berry, Theodore M. 31
Birch, Adolpho A., Jr. 85
Bishop, Sanford D., Jr. 24
Bolin, Jane 22, 59
Bolton, Terrell D. 25
Booker, Cory Anthony 68
Bosley, Freeman, Jr. 7
Boykin, Keith 14
Bradley, Thomas 2
Braun, Carol Moseley 4, 42
Brooke, Edward W. 8, 88
Brown, Byrd 49
Brown, Cora 33
Brown, Cupcake 63
Brown, Homer S. 47
Brown, Janice Rogers 43
Brown, Joe 29
Brown, Lee Patrick 1, 24

Brown, Ron 5
Bryant, Wayne R. 6
Bryant, William Benson 61
Bully-Cummings, Ella 48
Burke, Yvonne Brathwaite 42
Burris, Roland W. 25, 75
Butler, Louis 70
Butler, Paul D. 17
Bynoe, Peter C. B. 40
Campbell, Bill 9, 76
Carter, Pamela Lynn 67
Carter, Robert L. 51
Carter, Stephen L. 4
Cashin, Sheryll 63
Chambers, Julius 3
Chestnut, J. L., Jr. 73
Cleaver, Kathleen Neal 29
Clendenon, Donn 26, 56
Cochran, Johnnie 11, 39, 52
Coleman, James E., Jr. 79
Coleman, William T. 76
Colter, Cyrus J. 36
Conyers, John, Jr. 4, 45
Crenshaw, Kimberlé Williams 88
Darden, Christopher 13
Davis, Angela J. 88
Davis, Artur 41
Davis, Gordon J. 76
Days, Drew S., III 10
DeFrantz, Anita 37
Diggs-Taylor, Anna 20
Dillard, Godfrey J. 45
Dinkins, David 4
Dixon, Sharon Pratt 1
Edelman, Marian Wright 5, 42
Edley, Christopher 2, 48
Edley, Christopher F., Jr. 48
Ellington, E. David 11
Ephriam, Mablean 29
Ervin, Clark Kent 82
Espy, Mike 6
Evans, Warren C. 76
Farmer-Paellmann, Deadria 43
Feemster, Herbert 72
Fenty, Adrian 60, 88
Fields, Cleo 13
Finner-Williams, Paris Michele 62
Fisher, Ada Lois Sipuel 76
Ford, Wallace 58
Forman, James, Jr. 89
Foxx, Anthony 81
Frazier-Lyde, Jacqui 31
Freeman, Charles 19
Gaines, Lloyd 79
Gary, Willie E. 12
Gibson, Johnnie Mae 23
Glover, Nathaniel, Jr. 12
Gomez-Preston, Cheryl 9
Gordon-Reed, Annette 74
Gourdin, Edward O. 93
Graham, Lawrence Otis 12
Gray, Fred 37
Gray, Willie 46
Greenhouse, Bunnatine 57
Grimké, Archibald H. 9
Guinier, Lani 7, 30
Haley, George Williford Boyce 21
Hall, Elliott S. 24
Harris, Kamala D. 64
Harris, Maya Lakshmi 88
Harris, Patricia Roberts 2
Harvard, Beverly 11
Hassell, Leroy Rountree, Sr. 41

Hastie, William H. 8
Hastings, Alcee L. 16
Hatcher, Richard G. 55
Hatchett, Glenda 32
Hawkins, Augustus F. 68
Hawkins, Steven 14
Hayes, Dennis 54
Haywood, Margaret A. 24
Henderson, Thelton E. 68
Higginbotham, A. Leon, Jr. 13, 25
Hill, Anita 5, 65
Hillard, Terry 25
Hills, Oliver W. 24
Holder, Eric H., Jr. 9, 76
Hollowell, Donald L. 57
Holton, Hugh, Jr. 39
Hooks, Benjamin L. 2, 85
Houston, Charles Hamilton 4
Hubbard, Arnette Rhinehart 38
Hunter, Billy 22
Hurtt, Harold 46
Isaac, Julius 34
Jackson, Maynard 2, 41
Jackson Lee, Sheila 20
Johnson, Harry E. 57
Johnson, James Weldon 5
Johnson, Jeh C. 76
Johnson, Leroy R. 89
Johnson, Norma L. Holloway 17
Jones, Elaine R. 7, 45
Jones, Van 70
Jordan, Eddie 82
Jordan, Vernon E. 3, 35
Kearse, Amalya Lyle 12
Keith, Damon J. 16, 74
Kennard, William Earl 18
Kennedy, Florynce 12, 33
Kennedy, Randall 40
Kibaki, Mwai 60
Kirk, Ron 11, 75
Lafontant, Jewel Stradford 3, 51
Lewis, Delano 7
Lewis, Reginald F. 6
Lewis, William Henry 89
Lloyd, Reginald 64
Majette, Denise 41
Mallett, Conrad, Jr. 16
Mandela, Nelson 1, 14, 77
Marsh, Henry, III 32
Marshall, Thurgood 1, 44
Mathis, Greg 26
McAnulty, William E., Jr. 66
McCrary Anthony, Crystal 70
McDonald, Gabrielle Kirk 20
McDougall, Gay J. 11, 43
McKinnon, Isaiah 9
McKissick, Floyd B. 3
McPhail, Sharon 2
Meeks, Gregory 25
Melton, Harold D. 79
Mitchell, Arthur Wergs 91
Mitchell, Clarence M., Jr. 88
Moose, Charles 40
Morial, Ernest "Dutch" 26
Morton, Ferdinand Q. 90
Morton, Frederick A., Jr. 93
Motley, Constance Baker 10, 55
Muhammad, Ava 31
Murray, Pauli 38
Nance, Cynthia 71
Napoleon, Benny N. 23
Nash, Shannon King 84
Nelson, Sophia A. 93

Nix, Robert N. C., Jr. 51
Noble, Ronald 46
Nunn, Annetta 43
Obama, Michelle 61, 90
Ogletree, Charles, Jr. 12, 47
Ogunlesi, Adebayo O. 37
Oliver, Jerry 37
Page, Alan 7
Parker, Barrington D. 92
Parker, Kellis E. 30
Parks, Bernard C. 17
Parsons, James 14
Parsons, Richard Dean 11, 33
Pascal-Trouillot, Ertha 3
Paterson, Basil A. 69
Patrick, Deval 12
Payne, Ulice 42
Payton, John 48
Perry, Lowell 30
Philip, Marlene Nourbese 32
Pincham, R. Eugene, Sr. 69
Powell, Michael 32
Quince, Peggy A. 69
Ramsey, Charles H. 21, 69
Raoul, Kwame 55
Rawlinson, Johnnie B. 79
Ray, Charlotte E. 60
Redding, Louis L. 26
Reed, Kasim 82
Reynolds, Star Jones 10, 27, 61
Rice, Constance LaMay 60
Richie, Leroy C. 18
Robinson, Bishop L. 66
Robinson, Malcolm S. 44
Robinson, Randall 7, 46
Roundtree, Dovey 80
Russell-McCloud, Patricia 17
Sampson, Edith S. 4
Schmoke, Kurt 1, 48
Sears, Leah Ward 5, 79
Smith, DeMaurice 92
Solomon, Jimmie Lee 38
Sparks, Corinne Etta 53
Stokes, Louis 3
Stout, Juanita Kidd 24
Strautmanis, Michael 87
Sutton, Percy E. 42, 82
Taylor, John (David Beckett) 16
Thomas, Arthur Ray 52
Thomas, Clarence 2, 39, 65
Thomas, Franklin A. 5, 49
Thompson, Larry D. 39
Touré, Faya Ora Rose 56
Tubbs Jones, Stephanie 24, 72
Van Lierop, Robert 53
Vanzant, Iyanla 17, 47
Wagner, Annice 22
Wainwright, Joscelyn 46
Walker, Cora T. 68
Wallace, Perry E. 47
Ward, Benjamin 68
Washington, Harold 6
Watkins, Donald 35
Watt, Melvin 26
Wharton, Clifton Reginald, Sr. 36
Wilder, L. Douglas 3, 48
Wilkins, David 77
Williams, Ann Claire 82
Williams, Evelyn 10
Williams, Gregory 11
Williams, Patricia 11, 54
Williams, Willie L. 4
Wilson, Jimmy 45

Worthy, Kym **84**
Wright, Bruce McMarion **3, 52**
Wynn, Albert **25, 77**

Military

Abacha, Sani **11, 70**
Adams Early, Charity **13, 34**
Adams-Ender, Clara **40**
Alexander, Margaret Walker **22**
Amin, Idi **42**
Archer, Lee, Jr. **79**
Babangida, Ibrahim **4**
Baker, Vernon Joseph **65, 87**
Bashir, Omar al- **77**
Black, Barry C. **47**
Bolden, Charles Frank, Jr. **7, 78**
Brashear, Carl **29**
Brown, Anthony G. **72**
Brown, Erroll M. **23**
Brown, Jesse **6, 41**
Brown, Jesse Leroy **31**
Brown, Willa **40**
Bullard, Eugene **12**
Cadoria, Sherian Grace **14**
Chissano, Joaquim **7, 55, 67**
Christophe, Henri **9**
Clemmons, Reginal G. **41**
Compaore, Blaise **87**
Conté, Lansana **7, 76**
Cooke, Marcia **60**
Davis, Benjamin O., Jr. **2, 43**
Davis, Benjamin O., Sr. **4**
Drew, Alvin, Jr. **67**
Duggins, George **64**
Europe, James Reese **10**
Eyadéma, Gnassingbé **7, 52**
Fields, Evelyn J. **27**
Flipper, Henry O. **3**
Gravely, Samuel L., Jr. **5, 49**
Gregory, Frederick **8, 51**
Guéï, Robert **66**
Habré, Hissène **6**
Habyarimana, Juvenal **8**
Harris, Marcelite Jordan **16**
Healy, Michael **90**
Honoré, Russel L. **64**
Howard, Michelle **28**
Jackson, Fred James **25**
James, Daniel, Jr. **16**
Johnson, Hazel **22**
Johnson, Shoshana **47**
Julian, Hubert **90**
Kagame, Paul **54**
Kerekou, Ahmed (Mathieu) **1**
Kiir, Salva **85**
King, Teresa **80**
Laraque, Paul **67**
Lawrence, Robert H., Jr. **16**
Lyles, Lester **31**
Maceo, Antonio **82**
Magloire, Paul Eugène **68**
Matthews, Mark **59**
Miller, Dorie **29**
Nkunda, Laurent **75**
Nyanda, Siphiwe **21**
Obasanjo, Olusegun **5, 22**
Perry, Herman **89**
Petersen, Frank E. **31**
Powell, Colin **1, 28, 75**
Pratt, Geronimo **18**
Rawlings, Jerry **9**
Reason, J. Paul **19**
Rochon, Stephen W. **78**

Rogers, Alan G. **72**
Scantlebury, Janna **47**
Smalls, Robert **82**
Snow, Samuel **71**
Stanford, John **20**
Staupers, Mabel K. **7**
Stokes, Louis **3**
Touré, Amadou Toumani **18**
Von Lipsey, Roderick K. **11**
Watkins, Perry **12**
West, Togo, D., Jr. **16**
Wilson, Jimmy **45**
Wright, Lewin **43**
Young, Charles **77**

Music

Aaliyah **30**
Ace, Johnny **36**
Adams, Johnny **39**
Adams, Leslie **39**
Adams, Oleta **18**
Adams, Yolanda **17, 67**
Adderley, Julian "Cannonball" **30**
Adderley, Nat **29**
Ade, King Sunny **41**
Adebimpe, Tunde **75**
Afro, Teddy **78**
Akon **68**
Albright, Gerald **23**
Alert, Kool DJ **33**
Ali, Rashied **79**
Allen, Betty **83**
Allen, Geri **92**
Amerie **52**
Anderson, Carl **48**
Anderson, Fred **87**
Anderson, Marian **2, 33**
apl.de.ap **84**
Ardoin, Alphonse **65**
Armatrading, Joan **32**
Armstrong, Louis **2**
Armstrong, Vanessa Bell **24**
Arroyo, Marina **30**
Ashanti **37**
Ashford, Nickolas **21**
Ashong, Derrick **86**
Astatke, Mulatu **81**
Atkins, Juan **50**
Austin, Lovie **40**
Austin, Patti **24**
Avant, Clarence **19, 86**
Avant, Nicole A. **90**
Ayers, Roy **16**
Babyface **10, 31, 82**
Baca, Susana **80**
Badu, Erykah **22**
Bailey, Buster **38**
Bailey, DeFord **33**
Bailey, Philip **63**
Bailey Rae, Corinne **83**
Baiocchi, Regina Harris **41**
Baker, Anita **21, 48**
Baker, Josephine **3**
Baker, LaVern **26**
Ballard, Hank **41**
Bambaataa, Afrika **34**
Banner, David **55**
Banton, Buju **93**
Barker, Danny **32**
Barnes, Lloyd **77**
Barnes, Roosevelt "Booba" **33**
Barrino, Fantasia **53**
Basie, Count **23**

Bassey, Shirley **25**
Batiste, Alvin **66**
Battle, Kathleen **70**
Baylor, Helen **36**
Bebey, Francis **45**
Bechet, Sidney **18**
Beenie Man **32**
Belafonte, Harry **4, 65**
Belgrave, Marcus **77**
Belle, Regina **1, 51**
Benét, Eric **28, 77**
Benjamin, Andre **45**
Bennett, Estelle **77**
Bentley, Lamont **53**
Berry, Chuck **29**
Betts, Keter **85**
Beverly, Frankie **25**
Beyoncé **39, 70**
Bibb, Eric **49**
Big Daddy Kane **79**
Bivins, Michael **72**
Black Thought **63**
Blackman, Toni **86**
Blade, Brian **88**
Blake, Eubie **29**
Blakey, Art **37**
Blanchard, Terence **43**
Bland, Bobby "Blue" **36**
Bleu, Corbin **65**
Blige, Mary J. **20, 34, 60**
Blondy, Alpha **30**
Blow, Kurtis **31**
B.o.B. **91**
Bolden, Buddy **39**
Bond, Beverly **53**
Bonds, Margaret **39**
Bonga, Kuenda **13**
Bow Wow **35**
Boyz II Men **82**
Bradley, J. Robert **65**
Brae, C. Michael **61**
Brandy **14, 34, 72**
Braxton, Toni **15, 61, 91**
Bridgetower, George **78**
Bridgewater, Dee Dee **32, 92**
Brooks, Avery **9**
Brooks, Hadda **40**
Broonzy, Big Bill **82**
Brown, Angela M. **54**
Brown, Anne **76**
Brown, Bobby **58**
Brown, Carlinhos **81**
Brown, Charles **23**
Brown, Chris **74**
Brown, Chuck **78**
Brown, Clarence Gatemouth **59**
Brown, Clifford **86**
Brown, Foxy **25**
Brown, James **15, 60**
Brown, Melanie **73**
Brown, Nappy **73**
Brown, Oscar, Jr. **53**
Brown, Patrick "Sleepy" **50**
Brown, Ruth **90**
Brown, Uzee **42**
Brownlee, Lawrence **88**
Bumbry, Grace **5**
Burke, Solomon **31, 86**
Burleigh, Henry Thacker **56**
Burning Spear **79**
Burns, Eddie **44**
Burnside, R. L. **56**
Busby, Jheryl **3, 74**

Butler, George, Jr. **70**
Butler, Jerry **26**
Butler, Jonathan **28**
Caesar, Shirley **19**
Cage, Byron **53**
Calloway, Cab **1**
Campbell-Martin, Tisha **8, 42**
Cannon, Nick **47, 73**
Carey, Mariah **32, 53, 69**
Carr, Kurt **56**
Carr, Leroy **49**
Carroll, Diahann **9**
Carter, Benny **46**
Carter, Betty **19**
Carter, Nell **39**
Carter, Regina **23**
Carter, Warrick L. **27**
Cartiér, Xam Wilson **41**
Caymmi, Dorival **72**
Cee-Lo **70**
Chamillionaire **82**
Chanté, Keshia **50**
Chapman, Tracy **26**
Charlemagne, Manno **11**
Charles, Ray **16, 48**
Cheatham, Doc **17**
Checker, Chubby **28**
Chenault, John **40**
Christie, Angella **36**
Chuck D **9**
Ciara **56**
Clark, Mattie Moss **61**
Clark-Cole, Dorinda **66**
Clarke, Kenny **27**
Clark-Sheard, Karen **22**
Clemons, Clarence **41**
Cleveland, James **19**
Cliff, Jimmy **28, 92**
Clinton, George **9, 93**
Cole, Keyshia **63**
Cole, Nat "King" **17**
Cole, Natalie **17, 60, 84**
Coleman, Ornette **39, 69**
Coleridge-Taylor, Samuel **75**
Collins, Albert **12**
Collins, Bootsy **31**
Collins, Lyn **53**
Coltrane, Alice **70**
Coltrane, John **19**
Coltrane, Ravi **71**
Combs, Sean **17, 43, 92**
Common **31, 63**
Conrad, Barbara Smith **90**
Cook, Charles "Doc" **44**
Cook, Will Marion **40**
Cooke, Sam **17**
Coppola, Imani Francesca **82**
Cortez, Jayne **43**
Count Basie **23**
Cowboy Troy **54**
Cox, Deborah **28**
Cox, Ida **42**
Craig, Carl **31, 71**
Crawford, Hank **77**
Crawford, Randy **19**
Cray, Robert **30**
Creagh, Milton **27**
Crocker, Frankie **29**
Crothers, Scatman **19**
Crouch, Andraé **27**
Crowder, Henry **16**
Da Don, Polow **86**
Daemyon, Jerald **64**

D'Angelo 27
Danjah, Terror 91
Dara, Olu 35
Dash, Damon 31
Dash, Darien 29
David, Craig 31, 53
Davis, Anthony 11
Davis, Gary 41
Davis, Guy 36
Davis, Miles 4
Davis, Sammy, Jr. 18
Davis, Tyrone 54
Dawson, William Levi 39
de Passe, Suzanne 25
DeBarge, El 89
Deezer D 53
Dennard, Brazeal 37
Derülo, Jason 93
DeVaughn, Raheem 91
Dickenson, Vic 38
Diddley, Bo 39, 72
Dixon, Bill 87
Dixon, Dean 68
Dixon, Willie 4
DJ Jazzy Jeff 32
DMX 28, 64
Dobbs, Mattiwilda 34
Domino, Fats 20
Donegan, Dorothy 19
Dorsey, Lee 65
Dorsey, Thomas 15
Downing, Will 19
Drake 86
Dre, Dr. 10, 14, 30
Dube, Lucky 77
Duke, George 21
Dumas, Henry 41
Duncan, Todd 76
Dunner, Leslie B. 45
Duplechan, Larry 55
Dupri, Jermaine 13, 46
Durham, Bobby 73
Dworkin, Aaron P. 52
Earthquake 55
Eckstine, Billy 28
Edmonds, Tracey 16, 64
Edwards, Esther Gordy 43
Eldridge, Roy 37
Ellington, Duke 5
Elliott, Missy 31, 90
Ellis, Alton 74
Escobar, Damien 56
Escobar, Tourie 56
Estelle 75
Estes, Simon 28
Estes, Sleepy John 33
Eubanks, Kevin 15
Europe, James Reese 10
Evans, Faith 22
Eve 29
Evora, Cesaria 12
Fabolous 93
Falana, Lola 42
Farmer, Art 38
Fat Boys 92
Feemster, Herbert 72
Fela 1, 42
Ferrell, Rachelle 29
Ferrer, Ibrahim 41
Fiasco, Lupe 64
50 Cent 46, 83
Fiona, Melanie 84
Fitzgerald, Ella 8, 18

Flack, Roberta 19
Flanagan, Tommy 69
Flavor Flav 67
Flo Rida 78
Ford, T-Model 91
Ford, Vincent 75
Forté, John 74
Fortune, James 92
Foster, George "Pops" 40
Foster, William P. 88
Foxx, Jamie 15, 48
Franklin, Aretha 11, 44
Franklin, Kirk 15, 49
Franti, Michael 93
Freelon, Nnenna 32
Freeman, Paul 39
Freeman, Yvette 27
Fresh, Doug E. 93
Fuller, Blind Boy 86
Fuqua, Antoine 35
Fuqua, Harvey 90
Gaines, Grady 38
Gamble, Kenny 85
Garner, Erroll 76
Garrett, Sean 57
Gaye, Marvin 2
Gaye, Nona 56
Gaynor, Gloria 36
George, Zelma Watson 42
Ghostface Killah 90
Gibson, Althea 8, 43
Gibson, Tyrese 27, 62
Gil, Gilberto 53
Gill, Johnny 51
Gillespie, Dizzy 1
Ginuwine 35
Glover, Corey 34
Goapele 55
Golson, Benny 37
Goodman, Al 87
Gordon, Dexter 25
Gordy, Berry, Jr. 1
Gotti, Irv 39
Grae, Jean 51
Grandmaster Flash 33, 60
Graves, Denyce Antoinette 19, 57
Gray, F. Gary 14, 49
Gray, Macy 29
Greaves, William 38
Greely, M. Gasby 27
Green, Al 13, 47, 74
Green, Grant 56
Greene, Jimmy 74
Griffey, Dick 89
Griffin, Johnny 71
Griffin, LaShell 51
Griffiths, Marcia 29
Grist, Reri 84
Güines, Tata 69
Guru 84
Guy, Buddy 31
Haddon, Dietrick 55
Hailey, JoJo 22
Hailey, K-Ci 22
Hairston, Jester 88
Hall, Aaron 57
Hall, Juanita 62
Hamilton, Anthony 61
Hammond, Fred 23
Hammond, Lenn 34
Hampton, Lionel 17, 41
Hancock, Herbie 20, 67
Handy, W. C. 8

Hardin Armstrong, Lil 39
Harper, Ben 34, 62
Harrell, Andre 9, 30
Harris, Barry 68
Harris, Corey 39, 73
Hart, Alvin Youngblood 61
Hathaway, Donny 18
Hathaway, Lalah 57, 88
Hawkins, Coleman 9
Hawkins, Erskine 14
Hawkins, Screamin' Jay 30
Hawkins, Tramaine 16
Hawkins, Walter 87
Hayes, Isaac 20, 58, 73
Hayes, Roland 4
Hayes, Teddy 40
Haynes, Roy 87
Heavy D 58
Hemphill, Jessie Mae 33, 59
Henderson, Fletcher 32
Hendricks, Barbara 3, 67
Hendrix, Jimi 10
Hendryx, Nona 56
Henry, Clarence "Frogman" 46
Higginbotham, J. C. 37
Higginsen, Vy 65
Hill, Andrew 66
Hill, Lauryn 20, 53
Hilson, Keri 84
Hinderas, Natalie 5
Hines, Earl "Fatha" 39
Hinton, Milt 30
Holiday, Billie 1
Holland-Dozier-Holland 36
Holloway, Brenda 65
Holmes, Clint 57
Holt, Nora 38
Hooker, John Lee 30
Hopkins, Lightnin' 83
Horn, Shirley 32, 56
Horne, Lena 5, 86
Horton, Gladys 92
Houghton, Israel 92
House, Son 8
Houston, Cissy 20, 83
Houston, Whitney 7, 28, 83
Howell, Ayinde 91
Howlin' Wolf 9
Hubbard, Freddie 75
Hudson, Jennifer 63, 83
Huff, Leon 86
Humphrey, Bobbi 20
Hunter, Alberta 42
Hurt, Mississippi John 84
Hutch, Willie 62
Hyman, Phyllis 19
Ice Cube 8, 30, 60
Ice-T 6, 31
India.Arie 34
Ingram, James 84
Isaacs, Gregory 89
Isley, Marvin 87
Isley, Ronald 25, 56
Ja Rule 35, 91
Jackson, Fred James 25
Jackson, George 19
Jackson, Hal 41
Jackson, Isaiah 3
Jackson, Janet 6, 30, 68
Jackson, Jermaine 79
Jackson, John 36
Jackson, Mahalia 5
Jackson, Michael 19, 53, 76

Jackson, Millie 25
Jackson, Milt 26
Jackson, Randy 40
Jackson, Tito 81
Jacquet, Illinois 49
Jaheim 58
Jamal, Ahmad 69
Jamelia 51
Jamerson, James 59
James, Etta 13, 52
James, Rick 17
James, Skip 38
Jarreau, Al 21, 65
Jay-Z 27, 69
Jean, Wyclef 20, 86
Jefferson, Blind Lemon 81
Jenkins, Ella 15
Jennings, Lyfe 56, 69
Jerkins, Rodney 31
Jeter, Claude 75
Jimmy Jam 13
Johnson, Beverly 2
Johnson, Buddy 36
Johnson, Hall 90
Johnson, J. J. 37
Johnson, James Weldon 5
Johnson, Johnnie 56
Johnson, Lonnie 85
Johnson, Robert 2
Johnson-George, Tamara 79
Jones, Bobby 20
Jones, Booker T. 84
Jones, Donell 29
Jones, Elvin 14, 68
Jones, Etta 35
Jones, Hank 57, 86
Jones, Jonah 39
Jones, Quincy 8, 30
Jones, Robert G. 81
Jones, Sharon 86
Jones, Thad 68
Joplin, Scott 6
Jordan, Montell 23
Jordan, Ronny 26
Jorge, Seu 73
Joyner, Matilda Sissieretta 15
Kandi 83
Kay, Ulysses 37
Kee, John P. 43
Keita, Salif 83
Kelis 58
Kelley, Elijah 65
Kelly, R. 18, 44, 71
Kem 47
Kendricks, Eddie 22
Kenoly, Ron 45
Kenyatta, Robin 54
Keys, Alicia 32, 68
Khan, Chaka 12, 50
Kid Cudi 83
Kidjo, Angelique 50
Killings, Debra 57
King, B. B. 7
King, Coretta Scott 3, 57
King, Freddie 92
King Curtis 92
Kitt, Eartha 16, 75
Klugh, Earl 59
K'naan 76
Knight, Gladys 16, 66
Knight, Marie 80
Knight, Suge 11, 30
Knowles, Tina 61

Knuckles, Frankie 42
Kolosoy, Wendo 73
Kool Moe Dee 37
Kravitz, Lenny 10, 34
KRS-One 34
K-Swift 73
Kuti, Femi 47
Kweli, Talib 93
LaBelle, Patti 13, 30
Larrieux, Amel 63
Lateef, Yusef 91
Lattimore, Kenny 35
LaVette, Bettye 85
Laws, Hubert 90
Leadbelly 82
Ledisi 73
Lee, Consuela 84
Lefel, Edith 41
Legend, John 67
León, Tania 13
Lester, Julius 9
Levert, Eddie 70
Levert, Gerald 22, 59
Lewis, Ananda 28
Lewis, Butch 71
Lewis, Henry 38
Lewis, Leona 75
Lewis, Ramsey 35, 70
Lewis, Terry 13
Lil' Kim 28
Lil Wayne 66, 84
Liles, Kevin 42
Lincoln, Abbey 3, 88
Lipscomb, Mance 49
Lister, Marquita 65
Little Milton 36, 54
Little Richard 15
Little Walter 36
LL Cool J 16, 49
Locke, Eddie 44
Long, Huey 79
Lopes, Lisa "Left Eye" 36
Loueke, Lionel 88
Love, Darlene 23, 92
Love, Ed 58
Love, Laura 50
Lover, Ed 10
Lucie, Lawrence 80
Lucien, Jon 66
Luckett, Letoya 61
Ludacris 37, 60
Lymon, Frankie 22
Maal, Baaba 66
Madlib 88
Mahal, Taj 39
Mahlasela, Vusi 65
Maitreya, Sananda 85
Majors, Jeff 41
Makeba, Miriam 2, 50, 74
Mane, Gucci 91
Mann, Tamela 92
Mario 71
Marley, Bob 5
Marley, Rita 32, 70
Marley, Ziggy 41
Marrow, Queen Esther 24
Marsalis, Branford 34
Marsalis, Delfeayo 41
Marsalis, Ellis 90
Marsalis, Wynton 16, 90
Martelly, Michel 90
Martin, Roberta 58
Martin, Sara 38

Mary Mary 34, 92
Mase 24
Masekela, Hugh 1
Massenburg, Kedar 23
Master P 21
Mathis, Johnny 20
Matthews, Benjamin 93
Maxwell 20, 81
May, Derrick 41
Mayfield, Curtis 2, 43
Maynor, Dorothy 19
MC Breed 75
M.C. Hammer 20, 80
MC Lyte 34
McClendon, Lisa 61
McClurkin, Donnie 25
McCoo, Marilyn 53
McDaniel, Hattie 5
McFerrin, Bobby 68
McGill, Anthony 76
McGriff, Jimmy 72
McKee, Lonette 12
McKinney, Nina Mae 40
McKnight, Brian 18, 34
McLean, Jackie 78
McPherson, David 32
McRae, Carmen 77
McTell, Blind Willie 89
Memphis Minnie 33
Method Man 81
Miles, Buddy 69
Miller, Marcus 84
Mills, Stephanie 36
Minaj, Nicki 86
Mingus, Charles 15
Minott, Sugar 86
Mitchell, Leona 42
Mitchell, Nicole 66
Mo', Keb' 36
Monáe, Janelle 86
Monica 21
Monk, Thelonious 1
Montgomery, Wes 88
Moody, James 83
Moore, Chante 26
Moore, Dorothy Rudd 46
Moore, Johnny B. 38
Moore, LeRoi 72
Moore, Melba 21
Moore, Undine Smith 28
Moran, Jason 89
Morton, Jelly Roll 29
Mos Def 30
Moses, Gilbert 12
Moss, J 64
Moten, Etta 18
Moura, Paulo 87
Mowatt, Judy 38
Mullen, Nicole C. 45
Mumba, Samantha 29
Murphy, Eddie 4, 20, 61
Murray, Tai 47
Muse, Clarence Edouard 21
Musiq 37, 84
Mya 35
Nas 33
Nascimento, Milton 2, 64
Nash, Johnny 40
Nate Dogg 92
Ndegeocello, Meshell 15, 83
N'Dour, Youssou 1, 53, 79
Neal, Raful 44
Neale, Haydain 52

Nelly 32, 90
Neville, Aaron 21
Newman, David 76
Ne-Yo 65
Nicholas, Fayard 20, 57
Nicholas, Harold 20
Noah, Yannick 4, 60
Norman, Jessye 5
Notorious B.I.G. 20
Odetta 37, 74
Okosuns, Sonny 71
Ol' Dirty Bastard 52
Olatunji, Babatunde 36
Oliver, Joe "King" 42
O'Neal, Shaquille 8, 30
Ongala, Remmy 9, 91
Osborne, Jeffrey 26
Otis, Clyde 67
OutKast 35
Owens, Jack 38
Palmer, Keke 68
Palmer, Rissi 65
Parker, Charlie 20
Parker, Maceo 72
Parker, Ray, Jr. 85
Parks, Gordon 1, 35, 58
Patton, Antwan 45
Payne, Freda 58
Pena, Paul 58
Pendergrass, Teddy 22, 83
Peoples, Dottie 22
Perkins, Pinetop 70
Perren, Freddie 60
Perry, Ruth 19
Peterson, James 38
Peterson, Marvin "Hannibal" 27
Peterson, Oscar 52
Phillips, Helen L. 63
Phipps, Wintley 59
Pinkney, Fayette 80
Pleasure P 84
P.M. Dawn 54
Portuondo, Omara 53
Powell, Benny 87
Powell, Bud 24
Powell, Maxine 8
Pratt, Awadagin 31
Premice, Josephine 41
Preston, Billy 39, 59
Price, Florence 37
Price, Kelly 23
Price, Leontyne 1
Pride, Charley 26
Prince 18, 65
Pritchard, Robert Starling 21
Pryce, Trevor 89
Pryor, Rain 65
Purdie, Bernard 77
Queen Latifah 1, 16, 58
?uestlove 74
Ragin, Derek Lee 84
Rainey, Ma 33
Ralph, Sheryl Lee 18
Randall, Alice 38
Ranglin, Ernest 78
Rascal, Dizzee 82
Ray J 86
Razaf, Andy 19
Reagon, Bernice Johnson 7
Reagon, Toshi 76
Record, Eugene 60
Redman 81
Redman, Joshua 30

Reed, A. C. 36
Reed, Jimmy 38
Reese, Della 6, 20
Reeves, Dianne 32
Reeves, Martha 85
Reid, Antonio "L.A." 28
Reid, Vernon 34
Rhoden, Wayne 70
Rhone, Sylvia 2
Rhymes, Busta 31
Richard, Dawn 92
Richie, Lionel 27, 65
Rihanna 65
Riley, Boots 89
Riperton, Minnie 32
Roach, Max 21, 63
Roberts, Kimberly Rivers 72
Roberts, Marcus 19
Robeson, Paul 2
Robinson, Fenton 38
Robinson, Reginald R. 53
Robinson, Smokey 3, 49
Robinson, Sylvia 79
Rodríguez, Arsenio 87
Rogers, Jimmy 38
Rollins, Sonny 37
Ross, Diana 8, 27
Ross, Isaiah "Doc" 40
Ross, Rick 79
Roxanne Shante 33
Rucker, Darius 34, 74
Rudder, David 79
Ruffins, Kermit 85
Run 31, 73
Run-DMC 31, 75
RuPaul 17, 91
Rush, Bobby 78
Rush, Otis 38
Rushen, Patrice 12
Rushing, Jimmy 37
Russell, Brenda 52
RZA 80
Sade 15, 92
Sample, Joe 51
Sanders, Angelia 86
Sanders, Pharoah 64
Sangare, Oumou 18
Santamaria, Mongo 81
Sapp, Marvin 74
Scarlett, Millicent 49
Schuyler, Philippa 50
Scott, George 55
Scott, Hazel 66
Scott, Jill 29, 83
Scott, "Little" Jimmy 48
Seal 14, 75
Seals, Son 56
Sermon, Erick 81
Shaggy 31
Shakur, Afeni 67
Shakur, Tupac 14
Sheard, Kierra "Kiki 61
Shider, Garry 87
Shirley, George 33
Short, Bobby 52
Shorter, Wayne 75
Shorty, Ras, I 47
Siji 56
Silver, Horace 26
Simmons, Russell 1, 30
Simone, Nina 15, 41
Simpson, Valerie 21
Simpson-Hoffman, N'kenge 52

Sir Mix-A-Lot 82
Sisqo 30
Sissle, Noble 29
Sister Souljah 11
Slash 75
Sledge, Percy 39
Slick Rick 93
Slim Thug 86
Sly & Robbie 34
Smith, Bessie 3
Smith, Cladys "Jabbo" 32
Smith, Dr. Lonnie 49
Smith, Lonnie Liston 49
Smith, Mamie 32
Smith, Myrna 92
Smith, Stuff 37
Smith, Trixie 34
Smith, Will 8, 18, 53
Smith, Willow 92
Snoop Dogg 35, 84
Somi 85
Songz, Trey 88
Southern, Eileen 56
Sowande, Fela 39
Sparks, Jordin 66
Spector, Ronnie 77
Speech 82
Spence, Joseph 49
Stampley, Micah 54
Stanford, Olivia Lee Dilworth 49
Staples, Mavis 50, 88
Staples, "Pops" 32
Staton, Candi 27
Staton, Dakota 62
Steely 80
Steinberg, Martha Jean "The
   Queen" 28
Stew 69
Sticky Fingaz 86
Still, William Grant 37
Stone, Angie 31
Stone, Sly 85
Stoute, Steve 38
Strayhorn, Billy 31
Streeter, Sarah 45
Strong, Barrett 89
Studdard, Ruben 46
Sugarhill Gang, The 79
Sullivan, Jazmine 81
Sullivan, Maxine 37
Summer, Donna 25
Sun Ra 60
Sundiata, Sekou 66
Supremes, The 33
Sweat, Keith 19
Sykes, Roosevelt 20
Tait, Michael 57
Tamar-kali 63
Tamia 24, 55
Tampa Red 63
Tatum, Art 28
Taylor, Billy 23, 92
Taylor, Cecil 70
Taylor, Koko 40, 80
Tempations, The 33
Terrell, Tammi 32
Terry, Clark 39
Terry, Sonny 88
Tharpe, Rosetta 65
The-Dream 74
Thomas, Irma 29
Thomas, Rozonda 34, 78
Thomas, Rufus 20

Thornton, Big Mama 33
Three Mo' Tenors 35
Thurston, Stephen J. 49
Tillis, Frederick 40
Timbaland 32
Tinsley, Boyd 50
Tisdale, Wayman 50
TLC 34
Tonex 54
Tosh, Peter 9
Toussaint, Allen 60
T-Pain 73
Tresvant, Ralph 57
Tribbett, Tye 81
Turnbull, Walter 13, 60
Turner, Big Joe 92
Turner, Ike 68
Turner, Tina 6, 27
Tyner, McCoy 92
Uggams, Leslie 23
Ulmer, James 79
Usher 23, 56
Valdés, Bebo 75
Valdés, Chucho 89
Valentino, Bobby 62
Vandross, Luther 13, 48, 59
Vanity 67
Vaughan, Sarah 13
Vereen, Ben 4
Verrett, Shirley 66, 91
Wale 92
Walker, Albertina 10, 58, 89
Walker, Cedric 19
Walker, George 37
Walker, Hezekiah 34
Wallace, Sippie 1
Waller, Fats 29
Warwick, Dionne 18
Washington, Dinah 22
Washington, Grover, Jr. 17, 44
Waters, Benny 26
Waters, Ethel 7
Waters, Muddy 34
Watley, Jody 54
Watson, Johnny "Guitar" 18
Watts, Andre 42
Watts, Reggie 52
Webster, Katie 29
Wein, Joyce 62
Welch, Elisabeth 52
Wells, Mary 28
West, Kanye 52, 93
Whalum, Kirk 37, 64
White, Barry 13, 41
White, Josh 86
White, Josh, Jr. 52
White, Maurice 29
White, Willard 53
Whitfield, Norman 73
Wilkins, Thomas Alphonso 71
will.i.am 64
Williams, Bert 18
Williams, Clarence 33
Williams, Claude 80
Williams, Deniece 36
Williams, Denise 40
Williams, J. Mayo 83
Williams, Joe 5, 25
Williams, Mary Lou 15
Williams, Michelle 73
Williams, Nat D. 91
Williams, Pharrell 47, 82
Williams, Saul 31

Williams, Tony 67
Williams, Vanessa L. 4, 17
Williamson, Sonny Boy 84
Wilson, Cassandra 16
Wilson, Charlie 31, 77
Wilson, Gerald 49
Wilson, Jackie 60
Wilson, Mary 28
Wilson, Nancy 10
Wilson, Natalie 38
Wilson, Sunnie 7, 55
Winans, Angie 36
Winans, BeBe 14
Winans, CeCe 14, 43
Winans, David 77
Winans, Debbie 36
Winans, Marvin L. 17
Winans, Ronald 54
Winans, Vickie 24
Withers, Bill 61
Withers-Mendes, Elisabeth 64
Womack, Bobby 60, 92
Wonder, Stevie 11, 53
Woods, Georgie 57
Woods, Scott 55
Woodson, Ali Ollie 89
Wright, Timothy 74
Xzibit 78
Yabby You 83
Yarbrough, Camille 40
Yoba, Malik 11
York, Vincent 40
Young, Lee 72
Young, Lester 37
Young Jeezy 63

Religion

Abernathy, Ralph David 1
Adams, Yolanda 17, 67
Agyeman, Jaramogi Abebe 10, 63
Akinola, Peter Jasper 65
Akpan, Uwem 70
Al-Amin, Jamil Abdullah 6
Anthony, Wendell 25
Arinze, Francis 19
Aristide, Jean-Bertrand 6, 45
Armstrong, Vanessa Bell 24
Austin, Junius C. 44
Banks, William 11
Barrow, Willie T. 85
Baylor, Helen 36
Beauvoir, Max 74
Bell, Ralph S. 5
Ben-Israel, Ben Ami 11
Berry, Moses 84
Black, Barry C. 47
Blake, Charles E. 82
Blanks, Deborah K. 69
Bloomer, George 86
Bowen, John W. E., Sr. 89
Boyd, T. B., III 6
Braxton, Brad 77
Bryant, John R. 45
Burgess, John 46
Butts, Calvin O., III 9, 90
Bynum, Juanita 31, 71
Caesar, Shirley 19
Cage, Byron 53
Caldwell, Kirbyjon 55
Cannon, Katie 10
Cardozo, Francis L. 33
Carr, Kurt 56
Chavis, Benjamin 6

Chineworth, Mary Alice 79
Cleaver, Emanuel 4, 45, 68
Clements, George 2
Cleveland, James 19
Colemon, Johnnie 11
Collins, Janet 33, 64
Coltrane, Alice 70
Cone, James H. 3, 82
Cook, Suzan D. Johnson 22
Crouch, Andraé 27
Dandala, Mvume 77
DeLille, Henriette 30
Divine, Father 7
DuBois, Joshua 88
Dyson, Michael Eric 11, 40
Easton, Hosea 91
Ellis, Charles H., III 79
Elmore, Ronn 21
Fabre, Shelton 71
Farrakhan, Louis 2, 15
Fauntroy, Walter E. 11
Fisher, Miles Mark 91
Flake, Floyd H. 18
Forbes, James A., Jr. 71
Franklin, C. L. 68
Franklin, Kirk 15, 49
Franklin, Robert M. 13
Fuller, Thomas O. 90
Funnye, Capers C., Jr. 73
Gaither, Israel L. 65
Gantin, Bernardin 70
Gilmore, Marshall 46
Gomes, Peter J. 15, 93
Gray, Darius 69
Gray, William H., III 3
Green, Al 13, 47, 74
Gregory, Wilton 37
Grier, Roosevelt 13
Haddon, Dietrick 55
Haile Selassie 7
Harding, Vincent 67
Harris, Barbara 12
Hawkins, Tramaine 16
Hawkins, Walter 87
Hayes, James C. 10
Healy, James Augustine 30
Holsey, Lucius Henry 92
Hood, James Walker 91
Hooks, Benjamin L. 2, 85
Howard, M. William, Jr. 26
Jackson, Jesse 1, 27, 72
Jakes, Thomas "T. D." 17, 43
Jasper, John J. 91
Jean-Juste, Gérard 78
Jemison, Major L. 48
Johns, Vernon 38
Jones, Absalom 52
Jones, Alex 64
Jones, Bobby 20
Jones, E. Edward, Sr. 45
Jones, Robert Elijah 90
Jones, William A., Jr. 61
Kalbani, Adil 77
Karim, Benjamin 61
Kelly, Leontine 33
King, Barbara 22
King, Bernice 4, 81
King, Martin Luther, Jr. 1
King, Martin Luther, Sr. 89
Kobia, Samuel 43
Lawson, James M., Jr. 90
Lee, Eric P. 79
Lester, Julius 9

Lewis-Thornton, Rae 32
Lincoln, C. Eric 38
Little Richard 15
Loguen, J. W. 91
Long, Eddie L. 29, 89
Lowery, Joseph 2
Lowry, A. Leon 60
Lyons, Henry 12
Majors, Jeff 41
Marino, Eugene Antonio 30
Maxis, Theresa 62
Mays, Benjamin E. 7
McClellan, George Marion 91
McClurkin, Donnie 25
McGuire, George Alexander 80
McKenzie, Vashti M. 29
Meeks, James T. 92
Michaux, Solomon Lightfoot 91
Morgan, Gertrude 63
Moss, J 64
Moss, Otis, Jr. 72
Moss, Otis, III 72
Muhammad, Ava 31
Muhammad, Elijah 4
Muhammad, Jabir Herbert 72
Muhammad, Khallid Abdul 10, 31
Muhammed, W. Deen 27
Murray, Cecil 12, 47
Muzorewa, Abel 85
Okaalet, Peter 58
Otunga, Maurice Michael 55
Patterson, Gilbert Earl 41
Patterson, J. O., Jr. 80
Peterson, Jesse Lee 81
Phipps, Wintley 59
Pierre, Andre 17
Powell, Adam Clayton, Jr. 3
Price, Frederick K. C. 21
Redding, Ann Holmes 77
Reems, Ernestine Cleveland 27
Reese, Della 6, 20
Reverend Ike 79
Riley, Helen Caldwell Day 13
Rivers, Eugene F., III 81
Rogers, Alan G. 72
Roundtree, Dovey 80
Rugambwa, Laurean 20
Sapp, Marvin 74
Scott, George 55
Senghor, Augustin Diamancoune 66
Sentamu, John 58
Shabazz, Betty 7, 26
Sharpton, Al 21
Shaw, William J. 30
Shuttlesworth, Fred 47
Slocumb, Jonathan 52
Somé, Malidoma Patrice 10
Stallings, George A., Jr. 6
Stampley, Micah 54
Stanton, Alysa 78
Steinberg, Martha Jean "The Queen" 28
Stith, Charles R. 73
Sullivan, Leon H. 3, 30
Taylor, Gardner C. 76
Thurman, Howard 3
Tillard, Conrad 47
Tolton, Augustine 62
Tonex 54
Tribbett, Tye 81
Turner, Henry McNeal 5
Tutu, Desmond (Mpilo) 6, 44
Ukpabio, Helen 86

Vanity 67
Vanzant, Iyanla 17, 47
Waddles, Charleszetta "Mother" 10, 49
Walker, Hezekiah 34
Walker, John T. 50
Walker, Lucius, Jr. 88
Walker, Wyatt Tee 80
Washington, James Melvin 50
Waters, Ethel 7
Watkins, Joe 86
Weeks, Thomas, III 70
Weems, Renita J. 44
White, Reggie 6, 50
White-Hammond, Gloria 61
Williams, Frederick (B.) 63
Williams, Hosea Lorenzo 15, 31
Williams, Preston Warren, II 64
Wilson, Natalie 38
Winans, BeBe 14
Winans, CeCe 14, 43
Winans, Marvin L. 17
Winans, Ronald 54
Woods, Abraham, Jr. 74
Wright, Jeremiah A., Jr. 45, 69
Wright, Nathan, Jr. 56
Wright, Timothy 74
Wyatt, Addie L. 56
X, Malcolm 1
York, Dwight D. 71
Youngblood, Johnny Ray 8

Science and technology

Adams-Campbell, Lucille L. 60
Adkins, Rod 41
Adkins, Rutherford H. 21
Alcorn, George Edward, Jr. 59
Alexander, Archie Alphonso 14
Allen, Ethel D. 13
Allen, Will 74
Anderson, Charles Edward 37
Anderson, Michael P. 40
Anderson, Norman B. 45
Anderson, William G(ilchrist) 57
Atim, Julian 66
Auguste, Donna 29
Auguste, Rose-Anne 13
Bacon-Bercey, June 38
Banda, Hastings Kamuzu 6, 54
Banneker, Benjamin 93
Bashir, Halima 73
Bath, Patricia E. 37
Benjamin, Regina 20, 75
Benson, Angela 34
Black, Keith Lanier 18, 84
Blackwell, David 79
Bluford, Guy 2, 35
Bluitt, Juliann S. 14
Bolden, Charles Frank, Jr. 7, 78
Boykin, Otis 92
Branson, Herman 87
Brown, Vivian 27
Brown, Willa 40
Bullard, Eugene 12
Callender, Clive O. 3
Campbell, Donald J. 66
Canady, Alexa 28
Cargill, Victoria A. 43
Carroll, L. Natalie 44
Carruthers, George R. 40
Carson, Benjamin 1, 35, 76
Carter, Joye Maureen 41
Carter, Majora 77

Carver, George Washington 4
CasSelle, Malcolm 11
Chatard, Peter 44
Chinn, May Edward 26
Christian, Spencer 15
Clack, Zoanne 73
Clark, Mamie Phipps 79
Cobb, W. Montague 39
Cobbs, Price M. 9
Cole, Rebecca 38
Coleman, Bessie 9
Coleman, Ken 57
Comer, James P. 6
Coney, PonJola 48
Cooper, Edward S. 6
Cooper, Lisa 73
Cornwell, Edward E., III 70
Counter, S. Allen 74
Crosthwait, David 93
Crumpler, Rebecca Lee 89
Dabiri, John 93
Dailey, Ulysses Grant 87
Daly, Marie Maynard 37
Davis, Allison 12
Dean, Mark 35
Deas, Gerald 85
Deconge-Watson, Lovenia 55
Delany, Bessie 12
Delany, Martin R. 27
Dennis, Gary C. 91
Dickens, Helen Octavia 14, 64
Diop, Cheikh Anta 4
Drew, Alvin, Jr. 67
Drew, Charles Richard 7
Dunham, Katherine 4, 59
Dunston, Georgia Mae 48
Durham, James 90
Edwards, Lena Frances 76
Edwards, Willarda V. 59
Elders, Joycelyn 6
Ellington, E. David 11
Ellis, Clarence A. 38
Emeagwali, Dale 31
Emeagwali, Philip 30
Ericsson-Jackson, Aprille 28
Fennoy, Ilene 72
Fenton, Kevin 87
Fields, Evelyn J. 27
Fisher, Ada M. 76
Fisher, Rudolph 17
Flipper, Henry O. 3
Flowers, Sylester 50
Foster, Henry W., Jr. 26
Freeman, Harold P. 23
Fulani, Lenora 11
Fuller, A. Oveta 43
Fuller, Arthur 27
Fuller, Solomon Carter, Jr. 15
Gardere, Jeffrey 76
Gaston, Marilyn Hughes 60
Gates, Sylvester James, Jr. 15
Gayle, Helene D. 3, 46
Gibson, Kenneth Allen 6
Gibson, William F. 6
Giles, Roscoe C. 93
Gilliard, Steve 69
Goodlett, Carlton B. 91
Gourdine, Meredith 33
Grant, Augustus O. 71
Granville, Evelyn Boyd 36
Gray, Ida 41
Gregory, Frederick 8, 51
Grier, Eliza Ann 90

Griffin, Anthony 71
Griffin, Bessie Blout 43
Griffith, Patrick A. 64
Hall, Lloyd A. 8
Hamburg, Margaret 78
Hammonds, Evelynn 69
Hannah, Marc 10
Hansberry, Tony, II 93
Harris, Bernard A. 90
Harris, Gary L. 87
Harris, Mary Styles 31
Harris, Wesley L. 92
Haywood, Jimmy 58
Henderson, Cornelius Langston 26
Henderson, Henry Fairfax, Jr. 89
Henson, Matthew 2
Hillary, Barbara 65
Hinton, William Augustus 8
Holmes, Hamilton E. 82
Hopkins, Donald R. 89
Howard, Ayanna 65
Hughes, Dora 88
Hutcherson, Hilda Yvonne 54
Ibrahim, Mo 67
Imes, Elmer Samuel 39
Irving, Larry, Jr. 12
Jackson, Lisa 77
Jackson, Shirley Ann 12
Jarvis, Erich 67
Jawara, Dawda Kairaba 11
Jefferson, Mildred Fay 89
Jemison, Mae C. 1, 35
Jenifer, Franklyn G. 2
Johnson, Anthony M. 92
Johnson, Lonnie G. 32, 93
Jones, Edith Mae Irby 65
Jones, Frederick McKinley 68
Jones, Monty 66
Jones, Randy 35
Jones, Wayne 53
Joseph, Kathie-Ann 56
Julian, Hubert 90
Julian, Percy Lavon 6
Juma, Calestous 57
Just, Ernest Everett 3
Keith, Rachel Boone 63
Kenney, John A., Jr. 48
King, Reatha Clark 65
Kintaudi, Leon 62
Kittles, Rick 51
Knowling, Robert E., Jr. 38
Kong, B. Waine 50
Kountz, Samuel L. 10
Laroche, Joseph Philippe Lemercier 85
Laryea, Thomas Davies, III 67
Latimer, Lewis H. 4
Lavizzo-Mourey, Risa 48
Lawless, Theodore K. 8
Lawrence, Robert H., Jr. 16
Lee, Raphael C. 87
Leevy, Carrol M. 42
Leffall, Lasalle 3, 64
Lewis, Daurene 72
Lewis, Delano 7
Logan, Onnie Lee 14
Lushington, Augustus Nathaniel 56
Lyttle, Hulda Margaret 14
Madison, Romell 45
Malveaux, Floyd 54
Manley, Audrey Forbes 16
Massey, Walter E. 5, 45
Massie, Samuel P., Jr. 29

Maupin, John E., Jr. 92
Maxey, Randall 46
Mays, William G. 34
Mboup, Souleymane 10
McBay, Henry C. 91
McCoy, Elijah 8
McJunkin, George 93
McNair, Ronald 3, 58
Mensah, Thomas 48
Miller, Warren F., Jr. 53
Millines Dziko, Trish 28
Mills, Joseph C. 51
Morgan, Garrett 1
Mossell, Nathan Francis 91
Murray, Pauli 38
Nabrit, Samuel Milton 47
Naki, Hamilton 63
Neto, António Agostinho 43
Nour, Nawal M. 56
Ojikutu, Bisola 65
Olopade, Olufunmilayo Falusi 58
Osborne, Na'taki 54
Pace, Betty 59
Perry, Warren 56
Person, Waverly 9, 51
Peters, Lenrie 43
Pickett, Cecil 39
Pierre, Percy Anthony 46
Pinn, Vivian Winona 49
Pitt, David Thomas 10
Pitts, Derrick 77
Poindexter, Hildrus A. 87
Poussaint, Alvin F. 5, 67
Price, Richard 51
Prothrow-Stith, Deborah 10
Quarterman, Lloyd Albert 4
Rabb, Maurice F., Jr. 58
Randolph, Linda A. 52
Reece, E. Albert 63
Reese, Milous J., Jr. 51
Riley, Helen Caldwell Day 13
Rillieux, Norbert 92
Robeson, Eslanda Goode 13
Robinson, Rachel 16
Roker, Al 12, 49
Ross-Lee, Barbara 67
Samara, Noah 15
Satcher, David 7, 57
Seacole, Mary 54
Shabazz, Betty 7, 26
Shavers, Cheryl 31
Sigur, Wanda 44
Sinkford, Jeanne C. 13
Slaughter, John Brooks 53
Smith, Ian 62
Smith, Richard 51
Spencer, Michael G. 87
Staples, Brent 8
Staupers, Mabel K. 7
Stewart, Ella 39
Sullivan, Louis 8
Sweet, Ossian 68
Taylor, Susan C. 62
Terrell, Dorothy A. 24
Thomas, Vivien 9
Thornton, Yvonne S. 69
Thurston, Baratunde 79
Tuckson, Reed V. 71
Tyson, Neil deGrasse 15, 65
Walker, Arthur, II 87
Wambugu, Florence 42
Washington, Patrice Clarke 12
Watkins, Levi, Jr. 9

Wein, Joyce 62
Welsing, Frances Cress 5
West, James E. 87
Westbrooks, Bobby 51
White-Hammond, Gloria 61
Wilkens, J. Ernest, Jr. 43
Williams, Daniel Hale 2
Williams, David Rudyard 50
Williams, O. S. 13
Wilson, Donald E. 88
Wilson, Stephanie 72
Wisdom, Kimberlydawn 57
Witt, Edwin T. 26
Woods, Granville T. 5
Wright, Louis Tompkins 4
Young, Roger Arliner 29

Social issues
Abbott, Diane 9
Abbott, Robert Sengstacke 27
Abernathy, Ralph David 1
Abu-Jamal, Mumia 15
Achebe, Chinua 6
Adams, Sheila J. 25
Agyeman, Jaramogi Abebe 10, 63
Ake, Claude 30
Al-Amin, Jamil Abdullah 6
Alexander, Clifford 26
Alexander, Sadie Tanner Mossell
  22
Allen, Lucy 85
Allen, Will 74
Ali, Muhammad 2, 16, 52
Allen, Ethel D. 13
Amaker, Norman 63
Andrews, Benny 22, 59
Angelou, Maya 1, 15
Annan, Kofi Atta 15, 48
Anthony, Wendell 25
Appiah, Kwame Anthony 67
Arac de Nyeko, Monica 66
Archer, Dennis 7
Aristide, Jean-Bertrand 6, 45
Arnwine, Barbara 28
Asante, Molefi Kete 3
Ashe, Arthur 1, 18
Atyam, Angelina 55
Auguste, Rose-Anne 13
Autrey, Wesley 68
Avery, Byllye Y. 66
Azikiwe, Nnamdi 13
Ba, Mariama 30
Baisden, Michael 25, 66
Baker, Ella 5
Baker, Gwendolyn Calvert 9
Baker, Houston A., Jr. 6
Baker, Josephine 3
Baker, Thurbert 22
Baldwin, James 1
Banks, Paula A. 68
Barbee, Lloyd Augustus 71
Barlow, Roosevelt 49
Barnett, Etta Moten 56
Barrow, Willie T. 85
Bass, Charlotta Spears 40
Bates, Daisy 13
Beals, Melba Patillo 15
Bell, Derrick 6
Bell, Ralph S. 5
Berry, Bertice 8, 55
Berry, Edwin C. 81
Berry, Mary Frances 7
Berrysmith, Don Reginald 49

Bethune, Mary McLeod 4
Betsch, MaVynee 28
Betts, R. Dwayne 86
Bevel, James L. 75
Bibb, Henry and Mary 54
Biko, Steven 4
bin Wahad, Dhoruba 85
Birch, Glynn R. 61
Black, Albert 51
Blackwell, Unita 17
Blakely, Edward J. 88
Bobo, Lawrence 60
Bolin, Jane 22, 59
Bond, Julian 2, 35
Bonga, Kuenda 13
Booker, Cory Anthony 68
Bosley, Freeman, Jr. 7
Boyd, Gwendolyn 49
Boyd, John W., Jr. 20, 72
Boyd, T. B., III 6
Boykin, Keith 14
Bradley, David Henry, Jr. 39
Braun, Carol Moseley 4, 42
Bridges, Ruby 77
Broadbent, Hydeia 36
Brock, Roslyn McCallister 86
Brown, Byrd 49
Brown, Cora 33
Brown, Eddie C. 35
Brown, Elaine 8
Brown, Homer S. 47
Brown, Jesse 6, 41
Brown, Jim 11
Brown, Lee P. 1
Brown, Les 5
Brown, Lloyd Louis 10 42
Brown, Oscar, Jr. 53
Brown, Tony 3
Brown, Willa 40
Brown, Zora Kramer 12
Brutus, Dennis 38
Bryant, Wayne R. 6
Bullock, Steve 22
Bunch, Lonnie G., III 91
Bunche, Ralph J. 5
Burks, Mary Fair 40
Burroughs, Margaret Taylor 9
Butler, Paul D. 17
Butts, Calvin O., III 9, 90
Cameron, James 80
Campbell, Bebe Moore 6, 24, 59
Canada, Geoffrey 23
Carby, Hazel 27
Carmichael, Stokely 5, 26
Carr, Johnnie 69
Carr, Keela 74
Carter, Majora 77
Carter, Mandy 11
Carter, Robert L. 51
Carter, Rubin 26
Carter, Stephen L. 4
Cary, Lorene 3
Cary, Mary Ann Shadd 30
Catto, Octavius V. 83
Cayton, Horace 26
Chavis, Benjamin 6
Chestnut, J. L., Jr. 73
Chideya, Farai 14, 61
Childress, Alice 15
Chisholm, Daquan 93
Chissano, Joaquim 7, 55, 67
Christophe, Henri 9
Chuck D 9

Clark, Joe 1
Clark, Kenneth B. 5, 52
Clark, Septima 7
Clay, William Lacy 8
Clayton, Mayme Agnew 62
Claytor, Helen 14, 52
Cleaver, Eldridge 5
Cleaver, Kathleen Neal 29
Clements, George 2
Cobbs, Price M. 9
Cole, Johnnetta B. 5, 43
Cole, Lorraine 48
Coles, Alice 80
Collins, Patricia Hill 67
Colston, Hal 72
Comer, James P. 6
Compton-Rock, Malaak 86
Connerly, Ward 14
Conyers, John, Jr. 4, 45
Cook, Toni 23
Cooke, Marvel 31
Cooper, Anna Julia 20
Cooper, Edward S. 6
Cooper, Margaret J. 46
Correia, De'Jaun 93
Cosby, Bill 7, 26, 59
Cosby, Camille 14, 80
Cose, Ellis 5, 50
Cox, Donald Lee 93
Creagh, Milton 27
Crew, Spencer R. 55
Cruse, Harold 54
Cummings, Elijah E. 24
da Silva, Benedita 5
Davis, Angela 5
Davis, Artur 41
Davis, Danny K. 24
Dawson, Matel, Jr. 39
Dawson, Michael C. 63
DeBaptiste, George 32
Delany, Martin R. 27
Dellums, Ronald 2, 81
Dent, Thomas C. 50
Diallo, Amadou 27
Dickerson, Ernest 6
Dieudonné 67
Diop, Cheikh Anta 4
Dirie, Waris 56
Divine, Father 7
Dixon, Margaret 14
Dobbs, John Wesley 89
Dodson, Howard, Jr. 7, 52
Dortch, Thomas W., Jr. 45
Douglas, Derek 88
Douglass, Frederick 87
Drew, Charles Richard 7
Du Bois, W. E. B. 3
DuBois, Shirley Graham 21
Duggins, George 64
Dukes, Hazel Nell 56
Dumas, Henry 41
Dunham, Katherine 4, 59
Eagleson, William Lewis 90
Early, Gerald 15
Easton, Hosea 91
Edelin, Ramona Hoage 19
Edelman, Marian Wright 5, 42
Edley, Christopher 2, 48
Edwards, Harry 2
Edwards, Lena Frances 76
Elder, Larry 25
Elders, Joycelyn 6
Ellis-Lamkins, Phaedra 88

Ellison, Ralph **7**
Esposito, Giancarlo **9**
Espy, Mike **6**
Eugene-Richard, Margie **63**
Europe, James Reese **10**
Evers, Medgar **3**
Evers, Myrlie **8**
Farmer, James **2, 64**
Farrakhan, Louis **15**
Farris, Isaac Newton, Jr. **63**
Fauntroy, Walter E. **11**
Fauset, Jessie **7**
Fela **1, 42**
Fields, C. Virginia **25**
Finner-Williams, Paris Michele **62**
Flavor Flav **67**
Fletcher, Benjamin **90**
Fletcher, Bill, Jr. **41**
Forbes, James A., Jr. **71**
Forman, James **7, 51**
Fortune, T. Thomas **6**
Foster, Marie **48**
Franklin, C. L. **68**
Franklin, Hardy R. **9**
Franklin, John Hope **5, 77**
Franklin, Robert M. **13**
Frazier, E. Franklin **10**
Fulani, Lenora **11**
Fuller, Arthur **27**
Fuller, Charles **8**
Gaines, Ernest J. **7**
Gamble, Kenny **85**
Gardner, Chris **65**
Garvey, Marcus **1**
Gates, Henry Louis, Jr. **3, 38, 67**
Gayle, Helene D. **3**
Gbowee, Leymah **76**
George, Zelma Watson **42**
Gibson, Kenneth Allen **6**
Gibson, William F. **6**
Gilbert, Christopher **50**
Gist, Carole **1**
Goldberg, Whoopi **4, 33, 69**
Golden, Marita **19**
Golston, Allan C. **55**
Gomez, Jewelle **30**
Gomez-Preston, Cheryl **9**
Gomillion, Charles **90**
Goss, Carol A. **55**
Gossett, Louis, Jr. **7**
Graham, Lawrence Otis **12**
Granger, Lester B. **75**
Gray, Fred **37**
Greene, Petey **65**
Gregory, Dick **1, 54**
Gregory, Wilton **37**
Grier, Roosevelt **13**
Griffith, Mark Winston **8**
Grimké, Archibald H. **9**
Guinier, Lani **7, 30**
Guy, Rosa **5**
Hale, Lorraine **8**
Haley, Alex **4**
Hall, Elliott S. **24**
Hall, Stuart **78**
Hamblin, Ken **10**
Hamer, Fannie Lou **6**
Hampton, Fred **18**
Hampton, Henry **6**
Hani, Chris **6**
Hansberry, Lorraine **6**
Hansberry, William Leo **11**
Harding, Vincent **67**

Harper, Frances Ellen Watkins **11**
Harrington, Oliver W. **9**
Harris, Alice **7**
Harris, Leslie **6**
Harris, Marcelite Jordan **16**
Harris, Patricia Roberts **2**
Hastings, Alcee L. **16**
Hawkins, Augustus F. **68**
Hawkins, Steven **14**
Hayes, Dennis **54**
Haynes, George Edmund **8**
Hedgeman, Anna Arnold **22**
Height, Dorothy I. **2, 23, 78**
Henderson, Thelton E. **68**
Henderson, Wade J. **14**
Henderson, Zelma **71**
Henry, Aaron Edd **19**
Henry, Lenny **9, 52**
Henson, Josiah **90**
Hernandez, Aileen Clarke **13**
Herndon, Angelo **90**
Hernton, Calvin C. **51**
Hill, Anita **5, 65**
Hill, Jesse, Jr. **13**
Hill, Lauryn **20, 53**
Hill, Oliver W. **24, 63**
Hilliard, Asa Grant, III **66**
Hilliard, David **7**
Holland, Endesha Ida Mae **3, 57**
Holt Baker, Arlene **73**
Hood, James Walker **91**
hooks, bell **5, 90**
Hooks, Benjamin L. **2, 85**
Hope, Lugenia Burns **89**
Houston, Charles Hamilton **4**
Howard, M. William, Jr. **26**
Hoyte, Lenon **50**
Hubbard, Arnette Rhinehart **38**
Huggins, Nathan Irvin **52**
Hughes, Albert **7**
Hughes, Allen **7**
Hughes, Langston **4**
Hunt, Darnell **92**
Hunter-Gault, Charlayne **6, 31**
Hutchinson, Earl Ofari **24**
Hutson, Jean Blackwell **16**
Ibrahim, Mo **67**
Iceberg Slim **11**
Ice-T **6, 31**
Ingram, Rex **5**
Innis, Roy **5**
Irvis, K. Leroy **67**
Jackson, Edison O. **67**
Jackson, Fred James **25**
Jackson, George **14**
Jackson, Janet **6, 30, 68**
Jackson, Jesse **1, 27, 72**
Jackson, Judith D. **57**
Jackson, Mahalia **5**
Jacob, John E. **2**
Jagan, Cheddi **16**
James, Daniel, Jr. **16**
Jealous, Benjamin **70**
Jean, Wyclef **20, 86**
Jeffries, Leonard **8**
Jenkins, Ray **77**
Johnson, Charles S. **12**
Johnson, Earvin "Magic" **3, 39**
Johnson, James Weldon **5**
Johnson, Kevin **70**
Jolley, Willie **28**
Jones, Cullen **73**
Jones, Elaine R. **7, 45**

Jones, Eugene Kinckle **79**
Jones, John **89**
Jones, Van **70**
Jones, William A., Jr. **61**
Jordan, June **7, 35**
Jordan, Vernon E. **3, 35**
Joseph, Kathie-Ann **56**
Josey, E. J. **10**
Joyner, Marjorie Stewart **26**
Joyner, Tom **19, 90**
Julian, Percy Lavon **6**
Karim, Benjamin **61**
Kaunda, Kenneth **2**
Keita, Salif **83**
Kelley, Cliff **75**
Kennedy, Florynce **12, 33**
Khanga, Yelena **6**
Kidd, Mae Street **39**
Kimbro, Warren **76**
King, Bernice **4, 81**
King, Coretta Scott **3, 57**
King, Dexter **10**
King, Martin Luther, III **20**
King, Martin Luther, Jr. **1**
King, Martin Luther, Sr. **89**
King, Preston **28**
King, Robert Hillary **84**
King, Yolanda **6**
Kitwana, Bakari **86**
Kuzwayo, Ellen **68**
Ladner, Joyce A. **42**
LaGuma, Alex **30**
Lampkin, Daisy **19**
Lane, Charles **3**
Lane, Vincent **5**
Laraque, Paul **67**
Lawson, James M., Jr. **90**
Lee, Canada **8**
Lee, Eric P. **79**
Leland, Mickey **2**
Lester, Julius **9**
Lewis, Ananda **28**
Lewis, Delano **7**
Lewis, Thomas **19**
Lewis-Thornton, Rae **32**
Little, Robert L. **2**
Logan, Rayford W. **40**
Loguen, J. W. **91**
Lorde, Audre **6**
Louis, Errol T. **8**
Loving, Mildred **69**
Lowery, Joseph **2**
Lowry, A. Leon **60**
Lucas, John **7**
Lucy, William **50**
Lucy Foster, Autherine **35**
Maathai, Wangari **43**
Mabuza-Suttle, Felicia **43**
Madison, Joseph E. **17**
Makeba, Miriam **2, 50, 74**
Malone Jones, Vivian **59**
Malveaux, Julianne **32, 70**
Mandela, Nelson **1, 14, 77**
Mandela, Winnie **2, 35**
Manley, Audrey Forbes **16**
Marable, Manning **10**
Marshall, Paule **7, 77**
Marshall, Thurgood **1, 44**
Martin, Louis E. **16**
Masekela, Barbara **18**
Masekela, Hugh **1**
Mason, Biddy **89**
Mason, Ronald **27**

Mathabane, Mark **5**
Maynard, Robert C. **7**
Mays, Benjamin E. **7**
Mbeki, Thabo **14, 73**
McCabe, Jewell Jackson **10**
McCarty, Osceola **16**
McDougall, Gay J. **11, 43**
McKay, Claude **6**
McKenzie, Vashti M. **29**
McKinney Hammond, Michelle **51**
McKissick, Floyd B. **3**
McMurray, Georgia L. **36**
McQueen, Butterfly **6, 54**
McWhorter, John **35**
McWorter, Free Frank **91**
Meredith, James H. **11**
Mfume, Kweisi **6, 41**
Mhlaba, Raymond **55**
Micheaux, Oscar **7**
Millender-McDonald, Juanita **21, 61**
Miller-Travis, Vernice **64**
Millines Dziko, Trish **28**
Mitchell, Clarence M., Jr. **88**
Mkapa, Benjamin W. **16, 77**
Mongella, Gertrude **11**
Moore, Gwendolynne S. **55**
Moore, Harry T. **29**
Morgan, Irene **65**
Morial, Ernest "Dutch" **26**
Moses, Robert Parris **11**
Moss, Otis, Jr. **72**
Mossell, Gertrude Bustill **40**
Motley, Constance Baker **10, 55**
Moton, Robert Russa **83**
Moutoussamy-Ashe, Jeanne **7**
Mowry, Jess **7**
Muhammad, Elijah **4**
Muhammad, Khallid Abdul **10, 31**
Mukoko, Jestina **75**
Murphy, Laura M. **43**
Murray, Pauli **38**
Nash, Diane **72**
Ndadaye, Melchior **7**
Nelson, Jill **6, 54**
Newton, Huey **2**
Niane, Katoucha **70**
Nkoli, Simon **60**
Nkrumah, Kwame **3**
Noble, Gil **76**
Norman, Pat **10**
Nour, Nawal M. **56**
Nzo, Alfred **15**
Obasanjo, Olusegun **5**
Oglesby, Zena **12**
Ojikutu, Bisola **65**
Orange, James **74**
Ormes, Jackie **73**
Osborne, Na'taki **54**
Owens, Major **6**
Page, Alan **7**
Page, Clarence **4**
Parker, Kellis E. **30**
Parker, Pat **19**
Parks, Rosa **1, 35, 56**
Parr, Russ **51**
Patterson, Frederick Douglass **12**
Patterson, Louise **25**
Patterson, Orlando **4**
Patterson, P. J. **6, 20**
Perkins, Edward **5**
Perry, James **83**
Peterson, Jesse Lee **81**
Pitt, David Thomas **10**

Pleasant, Mary Ellen 9
Plessy, Homer Adolph 31
Pough, Terrell 58
Poussaint, Alvin F. 5, 67
Powell, Adam Clayton, Jr. 3
Powell, Kevin 31, 74
Pratt, Geronimo 18
Pressley, Condace L. 41
Price, Hugh B. 9, 54
Primus, Pearl 6
Pritchard, Robert Starling 21
Prothrow-Stith, Deborah 10
Quarles, Benjamin Arthur 18
Quigless, Helen G. 49
Ramaphosa, Cyril 3
Ramphele, Mamphela 29
Ramsey, Charles H. 21, 69
Rand, A. Barry 6
Randolph, A. Philip 3
Randolph, Linda A. 52
Rawlings, Nana Konadu Agyeman 13
Reagon, Bernice Johnson 7
Reed, Ishmael 8
Rice, Louise Allen 54
Rice, Norm 8
Richards, Hilda 49
Richardson, Julieanna 81
Richardson, Rupert 67
Riggs, Marlon 5
Riley, Boots 89
Riley, Helen Caldwell Day 13
Rivers, Eugene F., III 81
Roberts, Lillian 83
Robeson, Eslanda Goode 13
Robeson, Paul 2
Robinson, Jackie 6
Robinson, Rachel 16
Robinson, Randall 7, 46
Robinson, Sharon 22
Robinson, Spottswood W., III 22
Roble, Abdi 71
Rodriguez, Cheryl 64
Rowan, Carl T. 1, 30
Rowell, Victoria 13, 68
Ruffin, Josephine St. Pierre 75
Rusesabagina, Paul 60
Rustin, Bayard 4
Sampson, Edith S. 4
Sanders, Malika 48
Sané, Pierre Gabriel 21
Sapphire 14
Saro-Wiwa, Kenule 39
Satcher, David 7, 57
Savimbi, Jonas 2, 34
Sawyer, Amos 2
Sayles Belton, Sharon 9, 16
Scantlebury-White, Velma 64
Seacole, Mary 54
Seale, Bobby 3
Sears, Stephanie 53
Seele, Pernessa 46
Senghor, Léopold Sédar 12
Shabazz, Attallah 6
Shabazz, Betty 7, 26
Shadd, Abraham D. 81
Shakur, Afeni 67
Shakur, Assata 6
Shakur, Yusef 85
Sherrod, Shirley 87
Shinhoster, Earl 32
Shuttlesworth, Fred 47
Sifford, Charlie 4, 49

Simone, Nina 15, 41
Sisulu, Albertina 57
Sisulu, Sheila Violet Makate 24
Sleet, Moneta, Jr. 5
Smith, Anna Deavere 6
Smith, Barbara 28
Smith, Damu 54
Smith, Greg 28
Smith, Kemba 70
Smith, Marie F. 70
Smith, Nate 49
Snowden, Frank M., Jr. 67
Spriggs, William 67
Stallings, George A., Jr. 6
Staupers, Mabel K. 7
Steele, Claude Mason 13
Steele, Shelby 13, 82
Stewart, Alison 13
Stewart, Ella 39
Stewart, Maria W. Miller 19
Stone, Chuck 9
Sullivan, Leon H. 3, 30
Sweet, Ossian 68
Talbert, Mary B. 77
Tate, Eleanora E. 20, 55
Tatum, Wilbert 76
Taulbert, Clifton Lemoure 19
Taylor, Bo 72
Taylor, Mildred D. 26
Taylor, Recy 92
Terrell, Mary Church 9
Thomas, Arthur Ray 52
Thomas, Franklin A. 5, 49
Thomas, Jefferson 88
Thompson, Bennie G. 26
Thompson, Cynthia Bramlett 50
Thurman, Howard 3
Thurman, Wallace 16
Till, Emmett 7
Tobias, Channing H. 79
Toomer, Jean 6
Tosh, Peter 9
Touré, Askia (Muhammad Abu Bakr el) 47
Touré, Faya Ora Rose 56
Tribble, Israel, Jr. 8
Trotter, Donne E. 28
Trotter, Monroe 9
Tsvangirai, Morgan 26, 72
Tubman, Harriet 9
Tucker, C. Delores 12, 56
Tucker, Cynthia 15, 61
Tucker, Rosina 14
Tutu, Desmond 6
Tyree, Omar Rashad 21
Van Peebles, Melvin 7
Vanzant, Iyanla 17, 47
Vaughn, Viola 70
Vega, Marta Moreno 61
Velez-Rodriguez, Argelia 56
Vincent, Marjorie Judith 2
Waddles, Charleszetta "Mother" 10, 49
Walcott, Derek 5
Walker, A'lelia 14
Walker, Alice 1, 43
Walker, Bernita Ruth 53
Walker, Lucius, Jr. 88
Wall, Orindatus S. B. 92
Wallace, Joaquin 49
Wallace, Michele Faith 13
Wallace, Phyllis A. 9
Wallace, William 75

Washington, Booker T. 4
Washington, Ebonya 79
Washington, Fredi 10
Washington, Harold 6
Washington, Pauletta Pearson 86
Waters, Maxine 3, 67
Wattleton, Faye 9
Wells, Henrietta Bell 69
Wells, James Lesesne 10
Wells-Barnett, Ida B. 8
Welsing, Frances Cress 5
West, Cornel 5, 33, 80
White, Michael R. 5
White, Reggie 6, 50
White, Walter F. 4
White, Willye 67
White-Hammond, Gloria 61
Wilkins, Roy 4
Williams, Armstrong 29
Williams, Evelyn 10
Williams, Fannie Barrier 27
Williams, George Washington 18
Williams, Hosea Lorenzo 15, 31
Williams, Maggie 7, 71
Williams, Montel 4, 57
Williams, Patricia 11, 54
Williams, Robert F. 11
Williams, Stanley "Tookie" 29, 57
Williams, Walter E. 4
Williams, Willie L. 4
Wilson, August 7, 33, 55
Wilson, Margaret Bush 79
Wilson, Phill 9
Wilson, Sunnie 7, 55
Wilson, William Julius 22
Withers, Ernest C. 68, 88
Wiwa, Ken 67
Wolfe, George C. 6, 43
Woodson, Robert L. 10
Worrill, Conrad 12
Wright, Charles H. 35
Wright, Louis Tompkins 4
Wright, Nathan, Jr. 56
Wright, Richard 5
Wyatt, Addie L. 56
X, Malcolm 1
Xuma, Madie Hall 59
Yancy, Dorothy Cowser 42
Yarbrough, Camille 40
Yeboah, Emmanuel Ofosu 53
Yoba, Malik 11
Young, Andrew 3, 48
Young, Jean Childs 14
Young, Whitney M., Jr. 4
Youngblood, Johnny Ray 8
Zulu, Princess Kasune 54

Sports
Aaron, Hank 5
Abdul-Jabbar, Kareem 8
Abdur-Rahim, Shareef 28
Adams, Paul 50
Adu, Freddy 67
Alexander, Shaun 58
Ali, Laila 27, 63
Ali, Muhammad 2, 16, 52
Allen, Dick 85
Allen, Marcus 20
Allen, Ray 82
Amaker, Tommy 62
Amos, John 8, 62
Anderson, Elmer 25
Anderson, Jamal 22

Anderson, Mike 63
Anderson, Viv 58
Anthony, Carmelo 46
Archibald, Tiny 90
Arenas, Gilbert 84
Artest, Ron 52
Ashe, Arthur 1, 18
Ashford, Emmett 22
Ashford, Evelyn 63
Ashley, Maurice 15, 47
Baines, Harold 32
Baker, Dusty 8, 43, 72
Banks, Ernie 33
Barber, Ronde 41
Barber, Tiki 57
Barkley, Charles 5, 66
Barnes, Ernie 16, 78
Barnes, John 53
Barnes, Steven 54
Barney, Lem 26
Barnhill, David 30
Baugé, Grégory 86
Baylor, Don 6
Baylor, Elgin 93
Beamon, Bob 30
Beasley, Jamar 29
Bekele, Kenenisa 75
Bell, James "Cool Papa" 36
Belle, Albert 10
Bettis, Jerome 64
Bickerstaff, Bernie 21
Bing, Dave 3, 59, 78
Bivins, Michael 72
Black, Joe 75
Blair, Paul 36
Blake, James 43
Blanks, Billy 22
Blanton, Dain 29
Bogues, Tyrone "Muggsy" 56
Bol, Manute 1
Bolt, Usain 73
Bolton-Holifield, Ruthie 28
Bonaly, Surya 7
Bonds, Barry 6, 34, 63
Bonds, Bobby 43
Bonheur, Yannick 84
Bosh, Chris 85
Bowe, Riddick 6
Bramlett, Joseph 91
Brand, Elton 31
Brandon, Terrell 16
Branham, George, III 50
Brashear, Donald 39
Brathwaite, Fred 35
Briscoe, Marlin 37
Brock, Lou 18
Brooks, Aaron 33
Brooks, Derrick 43
Brown, Antron 85
Brown, James 22
Brown, Jim 11
Brown, Mike 77
Brown, Sean 52
Brown, Willard 36
Bruce, Isaac 26
Bryant, Cullen 81
Bryant, Kobe 15, 31, 71
Buchanan, Ray 32
Bush, Reggie 59, 88
Butler, Leroy, III 17
Bynoe, Peter C. B. 40
Caldwell, Jim 81
Campanella, Roy 25

Carew, Rod **20**
Carnegie, Herbert **25**
Carter, Anson **24**
Carter, Butch **27**
Carter, Cris **21**
Carter, Joe **30**
Carter, Kenneth **53**
Carter, Rubin **26**
Carter, Vince **26**
Cash, Swin **59**
Catchings, Tamika **43**
Chamberlain, Wilt **18, 47**
Chaney, John **67**
Charleston, Oscar **39**
Cheeks, Maurice **47**
Cherry, Deron **40**
Cheruiyot, Robert **69**
Christie, Linford **8**
Claiborne, Loretta **34**
Clay, Bryan **57, 74**
Clemons, Michael "Pinball" **64**
Clendenon, Donn **26, 56**
Clifton, Nathaniel "Sweetwater" **47**
Coachman, Alice **18**
Coleman, Leonard S., Jr. **12**
Cooper, Andy "Lefty" **63**
Cooper, Charles "Chuck" **47**
Cooper, Michael **31**
Cooper-Dyke, Cynthia **17, 89**
Copeland, Michael **47**
Corley, Tony **62**
Cottrell, Comer **11**
Cox, Bryan **83**
Crawford, Carl **90**
Crennel, Romeo **54**
Crooks, Garth **53**
Croom, Sylvester **50**
Culpepper, Daunte **32, 85**
Cunningham, Randall **23**
Curry, Michael **85**
Dandridge, Ray **36**
Dantley, Adrian **72**
Davis, Ernie **48**
Davis, Mike **41**
Davis, Milt **74**
Davis, Piper **19**
Davis, Shani **58, 84**
Davis, Terrell **20**
Dawes, Dominique **11**
Dawson, Andre **85**
Day, Leon **39**
DeFrantz, Anita **37**
DeGale, James **74**
Delaney, Joe **76**
Devers, Gail **7, 87**
Dibaba, Tirunesh **73**
Dickerson, Eric **27**
Dixon, George **52**
Doby, Lawrence Eugene, Sr. **16, 41**
Doig, Jason **45**
Dorrell, Karl **52**
dos Santos, Manuel Francisco **65**
Drew, Charles Richard **7**
Drexler, Clyde **4, 61**
Drogba, Didier **78**
Duerson, Dave **93**
Dumars, Joe **16, 65**
Duncan, Tim **20, 91**
Dungy, Tony **17, 42, 59**
Dunn, Jerry **27**
Dunn, Warrick **90**
Durant, Kevin **76**
Dye, Jermaine **58**

Edwards, Harry **2**
Edwards, Herman **51**
Edwards, Teresa **14**
Elder, Lee **6**
Ellerbe, Brian **22**
Elliott, Sean **26**
Ellis, Dock **78**
Ellis, Jimmy **44**
Ervin, Anthony **66**
Erving, Julius **18, 47**
Eto'o, Samuel **73**
Ewing, Patrick **17, 73**
Farr, Mel **24**
Faulk, Marshall **35**
Felix, Allyson **48**
Ferdinand, Rio **82**
Fielder, Cecil **2**
Fielder, Prince Semien **68**
Flood, Curt **10, 93**
Flowers, Vonetta **35**
Ford, Cheryl **45**
Foreman, George **1, 15**
Forrest, Vernon **40, 79**
Foster, Andrew **79**
Fowler, Reggie **51**
Fox, Rick **27**
Frazier, Joe **19**
Frazier, Walt **91**
Frazier-Lyde, Jacqui **31**
Freeman, Cathy **29**
Freeman, Marianna **23**
Fuhr, Grant **1, 49**
Fuller, Vivian **33**
Futch, Eddie **33**
Gaines, Clarence E., Sr. **55**
Gaither, Alonzo Smith (Jake) **14**
Gans, Joe **91**
Garnett, Kevin **14, 70**
Garrison, Zina **2**
Gaston, Cito **71**
Gebrselassie, Haile **70**
Gentry, Alvin **23**
George, Eddie **80**
Gervin, George **80**
Gibson, Althea **8, 43**
Gibson, Bob **33**
Gibson, Josh **22**
Gibson, Truman K., Jr. **60**
Gill, Turner **83**
Gilliam, Frank **23**
Gilliam, Joe **31**
Glanville, Douglas Metunwa **82**
Gooden, Dwight **20**
Gorden, W. C. **71**
Goss, Tom **23**
Gourdine, Meredith **33**
Gourdine, Simon **11**
Graham, Trevor **84**
Granderson, Curtis **66**
Grand-Pierre, Jean-Luc **46**
Gray, Yeshimbra "Shimmy" **55**
Green, A. C. **32**
Green, Darrell **39, 74**
Green, Dennis **5, 45**
Greene, Joe **10**
Greene, Maurice **27, 77**
Greer, Hal **92**
Gregg, Eric **16**
Gregory, Ann **63**
Grier, Mike **43**
Grier, Roosevelt **1**
Griffey, Ken, Jr. **12, 73**
Griffith, Yolanda **25**

Griffith-Joyner, Florence **28**
Gumbel, Greg **8**
Gwynn, Tony **18, 83**
Gyan, Asamoah **87**
Hairston, Sam **88**
Hamilton, Lewis **66**
Haney, Lee **77**
Hardaway, Anfernee (Penny) **13**
Hardaway, Tim **35**
Harris, James **79**
Harris, Sylvia **70**
Harrison, Alvin **28**
Harrison, Calvin **28**
Harris-Stewart, Lusia **90**
Haskins, Clem **23**
Hawkins, Connie **91**
Haye, David **82**
Hayes, Bob **77**
Hayes, Elvin **93**
Heard, Gar **25**
Hearns, Thomas **29**
Henderson, Rickey **28, 78**
Henry, Thierry **66**
Hickman, Fred **11**
Hill, Calvin **19**
Hill, Grant **13**
Hillary, Barbara **65**
Hilliard, Wendy **53**
Hines, Garrett **35**
Holdsclaw, Chamique **24**
Holland, Kimberly N. **62**
Holmes, Kelly **47**
Holmes, Larry **20, 68**
Holmes, Santonio **87**
Holyfield, Evander **6**
Hopkins, Bernard **35, 69**
Horton, Andre **33**
Horton, Suki **33**
Howard, Desmond **16, 58**
Howard, Juwan **15**
Howard, Ryan **65**
Howard, Sherri **36**
Hunter, Billy **22**
Hunter, Torii **43**
Hyde, Cowan F. "Bubba" **47**
Iginla, Jarome **35**
Ince, Paul **83**
Irvin, Michael **64**
Irvin, Monte **31**
Isaacs, John **76**
Iverson, Allen **24, 46**
Ivey, Phil **72**
Jackson, Jamea **64**
Jackson, Mannie **14**
Jackson, Rampage **83**
Jackson, Reggie **15**
Jackson, Rickey **88**
Jackson, Tom **70**
Jacobs, Regina **38**
James, David **84**
James, G. Larry **74**
James, LeBron **46, 78**
James, Vanessa **84**
Jenkins, Fergie **46**
Jeter, Derek **27, 93**
Johnson, Avery **62**
Johnson, Ben **1**
Johnson, Chris **92**
Johnson, Clifford "Connie" **52**
Johnson, Dennis **89**
Johnson, Earvin "Magic" **3, 39**
Johnson, Gus **92**
Johnson, Jack **8**

Johnson, Kevin **70**
Johnson, Keyshawn **91**
Johnson, Larry **28**
Johnson, Levi **48**
Johnson, Mamie "Peanut" **40**
Johnson, Michael **13**
Johnson, Rafer **33**
Johnson, Rodney Van **28**
Jones, Cobi N'Gai **18**
Jones, Cullen **73**
Jones, Deacon **92**
Jones, Ed "Too Tall" **46**
Jones, K. C. **83**
Jones, Lou **64**
Jones, Marion **21, 66**
Jones, Merlakia **34**
Jones, Randy **35**
Jones, Roy, Jr. **22**
Jones, Sam **85**
Jordan, Eddie **83**
Jordan, Michael **6, 21**
Joyce, Dru **81**
Joyner-Kersee, Jackie **5**
Justice, David **18**
Kaiser, Cecil **42**
Kanouté, Fred **68**
Keflezighi, Meb **49**
Keith, Floyd A. **61**
Kellogg, Clark **64**
Kennedy-Overton, Jayne Harris **46**
Kerry, Leon G. **46**
Kidd, Jason **86**
Kimbro, Henry A. **25**
King, Don **14**
Lacy, Sam **30, 46**
Ladd, Ernie **64**
Lane, Dick **92**
Lanier, Bob **47**
Lanier, Willie **33**
Lankford, Ray **23**
Laraque, Georges **48**
Larkin, Barry **24**
Lashley, Bobby **63**
Lassiter, Roy **24**
Lee, Canada **8**
Lennox, Betty **31**
Leonard, Buck **67**
Leonard, Sugar Ray **15**
Leslie, Lisa **16, 73**
Lester, Bill **42, 85**
Lewis, Butch **71**
Lewis, Carl **4**
Lewis, Denise **33**
Lewis, Lennox **27**
Lewis, Marvin **51, 87**
Lewis, Oliver **56**
Lewis, Ray **33**
Liston, Sonny **33**
Little, Floyd **86**
Little, Larry **90**
Littlepage, Craig **35**
Lloyd, Earl **26**
Lloyd, John Henry "Pop" **30**
Lofton, James **42**
Lofton, Kenny **12**
Lopes, Davey **92**
Loroupe, Tegla **59**
Lott, Ronnie **9**
Louis, Joe **5**
Love, Nat **9**
Love, Reggie **77**
Lowe, Sidney **64**
Lucas, John **7**

Mackey, Biz 82
Mahorn, Rick 60
Malone, Karl 18, 51, 90
Malone, Moses 79
Manigault, Earl "The Goat" 15
Mariner, Jonathan 41
Martinez, Pedro 81
Master P 21
Matson, Ollie 93
Mayers, Jamal 39
Mayhew, Martin R. 76
Mays, Willie 3
Mayweather, Floyd, Jr. 57
McAdoo, Bob 75
McBride, Bryant 18
McCarthy, Sandy 64
McCray, Nikki 18
McDaniel, Randall Cornell 81
McGrady, Tracy 80
McGriff, Fred 24
McKegney, Tony 3
McLendon, John B., Jr. 89
McNabb, Donovan 29
McNair, Steve 22, 47, 79
McNeil, Lori 1
McRae, Hal 84
Mello, Breno 73
Mensah, John 87
Metcalfe, Ralph 26
Milla, Roger 2
Miller, Cheryl 10, 74
Miller, Larry G. 72
Miller, Reggie 33
Mills, Sam 33
Milton, DeLisha 31
Minor, DeWayne 32
Minoso, Minnie 89
Mitchell, Sam 82
Mohammed, Nazr 64
Monk, Art 38, 73
Monroe, Earl 89
Montgomery, Tim 41
Moon, Warren 8, 66
Moorer, Michael 19
Morgan, Joe Leonard 9
Morris, Raheem 77
Moses, Edwin 8
Mosley, Shane 32
Moss, Randy 23, 90
Motley, Marion 26
Mourning, Alonzo 17, 44
Muhammad, Jabir Herbert 72
Mundine, Anthony 56
Murray, Eddie 12
Murray, Lenda 10
Mutola, Maria 12
Mutombo, Dikembe 7
Nakhid, David 25
Newcombe, Don 24
Newsome, Ozzie 26
Noah, Yannick 4, 60
Odom, Lamar 81
Olajuwon, Hakeem 2, 72
Oliver, Pam 54
O'Neal, Shaquille 8, 30
O'Neil, Buck 19, 59
Onyewu, Oguchi 60
O'Ree, Willie 5
Ortiz, David 52, 82
Owens, Jesse 2
Owens, Terrell 53
Pace, Orlando 21
Page, Alan 7

Page, Greg 78
Paige, Satchel 7
Palmer, Violet 59
Parish, Robert 43
Parker, Candace 74
Parker, Jim 64
Parker, Tony 75
Patterson, Floyd 19, 58
Paul, Chris 84
Payne, Ulice 42
Payton, Walter 11, 25
Peck, Carolyn 23
Peete, Calvin 11
Peete, Rodney 60
Pelé 7
Perrot, Kim 23
Perry, Lowell 30
Peters, Margaret 43
Peters, Matilda 43
Phillips, Teresa L. 42
Pickett, Bill 11
Pierce, Paul 71
Pippen, Scottie 15, 89
Pollard, Fritz 53
Porter, Terry 75
Powell, Mike 7
Powell, Renee 34
Powell, William J. 82
Pride, Charley 26
Prince, Ron 64
Prince, Tayshaun 68
Pryce, Trevor 89
Puckett, Kirby 4, 58
Quirot, Ana 13
Radcliffe, Ted 74
Randle, John 87
Randolph, Willie 53
Rashad, Ahmad 18
Ready, Stephanie 33
Reed, Willis, Jr. 86
Reese, Pokey 28
Regis, Cyrille 51
Reynolds, Harold 77
Rhoden, William C. 67
Rhodes, Ray 14
Ribbs, Willy T. 2
Rice, Jerry 5, 55, 89
Rice, Jim 75
Richard, J. R. 87
Richards, Sanya 66
Richardson, Donna 39
Richardson, Nolan 9
Richmond, Mitch 19
Rivers, Doc 25, 81
Robertson, Oscar 26
Robinson, David 24, 90
Robinson, Eddie G. 10, 61
Robinson, Frank 9, 87
Robinson, Jackie 6
Robinson, Sugar Ray 18
Robinson, Will 51, 69
Rodman, Dennis 12, 44
Rollins, Jimmy 70
Ronaldinho 69
Rose, Derrick 82
Rose, Lionel 56
Rubin, Chanda 37
Rudolph, Wilma 4
Russell, Bill 8
Sabathia, CC 74
St. Julien, Marlon 29
Salvador, Bryce 51
Sampson, Charles 13

Sanders, Barry 1, 53
Sanders, Bob 72
Sanders, Deion 4, 31
Sanders, Satch 77
Sapp, Warren 38
Sayers, Gale 28
Scott, Stuart 34
Scott, Wendell Oliver, Sr. 19
Scurry, Briana 27
Shannon, Randy 82
Sharper, Darren 32
Sheffield, Gary 16
Shell, Art 1, 66
Shippen, John 43
Showers, Reggie 30
Sifford, Charlie 4, 49
Silas, Paul 24
Simmons, Bob 29
Simpson, O. J. 15
Singletary, Mike 4, 76
Slice, Kimbo 73
Smith, Bruce 80
Smith, Emmitt 7, 87
Smith, Hilton 29
Smith, Lovie 66
Smith, Ozzie 77
Smith, Randy 81
Smith, Rick 72
Smith, Stephen A. 69
Smith, Tubby 18, 83
Solomon, Jimmie Lee 38
Sono, Jomo 86
Sosa, Sammy 21, 44
Spiller, Bill 64
Sprewell, Latrell 23
Stackhouse, Jerry 30
Staley, Dawn 57
Stargell, Willie 29
Stearns, Norman "Turkey" 31
Steward, Emanuel 18
Stewart, James "Bubba," Jr. 60
Stewart, Kordell 21
Stingley, Darryl 69
Stith, Tom 93
Stone, Toni 15
Stoudemire, Amaré 59
Strahan, Michael 35, 81
Strawberry, Darryl 22
Stringer, C. Vivian 13, 66
Stringer, Korey 35
Swann, Lynn 28
Swoopes, Sheryl 12, 56
Tatum, Jack 87
Taylor, Jason 70
Taylor, Jermain 60
Taylor, Lawrence 25
Taylor, Marshall Walter "Major" 62
Tergat, Paul 59
Terrell-Kearney, Kim 83
Thomas, Debi 26
Thomas, Derrick 25
Thomas, Emmitt 71
Thomas, Frank 12, 51
Thomas, Isiah 7, 26, 65
Thomas, Thurman 75
Thompson, Tina 25, 75
Thrower, Willie 35
Thugwane, Josia 21
Thurmond, Nate 88
Tirico, Mike 68
Tisdale, Wayman 50
Toler, Burl 80
Tomlinson, LaDainian 65

Toney, James 89
Trouppe, Quincy Thomas, Sr. 84
Tunnell, Emlen 54
Tyson, Mike 28, 44, 93
Unseld, Wes 23
Upshaw, Gene 18, 47, 72
Ussery, Terdema, II 29
Vanessa James and Yannick Bon-
    heur 84
Vick, Michael 39
Vincent, Troy 91
Virgil, Ozzie 48
Wade, Dwyane 61
Walker, Herschel 1, 69
Wallace, Ben 54
Wallace, Perry E. 47
Wallace, Rasheed 56
Ward, Andre 62
Ward, Hines 84
Ware, Andre 37
Ware, DeMarcus 92
Washington, Gene 63
Washington, Kenny 50
Washington, MaliVai 8
Watson, Bob 25
Watts, J. C., Jr. 14, 38
Weah, George 58
Weathers, Carl 10
Webber, Chris 15, 30, 59
Weekes, Kevin 67
Wells, Vernon 91
Westbrook, Peter 20
Whitaker, Pernell 10, 89
White, Bill 1, 48
White, Jesse 22, 75
White, Reggie 6, 50
White, Willye 67
Whitfield, Fred 23
Whitfield, Mal 60
Wilbon, Michael 68
Wilkens, Lenny 11, 88
Wilkins, Dominique 74
Williams, Billy 86
Williams, Deron 92
Williams, Doug 22
Williams, J. Mayo 83
Williams, Ken 68
Williams, Lauryn 58
Williams, Natalie 31
Williams, Ricky 85
Williams, Serena 20, 41, 73
Williams, Stevie 71
Williams, Venus 17, 34, 62
Williamson, Fred 67
Willingham, Tyrone 43
Willis, Bill 68
Willis, Dontrelle 55
Wills, Harry 80
Wills, Maury 73
Wilson, Sunnie 7, 55
Winfield, Dave 5, 91
Winkfield, Jimmy 42
Winslow, Kellen 83
Wolfe, Ann 82
Woodard, Lynette 67
Woodruff, John 68
Woods, Tiger 14, 31, 81
Woodson, Mike 78
Woodson, Rod 79
Worthy, James 49
Wright, Rayfield 70
Yeboah, Emmanuel Ofosu 53
Young, Donald, Jr. 57

Young, Jimmy **54**

Television

Akil, Mara Brock **60, 82**
Akinnuoye-Agbaje, Adewale **56**
Alexander, Khandi **43**
Ali, Tatyana **73**
Allen, Byron **3**
Allen, Debbie **13, 42**
Allen, Marcus **20**
Alonso, Laz **87**
Amos, John **8, 62**
Anderson, Anthony **51, 77**
Anderson, Eddie "Rochester" **30**
Andrews, Tina **74**
Arkadie, Kevin **17**
Arnez J **53**
Arnold, Tichina **63**
Babatunde, Obba **35**
Banks, Michelle **59**
Banks, William **11**
Barclay, Paris **37**
Bassett, Angela **6, 23, 62**
Beach, Michael **26**
Beaton, Norman **14**
Beauvais, Garcelle **29**
Bellamy, Bill **12**
Bennett, Louise **69**
Bentley, Lamont **53**
Berry, Bertice **8, 55**
Berry, Fred "Rerun" **48**
Blackmon, Brenda **58**
Blackwood, Maureen **37**
Blacque, Taurean **58**
Blake, Asha **26**
Bleu, Corbin **65**
Bonet, Lisa **58**
Boston, Kelvin E. **25**
Bowser, Yvette Lee **17**
Bradley, Ed **2, 59**
Brady, Wayne **32, 71**
Brandy **14, 34, 72**
Braugher, Andre **13, 58, 91**
Bridges, Todd **37**
Brooks, Avery **9**
Brooks, Golden **62**
Brooks, Hadda **40**
Brooks, Mehcad **62**
Brown, Chris **74**
Brown, James **22**
Brown, Joe **29**
Brown, Les **5**
Brown, Tony **3**
Brown, Vivian **27**
Brown, Warren **61**
Browne, Roscoe Lee **66**
Bruce, Bruce **56**
Burnett, Charles **16, 68**
Burton, LeVar **8**
Byrd, Eugene **64**
Byrd, Robert **11**
Caldwell, Benjamin **46**
Cameron, Earl **44**
Campbell, Naomi **1, 31**
Campbell-Martin, Tisha **8, 42**
Cannon, Nick **47, 73**
Cannon, Reuben **50**
Cara, Irene **77**
Carroll, Rocky **74**
Carroll, Diahann **9**
Carson, Lisa Nicole **21**
Carter, Nell **39**
Cash, Rosalind **28**

Cedric the Entertainer **29, 60**
Chappelle, Dave **50**
Cheadle, Don **19, 52**
Chestnut, Morris **31**
Chideya, Farai **14, 61**
Christian, Spencer **15**
Ciara, Barbara **69**
Clack, Zoanne **73**
Clash, Kevin **14, 93**
Clayton, Xernona **3, 45**
CoCo Brother **93**
Cole, Nat "King" **17**
Coleman, Gary **35, 86**
Corbi, Lana **42**
Cornelius, Don **4**
Cosby, Bill **7, 26, 59**
Crothers, Scatman **19**
Curry, Mark **17**
Curtis-Hall, Vondie **17**
Davidson, Tommy **21**
Davis, Eisa **68**
Davis, Ossie **5, 50**
Davis, Viola **34, 76**
de Passe, Suzanne **25**
De Shields, André **72**
Dee, Ruby **8, 50, 68**
Deezer D **53**
Devine, Loretta **24**
Dickerson, Eric **27**
Dickerson, Ernest **6**
Diggs, Taye **25, 63**
Dixon, Ivan **69**
Dourdan, Gary **37**
Drake **86**
Dre, Dr. **10**
Duke, Bill **3**
Dungey, Merrin **62**
Dutton, Charles S. **4, 22**
Earthquake **55**
Ejiofor, Chiwetel **67**
Elba, Idris **49, 89**
Elder, Larry **25**
Elise, Kimberly **32**
Emmanuel, Alphonsia **38**
Ephriam, Mablean **29**
Epperson, Sharon **54**
Erving, Julius **18, 47**
Esposito, Giancarlo **9**
Eubanks, Kevin **15**
Evans, Harry **25**
Faison, Donald **50**
Faison, Frankie **55**
Falana, Lola **42**
Fales-Hill, Susan **88**
Fargas, Antonio **50**
Fields, Kim **36**
Fishburne, Laurence **4, 22, 70**
Fisher, Gail **85**
Flavor Flav **67**
Fox, Rick **27**
Foxx, Jamie **15, 48**
Foxx, Redd **2**
Frazier, Kevin **58**
Freeman, Aaron **52**
Freeman, Al, Jr. **11**
Freeman, Morgan **2, 20, 62**
Freeman, Yvette **27**
Gaines, Ernest J. **7**
Gardere, Jeffrey **76**
Garvin, Gerry **78**
Gibbs, Marla **86**
Gibson, Tyrese **27, 62**
Givens, Adele **62**

Givens, Robin **4, 25, 58**
Glover, Danny **3, 24**
Glover, Donald **85**
Glover, Savion **14**
Goldberg, Whoopi **4, 33, 69**
Goode, Mal **13**
Gooding, Cuba, Jr. **16, 62**
Gordon, Carl **87**
Gordon, Ed **10, 53**
Gossett, Louis, Jr. **7**
Gray, Darius **69**
Greely, M. Gasby **27**
Greene, Petey **65**
Grier, David Alan **28**
Grier, Pam **9, 31, 86**
Griffin, Angela **80**
Guillaume, Robert **3, 48**
Gumbel, Bryant **14, 80**
Gumbel, Greg **8**
Gunn, Moses **10**
Gurira, Danai **73**
Guy, Jasmine **2**
Hairston, Jester **88**
Haley, Alex **4**
Hall, Arsenio **58**
Hamilton, Lisa Gay **71**
Hampton, Henry **6**
Hardison, Kadeem **22**
Harewood, David **52**
Harper, Hill **32, 65**
Harrell, Andre **9, 30**
Harris, Naomie **55**
Harris, Robin **7**
Harvey, Steve **18, 58**
Hatchett, Glenda **32**
Hayes, Isaac **20, 58, 73**
Haynes, Trudy **44**
Haysbert, Dennis **42**
Hemsley, Sherman **19**
Henderson, Jeff **72**
Henriques, Julian **37**
Henry, Lenny **9, 52**
Henson, Darrin **33**
Henson, Taraji P. **58, 77**
Hickman, Fred **11**
Hill, Dulé **29**
Hill, Lauryn **20, 53**
Hill, Marc Lamont **80**
Hinderas, Natalie **5**
Hines, Gregory **1, 42**
Holmes, Amy **69**
Holt, Lester **66**
Hooks, Robert **76**
Hounsou, Djimon **19, 45**
Howard, Sherri **36**
Howard, Terrence **59**
Hudson, Ernie **72**
Huggins, Edie **71**
Hughley, D. L. **23, 76**
Hunter-Gault, Charlayne **6, 31**
Hyman, Earle **25, 79**
Ice-T **6, 31**
Ifill, Gwen **28**
Ingram, Rex **5**
Jackson, George **19**
Jackson, Janet **6, 30, 68**
Jackson, Randy **40**
Jackson, Tom **70**
Jarrett, Vernon D. **42**
Joe, Yolanda **21**
Johnson, Beverly **2**
Johnson, Linton Kwesi **37**
Johnson, Robert L. **3, 39**

Johnson, Rodney Van **28**
Jones, Bobby **20**
Jones, James Earl **3, 49, 79**
Jones, Orlando **30**
Jones, Quincy **8, 30**
Kandi **83**
Kaufman, Monica **66**
Kelley, Malcolm David **59**
Kennedy-Overton, Jayne Harris **46**
Keys, Alicia **32, 68**
Kid Cudi **83**
King, Gayle **19**
King, Regina **22, 45**
King, Woodie, Jr. **27**
Kirby, George **14**
Kitt, Eartha **16, 75**
Knight, Gladys **16, 66**
Kodjoe, Boris **34, 89**
Kotto, Yaphet **7**
Kwei-Armah, Kwame **84**
La Salle, Eriq **12**
LaBelle, Patti **13, 30**
Langhart Cohen, Janet **19, 60**
Lathan, Sanaa **27**
Lawrence, Martin **6, 27, 60**
Lawson, Jennifer **1, 50**
Lee, Leslie **85**
Lemmons, Kasi **20**
Lesure, James **64**
Lewis, Ananda **28**
Lewis, Byron E. **13**
Lewis, Emmanuel **36**
Lil' Kim **28**
Lindo, Delroy **18, 45**
LisaRaye **27**
LL Cool J **16, 49**
Lofton, James **42**
Long, Loretta **58**
Long, Nia **17**
Lover, Ed **10**
Luke, Derek **61**
Lumbly, Carl **47**
Mabrey, Vicki **26**
Mabuza-Suttle, Felicia **43**
Mac, Bernie **29, 61, 72**
Madison, Paula **37**
Malco, Romany **71**
Malveaux, Suzanne **88**
Manigault-Stallworth, Omarosa **69**
Mann, Tamela **92**
Martin, Helen **31**
Martin, Jesse L. **31**
Mathis, Greg **26**
Mayo, Whitman **32**
Mbatha-Raw, Gugu **89**
McBride, Chi **73**
McCrary Anthony, Crystal **70**
McDaniel, Hattie **5**
McDaniels, Ralph **79**
McEwen, Mark **5**
McFarland, Roland **49**
McGlowan, Angela **64, 86**
McKee, Lonette **12**
McKenzie, Vashti M. **29**
McKinney, Nina Mae **40**
McQueen, Butterfly **6, 54**
Meadows, Tim **30**
Mello, Breno **73**
Melton, Frank **81**
Mercado-Valdes, Frank **43**
Merkerson, S. Epatha **47, 83**
Michele, Michael **31**
Mickelbury, Penny **28**

Miller, Omar Benson 93
Miller, Wentworth 75
Mitchell, Brian Stokes 21
Mitchell, Kel 66
Mitchell, Russ 21, 73
Mokae, Zakes 80
Mo'Nique 35, 84
Mooney, Paul 37
Moore, Chante 26
Moore, Melba 21
Moore, Shemar 21
Morgan, Joe Leonard 9
Morgan, Tracy 61
Morris, Garrett 31
Morris, Greg 28
Morton, Frederick A., Jr. 93
Morton, Joe 18
Mos Def 30
Moses, Gilbert 12
Moss, Carlton 17
Mowry, Tamera 79
Mowry, Tia 78
Murphy, Eddie 4, 20, 61
Muse, Clarence Edouard 21
Myles, Kim 69
Nash, Johnny 40
Nash, Niecy 66
Neal, Elise 29
Nicholas, Denise 82
Nichols, Nichelle 11
Nissel, Angela 42
Neville, Arthel 53
Noble, Gil 76
Norman, Christina 47
Norman, Maidie 20
O'Brien, Soledad 88
Odetta 37, 74
Okonedo, Sophie 67
Oliver, Pam 54
Onwurah, Ngozi 38
Orman, Roscoe 55
Palmer, Keke 68
Parker, Nicole Ari 52
Parr, Russ 51
Payne, Allen 13
Peete, Holly Robinson 20
Peete, Rodney 60
Perkins, Tony 24
Perrineau, Harold, Jr. 51
Perry, Lowell 30
Perry, Tyler 40
Phifer, Mekhi 25
Phillips, Joseph C. 73
Pickens, James, Jr. 59
Pierce, Wendell 90
Pinckney, Sandra 56
Pinkett Smith, Jada 10, 41
Pinkston, W. Randall 24
Pitts, Byron 71
Poitier, Sydney Tamiia 65
Pounder, CCH 72
Poussaint, Renee 78
Price, Frederick K. C. 21
Price, Hugh B. 9, 54
Prince-Bythewood, Gina 31, 77
Pugh, Charles 81
Quarles, Norma 25
Queen Latifah 1, 16, 58
Quivers, Robin 61
Ralph, Sheryl Lee 18
Randle, Theresa 16
Rashad, Ahmad 18
Rashad, Phylicia 21

Raven 44
Ray, Gene Anthony 47
Ray J 86
Reddick, Lance 52
Reed Hall, Alaina 83
Reese, Della 6, 20
Reid, Tim 56
Reuben, Gloria 15
Reynolds, Star Jones 10, 27, 61
Rhimes, Shonda Lynn 67
Ribeiro, Alfonso 17
Richards, Beah 30
Richardson, Donna 39
Richardson, LaTanya 71
Richardson, Salli 68
Ridley, John 69
Roberts, Deborah 35
Roberts, Robin 16, 54
Robinson, Matt 69
Robinson, Max 3
Robinson, Shaun 36
Rochon, Lela 16
Rock, Chris 3, 22, 66
Rodgers, Johnathan 6, 51
Rodrigues, Percy 68
Roker, Al 12, 49
Roker, Roxie 68
Rolle, Esther 13, 21
Rollins, Howard E., Jr. 16
Ross, Diana 8, 27
Ross, Tracee Ellis 35
Roundtree, Richard 27
Rowan, Carl T. 1, 30
Rowell, Victoria 13, 68
Rudolph, Maya 46
Run 31, 73
RuPaul 17, 91
Russell, Bill 8
Russell, Nipsey 66
Rust, Art, Jr. 83
St. Jacques, Raymond 8
St. John, Kristoff 25
St. Patrick, Mathew 48
Saldana, Zoe 72
Salters, Lisa 71
Sands, Diana 87
Sanford, Isabel 53
Santiago-Hudson, Ruben 85
Schultz, Michael A. 6
Scott, Hazel 66
Scott, Jill 29, 83
Scott, Stuart 34
Shaw, Bernard 2, 28
Shepherd, Sherri 55
Simmons, Henry 55
Simmons, Jamal 72
Simmons, Kimora Lee 51, 83
Simpson, Carole 6, 30
Simpson, O. J. 15
Sinbad 1, 16
Sinclair, Madge 78
Smiley, Tavis 20, 68
Smith, Anjela Lauren 44
Smith, B(arbara) 11
Smith, Ian 62
Smith, Roger Guenveur 12
Smith, Tasha 73
Smith, Will 8, 18, 53
Stewart, Alison 13
Stewart, Nzingha 89
Stokes, Carl 10, 73
Stone, Chuck 9
Strahan, Michael 35, 81

Stuart, Moira 82
Sykes, Wanda 48, 81
Syler, Rene 53
Swann, Lynn 28
Tate, Larenz 15
Taylor, Jason 70
Taylor, Karin 34
Taylor, Meshach 4
Taylor, Regina 9, 46
Thigpen, Lynne 17, 41
Thomas-Graham, Pamela 29
Thomason, Marsha 47
Thompson, Kenan 52
Thoms, Tracie 61
Tirico, Mike 68
Torres, Gina 52
Torry, Guy 31
Toussaint, Lorraine 32
Townsend, Robert 4, 23
True, Rachel 82
Tucker, Chris 13, 23, 62
Tunie, Tamara 63
Tyler, Aisha N. 36
Tyson, Cicely 7, 51
Uggams, Leslie 23
Underwood, Blair 7, 27, 76
Union, Gabrielle 31, 92
Usher 23, 56
Van Peebles, Mario 2, 51
Van Peebles, Melvin 7
Vaughn, Countess 53
Vereen, Ben 4
Walker, Eamonn 37
Ware, Andre 37
Warfield, Marsha 2
Warner, Malcolm-Jamal 22, 36
Warren, Michael 27
Warwick, Dionne 18
Washington, Denzel 1, 16, 93
Washington, Hayma 86
Washington, Isaiah 62
Watson, Carlos 50
Wattleton, Faye 9
Watts, Rolonda 9
Wayans, Damien 78
Wayans, Damon 8, 41
Wayans, Kim 80
Wayans, Keenen Ivory 18
Wayans, Marlon 29, 82
Wayans, Shawn 29
Weathers, Carl 10
Wesley, Richard 73
Whack, Rita Coburn 36
Whitfield, Lynn 1, 18
Wilbon, Michael 68
Williams, Armstrong 29
Williams, Billy Dee 8
Williams, Clarence, III 26
Williams, Juan 35, 80
Williams, Malinda 57
Williams, Montel 4, 57
Williams, Russell, II 70
Williams, Samm-Art 21
Williams, Vanessa A. 32, 66
Williams, Vanessa L. 4, 17
Williams, Wendy 62
Williamson, Mykelti 22
Wills, Maury 73
Wilson, Chandra 57
Wilson, Debra 38
Wilson, Dorien 55
Wilson, Flip 21
Winfield, Paul 2, 45

Winfrey, Oprah 2, 15, 61
Witherspoon, John 38
Wright, Jeffrey 54
Yarbrough, Cedric 51
Yoba, Malik 11

Theater
Adams, Osceola Macarthy 31
Ailey, Alvin 8
Alexander, Khandi 43
Allen, Debbie 13, 42
Amos, John 8, 62
Anderson, Carl 48
Andrews, Bert 13
Angelou, Maya 1, 15
Anthony, Trey 63
Arkadie, Kevin 17
Armstrong, Vanessa Bell 24
Arnez J 53
Babatunde, Obba 35
Bandele, Biyi 68
Baraka, Amiri 1, 38
Barnett, Etta Moten 56
Barrett, Lindsay 43
Bassett, Angela 6, 23, 62
Beach, Michael 26
Beaton, Norman 14
Belafonte, Harry 4, 65
Belgrave, Cynthia 75
Bennett, Louise 69
Borders, James 9
Branch, William Blackwell 39
Braugher, Andre 13, 58, 91
Brooks, Avery 9
Brown, Oscar, Jr. 53
Brown, Ruth 90
Browne, Roscoe Lee 66
Bruce, Bruce 56
Caldwell, Benjamin 46
Calloway, Cab 14
Cameron, Earl 44
Campbell, Naomi 1
Cara, Irene 77
Carroll, Diahann 9
Carroll, Rocky 74
Carroll, Vinnette 29
Carter, Nell 39
Cash, Rosalind 28
Cheadle, Don 19, 52
Chenault, John 40
Childress, Alice 15
Clarke, Hope 14
Cleage, Pearl 17, 64
Cook, Will Marion 40
Cooper, Chuck 75
Corthron, Kia 43
Curtis-Hall, Vondie 17
Dadié, Bernard 34
David, Keith 27
Davis, Altovise 76
Davis, Eisa 68
Davis, Ossie 5, 50
Davis, Sammy, Jr. 18
Davis, Viola 34, 76
Dawn, Marpessa 75
De Shields, André 72
Dee, Ruby 8, 50, 68
Devine, Loretta 24
Dieudonné 67
Diggs, Taye 25, 63
Dixon, Ivan 69
Dodson, Owen Vincent 38
Duke, Bill 3

Dunham, Katherine **4, 59**
Dutton, Charles S. **4, 22**
Ejiofor, Chiwetel **67**
Elba, Idris **49, 89**
Elder, Lonne, III **38**
Emmanuel, Alphonsia **38**
Epps, Mike **60**
Esposito, Giancarlo **9**
Europe, James Reese **10**
Faison, Frankie **55**
Falana, Lola **42**
Fargas, Antonio **50**
Fields, Felicia P. **60**
Fishburne, Laurence **4, 22, 70**
Francis, Thais **93**
Franklin, J. E. **44**
Freeman, Aaron **52**
Freeman, Al, Jr. **11**
Freeman, Morgan **2, 20, 62**
Freeman, Yvette **27**
Fuller, Charles **8**
Gibson, John Trusty **87**
Gilpin, Charles Sidney **81**
Givens, Adele **62**
Glover, Danny **1, 24**
Glover, Keith **79**
Glover, Savion **14**
Goldberg, Whoopi **4, 33, 69**
Gordone, Charles **15**
Gossett, Louis, Jr. **7**
Graves, Denyce Antoinette **19, 57**
Greaves, William **38**
Grier, Pam **9, 31, 86**
Guillaume, Robert **3, 48**
Gunn, Moses **10**
Gurira, Danai **73**
Hall, Juanita **62**
Hamilton, Lisa Gay **71**
Hamlin, Larry Leon **49, 62**
Hansberry, Lorraine **6**
Harewood, David **52**
Harris, Bill **72**
Harris, Robin **7**
Hayes, Teddy **40**
Hemsley, Sherman **19**
Higginsen, Vy **65**
Hill, Dulé **29**
Hill, Errol **40**
Hill, Hugh Morgan **83**
Hines, Gregory **1, 42**
Holder, Geoffrey **78**
Holder, Laurence **34**
Holland, Endesha Ida Mae **3, 57**
Hooks, Robert **76**
Hyman, Earle **25, 79**
Hyman, Phyllis **19**
Ingram, Rex **5**
Jackson, Millie **25**
Jackson, Samuel **8, 19, 63**
Jamison, Judith **7, 67**
Jean-Baptiste, Marianne **17, 46**
Johnson, Je'Caryous **63**
Jones, James Earl **3, 49, 79**
Jones, Sarah **39**
Joyner, Matilda Sissieretta **15**
Kente, Gibson **52**
Khumalo, Leleti **51**
King, Woodie, Jr. **27**
King, Yolanda **6**
Kitt, Eartha **16, 75**
Kotto, Yaphet **7**
Kwei-Armah, Kwame **84**
La Salle, Eriq **12**

LaChanze **93**
Lampley, Oni Faida **43, 71**
Lathan, Sanaa **27**
Lee, Canada **8**
Lee, Leslie **85**
Leggs, Kingsley **62**
LeNoire, Rosetta **37**
Lenox, Adriane **59**
Leon, Kenny **10**
Lester, Adrian **46**
Letson, Al **39**
Lindo, Delroy **18, 45**
Lister, Marquita **65**
Mann, Tamela **92**
Marrow, Queen Esther **24**
Martin, Helen **31**
Martin, Jesse L. **31**
Mbatha-Raw, Gugu **89**
McClinton, Marion Isaac **77**
McDaniel, Hattie **5**
McDonald, Audra **20, 62**
McFarlan, Tyron **60**
McKee, Lonette **12**
McQueen, Butterfly **6, 54**
Merkerson, S. Epatha **47, 83**
Mickelbury, Penny **28**
Mills, Florence **22**
Milner, Ron **39**
Mitchell, Brian Stokes **21**
Mokae, Zakes **80**
Mollel, Tololwa **38**
Moore, Melba **21**
Morgan, Tracy **61**
Moses, Gilbert **12**
Moss, Carlton **17**
Moss, Preacher **63**
Moten, Etta **18**
Muse, Clarence Edouard **21**
Nascimento, Abdias do **93**
Ngaujah, Sahr **86**
Nicholas, Fayard **20, 57**
Nicholas, Harold **20**
Norman, Maidie **20**
Nottage, Lynn **66**
Ntshona, Winston **52**
Okonedo, Sophie **67**
Orlandersmith, Dael **42**
Oyelowo, David **82**
Payne, Allen **13**
Perrineau, Harold, Jr. **51**
Perry, Tyler **54**
Pierce, Wendell **90**
Pounder, CCH **72**
Powell, Maxine **8**
Power, Will **83**
Preer, Evelyn **82**
Premice, Josephine **41**
Primus, Pearl **6**
Pryor, Rain **65**
Ralph, Sheryl Lee **18**
Randle, Theresa **16**
Rashad, Phylicia **21**
Raven **44**
Redwood, John Henry **78**
Reese, Della **6, 20**
Reid, Tim **56**
Rhames, Ving **14, 50**
Richards, Beah **30**
Richards, Lloyd **2**
Richardson, Desmond **39**
Richardson, LaTanya **71**
Robeson, Paul **2**

Rolle, Esther **13, 21**
Rollins, Howard E., Jr. **16**
Rose, Anika Noni **70**
Rotimi, Ola **1**
St. Jacques, Raymond **8**
Salter, Nikkole **73**
Sands, Diana **87**
Sanford, Isabel **53**
Santiago-Hudson, Ruben **85**
Schultz, Michael A. **6**
Scott, Harold Russell, Jr. **61**
Shabazz, Attallah **6**
Slocumb, Jonathan **52**
Smiley, Rickey **59**
Smith, Anjela Lauren **44**
Smith, Anna Deavere **6, 44**
Smith, Roger Guenveur **12**
Snipes, Wesley **3, 24, 67**
Sommore **61**
Soyinka, Wole **4, 93**
Stew **69**
Stewart, Tonea Harris **78**
Sundiata, Sekou **66**
Talbert, David E. **34, 93**
Taylor, Meshach **4**
Taylor, Regina **9, 46**
Taylor, Ron **35**
Teer, Barbara Ann **81**
Thigpen, Lynne **17, 41**
Thompson, John Douglas **81**
Thompson, Tazewell **13**
Thurman, Wallace **16**
Torres, Gina **52**
Toussaint, Lorraine **32**
Townsend, Robert **4, 23**
Tyson, Cicely **7, 51**
Uggams, Leslie **23**
Underwood, Blair **7, 27, 76**
Van Peebles, Melvin **7**
Vance, Courtney B. **15, 60**
Vereen, Ben **4**
Walcott, Derek **5**
Walker, Eamonn **37**
Ward, Douglas Turner **42**
Washington, Fredi **10**
Waters, Ethel **7**
Watts, Reggie **52**
Whitaker, Forest **2, 49, 67**
White, Terri **82**
White, Willard **53**
Whitfield, Lynn **18**
Williams, Bert **18**
Williams, Billy Dee **8**
Williams, Clarence, III **26**
Williams, Michelle **73**
Williams, Samm-Art **21**
Williamson, Mykelti **22**
Wilson, August **7, 33, 55**
Wilson, Dorien **55**
Wilson, Tracey Scott **777**
Winfield, Paul **2, 45**
Withers-Mendes, Elisabeth **64**
Wolfe, George C. **6, 43**
Woodard, Alfre **9**
Wright, Jeffrey **54**
Yarbrough, Cedric **51**

Writing
Abani, Chris **77**
Abrahams, Peter **39**
Abu-Jamal, Mumia **15**
Achebe, Chinua **6**
Adams, Jenoyne **60**

Adams-Ender, Clara **40**
Adichie, Chimamanda Ngozi **64**
Aidoo, Ama Ata **38**
Ake, Claude **30**
Akpan, Uwem **70**
Al-Amin, Jamil Abdullah **6**
Alexander, Elizabeth **75**
Alexander, Margaret Walker **22**
Ali, Ayaan Hirsi **58, 92**
Ali, Hana Yasmeen **52**
Ali, Mohammed Naseehu **60**
Allen, Robert L. **38**
Allen, Samuel W. **38**
Amadi, Elechi **40**
Ames, Wilmer **27**
Anderson, Ho Che **54**
Andrews, Raymond **4**
Andrews, Tina **74**
Angelou, Maya **1, 15**
Ansa, Tina McElroy **14**
Anthony, Michael **29**
Appiah, Kwame Anthony **67**
Arac de Nyeko, Monica **66**
Aristide, Jean-Bertrand **6, 45**
Arkadie, Kevin **17**
Armah, Ayi Kwei **49**
Armah, Esther **87**
Asante, Molefi Kete **3**
Ashley-Ward, Amelia **23**
Asim, Jabari **71**
Atkins, Cholly **40**
Atkins, Russell **45**
Aubert, Alvin **41**
Auguste, Arnold A. **47**
Awoonor, Kofi **37**
Azikiwe, Nnamdi **13**
Ba, Mariama **30**
Bahati, Wambui **60**
Bailey, Chauncey **68**
Baiocchi, Regina Harris **41**
Baisden, Michael **25, 66**
Baker, Augusta **38**
Baker, Houston A., Jr. **6**
Baldwin, James **1**
Ballard, Allen Butler, Jr. **40**
Bambara, Toni Cade **10**
Bandele, Asha **36**
Bandele, Biyi **68**
Baquet, Dean **63**
Baraka, Amiri **1, 38**
Barnes, Steven **54**
Barnett, Amy Du Bois **46**
Barrax, Gerald William **45**
Barrett, Lindsay **43**
Bashir, Halima **73**
Bass, Charlotta Spears **40**
Baszile, Jennifer **79**
Bates, Karen Grigsby **40**
Beah, Ishmael **69**
Beals, Melba Patillo **15**
Bebey, Francis **45**
Beckham, Barry **41**
Bell, Derrick **6**
Bell, James Madison **40**
Benberry, Cuesta **65**
Bennett, George Harold **45**
Bennett, Gwendolyn B. **59**
Bennett, Lerone, Jr. **5, 84**
Bennett, Louise **69**
Benson, Angela **34**
Berry, James **41**
Berry, Mary Frances **7**
Best, Carrie **80**

Beti, Mongo 36
Betts, R. Dwayne 86
Bishop, Maurice 39
Blackman, Toni 86
Blair, Jayson 50
Bland, Eleanor Taylor 39
Blassingame, John Wesley 40
Blockson, Charles L. 42
Blow, Charles M. 73
Bluitt, Juliann S. 14
Bolden, Tonya 32
Bontemps, Arna 8
Booker, Simeon 23
Borders, James 9
Boston, Lloyd 24
Boyd, Gerald M. 32, 59
Boyd, Melba Joyce 86
Boyd, Suzanne 52
Bradley, David Henry, Jr. 39
Bradley, Ed 2, 59
Braithwaite, William Stanley 52
Branch, William Blackwell 39
Brand, Dionne 32
Brathwaite, Kamau 36
Brawley, Benjamin 44
Breeze, Jean "Binta" 37
Bridges, Sheila 36
Brimmer, Andrew F. 2, 48
Briscoe, Connie 15
Britt, Donna 28
Brooks, Gwendolyn 1, 28
Brower, William 49
Brown, Cecil M. 46
Brown, Claude 38
Brown, Elaine 8
Brown, Les 5
Brown, Lloyd Louis 10, 42
Brown, Marie Dutton 12
Brown, Sterling Allen 10, 64
Brown, Tony 3
Brown, Wesley 23
Broyard, Anatole 68
Broyard, Bliss 68
Brutus, Dennis 38
Bryan, Ashley F. 41
Buckley, Gail Lumet 39
Bullins, Ed 25
Bunche, Ralph J. 5
Bunkley, Anita Richmond 39
Burgess, Marjorie L. 55
Burroughs, Margaret Taylor 9
Burwell, Bryan 83
Butler, Octavia 8, 43, 58
Bynum, Juanita 31, 71
Caldwell, Earl 60
Calhoun, Lillian Scott 87
Campbell, Bebe Moore 6, 24, 59
Carby, Hazel 27
Carmichael, Stokely 5, 26
Carroll, Vinnette 29
Carter, Joye Maureen 41
Carter, Martin 49
Carter, Stephen L. 4
Cartey, Wilfred 47
Cartiér, Xam Wilson 41
Cary, Lorene 3
Cary, Mary Ann Shadd 30
Cayton, Horace 26
Césaire, Aimé 48, 69
Chadiha, Jeffri 57
Channer, Colin 36
Chase-Riboud, Barbara 20, 46
Chenault, John 40

Cheney-Coker, Syl 43
Chesnutt, Charles 29
Chideya, Farai 14, 61
Childress, Alice 15
Christian, Barbara T. 44
Churchwell, Robert, Sr. 76
Clack, Zoanne 73
Clark, Kenneth B. 5, 52
Clark, Septima 7
Clark-Bekedermo, J. P. 44
Clarke, Austin C. 32
Clarke, Cheryl 32
Clarke, George 32
Cleage, Pearl 17, 64
Cleaver, Eldridge 5
Cliff, Michelle 42
Clifton, Lucille 14, 64, 91
Coates, Ta-Nehisi 76
Cobb, William Jelani 59
Cobbs, Price M. 9
Cohen, Anthony 15
Cole, Johnnetta B. 5, 43
Coleman, Wanda 48
Collins, Patricia Hill 67
Colter, Cyrus J. 36
Comer, James P. 6
Common 31, 63
Contee, Cheryl 88
Cook, Suzan D. Johnson 22
Cooke, Marvel 31
Coombs, Orde M. 44
Cooper, Afua 53
Cooper, Andrew W. 36
Cooper, Anna Julia 20
Cooper, Helene 74
Cooper, J. California 12, 85
Cornish, Sam 50
Cortez, Jayne 43
Cosby, Bill 7, 26, 59
Cose, Ellis 5, 50
Cotter, Joseph Seamon, Sr. 40
Couto, Mia 45
Cox, Joseph Mason Andrew 51
Creagh, Milton 27
Croal, N'Gai 76
Crouch, Stanley 11, 87
Cruse, Harold 54
Crutchfield, James N. 55
Cullen, Countee 8
Cuney, William Waring 44
Cunningham, Evelyn 23, 85
Curry, George E. 23
Curtis, Christopher Paul 26
Curtis-Hall, Vondie 17
Dabydeen, David 48
Dadié, Bernard 34
D'Aguiar, Fred 50
Damas, Léon-Gontran 46
Dandridge, Raymond Garfield 45
Danner, Margaret Esse 49
Danquah, Meri Nana Ama 93
Danticat, Edwidge 15, 68
Dash, Leon 47
Datcher, Michael 60
Dathorne, O. R. 52
Davis, Allison 12
Davis, Angela 5
Davis, Charles T. 48
Davis, Eisa 68
Davis, Frank Marshall 47
Davis, George 36
Davis, Nolan 45
Davis, Ossie 5, 50

Davis, Thulani 61
Dawkins, Wayne 20
de Passe, Suzanne 25
De Veaux, Alexis 44
Deggans, Eric 71
Delany, Martin R. 27
Delany, Samuel R., Jr. 9
DeLoach, Nora 30
Demby, William 51
Dent, Thomas C. 50
Dickerson, Debra J. 60
Dickey, Eric Jerome 21, 56
Diop, Birago 53
Diop, Cheikh Anta 4
Dodson, Howard, Jr. 7, 52
Dodson, Owen Vincent 38
Douglass, Frederick 87
Dove, Rita 6, 78
Draper, Sharon Mills 16, 43
Driskell, David C. 7
Driver, David E. 11
Drummond, William J. 40
Du Bois, David Graham 45
Du Bois, W. E. B. 3
DuBois, Shirley Graham 21
Due, Tananarive 30
Dumas, Henry 41
Dunbar, Paul Laurence 8
Dunbar-Nelson, Alice Ruth Moore 44
Dungy, Camille 86
Dunham, Katherine 4, 59
Dunnigan, Alice Allison 41
Duplechan, Larry 55
Dyson, Michael Eric 11, 40
Eagleson, William Lewis 90
Edmonds, Terry 17
Ekwensi, Cyprian 37
Elder, Lonne, III 38
Elliot, Lorris 37
Ellison, Ralph 7
Elmore, Ronn 21
Emanuel, James A. 46
Emecheta, Buchi 30
Equiano, Olaudah 78
Estes, Rufus 29
Evans, Diana 72
Evans, Mari 26
Everett, Percival 93
Fabio, Sarah Webster 48
Fair, Ronald L. 47
Fales-Hill, Susan 88
Fanon, Frantz 44
Farah, Nuruddin 27
Farley, Christopher John 54
Farrakhan, Louis 15
Fauset, Jessie 7
Feelings, Muriel 44
Feelings, Tom 11, 47
Fields, Julia 45
Figueroa, John J. 40
Files, Lolita 35
Finner-Williams, Paris Michele 62
Fisher, Antwone 40
Fisher, Rudolph 17
Fleming, Raymond 48
Fletcher, Bill, Jr. 41
Fletcher, Geoffrey 85
Forbes, Calvin 46
Ford, Clyde W. 40
Ford, Nick Aaron 44
Ford, Wallace 58
Forman, James 7, 51

Forrest, Leon 44
Fortune, T. Thomas 6
Foster, Cecil 32
Foster, Jylla Moore 45
Franklin, John Hope 5, 77
Franklin, Robert M. 13
Frazier, E. Franklin 10
Frazier, Oscar 58
French, Albert 18
Fuller, Charles 8
Fuller, Hoyt 44
Gabre-Medhin, Tsegaye 64
Gaines, Ernest J. 7
Gaiter, Dorothy J. 80
Gardner, Chris 65
Gaston, Marilyn Hughes 60
Gates, Henry Louis, Jr. 3, 38, 67
Gayle, Addison, Jr. 41
George, Nelson 12
Gibson, Donald Bernard 40
Giddings, Paula 11
Gilbert, Christopher 50
Gilliard, Steve 69
Giovanni, Nikki 9, 39, 85
Givhan, Robin Deneen 72
Gladwell, Malcolm 62
Gloster, Hugh Morris, Sr. 90
Glover, Donald 85
Goines, Donald 19
Golden, Marita 19
Gomez, Jewelle 30
Goodison, Lorna 71
Goodlett, Carlton B. 91
Gordon-Reed, Annette 74
Graham, Lawrence Otis 12
Graham, Lorenz 48
Grant, Gwendolyn Goldsby 28
Gray, Darius 69
Greaves, William 38
Greenfield, Eloise 9
Greenlee, Sam 48
Greenwood, Monique 38
Griffith, Mark Winston 8
Grimké, Archibald H. 9
Guinier, Lani 7, 30
Guy, Rosa 5
Guy-Sheftall, Beverly 13, 92
Haley, Alex 4
Halliburton, Warren J. 49
Hamblin, Ken 10
Hamilton, Virginia 10
Hansberry, Lorraine 6
Harding, Vincent 67
Hare, Nathan 44
Harkless, Necia Desiree 19
Harper, Frances Ellen Watkins 11
Harper, Michael S. 34
Harper, Rachel M. 92
Harrington, Oliver W. 9
Harris, Bill 72
Harris, Claire 34
Harris, Eddy L. 18
Harris, Jay 19
Harris, Jessica B. 91
Harris, Leslie 6
Harris, Monica 18
Harrison, Alvin 28
Harrison, Calvin 28
Haskins, James 36, 54
Hayden, Robert 12
Hayes, Teddy 40
Haygood, Wil 83
Haywood, Gar Anthony 43

Head, Bessie 28
Heard, Nathan C. 45
Hearne, John Edgar Caulwell 45
Hemphill, Essex 10
Henderson, David 53
Henderson, Stephen E. 45
Henries, A. Doris Banks 44
Henriques, Julian 37
Henry, Lenny 9, 52
Henson, Josiah 90
Henson, Matthew 2
Herbert, Bob 63
Hercules, Frank 44
Herndon, Angelo 90
Hernton, Calvin C. 51
Hill, Donna 32
Hill, Errol 40
Hill, Leslie Pinckney 44
Hilliard, David 7
Hoagland, Everett H. 45
Hobson, Julius W. 44
Holland, Endesha Ida Mae 3, 57
Holmes, Shannon 70
Holt, Nora 38
Holton, Hugh, Jr. 39
hooks, bell 5, 90
Horne, Frank 44
Hrabowski, Freeman A., III 22
Hudlin, Reginald 9, 86
Hudson, Cheryl 15
Hudson, Wade 15
Hughes, Langston 4
Hull, Akasha Gloria 45
Hunter-Gault, Charlayne 6, 31
Hurston, Zora Neale 3
Iceberg Slim 11
Ifill, Gwen 28
Ilibagiza, Immaculée 66
Jackson, Brenda 87
Jackson, Fred James 25
Jackson, George 14
Jackson, James A. 90
Jackson, Sheneska 18
James, Marlon 85
Jarrett, Vernon D. 42
Jasper, Kenji 39
Jenkins, Beverly 14
Joachim, Paulin 34
Joe, Yolanda 21
Johnson, Angela 52
Johnson, Charles 1, 82
Johnson, Charles S. 12
Johnson, Fenton 91
Johnson, Georgia Douglas 41
Johnson, James Weldon 5
Johnson, John H. 3, 54
Johnson, Linton Kwesi 37
Johnson, Mat 31
Johnson, R. M. 36
Johnson, William 91
Jolley, Willie 28
Jones, Edward P. 43, 67
Jones, Gayl 37
Jones, Orlando 30
Jones, Sarah 39
Jordan, June 7, 35
Josey, E. J. 10
July, William 27
Just, Ernest Everett 3
Kamau, Kwadwo Agymah 28
Karenga, Maulana 10, 71
Kariuki, J. M. 67
Kay, Jackie 37

Kayira, Legson 40
Kearney, Janis 54
Keckley, Elizabeth 90
Keene, John 73
Kendrick, Erika 57
Kennedy, Adrienne 11
Kennedy, Florynce 12, 33
Kennedy, Randall 40
Khanga, Yelena 6
Killens, John O. 54
Kimbro, Dennis 10
Kincaid, Jamaica 4
King, Colbert I. 69
King, Coretta Scott 3, 57
King, Preston 28
King, Woodie, Jr. 27
King, Yolanda 6
Kitt, Sandra 23
Kitwana, Bakari 86
Knight, Etheridge 37
Kobia, Samuel 43
Komunyakaa, Yusef 9
Kunjufu, Jawanza 3, 50
Lacy, Sam 30, 46
Ladner, Joyce A. 42
Laferriere, Dany 33
LaGuma, Alex 30
Lamming, George 35
Lampley, Oni Faida 43, 71
Lane, Lunsford 93
Larsen, Nella 10
Lateef, Yusef 91
Lattany, Kristin Hunter 88
Lawrence, Martin 6, 27, 60
Lawrence-Lightfoot, Sara 10
Lemmons, Kasi 20
Lester, Julius 9
Letson, Al 39
Lewis, David Levering 9
Lewis, Samella 25
Lincoln, C. Eric 38
Little, Benilde 21
Locke, Alain 10
Locke, Attica 85
Lomax, Louis E. 90
Lorde, Audre 6
Louis, Errol T. 8
Loury, Glenn 36
Lowe, Herbert 57
Mabry, Marcus 70
Mabuza-Suttle, Felicia 43
Machado de Assis 74
Mackey, Nathaniel 75
Madhubuti, Haki 7, 85
Madison, Paula 37
Major, Clarence 9
Makeba, Miriam 2, 50, 74
Malveaux, Julianne 32, 70
Manley, Ruth 34
Marechera, Dambudzo 39
Markham, E. A. 37
Marshall, Paule 7, 77
Martin, Roland S. 49, 84
Mason, Felicia 31
Mason, Herman, Jr. 83
Massaquoi, Hans J. 30
Matejka, Adrian 87
Mathabane, Mark 5
Maynard, Nancy Hicks 73
Maynard, Robert C. 7
Mays, Benjamin E. 7
Mbaye, Mariétou 31
McBride, James 35, 87

McCall, Nathan 8
McCauley, Gina 76
McClellan, George Marion 91
McCrary Anthony, Crystal 70
McDuffie, Dwayne 62
McFadden, Bernice L. 39
McGruder, Robert 22, 35
McKay, Claude 6
McKinney Hammond, Michelle 51
McKinney-Whetstone, Diane 27
McMillan, Rosalynn A. 36
McMillan, Terry 4, 17, 53
McMillan, Tracy 93
McPherson, James Alan 70
Memmi, Albert 37
Menard, John Willis 90
Mengestu, Dinaw 66
Meredith, James H. 11
Mfume, Kweisi 6, 41
Micheaux, Oscar 7
Mickelbury, Penny 28
Millner, Denene 76
Milner, Ron 39
Mitchell, Elvis 67
Mitchell, Loften 31
Mitchell, Russ 21, 73
Mitchell, Sharon 36
Mofolo, Thomas Mokopu 37
Mollel, Tololwa 38
Monroe, Bryan 71
Monroe, Mary 35
Moore, Jessica Care 30
Moore, Wes 86
Morrison, Toni 2, 15, 86
Mosley, Walter 5, 25, 68
Moss, Carlton 17
Mossell, Gertrude Bustill 40
Moutoussamy-Ashe, Jeanne 7
Mowry, Jess 7
Mphalele, Es'kia (Ezekiel) 40
Mudimbe, V.Y. 61
Mugo, Micere Githae 32
Mullen, Harryette 34
Murphy, John H. 42
Murray, Albert L. 33
Murray, Pauli 38
Mwangi, Meja 40
Myers, Walter Dean 8, 70
Nash, Shannon King 84
Naylor, Gloria 10, 42
Neal, Larry 38
Neal, Mark Anthony 74
Nelson, Jill 6, 54
Neto, António Agostinho 43
Newkirk, Pamela 69
Newton, Huey 2
Ngugi wa Thiong'o 29, 61
Nissel, Angela 42
Njawe, Pius 87
Nkosi, Lewis 46
Norris, Michele 83
Norton, Meredith 72
Nugent, Richard Bruce 39
Nunez, Elizabeth 62
Ojikutu, Bayo 66
Okara, Gabriel 37
Oliver, John J., Jr. 48
Onwueme, Tess Osonye 23
Orlandersmith, Dael 42
Oyono, Ferdinand 38
Packer, Z. Z. 64
Page, Clarence 4
Painter, Nell Irvin 24, 88

Palmer, Everard 37
Parker, Pat 19
Parker, Star 70
Parks, Suzan-Lori 34, 85
Patterson, Orlando 4
Payne, Ethel L. 28
Payne, Les 89
Peters, Lenrie 43
Petry, Ann 19
Philip, Marlene Nourbese 32
Phillips, Joseph C. 73
Piper, Adrian 71
Pitts, Leonard, Jr. 54, 85
Plaatje, Sol. T. 80
Polite, Carlene Hatcher 82
Poussaint, Alvin F. 5, 67
Poussaint, Renee 78
Powell, Adam Clayton, Jr. 3
Powell, Kevin 31, 74
Power, Will 83
Pressley, Condace L. 41
Prince, Richard E. 71
Pryce, Trevor 89
Pryor, Rain 65
Pryor, Richard 3, 24, 56
Quarles, Benjamin Arthur 18
Rahman, Aishah 37
Randall, Alice 38
Randall, Dudley 8, 55
Rapier, James T. 82
Raspberry, William 2
Reagon, Bernice Johnson 7
Reddick, Lawrence Dunbar 20
Redding, J. Saunders 26
Redmond, Eugene 23
Reed, Ishmael 8
Rhimes, Shonda Lynn 67
Rhoden, William C. 67
Rhodes, Jewell Parker 84
Rhone, Trevor 80
Richards, Beah 30
Ridley, John 69
Riggs, Marlon 5
Riley, Rochelle 50
Ringgold, Faith 4, 81
Robertson, Gil L., IV 85
Robeson, Eslanda Goode 13
Robinson, Aminah 50
Robinson, Eugene 77
Robinson, Matt 69
Roby, Kimberla Lawson 86
Rogers, Joel Augustus 30
Rollins, Charlamae Hill 27
Rotimi, Ola 1
Rowan, Carl T. 1, 30
Ruffin, Josephine St. Pierre 75
Run 31, 73
Rust, Art, Jr. 83
Sadlier, Rosemary 62
Saint James, Synthia 12
St. John, Kristoff 25
Salih, Al-Tayyib 37
Sanchez, Sonia 17, 51
Sanders, Dori 8
Sapphire 14
Saro-Wiwa, Kenule 39
Shelton, Paula Young 86
Schomburg, Arthur Alfonso 9
Schuyler, George Samuel 40
Seale, Bobby 3
Sembène, Ousmane 13, 62
Senghor, Léopold Sédar 12, 66
Sengstacke, John 18

Senior, Olive 37
Senna, Danzy 93
Shabazz, Attallah 6
Shabazz, Ilyasah 36
Shakur, Assata 6
Shakur, Yusef 85
Shange, Ntozake 8, 89
Shaw, Bernard 2, 28
Shipp, E. R. 15
Shockley, Ann Allen 84
Simone, Nina 15, 41
Simpson, Carole 6, 30
Singletary, Mike 4, 76
Singleton, John 2, 30
Sister Souljah 11
Skinner, Kiron K. 65
Smiley, Tavis 20, 68
Smith, Anna Deavere 6
Smith, B(arbara) 11
Smith, Barbara 28
Smith, Bruce W. 53
Smith, Danyel 40
Smith, Jessie Carney 35
Smith, Mary Carter 26
Smith, Stephen A. 69
Smith, Zadie 51
Snowden, Frank M., Jr. 67
Somé, Malidoma Patrice 10
Southgate, Martha 58
Sowell, Thomas 2
Soyinka, Wole 4, 93
Spencer, Anne 27
Spriggs, William 67
Staples, Brent 8
Stewart, Alison 13
Stone, Chuck 9
Stringer, Vickie 58

Sundiata, Sekou 66
Tademy, Lalita 36
Talbert, David E. 34, 93
Talley, André Leon 56
Tate, Eleanora E. 20, 55
Tatum, Beverly Daniel 42, 84
Tatum, Elinor R. 78
Tatum, Wilbert 76
Taulbert, Clifton Lemoure 19
Taylor, Kristin Clark 8
Taylor, Mildred D. 26
Taylor, Susan C. 62
Taylor, Susan L. 10, 86
Teasley, Lisa 92
Thomas, Michael 69
Thomas, Trisha R. 65
Thomas-Graham, Pamela 29
Thornton, Yvonne S. 69
Thurman, Howard 3
Thurston, Baratunde 79
Tillis, Frederick 40
Tolson, Melvin 37
Toomer, Jean 6
Touré, Askia (Muhammad Abu Bakr el) 47
Townsend, Robert 4
Trotter, Monroe 9
Troupe, Quincy 83
Tucker, Cynthia 15, 61
Turner, Henry McNeal 5
Tutuola, Amos 30
Tyree, Omar Rashad 21
Tyson, Asha 39
Tyson, Neil deGrasse 15, 65
Van Peebles, Melvin 7
van Sertima, Ivan 25
Vega, Marta Moreno 61

Vera, Yvonne 32
Verdelle, A. J. 26
Wade-Gayles, Gloria Jean 41
Walcott, Derek 5
Walker, Alice 1, 43
Walker, Margaret 29
Walker, Rebecca 50
Wallace, Michele Faith 13
Wallace, Phyllis A. 9
Walters, Ronald 83
Ward, Douglas Turner 42
Washington, Booker T. 4
Washington, Elsie B. 78
Washington, Harriet A. 69
Washington, James, Jr. 38
Washington, Laura S. 18
Wattleton, Faye 9
Wayans, Damon 8, 41
Weaver, Afaa Michael 37
Webb, Veronica 10
Weems, Renita J. 44
Wells-Barnett, Ida B. 8
Wesley, Dorothy Porter 19
Wesley, Richard 73
Wesley, Valerie Wilson 18
West, Cornel 5, 33, 80
West, Dorothy 12, 54
Whack, Rita Coburn 36
Wharton, Clifton R., Jr. 7
Whitaker, Mark 21, 47
White, Armond 80
White, Walter F. 4
Whitehead, Colson 77
Whitfield, LeRoy 84
Whitfield, Van 34
Whitlock, Jason 78
Wideman, John Edgar 5, 87

Wilbekin, Emil 63
Wiley, Ralph 8, 78
Wilkerson, Isabel 71
Wilkins, Roger 2, 84
Wilkins, Roy 4
Williams, Armstrong 29
Williams, George Washington 18
Williams, John A. 27
Williams, Juan 35, 80
Williams, Patricia 11, 54
Williams, Robert F. 11
Williams, Roy 89
Williams, Samm-Art 21
Williams, Saul 31
Williams, Sherley Anne 25
Williams, Stanley "Tookie" 29, 57
Williams, Wendy 62
Wilson, August 7, 33, 55
Wilson, Mary 28
Wilson, William Julius 22
Winans, Marvin L. 17
Wiwa, Ken 67
Wolfe, George C. 6, 43
Woods, Mattiebelle 63
Woods, Scott 55
Woods, Teri 69
Woodson, Carter G. 2
Worrill, Conrad 12
Wright, Bruce McMarion 3, 52
Wright, Richard 5
X, Marvin 45
Yarbrough, Camille 40
Yette, Samuel F. 63
Young, Al 82
Young, Whitney M., Jr. 4
Youngblood, Shay 32
Zane 71
Zook, Kristal Brent 62

Cumulative Subject Index

Volume numbers appear in **bold**

A cappella
Cooke, Sam **17**
Reagon, Bernice Johnson **7**

AA
See Alcoholics Anonymous

AAAS
See American Association for the
Advancement of Science

AARP
Dixon, Margaret **14**
Smith, Marie F. **70**

ABC
See American Broadcasting Company

Abstract expressionism
Lewis, Norman **39**

Academy awards
Austin, Patti **24**
Cara, Irene **77**
Fletcher, Geoffrey **85**
Freeman, Morgan **2, 20, 62**
Goldberg, Whoopi **4, 33, 69**
Gooding, Cuba, Jr. **16, 62**
Gossett, Louis, Jr. **7**
Jean-Baptiste, Marianne **17, 46**
McDaniel, Hattie **5**
Mo'Nique **35, 84**
Poitier, Sidney **11, 36**
Prince **18, 65**
Richie, Lionel **27, 65**
Washington, Denzel **1, 16, 93**
Whitaker, Forest **2, 49, 67**
Williams, Russell, II **70**
Wonder, Stevie **11, 53**

ACLU
See American Civil Liberties Union

Acquired immune deficiency syndrome (AIDS)
Ashe, Arthur **1, 18**
Atim, Julian **66**
Broadbent, Hydeia **36**
Cargill, Victoria A. **43**
Fenton, Kevin **87**
Gayle, Helene D. **3, 46**
Hale, Lorraine **8**
Johnson, Earvin "Magic" **3, 39**
Lewis-Thornton, Rae **32**
Mboup, Souleymane **10**

Moutoussamy-Ashe, Jeanne **7**
Norman, Pat **10**
Ojikutu, Bisola **65**
Okaalet, Peter **58**
Pickett, Cecil **39**
Riggs, Marlon **5, 44**
Satcher, David **7, 57**
Seele, Pernessa **46**
Whitfield, LeRoy **84**
Wilson, Phill **9**
Zulu, Princess Kasune **54**

ACT UP
See AIDS Coalition to Unleash
Power

Acting
Aaliyah **30**
Aaron, Quinton **82**
Adams, Osceola Macarthy **31**
Adebimpe, Tunde **75**
Akinnuoye-Agbaje, Adewale **56**
Alexander, Khandi **43**
Ali, Tatyana **73**
Allen, Debbie **13, 42**
Alonso, Laz **87**
Amos, John **8, 62**
Anderson, Anthony **51, 77**
Anderson, Carl **48**
Anderson, Eddie "Rochester" **30**
Andrews, Tina **74**
Angelou, Maya **1, 15**
Armstrong, Vanessa Bell **24**
Ashanti **37**
Babatunde, Obba **35**
Bahati, Wambui **60**
Baker, Josephine **3**
Banks, Michelle **59**
Banks, Tyra **11, 50**
Barnett, Etta Moten **56**
Bassett, Angela **6, 23, 62**
Beach, Michael **26**
Beals, Jennifer **12**
Beaton, Norman **14**
Beauvais, Garcelle **29**
Belgrave, Cynthia **75**
Bennett, Louise **69**
Bentley, Lamont **53**
Berry, Fred "Rerun" **48**
Berry, Halle **4, 19, 57, 91**
Beyoncé **39, 70**
Bivins, Michael **72**
Blacque, Taurean **58**
Blanks, Billy **22**

Blige, Mary J. **20, 34, 60**
Bonet, Lisa **58**
Borders, James **9**
Bow Wow **35**
Brady, Wayne **32, 71**
Branch, William Blackwell **39**
Braugher, Andre **13, 58, 91**
Bridges, Todd **37**
Brooks, Avery **9**
Brooks, Golden **62**
Brooks, Mehcad **62**
Brown, Chris **74**
Brown, Jim **11**
Browne, Roscoe Lee **66**
Byrd, Eugene **64**
Caesar, Shirley **19**
Calloway, Cab **14**
Cameron, Earl **44**
Campbell, Naomi **1, 31**
Campbell-Martin, Tisha **8, 42**
Cannon, Nick **47, 73**
Cara, Irene **77**
Carroll, Diahann **9**
Carroll, Rocky **74**
Carson, Lisa Nicole **21**
Carey, Mariah **32, 53, 69**
Cash, Rosalind **28**
Cedric the Entertainer **29, 60**
Cheadle, Don **19, 52**
Chestnut, Morris **31**
Childress, Alice **15**
Chong, Rae Dawn **62**
Chweneyagae, Presley **63**
Clarke, Hope **14**
Cole, Nat "King" **17**
Coleman, Gary **35, 86**
Combs, Sean **17, 43, 92**
Cooper, Chuck **75**
Cosby, Bill **7, 26, 59**
Crothers, Scatman **19**
Curry, Mark **17**
Curtis-Hall, Vondie **17**
Dandridge, Dorothy **3**
David, Keith **27**
Davidson, Jaye **5**
Davis, Altovise **76**
Davis, Eisa **68**
Davis, Guy **36**
Davis, Ossie **5, 50**
Davis, Sammy, Jr. **18**
Davis, Viola **34, 76**
Dawn, Marpessa **75**
Dawson, Rosario **72**
De Bankolé, Isaach **78**

De Shields, André **72**
Dee, Ruby **8, 50, 68**
Devine, Loretta **24**
Diesel, Vin **29**
Diggs, Taye **25, 63**
Dixon, Ivan **69**
DMX **28, 64**
Dourdan, Gary **37**
Duke, Bill **3**
Duncan, Michael Clarke **26**
Dungey, Merrin **62**
Dutton, Charles S. **4, 22**
Ejiofor, Chiwetel **67**
Elba, Idris **49, 89**
Elise, Kimberly **32**
Emmanuel, Alphonsia **38**
Epps, Mike **60**
Epps, Omar **23, 59**
Esposito, Giancarlo **9**
Everett, Francine **23**
Faison, Donald **50**
Faison, Frankie **55**
Falana, Lola **42**
Fargas, Antonio **50**
Fetchit, Stepin **32**
Fields, Felicia P. **60**
Fields, Kim **36**
Fishburne, Laurence **4, 22, 70**
Fisher, Gail **85**
Fox, Rick **27**
Fox, Vivica A. **15, 53**
Foxx, Jamie **15, 48**
Foxx, Redd **2**
Francis, Thais **93**
Freeman, Al, Jr. **11**
Freeman, Morgan **2, 20, 62**
Freeman, Yvette **27**
Gaye, Nona **56**
Gibbs, Marla **86**
Gibson, Tyrese **27, 62**
Gilpin, Charles Sidney **81**
Ginuwine **35**
Givens, Adele **62**
Givens, Robin **4, 25, 58**
Glover, Danny **1, 24**
Glover, Donald **85**
Goldberg, Whoopi **4, 33, 69**
Gooding, Cuba, Jr. **16, 62**
Gordon, Dexter **25**
Gossett, Louis, Jr. **7**
Greaves, William **38**
Grier, David Alan **28**
Grier, Pam **9, 31, 86**
Griffin, Angela **80**

Guillaume, Robert 3, 48
Gunn, Moses 10
Gurira, Danai 73
Guy, Jasmine 2
Hairston, Jester 88
Hall, Arsenio 58
Hamilton, Lisa Gay 71
Hamlin, Larry Leon 49, 62
Hammond, Fred 23
Hardison, Kadeem 22
Harewood, David 52
Harper, Hill 32, 65
Harris, Naomie 55
Harris, Robin 7
Harvey, Steve 18, 58
Hawkins, Screamin' Jay 30
Hayes, Isaac 20, 58, 73
Haysbert, Dennis 42
Hemsley, Sherman 19
Henry, Lenny 9, 52
Henson, Taraji P. 58, 77
Hill, Dulé 29
Hill, Lauryn 20, 53
Hines, Gregory 1, 42
Holder, Geoffrey 78
Hooks, Robert 76
Horne, Lena 5, 86
Hounsou, Djimon 19, 45
Houston, Whitney 7, 28, 83
Howard, Sherri 36
Howard, Terrence 59
Howell, Ayinde 91
Hudson, Ernie 72
Hudson, Jennifer 63, 83
Hughley, D. L. 23, 76
Hyman, Earle 25, 79
Ice Cube 8, 30, 60
Ingram, Rex 5
Jackson, Millie 25
Jackson, Samuel 8, 19, 63
Jean-Baptiste, Marianne 17, 46
Jean-Louis, Jimmy 76
Johnson, Rafer 33
Johnson, Rodney Van 28
Jones, James Earl 3, 49, 79
Jones, Orlando 30
Jorge, Seu 73
Kelley, Elijah 65
Kelley, Malcolm David 59
Kennedy-Overton, Jayne Harris 46
Khumalo, Leleti 51
Kid Cudi 83
King, Regina 22, 45
King, Woodie, Jr. 27
Kirby, George 14
Kitt, Eartha 16, 75
Knight, Gladys 16, 66
Kodjoe, Boris 34, 89
Kotto, Yaphet 7
La Salle, Eriq 12
LaBelle, Patti 13, 30
LaChanze 93
Lampley, Oni Faida 43, 71
Lane, Charles 3
Lassiter, Roy 24
Lathan, Sanaa 27
Lawrence, Martin 6, 27, 60
Lee, Canada 8
Lee, Joie 1
Leggs, Kingsley 62
Lemmons, Kasi 20
LeNoire, Rosetta 37
Lenox, Adriane 59

Lester, Adrian 46
Lesure, James 64
Lewis, Emmanuel 36
Lil' Kim 28
Lincoln, Abbey 3, 88
Lindo, Delroy 18, 45
LisaRaye 27
LL Cool J 16, 49
Luke, Derek 61
Lumbly, Carl 47
Mabley, Jackie "Moms" 15
Mac, Bernie 29, 61, 72
Malco, Romany 71
Mann, Tamela 92
Mario 71
Marrow, Queen Esther 24
Martin, Helen 31
Martin, Jesse L. 31
Master P 21
Mayo, Whitman 32
Mbatha-Raw, Gugu 89
M.C. Hammer 20, 80
McBride, Chi 73
McClinton, Marion Isaac 77
McDaniel, Hattie 5
McDonald, Audra 20, 62
McKee, Lonette 12
McKinney, Nina Mae 40
McQueen, Butterfly 6, 54
Meadows, Tim 30
Mello, Breno 73
Merkerson, S. Epatha 47, 83
Michele, Michael 31
Miller, Omar Benson 93
Miller, Wentworth 75
Mitchell, Brian Stokes 21
Mitchell, Kel 66
Mokae, Zakes 80
Mo'Nique 35, 84
Moore, Chante 26
Moore, Juanita 83
Moore, Shemar 21
Morris, Garrett 31
Morris, Greg 28
Morton, Joe 18
Mos Def 30
Moten, Etta 18
Mowry, Tamera 79
Mowry, Tia 78
Murphy, Eddie 4, 20, 61
Muse, Clarence Edouard 21
Nash, Johnny 40
Nash, Niecy 66
Neal, Elise 29
Newton, Thandie 26
Ngaujah, Sahr 86
Nicholas, Fayard 20, 57
Nicholas, Harold 20
Nichols, Nichelle 11
Norman, Maidie 20
Notorious B.I.G. 20
Ntshona, Winston 52
Okonedo, Sophie 67
O'Neal, Ron 46
Orlandersmith, Dael 42
Orman, Roscoe 55
Oyelowo, David 82
Parker, Nicole Ari 52
Patton, Paula 62
Payne, Allen 13
Payne, Freda 58
Peete, Holly Robinson 20
Perrineau, Harold, Jr. 51

Perry, Tyler 40, 54
Phifer, Mekhi 25
Phillips, Joseph C. 73
Pickens, James, Jr. 59
Pierce, Wendell 90
Pinkett Smith, Jada 10, 41
Poitier, Sidney 11, 36
Poitier, Sydney Tamiia 65
Pounder, CCH 72
Pratt, Kyla 57
Preer, Evelyn 82
Premice, Josephine 41
Prince 18, 65
Pryor, Rain 65
Pryor, Richard 3, 24, 56
Queen Latifah 1, 16, 58
Randle, Theresa 16
Rashad, Phylicia 21
Raven 44
Ray, Gene Anthony 47
Reddick, Lance 52
Reed Hall, Alaina 83
Reese, Della 6, 20
Reid, Tim 56
Reuben, Gloria 15
Rhames, Ving 14, 50
Rhymes, Busta 31
Ribeiro, Alfonso 17
Richards, Beah 30
Richards, Lloyd 2
Richardson, LaTanya 71
Richardson, Salli 68
Robeson, Paul 2
Robinson, Shaun 36
Rock, Chris 3, 22, 66
Rock, The 29 66
Rodgers, Rod 36
Rodrigues, Percy 68
Roker, Roxie 68
Rolle, Esther 13, 21
Rose, Anika Noni 70
Ross, Diana 8, 27
Ross, Tracee Ellis 35
Roundtree, Richard 27
Rowell, Victoria 13, 68
Rudolph, Maya 46
Russell, Nipsey 66
St. Jacques, Raymond 8
St. John, Kristoff 25
St. Patrick, Mathew 48
Saldana, Zoe 72
Salter, Nikkole 73
Sands, Diana 87
Santiago-Hudson, Ruben 85
Scott, Hazel 66
Scott, Jill 29, 83
Shakur, Tupac 14
Short, Columbus 79
Sidibe, Gabourey 84
Simmons, Henry 55
Sinbad 1, 16
Sinclair, Madge 78
Sisqo 30
Smith, Anjela Lauren 44
Smith, Anna Deavere 6, 44
Smith, B(arbara) 11
Smith, Jaden 82
Smith, Roger Guenveur 12
Smith, Tasha 73
Smith, Will 8, 18, 53
Smith, Willow 92
Snipes, Wesley 3, 24, 67
Snoop Dogg 35, 84

Sommore 61
Stewart, Tonea Harris 78
Sticky Fingaz 86
Tamia 24, 55
Tate, Larenz 15
Taylor, Meshach 4
Taylor, Regina 9, 46
Taylor, Ron 35
Thomas, Sean Patrick 35
Thomason, Marsha 47
Thompson, John Douglas 81
Thompson, Kenan 88
Thompson, Tazewell 13
Thoms, Tracie 61
Torres, Gina 52
Torry, Guy 31
Toussaint, Lorraine 32
Townsend, Robert 4, 23
True, Rachel 82
Tucker, Chris 13, 23, 62
Tunie, Tamara 63
Turner, Tina 6, 27
Tyler, Aisha N. 36
Tyson, Cicely 7, 51
Uggams, Leslie 23
Underwood, Blair 7, 27, 76
Union, Gabrielle 31, 92
Usher 23, 56
Van Peebles, Mario 2, 51
Van Peebles, Melvin 7
Vance, Courtney B. 15, 60
Vanity 67
Vereen, Ben 4
Walker, Eamonn 37
Ward, Douglas Turner 42
Warfield, Marsha 2
Warner, Malcolm-Jamal 22, 36
Warren, Michael 27
Washington, Denzel 1, 16, 93
Washington, Fredi 10
Washington, Isaiah 62
Washington, Kerry 46
Waters, Ethel 7
Wayans, Damon 8, 41
Wayans, Keenen Ivory 18
Wayans, Kim 80
Wayans, Marlon 29, 82
Wayans, Shawn 29
Weathers, Carl 10
Webb, Veronica 10
Whitaker, Forest 2, 49, 67
White, Michael Jai 71
White, Terri 82
Whitfield, Lynn 18
Williams, Bert 18
Williams, Billy Dee 8
Williams, Clarence, III 26
Wilson, Chandra 57
Wilson, Dorien 55
Williams, Joe 5, 25
Williams, Malinda 57
Williams, Samm-Art 21
Williams, Saul 31
Williams, Vanessa A. 32, 66
Williams, Vanessa L. 4, 17
Williamson, Fred 67
Williamson, Mykelti 22
Wilson, Debra 38
Wilson, Flip 21
Winfield, Paul 2, 45
Winfrey, Oprah 2, 15, 61
Withers-Mendes, Elisabeth 64
Witherspoon, John 38

Woodard, Alfre **9**
Woodson, Ali Ollie **89**
Wright, Jeffrey **54**
Yarbrough, Cedric **51**
Yoba, Malik **11**

Adoption and foster care
Clements, George **2**
Hale, Clara **16**
Hale, Lorraine **8**
Oglesby, Zena **12**
Rowell, Victoria **13, 68**

Advertising
Barboza, Anthony **10**
Boyd, Edward **70**
Burrell, Tom **21, 51**
Campbell, E. Simms **13**
Chisholm, Samuel J. **32**
Coleman, Donald **24, 62**
Cullers, Vincent T. **49**
Gaskins, Rudy **74**
Johnson, Beverly **2**
Jones, Caroline R. **29**
Jordan, Montell **23**
Lewis, Byron E. **13**
McKinney Hammond, Michelle **51**
Mingo, Frank **32**
Olden, Georg(e) **44**
Pinderhughes, John **47**
Roche, Joyce M. **17**

Affirmative action
Arnwine, Barbara **28**
Berry, Mary Frances **7**
Coleman, William T. **76**
Edley, Christopher F., Jr. **48**
Higginbotham, A. Leon, Jr. **13, 25**
Maynard, Robert C. **7**
Rand, A. Barry **6**
Thompson, Bennie G. **26**
Waters, Maxine **3, 67**

AFL-CIO
See American Federation of Labor and Congress of Industrial Organizations

African American art
Jones, Paul R. **76**

African American Dance Ensemble
Davis, Chuck **33**

African American folklore
Bailey, Xenobia **11**
Brown, Sterling Allen **10, 64**
Driskell, David C. **7**
Ellison, Ralph **7**
Gaines, Ernest J. **7**
Hamilton, Virginia **10**
Hughes, Langston **4**
Hurston, Zora Neale **3**
Lester, Julius **9**
Primus, Pearl **6**
Tillman, George, Jr. **20**
Williams, Bert **18**
Yarbrough, Camille **40**

African American history
Appiah, Kwame Anthony **67**
Benberry, Cuesta **65**
Bennett, Lerone, Jr. **5, 84**
Berry, Mary Frances **7**

Blackshear, Leonard **52**
Blockson, Charles L. **42**
Burroughs, Margaret Taylor **9**
Camp, Kimberly **19**
Chase-Riboud, Barbara **20, 46**
Cheadle, Don **19, 52**
Clarke, John Henrik **20**
Clayton, Mayme Agnew **62**
Cobb, William Jelani **59**
Coombs, Orde M. **44**
Cooper, Anna Julia **20**
Dodson, Howard, Jr. **7, 52**
Douglas, Aaron **7**
Du Bois, W. E. B. **3**
DuBois, Shirley Graham **21**
Dyson, Michael Eric **11, 40**
Feelings, Tom **11, 47**
Franklin, John Hope **5, 77**
Gaines, Ernest J. **7**
Gates, Henry Louis, Jr. **3, 38, 67**
Gill, Gerald **69**
Gordon-Reed, Annette **74**
Haley, Alex **4**
Halliburton, Warren J. **49**
Harkless, Necia Desiree **19**
Harris, Richard E. **61**
Hine, Darlene Clark **24**
Hughes, Langston **4**
Johnson, James Weldon **5**
Jones, Edward P. **43, 67**
Lewis, David Levering **9**
Marable, Manning **10**
Mason, Herman, Jr. **83**
Painter, Nell Irvin **24, 88**
Pritchard, Robert Starling **21**
Putney, Martha S. **75**
Quarles, Benjamin Arthur **18**
Reagon, Bernice Johnson **7**
Richardson, Julieanna **81**
Schomburg, Arthur Alfonso **9**
Shadd, Abraham D. **81**
Southern, Eileen **56**
Tancil, Gladys Quander **59**
Wilson, August **7, 33, 55**
Woodson, Carter G. **2**
Yarbrough, Camille **40**

African American literature
Andrews, Raymond **4**
Angelou, Maya **1, 15**
Appiah, Kwame Anthony **67**
Baisden, Michael **25, 66**
Baker, Houston A., Jr. **6**
Baldwin, James **1**
Bambara, Toni Cade **1**
Baraka, Amiri **1, 38**
Bennett, George Harold "Hal" **45**
Bontemps, Arna **8**
Briscoe, Connie **15**
Brooks, Gwendolyn **1, 28**
Brown, Claude **38**
Brown, Wesley **23**
Burroughs, Margaret Taylor **9**
Campbell, Bebe Moore **6, 24, 59**
Cary, Lorene **3**
Childress, Alice **15**
Cleage, Pearl **17, 64**
Cullen, Countee **8**
Curtis, Christopher Paul **26**
Davis, Arthur P. **41**
Davis, Nolan **45**
Dickey, Eric Jerome **21, 56**
Dove, Rita **6, 78**

Du Bois, W. E. B. **3**
Dunbar, Paul Laurence **8**
Ellison, Ralph **7**
Evans, Mari **26**
Fair, Ronald L. **47**
Fauset, Jessie **7**
Feelings, Tom **11, 47**
Fisher, Rudolph **17**
Ford, Nick Aaron **44**
Fuller, Charles **8**
Gaines, Ernest J. **7**
Gates, Henry Louis, Jr. **3, 38, 67**
Gayle, Addison, Jr. **41**
Gibson, Donald Bernard **40**
Giddings, Paula **11**
Giovanni, Nikki **9, 39, 85**
Goines, Donald **19**
Golden, Marita **19**
Guy, Rosa **5**
Haley, Alex **4**
Hansberry, Lorraine **6**
Harper, Frances Ellen Watkins **11**
Heard, Nathan C. **45**
Himes, Chester **8**
Holland, Endesha Ida Mae **3, 57**
Holmes, Shannon **70**
Hughes, Langston **4**
Hull, Akasha Gloria **45**
Hurston, Zora Neale **3**
Iceberg Slim **11**
Joe, Yolanda **21**
Johnson, Charles **1, 82**
Johnson, James Weldon **5**
Jones, Gayl **37**
Jordan, June **7, 35**
July, William **27**
Kitt, Sandra **23**
Larsen, Nella **10**
Lester, Julius **9**
Little, Benilde **21**
Lorde, Audre **6**
Madhubuti, Haki **7, 85**
Major, Clarence **9**
Marshall, Paule **7, 77**
McKay, Claude **6**
McKay, Nellie Yvonne **17, 57**
McKinney-Whetstone, Diane **27**
McMillan, Terry **4, 17, 53**
McPherson, James Alan **70**
Morrison, Toni **2, 15, 86**
Mowry, Jess **7**
Myers, Walter Dean **8, 20**
Naylor, Gloria **10, 42**
Petry, Ann **19**
Pinkney, Jerry **15**
Rahman, Aishah **37**
Randall, Dudley **8, 55**
Redding, J. Saunders **26**
Redmond, Eugene **23**
Reed, Ishmael **8**
Ringgold, Faith **4, 81**
Sanchez, Sonia **17, 51**
Schomburg, Arthur Alfonso **9**
Schuyler, George Samuel **40**
Shange, Ntozake **8, 89**
Smith, Mary Carter **26**
Taylor, Mildred D. **26**
Thomas, Trisha R. **65**
Thurman, Wallace **16**
Toomer, Jean **6**
Tyree, Omar Rashad **21**
Van Peebles, Melvin **7**
Verdelle, A. J. **26**

Villarosa, Clara **85**
Walker, Alice **1, 43**
Wesley, Valerie Wilson **18**
Wideman, John Edgar **5, 87**
Williams, John A. **27**
Williams, Sherley Anne **25**
Wilson, August **7, 33, 55**
Wolfe, George C. **6, 43**
Wright, Richard **5**
Yarbrough, Camille **40**

African American studies
Alexander, Elizabeth **75**
Baszile, Jennifer **79**
Brawley, Benjamin **44**
Carby, Hazel **27**
Christian, Barbara T. **44**
De Veaux, Alexis **44**
Ford, Nick Aaron **44**
Hare, Nathan **44**
Harris-Lacewell, Melissa **81**
Henderson, Stephen E. **45**
Huggins, Nathan Irvin **52**
Long, Richard Alexander **65**
Neal, Mark Anthony **74**
Peterson, James **81**
West, Cornel **5, 33, 80**

African Burial Ground Project
Perry, Warren **56**

African Canadian literature
Elliott, Lorris **37**
Foster, Cecil **32**
Senior, Olive **37**

African dance
Acogny, Germaine **55**
Adams, Jenoyne **60**
Ailey, Alvin **8**
Davis, Chuck **33**
Fagan, Garth **18**
Primus, Pearl **6**

African history
Appiah, Kwame Anthony **67**
Chase-Riboud, Barbara **20, 46**
Clarke, John Henrik **20**
Counter, S. Allen **74**
Diop, Cheikh Anta **4**
Dodson, Howard, Jr. **7, 52**
DuBois, Shirley Graham **21**
Feelings, Muriel **44**
Halliburton, Warren J. **49**
Hansberry, William Leo **11**
Harkless, Necia Desiree **19**
Henries, A. Doris Banks **44**
Hilliard, Asa Grant, III **66**
Jawara, Dawda Kairaba **11**
Marshall, Paule **7, 77**
van Sertima, Ivan **25**

African literature
Aidoo, Ama Ata **38**
Akpan, Uwem **70**
Appiah, Kwame Anthony **67**
Arac de Nyeko, Monica **66**
Armah, Ayi Kwei **49**
Awoonor, Kofi **37**
Bandele, Biyi **68**
Cartey, Wilfred **47**
Cheney-Coker, Syl **43**
Couto, Mia **45**
Dadié, Bernard **34**
Dathorne, O. R. **52**

Ekwensi, Cyprian 37
Farah, Nuruddin 27
Gabre-Medhin, Tsegaye 64
Head, Bessie 28
Kayira, Legson 40
Memmi, Albert 37
Mphalele, Es'kia 40
Mwangi, Meja 40
Oyono, Ferdinand 38
Peters, Lenrie 43
Salih, Al-Tayyib 37

African Methodist Episcopal Church (AME)
Blanks, Deborah K. 69
Bryant, John R. 45
Flake, Floyd H. 18
Loguen, J. W. 91
McKenzie, Vashti M. 29
Mudimbe, V. Y. 61
Murray, Cecil 12, 47
Roundtree, Dovey 80
Shuttlesworth, Fred 47
Turner, Henry McNeal 5
Youngblood, Johnny Ray 8

African music
Ade, King Sunny 41
Afro, Teddy 78
Ashong, Derrick 86
Fela 1, 42
Keita, Salif 83
Kidjo, Angelique 50
Kolosoy, Wendo 73
Kuti, Femi 47
Maal, Baaba 66
Mahlasela, Vusi 65
Makeba, Miriam 2, 50, 74
Nascimento, Milton 2 64
Somi 85

African National Congress (ANC)
Baker, Ella 5
Hani, Chris 6
Ka Dinizulu, Mcwayizeni 29
Kaunda, Kenneth 2
Kuzwayo, Ellen 68
Luthuli, Albert 13
Mandela, Nelson 1, 14, 77
Mandela, Winnie 2, 35
Masekela, Barbara 18
Mbeki, Govan A. 80
Mbeki, Thabo 14, 73
Mhlaba, Raymond 55
Motlanthe, Kgalema 74
Nkomo, Joshua 4, 65
Nyanda, Siphiwe 21
Nzo, Alfred 15
Ramaphosa, Cyril 3
Sisulu, Albertina 57
Sisulu, Walter 47
Tutu, Desmond Mpilo 6, 44
Weems, Renita J. 44
Xuma, Madie Hall 59
Zuma, Jacob 33, 75
Zuma, Nkosazana Dlamini 34

Afro-Beat music
Fela 1, 42

Afro-Brazilian music
Brown, Carlinhos 81
Caymmi, Dorival 72

Gil, Gilberto 53
Jorge, Seu 73
Moura, Paulo 87

Afrocentricity
Asante, Molefi Kete 3
Biggers, John 20, 33
Diop, Cheikh Anta 4
Hansberry, Lorraine 6
Hansberry, William Leo 11
Sanchez, Sonia 17, 51
Turner, Henry McNeal 5

Afro-Cuban music
Lefel, Edith 41
Rodríguez, Arsenio 87
Santamaria, Mongo 81

Afro-Peruvian music
Baca, Susana 80

Agency for International Development (AID)
Gayle, Helene D. 3, 46
Perkins, Edward 5

Agriculture
Allen, Will 74
Boyd, John W., Jr. 20, 72
Carver, George Washington 4
Hall, Lloyd A. 8
Jones, Monty 66
Masire, Quett 5
Sanders, Dori 8
Wambugu, Florence 42

AHA
See American Heart Association

AID
See Agency for International Development

AIDS
See Acquired immune deficiency syndrome

AIDS Coalition to Unleash Power (ACT UP)
Norman, Pat 10

Akron Beacon Journal
Crutchfield, James N. 55

ALA
See American Library Association

Alabama state government
Davis, Artur 41
Ford, Johnny 70
Gray, Fred 37
Rapier, James T. 82

Alcoholics Anonymous (AA)
Hilliard, David 7
Lucas, John 7

All Afrikan People's Revolutionary Party
Carmichael, Stokely 5, 26
Moses, Robert Parris 11

Allied Arts Academy
Bonds, Margaret 39

Alpha & Omega Ministry
White, Reggie 6, 50

Alpha Kappa Alpha Sorority
White, Linda M. 45

Alvin Ailey American Dance Theater
Ailey, Alvin 8
Clarke, Hope 14
Dove, Ulysses 5
Faison, George 16
Jamison, Judith 7, 67
Jefferson, Denise 87
Primus, Pearl 6
Rhoden, Dwight 40
Richardson, Desmond 39
Spears, Warren 52
Tyson, Andre 40
Williams, Dudley 60

Alvin Ailey Repertory Ensemble
Ailey, Alvin 8
Miller, Bebe 3

Ambassadors
Avant, Nicole A. 90
Braun, Carol Moseley 4, 42
Carson, Johnnie 85
Cook, Mercer 40
Davis, Ruth 37
Dudley, Edward R. 58
Dymally, Mervyn 42
Frazer, Jendayi 68
Mbuende, Kaire 12
Poitier, Sidney 11, 36
Smythe Haith, Mabel 61
Spearman, Leonard H. O., Sr. 81
Stith, Charles R. 73
Todman, Terence A. 55
Watson, Diane 41
Wharton, Clifton Reginald, Sr. 36
Whitfield, Mal 60

AME
See African Methodist Episcopal Church

American Academy of Arts and Sciences
Loury, Glenn 36

American Art Award
Simpson, Lorna 4, 36

American Association for the Advancement of Science (AAAS)
Cobb, W. Montague 39
Massey, Walter E. 5, 45
Pickett, Cecil 39

American Association of University Women
Granville, Evelyn Boyd 36

American Ballet Theatre
Dove, Ulysses 5
Richardson, Desmond 39

American Bar Association
Archer, Dennis 7, 36
Pincham, R. Eugene, Sr. 69
Thompson, Larry D. 39
Walker, Cora T. 68

American Beach
Betsch, MaVynee 28

American Book Award
Baraka, Amiri 1, 38
Bates, Daisy 13
Bradley, David Henry, Jr. 39
Clark, Septima 7
Gates, Henry Louis, Jr. 3, 38, 67
Lorde, Audre 6
Loury, Glenn 36
Marshall, Paule 7, 77
Sanchez, Sonia 17, 51
Troupe, Quincy 83
Walker, Alice 1, 43

American Broadcasting Company (ABC)
Christian, Spencer 15
Goode, Mal 13
Mickebury, Penny 28
Reynolds, Star Jones 10, 27, 61
Roberts, Robin 16, 54
Robinson, Max 3
Simpson, Carole 6, 30

American Cancer Society
Ashe, Arthur 1, 18
Leffall, Lasalle 3, 64
Riperton, Minnie 32
Thomas, Arthur Ray 52

American Choral Directors Association
Adams, Leslie 39

American Civil Liberties Union (ACLU)
Baugh, David 23
Harris, Maya Lakshmi 88
Murphy, Laura M. 43
Murray, Pauli 38
Pincham, R. Eugene, Sr. 69

American Community Housing Associates, Inc.
Lane, Vincent 5

American Composers Alliance
Tillis, Frederick 40

American Counseling Association
Mitchell, Sharon 36

American Economic Association
Loury Glenn 36

American Enterprise Institute
Woodson, Robert L. 10

American Express Company
Adams, Eula L. 39
Chenault, Kenneth I. 4, 36

American Federation of Labor and Congress of Industrial Organizations (AFL-CIO)
Fletcher, Bill, Jr. 41
Holt Baker, Arlene 73
Randolph, A. Philip 3

American Guild of Organists
Adams, Leslie 39

American Heart Association (AHA)
Cooper, Edward S. 6
Grant, Augustus O. 71

Richardson, Donna **39**

American Idol
Hudson, Jennifer **63, 83**
Jackson, Randy **40**

American Institute for the Prevention of Blindness
Bath, Patricia E. **37**

American Library Association (ALA)
Franklin, Hardy R. **9, 87**
Hayden, Carla D. **47**
Jones, Clara Stanton **51**
Josey, E. J. **10**
McFadden, Bernice L. **39**
Rollins, Charlemae Hill **27**
Wedgeworth, Robert W. **42**

American Negro Academy
Grimké, Archibald H. **9**
Schomburg, Arthur Alfonso **9**

American Negro Theater
Martin, Helen **31**

American Nuclear Society
Wilkens, J. Ernest, Jr. **43**

American Nurses Association (ANA)
Kennedy, Adrienne **11**
Staupers, Mabel K. **7**

American Postal Workers Union
Burrus, William Henry "Bill" **45**

American Psychological Association (APA)
Anderson, Norman B. **45**
Mitchell, Sharon **36**

American Red Cross
Bullock, Steve **22**
Drew, Charles Richard **7**

American Society of Magazine Editors
Curry, George E. **23**

American Tennis Association
Gibson, Althea **8, 43**
Peters, Margaret and Matilda **43**

American Writers Association
Schuyler, George Samuel **40**

Amsterdam News
Cooper, Andrew W. **36**
Holt, Nora **38**
Tatum, Elinor R. **78**
Tatum, Wilbert **76**

ANA
See American Nurses Association

ANC
See African National Congress

Anglican Church hierarchy
Akinola, Peter Jasper **65**
Tutu, Desmond Mpilo **6, 44**

Angolan government
dos Santos, José Eduardo **43**
Neto, António Agostinho **43**

Anheuser-Busch distribution
Cherry, Deron **40**

Anthropology
Asante, Molefi Kete **3**
Bunche, Ralph J. **5**
Cole, Johnnetta B. **5, 43**
Davis, Allison **12**
Diop, Cheikh Anta **4**
Dunham, Katherine **4, 59**
Hansberry, William Leo **11**
Primus, Pearl **6**
Robeson, Eslanda Goode **13**
Rodriguez, Cheryl **64**

Antoinette Perry awards
See Tony awards

APA
See American Psychological Association

Apartheid
Abrahams, Peter **39**
Ashe, Arthur **18**
Berry, Mary Frances **7**
Biko, Steven **4**
Brutus, Dennis **38**
Butler, Jonathan **28**
Howard, M. William, Jr. **26**
Ka Dinizulu, Mcwayizeni **29**
Kuzwayo, Ellen **68**
LaGuma, Alex **30**
Luthuli, Albert **13**
Mahlasela, Vusi **65**
Makeba, Miriam **2, 50, 74**
Mandela, Nelson **1, 14, 77**
Mandela, Winnie **2, 35**
Masekela, Hugh **1**
Mathabane, Mark **5**
Mbeki, Thabo **14, 73**
Mbuende, Kaire **12**
McDougall, Gay J. **11, 43**
Mhlaba, Raymond **55**
Mphalele, Es'kia **40**
Nkoli, Simon **60**
Ntshona, Winston **52**
Nyanda, Siphiwe **21**
Nzo, Alfred **15**
Plaatje, Sol. T. **80**
Ramaphosa, Cyril **3**
Ramphele, Maphela **29**
Robinson, Randall **7, 46**
Sisulu, Albertina **57**
Sisulu, Walter **47**
Sullivan, Leon H. **13, 30**
Tutu, Desmond Mpilo **6, 44**

Apollo
Williams, O. S. **13**

Apollo Theater
Sims, Howard **48**
Sutton, Percy E. **42, 82**

APWU
See American Postal Workers Union

Archaeology
Gilbert, John Wesley **91**
McJunkin, George **93**

Architecture
Abele, Julian **55**
Adjaye, David **38, 78**

Bond, J. Max, Jr. 76
Gantt, Harvey **1**
Johnson, Jeh Vincent **44**
King, Robert Arthur **58**
McKissack, Leatrice **80**
Sklarek, Norma Merrick **25**
Taylor, Robert Robinson **80**
Williams, Paul R. **9**

Argonne National Laboratory
Massey, Walter E. **5, 45**
Quarterman, Lloyd Albert **4**

Ariel Capital Management
Hobson, Mellody **40**
Rogers, John W., Jr. **5, 52**

Arista Records
Lattimore, Kenny **35**
Reid, Antonio "L.A." **28**

Arkansas government
Elders, Joycelyn **6**

Art history
Amaki, Amalia **76**
Benjamin, Tritobia Hayes **53**
Campbell, Mary Schmidt **43**

Arthur Andersen
Scott, Milton **51**

Astronauts
Anderson, Michael P. **40**
Bluford, Guy **2, 35**
Bolden, Charles Frank, Jr. **7, 78**
Gregory, Frederick **8, 51**
Harris, Bernard A. **90**
Jemison, Mae C. **1, 35**
Lawrence, Robert H., Jr. **16**
McNair, Ronald **3, 58**
Wilson, Stephanie **72**

Astronomy
Banneker, Benjamin **93**
Pitts, Derrick **77**

Astrophysics
Alcorn, George Edward, Jr. **59**
Carruthers, George R. **40**
Walker, Arthur, II **87**

Atco-EastWest
Rhone, Sylvia **2**

ATD Publishing
Tyson, Asha **39**

Athletic administration
Goss, Tom **23**
Littlepage, Craig **35**

Atlanta Baptist College
See Morehouse College

Atlanta Board of Education
Mays, Benjamin E. **7**

Atlanta Braves baseball team
Aaron, Hank **5**
Baker, Dusty **8, 43, 72**
Justice, David **18**
McGriff, Fred **24**
Sanders, Deion **4, 31**

Atlanta city government
Campbell, Bill **9, 76**
Franklin, Shirley **34, 80**

Jackson, Maynard **2, 41**
Pitts, Robb **84**
Reed, Kasim **82**
Williams, Hosea Lorenzo **15, 31**
Young, Andrew **3, 48**

Atlanta Falcons football team
Anderson, Jamal **22**
Buchanan, Ray **32**
Sanders, Deion **4, 31**
Vick, Michael **39, 65**

Atlanta Police Department
Brown, Lee Patrick **1, 24**
Harvard, Beverly **11**

Audelco awards
Holder, Laurence **34**
Rodgers, Rod **36**
Wesley, Richard **73**

Aurelian Honor Society Award
Lewis, William M., Jr. **40**

Authors Guild
Davis, George **36**
Gayle, Addison, Jr. **41**
Schuyler, George Samuel **40**

Authors League of America
Abrahams, Peter **39**
Cotter, Joseph Seamon, Sr. **40**
Davis, George **36**
Gayle, Addison, Jr. **41**

Automobile dealership
Farr, Mel **24**
Gidron, Richard D. **68**
Parker, Jim **64**

Aviation
Brown, Jesse Leroy **31**
Brown, Willa **40**
Bullard, Eugene **12**
Coleman, Bessie **9**
Julian, Hubert **90**
McLeod, Gus **27**
Petersen, Frank E. **31**
Roy, Kenny **51**

"Back to Africa" movement
Turner, Henry McNeal **5**

Bahamian government
Christie, Perry Gladstone **53**
Pindling, Lynden **81**

Ballet
Ailey, Alvin **8**
Allen, Debbie **13, 42**
Anderson, Lauren **72**
Collins, Janet **33, 64**
Dove, Ulysses **5**
Faison, George **16**
Jamison, Judith **7, 67**
Johnson, Virginia **9**
Jones, Doris W. **62**
Mitchell, Arthur **2, 47**
Nichols, Nichelle **11**
Parks, Gordon **1, 35, 58**
Rhoden, Dwight **40**
Richardson, Desmond **39**
Rowell, Victoria **13, 68**

Tyson, Andre **40**

Balm in Gilead, The
Seele, Pernessa **46**

Baltimore Black Sox baseball team
Day, Leon **39**

Baltimore city government
Dixon, Sheila **68**
Rawlings-Blake, Stephanie **93**
Robinson, Bishop L. **66**
Schmoke, Kurt **1, 48**

Baltimore Colts football team
Davis, Milt **74**
Parker, Jim **64**

Baltimore Elite Giants baseball team
Campanella, Roy **25**
Day, Leon **39**
Kimbro, Henry A. **25**

Baltimore Orioles baseball team
Baylor, Don **6**
Blair, Paul **36**
Carter, Joe **30**
Jackson, Reggie **15**
Robinson, Frank **9, 87**

Banking
Blaylock, Ronald **86**
Boyd, T. B., III **6**
Bradley, Jennette B. **40**
Bridgforth, Glinda **36**
Brimmer, Andrew F. **2, 48**
Bryant, John **26**
Chapman, Nathan A., Jr. **21**
Chappell, Emma **18**
Ferguson, Roger W. **25**
Forte, Linda Diane **54**
Funderburg, I. Owen **38**
Greene, Richard Thaddeus, Sr. **67**
Griffith, Mark Winston **8**
Harris, Carla A. **67**
Lawless, Theodore K. **8**
Louis, Errol T. **8**
March, William Carrington **56**
McGuire, Raymond J. **57**
Morgan, Rose **11**
Parsons, Richard Dean **11**
Utendahl, John **23**
Walker, Maggie Lena **17**
Watkins, Donald **35**
Watkins, Walter C. **24**
Willie, Louis, Jr. **68**
Wright, Deborah C. **25**

Baptist
Austin, Junius C. **44**
Bradley, J. Robert **65**
Braxton, Brad **77**
Butts, Calvin O., III **9, 90**
Davis, Gary **41**
Forbes, James A., Jr. **71**
Franklin, C. L. **68**
Fuller, Thomas O. **90**
Gomes, Peter J. **15, 93**
Hooks, Benjamin L. **2, 85**
Jasper, John J. **91**
Jemison, Major L. **48**
Jones, E. Edward, Sr. **45**

King, Martin Luther, Sr. **89**
Long, Eddie L. **29, 89**
Meeks, James T. **92**
Moss, Otis, Jr. **72**
Rogers, Alan G. **72**
Taylor, Gardner C. **76**
Thurston, Stephen J. **49**
Walker, Lucius, Jr. **88**
Walker, Wyatt Tee **80**

Baseball
Aaron, Hank **5**
Allen, Dick **85**
Anderson, Elmer **25**
Ashford, Emmett **22**
Baines, Harold **32**
Baker, Dusty **8, 43, 72**
Banks, Ernie **33**
Barnhill, David **30**
Baylor, Don **6**
Bell, James "Cool Papa" **36**
Belle, Albert **10**
Black, Joe **75**
Blair, Paul **36**
Bonds, Barry **6, 34, 63**
Bonds, Bobby **43**
Brock, Lou **18**
Brown, Willard **36**
Campanella, Roy **25**
Carew, Rod **20**
Carter, Joe **30**
Charleston, Oscar **39**
Clendenon, Donn **26, 56**
Coleman, Leonard S., Jr. **12**
Cooper, Andy "Lefty" **63**
Cottrell, Comer **11**
Crawford, Carl **90**
Dandridge, Ray **36**
Davis, Piper **19**
Dawson, Andre **85**
Day, Leon **39**
Doby, Lawrence Eugene, Sr. **16**
Dye, Jermaine **58**
Ellis, Dock **78**
Fielder, Cecil **2**
Fielder, Prince Semien **68**
Flood, Curt **10, 93**
Foster, Andrew **79**
Gaston, Cito **71**
Gibson, Bob **33**
Gibson, Josh **22**
Glanville, Douglas Metunwa **82**
Gooden, Dwight **20**
Granderson, Curtis **66**
Gregg, Eric **16**
Griffey, Ken, Jr. **12, 73**
Gwynn, Tony **18, 83**
Henderson, Rickey **28, 78**
Howard, Ryan **65**
Hunter, Torii **43**
Hyde, Cowan F. "Bubba" **47**
Irvin, Monte **31**
Jackson, Reggie **15**
Jenkins, Fergie **46**
Jeter, Derek **27, 93**
Johnson, Clifford "Connie" **52**
Johnson, Mamie "Peanut" **40**
Justice, David **18**
Kaiser, Cecil **42**
Kimbro, Henry A. **25**
Lacy, Sam **30, 46**
Lankford, Ray **23**
Larkin, Barry **24**

Lloyd, John Henry "Pop" **30**
Lofton, Kenny **12**
Lopes, Davey **92**
Mackey, Biz **82**
Mariner, Jonathan **41**
Martinez, Pedro **81**
Mays, Willie **3**
McGriff, Fred **24**
McRae, Hal **84**
Minoso, Minnie **89**
Morgan, Joe **9**
Murray, Eddie **12**
Newcombe, Don **24**
O'Neil, Buck **19, 59**
Ortiz, David **52, 82**
Paige, Satchel **7**
Payne, Ulice **42**
Pride, Charley **26**
Puckett, Kirby **4, 58**
Radcliffe, Ted **74**
Randolph, Willie **53**
Reese, Pokey **28**
Reynolds, Harold **77**
Rice, Jim **75**
Richard, J. R. **87**
Robinson, Frank **9, 87**
Robinson, Jackie **6**
Robinson, Sharon **22**
Rollins, Jimmy **70**
Sabathia, CC **74**
Sanders, Deion **4, 31**
Sheffield, Gary **16**
Smith, Hilton **29**
Smith, Ozzie **77**
Sosa, Sammy **21, 44**
Stargell, Willie **29**
Stearnes, Norman "Turkey" **31**
Stone, Toni **15**
Strawberry, Darryl **22**
Thomas, Frank **12, 51**
Trouppe, Quincy Thomas, Sr. **84**
Vaughn, Mo **16**
Virgil, Ozzie **48**
Watson, Bob **25**
Wells, Vernon **91**
White, Bill **1, 48**
Williams, Billy **86**
Williams, Ken **68**
Willis, Dontrelle **55**
Wills, Maury **73**
Winfield, Dave **5, 91**

Baseball Hall of Fame
Banks, Ernie **33**
Bell, James "Cool Papa" **36**
Brown, Willard **36**
Campanella, Roy **25**
Charleston, Oscar **39**
Dandridge, Ray **36**
Dawson, Andre **85**
Day, Leon **39**
Doby, Lawrence Eugene, Sr. **16, 41**
Gibson, Josh **22**
Gwynn, Tony **18, 83**
Henderson, Rickey **28, 78**
Irvin, Monte **31**
Leonard, Buck **67**
Lloyd, John Henry "Pop" **30**
Morgan, Joe **9**
Paige, Satchel **7**
Rice, Jim **75**
Robinson, Frank **9, 87**
Robinson, Jackie **6**

Smith, Hilton **29**
Smith, Ozzie **77**
Stearnes, Norman "Turkey" **31**
Williams, Billy **86**
Winfield, Dave **5, 91**

Barbadian government
Adams, Grantley **82**
Arthur, Owen **33**

Basket making
Jackson, Mary **73**

Basketball
Abdul-Jabbar, Kareem **8**
Abdur-Rahim, Shareef **28**
Allen, Ray **82**
Amaker, Tommy **62**
Anderson, Mike **63**
Anthony, Carmelo **46**
Archibald, Tiny **90**
Arenas, Gilbert **84**
Artest, Ron **52**
Barkley, Charles **5, 66**
Baylor, Elgin **93**
Bing, Dave **3, 59, 78**
Bogues, Tyrone "Muggsy" **56**
Bol, Manute **1**
Bolton-Holifield, Ruthie **28**
Bosh, Chris **85**
Brand, Elton **31**
Brandon, Terrell **16**
Brown, Mike **77**
Bryant, Kobe **15, 31, 71**
Bynoe, Peter C. B. **40**
Carter, Butch **27**
Carter, Kenneth **53**
Carter, Vince **26**
Catchings, Tamika **43**
Chamberlain, Wilt **18, 47**
Chaney, John **67**
Cheeks, Maurice **47**
Clifton, Nathaniel "Sweetwater" **47**
Cooper, Charles "Chuck" **47**
Cooper, Michael **31**
Cooper-Dyke, Cynthia **17, 89**
Curry, Michael **85**
Dantley, Adrian **72**
Davis, Mike **41**
Drexler, Clyde **4, 61**
Dumars, Joe **16, 65**
Duncan, Tim **20, 91**
Dunn, Jerry **27**
Durant, Kevin **76**
Edwards, Teresa **14**
Ellerbe, Brian **22**
Elliott, Sean **26**
Erving, Julius **18, 47**
Ewing, Patrick **17, 73**
Fox, Rick **27**
Frazier, Walt **91**
Freeman, Marianna **23**
Gaines, Clarence E., Sr. **55**
Garnett, Kevin **14, 70**
Gentry, Alvin **23**
Gossett, Louis, Jr. **7**
Gourdine, Simon **11**
Gray, Yeshimbra "Shimmy" **55**
Green, A. C. **32**
Greer, Hal **92**
Griffith, Yolanda **25**
Hardaway, Anfernee (Penny) **13**
Hardaway, Tim **35**
Harris-Stewart, Lusia **90**

Haskins, Clem 23
Hawkins, Connie 91
Hayes, Elvin 93
Haynes, Marques 22
Heard, Gar 25
Hill, Grant 13
Holdsclaw, Chamique 24
Howard, Juwan 15
Hunter, Billy 22
Isaacs, John 76
Iverson, Allen 24, 46
James, LeBron 46, 78
Johnson, Avery 62
Johnson, Dennis 89
Johnson, Earvin "Magic" 3, 39
Johnson, Gus 92
Johnson, Kevin 70
Johnson, Larry 28
Jones, K. C. 83
Jones, Merlakia 34
Jones, Roy, Jr. 22
Jones, Sam 85
Jordan, Eddie 83
Jordan, Michael 6, 21
Joyce, Dru 81
Justice, David 18
Kellogg, Clark 64
Kidd, Jason 86
Lanier, Bob 47
Lennox, Betty 31
Leslie, Lisa 16, 73
Lloyd, Earl 26
Lofton, Kenny 12
Lowe, Sidney 64
Lucas, John 7
Mahorn, Rick 60
Malone, Karl 18, 51, 90
Malone, Moses 79
Manigault, Earl "The Goat" 15
Master P 21
McAdoo, Bob 75
McGrady, Tracy 80
McLendon, John B., Jr. 89
Miller, Cheryl 10, 74
Milton, DeLisha 31
Mitchell, Sam 82
Mohammed, Nazr 64
Monroe, Earl 89
Mourning, Alonzo 17, 44
Mutombo, Dikembe 7
Odom, Lamar 81
Olajuwon, Hakeem 2, 72
O'Neal, Shaquille 8, 30
Palmer, Violet 59
Parish, Robert 43
Parker, Candace 74
Parker, Tony 75
Paul, Chris 84
Peck, Carolyn 23
Phillips, Teresa L. 42
Pierce, Paul 71
Pippen, Scottie 15, 89
Porter, Terry 75
Prince, Tayshaun 68
Reed, Willis, Jr. 86
Richardson, Nolan 9
Richmond, Mitch 19
Rivers, Doc 25, 81
Robertson, Oscar 26
Robinson, David 24, 90
Robinson, Will 51, 69
Rodman, Dennis 12, 44
Rose, Derrick 82

Russell, Bill 8
Sanders, Satch 77
Silas, Paul 24
Smith, Randy 81
Smith, Stephen A. 69
Smith, Tubby 18, 83
Sprewell, Latrell 23
Stackhouse, Jerry 30
Staley, Dawn 57
Stith, Tom 93
Stoudemire, Amaré 59
Stringer, C. Vivian 13, 66
Swoopes, Sheryl 12, 56
Ussery, Terdema, II 29
Thomas, Isiah 7, 26, 65
Thompson, Tina 25, 75
Thurmond, Nate 88
Tisdale, Wayman 50
Unseld, Wes 23
Wade, Dwyane 61
Wallace, Ben 54
Wallace, Perry E. 47
Wallace, Rasheed 56
Webber, Chris 15, 30, 59
Wilkens, Lenny 11, 88
Williams, Deron 92
Williams, Natalie 31
Woodard, Lynette 67
Woodson, Mike 78
Worthy, James 49

Basketball Hall of Fame
Abdul-Jabbar, Kareem 8
Archibald, Tiny 90
Barkley, Charles 5, 66
Baylor, Elgin 93
Bing, Dave 3, 59, 78
Chamberlain, Wilt 18, 47
Chaney, John 67
Cooper-Dyke, Cynthia 17, 89
Dantley, Adrian 72
Drexler, Clyde 4, 61
Dumars, Joe 16, 65
Ewing, Patrick 17, 73
Frazier, Walt 91
Gaines, Clarence E., Sr. 55
Gervin, George 80
Greer, Hal 92
Harris-Stewart, Lusia 90
Hawkins, Connie 91
Hayes, Elvin 93
Haynes, Marques 22
Johnson, Dennis 89
Johnson, Earvin "Magic"
Johnson, Gus 92
Jones, K. C. 83
Jones, Sam 85
Lanier, Bob 47
Lloyd, Earl 26
Malone, Karl 18, 51, 90
Malone, Moses 79
McAdoo, Bob 75
McLendon, John B., Jr. 89
Miller, Cheryl 10, 74
Monroe, Earl 89
Olajuwon, Hakeem 2, 72
Parish, Robert 43
Pippen, Scottie 15, 89
Reed, Willis, Jr. 86
Robertson, Oscar 26
Robinson, David 24, 90
Russell, Bill 8
Sanders, Satch 77

Thomas, Isiah 7, 26, 65
Thurmond, Nate 88
Unseld, Wes 23
Wilkens, Lenny 11, 88
Wilkins, Dominique 74
Woodard, Lynette 67
Worthy, James 49

Bass
Foster, George "Pops" 40
Isley, Marvin 87
Jamerson, James 59

BBC
See British Broadcasting Company

Beale Streeters
Ace, Johnny 36
Bland, Bobby "Blue" 36
King, B. B. 7

Beatrice International
See TLC Beatrice International
   Holdings, Inc.

Beauty salons and products
Fine, Sam 60
Gibson, Ted 66
Stanford, Olivia Lee Dilworth 49

Bebop
Carter, Betty 19
Clarke, Kenny 27
Coltrane, John 19
Davis, Miles 4
Eckstine, Billy 28
Fitzgerald, Ella 8, 18
Gillespie, Dizzy 1
Gordon, Dexter 25
Hancock, Herbie 20, 67
Harris, Barry 68
Hawkins, Coleman 9
Jackson, Milt 26
Parker, Charlie 20
Powell, Bud 24
Roach, Max 21, 63
Vaughan, Sarah 13

**Ben & Jerry's Homemade Ice
Cream, Inc.**
Holland, Robert, Jr. 11

Bennett College
Cole, Johnnetta B. 5, 43
Player, Willa B. 43

Benin government
Kerekou, Ahmed 1
Soglo, Nicéphore 15
Yayi, Boni T. 84

Bessie award
Richardson, Desmond 39

BET
See Black Entertainment Television

Bethune-Cookman College
Bethune, Mary McLeod 4
Joyner, Marjorie Stewart 26

A Better Chance
Lewis, William M., Jr. 40

Big Easy Award
Adams, Johnny 39

**Bill and Melinda Gates Foun-
dation**
Golston, Allan C. 55

**Billy Graham Evangelistic As-
sociation**
Bell, Ralph S. 5
Waters, Ethel 7

Bing Group, The
Bing, Dave 3, 59, 78
Lloyd, Earl 26

Biology
Cobb, Jewel Plummer 42
Emeagwali, Dale 31
Jarvis, Erich 67
Just, Ernest Everett 3
Malveaux, Floyd 54
Pickett, Cecil 39

Biotechnology
Dabiri, John 93
Juma, Calestous 57
Wambugu, Florence 42

**Birmingham (AL) city govern-
ment**
Kincaid, Bernard 28
Langford, Larry P. 74
Nunn, Annetta 43

**Birmingham (AL) Police De-
partment**
Nunn, Annetta 43
Woods, Abraham, Jr. 74

Birth control
Elders, Joycelyn 6
Williams, Maggie 7, 71

Bishop College
Cottrell, Comer 11

**Black Academy of Arts & Let-
ters**
White, Charles 39

**Black Alliance for Educational
Options**
Fuller, Howard L. 37

Black American West Museum
Stewart, Paul Wilbur 12

**Black Americans for Family
Values**
Foster, Ezola 28

Black arts movement
Barrett, Lindsay 43
Caldwell, Benjamin 46
Cornish, Sam 50
Cortez, Jayne 43
Cruse, Harold 54
Dent, Thomas C. 50
Donaldson, Jeff 46
Dumas, Henry 41
Gayle, Addison, Jr. 41
Giovanni, Nikki 9, 39, 85
Henderson, David 53
Hoagland, Everett H. 45
Neal, Larry 38
Pomare, Eleo 72
Smith, Vincent D. 48
Touré, Askia (Muhammad Abu Bakr
   el) 47

X, Marvin 45

Black Cabinet
Hastie, William H. 8

Black Coaches Association (BCA)
Freeman, Marianna 23
Keith, Floyd A. 61

Black Consciousness movement
Biko, Steven 4
Fanon, Frantz 44
Fuller, Hoyt 44
Muhammad, Elijah 4
Ramaphosa, Cyril 3
Ramphele, Maphela 29
Tutu, Desmond Mpilo 6, 44

Black Economic Union (BEU)
Brown, Jim 11

Black Enterprise magazine
Brimmer, Andrew F. 2, 48
Graves, Butch 77
Graves, Earl G. 1, 35
Wallace, Phyllis A. 9

Black Entertainment Television (BET)
Ames, Wilmer 27
Gordon, Ed 10, 53
Greely, M. Gasby 27
Johnson, Robert L. 3, 39
Johnson, Sheila Crump 48
Jones, Bobby 20
Lee, Debra L. 62
McCrary Anthony, Crystal 70
Smiley, Tavis 20, 68

Black Filmmakers Hall of Fame
Browne, Roscoe Lee 66
Dee, Ruby 8, 50, 68
Dixon, Ivan 69
McKinney, Nina Mae 40

Black History Month
Woodson, Carter G. 2

Black Horizons on the Hill
Wilson, August 7, 33, 55

Black Manifesto
Forman, James 7, 51

Black Music Center
Moore, Undine Smith 28

Black Muslims
Abdul-Jabbar, Kareem 8
Ali, Muhammad 2, 16, 52
Farrakhan, Louis 2
Muhammad, Elijah 4
Muhammed, W. Deen 27
Redding, Ann Holmes 77
X, Malcolm 1

Black nationalism
Baker, Houston A., Jr. 6
Baraka, Amiri 1, 38
Caldwell, Benjamin 46
Carmichael, Stokely 5, 26
Donaldson, Jeff 46
Farrakhan, Louis 2
Forman, James 7, 51

Garvey, Marcus 1
Heard, Nathan C. 45
Innis, Roy 5
Muhammad, Elijah 4
Obadele, Imari 84
Turner, Henry McNeal 5
X, Malcolm 1
York, Dwight D. 71

Black Panther Party (BPP)
Abu-Jamal, Mumia 15
Al-Amin, Jamil Abdullah 6
bin Wahad, Dhoruba 85
Brown, Elaine 8
Carmichael, Stokely 5
Cleaver, Eldridge 5
Cleaver, Kathleen Neal 29
Coates, Ta-Nehisi 76
Cox, Donald Lee 93
Davis, Angela 5
Douglas, Emory 89
Forman, James 7, 51
Hampton, Fred 18
Hilliard, David 7
Jackson, George Lester 14
Kimbro, Warren 76
Neal, Larry 38
Newton, Huey 2
Pratt, Geronimo 18
Rush, Bobby 26, 76
Seale, Bobby 3
Shakur, Afeni 67
Shakur, Assata 6

Black Power movement
Al-Amin, Jamil Abdullah 6
Baker, Houston A., Jr. 6
Brown, Elaine 8
Carmichael, Stokely 5, 26
Dodson, Howard, Jr. 7, 52
Donaldson, Jeff 46
Dumas, Henry 41
Hare, Nathan 44
McKissick, Floyd B. 3
Stone, Chuck 9

Black Think Tank
Hare, Nathan 44

Blackvoices.com
Cooper, Barry 33

Blackwell Consulting Services
Blackwell, Robert D., Sr. 52

Black World magazine
See Negro Digest magazine

Black Writers Conference
McMillan, Rosalynn A. 36

Blind Boys of Alabama
Scott, George 55

Blogging
Contee, Cheryl 88

Blues
Ace, Johnny 36
Austin, Lovie 40
Barnes, Roosevelt "Booba" 33
Bibb, Eric 49
Bland, Bobby "Blue" 36
Broonzy, Big Bill 82
Brown, Charles 23
Brown, Nappy 73

Burns, Eddie 44
Burnside, R. L. 56
Carr, Leroy 49
Clarke, Kenny 27
Collins, Albert 12
Cox, Ida 42
Cray, Robert 30
Davis, Gary 41
Davis, Guy 36
Davis, Tyrone 54
Dixon, Willie 4
Dorsey, Thomas 15
Estes, Sleepy John 33
Evora, Cesaria 12
Ford, T-Model 91
Freeman, Yvette 27
Fuller, Blind Boy 86
Gaines, Grady 38
Guy, Buddy 31
Handy, W. C. 8
Harris, Corey 39, 73
Hemphill, Jessie Mae 33, 59
Holiday, Billie 1
Hooker, John Lee 30
Hopkins, Lightnin' 83
House, Son 8
Howlin' Wolf 9
Hunter, Alberta 42
Hurt, Mississippi John 84
Jackson, John 36
James, Skip 38
Jefferson, Blind Lemon 81
Johnson, Buddy 36
Johnson, Lonnie 85
King, B. B. 7
King, Freddie 92
LaVette, Bettye 85
Leadbelly 82
Lipscomb, Mance 49
Little Milton 36
Little Walter 36
Mahal, Taj 39
Martin, Sara 38
McGriff, Jimmy 72
McTell, Blind Willie 89
Mo', Keb' 36
Moore, Johnny B. 38
Muse, Clarence Edouard 21
Neal, Raful 44
Odetta 37, 74
Owens, Jack 38
Parker, Charlie 20
Pena, Paul 58
Perkins, Pinetop 70
Peterson, James 38
Rawls, Lou 17, 57
Reed, A. C. 36
Reed, Jimmy 38
Reese, Della 6, 20
Robinson, Fenton 38
Rogers, Jimmy 38
Ross, Isaiah "Doc" 40
Rush, Bobby 78
Rush, Otis 38
Seals, Son 56
Smith, Bessie 3
Smith, Mamie 32
Smith, Trixie 34
Streeter, Sarah 45
Sykes, Roosevelt 20
Tampa Red 63
Taylor, Koko 40, 80
Terry, Sonny 88

Turner, Big Joe 92
Turner, Ike 68
Wallace, Sippie 1
Washington, Dinah 22
Waters, Ethel 7
Waters, Muddy 34
Watson, Johnny "Guitar" 18
Webster, Katie 29
White, Josh, Jr. 52
Williams, Joe 5, 25
Williamson, Sonny Boy 84
Wilson, August 7, 33, 55

Blues Hall of Fame
Broonzy, Big Bill 82
Hopkins, Lightnin' 83
Hunter, Alberta 42
Hurt, Mississippi John 84
Little Milton 36
Williamson, Sonny Boy 84

Blues vernacular
Baker, Houston A., Jr. 6

Bobsledding
Flowers, Vonetta 35
Hines, Garrett 35
Jones, Randy 35
Moses, Edwin 8

Bodybuilding
Haney, Lee 77
Murray, Lenda 10

Boeing Company, The
Bell, James A. 50
Grooms, Henry R(andall) 50
Mills, Joseph C. 51

Bola Press
Cortez, Jayne 43

Bolero music
Ferrer, Ibrahim 41

Boogie music
Brooks, Hadda 40

The Boondocks
McGruder, Aaron 28, 56

Boston Bruins hockey team
O'Ree, Willie 5

Boston Celtics basketball team
Allen, Ray 82
Cooper, Charles "Chuck" 47
Fox, Rick 27
Garnett, Kevin 14, 70
Parish, Robert 43
Pierce, Paul 71
Rivers, Doc 25, 81
Russell, Bill 8
Sanders, Satch 77
Silas, Paul 24

Boston Red Sox baseball team
Baylor, Don 6
Ortiz, David 52, 82
Rice, Jim 75
Vaughn, Mo 16

Boston University
Loury, Glenn 36
Mitchell, Sharon 36

Botswanan government
Masire, Quett 5
Mogae, Festus Gontebanye 19, 79

Bowling
Branham, George, III 50
Terrell-Kearney, Kim 83

Boxing
Ali, Laila 27, 63
Ali, Muhammad 2, 16, 52
Bowe, Riddick 6
Carter, Rubin 26
DeGale, James 74
Dixon, George 52
Ellis, Jimmy 44
Foreman, George 1, 15
Forrest, Vernon 40, 79
Frazier, Joe 19
Frazier-Lyde, Jacqui 31
Futch, Eddie 33
Gans, Joe 91
Gibson, Truman K., Jr. 60
Haye, David 82
Hearns, Thomas 29
Holmes, Larry 20, 68
Holyfield, Evander 6
Hopkins, Bernard 35, 69
Johnson, Jack 8
Jones, Roy, Jr. 22
King, Don 14
Lee, Canada 8
Leonard, Sugar Ray 15
Lewis, Butch 71
Lewis, Lennox 27
Louis, Joe 5
Mayweather, Floyd, Jr. 57
Moorer, Michael 19
Mosley, Shane 32
Muhammad, Jabir Herbert 72
Mundine, Anthony 56
Page, Greg 78
Patterson, Floyd 19, 58
Robinson, Sugar Ray 18
Rose, Lionel 56
Steward, Emanuel 18
Taylor, Jermain 60
Toney, James 89
Tyson, Mike 28, 44, 93
Ward, Andre 62
Whitaker, Pernell 10, 89
Wills, Harry 80
Wolfe, Ann 82
Young, Jimmy 54

Boys and Girls Clubs
Brooks, Derrick 43
Gaines, Brenda 41

Boys Choir of Harlem
Turnbull, Walter 13, 60

BPP
See Black Panther Party

Brazilian government
da Silva, Benedita 5
Nascimento, Abdias do 93
Silva, Marina 80

Breast cancer awareness
Brown, Zora Kramer 12
Norton, Meredith 72

Riperton, Minnie 32

Bristol-Myers Squibb Inc.
Potter, Myrtle 40

British Broadcasting Company (BBC)
Armah, Esther 87
Figueroa, John J. 40
Stuart, Moira 82

British Film Institute
Akomfrah, John 37

British government
Abbott, Diane 9
Amos, Valerie 41
Boateng, Paul Yaw 56
Grant, Bernie 57
King, Oona 27
Pitt, David Thomas 10

British Virgin Islands government
Stoutt, H. Lavity 83

Broadcasting
Allen, Byron 3, 24
Ashley, Maurice 15, 47
Banks, William 11
Bettis, Jerome 64
Blackmon, Brenda 58
Bradley, Ed 2, 59
Branch, William Blackwell 39
Brown, Les 5
Brown, Tony 3
Brown, Vivian 27
Brunson, Dorothy 1, 87
Clayton, Xernona 3, 45
Cornelius, Don 4
Dee, Merri 55
Elder, Larry 25
Evans, Harry 25
Figueroa, John J. 40
Freeman, Aaron 52
Goode, Mal 13
Gumbel, Bryant 14, 80
Gumbel, Greg 8
Hamblin, Ken 10
Hickman, Fred 11
Holt, Lester 66
Hunter-Gault, Charlayne 6, 31
Jackson, Hal 41
Johnson, Rafer 33
Johnson, Robert L. 3, 39
Jones, Bobby 20
Joyner, Tom 19, 90
Kellogg, Clark 64
Kennedy-Overton, Jayne Harris 46
Langhart Cohen, Janet 19, 60
Lawson, Jennifer 1, 50
Lewis, Delano 7
Lofton, James 42
Lomax, Louis E. 90
Mabrey, Vicki 26
Madison, Joseph E. 17
Madison, Paula 37
McEwen, Mark 5
McFarland, Roland 49
Melton, Frank 81
Mickelbury, Penny 28
Miller, Cheryl 10, 74
Mitchell, Russ 21, 73
Morgan, Joe 9
Morton, Frederick A., Jr. 93

Neville, Arthel 53
Peete, Rodney 60
Pinckney, Sandra 56
Pinkston, W. Randall 24
Quarles, Norma 25
Reynolds, Star Jones 10, 27, 61
Roberts, Deborah 35
Roberts, Robin 16, 54
Rodgers, Johnathan 6, 51
Russell, Bill 8
Shaw, Bernard 2, 28
Simmons, Jamal 72
Simpson, Carole 6, 30
Simpson, O. J. 15
Smiley, Tavis 20, 68
Stewart, Alison 13
Swann, Lynn 28
Syler, Rene 53
Tirico, Mike 68
Watts, Rolonda 9
White, Bill 1, 48
Williams, Armstrong 29
Williams, Juan 35, 80
Williams, Montel 4, 57
Winfrey, Oprah 2, 15, 61

Broadside Press
Hoagland, Everett H. 45
Randall, Dudley 8, 55

Brookings Institute
Ladner, Joyce A. 42

Brooklyn Academy of Music
Miller, Bebe 3

Brooklyn Dodgers baseball team
Black, Joe 75
Campanella, Roy 25
Newcombe, Don 24
Robinson, Jackie 6

Brooklyn Eagles baseball team
Day, Leon 39

Brotherhood of Sleeping Car Porters
Randolph, A. Philip 3
Tucker, Rosina 14

Brown University
Beckham, Barry 41
Gibson, Donald Bernard 40
Simmons, Ruth 13, 38

Brown v. Board of Education of Topeka
Bell, Derrick 6
Carter, Robert L. 51
Clark, Kenneth B. 5, 52
Franklin, John Hope 5, 77
Henderson, Zelma 71
Hill, Oliver W. 24, 63
Houston, Charles Hamilton 4
Malone Jones, Vivian 59
Marshall, Thurgood 1, 44
Motley, Constance Baker 10, 55
Redding, Louis L. 26
Robinson, Spottswood W., III 22

Buena Vista Social Club
Ferrer, Ibrahim 41

Buffalo Bills football team
Lofton, James 42
Simpson, O. J. 15
Smith, Bruce 80
Thomas, Thurman 75

Bull-riding
Sampson, Charles 13

Burundian government
Ndadaye, Melchior 7
Nkurunziza, Pierre 78
Ntaryamira, Cyprien 8

Busing (anti-busing legislation)
Bosley, Freeman, Jr. 7

Cabinet
See U.S. Cabinet

Cable News Network (CNN)
Chideya, Farai 14, 61
Hickman, Fred 11
Malveaux, Suzanne 88
O'Brien, Soledad 88
Quarles, Norma 25
Shaw, Bernard 2, 28
Watson, Carlos 50

Calabash International Literary Festival
Channer, Colin 36

Calgary Flames hockey team
Iginla, Jarome 35

California Angels baseball team
See Los Angeles Angels baseball team

California Eagle newspaper
Bass, Charlotta Spears 40
Jackson, Vera 40

California state government
Bass, Karen 70
Brown, Janice Rogers 43
Brown, Willie 7, 85
Dixon, Julian C. 24
Dymally, Mervyn 42
Hawkins, Augustus F. 68
Lee, Barbara 25
Millender-McDonald, Juanita 21, 61
Richardson, Laura 81
Riles, Wilson C. 79
Waters, Maxine 3, 67
Watson, Diane 41

California State University
Cobb, Jewel Plummer 42
Granville, Evelyn Boyd 36
Karenga, Maulana 10, 71

California Supreme Court
Brown, Janice Rogers 43

Calypso
Belafonte, Harry 4, 65
Premice, Josephine 41
Rhoden, Wayne 70
Rudder, David 79

Cameroonian government
Ahidjo, Ahmadou 81
Biya, Paul 28

Oyono, Ferdinand 38

Canadian Football League (CFL)
Clemons, Michael "Pinball" 64
Gilliam, Frank 23
Moon, Warren 8, 66
Thrower, Willie 35
Weathers, Carl 10

Canadian government
Augustine, Jean 53
Brown, Rosemary 62
Cools, Anne 64
Jean, Michaëlle; 70
Lewis, Daurene 72
Sparks, Corinne Etta 53

Cancer research
Adams-Campbell, Lucille L. 60
Chinn, May Edward 26
Clark, Celeste 15
Daly, Marie Maynard 37
Dunston, Georgia Mae 48
Freeman, Harold P. 23
Leffall, Lasalle 3, 64
Olopade, Olufunmilayo Falusi 58

Capital punishment
Correia, De'Jaun 93
Hawkins, Steven 14

Cardiac research
Watkins, Levi, Jr. 9

CARE
Gossett, Louis, Jr. 7
Stone, Chuck 9

Caribbean Artists' Movement
Brathwaite, Kamau 36

Caribbean dance
Ailey, Alvin 8
Dunham, Katherine 4, 59
Fagan, Garth 18
Nichols, Nichelle 11
Primus, Pearl 6

Caribbean literature
Breeze, Jean "Binta" 37
Carter, Martin 49
Cartey, Wilfred 47
Dabydeen, David 48
Hearne, John Edgar Caulwell 45

Caribbean music
Ellis, Alton 74
Lefel, Edith 41
Ranglin, Ernest 78

Casting
Cannon, Reuben 50

Cartoonists
Armstrong, Robb 15
Bell, Darrin 77
Brandon, Barbara 3
Brown, Robert 65
Campbell, E. Simms 13
Fax, Elton 48
Harrington, Oliver W. 9
McDuffie, Dwayne 62
McGruder, Aaron 28, 56
Ormes, Jackie 73

Smith, Bruce W. 53

Catering
See Restaurants/Catering/Cooking

Catholicism
See Roman Catholic Church

CBC
See Congressional Black Caucus

CBS
See Columbia Broadcasting System

CDC
See Centers for Disease Control and Prevention

CDF
See Children's Defense Fund

Celebrities for a Drug-Free America
Vereen, Ben 4

Censorship
Butts, Calvin O., III 9, 90
Ice-T 6, 31

Centers for Disease Control and Prevention (CDC)
Fenton, Kevin 87
Gayle, Helene D. 3
Satcher, David 7, 57
Wisdom, Kimberlydawn 57

Central Intercollegiate Athletic Association (CIAA)
Kerry, Leon G. 46
Yancy, Dorothy Cowser 42

Certified public accountant
Jones, Thomas W. 41
Washington, Mary T. 57

CFL
See Canadian Football League

Chadian government
Déby, Idriss 30
Habré, Hissène 6

Challenged Athletes Foundation
Yeboah, Emmanuel Ofosu 53

Challenger
McNair, Ronald 3, 58

Challenger Air Pilot's Association
Brown, Willa 40

Chama Cha Mapinduzi (Tanzania; Revolutionary Party)
Kikwete, Jakaya Mrisho 73
Mkapa, Benjamin W. 16, 77
Mongella, Gertrude 11
Mwinyi, Ali Hassan 1, 77
Nyerere, Julius 5

Charles H. Wright Museum of African American History
Wright, Charles H. 35

Charles R. Drew University
Bath, Patricia E. 37

Charlotte Hornets basketball team
Bryant, Kobe 15, 31, 71
Parish, Robert 43

Charter Schools USA
Mariner, Jonathan 41

Chemistry
Daly, Marie Maynard 37
Donald, Arnold Wayne 36
Hall, Lloyd A. 8
Humphries, Frederick 20
Julian, Percy Lavon 6
King, Reatha Clark 65
Massie, Samuel Proctor, Jr. 29
Mays, William G. 34
McBay, Henry C. 91
Mensah, Thomas 48
Quarterman, Lloyd Albert 4

Chesapeake and Potomac Telephone Company
Lewis, Delano 7

Chess
Ashley, Maurice 15, 47

Chicago American Giants baseball team
Bell, James "Cool Papa" 36
Charleston, Oscar 39

Chicago Art League
Wilson, Ellis 39

Chicago Bears football team
Page, Alan 7
Payton, Walter 11, 25
Sayers, Gale 28
Singletary, Mike 4, 76
Thrower, Willie 35

Chicago Black Arts Movement
Cortor, Eldzier 42
Sebree, Charles 40

Chicago Bulls basketball team
Brand, Elton 31
Jordan, Michael 6, 21
Parish, Robert 43

Chicago city government
Berry, Edwin C. 81
De Priest, Oscar Stanton 80
Jones, Emil, Jr. 74
Jones, John 89
Kelley, Cliff 75
Lane, Vincent 5
Metcalfe, Ralph 26
Sawyer, Eugene 81
Tillman, Dorothy 76
Washington, Harold 6

Chicago Cubs baseball team
Baker, Dusty 8, 43, 72
Banks, Ernie 33
Bonds, Bobby 43
Carter, Joe 30
Sosa, Sammy 21, 44
Williams, Billy 86

Chicago Defender
Abbott, Robert Sengstacke 27
Holt, Nora 38
Martin, Roland S. 49, 84

Ormes, Jackie 73
Payne, Ethel L. 28

Chicago Defender Charities
Joyner, Marjorie Stewart 26

Chicago Eight
Seale, Bobby 3

Chicago Library Board
Williams, Fannie Barrier 27

Chicago Negro Chamber of Commerce
Fuller, S. B. 13

Chicago Police Department
Hillard, Terry 25
Holton, Hugh, Jr. 39

Chicago Reporter
Calhoun, Lillian Scott 87
Washington, Laura S. 18

Chicago Tribune
Page, Clarence 4

Chicago White Sox baseball team
Baines, Harold 32
Bonds, Bobby 43
Doby, Lawrence Eugene, Sr. 16, 41
Johnson, Clifford "Connie" 52
Thomas, Frank 12, 51
Williams, Ken 68

Chicago Women's Club
Williams, Fannie Barrier 27

Children's Defense Fund (CDF)
Edelman, Marian Wright 5, 42
Williams, Maggie 7, 71

Children's literature
Asim, Jabari 71
Berry, James 41
Bryan, Ashley F. 41
Common 31, 63
De Veaux, Alexis 44
Feelings, Muriel 44
Graham, Lorenz 48
Greenfield, Eloise 9
Johnson, Angela 52
Mollel, Tololwa 38
Myers, Walter Dean 8, 20
Okara, Gabriel 37
Palmer, Everard 37
Shelton, Paula Young 86
Yarbrough, Camille 40

Chi-Lites
Record, Eugene 60

Chiropractics
Ford, Clyde W. 40
Reese, Milous J., Jr. 51
Westbrooks, Bobby 51

Chisholm-Mingo Group, Inc.
Chisholm, Samuel J. 32
Mingo, Frank 32

Choreography
Acogny, Germaine 55
Ailey, Alvin 8
Alexander, Khandi 43

Allen, Debbie **13, 42**
Atkins, Cholly **40**
Babatunde, Obba **35**
Beatty, Talley **35**
Brooks, Avery **9**
Brown, Ronald K. **91**
Byrd, Donald **10**
Campbell-Martin, Tisha **8, 42**
Collins, Janet **33, 64**
Davis, Chuck **33**
de Lavallade, Carmen **78**
de Passe, Suzanne **25**
De Shields, André **72**
Dove, Ulysses **5**
Dunham, Katherine **4, 59**
Ellington, Mercedes **34**
Fagan, Garth **18**
Faison, George **16**
Glover, Savion **14**
Hall, Arthur **39**
Henson, Darrin **33**
Jamison, Judith **7, 67**
Johnson, Virginia **9**
Jones, Bill T. **1, 46, 80**
King, Alonzo **38**
LeTang, Henry **66**
Manning, Frankie **78**
Miller, Bebe **3**
Mitchell, Arthur **2, 47**
Nicholas, Fayard **20, 57**
Nicholas, Harold **20**
Pomare, Eleo **72**
Primus, Pearl **6**
Rhoden, Dwight **40**
Richardson, Desmond **39**
Robinson, Cleo Parker **38**
Robinson, Fatima **34**
Rodgers, Rod **36**
Spears, Warren **52**
Tyson, Andre **40**
Zollar, Jawole **28**

Christian Financial Ministries, Inc.
Ross, Charles **27**

Christian Science Monitor
Khanga, Yelena **6**

Chrysler Corporation
Colbert, Virgis William **17**
Farmer, Forest **1**
Gilles, Ralph **61**
Richie, Leroy C. **18**

Church of God in Christ
Blake, Charles E. **82**
Franklin, Robert M. **13**
Hayes, James C. **10**
Patterson, Gilbert Earl **41**

CIAA
See Central Intercollegiate Athletic Association

Cincinnati city government
Berry, Theodore M. **31**
Mallory, Mark **62**

Cincinnati Reds baseball team
Baker, Dusty **8, 43, 72**
Blair, Paul **36**
Larkin, Barry **24**
Morgan, Joe **9**
Reese, Pokey **28**

Robinson, Frank **9, 87**
Sanders, Deion **4, 31**

Cinematography
Dickerson, Ernest **6, 17**

Circus
McFarlan, Tyron **60**
Walker, Cedric "Ricky" **19**

Citadel Press
Achebe, Chinua **6**

Citigroup
Gaines, Brenda **41**
Jones, Thomas W. **41**
McGuire, Raymond J. **57**

City government--U.S.
Bell, Michael **40**
Bellamy, Terry **58**
Bobb, Robert C. **83**
Bradley, Jennette B. **40**
Brown, Lee P. **1, 24**
Brown, Willie **7, 85**
Burris, Chuck **21**
Bush, Gordon **82**
Caesar, Shirley **19**
Clayton, Constance **1**
Cleaver, Emanuel **4, 45, 68**
Coleman, Michael **28, 79**
Craig-Jones, Ellen Walker **44**
Dellums, Ronald **2, 81**
Ford, Jack **39**
Ford, Johnny **70**
Foxx, Anthony **81**
Hatcher, Richard G. **55**
Hayes, James C. **10**
Herenton, Willie W. **24, 81**
Johnson, Harvey, Jr. **24, 82**
Lowery, Myron **80**
Mallett, Conrad, Jr. **16**
Marsh, Henry **32**
McPhail, Sharon **2**
Melton, Frank **81**
Millender-McDonald, Juanita **21, 61**
Morial, Ernest "Dutch" **26**
Morial, Marc H. **20, 51**
Murrell, Sylvia Marilyn **49**
Patterson, J. O., Jr. **80**
Perkins, James, Jr. **55**
Powell, Adam Clayton, Jr. **3**
Powell, Debra A. **23**
Redd, Dana **93**
Usry, James L. **23**

City Sun newspaper
Cooper, Andrew W. **36**

City University of New York
Ballard, Allen Butler, Jr. **40**
Davis, George **36**
Gayle, Addison, Jr. **41**
Shabazz, Ilyasah **36**

Civil rights
Abbott, Diane **9**
Abernathy, Ralph **1**
Agyeman, Jaramogi Abebe **10, 63**
Al-Amin, Jamil Abdullah **6**
Alexander, Clifford **26**
Ali, Muhammad **2, 16, 52**
Amaker, Norman **63**
Angelou, Maya **1, 15**
Anthony, Wendell **25**

Aristide, Jean-Bertrand **6, 45**
Arnwine, Barbara **28**
Baker, Ella **5**
Baker, Houston A., Jr. **6**
Baker, Josephine **3**
Ballance, Frank W. **41**
Barbee, Lloyd Augustus **71**
Barrow, Willie T. **85**
Bashir, Halima **73**
Bass, Charlotta Spears **40**
Bates, Daisy **13**
Baugh, David **23**
Beals, Melba Patillo **15**
Belafonte, Harry **4, 65**
Bell, Derrick **6**
Bell, James Madison **40**
Berry, Mary Frances **7**
Berry, Theodore M. **31**
Bevel, James L. **75**
Biko, Steven **4**
Bishop, Sanford D., Jr. **24**
Bond, Julian **2, 35**
Booker, Simeon **23**
Boyd, John W., Jr. **20, 72**
Bradle, David Henry, Jr. **39**
Bridges, Ruby **77**
Brock, Roslyn McCallister **86**
Brooks, Tyrone **59**
Brown, Byrd **49**
Brown, Elaine **8**
Brown, Homer S. **47**
Brown, Tony **3**
Brown, Wesley **23**
Brown, Willa **40**
Burks, Mary Fair **40**
Caldwell, Earl **60**
Cameron, James **80**
Campbell, Bebe Moore **6, 24, 59**
Carmichael, Stokely **5, 26**
Carr, Johnnie **69**
Carter, Mandy **11**
Carter, Rubin **26**
Cary, Mary Ann Shadd **30**
Catto, Octavius V. **83**
Cayton, Horace **26**
Chambers, Julius **3**
Chavis, Benjamin **6**
Chestnut, J. L., Jr. **73**
Clark, Septima **7**
Clay, William Lacy **8**
Cleaver, Eldridge **5**
Cleaver, Kathleen Neal **29**
Clyburn, James E. **21, 71**
Cobb, W. Montague **39**
Cobbs, Price M. **9**
Cockrel, Kenneth Vern, Sr. **79**
Coleman, James E., Jr. **79**
Cooper, Anna Julia **20**
Cosby, Bill **7, 26, 59**
Crockett, George W., Jr. **10, 64**
Cunningham, Evelyn **23, 85**
Davis, Angela **5**
Davis, Artur **41**
Davis, James E. **50**
Days, Drew S., III **10**
Dee, Ruby **8, 50, 68**
Dent, Thomas C. **50**
Diallo, Amadou **27**
Diggs, Charles C. **21**
Diggs-Taylor, Anna **20**
Divine, Father **7**
Dobbs, John Wesley **89**
Dodson, Howard, Jr. **7, 52**

Douglass, Frederick **87**
Du Bois, W. E. B. **3**
Dudley, Edward R. **58**
Dukes, Hazel Nell **56**
Dumas, Henry **41**
Eagleson, William Lewis **90**
Edelman, Marian Wright **5, 42**
Ellison, Ralph **7**
Evers, Medgar **3**
Evers, Myrlie **8**
Farmer, James **2, 64**
Farmer-Paellmann, Deadria **43**
Fauntroy, Walter E. **11**
Fisher, Ada Lois Sipuel **76**
Fletcher, Bill, Jr. **41**
Forman, James **7, 51**
Fortune, T. Thomas **6**
Foster, Marie **48**
Franklin, C. L. **68**
Franklin, John Hope **5, 77**
Gaines, Ernest J. **7**
Gaines, Lloyd **79**
George, Zelma Watson **42**
Gibson, William F. **6**
Gomillion, Charles **90**
Granger, Lester B. **75**
Gray, Fred **37**
Gregory, Dick **1, 54**
Grimké, Archibald H. **9**
Guinier, Lani **7, 30**
Haley, Alex **4**
Haley, George Williford Boyce **21**
Hall, Elliott S. **24**
Hamer, Fannie Lou **6**
Hampton, Fred **18**
Hampton, Henry **6**
Hansberry, Lorraine **6**
Harding, Vincent **67**
Harper, Frances Ellen Watkins **11**
Harris, Patricia Roberts **2**
Hastie, William H. **8**
Hatcher, Richard G. **55**
Hawkins, Augustus F. **68**
Hawkins, Steven **14**
Hayes, Dennis **54**
Hedgeman, Anna Arnold **22**
Height, Dorothy I. **2, 23, 78**
Henderson, Thelton E. **68**
Henderson, Wade J. **14**
Henry, Aaron **19**
Higginbotham, A. Leon, Jr. **13, 25**
Hill, Jesse, Jr. **13**
Hill, Oliver W. **24, 63**
Hilliard, David **7**
Hobson, Julius W. **44**
Holland, Endesha Ida Mae **3, 57**
Hollowell, Donald L. **57**
Hooks, Benjamin L. **2, 85**
Hope, Lugenia Burns **89**
Houston, Charles Hamilton **4**
Howard, M. William, Jr. **26**
Innis, Roy **5**
Irvis, K. Leroy **67**
Jackson, Alexine Clement **22**
Jackson, Jesse **1, 27, 72**
James, Daniel, Jr. **16**
Jarrett, Vernon D. **42**
Jenkins, Ray **77**
Johns, Vernon **38**
Johnson, Georgia Douglas **41**
Johnson, James Weldon **5**
Johnson, Norma L. Holloway **17**
Jones, Elaine R. **7, 45**

Jones, John 89
Jones, William A., Jr. 61
Jordan, Barbara 4, 78
Jordan, June 7, 35
Jordan, Vernon E. 3, 35
Julian, Percy Lavon 6
Karim, Benjamin 61
Kennedy, Florynce 12, 33
Kenyatta, Jomo 5
Kidd, Mae Street 39
King, Bernice 4, 81
King, Coretta Scott 3, 57
King, Martin Luther, III 20
King, Martin Luther, Jr. 1
King, Martin Luther, Sr. 89
King, Preston 28
King, Robert Hillary 84
King, Yolanda 6
Ladner, Joyce A. 42
Lampkin, Daisy 19
Lawson, James M., Jr. 90
Lester, Julius 9
Lewis, John 2, 46, 83
Lewis, William Henry 89
Logan, Rayford W. 40
Lorde, Audre 6
Loving, Mildred 69
Lowery, Joseph 2
Lowry, A. Leon 60
Lucy Foster, Autherine 35
Makeba, Miriam 2, 50, 74
Malone Jones, Vivian 59
Mandela, Nelson 1, 14, 77
Mandela, Winnie 2, 35
Martin, Louis E. 16
Martin, Ruby Grant 49
Mays, Benjamin E. 7
Mbeki, Thabo 14, 73
McDonald, Gabrielle Kirk 20
McDougall, Gay J. 11, 43
McKissick, Floyd B. 3
Meredith, James H. 11
Metcalfe, Ralph 26
Mitchell, Clarence M., Jr. 88
Morgan, Irene 65
Moore, Barbara C. 49
Moore, Harry T. 29
Morial, Ernest "Dutch" 26
Moses, Robert Parris 11
Moss, Otis, Jr. 72
Motley, Constance Baker 10, 55
Mowry, Jess 7
Mukoko, Jestina 75
Murphy, Laura M. 43
Murray, Pauli 38
Nash, Diane 72
Ndadaye, Melchior 7
Nelson, Jill 6, 54
Newton, Huey 2
Nkoli, Simon 60
Nkomo, Joshua 4, 65
Noble, Gil 76
Norman, Pat 10
Nunn, Annetta 43
Nzo, Alfred 15
Orange, James 74
Parker, Kellis E. 30
Parks, Rosa 1, 35, 56
Patrick, Deval 12, 61
Patterson, Louise 25
Patterson, Orlando 4
Perkins, Edward 5
Pincham, R. Eugene, Sr. 69

Pinchback, P. B. S. 9
Player, Willa B. 43
Pleasant, Mary Ellen 9
Plessy, Homer Adolph 31
Poitier, Sidney 11, 36
Powell, Adam Clayton, Jr. 3
Price, Hugh B. 9, 54
Ramaphosa, Cyril 3
Randolph, A. Philip 3
Reagon, Bernice Johnson 7
Redding, Louis L. 26
Riggs, Marlon 5, 44
Rivers, Eugene F., III 81
Robeson, Paul 2
Robinson, Jackie 6
Robinson, Rachel 16
Robinson, Randall 7, 46
Robinson, Sharon 22
Robinson, Spottswood W., III 22
Roundtree, Dovey 80
Rowan, Carl T. 1, 30
Rush, Bobby 26, 76
Rustin, Bayard 4
Sadlier, Rosemary 62
Sanders, Malika 48
Sané, Pierre Gabriel 21
Saro-Wiwa, Kenule 39
Seale, Bobby 3
Shabazz, Attallah 6
Shabazz, Betty 7, 26
Shakur, Assata 6
Shelton, Paula Young 86
Shinhoster, Earl 32
Shuttlesworth, Fred 47
Simone, Nina 15, 41
Sisulu, Albertina 57
Sisulu, Sheila Violet Makate 24
Sleet, Moneta, Jr. 5
Smith, Barbara 28
Staupers, Mabel K. 7
Sullivan, Leon H. 3, 30
Sutton, Percy E. 42, 82
Sweet, Ossian 68
Taylor, Recy 92
Thompson, Bennie G. 26
Thurman, Howard 3
Till, Emmett 7
Tillman, Dorothy 76
Tolson, Melvin B. 37
Touré, Faya Ora Rose 56
Trotter, Monroe 9
Tsvangirai, Morgan 26, 72
Turner, Henry McNeal 5
Tutu, Desmond Mpilo 6, 44
Underwood, Blair 7, 27, 76
Walker, Rebecca 50
Washington, Booker T. 4
Washington, Fredi 10
Watt, Melvin 26
Weaver, Robert C. 8, 46
Wells, James Lesesne 10
Wells-Barnett, Ida B. 8
White, Walter F. 4
Wilkins, Roy 4
Williams, Evelyn 10
Williams, Fannie Barrier 27
Williams, Hosea Lorenzo 15, 31
Williams, Robert F. 11
Williams, Walter E. 4
Wilson, August 7, 33, 55
Wilson, Sunnie 7, 55
Wilson, William Julius 22
Woods, Abraham, Jr. 74

Woodson, Robert L. 10
Wright, Nathan, Jr. 56
X, Malcolm 1
Yoba, Malik 11
Young, Andrew 3, 48
Young, Jean Childs 14
Young, Whitney M., Jr. 4

Civilian Pilots Training Program
Brown, Willa 40

Clarinet
Bechet, Sidney 18
McGill, Anthony 76

Classical music
Adams, Leslie 39
Baiocchi, Regina Harris 41
Bonds, Margaret 39
Brown, Uzee 42
Burleigh, Henry Thacker 56
Coleridge-Taylor, Samuel 75
Cook, Will Marion 40
Dawson, William Levi 39
DePreist, James 37
Dixon, Dean 68
Dunner, Leslie B. 45
Freeman, Paul 39
Kay, Ulysses 37
Lewis, Henry 38
McFerrin, Bobby 68
McGill, Anthony 76
Moore, Dorothy Rudd 46
Murray, Tai 47
Pratt, Awadagin 31
Price, Florence 37
Schuyler, Philippa 50
Sowande, Fela 39
Still, William Grant 37
Tillis, Frederick 40
Walker, George 37
Wilkins, Thomas Alphonso 71
Williams, Denise 40

Classical singers
Anderson, Marian 2, 33
Battle, Kathleen 70
Bumbry, Grace 5
Burleigh, Henry Thacker 56
Hayes, Roland 4
Hendricks, Barbara 3, 67
Lister, Marquita 65
Norman, Jessye 5
Price, Leontyne 1
Three Mo' Tenors 35
Williams, Denise 40

Clearview Golf Club
Powell, Renee 34

Cleo Parker Robinson Dance Ensemble
Robinson, Cleo Parker 38

Clergy
Agyeman, Jaramogi Abebe 10, 63
Anthony, Wendell 25
Austin, Junius C. 44
Berry, Moses 84
Black, Barry C. 47
Bloomer, George 86
Bowen, John W. E., Sr. 89
Burgess, John 46
Bynum, Juanita 31, 71

Caesar, Shirley 19
Caldwell, Kirbyjon 55
Cleveland, James 19
Cook, Suzan D. Johnson 22
Dyson, Michael Eric 11, 40
Easton, Hosea 91
Ellis, Charles H., III 79
Falana, Lola 42
Gilmore, Marshall 46
Gregory, Wilton 37
Henson, Josiah 90
Holsey, Lucius Henry 92
Hood, James Walker 91
Howard, M. William, Jr. 26
Jakes, Thomas "T. D." 17, 43
James, Skip 38
Jemison, Major L. 48
Johns, Vernon 38
Jones, Absalom 52
Jones, Alex 64
Jones, Robert Elijah 90
Jones, William A., Jr. 61
Karim, Benjamin 61
Kee, John P. 43
Kelly, Leontine 33
King, Barbara 22
King, Bernice 4, 81
Kobia, Samuel 43
Lee, Eric P. 79
Lincoln, C. Eric 38
Maxis, Theresa 62
McClurkin, Donnie 25
McGuire, George Alexander 80
McKenzie, Vashti M. 29
Michaux, Solomon Lightfoot 91
Morgan, Gertrude 63
Okaalet, Peter 58
Otunga, Maurice Michael 55
Peterson, Jesse Lee 81
Phipps, Wintley 59
Reems, Ernestine Cleveland 27
Reese, Della 6, 20
Reverend Ike 79
Sentamu, John 58
Shuttlesworth, Fred 47
Taylor, Gardner C. 76
Thurman, Howard 3
Thurston, Stephen J. 49
Tillard, Conrad 47
Tolton, Augustine 62
Ukpabio, Helen 86
Walker, John T. 50
Washington, James Melvin 50
Watkins, Joe 86
Weeks, Thomas, III 70
Weems, Renita J. 44
White-Hammond, Gloria 61
Williams, David Rudyard 50
Williams, Frederick (B.) 63
Williams, Preston Warren, II 64
Winans, Marvin L. 17
Wright, Nathan, Jr. 56

Cleveland Browns football team
Brown, Jim 11
Crennel, Romeo 54
Hill, Calvin 19
Motley, Marion 26
Newsome, Ozzie 26

Willis, Bill 68

Cleveland city government
Jackson, Frank G. 76
Stokes, Carl 10, 73
White, Michael R. 5

Cleveland Foundation
Adams, Leslie 39

Cleveland Indians baseball team
Belle, Albert 10
Bonds, Bobby 43
Carter, Joe 30
Doby, Lawrence Eugene, Sr. 16, 41
Justice, David 18
Lofton, Kenny 12
Murray, Eddie 12
Paige, Satchel 7
Robinson, Frank 9, 87
Sabathia, CC 74

CLIO Awards
Lewis, Emmanuel 36

Clothing design
Aberra, Amsale 67
Bailey, Xenobia 11
Burrows, Stephen 31
Gaskins, Eric 64
Henderson, Gordon 5
John, Daymond 23
Jones, Carl 7
Kani, Karl 10
Kelly, Patrick 3
Lars, Byron 32
Malone, Maurice 32
Pinkett Smith, Jada 10, 41
Robinson, Patrick 19, 71
Smith, Willi 8
Walker, T. J. 7
Williams, Serena 20, 41, 73

CNBC
Epperson, Sharon 54
Thomas-Graham, Pamela 29

CNN
See Cable News Network

Coaching
Amaker, Tommy 62
Anderson, Mike 63
Ashley, Maurice 15, 47
Baker, Dusty 8, 43, 72
Baylor, Don 6
Bickerstaff, Bernie 21
Bonds, Bobby 43
Brown, Mike 77
Caldwell, Jim 81
Campanella, Roy 25
Carew, Rod 20
Carter, Butch 27
Carter, Kenneth 53
Chaney, John 67
Cheeks, Maurice 47
Cooper, Michael 31
Cox, Bryan 83
Crennel, Romeo 54
Curry, Michael 85
Davis, Mike 41
Dorrell, Karl 52
Dungy, Tony 17, 42, 59
Dunn, Jerry 27

Edwards, Herman 51
Ellerbe, Brian 22
Freeman, Marianna 23
Gaines, Clarence E., Sr. 55
Gaither, Alonzo Smith (Jake) 14
Gaston, Cito 71
Gentry, Alvin 23
Gibson, Althea 8, 43
Gibson, Bob 33
Gill, Turner 83
Gorden, W. C. 71
Graham, Trevor 84
Gray, Yeshimbra "Shimmy" 55
Green, Dennis 5, 45
Greene, Joe 10
Haskins, Clem 23
Heard, Gar 25
Johnson, Avery 62
Jordan, Eddie 83
Joyce, Dru 81
Keith, Floyd A. 61
Lewis, Marvin 51, 87
Lofton, James 42
Miller, Cheryl 10, 74
Mitchell, Sam 82
Morris, Raheem 77
O'Neil, Buck 19, 59
Parish, Robert 43
Phillips, Teresa L. 42
Rhodes, Ray 14
Richardson, Nolan 9
Rivers, Doc 25, 81
Robinson, Eddie G. 10, 61
Robinson, Frank 9, 87
Robinson, Will 51, 69
Russell, Bill 8
Sanders, Satch 77
Shannon, Randy 82
Shell, Art 1, 66
Silas, Paul 24
Simmons, Bob 29
Singletary, Mike 4, 76
Smith, Lovie 66
Smith, Tubby 18, 83
Stringer, C. Vivian 13, 66
Thomas, Emmitt 71
Tunnell, Emlen 54
White, Jesse 22, 75
Williams, Doug 22
Willingham, Tyrone 43
Wills, Maury 73

Coalition of Black Trade Unionists
Lucy, William 50
Wyatt, Addie L. 56

Coca-Cola Company
Llewellyn, J. Bruce 13, 85
Ware, Carl T. 30

Coca-Cola Foundation
Jones, Ingrid Saunders 18

Collage
Andrews, Benny 22, 59
Bearden, Romare 2, 50
Bradford, Mark 89
Driskell, David C. 7
Pindell, Howardena 55
Pinder, Jefferson 77
Robinson, Aminah 50
Saar, Betye 80
Thomas, Mickalene 61

Verna, Gelsy 70

College and university administration
Ammons, James H. 81
Archie-Hudson, Marguerite 44
Barnett, Marguerite 46
Bromery, Randolph Wilson 85
Burnim, Mickey L. 48
Christian, Barbara T. 44
Cross, Dolores E. 23
Davis, Erroll B., Jr. 57
Dogan, Matthew Winifred 91
Ford, Nick Aaron 44
Gilbert, John Wesley 91
Hill, Leslie Pinckney 44
Hogan, Beverly Wade 50
Horne, Frank 44
Jackson, Edison O. 67
King, Reatha Clark 65
Lee, Joe A. 45
Lewis, Shirley A. R. 14
Mason, Ronald 27
Massey, Walter E. 5, 45
Maupin, John E., Jr. 92
Mell, Patricia 49
Moody-Adams, Michele 76
Morón, Alonzo G. 91
Nance, Cynthia 71
Newman, Lester C. 51
Page, Inman 82
Pollard, William L. 91
Ribeau, Sidney 70
Trueheart, William E. 49

Colorado Rockies baseball team
Baylor, Don 6

Colorado state government
Brown, George Leslie 62
Rogers, Joe 27

Columbia Broadcasting System (CBS)
Bradley, Ed 2, 59
Kellogg, Clark 64
Mabrey, Vicki 26
McEwen, Mark 5
Mitchell, Russ 21, 73
Olden, Georg(e) 44
Pinkston, W. Randall 24
Pitts, Byron 71
Rodgers, Johnathan 6, 51
Ware, Andre 37

Columbia Records
Jackson, Randy 40
Knowles, Tina 61
Olatunji, Babatunde 36
Williams, Deniece 36

Columbia University
Huggins, Nathan Irvin 52
Marable, Manning 10
Moody-Adams, Michele 76

Comedy
Allen, Byron 3, 24
Amos, John 8, 62
Anderson, Anthony 51, 77
Anderson, Eddie "Rochester" 30
Anthony, Trey 63
Arnez J 53
Beaton, Norman 14

Bellamy, Bill 12
Berry, Bertice 8, 55
Brady, Wayne 32, 71
Bruce, Bruce 56
Cannon, Nick 47, 73
Cedric the Entertainer 29, 60
Chappelle, Dave 50
Cosby, Bill 7, 26, 59
Curry, Mark 17
Davidson, Tommy 21
Davis, Sammy, Jr. 18
Dieudonné 67
Earthquake 55
Epps, Mike 60
Foxx, Jamie 15, 48
Foxx, Redd 2
Freeman, Aaron 52
Givens, Adele 62
Glover, Donald 85
Goldberg, Whoopi 4, 33, 69
Harris, Robin 7
Harvey, Steve 18, 58
Henry, Lenny 9, 52
Hughley, D. L. 23, 76
Kirby, George 14
Lawrence, Martin 6, 27, 60
Mabley, Jackie "Moms" 15
Mac, Bernie 29, 61, 72
Mayo, Whitman 32
McEwen, Mark 5
Meadows, Tim 30
Mooney, Paul 37
Morgan, Tracy 61
Morris, Garrett 31
Moss, Preacher 63
Murphy, Eddie 4, 20, 61
Nash, Niecy 66
Perry, Tyler 40, 54
Pryor, Richard 3, 24, 56
Rock, Chris 3, 22, 66
Russell, Nipsey 66
Schultz, Michael A. 6
Slocumb, Jonathan 52
Smiley, Rickey 59
Sommore 61
Sykes, Wanda 48, 81
Thompson, Kenan 52
Thurston, Baratunde 79
Torry, Guy 31
Townsend, Robert 4, 23
Tucker, Chris 13, 23, 62
Tyler, Aisha N. 36
Wayans, Damon 8, 41
Wayans, Keenen Ivory 18
Wayans, Kim 80
Wayans, Marlon 29, 82
Wayans, Shawn 29
Wilson, Debra 38
Wilson, Flip 21
Witherspoon, John 38
Yarbrough, Cedric 51

Comerica Bank
Forte, Linda Diane 54

Commercial art
Freeman, Leonard 27

Communist Party
Brown, Lloyd Louis 42
Davis, Angela 5
Du Bois, W. E. B. 3
Herndon, Angelo 90
Jagan, Cheddi 16

Patterson, Louise 25
Wright, Richard 5

Community activism
Kimbro, Warren 76
Shakur, Yusef 85

Complete Energy Partners
Scott, Milton 51

Complexions dance troupe
Rhoden, Dwight 40
Richardson, Desmond 39
Tyson, Andre 40

Computer graphics
Coleman, Ken 57
Hannah, Marc 10

Computer science
Adkins, Rod 41
Auguste, Donna 29
Dean, Mark 35
Easley, Annie J. 61
Ellis, Clarence 38
Emeagwali, Philip 30
Hannah, Marc 10
Irvin, Vernon 65
Laryea, Thomas Davies, III 67
Mensah, Thomas 48
Millines Dziko, Trish 28
Zollar, Alfred 40

Conceptual art
Allen, Tina 22, 75
Bailey, Xenobia 11
Harris, Lyle Ashton 83
O'Grady, Lorraine 73
Piper, Adrian 71
Pope.L, William 72
Robinson, Aminah 50
Shonibare, Yinka 58
Simpson, Lorna 4, 36

Conductors
Calloway, Cab 14
Cook, Will Marion 40
Dawson, William Levi 39
DePreist, James 37
Dixon, Dean 68
Dunner, Leslie B. 45
Foster, William P. 88
Freeman, Paul 39
Hairston, Jester 88
Jackson, Isaiah 3
León, Tania 13
Lewis, Henry 38

Congress of Racial Equality (CORE)
Dee, Ruby 8, 50, 68
Farmer, James 2, 64
Hobson, Julius W. 44
Innis, Roy 5
Jackson, Jesse 1, 27, 72
McKissick, Floyd B. 3
Rustin, Bayard 4

Congressional Black Caucus (CBC)
Christian-Green, Donna M. 17
Clay, William Lacy 8
Clyburn, James E. 21, 71
Collins, Cardiss 10, 80
Conyers, John, Jr. 4, 45

Dellums, Ronald 2, 81
Diggs, Charles C. 21
Fauntroy, Walter E. 11
Gray, William H., III 3
Hastings, Alcee L. 16
Hawkins, Augustus F. 68
Johnson, Eddie Bernice 8, 90
Mfume, Kweisi 6, 41
Mitchell, Parren J. 42, 66
Owens, Major 6
Payton, John 48
Rangel, Charles B. 3, 52, 85
Scott, Robert C. 23
Stokes, Louis 3
Thompson, Bennie G. 26
Towns, Edolphus 19, 75

Contemporary Christian music
Griffin, LaShell 51
Tait, Michael 57

Continental Basketball Association (CBA)
Davis, Mike 41
Thomas, Isiah 7, 26, 65
Ussery, Terdema, II 29

Cooking
See Restaurants/Catering/Cooking

Coppin State College
Blair, Paul 36

CORE
See Congress of Racial Equality

Coretta Scott King Awards
Clifton, Lucille 14, 64, 91
Curtis, Christopher Paul 26
Draper, Sharon Mills 16, 43
Fax, Elton 48
Greenfield, Eloise 9
Hamilton, Virginia 10
Haskins, James 36, 54
Johnson, Angela 52
Lester, Julius 9
Morrison, Toni 2, 15, 86
Rollins, Charlemae Hill 27
Taylor, Mildred D. 26

Coronet
Oliver, Joe "King" 42

Corporation for Public Broadcasting (CPB)
Brown, Tony 3

Cosmetology
Cottrell, Comer 11
Fuller, S. B. 13
McGrath, Pat 72
Morgan, Rose 11
Powell, Maxine 8
Roche, Joyce M. 17
Walker, A'lelia 14
Walker, Madame C. J. 7

Cotton Club Revue
Johnson, Buddy 36

Council on Legal Education Opportunities (CLEO)
Henderson, Wade J. 14
Henry, Aaron 19

Count Basie Orchestra
Eldridge, Roy 37
Johnson, J. J. 37
Powell, Benny 87
Rushing, Jimmy 37
Williams, Joe 5, 25
Young, Lester 37

Country music
Bailey, DeFord 33
Cowboy Troy 54
Palmer, Rissi 65
Pride, Charley 26
Randall, Alice 38
Rucker, Darius 34, 74

Covad Communications
Knowling, Robert 38

Cowboys
Love, Nat 9
Pickett, Bill 11

CPB
See Corporation for Public Broadcasting

Craftwork
Hill, Peter 92

Creative Artists Agency
Nelson Meigs, Andrea 48

Credit Suisse First Boston, Inc.
Ogunlesi, Adebayo 37

Creole music
Ardoin, Alphonse 65

Cricket
Adams, Paul 50

Critics' Choice Award
Channer, Colin 36

Critical race theory
Crenshaw, Kimberlé Williams 88
Williams, Patricia 11, 54

Cross Colours
Jones, Carl 7
Kani, Karl 10
Walker, T. J. 7

Crown Media
Corbi, Lana 42

Crusader
Williams, Robert F. 11

Cuban League
Charleston, Oscar 39
Day, Leon 39

Cuban military
Maceo, Antonio 82

Cuban music
Ferrer, Ibrahim 41
Portuondo, Omara 53
Valdés, Bebo 75
Valdés, Chucho 89

Cubism
Bearden, Romare 2, 50
Green, Jonathan 54

Culinary arts
Allen, Eugene 79
Brown, Warren 61

Calabrese, Karyn 89
Chase, Leah 57
Clark, Patrick 14
Estes, Rufus 29
Evans, Darryl 22
Garvin, Gerry 78
Henderson, Jeff 72
Ouattara, Morou 74
Samuelsson, Marcus 53

Cultural Hangups
Ham, Cynthia Parker 58

Cultural pluralism
Locke, Alain 10

Curator/exhibition designer
Amaki, Amalia 76
Camp, Kimberly 19
Campbell, Mary Schmidt 43
Golden, Thelma 10, 55
Hoyte, Lenon 50
Hutson, Jean Blackwell 16
Pindell, Howardena 55
Sanders, Joseph R., Jr. 11
Sims, Lowery Stokes 27
Stewart, Paul Wilbur 12

Cy Young Award
Gibson, Bob 33
Gooden, Dwight 20
Jenkins, Fergie 46
Martinez, Pedro 81
Newcombe, Don 24
Sabathia, CC 74

Cycling
Baugé, Grégory 86
Taylor, Marshall Walter "Major" 62
Yeboah, Emmanuel Ofosu 53

Cytogenetics
Satcher, David 7, 57

Dallas city government
Kirk, Ron 11, 75

Dallas Cowboys football team
Hayes, Bob 77
Hill, Calvin 19
Irvin, Michael 64
Jones, Ed "Too Tall" 46
Sanders, Deion 4, 31
Smith, Emmitt 7, 87
Wright, Rayfield 70

Dallas Police Department
Bolton, Terrell D. 25

DanceAfrica
Davis, Chuck 33

Dance Theatre of Harlem
Johnson, Virginia 9
King, Alonzo 38
Mitchell, Arthur 2, 47
Nicholas, Fayard 20, 57
Nicholas, Harold 20
Tyson, Cicely 7, 51

DAV
See Disabled American Veterans

Daytona Institute
See Bethune-Cookman College

D.C. sniper
Moose, Charles **40**

Death Row Records
Dre, Dr. **10, 14, 30**
Knight, Suge **11, 30**
Shakur, Tupac **14**

Decca Records
Hardin Armstrong, Lil **39**

Def Jam Records
Jay-Z **27, 69**
Liles, Kevin **42**
Simmons, Russell **1, 30**

Defense Communications Agency
Gravely, Samuel L., Jr. **5, 49**

Delta Sigma Theta Sorority
Rice, Louise Allen **54**

Democratic National Committee (DNC)
Brown, Ron **5**
Dixon, Sharon Pratt **1**
Fattah, Chaka **11, 70**
Hamer, Fannie Lou **6**
Horsford, Steven **88**
Jackson, Maynard **2, 41**
Jordan, Barbara **4, 78**
Joyner, Marjorie Stewart **26**
Mallett, Conrad, Jr. **16**
Martin, Louis E. **16**
Moore, Minyon **45**
Waters, Maxine **3, 67**
Williams, Maggie **7, 71**

Dentistry
Bluitt, Juliann S. **14**
Delany, Bessie **12**
Gray, Ida **41**
Madison, Romell **45**
Maupin, John E., Jr. **92**
Sinkford, Jeanne C. **13**

Denver Broncos football team
Barnes, Ernie **16, 78**
Briscoe, Marlin **37**
Davis, Terrell **20**
Jackson, Tom **70**
Little, Floyd **86**

Denver city government
Webb, Wellington **3, 81**

Denver Nuggets basketball team
Bickerstaff, Bernie **21**
Bynoe, Peter C. B. **40**
Hardaway, Tim **35**
Lee, Bertram M., Sr. **46**
Mutombo, Dikembe **7**

DePaul University
Braun, Carol Moseley **4, 42**
Sizemore, Barbara A. **26**

Depression/The Great Depression
Hampton, Henry **6**

Dermatology
Taylor, Susan C. **62**

Desert Shield/Desert Storm
See Operation Desert Shield/Operation Desert Storm

Destiny's Child
Beyoncé **39, 70**
Knowles, Tina **61**
Luckett, Letoya **61**
Williams, Michelle **73**

Detective fiction
See Mystery/Detective fiction

Detroit city government
Archer, Dennis **7, 36**
Bing, Dave **3, 59, 78**
Cockrel, Kenneth V., Jr. **79**
Cockrel, Kenneth Vern, Sr. **79**
Collins, Barbara-Rose **7, 87**
Conyers, Monica **85**
Crockett, George W., Jr. **10, 64**
Evans, Warren C. **76**
Garrett, Joyce Finley **59**
Kilpatrick, Kwame **34, 71**
Marshall, Bella **22**
Pugh, Charles **81**
Reeves, Martha **85**
Young, Coleman **1, 20**

Detroit Golden Gloves
Wilson, Sunnie **7, 55**

Detroit Lions football team
Barney, Lem **26**
Farr, Mel **24**
Johnson, Levi **48**
Mayhew, Martin R. **76**
Sanders, Barry **1, 53**
Ware, Andre **37**

Detroit Pistons basketball team
Bing, Dave **3, 59, 78**
Dumars, Joe **16, 65**
Gentry, Alvin **23**
Hill, Grant **13**
Lanier, Bob **47**
Lloyd, Earl **26**
Lowe, Sidney **64**
Mahorn, Rick **60**
Mohammed, Nazr **64**
Prince, Tayshaun **68**
Robinson, Will **51, 69**
Stackhouse, Jerry **30**
Thomas, Isiah **7, 26, 65**
Wallace, Ben **54**
Webber, Chris **15, 30, 59**

Detroit Police Department
Bully-Cummings, Ella **48**
Gomez-Preston, Cheryl **9**
McKinnon, Isaiah **9**
Napoleon, Benny N. **23**

Detroit Public Schools
Coleman, William F., III **61**

Detroit Tigers baseball team
Fielder, Cecil **2**
Granderson, Curtis **66**
Virgil, Ozzie **48**

Diabetes
Fennoy, Ilene **72**
Wisdom, Kimberlydawn **57**

Diamond mining
Masire, Quett **5**

Dictators
Abacha, Sani **11, 70**
Ahidjo, Ahmadou **81**
Amin, Idi **42**
Biya, Paul **28**
Compaore, Blaise **87**
Eyadéma, Gnassingbé **7, 52**
Gbagbo, Laurent **43, 90**
Habré, Hissène **6**
Kabila, Laurent **20**
Meles Zenawi **3**
Mengistu, Haile Mariam **65**
Moi, Daniel Arap **1, 35**
Mswati III **56**
Mugabe, Robert **10, 71**
Touré, Sekou **6**

Digital divide
Adkins, Rod **41**

Dillard University
Cook, Samuel DuBois **14**
Lomax, Michael L. **58**

Dime Savings Bank
Parsons, Richard Dean **11**

Diner's Club
Gaines, Brenda **41**

Diplomatic Corps
See U.S. Department of State

Director's Guild of America
Barclay, Paris **37**

Disabled American Veterans (DAV)
Brown, Jesse **6, 41**

Disco
Gaynor, Gloria **36**
Payne, Freda **58**
Perren, Freddie **60**
Staton, Candi **27**
Summer, Donna **25**

Distance running
Cheruiyot, Robert **69**
Loroupe, Tegla **59**
Tergat, Paul **59**

Diving
Brashear, Carl **29**

DJ
Alert, Kool DJ Red **32**
Atkins, Juan **50**
Bond, Beverly **53**
DJ Jazzy Jeff **32**
Grandmaster Flash **33, 60**
Knuckles, Frankie **42**
Love, Ed **58**

DNC
See Democratic National Committee

Documentary film
Billops, Camille **82**
Blackwood, Maureen **37**
Branch, William Blackwell **39**
Byrd, Robert **11**
Dash, Julie **4**

Diamond mining — Davis, Ossie **5, 50**
Gray, Darius **69**
Greaves, William **38**
Hampton, Henry **6**
Henry, Lenny **9, 52**
Hudlin, Reginald **9, 86**
Hudlin, Warrington **9**
Hurt, Byron **61**
Jean, Michaëlle; **70**
Julien, Isaac **3**
Lynch, Shola **61**
Nelson, Stanley **92**
Peck, Raoul **32**
Riggs, Marlon **5, 44**
Roberts, Kimberly Rivers **72**
Whack, Rita Coburn **36**
Williams, Marco **53**

Dollmaking
El Wilson, Barbara **35**

Dominica government
Charles, Mary Eugenia **10, 55**
Charles, Pierre **52**
Skerrit, Roosevelt **72**

Dove Award
Baylor, Helen **36**
Winans, CeCe **14, 43**

Down Beat Jazz Hall of Fame
Terry, Clark **39**

Drama Desk Awards
Carter, Nell **39**
Taylor, Ron **35**
Wesley, Richard **73**

Dreamland Orchestra
Cook, Charles "Doc" **44**

Drug abuse prevention
Clements, George **2**
Creagh, Milton **27**
Hale, Lorraine **8**
Harris, Alice **7**
Lucas, John **7**

Drug synthesis
Julian, Percy Lavon **6**
Pickett, Cecil **39**

Drums
Ali, Rashied **79**
Blade, Brian **88**
Blakey, Art **37**
Brown, Carlinhos **81**
Durham, Bobby **73**
Güines, Tata **69**
Haynes, Roy **87**
Jones, Elvin **14, 68**
Locke, Eddie **44**
Miles, Buddy **69**
Purdie, Bernard **77**
Rodríguez, Arsenio **87**
Williams, Tony **67**
Young, Lee **72**

Duke Ellington School of Arts
Cooper Cafritz, Peggy **43**

Duke Records
Bland, Bobby "Blue" **36**

Dunham Dance Company
Dunham, Katherine **4, 59**

DuSable Museum of African American History
Burroughs, Margaret Taylor 9
Wright, Antoinette 60

Dynegy
Scott, Milton 51

E Street Band
Clemons, Clarence 41

East Harlem School at Exodus House
Hageman, Hans 36
Hageman, Ivan 36

Ebonics
Cook, Toni 23

Ebony magazine
Bennett, Lerone, Jr. 5, 84
Branch, William Blackwell 39
Cullers, Vincent T. 49
Fuller, Hoyt 44
Johnson, Eunice W. 83
Johnson, John H. 3, 54
Massaquoi, Hans J. 30
Rice, Linda Johnson 9, 41
Sleet, Moneta, Jr. 5

Ebony Museum of African American History
See DuSable Museum of African American History

Economic Community of West African States (ECOWAS)
Sawyer, Amos 2

Economic Regulatory Administration
O'Leary, Hazel 6

Economics
Ake, Claude 30
Arthur, Owen 33
Boyd, T. B., III 6
Brimmer, Andrew F. 2, 48
Brown, Tony 3
Divine, Father 7
Fryer, Roland G. 56
Gibson, William F. 6
Hamer, Fannie Lou 6
Hampton, Henry 6
Juma, Calestous 57
Machel, Graca Simbine 16
Malveaux, Julianne 32, 70
Masire, Quett 5
Moyo, Dambisa 76
Pitta, Celso 17
Raines, Franklin Delano 14
Robinson, Randall 7, 46
Sowell, Thomas 2
Spriggs, William 67
Sullivan, Leon H. 3, 30
Van Peebles, Melvin 7
Wallace, Phyllis A. 9
Washington, Ebonya 79
Wharton, Clifton R., Jr. 7
White, Michael R. 5
Williams, Walter E. 4
Woodson, Robert L. 10

ECOWAS
See Economic Community of West African States

Editing
Abani, Chris 77
Aubert, Alvin 41
Bass, Charlotta Spears 40
Brown, Lloyd Louis 42
Curry, George E. 23
Delany, Martin R. 27
Dumas, Henry 41
Murphy, John H. 42
Schuyler, George Samuel 40

Edmonton Oilers hockey team
Fuhr, Grant 1, 49
Grier, Mike 43
Laraque, Georges 48

Educational Testing Service
Stone, Chuck 9

EEC
See European Economic Community

EEOC
See Equal Employment Opportunity Commission

Egyptology
Diop, Cheikh Anta 4

Elder Foundation
Elder, Lee 6

Electronic music
Craig, Carl 31, 71

Elektra Records
McPherson, David 32

Emerge (Savoy) magazine
Ames, Wilmer 27
Curry, George E. 23

Emmy awards
Allen, Debbie 13, 42
Amos, John 8, 62
Ashe, Arthur 1, 18
Barclay, Paris 37
Belafonte, Harry 4, 65
Bradley, Ed 2, 59
Branch, William Blackwell 39
Brown, James 22
Brown, Les 5
Browne, Roscoe Lee 66
Carter, Nell 39
Clayton, Xernona 3, 45
Cosby, Bill 7, 26, 59
Curtis-Hall, Vondie 17
De Shields, André 72
Dee, Ruby 8, 50, 68
Fisher, Gail 85
Foxx, Redd 2
Freeman, Al, Jr. 11
Goldberg, Whoopi 4, 33, 69
Gossett, Louis, Jr. 7
Guillaume, Robert 3, 48
Gumbel, Greg 8
Hunter-Gault, Charlayne 6, 31
Jones, James Earl 3, 49, 79
Kitt, Eartha 16, 75
La Salle, Eriq 12
Mabrey, Vicki 26
McQueen, Butterfly 6, 54
Moore, Shemar 21
Parks, Gordon 1, 35, 58
Pinkston, W. Randall 24

Quarles, Norma 25
Richards, Beah 30
Robinson, Max 3
Rock, Chris 3, 22, 66
Rolle, Esther 13, 21
St. John, Kristoff 25
Taylor, Billy 23, 92
Thigpen, Lynne 17, 41
Tyson, Cicely 7, 51
Uggams, Leslie 23
Washington, Hayma 86
Wayans, Damon 8, 41
Whack, Rita Coburn 36
Whitfield, Lynn 18
Williams, Montel 4, 57
Williams, Russell, II 70
Williams, Sherley Anne 25
Winfrey, Oprah 2, 15, 61
Woodard, Alfre 9

Emory University
Cole, Johnnetta B. 5, 43

Endocrinology
Elders, Joycelyn 6
Fennoy, Ilene 72

Energy
Cose, Ellis 5, 50
Lawal, Kase L. 45
O'Leary, Hazel 6

Engineering
Alexander, Archie Alphonso 14
Anderson, Charles Edward 37
Auguste, Donna 29
Benson, Angela 34
Boyd, Gwendolyn 49
Boykin, Otis 92
Burns, Ursula 60
Crosthwait, David 93
Dabiri, John 93
Emeagwali, Philip 30
Ericsson-Jackson, Aprille 28
Gibson, Kenneth Allen 6
Gourdine, Meredith 33
Grooms, Henry R(andall) 50
Hannah, Marc 10
Harris, Gary L. 87
Harris, Wesley L. 92
Henderson, Cornelius Langston 26
Henderson, Henry Fairfax, Jr. 89
Howard, Ayanna 65
Johnson, Anthony M. 92
Jones, Wayne 53
Laroche, Joseph Philippe Lemercier 85
Laryea, Thomas Davies, III 67
McCoy, Elijah 8
Miller, Warren F., Jr. 53
Mills, Joseph C. 51
O'Neal, Rodney 88
Pierre, Percy Anthony 46
Price, Richard 51
Rillieux, Norbert 92
Sigur, Wanda 44
Slaughter, John Brooks 53
Spencer, Michael G. 87
Trotter, Lloyd G. 56
West, James E. 87
Wilkens, J. Ernest, Jr. 43

Williams, O. S. 13

Entertainment promotion
Bowen, Ruth 83
Lewis, Butch 71

Entrepreneur
Barden, Donald H. 9, 20, 89
Chenault, Kenneth I. 5, 36
Downing, George T. 91
Fletcher, Alphonse, Jr. 16
Fudge, Ann (Marie) 11, 55
Gardner, Edward G. 45
Gaston, Arthur George 3, 38, 59
Gordy, Berry, Jr. 1
Graves, Earl G. 1, 35
Henderson, Henry Fairfax, Jr. 89
Herndon, Alonzo Franklin 89
Johnson, John H. 3, 54
Lewis, Reginald F. 6
McCann, Renetta 44
Otis, Clarence, Jr. 55
Parks, Henry Green, Jr. 89
Payton, Philip A., Jr. 88
Perry, Tyler 40, 54
Spaulding, Charles Clinton 9
Steward, David L. 36
Walker, Madame C. J. 7
Walker, Maggie Lena 17
Winfrey, Oprah 2, 15, 61
Woods, Granville T. 5

Environmental issues
Carter, Majora 77
Ellis-Lamkins, Phaedra 88
Eugene-Richard, Margie 63
Hill, Bonnie Guiton 20
Jackson, Lisa 77
Jones, Van 70
Miller-Travis, Vernice 64
Osborne, Na'taki 54
Saro-Wiwa, Kenule 39

Epic Records
McPherson, David 32
Mo', Keb' 36

Epidemiology
Fenton, Kevin 87
Gayle, Helene D. 3
Poindexter, Hildrus A. 87

Episcopalian
Burgess, John 46
Harris, Barbara 12
Jones, Absalom 52
Redding, Ann Holmes 77
Walker, John T. 50
Williams, Frederick (B.) 63

Equal Employment Opportunity Commission (EEOC)
Alexander, Clifford 26
Berrien, Jacqueline A. 93
Hill, Anita 5, 65
Lewis, Delano 7
Norton, Eleanor Holmes 7, 93
Thomas, Clarence 2, 39, 65
Wallace, Phyllis A. 9

Esalen Institute
Olatunji, Babatunde 36

ESPN
Jackson, Tom 70
Roberts, Robin 16, 54

Salters, Lisa **71**
Scott, Stuart **34**
Smith, Stephen A. **69**
Tirico, Mike **68**
Wilbon, Michael **68**

Essence magazine
Bandele, Asha **36**
Burt-Murray, Angela **59**
Channer, Colin **36**
De Veaux, Alexis **44**
Ebanks, Michelle **60**
Grant, Gwendolyn Goldsby **28**
Greenwood, Monique **38**
Lewis, Edward T. **21**
Parks, Gordon **1, 35, 58**
Smith, Clarence O. **21**
Taylor, Susan L. **10, 86**
Wesley, Valerie Wilson **18**

Essence Award
Broadbent, Hydeia **36**
McMurray, Georgia L. **36**

Ethiopian government
Haile Selassie **7**
Meles Zenawi **3**
Mengistu, Haile Mariam **65**

Etiquette
Bates, Karen Grigsby **40**

Eugene O'Neill Theater
Richards, Lloyd **2**

European Economic Community (EEC)
Diouf, Abdou **3**

Event planning
Bailey, Preston **64**
Williams, Lindsey **75**

Executive Leadership Council
Jackson, Mannie **14**

Exiled heads of state
Amin, Idi **42**
Aristide, Jean-Bertrand **6, 45**
Mengistu, Haile Mariam **65**
Mobutu Sese Seko **1, 56**

Exploration
Henson, Matthew **2**

Famine relief
See World hunger

FAN
See Forces Armées du Nord (Chad)

Fannie Mae
Jackson, Maynard **2, 41**
Raines, Franklin Delano **14**

Fashion
Aberra, Amsale **67**
Biya, Chantal **89**
Boateng, Ozwald **35**
Boyd, Suzanne **52**
Chanticleer, Raven **91**
Darego, Agbani **52**
Delice, Ronald **48**
Delice, Rony **48**
Evans, Etu **55**
Fine, Sam **60**

Gaskins, Eric **64**
Givhan, Robin Deneen **72**
Hall, Kevan **61**
Hendy, Francis **47**
Keckley, Elizabeth **90**
Knowles, Tina **61**
Lars, Byron **32**
Luna, Donyale **88**
Malone, Maurice **32**
McGrath, Pat **72**
Reese, Tracy **54**
Simmons, Kimora Lee **51, 83**
Smaltz, Audrey **12**
Steele, Lawrence **28**
Stoney, Michael **50**
Sy, Oumou **65**
Talley, André Leon **56**
White, Jessica **83**

Fashion Institute of Technology (FIT)
Brown, Joyce F. **25**

FCC
See Federal Communications Commission

Federal Bureau of Investigation (FBI)
Gibson, Johnnie Mae **23**
Harvard, Beverly **11**

Federal Communications Commission (FCC)
Barrett, Andrew C. **12**
Clyburn, Mignon **78**
Hughes, Cathy **27**
Kennard, William Earl **18**
Powell, Michael **32**
Russell-McCloud, Patricia A. **17**

Federal Court of Canada
Isaac, Julius **34**

Federal Energy Administration
O'Leary, Hazel **6**

Federal Reserve Bank
Brimmer, Andrew F. **2, 48**
Ferguson, Roger W. **25**
Layton, William **87**

Federation of Nigeria
Sowande, Fela **39**

Feed the Hungry program
Williams, Hosea Lorenzo **15, 31**

Fellowship of Reconciliation (FOR)
Farmer, James **2, 64**
Rustin, Bayard **4**

Fencing
Westbrook, Peter **20**

Fiction
Adams, Jenoyne **60**
Adichie, Chimamanda Ngozi **64**
Alexander, Margaret Walker **22**
Ali, Mohammed Naseehu **60**
Amadi, Elechi **40**
Anthony, Michael **29**
Ansa, Tina McElroy **14**
Armah, Ayi Kwei **49**
Ba, Mariama **30**

Baiocchi, Regina Harris **41**
Baisden, Michael **25, 66**
Ballard, Allen Butler, Jr. **40**
Bandele, Biyi **68**
Barrett, Lindsay **43**
Bates, Karen Grigsby **40**
Beckham, Barry **41**
Benson, Angela **34**
Berry, James **41**
Bland, Eleanor Taylor **39**
Bolden, Tonya **32**
Bradley, David Henry, Jr. **39**
Brand, Dionne **32**
Briscoe, Connie **15**
Brown, Cecil M. **46**
Brown, Lloyd Louis **42**
Bunkley, Anita Richmond **39**
Butler, Octavia **8, 43, 58**
Campbell, Bebe Moore **6, 24, 59**
Cartiér, Xam Wilson **41**
Chase-Riboud, Barbara **20, 46**
Cheney-Coker, Syl **43**
Chesnutt, Charles **29**
Clarke, Austin **32**
Cleage, Pearl **17, 64**
Cliff, Michelle **42**
Cooper, J. California **12, 85**
Creagh, Milton **27**
Curtis, Christopher Paul **26**
Danticat, Edwidge **15, 68**
Dathorne, O. R. **52**
Demby, William **51**
Diop, Birago **53**
Draper, Sharon Mills **16, 43**
Due, Tananarive **30**
Dumas, Henry **41**
Dunbar-Nelson, Alice Ruth Moore **44**
Duplechan, Larry **55**
Emecheta, Buchi **30**
Evans, Diana **72**
Everett, Percival **93**
Fair, Ronald L. **47**
Fales-Hill, Susan **88**
Farah, Nuruddin **27**
Farley, Christopher John **54**
Files, Lolita **35**
Ford, Nick Aaron **44**
Ford, Wallace **58**
Forrest, Leon **44**
Gomez, Jewelle **30**
Gray, Darius **69**
Greenlee, Sam **48**
Harper, Rachel M. **92**
Harris, E. Lynn **12, 33**
Haywood, Gar Anthony **43**
Hercules, Frank **44**
Hill, Donna **32**
Holton, Hugh, Jr. **39**
Horne, Frank **44**
Jackson, Sheneska **18**
Jakes, Thomas "T. D." **17, 43**
James, Marlon **85**
Jasper, Kenji **39**
Jenkins, Beverly **14**
Johnson, Georgia Douglas **41**
Johnson, Mat **31**
Jones, Edward P. **43, 67**
Jones, Gayl **37**
Kamau, Kwadwo Agymah **28**
Kay, Jackie **37**
Kayira, Legson **40**
Keene, John **73**

Kendrick, Erika **57**
Killens, John O. **54**
Laferriere, Dany **33**
LaGuma, Alex **30**
Lamming, George **35**
Lattany, Kristin Hunter **88**
Locke, Attica **85**
Machado de Assis **74**
Marechera, Dambudzo **39**
Markham, E. A. **37**
Mason, Felicia **31**
Mbaye, Mariétou **31**
McCrary Anthony, Crystal **70**
McFadden, Bernice L. **39**
McKinney-Whetstone, Diane **27**
McMillan, Terry **4, 17, 53**
Memmi, Albert **37**
Mengestu, Dinaw **66**
Monroe, Mary **35**
Mosley, Walter **5, 25, 68**
Mossell, Gertrude Bustill **40**
Mphalele, Es'kia **40**
Mwangi, Meja **40**
Naylor, Gloria **10, 42**
Ngugi wa Thiong'o **29, 61**
Nkosi, Lewis **46**
Nugent, Richard Bruce **39**
Nunez, Elizabeth **62**
Okara, Gabriel **37**
Ojikutu, Bayo **66**
Packer, Z. Z. **64**
Peters, Lenrie **43**
Philip, Marlene Nourbese **32**
Polite, Carlene Hatcher **82**
Randall, Alice **38**
Ridley, John **69**
Roby, Kimberla Lawson **86**
Schuyler, George Samuel **40**
Senior, Olive **37**
Senna, Danzy **93**
Smith, Danyel **40**
Smith, Zadie **51**
Southgate, Martha **58**
Tate, Eleanora E. **20, 55**
Taylor, Mildred D. **26**
Teasley, Lisa **92**
Thomas, Michael **69**
Thomas-Graham, Pamela **29**
Tutuola, Amos **30**
Vera, Yvonne **32**
Verdelle, A. J. **26**
Walker, Margaret **29**
Weaver, Afaa Michael **37**
Whitehead, Colson **77**
Whitfield, Van **34**
Williams, Sherley Anne **25**
Williams, Stanley "Tookie" **29, 57**
Woods, Teri **69**
Yarbrough, Camille **40**
Young, Al **82**
Youngblood, Shay **32**
Zane **71**

Figure skating
Bonaly, Surya **7**
Bonheur, Yannick **84**
James, Vanessa **84**
Thomas, Debi **26**
Vanessa James and Yannick Bonheur **84**

Film criticism
Mitchell, Elvis **67**

Film direction/video direction

Akomfrah, John 37
Allain, Stephanie 49
Barclay, Paris 37
Blackwood, Maureen 37
Burnett, Charles 16, 68
Byrd, Robert 11
Cortez, Jayne 43
Curtis-Hall, Vondie 17
Daniels, Lee 36, 76
Dash, Julie 4
Davis, Ossie 5, 50
Dickerson, Ernest 6, 17
Duke, Bill 3
Franklin, Carl 11
Freeman, Al, Jr. 11
Fuqua, Antoine 35
Gerima, Haile 38, 80
Gray, Darius 69
Gray, F. Gary 14, 49
Greaves, William 38
Hamilton, Tanya 93
Harris, Leslie 6
Hayes, Teddy 40
Henriques, Julian 37
Hines, Gregory 1, 42
Hudlin, Reginald 9, 86
Hudlin, Warrington 9
Hughes, Albert 7
Hughes, Allen 7
Hurt, Byron 61
Jackson, George 19
Julien, Isaac 3
Lane, Charles 3
Lee, Malcolm D. 75
Lee, Spike 5, 19, 86
Lemmons, Kasi 20
Lewis, Samella 25
Martin, Darnell 43, 78
McQueen, Steve 84
Micheaux, Oscar 7
Morton, Joe 18
Moses, Gilbert 12
Moss, Carlton 17
Mwangi, Meja 40
Onwurah, Ngozi 38
Peck, Raoul 32
Perry, Tyler 40, 54
Pinkett Smith, Jada 10, 41
Poitier, Sidney 11, 36
Prince-Bythewood, Gina 31, 77
Riggs, Marlon 5, 44
Roberts, Darryl 70
St. Jacques, Raymond 8
Schultz, Michael A. 6
Sembène, Ousmane 13, 62
Singleton, John 2, 30
Smith, Roger Guenveur 12
Souleymane, Mahamane 78
Tillman, George, Jr. 20
Townsend, Robert 4, 23
Tyler, Aisha N. 36
Underwood, Blair 7, 27, 76
Van Peebles, Mario 2, 51
Van Peebles, Melvin 7
Wallace, William 75
Ward, Douglas Turner 42
Wayans, Damon 8, 41
Wayans, Keenen Ivory 18
Whitaker, Forest 2, 49, 67

Film production

Allain, Stephanie 49
Chase, Debra Martin 49
Daniels, Lee 36, 76
Gerima, Haile 38, 80
Greaves, William 38
Julian, Hubert 90
Morrison, Vanessa 84
Onwurah, Ngozi 38
Packer, Will 71
Patton, Paula 62
Randall, Alice 38
Robinson, Matt 69
Stewart, Nzingha 89
Tyler, Aisha N. 36
Van Lierop, Robert 53
Ward, Douglas Turner 42
Wayans, Damien 78
Whitaker, Forest 2, 49, 67
Williams, Marco 53
Williams, Russell, II 70
Williamson, Fred 67

Film scores

Blanchard, Terence 43
Crouch, Andraé 27
Hancock, Herbie 20, 67
Jones, Quincy 8, 30
Prince 18, 65
RZA 80

Finance

Adams, Eula L. 39
Banks, Jeffrey 17
Bell, James A. 50
Boston, Kelvin E. 25
Brown, Eddie C. 35
Bryant, John 26
Chapman, Nathan A., Jr. 21
Doley, Harold, Jr. 26
Epperson, Sharon 54
Ferguson, Roger W. 25
Fletcher, Alphonse, Jr. 16
Funderburg, I. Owen 38
Gaines, Brenda 41
Griffith, Mark Winston 8
Hall, Alvin D. 86
Harris, Carla A. 67
Hobson, Mellody 40
Jones, Thomas W. 41
Lawless, Theodore K. 8
Lewis, William M., Jr. 40
Louis, Errol T. 8
Marshall, Bella 22
Moyo, Dambisa 76
Nash, Shannon King 84
O'Neal, Stanley 38, 67
Rogers, John W., Jr. 5, 52
Ross, Charles 27
Shank, Suzanne F. 77
Taylor, Ephren W., II 61
Thompson, William C. 35

Firefighters

Barlow, Roosevelt 49
Bell, Michael 40

First Data Corporation

Adams, Eula L. 39

Fisk University

Harvey, William R. 42
Imes, Elmer Samuel 39
Johnson, Charles S. 12

Phillips, Teresa L. 42
Smith, John L. 22

Fitness

Richardson, Donna 39
Smith, Ian 62

Florida A & M University

Ammons, James H. 81
Foster, William P. 88
Gaither, Alonzo Smith (Jake) 14
Humphries, Frederick 20

Florida Marlins baseball team

Mariner, Jonathan 41

Florida state government

Brown, Corrine 24, 90
Meek, Carrie 6, 36
Meek, Kendrick 41, 89
Menard, John Willis 90
Tribble, Israel, Jr. 8
Wilson, Frederica 92

Florida State Supreme Court

Quince, Peggy A. 69

Flute

Laws, Hubert 90

Folk music

Bailey, DeFord 33
Broonzy, Big Bill 82
Chapman, Tracy 26
Charlemagne, Manno 11
Cuney, William Waring 44
Davis, Gary 41
Dawson, William Levi 39
Handy, W. C. 8
Harper, Ben 34, 62
House, Son 8
Jenkins, Ella 15
Johnson, James Weldon 5
Lester, Julius 9
Love, Laura 50
Odetta 37, 74
Reagon, Toshi 76
Southern, Eileen 56
Spence, Joseph 49
White, Josh 86
Williams, Denise 40

Food products

Amos, Wally 9
Briggs, Curtis 84
Parks, Henry Green, Jr. 89

Football

Buchanan, Ray 32
Carter, Cris 21
Clemons, Michael "Pinball" 64
Davis, Ernie 48
Dorrell, Karl 52
Dungy, Tony 17, 42, 59
Gaither, Alonzo Smith (Jake) 14
Gill, Turner 83
Gorden, W. C. 71
Grier, Roosevelt 13
Jones, Ed "Too Tall" 46
Keith, Floyd A. 61
Lanier, Willie 33
Lewis, Marvin 51, 87
Lewis, William Henry 89
McNabb, Donovan 29
Parker, Jim 64

Perry, Lowell 30
Pollard, Fritz 53
Prince, Ron 64
Robinson, Eddie G. 10, 61
Shannon, Randy 82
Simmons, Bob 29
Smith, Lovie 66
Watts, J. C., Jr. 14, 38
Weathers, Carl 10
Willingham, Tyrone 43
Willis, Bill 68
Woodson, Rod 79

Football Hall of Fame, professional

Allen, Marcus 20
Barney, Lem 26
Briscoe, Marlin 37
Brown, Jim 11
Dickerson, Eric 27
Faulk, Marshall 35
Green, Darrell 39, 74
Greene, Joe 10
Hayes, Bob 77
Irvin, Michael 64
Jackson, Rickey 88
Jones, Deacon 92
Lane, Dick 92
Lanier, Willie 33
Little, Floyd 86
Little, Larry 90
Lofton, James 42
Lott, Ronnie 9
Matson, Ollie 93
McDaniel, Randall Cornell 81
Monk, Art 38, 73
Moon, Warren 8, 66
Motley, Marion 26
Newsome, Ozzie 26
Page, Alan (Cedric) 7
Parker, Jim 64
Payton, Walter (Jerry) 11, 25
Pollard, Fritz 53
Randle, John 87
Rice, Jerry 5, 55, 89
Sanders, Barry 1, 53
Sanders, Deion 4, 31
Sayers, Gale 28
Shell, Art 1, 66
Simpson, O. J. 15
Singletary, Mike 4, 76
Smith, Bruce 80
Smith, Emmitt 7, 87
Swann, Lynn 28
Taylor, Lawrence 25
Thomas, Derrick 25
Thomas, Emmitt 71
Thomas, Thurman 75
Tunnell, Emlen 54
Upshaw, Gene 18, 47, 72
White, Reggie 6, 50
Willis, Bill 68
Winslow, Kellen 83
Woodson, Rod 79
Wright, Rayfield 70

FOR

See Fellowship of Reconciliation

Forces Armées du Nord (Chad; FAN)

Déby, Idriss 30
Habré, Hissène 6

Ford Foundation
Franklin, Robert M. 13
Thomas, Franklin A. 5, 49

Ford Motor Company
Cherry, Deron 40
Dawson, Matel, Jr. 39
Goldsberry, Ronald 18
Hazel, Darryl B. 50
McMillan, Rosalynn A. 36

Fordham University
Blair, Paul 36
McMurray, Georgia L. 36

Foreign investment
Amoudi, Mohammed al- 88

Foreign policy
Bunche, Ralph J. 5
Frazer, Jendayi 68
Rice, Condoleezza 3, 28, 72
Robinson, Randall 7, 46

Forensic science
Griffin, Bessie Blout 43

Forest Club
Wilson, Sunnie 7, 55

Foster care
Hale, Clara 16
Hale, Lorraine 8

Fox Broadcasting Company
Corbi, Lana 42
McFarland, Roland 49
Oliver, Pam 54
Strahan, Michael 35, 81

Franklin H. Williams Caribbean Cultural Center African Diaspora Institute
Vega, Marta Moreno 61

Freddie Mac
Baker, Maxine 28

Frederick Douglass Caring Award
Broadbent, Hydeia 36

French West Africa
Camara, Moussa Dadis 76
Diouf, Abdou 3
Ndiaye, Iba 74

Funeral homes
March, William Carrington 56

Funk music
Ayers, Roy 16
Brown, James 15, 60
Clinton, George 9, 93
Collins, Bootsy 31
Collins, Lyn 53
Love, Laura 50
Monáe, Janelle 86
Parker, Maceo 72
Parker, Ray, Jr. 85
Purdie, Bernard 77
Richie, Lionel 27, 65
Shider, Garry 87
Stone, Sly 85

Watson, Johnny "Guitar" 18

Fusion
Davis, Miles 4
Jones, Quincy 8, 30
Williams, Tony 67

Gabonese government
Bongo, Ali Ben 80
Bongo, Omar 1, 79

Gambling
Ivey, Phil 72

Gangs
Taylor, Bo 72
Shakur, Yusef 85
Williams, Stanley "Tookie" 29, 57

Gary Post-Tribune
Ross, Don 27

Gassaway, Crosson, Turner & Parsons
Parsons, James 14

Gay and lesbian activism
De Veaux, Alexis 44

Gay Men of Color Consortium
Wilson, Phill 9

Genealogy
Allen, Lucy 85
Blockson, Charles L. 42
Dash, Julie 4
Haley, Alex 4

General Hospital TV series
Cash, Rosalind 28

General Motors Corporation
O'Neal, Stanley 38, 67
Roberts, Roy S. 14
Welburn, Edward T. 50

Genetech
Potter, Myrtle 40

Genetics
Dunston, Georgia Mae 48
Harris, Mary Styles 31
Kittles, Rick 51
Olopade, Olufunmilayo Falusi 58

Geometric symbolism
Douglas, Aaron 7

Geophysics
Person, Waverly 9, 51

George Foster Peabody Broadcasting Award
Bradley, Ed 2, 59
Hunter-Gault, Charlayne 6, 31
Mac, Bernie 29, 61, 72
Shaw, Bernard 2

George Mason University
Dunn, Jerry 27
Wilkins, Roger 2, 84

George Washington University
Carter, Joye Maureen 41

Georgia state government
Baker, Thurbert 22
Bishop, Sanford D., Jr. 24

Bond, Julian 2, 35
Brooks, Tyrone 59
Johnson, Hank, Jr. 80
Johnson, Leroy R. 89
Majette, Denise 41
McKinney, Cynthia 11, 52, 74
Reed, Kasim 82
Scott, David 41
Smyre, Calvin 90
Williams, Hosea Lorenzo 15, 31

Georgia State Supreme Court
Benham, Robert 78
Melton, Harold D. 79
Sears, Leah Ward 5, 79

Ghanaian government
Atta Mills, John 75
Awoonor, Kofi 37
Bartels, Peggielene 80
Kufuor, John Agyekum 54, 82
Nkrumah, Kwame 3
Rawlings, Jerry 9

Girl Scouts of the USA
Thompson, Cynthia Bramlett 50

Goddard Space Flight Center
Ericsson-Jackson, Aprille 28

Golden Globe awards
Allen, Debbie 13, 42
Bassett, Angela 6, 23, 62
Cara, Irene 77
Carroll, Diahann 9
Fisher, Gail 85
Freeman, Morgan 2, 20, 62
Ross, Diana 8, 27
Taylor, Regina 9, 46

Golden Pen award
McFadden, Bernice L. 39

Golden State Warriors basketball team
Parish, Robert 43
Sprewell, Latrell 23

Golf
Bramlett, Joseph 91
Elder, Lee 6
Gibson, Althea 8, 43
Gregory, Ann 63
Jackson, Fred James 25
Peete, Calvin 11
Powell, William J. 82
Richmond, Mitch 19
Shippen, John 43
Sifford, Charlie 4, 49
Spiller, Bill 64
Woods, Tiger 14, 31, 81

Goodwill ambassador
Terry, Clark 39

Gospel music
Adams, Oleta 18
Adams, Yolanda 17, 67
Armstrong, Vanessa Bell 24
Baylor Helen 36
Bonds, Margaret 39
Bradley, J. Robert 65
Caesar, Shirley 19
Cage, Byron 53
Clark, Mattie Moss 61
Clark-Cole, Dorinda 66

Clark-Sheard, Karen 22
Cleveland, James 19
Christie, Angella 36
Cooke, Sam 17
Crouch, Andraé 27
Davis, Gary 41
Dorsey, Thomas 15
Fortune, James 92
Franklin, Aretha 11, 44
Franklin, Kirk 15, 49
Gaynor, Gloria 71
Green, Al 13, 47, 74
Haddon, Dietrick 55
Hammond, Fred 23
Hawkins, Tramaine 16
Hawkins, Walter 87
Higginsen, Vy 65
Houghton, Israel 92
Houston, Cissy 20, 83
Jackson, Mahalia 5
Jakes, Thomas "T. D." 17, 43
Jeter, Claude 75
Jones, Bobby 20
Kee, John P. 43
Kenoly, Ron 45
Killings, Debra 57
Knight, Gladys 16, 66
Knight, Marie 80
Lassiter, Roy 24
Little Richard 15
Majors, Jeff 41
Mann, Tamela 92
Marrow, Queen Esther 24
Martin, Roberta 58
Mary Mary 34, 92
Mayfield, Curtis 2, 43
McClendon, Lisa 61
McClurkin, Donnie 25
Mills, Stephanie 36
Monica 21
Moss, J 64
Mullen, Nicole C. 45
Peoples, Dottie 22
Phipps, Wintley 59
Preston, Billy 39, 59
Reagon, Bernice Johnson 7
Reese, Della 6, 20
Sapp, Marvin 74
Scott, George 55
Sheard, Kierra "Kiki" 61
Stampley, Micah 54
Staples, Mavis 50, 88
Staples, "Pops" 32
Staton, Candi 27
Steinberg, Martha Jean "The Queen" 28
Tharpe, Rosetta 65
Tonex 54
Tribbett, Tye 81
Walker, Albertina 10, 58, 89
Walker, Hezekiah 34
Washington, Dinah 22
Whalum, Kirk 37, 64
Williams, Deniece 36
Williams, Michelle 73
Wilson, Natalie 38
Winans, Angie 36
Winans, BeBe 14
Winans, CeCe 14, 43
Winans, David 77
Winans, Debbie 36
Winans, Marvin L. 17
Winans, Ronald 54

Winans, Vickie **24**
Wright, Timothy **74**

Graffiti art
White, Dondi **34**

Grambling State University
Favors, Steve **23**

Grammy awards
Adams, Oleta **18**
Adderley, Nat **29**
Babyface **10**, **31**, **82**
Badu, Erykah **22**
Battle, Kathleen **70**
Belafonte, Harry **4**, **65**
Beyoncé **39**, **70**
Blade, Brian **88**
Blige, Mary J. **20**, **34**, **60**
Brandy **14**, **34**, **72**
Caesar, Shirley **19**
Cara, Irene **77**
Chapman, Tracy **26**
Cleveland, James **19**
Cole, Natalie **17**, **60**, **84**
Combs, Sean **17**, **43**, **92**
Cosby, Bill **7**, **26**, **59**
Cray, Robert **30**
Crouch, Andraé **27**
Davis, Miles **4**
Dee, Ruby **8**, **50**, **68**
Ellington, Duke **5**
Estelle **75**
Ferrer, Ibrahim **41**
Fitzgerald, Ella **8**
Forté, John **74**
Franklin, Aretha **11**, **44**
Gamble, Kenny **85**
Gaye, Marvin **2**
Gaynor, Gloria **36**
Gibson, Tyrese **27**, **62**
Glover, Corey **34**
Goldberg, Whoopi **4**, **33**, **69**
Gray, Macy **29**
Guy, Buddy **31**
Hathaway, Donny **18**
Hawkins, Tramaine **16**
Hawkins, Walter **87**
Hayes, Isaac **20**, **58**, **73**
Hill, Lauryn **20**, **53**
Holland-Dozier-Holland **36**
Hooker, John Lee **30**
Houston, Cissy **20**, **83**
Houston, Whitney **7**, **28**, **83**
Hubbard, Freddie **75**
Isley, Ronald **25**, **56**
Jackson, Janet **6**, **30**, **68**
Jackson, Michael **19**, **53**, **76**
James, Etta **13**, **52**
Jay-Z **27**, **69**
Jean, Wyclef **20**, **86**
Jimmy Jam **13**
Jones, Bobby **20**
Jones, Quincy **8**, **30**
Kee, John P. **43**
Kelly, R. **18**, **44**, **71**
Keys, Alicia **32**, **68**
Knight, Gladys **16**, **66**
Knuckles, Frankie **42**
LaBelle, Patti **13**, **30**
Legend, John **67**
Lewis, Terry **13**
Lopes, Lisa "Left Eye" **36**
Mahal, Taj **39**

Maitreya, Sananda **85**
Makeba, Miriam **2**, **50**, **74**
Marley, Ziggy **41**
Marsalis, Branford **34**
M.C. Hammer **20**, **80**
Method Man **81**
Mills, Stephanie **36**
Mo', Keb' **36**
Moore, LeRoi **72**
Murphy, Eddie **4**, **20**, **61**
Norman, Jessye **5**
Olatunji, Babatunde **36**
Perkins, Pinetop **70**
Poitier, Sidney **11**, **36**
Price, Leontyne **1**
Pride, Charley **26**
Prince **18**, **65**
Queen Latifah **1**, **16**, **58**
?uestlove **74**
Reagon, Bernice Johnson **7**
Redding, Otis **16**
Reid, Vernon **34**
Richie, Lionel **27**, **65**
Robinson, Smokey **3**, **49**
Ross, Isaiah "Doc" **40**
Rucker, Darius **34**, **74**
Sade **15**, **92**
Scott, Jill **29**, **83**
Seal **14**, **75**
Shaggy **31**
Shorter, Wayne **75**
Slash **75**
Smith, Will **8**, **18**
Summer, Donna **25**
Turner, Tina **6**, **27**
Walker, Hezekiah **34**
Warwick, Dionne **18**
West, Kanye **52**, **93**
White, Barry **13**, **41**
White, Maurice **29**
Whitfield, Norman **73**
Williams, Deniece **36**
Williams, Joe **5**, **25**
Williams, Michelle **73**
Wilson, Nancy **10**
Winans, CeCe **14**, **43**
Winans, Marvin L. **17**
Wonder, Stevie **11**, **53**

Grand Ole Opry
Bailey, DeFord **33**

Graphic novels
Anderson, Ho Che **54**
McDuffie, Dwayne **62**
Tooks, Lance **62**

Green Bay Packers football team
Brooks, Aaron **33**
Butler, Leroy, III **17**
Howard, Desmond **16**, **58**
Lofton, James **42**
Sharper, Darren **32**
White, Reggie **6**, **50**

Green Belt Movement
Maathai, Wangari **43**

Green Party
Clemente, Rosa **74**
McKinney, Cynthia **11**, **52**, **74**

Grenadian government
Bishop, Maurice **39**
Gairy, Eric Matthew **83**

Mitchell, Keith **82**

Groupe de Recherche Chorégraphique de
Dove, Ulysses **5**

Guardian
Trotter, Monroe **9**

Guggenheim fellowship
Pope.L, William **72**
Rollins, Sonny **37**
Taylor, Cecil **70**
Wilson, Ellis **39**

Guinea government
Camara, Moussa Dadis **76**
Conté, Lansana **7**, **76**
Touré, Sekou **6**

Guinea-Bissau government
Sanhá Malam Bacai **84**
Vieira, João **14**, **84**

Guitar
Ade, King Sunny **41**
Barker, Danny **32**
Barnes, Roosevelt "Booba" **33**
Bibb, Eric **49**
Brown, Clarence Gatemouth **59**
Butler, Jonathan **28**
Burns, Eddie **44**
Burnside, R. L. **56**
Caymmi, Dorival **72**
Collins, Bootsy **31**
Cray, Robert **30**
Davis, Gary **41**
Diddley, Bo **39**, **72**
Estes, Sleepy John **33**
Fuller, Blind Boy **86**
Green, Grant **56**
Guy, Buddy **31**
Harris, Corey **39**, **73**
Hemphill, Jessie Mae **33**, **59**
Hendrix, Jimi **10**
House, Son **8**
Hooker, John Lee **30**
Hopkins, Lightnin' **83**
Howlin' Wolf **9**
Johnson, Robert **2**
Jordan, Ronny **26**
Killings, Debra **57**
King, B. B. **7**
King, Freddie **92**
Klugh, Earl **59**
Kolosoy, Wendo **73**
Kravitz, Lenny **10**, **34**
Leadbelly **82**
Lipscomb, Mance **49**
Long, Huey **79**
Loueke, Lionel **88**
Marley, Bob **5**
Mayfield, Curtis **2**, **43**
McTell, Blind Willie **89**
Montgomery, Wes **88**
Ndegeocello, Meshell **15**, **83**
Ongala, Remmy **9**, **91**
Parker, Ray, Jr. **85**
Pena, Paul **58**
Ranglin, Ernest **78**
Rodríguez, Arsenio **87**
Rush, Bobby **78**
Seals, Son **56**
Shider, Garry **87**
Slash **75**

Spence, Joseph **49**
Ulmer, James **79**
Watson, Johnny "Guitar" **18**
White, Josh **86**

Gulf War
Powell, Colin **1**, **28**, **75**
Shaw, Bernard **2**
Von Lipsey, Roderick K. **11**

Gurdjieff Institute
Toomer, Jean **6**

Guyanese government
Burnham, Forbes **66**

Gymnastics
Dawes, Dominique **11**
Hilliard, Wendy **53**
White, Jesse **22**, **75**

Hair care
Cottrell, Comer **11**
Fuller, S. B. **13**
Gardner, Edward G. **45**
Gibson, Ted **66**
Johnson, George E. **29**
Johnson, William **91**
Joyner, Marjorie Stewart **26**
Malone, Annie **13**
Roche, Joyce M. **17**
Walker, Madame C. J. **7**

Haitian government
Aristide, Jean-Bertrand **6**, **45**
Manigat, Mirlande **90**
Martelly, Michel **90**
Pascal-Trouillot, Ertha **3**
Pierre-Louis, Michèle **75**
Préval, René **87**

Hale House
Hale, Clara **16**
Hale, Lorraine **8**

Hallmark Channel
Corbi, Lana **42**

Hampton University
Harvey, William R. **42**

Handy Award
Hunter, Alberta **42**

Harlem Artist Guild
Nugent, Richard Bruce **39**
Wilson, Ellis **39**

Harlem Globetrotters
Chamberlain, Wilt **18**, **47**
Haynes, Marques **22**
Jackson, Mannie **14**
Woodard, Lynette **67**

Harlem Renaissance
Alexander, Margaret Walker **22**
Bennett, Gwendolyn B. **59**
Christian, Barbara T. **44**
Crichlow, Ernest **75**
Cullen, Countee **8**
Cuney, William Waring **44**
Dandridge, Raymond Garfield **45**
Davis, Arthur P. **41**
Delaney, Beauford **19**
Ellington, Duke **5**
Fauset, Jessie **7**
Fisher, Rudolph **17**

Frazier, E. Franklin 10
Horne, Frank 44
Hughes, Langston 4
Hurston, Zora Neale 3
Imes, Elmer Samuel 39
Johnson, Georgia Douglas 41
Johnson, James Weldon 5
Johnson, William Henry 3
Larsen, Nella 10
Locke, Alain 10
McKay, Claude 6
Mills, Florence 22
Morton, Ferdinand Q. 90
Nail, John E. 92
Nugent, Richard Bruce 39
Payton, Philip A., Jr. 88
Petry, Ann 19
Thurman, Wallace 16
Toomer, Jean 6
VanDerZee, James 6
West, Dorothy 12, 54
Wilson, Ellis 39

Harlem Writers Guild
Guy, Rosa 5
Killens, John O. 54
Wesley, Valerie Wilson 18

Harlem Youth Opportunities Unlimited (HARYOU)
Clark, Kenneth B. 5, 52

Harmonica
Bailey, DeFord 33
Barnes, Roosevelt "Booba" 33
Burns, Eddie 44
Howlin' Wolf 9
Neal, Raful 44
Ross, Isaiah "Doc" 40
Terry, Sonny 88

Harness racing
Minor, DeWayne 32

Harp
Coltrane, Alice 70
Majors, Jeff 41

Harvard Law School
Bell, Derrick 6
Dickerson, Debra J. 60
Ogletree, Charles, Jr. 12, 47
Wilkins, David 77

Harvard University
Amaker, Tommy 62
Epps, Archie C., III 45
Ferguson, Ronald F. 75
Gomes, Peter J. 15, 93
Hammonds, Evelynn 69
Huggins, Nathan Irvin 52
Loury, Glenn 36
Poindexter, Hildrus A. 87

HARYOU
See Harlem Youth Opportunities Unlimited

Hazelitt Award for Excellence in Arts
Bradley, David Henry, Jr. 39

Head Start
Edelman, Marian Wright 5, 42
Taylor, Helen 30

Health care reform
Adams-Campbell, Lucille L. 60
Berrysmith, Don Reginald 49
Brown, Jesse 6, 41
Carroll, L. Natalie 44
Cole, Lorraine 48
Cooper, Edward S. 6
Dirie, Waris 56
Gibson, Kenneth A. 6
Hughes, Dora 88
Hughes, Ebony 57
Kintaudi, Leon 62
Lavizzo-Mourey, Risa 48
Norman, Pat 10
Potter, Myrtle 40
Richardson, Rupert 67
Satcher, David 7, 57
Tuckson, Reed V. 71
Vaughn, Viola 70
Williams, Daniel Hale 2
Williams, David Rudyard 50

Heart disease
Cooper, Edward S. 6
Grant, Augustus O. 71

Heidelberg Project
Guyton, Tyree 9

Heisman Trophy
Allen, Marcus 20
Bush, Reggie 59, 88
Davis, Ernie 48
George, Eddie 80
Howard, Desmond 16, 58
Sanders, Barry 1, 53
Simpson, O. J. 15
Walker, Herschel 1, 69
Ware, Andre 37
Williams, Ricky 85

Heritage Network, The
Mercado-Valdes, Frank 43

Heroism
Autrey, Wesley 68
Delaney, Joe 76

HEW
See U.S. Department of Health, Education, and Welfare

HHS
See U.S. Department of Health and Human Services

Hip-hop music
Akon 68
apl.de.ap 84
Ashanti 37
Benjamin, Andre 45
Blackman, Toni 86
B.o.B. 91
Combs, Sean 17, 43, 92
Elliott, Missy 31, 90
Estelle 75
Fabolous 93
Fat Boys 92
Fiasco, Lupe 64
Forté, John 74
Franti, Michael 93
Fresh, Doug E. 93
Garrett, Sean 57
Ghostface Killah 90
Guru 84

Jean, Wyclef 20, 86
Jennings, Lyfe 56, 69
Kid Cudi 83
Kitwana, Bakari 86
K-Swift 73
Kweli, Talib 93
Lil Wayne 66, 84
Madlib 88
Mane, Gucci 91
Method Man 81
Minaj, Nicki 86
Nelly 32, 90
Nate Dogg 92
Patton, Antwan 45
Peterson, James 81
?uestlove 74
Rascal, Dizzee 82
Redman 81
Run 31, 73
Sermon, Erick 81
Slick Rick 93
Smith, Danyel 40
Wale 92
West, Kanye 52, 93
will.i.am 64
Williams, Pharrell 47, 82

Hip-hop theater
Power, Will 83

Historians
Ballard, Allen Butler, Jr. 40
Berry, Mary Frances 7
Blassingame, John Wesley 40
Blockson, Charles L. 42
Bogle, Donald 34
Chase-Riboud, Barbara 20, 46
Cooper, Afua 53
Cooper, Anna Julia 20
Cruse, Harold 54
Diop, Cheikh Anta 4
Dodson, Howard, Jr. 7, 52
Du Bois, W. E. B. 3
Fisher, Miles Mark 91
Franklin, John Hope 5, 77
Gates, Henry Louis, Jr. 3, 38, 67
Giddings, Paula 11
Gill, Gerald 69
Gordon-Reed, Annette 74
Hammonds, Evelynn 69
Hansberry, William Leo 11
Harkless, Necia Desiree 19
Harris, Jessica B. 91
Hine, Darlene Clark 24
Horton, James Oliver 58
Huggins, Nathan Irvin 52
Logan, Rayford W. 40
Nash, Joe 55
Marable, Manning 10
Moore, Wes 86
Painter, Nell Irvin 24, 88
Patterson, Orlando 4
Quarles, Benjamin Arthur 18
Querino, Manuel Raimundo 84
Reagon, Bernice Johnson 7
Reddick, Lawrence Dunbar 20
Rogers, Joel Augustus 30
Sadlier, Rosemary 62
Schomburg, Arthur Alfonso 9
Skinner, Kiron K. 65
Snowden, Frank M., Jr. 67
van Sertima, Ivan 25
Washington, James Melvin 50

Williams, George Washington 18
Williams, Rhonda Y. 86
Woodson, Carter G. 2

Hitman Records
Brae, C. Michael 61

Hockey
Carnegie, Herbert 25
Doig, Jason 45
Grand-Pierre, Jean-Luc 46

Homosexuality
Carter, Mandy 11
Clarke, Cheryl 32
Delany, Samuel R., Jr. 9
Harris, E. Lynn 12, 33
Hemphill, Essex 10
Julien, Isaac 3
Norman, Pat 10
Nugent, Richard Bruce 39
Parker, Pat 19
Riggs, Marlon 5, 44
RuPaul 17, 91
Wilson, Phill 9

Honeywell Corporation
Jackson, Mannie 14

Horse racing
Harris, Sylvia 70
St. Julien, Marlon 29
Winkfield, Jimmy 42

House of Representatives
See U.S. House of Representatives

Houston Astros baseball team
Morgan, Joe 9
Richard, J. R. 87
Watson, Bob 25

Houston Oilers football team
McNair, Steve 22, 47, 79
Moon, Warren 8, 66

Houston Rockets basketball team
Lucas, John 7
Olajuwon, Hakeem 2, 72

Howard University
Adams-Campbell, Lucille L. 60
Benjamin, Tritobia Hayes 53
Branson, Herman 87
Cardozo, Francis L. 33
Carter, Joye Maureen 41
Cobb, W. Montague 39
Davis, Arthur P. 41
Dodson, Owen 38
Gerima, Haile 38, 80
Harris, Gary L. 87
Jenifer, Franklyn G. 2
Johnson, Mordecai Wyatt 79
Ladner, Joyce A. 42
Locke, Alain 10
Logan, Rayford W. 40
Malveaux, Floyd 54
Mays, Benjamin E. 7
Neal, Larry 38
Payton, Benjamin F. 23
Porter, James A. 11
Reid, Irvin D. 20
Ribeau, Sidney 70
Robinson, Spottswood W., III 22
Snowden, Frank M., Jr. 67

Sowande, Fela **39**
Spriggs, William **67**
Swygert, H. Patrick **22**
Wells, James Lesesne **10**
Wesley, Dorothy Porter **19**
White, Charles **39**
Young, Roger Arliner **29**

HUD
See U.S. Department of Housing and Urban Development

Hugo awards
Butler, Octavia **8, 43, 58**
Delany, Samuel R., Jr. **9**

Human resources
Howroyd, Janice Bryant **42**

Human rights
Atyam, Angelina **55**
Bond, Julian **2, 35**
Carter, Mandy **11**
McDougall, Gay J. **11, 43**
Williams, Robert F. **11**

Hunter College
DeCarava, Roy **42, 81**
Mayhew, Richard **39**
Thomas, Michael **69**

IBM
Adkins, Rod **41**
Blackwell, Robert D., Sr. **52**
Chenault, Kenneth I. **5, 36**
Dean, Mark **35**
Foster, Jylla Moore **45**
Thompson, John W. **26**
Zollar, Alfred **40**

Ice Hockey in Harlem
Mayers, Jamal **39**

Ice skating
See Figure skating

Igbo people/traditions
Achebe, Chinua **6**

Illinois state government
Braun, Carol Moseley **4, 42**
Burris, Roland W. **25, 75**
Colter, Cyrus J. **36**
Jones, Emil, Jr. **74**
Meeks, James T. **92**
Obama, Barack **49, 74, 91**
Raoul, Kwame **55**
Trotter, Donne E. **28**
Washington, Harold **6**
White, Jesse **22, 75**

Illustrations
Anderson, Ho Che **54**
Baker, Matt **76**
Biggers, John **20, 33**
Bryan, Ashley F. **41**
Campbell, E. Simms **13**
Crichlow, Ernest **75**
Fax, Elton **48**
Honeywood, Varnette P. **54, 88**
Hudson, Cheryl **15**
Kitt, Sandra **23**
Pinkney, Jerry **15**
Ransome, James E. **88**
Saint James, Synthia **12**

Simmons, Gary **58**

IMF
See International Monetary Fund

Indecorp, Inc.
Johnson, George E. **29**

Indiana state government
Carson, Julia **23, 69**
Carter, Pamela Lynn **67**

Indianapolis Colts football team
Caldwell, Jim **81**
Dickerson, Eric **27**
Dungy, Tony **17, 42, 59**
Sanders, Bob **72**

Indianapolis 500
Ribbs, Willy T. **2**

Industrial design
Harrison, Charles **72**

Information technology
Blackwell, Robert D., Sr. **52**
Coleman, Ken **57**
Pinkett, Randal **61**
Smith, Joshua **10**
Steward, David L. **36**
Woods, Jacqueline **52**
Zollar, Alfred **40**

Insurance
Gaston, Arthur George **3, 38, 59**
Herndon, Alonzo Franklin **89**
Hill, Jesse, Jr. **13**
Holstein, Casper **89**
James, Donna A. **51**
Kidd, Mae Street **39**
Killingsworth, Cleve, Jr. **54**
Procope, Ernesta **23**
Procope, John Levy **56**
Scott, Tim **87**
Spaulding, Charles Clinton **9**
Vaughns, Cleopatra **46**
Williams, Ronald A. **57**
Willie, Louis, Jr. **68**

Interior design
Ashford, Calvin, Jr. **74**
Bridges, Sheila **36**
De' Alexander, Quinton **57**
Ham, Cynthia Parker **58**
Hayes, Cecil N. **46**
King, Robert Arthur **58**
Myles, Kim **69**
Steave-Dickerson, Kia **57**
Taylor, Karin **34**

Internal Revenue Service
Colter, Cyrus J. **36**

International Association of Fire Chiefs
Bell, Michael **40**
Day, Leon **39**

International Federation of Library Associations and Institutions
Wedgeworth, Robert W. **42**

International Free and Accepted Masons and Eastern

Star
Banks, William **11**

International Ladies' Auxiliary
Tucker, Rosina **14**

International law
Payne, Ulice **42**

International Monetary Fund (IMF)
Babangida, Ibrahim **4**
Chissano, Joaquim **7, 55, 67**
Diouf, Abdou **3**
Patterson, P. J. **6, 20**

International Workers Organization (IWO)
Patterson, Louise **25**

Internet
CasSelle, Malcolm **11**
Cooper, Barry **33**
Ellington, E. David **11**
Gilliard, Steve **69**
Knowling, Robert **38**
Mitchell, Shireen **89**
Thomas-Graham, Pamela **29**
Thompson, John W. **26**

Interpol
Noble, Ronald **46**

Interscope Geffen A & M Records
Stoute, Steve **38**

In the Black television show
Jones, Caroline R. **29**

Inventions
Chisholm, Daquan **93**
Johnson, Lonnie G. **32, 93**
Jones, Frederick McKinley **68**
Julian, Percy Lavon **6**
Latimer, Lewis H. **4**
Matzeliger, Jan **93**
McCoy, Elijah **8**
Morgan, Garrett **1**
West, James E. **87**
Woods, Granville T. **5**

Investment management
Beal, Bernard B. **46**
Bryant, John **26**
Ford, Wallace **58**
Gardner, Chris **65**
Goings, Russell **59**
Green, Isaac H. **79**
Harris, Carla A. **67**
Procope, Ernesta **23**
Rogers, John W., Jr. **5, 52**
Utendahl, John **23**

Islam
Ali, Ayaan Hirsi **58, 92**
Kalbani, Adil **77**
Muhammed, W. Deen **27**

Ivory Coast government
Gbagbo, Laurent **43, 90**
Guéï, Robert **66**
Ouattara, Alassane **90**

Jackie Robinson Foundation
Robinson, Rachel **16**

Jackson State University
Mason, Ronald **27**

Jamaican government
Golding, Bruce **78**
Simpson-Miller, Portia **62**

Jazz
Adderley, Julian "Cannonball" **30**
Adderley, Nat **29**
Albright, Gerald **23**
Ali, Rashied **79**
Allen, Geri **92**
Anderson, Carl **48**
Anderson, Fred **87**
Armstrong, Louis **2**
Astatke, Mulatu **81**
Austin, Lovie **40**
Austin, Patti **24**
Ayers, Roy **16**
Bailey, Buster **38**
Bailey, Philip **63**
Barker, Danny **32**
Basie, Count **23**
Batiste, Alvin **66**
Bechet, Sidney **18**
Belgrave, Marcus **77**
Belle, Regina **1, 51**
Betts, Keter **85**
Blade, Brian **88**
Blakey, Art **37**
Blanchard, Terence **43**
Bolden, Buddy **39**
Bridgewater, Dee Dee **32, 92**
Brooks, Avery **9**
Brown, Clifford **86**
Butler, Jonathan **28**
Calloway, Cab **14**
Carter, Benny **46**
Carter, Betty **19**
Carter, Regina **23**
Carter, Warrick L. **27**
Cartiér, Xam Wilson **41**
Charles, Ray **16, 48**
Cheatham, Doc **17**
Clarke, Kenny **27**
Cole, Nat "King" **17**
Cole, Natalie **17, 60, 84**
Coleman, Ornette **39, 69**
Coltrane, Alice **70**
Coltrane, John **19**
Coltrane, Ravi **71**
Cook, Charles "Doc" **44**
Count Basie **23**
Crawford, Hank **77**
Crawford, Randy **19**
Crothers, Scatman **19**
Crouch, Stanley **11, 87**
Crowder, Henry **16**
Daemyon, Jerald **64**
Dara, Olu **35**
Davis, Anthony **11**
Davis, Frank Marshall **47**
Davis, Miles **4**
Dickenson, Vic **38**
Dixon, Bill **87**
Donegan, Dorothy **19**
Downing, Will **19**
Duke, George **21**
Dumas, Henry **41**
Durham, Bobby **73**
Eckstine, Billy **28**
Eldridge, Roy **37**

Ellington, Duke 5
Ellison, Ralph 7
Eubanks, Kevin 15
Farmer, Art 38
Ferrell, Rachelle 29
Fitzgerald, Ella 8, 18
Flanagan, Tommy 69
Foster, George "Pops" 40
Freelon, Nnenna 32
Freeman, Yvette 27
Fuller, Arthur 27
Garner, Erroll 76
Gillespie, Dizzy 1
Golson, Benny 37
Gordon, Dexter 25
Green, Grant 56
Greene, Jimmy 74
Griffin, Johnny 71
Güines, Tata 69
Hampton, Lionel 17, 41
Hancock, Herbie 20, 67
Hardin Armstrong, Lil 39
Harris, Barry 68
Hawkins, Coleman 9
Haynes, Roy 87
Henderson, Fletcher 32
Higginbotham, J. C. 37
Hill, Andrew 66
Hines, Earl "Fatha" 39
Hinton, Milt 30
Holiday, Billie 1
Horn, Shirley 32, 56
Hubbard, Freddie 75
Hyman, Phyllis 19
Jackson, Milt 26
Jacquet, Illinois 49
Jamal, Ahmad 69
James, Etta 13, 52
Jarreau, Al 21, 65
Johnson, Buddy 36
Johnson, J. J. 37
Johnson, Lonnie 85
Jones, Elvin 14, 68
Jones, Etta 35
Jones, Hank 57, 86
Jones, Jonah 39
Jones, Quincy 8, 30
Jones, Thad 68
Jordan, Ronny 26
Kenyatta, Robin 54
Klugh, Earl 59
Lateef, Yusef 91
Laws, Hubert 90
Ledisi 73
Lee, Consuela 84
Lewis, Ramsey 35, 70
Lincoln, Abbey 3, 88
Locke, Eddie 44
Long, Huey 79
Loueke, Lionel 88
Lucie, Lawrence 80
Lucien, Jon 66
Marsalis, Branford 34
Marsalis, Delfeayo 41
Marsalis, Ellis 90
Marsalis, Wynton 16, 90
McBride, James 35, 87
McGriff, Jimmy 72
McLean, Jackie 78
McRae, Carmen 77
Miller, Marcus 84
Mills, Florence 22
Mingus, Charles 15

Mitchell, Nicole 66
Monk, Thelonious 1
Montgomery, Wes 88
Moody, James 83
Moore, Melba 21
Moran, Jason 89
Morton, Jelly Roll 29
Muse, Clarence Edouard 21
Nascimento, Milton 2, 64
Newman, David 76
Oliver, Joe "King" 42
Parker, Charlie 20
Parker, Maceo 72
Payne, Freda 58
Peterson, Marvin "Hannibal" 27
Peterson, Oscar 52
Powell, Benny 87
Powell, Bud 24
Purdie, Bernard 77
Redman, Joshua 30
Reese, Della 6, 20
Reeves, Dianne 32
Roach, Max 21, 63
Roberts, Marcus 19
Rollins, Sonny 37
Ruffins, Kermit 85
Rushing, Jimmy 37
Sample, Joe 51
Santamaria, Mongo 81
Scarlett, Millicent 49
Scott, Hazel 66
Scott, "Little" Jimmy 48
Shorter, Wayne 75
Silver, Horace 26
Simpson-Hoffman, N'kenge 52
Sissle, Noble 29
Smith, Bessie 3
Smith, Cladys "Jabbo" 32
Smith, Dr. Lonnie 49
Smith, Lonnie Liston 49
Smith, Stuff 37
Somi 85
Staton, Dakota 62
Strayhorn, Billy 31
Sullivan, Maxine 37
Sun Ra 60
Swann, Lynn 28
Tampa Red 63
Taylor, Billy 23, 92
Taylor, Cecil 70
Terry, Clark 39
Tisdale, Wayman 50
Tyner, McCoy 92
Ulmer, James 79
Valdés, Bebo 75
Valdés, Chucho 89
Vaughan, Sarah 13
Waller, Fats 29
Washington, Dinah 22
Washington, Grover, Jr. 17, 44
Waters, Benny 26
Watson, Johnny "Guitar" 18
Watts, Reggie 52
Webster, Katie 29
Wein, Joyce 62
Whalum, Kirk 37, 64
White, Maurice 29
Williams, Claude 80
Williams, Joe 5, 25
Williams, Mary Lou 15
Williams, Tony 67
Wilson, Cassandra 16
Wilson, Gerald 49

Wilson, Nancy 10
York, Vincent 40
Young, Lee 72
Young, Lester 37

Jet magazine
Johnson, John H. 3, 54
Massaquoi, Hans J. 30
Sleet, Moneta, Jr. 5

Jive Records
McPherson, David 32

Jockeys
Harris, Sylvia 70
Lewis, Oliver 56
Winkfield, Jimmy 42

Johnson C. Smith University
Yancy, Dorothy Cowser 42

Johnson Products
Johnson, George E. 29

Johnson Publishing Company, Inc.
Booker, Simeon 23
Johnson, Eunice W. 83
Johnson, John H. 3, 54
Monroe, Bryan 71
Rice, Linda Johnson 9, 41
Rogers, Desirée 88
Sleet, Moneta, Jr. 5

Joint Center for Political Studies
Williams, Eddie N. 44

Joint Chiefs of Staff
See U.S. Joint Chiefs of Staff

Jones Haywood School of Ballet
Jones, Doris W. 62

Journalism
Abbott, Robert Sengstacke 27
Abrahams, Peter 39
Abu-Jamal, Mumia 15
Ansa, Tina McElroy 14
Ashley-Ward, Amelia 23
Asim, Jabari 71
Auguste, Arnold A. 47
Azikiwe, Nnamdi 13
Bailey, Chauncey 68
Baquet, Dean 63
Barnett, Amy Du Bois 46
Barrett, Lindsay 43
Bass, Charlotta Spears 40
Bates, Karen Grigsby 40
Bennett, Gwendolyn B. 59
Bennett, Lerone, Jr. 5, 84
Best, Carrie 80
Blair, Jayson 50
Blake, Asha 26
Blow, Charles M. 73
Bolden, Frank E. 44
Booker, Simeon 23
Borders, James 9
Boyd, Gerald M. 32, 59
Boyd, Suzanne 52
Bradley, Ed 2, 59
Britt, Donna 28
Brower, William 49
Brown, George Leslie 62
Brown, Lloyd Louis 42

Brown, Tony 3
Buckley, Gail Lumet 39
Burt-Murray, Angela 59
Burwell, Bryan 83
Caldwell, Earl 60
Campbell, Bebe Moore 6, 24, 59
Cary, Mary Ann Shadd 30
Cayton, Horace 26
Chadiha, Jeffri 57
Chideya, Farai 14, 61
Churchwell, Robert, Sr. 76
Ciara, Barbara 69
Cooke, Marvel 31
Cooper, Barry 33
Cooper, Helene 74
Cose, Ellis 5, 50
Croal, N'Gai 76
Crouch, Stanley 11, 87
Crutchfield, James N. 55
Cullen, Countee 8
Cunningham, Evelyn 23, 85
Dash, Leon 47
Datcher, Michael 60
Davis, Belva 61
Davis, Frank Marshall 47
Davis, Thulani 61
Dawkins, Wayne 20
Deggans, Eric 71
Douglass, Frederick 87
Drummond, William J. 40
Due, Tananarive 30
Dunbar, Paul Laurence 8
Dunnigan, Alice Allison 41
Eagleson, William Lewis 90
Edmonds, Terry 17
Epperson, Sharon 54
Farley, Christopher John 54
Forman, James 7, 51
Fortune, T. Thomas 6
Fuller, Hoyt 44
Gaiter, Dorothy J. 80
Giddings, Paula 11
Gilliard, Steve 69
Givhan, Robin Deneen 72
Goode, Mal 13
Gordon, Ed 10, 53
Grimké, Archibald H. 9
Gumbel, Bryant 14, 80
Gumbel, Greg 8
Hansberry, Lorraine 6
Hare, Nathan 44
Harrington, Oliver W. 9
Harris, Claire 34
Harris, Jay 19
Harris, Richard E. 61
Hatcher, Andrew T. 90
Haygood, Wil 83
Haynes, Trudy 44
Henriques, Julian 37
Herbert, Bob 63
Hickman, Fred 11
Holt, Lester 66
Huggins, Edie 71
Hunter-Gault, Charlayne 6, 31
Ifill, Gwen 28
Jackson, James A. 90
Jarrett, Vernon D. 42
Jasper, Kenji 39
Jealous, Benjamin 70
Joachim, Paulin 34
Johnson, Georgia Douglas 41
Johnson, James Weldon 5
Kaufman, Monica 66

Kearney, Janis **54**
Khanga, Yelena **6**
Killens, John O. **54**
King, Colbert I. **69**
Kitwana, Bakari **86**
Knight, Etheridge **37**
LaGuma, Alex **30**
Lacy, Sam **30, 46**
Lampkin, Daisy **19**
Leavell, Dorothy R. **17**
Lewis, Edward T. **21**
Lomax, Louis E. **90**
Lowe, Herbert **57**
Mabrey, Vicki **26**
Mabry, Marcus **70**
Mabuza-Suttle, Felicia **43**
Madison, Paula **37**
Malveaux, Suzanne **88**
Martin, Louis E. **16**
Mason, Felicia **31**
Maynard, Nancy Hicks **73**
Maynard, Robert C. **7**
Mbeki, Govan A. **80**
McBride, James **35, 87**
McCall, Nathan **8**
McGruder, Robert **22, 35**
McKay, Claude **6**
Mickelbury, Penny **28**
Mitchell, Elvis **67**
Mitchell, Russ **21, 73**
Mkapa, Benjamin W. **16, 77**
Monroe, Bryan **71**
Mossell, Gertrude Bustill **40**
Mukoko, Jestina **75**
Murphy, John H. **42**
Murray, Pauli **38**
Nelson, Jill **6, 54**
Neville, Arthel **53**
Newkirk, Pamela **69**
Njawe, Pius **87**
Nkosi, Lewis **46**
Noble, Gil **76**
Norris, Michele **83**
O'Brien, Soledad **88**
Oliver, Pam **54**
Olojede, Dele **59**
Page, Clarence **4**
Palmer, Everard **37**
Parham, Marjorie B. **71**
Parker, Star **70**
Parks, Gordon **1, 35, 58**
Payne, Ethel L. **28**
Payne, Les **89**
Perez, Anna **1**
Perkins, Tony **24**
Phillips, Joseph C. **73**
Pinkston, W. Randall **24**
Pitts, Byron **71**
Pitts, Leonard, Jr. **54, 85**
Plaatje, Sol. T. **80**
Poussaint, Renee **78**
Pressley, Condace L. **41**
Price, Hugh B. **9, 54**
Prince, Richard E. **71**
Pugh, Charles **81**
Quarles, Norma **25**
Rapier, James T. **82**
Raspberry, William **2**
Reed, Ishmael **8**
Reeves, Rachel J. **23**
Rhoden, William C. **67**
Riley, Rochelle **50**
Roberts, Robin **16, 54**

Robertson, Gil L., IV **85**
Robinson, Eugene **77**
Robinson, Max **3**
Rodgers, Johnathan **6, 51**
Rowan, Carl T. **1, 30**
Rust, Art, Jr. **83**
Salih, Al-Tayyib **37**
Salters, Lisa **71**
Sanders, Pharoah **64**
Schuyler, George Samuel **40**
Schuyler, Philippa **50**
Senior, Olive **37**
Shaw, Bernard **2, 28**
Shipp, E. R. **15**
Simpson, Carole **6, 30**
Smith, Clarence O. **21**
Smith, Danyel **40**
Smith, Stephen A. **69**
Sowell, Thomas **2**
Staples, Brent **8**
Stewart, Alison **13**
Stokes, Carl **10, 73**
Stone, Chuck **9**
Syler, Rene **53**
Tate, Eleanora E. **20, 55**
Tatum, Elinor R. **78**
Tatum, Wilbert **76**
Taylor, Kristin Clark **8**
Thurman, Wallace **16**
Tolson, Melvin B. **37**
Trotter, Monroe **9**
Tucker, Cynthia **15, 61**
Wallace, Michele Faith **13**
Washington, Elsie B. **78**
Washington, Harriet A. **69**
Watson, Carlos **50**
Watts, Rolonda **9**
Webb, Veronica **10**
Wells-Barnett, Ida B. **8**
Wesley, Valerie Wilson **18**
Whitaker, Mark **21, 47**
White, Armond **80**
Whitfield, LeRoy **84**
Whitlock, Jason **78**
Wilbekin, Emil **63**
Wilbon, Michael **68**
Wiley, Ralph **8, 78**
Wilkerson, Isabel **71**
Wilkins, Roger **2, 84**
Williams, Armstrong **29**
Williams, Clarence **70**
Williams, Juan **35, 80**
Wiwa, Ken **67**
Woods, Mattiebelle **63**
Yette, Samuel F. **63**
Zook, Kristal Brent **62**

Judaism
Funnye, Capers C., Jr. **73**
Stanton, Alysa **78**

Judiciary
Hatchett, Glenda **32**
Hubbard, Arnette **38**
Sampson, Edith S. **4**

Just Us Books
Hudson, Cheryl **15**
Hudson, Wade **15**

Kansas City Chiefs football team
Allen, Marcus **20**
Cherry, Deron **40**

Delaney, Joe **76**
Dungy, Tony **17, 42, 59**
Thomas, Derrick **25**
Thomas, Emmitt **71**

Kansas City (MO) government
Cleaver, Emanuel **4, 45, 68**

Kansas City Monarchs baseball team
Bell, James "Cool Papa" **36**
Brown, Willard **36**

Kansas State University
Prince, Ron **64**

KANU
See Kenya African National Union

Kappa Alpha Psi
Hamilton, Samuel C. **47**

Kentucky Derby
Winkfield, Jimmy **42**

Kentucky Negro Educational Association
Cotter, Joseph Seamon, Sr. **40**

Kentucky state government
Kidd, Mae Street **39**

Kenya African National Union (KANU)
Kariuki, J. M. **67**
Kenyatta, Jomo **5**
Kibaki, Mwai **60**
Moi, Daniel Arap **1, 35**
Ngilu, Charity **58**
Odinga, Raila **67**

Kenya National Council of Churches (NCCK)
Kobia, Samuel **43**

Kenyan government
Kariuki, J. M. **67**
Kibaki, Mwai **60**
Maathai, Wangari **43**
Moi, Daniel Arap **1, 35**
Ngilu, Charity **58**
Odinga, Raila **67**

King Center
See Martin Luther King Jr. Center for Nonviolent Social Change

King Oliver's Creole Band
Armstrong, Louis **2**
Hardin Armstrong, Lil **39**
Oliver, Joe "King" **42**

King's Troop of the Royal Horse Artillery
Scantlebury, Janna **47**

Kraft General Foods
Fudge, Ann (Marie) **11, 55**
Sneed, Paula A. **18**

Kunta Kinte–Alex Haley Foundation
Blackshear, Leonard **52**

Kwanzaa
Karenga, Maulana **10, 71**

Kwazulu Territorial Authority
Buthelezi, Mangosuthu Gatsha **9**

Labour Party
Amos, Valerie **41**

Ladies Professional Golfers' Association (LPGA)
Gibson, Althea **8, 43**
Powell, Renee **34**

LaFace Records
Babyface **10, 31, 82**
Benjamin, Andre **45**
OutKast **35**
Patton, Antwan **45**
Reid, Antonio "L.A." **28**

LAPD
See Los Angeles Police Department

Latin American folk music
Nascimento, Milton **2, 64**

Latin baseball leagues
Kaiser, Cecil **42**

Law education
Bell, Derrick **6**
Carter, Stephen L. **4**
Forman, James, Jr. **89**
Guinier, Lani **7, 30**
Williams, Patricia **11, 54**

Law enforcement
Alexander, Joyce London **18**
Barrett, Jacquelyn **28**
Bolton, Terrell D. **25**
Bradley, Thomas **2, 20**
Brown, Lee P. **1, 24**
Bully-Cummings, Ella **48**
Evans, Warren C. **76**
Feemster, Herbert **72**
Freeman, Charles **19**
Gibson, Johnnie Mae **23**
Glover, Nathaniel, Jr. **12**
Gomez-Preston, Cheryl **9**
Harvard, Beverly **11**
Hillard, Terry **25**
Holton, Hugh, Jr. **39**
Hurtt, Harold **46**
Johnson, Norma L. Holloway **17**
Johnson, Robert T. **17**
Jordan, Eddie **82**
McKinnon, Isaiah **9**
Moose, Charles **40**
Napoleon, Benny N. **23**
Noble, Ronald **46**
Oliver, Jerry **37**
Parks, Bernard C. **17**
Ramsey, Charles H. **21, 69**
Robinson, Bishop L. **66**
Schmoke, Kurt **1, 48**
Smith, Richard **51**
Thomas, Franklin A. **5, 49**
Wainwright, Joscelyn **46**
Ward, Benjamin **68**
Williams, Willie L. **4**
Wilson, Jimmy **45**

LDF
See NAACP Legal Defense and Educational Fund

League of Nations
Haile Selassie 7

Legal Defense Fund
See NAACP Legal Defense and
Educational Fund

Lexicography
Major, Clarence 9

Liberian government
Henries, A. Doris Banks 44
Sawyer, Amos 2
Sirleaf, Ellen Johnson 71
Weah, George 58

**Liberians United for Recon-
ciliation and Democracy
(LURD)**
Conneh, Sekou Damate, Jr. 51

Library science
Bontemps, Arna 8
Franklin, Hardy R. 9, 87
Harsh, Vivian Gordon 14
Hutson, Jean Blackwell 16
Jones, Clara Stanton 51
Josey, E. J. 10
Kitt, Sandra 23
Larsen, Nella 10
Morrison, Sam 50
Owens, Major 6
Rollins, Charlemae Hill 27
Schomburg, Arthur Alfonso 9
Shockley, Ann Allen 84
Smith, Jessie Carney 35
Spencer, Anne 27
Wedgeworth, Robert W. 42
Wesley, Dorothy Porter 19

Librettos
Chenault, John 40

Lincoln University (MO)
Page, Inman 82
Randall, Dudley 8, 55

Lincoln University (PA)
Cuney, William Waring 44
Sudarkasa, Niara 4

**Literacy Volunteers of
America**
Amos, Wally 9

Literary criticism
Baker, Houston A., Jr. 6
Braithwaite, William Stanley 52
Brown, Sterling Allen 10, 64
Broyard, Anatole 68
Cartey, Wilfred 47
Christian, Barbara T. 44
Cook, Mercer 40
De Veaux, Alexis 44
Emanuel, James A. 46
Fleming, Raymond 48
Ford, Nick Aaron 44
Joachim, Paulin 34
Mackey, Nathaniel 75
Mugo, Micere Githae 32
Ngugi wa Thiong'o 29, 61
Redding, J. Saunders 26
Reed, Ishmael 8
Smith, Barbara 28
Wesley, Valerie Wilson 18

West, Cornel 5, 33, 80

**Literary Hall of Fame for Writ-
ers of African Descent**
Colter, Cyrus J. 36

Lithography
White, Charles 39

Litigation
Allen, Lucy 85
Baldwin, Cynthia A. 74
Cochran, Johnnie 11, 39, 52
Gary, Willie E. 12
Worthy, Kym 84

"Little Rock Nine"
Bates, Daisy 13
Thomas, Jefferson 88

Liver research
Leevy, Carrol M. 42

Lobbying
Boyd, John W., Jr. 20, 72
Brown, Elaine 8
Brown, Jesse 6, 41
Brown, Ron 5
Christie, Ron 83
Edelman, Marian Wright 5, 42
Lee, Canada 8
Mallett, Conrad, Jr. 16
Reeves, Gregory 49
Robinson, Randall 7, 46
Wynn, Albert R. 25, 77

**Los Angeles Angels baseball
team**
Baylor, Don 6
Bonds, Bobby 43

Los Angeles city government
Bradley, Thomas 2, 20
Evers, Myrlie 8

**Los Angeles Clippers basket-
ball team**
Baylor, Elgin 93
Brand, Elton 31

**Los Angeles Dodgers base-
ball team**
Baker, Dusty 8, 43, 72
Newcombe, Don 24
Strawberry, Darryl 22
Wills, Maury 73

**Los Angeles Lakers basket-
ball team**
Abdul-Jabbar, Kareem 8
Baylor, Elgin 93
Bryant, Kobe 15, 31, 71
Chamberlain, Wilt 18, 47
Fox, Rick 27
Green, A. C. 32
Johnson, Earvin "Magic" 3, 39
Odom, Lamar 81
O'Neal, Shaquille 8, 30
Worthy, James 49

Los Angeles Philharmonic
Lewis, Henry 38

**Los Angeles Police Depart-
ment (LAPD)**
Parks, Bernard C. 17
Smith, Richard 51

Williams, Willie L. 4

**Los Angeles Raiders football
team**
Allen, Marcus 20
Lofton, James 42
Lott, Ronnie 9
Shell, Art 1, 66

**Los Angeles Rams football
team**
Bryant, Cullen 81
Dickerson, Eric 27
Washington, Kenny 50

Los Angeles Times newspaper
Baquet, Dean 63
Drummond, William J. 40

Lost-Found Nation of Islam
Ali, Muhammad 2, 16, 52
Ellison, Keith 59
Farrakhan, Louis 2, 15
Heard, Nathan C. 45
Karim, Benjamin 61
Muhammad, Ava 31
Muhammad, Elijah 4
Muhammad, Jabir Herbert 72
Muhammad, Khallid Abdul 10, 31
Muhammed, W. Deen 27
Sutton, Percy E. 42, 82
Tillard, Conrad 47
X, Malcolm 1
X, Marvin 45

Louisiana state government
Fields, Cleo 13
Francis, Norman (C.) 60
Jefferson, William J. 25, 72
Morial, Ernest "Dutch" 26
Peterson, Karen Carter 90
Pinchback, P. B. S. 9
Richardson, Rupert 67
Richmond, Cedric 93

LPGA
See Ladies Professional Golfers'
Association

**Lunar surface ultraviolet cam-
era**
See Ultraviolet
camera/spectrograph

**Lynching (anti-lynching legis-
lation)**
Johnson, James Weldon 5
Moore, Harry T. 29
Till, Emmett 7

Lyrics
Crouch, Andraé 27
D'Angelo 27
Dunbar, Paul Laurence 8
Fitzgerald, Ella 8
Jefferson, Blind Lemon 81
Johnson, James Weldon 5
KRS-One 34
Lil' Kim 28
MC Lyte 34
Randall, Alice 38
Run-DMC 31, 75

**MacArthur Foundation Fellow-
ship**
Allen, Will 74
Benjamin, Regina 20, 75

Butler, Octavia 8, 43, 58
Carter, Majora 77
Carter, Regina 23
Cooper, Lisa 73
Dabiri, John 93
Gordon-Reed, Annette 74
Hammons, David 69
Harris, Corey 39, 73
Jackson, Mary 73
Johnson, Angela 52
Johnson, Charles 1, 82
Jones, Edward P. 43, 67
Lee, Raphael C. 87
Lindsey, Tommie 51
Lovell, Whitfield 74
Mehretu, Julie 85
Moran, Jason 89
Nelson, Stanley 92
Olopade, Olufunmilayo Falusi 58
Parks, Suzan-Lori 34, 85
Robinson, Aminah 50
Taylor, Cecil 70
Whitehead, Colson 77
Williams, Patricia 11, 54

MacNeil/Lehrer NewsHour
Hunter-Gault, Charlayne 6, 31

Mad TV
Jones, Orlando 30
Wilson, Debra 38

**Madame C. J. Walker Manu-
facturing Company**
Joyner, Marjorie Stewart 26
Walker, A'lelia 14
Walker, Madame C. J. 7

**Major League Baseball admin-
istration**
Solomon, Jimmie Lee 38

Malaco Records
Bland, Bobby "Blue" 36

Malawi Congress Party (MCP)
Banda, Hastings Kamuzu 6, 54

Malawian government
Muluzi, Bakili 14, 76

Manhattan Project
Quarterman, Lloyd Albert 4
Wilkens, J. Ernest, Jr. 43

MARC Corp.
See Metropolitan Applied Research
Center

**March on
Washington/Freedom March**
Baker, Josephine 3
Belafonte, Harry 4, 65
Bunche, Ralph J. 5
Davis, Ossie 5, 50
Fauntroy, Walter E. 11
Forman, James 7, 51
Franklin, John Hope 5, 77
Hedgeman, Anna Arnold 22
Jackson, Mahalia 5
King, Coretta Scott 3, 57
King, Martin Luther, Jr. 1
Lewis, John 2, 46, 83
Meredith, James H. 11
Randolph, A. Philip 3
Rustin, Bayard 4

Sleet, Moneta, Jr. **5**
Wilkins, Roy **4**
Woods, Abraham, Jr. **74**
Young, Whitney M., Jr. **4**

Marketing
DeVard, Jerri **61**
Edwards, Trevor **54**
Fils-Aimé, Reggie **74**
Gaskins, Rudy **74**
Jackson, James A. **90**
Kaigler, Denise **63**
Kendrick, Erika **57**
Moyo, Karega Kofi **36**
Moyo, Yvette Jackson **36**

Martial arts
Barnes, Steven **54**
Copeland, Michael **47**
Slice, Kimbo **73**

Martin Luther King Jr. Center for Nonviolent Social Change
Dodson, Howard, Jr. **7, 52**
Farris, Isaac Newton, Jr. **63**
King, Bernice **4, 81**
King, Coretta Scott **3, 57**
King, Dexter **10**
King, Martin Luther, Jr. **1**
King, Yolanda **6**

Martin Luther King Jr. Drum Major Award
Broadbent, Hydeia **36**
Mfume, Kweisi **6, 41**

Martin Luther King Jr. National Memorial Project
Johnson, Harry E. **57**

Marxism
Baraka, Amiri **1, 38**
Bishop, Maurice **39**
Jagan, Cheddi **16**
Machel, Samora Moises **8**
Nkrumah, Kwame **3**
Sankara, Thomas **17**

Maryland state government
Brown, Anthony G. **72**
Currie, Ulysses **73**
Steele, Michael **38, 73, 91**

Massachusetts state government
Brooke, Edward W. **8, 88**
Gourdin, Edward O. **93**
Lewis, William Henry **89**
Patrick, Deval **12, 61**

Masters Golf Tournament
Elder, Lee **6**
Woods, Tiger **14, 31, 81**

Mathematics
Alcorn, George Edward, Jr. **59**
Banneker, Benjamin **93**
Blackwell, David **79**
Deconge-Watson, Lovenia **55**
Emeagwali, Philip **30**
Falconer, Etta Zuber **59**
Gates, Sylvester James, Jr. **15**
Johnson, Katherine (Coleman Goble) **61**
Price, Richard **51**

Wilkens, J. Ernest, Jr. **43**

MAXIMA Corporation
Smith, Joshua **10**

Maxwell House Coffee Company
Fudge, Ann (Marie) **11, 55**

McDonald's Corporation
Thompson, Don **56**

McGill University (Canada)
Elliott, Lorris **37**

MCP
See Malawi Congress Party

Medical examiners
Carter, Joye Maureen **41**

Medicine
Adams-Campbell, Lucille L. **60**
Anderson, William G(ilchrist) **57**
Atim, Julian **66**
Banda, Hastings Kamuzu **6, 54**
Bashir, Halima **73**
Benjamin, Regina **20, 75**
Black, Keith Lanier **18, 84**
Callender, Clive O. **3**
Canady, Alexa **28**
Carroll, L. Natalie **44**
Carson, Benjamin **1, 35, 76**
Carter, Joye Maureen **41**
Chatard, Peter **44**
Chinn, May Edward **26**
Christian-Green, Donna M. **17**
Cobb, W. Montague **39**
Cole, Rebecca **38**
Comer, James P. **6**
Coney, PonJola **48**
Cooper, Edward S. **6**
Cooper, Lisa **73**
Cornwell, Edward E., III **70**
Counter, S. Allen **74**
Crumpler, Rebecca Lee **89**
Dailey, Ulysses Grant **87**
Deas, Gerald **85**
Dickens, Helen Octavia **14, 64**
Drew, Charles Richard **7**
Durham, James **90**
Edwards, Lena Frances **76**
Edwards, Willarda V. **59**
Elders, Joycelyn **6**
Fennoy, Ilene **72**
Fisher, Ada M. **76**
Fisher, Rudolph **17**
Flowers, Sylester **50**
Foster, Henry W., Jr. **26**
Freeman, Harold P. **23**
Fuller, Solomon Carter, Jr. **15**
Gayle, Helene D. **3**
Gibson, William F. **6**
Giles, Roscoe C. **93**
Goodlett, Carlton B. **91**
Grant, Augustus O. **71**
Grier, Eliza Ann **90**
Griffin, Anthony **71**
Griffith, Patrick A. **64**
Hamburg, Margaret **78**
Hansberry, Tony, II **93**
Harris, Bernard A. **90**
Hinton, William Augustus **8**
Holmes, Hamilton E. **82**
Hopkins, Donald R. **89**

Hutcherson, Hilda Yvonne **54**
Jefferson, Mildred Fay **89**
Jemison, Mae C. **1, 35**
Johnson, R. M. **36**
Jones, Edith Mae Irby **65**
Joseph, Kathie-Ann **56**
Keith, Rachel Boone **63**
Kenney, John A., Jr. **48**
Kintaudi, Leon **62**
Kong, B. Waine **50**
Kountz, Samuel L. **10**
Lavizzo-Mourey, Risa **48**
Lawless, Theodore K. **8**
Lee, Raphael C. **87**
Leffall, Lasalle **3, 64**
Logan, Onnie Lee **14**
Malveaux, Floyd **54**
Maxey, Randall **46**
Mossell, Nathan Francis **91**
Naki, Hamilton **63**
Nour, Nawal M. **56**
Okaalet, Peter **58**
Olopade, Olufunmilayo Falusi **58**
Pace, Betty **59**
Pinn, Vivian Winona **49**
Pitt, David Thomas **10**
Poussaint, Alvin F. **5, 67**
Rabb, Maurice F., Jr. **58**
Randolph, Linda A. **52**
Reece, E. Albert **63**
Ross-Lee, Barbara **67**
Satcher, David **7, 57**
Scantlebury-White, Velma **64**
Smith, Ian **62**
Stewart, Ella **39**
Sullivan, Louis **8**
Sweet, Ossian **68**
Taylor, Susan C. **62**
Thomas, Claudia Lynn **64**
Thomas, Vivien **9**
Thornton, Yvonne S. **69**
Tuckson, Reed V. **71**
Washington, Harriet A. **69**
Watkins, Levi, Jr. **9**
Welsing, Frances Cress **5**
White-Hammond, Gloria **61**
Williams, Daniel Hale **2**
Wilson, Donald E. **88**
Witt, Edwin T. **26**
Wright, Charles H. **35**
Wright, Louis Tompkins **4**

Meharry Medical College
Coney, PonJola **48**
Foster, Henry W., Jr. **26**
Griffith, Patrick A. **64**
Lyttle, Hulda Margaret **14**

Melody Makers
Marley, Ziggy **41**

Men's movement
Somé, Malidoma Patrice **10**

Merce Cunningham Dance Company
Dove, Ulysses **5**

Merrill Lynch & Co., Inc.
Ford, Harold E(ugene), Jr. **16, 70**
Matthews Shatteen, Westina **51**

O'Neal, Stanley **38, 67**

Meteorology
Anderson, Charles Edward **37**
Bacon-Bercey, June **38**

Metropolitan Applied Research Center (MARC Corp.)
Clark, Kenneth B. **5, 52**

Mexican baseball league
Bell, James "Cool Papa" **36**
Dandridge, Ray **36**

Miami Dolphins football team
Cox, Bryan **83**
Greene, Joe **10**
Little, Larry **90**
Williams, Ricky **85**

Michigan state government
Brown, Cora **33**
Collins, Barbara-Rose **7, 87**
Kilpatrick, Carolyn Cheeks **16**
Kilpatrick, Kwame **34, 71**
Reeves, Triette Lipsey **27**
Wisdom, Kimberlydawn **57**

Michigan State Supreme Court
Archer, Dennis **7, 36**
Mallett, Conrad, Jr. **16**

Michigan State University
Wharton, Clifton R., Jr. **7**
Willingham, Tyrone **43**

Microsoft Corporation
Millines Dziko, Trish **28**

Midwest Stamping
Thompson, Cynthia Bramlett **50**

Midwifery
Logan, Onnie Lee **14**
Mason, Biddy **89**
Robinson, Sharon **22**

Military police
Cadoria, Sherian Grace **14**

Militia
Nkunda, Laurent **75**

Millennium Digital Media
Westbrook, Kelvin **50**

Miller Brewing Company
Colbert, Virgis William **17**
Shropshire, Thomas B. **49**

Millinery
Bailey, Xenobia **11**

Million Man March
Farrakhan, Louis **2, 15**
Hawkins, La-Van **17, 54**
Worrill, Conrad **12**

Milwaukee Brewers baseball team
Aaron, Hank **5**
Baylor, Don **6**
Fielder, Prince Semien **68**
Payne, Ulice **42**

Sheffield, Gary **16**

Milwaukee Bucks basketball team
Abdul-Jabbar, Kareem **8**
Robertson, Oscar **26**

Mingo-Jones Advertising
Chisholm, Samuel J. **32**
Jones, Caroline R. **29**
Mingo, Frank **32**

Minneapolis city government
Sayles Belton, Sharon **9, 16**

Minnesota State Supreme Court
Page, Alan **7**

Minnesota Timberwolves basketball team
Garnett, Kevin **14, 70**

Minnesota Twins baseball team
Baylor, Don **6**
Carew, Rod **20**
Hunter, Torii **43**
Puckett, Kirby **4, 58**

Minnesota Vikings football team
Carter, Cris **21**
Culpepper, Daunte **32, 85**
Cunningham, Randall **23**
Dungy, Tony **17, 42, 59**
Fowler, Reggie **51**
Gilliam, Frank **23**
Green, Dennis **5, 45**
McDaniel, Randall Cornell **81**
Moon, Warren **8, 66**
Moss, Randy **23, 90**
Page, Alan **7**
Randle, John **87**
Rashad, Ahmad **18**
Stringer, Korey **35**

Minority Business Enterprise Legal Defense and Education Fund
Mitchell, Parren J. **42, 66**

Minstrel shows
Lane, William Henry **90**
McDaniel, Hattie **5**

Miracle Network Telethon
Warner, Malcolm-Jamal **22, 36**

Miss America
Dunlap, Ericka **55**
Harold, Erika **54**
Vincent, Marjorie Judith **2**
Williams, Vanessa L. **4, 17**

Miss USA
Gist, Carole **1**

Miss World
Darego, Agbani **52**

Mississippi state government
Anderson, Reuben V. **81**
Fleming, Erik R. **75**

Hamer, Fannie Lou **6**

Missouri state government
Wilson, Margaret Bush **79**

Mixed martial arts
Jackson, Rampage **83**

MLA
See Modern Language Association of America

Model Inner City Community Organization (MICCO)
Fauntroy, Walter E. **11**

Modeling
Allen-Buillard, Melba **55**
Banks, Tyra **11, 50**
Beckford, Tyson **11, 68**
Berry, Halle **4, 19, 57, 91**
Campbell, Naomi **1, 31**
Darego, Agbani **52**
Dirie, Waris **56**
Ebanks, Selita **67**
Gibson, Tyrese **27, 62**
Hardison, Bethann **12**
Hounsou, Djimon **19, 45**
Iman **4, 33, 87**
Iman, Chanel **66**
Johnson, Beverly **2**
Kebede, Liya **59**
Kodjoe, Boris **34, 89**
Langhart Cohen, Janet **19, 60**
Leslie, Lisa **16, 73**
LisaRaye **27**
McKenzie, Jaunel **73**
Michele, Michael **31**
Niane, Katoucha **70**
Onwurah, Ngozi **38**
Powell, Maxine **8**
Rochon, Lela **16**
RuPaul **17, 91**
Simmons, Kimora Lee **51, 83**
Sims, Naomi **29, 79**
Smith, B(arbara) **11**
Tamia **24, 55**
Taylor, Karin **34**
Tyson, Cicely **7, 51**
Watley, Jody **54**
Webb, Veronica **10**
Wek, Alek **18, 63**

Modern dance
Ailey, Alvin **8**
Allen, Debbie **13, 42**
Brown, Ronald K. **91**
Byrd, Donald **10**
Collins, Janet **33, 64**
Davis, Chuck **33**
Diggs, Taye **25, 63**
Dove, Ulysses **5**
Fagan, Garth **18**
Faison, George **16**
Henson, Darrin **33**
Jamison, Judith **7, 67**
Jones, Bill T. **1, 46, 80**
King, Alonzo **38**
Kitt, Eartha **16, 75**
Miller, Bebe **3**
Pomare, Eleo **72**
Primus, Pearl **6**
Spears, Warren **52**
Vereen, Ben **4**

Williams, Dudley **60**

Modern Language Association of America (MLA)
Baker, Houston A., Jr. **6**

Modern Records
Brooks, Hadda **40**

Montgomery bus boycott
Abernathy, Ralph David **1**
Baker, Ella **5**
Burks, Mary Fair **40**
Carr, Johnnie **69**
Jackson, Mahalia **5**
Killens, John O. **54**
King, Martin Luther, Jr. **1**
Parks, Rosa **1, 35, 56**
Rustin, Bayard **4**

Montgomery County (MD) Police Department
Moose, Charles **40**

Montreal Canadiens hockey team
Brashear, Donald **39**

Montreal Expos baseball team
Dawson, Andre **85**
Doby, Lawrence Eugene, Sr. **16, 41**

Morehouse College
Brown, Uzee **42**
Gloster, Hugh Morris, Sr. **90**
Hope, John **8**
Mays, Benjamin E. **7**

Morgan Stanley
Lewis, William M., Jr. **40**

Moscow World News
Khanga, Yelena **6**
Sullivan, Louis **8**

Motivational speaking
Bahati, Wambui **60**
Baisden, Michael **66**
Brown, Les **5**
Bunkley, Anita Richmond **39**
Creagh, Milton **27**
Gardner, Chris **65**
Grant, Gwendolyn Goldsby **28**
Gray, Farrah **59**
Jolley, Willie **28**
July, William **27**
Kimbro, Dennis **10**
Russell-McCloud, Patricia **17**
Tyson, Asha **39**

Motorcycle racing
Brown, Antron **85**
Showers, Reggie **30**
Stewart, James "Bubba," Jr. **60**

Motown Records
Atkins, Cholly **40**
Avant, Clarence **19, 86**
Bizimungu, Pasteur **19**
Busby, Jheryl **3, 74**
de Passe, Suzanne **25**
Edwards, Esther Gordy **43**
Gaye, Marvin **2**
Gordy, Berry, Jr. **1**
Harrell, Andre **9, 30**
Holland-Dozier-Holland **36**

Holloway, Brenda **65**
Hutch, Willie **62**
Jackson, George **19**
Jamerson, James **59**
Jones, Robert G. **81**
Kendricks, Eddie **22**
Knight, Gladys **16, 66**
Massenburg, Kedar **23**
Powell, Maxine **8**
Richie, Lionel **27, 65**
Robinson, Smokey **3, 49**
Ross, Diana **8, 27**
Sanders, Angelia **86**
Terrell, Tammi **32**
Wells, Mary **28**
Whitfield, Norman **73**
Wilson, Mary **28**
Wonder, Stevie **11, 53**

Mount Holyoke College
Tatum, Beverly Daniel **42, 84**

Movement for Democratic Change (MDC)
Moyo, Lovemore **76**
Tsvangirai, Morgan **26, 72**

Movimento Popular de Libertação de Angola (MPLA)
dos Santos, José Eduardo **43**
Neto, António Agostinho **43**

Mozambican government
Chissano, Joaquim **7, 55, 67**
Diogo, Luisa Dias **63**
Guebuza, Armando **81**
Machel, Samora Moises **8**

MPLA
See Movimento Popular de Libertação de Angola

Multimedia art
Amaki, Amalia **76**
Bailey, Xenobia **11**
Lovell, Whitfield **74**
Pinder, Jefferson **77**
Robinson, Aminah **50**
Simpson, Lorna **4, 36**

Muppets, The
Clash, Kevin **14, 93**

Murals
Alston, Charles **33**
Biggers, John **20, 33**
Douglas, Aaron **7**
Lee-Smith, Hughie **5**
Walker, Kara **16, 80**

Museum of Modern Art
Pindell, Howardena **55**

Music Critics Circle
Holt, Nora **38**

Music One, Inc.
Majors, Jeff **41**

Music publishing
Avant, Nicole A. **90**
Edmonds, Tracey **16, 64**
Griffey, Dick **89**
Handy, W. C. **8**
Holland-Dozier-Holland **36**
Humphrey, Bobbi **20**
Jackson, George **19**

James, Rick **17**
Knight, Suge **11, 30**
Master P **21**
Mayfield, Curtis **2, 43**
Otis, Clyde **67**
Pryce, Trevor **89**
Redding, Otis **16**
Riley, Boots **89**
Shakur, Afeni **67**
Shorty, Ras, I **47**
Strong, Barrett **89**

Music Television (MTV)
Bellamy, Bill **12**
Chideya, Farai **14, 61**
Morton, Frederick A., Jr. **93**
Norman, Christina **47**
Powell, Kevin **31, 74**
Run **31, 73**

Musical composition
Armatrading, Joan **32**
Ashford, Nickolas **21**
Baiocchi, Regina Harris **41**
Ballard, Hank **41**
Bebey, Francis **45**
Blanchard, Terence **43**
Blige, Mary J. **20, 34, 60**
Bonds, Margaret **39**
Bonga, Kuenda **13**
Bridgetower, George **78**
Brown, Patrick "Sleepy" **50**
Brown, Uzee **42**
Burke, Solomon **31, 86**
Burleigh, Henry Thacker **56**
Caesar, Shirley **19**
Carter, Warrick L. **27**
Chapman, Tracy **26**
Charlemagne, Manno **11**
Charles, Ray **16, 48**
Cleveland, James **19**
Cole, Natalie **17, 60, 84**
Coleman, Ornette **39, 69**
Collins, Bootsy **31**
Cook, Will Marion **40**
Davis, Anthony **11**
Davis, Miles **4**
Davis, Sammy, Jr. **18**
Dawson, William Levi **39**
Diddley, Bo **39, 72**
Domino, Fats **20**
Ellington, Duke **5**
Europe, James Reese **10**
Evans, Faith **22**
Freeman, Paul **39**
Fuller, Arthur **27**
Gamble, Kenny **85**
Garrett, Sean **57**
Gaynor, Gloria **36**
George, Nelson **12**
Gillespie, Dizzy **1**
Golson, Benny **37**
Green, Al **13, 47, 74**
Hailey, JoJo **22**
Hailey, K-Ci **22**
Handy, W. C. **8**
Harris, Corey **39, 73**
Hathaway, Donny **18**
Hayes, Isaac **20, 58, 73**
Hayes, Teddy **40**
Hill, Lauryn **20, 53**
Holland-Dozier-Holland **36**
Holmes, Clint **57**

Holt, Nora **38**
Humphrey, Bobbi **20**
Hutch, Willie **62**
Isley, Ronald **25, 56**
Jackson, Fred James **25**
Jackson, Michael **19, 53, 76**
Jackson, Randy **40**
James, Rick **17**
Jerkins, Rodney **31**
Johnson, Buddy **36**
Johnson, Georgia Douglas **41**
Jones, Jonah **39**
Jones, Quincy **8, 30**
Jones, Thad **68**
Joplin, Scott **6**
Jordan, Montell **23**
Jordan, Ronny **26**
Kay, Ulysses **37**
Kee, John P. **43**
Kelly, R. **18, 44, 71**
Keys, Alicia **32, 68**
Kidjo, Angelique **50**
Killings, Debra **57**
King, B. B. **7**
León, Tania **13**
Little Milton **36, 54**
Little Walter **36**
Lopes, Lisa "Left Eye" **36**
Mahlasela, Vusi **65**
Majors, Jeff **41**
Marsalis, Delfeayo **41**
Martin, Roberta **58**
Master P **21**
Maxwell **20, 81**
Mayfield, Curtis **2, 43**
M.C. Hammer **20, 80**
McClurkin, Donnie **25**
McFerrin, Bobby **68**
Mills, Stephanie **36**
Mitchell, Brian Stokes **21**
Mo', Keb' **36**
Monica **21**
Moore, Chante **26**
Moore, Dorothy Rudd **46**
Moore, Undine Smith **28**
Muse, Clarence Edouard **21**
Nash, Johnny **40**
Ndegeocello, Meshell **15, 83**
Osborne, Jeffrey **26**
Otis, Clyde **67**
Parker, Ray, Jr. **85**
Pratt, Awadagin **31**
Price, Florence **37**
Prince **18, 65**
Pritchard, Robert Starling **21**
Reagon, Bernice Johnson **7**
Redding, Otis **16**
Reed, A. C. **36**
Reid, Antonio "L.A." **28**
Roach, Max **21, 63**
Robinson, Reginald R. **53**
Run-DMC **31, 75**
Rushen, Patrice **12**
Russell, Brenda **52**
Sangare, Oumou **18**
Seal **14, 75**
Shorty, Ras, I **47**
Silver, Horace **26**
Simone, Nina **15, 41**
Simpson, Valerie **21**
Somi **85**
Sowande, Fela **39**
Still, William Grant **37**

Strayhorn, Billy **31**
Sundiata, Sekou **66**
Sweat, Keith **19**
Tillis, Frederick **40**
Usher **23, 56**
Van Peebles, Melvin **7**
Walker, George **37**
Warwick, Dionne **18**
Washington, Grover, Jr. **17, 44**
Williams, Deniece **36**
Williams, Tony **67**
Winans, Angie **36**
Winans, Debbie **36**
Withers, Bill **61**

Musicology
George, Zelma Watson **42**

Mysteries
Bland, Eleanor Taylor **39**
Creagh, Milton **27**
DeLoach, Nora **30**
Himes, Chester **8**
Holton, Hugh, Jr. **39**
Mickelbury, Penny **28**
Mosley, Walter **5, 25, 68**
Thomas-Graham **29**
Wesley, Valerie Wilson **18**

Mystery/Detective fiction
Bates, Karen Grigsby **40**
Bland, Eleanor Taylor **39**
DeLoach, Nora **30**
Hayes, Teddy **40**
Haywood, Gar Anthony **43**
Himes, Chester **8**
Holton, Hugh, Jr. **39**
Mosley, Walter **5, 25, 68**
Wesley, Valerie Wilson **18**

Mystic Seaport Museum
Pinckney, Bill **42**

NAACP
See National Association for the
 Advancement of Colored People

NAACP Image Awards
Brandy **14, 34, 72**
Fields, Kim **36**
Lawrence, Martin **6, 27, 60**
Mac, Bernie **29, 61, 72**
McRae, Carmen **77**
Okonedo, Sophie **67**
Prince-Bythewood, Gina **31, 77**
Rhimes, Shonda Lynn **67**
Warner, Malcolm-Jamal **22, 36**
Wesley, Richard **73**

**NAACP Legal Defense and
Educational Fund (LDF)**
Bell, Derrick **6**
Berrien, Jacqueline A. **93**
Carter, Robert L. **51**
Chambers, Julius **3**
Coleman, James E., Jr. **79**
Coleman, William T. **76**
Edelman, Marian Wright **5, 42**
Fisher, Ada Lois Sipuel **76**
Guinier, Lani **7, 30**
Jones, Elaine R. **7, 45**
Julian, Percy Lavon **6**
Marshall, Thurgood **1, 44**
Motley, Constance Baker **10, 55**
Rice, Constance LaMay **60**

Smith, Kemba **70**
Smythe Haith, Mabel **61**

NABJ
See National Association of Black
 Journalists

NAC
See Nyasaland African Congress

NACW
See National Association of Colored Women

Namibian government
Mbuende, Kaire **12**
Nujoma, Samuel **10**

NASA
See National Aeronautics and
 Space Administration

NASCAR
See National Association of Stock
 Car Auto Racing

Nation of Islam
See Lost-Found Nation of Islam

National Academy of Design
White, Charles **39**

**National Action Council for
Minorities in Engineering**
Pierre, Percy Anthony **46**
Slaughter, John Brooks **53**

National Action Network
Sharpton, Al **21**

**National Aeronautics and
Space Administration (NASA)**
Anderson, Michael P. **40**
Bluford, Guy **2, 35**
Bolden, Charles Frank, Jr. **7, 78**
Campbell, Donald J. **66**
Carruthers, George R. **40**
Drew, Alvin, Jr. **67**
Easley, Annie J. **61**
Gregory, Frederick **8, 51**
Harris, Bernard A. **90**
Jemison, Mae C. **1, 35**
Johnson, Katherine (Coleman
 Goble) **61**
Johnson, Lonnie G. **32, 93**
McNair, Ronald **3, 58**
Mills, Joseph C. **51**
Nichols, Nichelle **11**
Sigur, Wanda **44**
Wilson, Stephanie **72**

**National Afro-American Coun-
cil**
Fortune, T. Thomas **6**
Mossell, Gertrude Bustill **40**

**National Airmen's Association
of America**
Brown, Willa **40**

**National Alliance of Postal
and Federal Employees**
McGee, James Madison **46**

**National Association for the
Advancement of Colored
People (NAACP)**
Anderson, Reuben V. **81**
Anderson, William G(ilchrist) **57**

Anthony, Wendell 25
Austin, Junius C. 44
Baker, Ella 5
Ballance, Frank W. 41
Bates, Daisy 13
Bell, Derrick 6
Bond, Julian 2, 35
Bontemps, Arna 8
Brock, Roslyn McCallister 86
Brooks, Gwendolyn 1
Brown, Homer S. 47
Bunche, Ralph J. 5
Chambers, Julius 3
Chavis, Benjamin 6
Clark, Kenneth B. 5, 52
Clark, Septima 7
Cobb, W. Montague 39
Colter, Cyrus, J. 36
Cotter, Joseph Seamon, Sr. 40
Creagh, Milton 27
Days, Drew S., III 10
Dee, Ruby 8, 50, 68
Du Bois, W. E. B. 3
DuBois, Shirley Graham 21
Dukes, Hazel Nell 56
Edelman, Marian Wright 5, 42
Evers, Medgar 3
Evers, Myrlie 8
Farmer, James 2, 64
Ford, Clyde W. 40
Fuller, S. B. 13
Grimké, Archibald H. 9
Hampton, Fred 18
Harrington, Oliver W. 9
Hayes, Dennis 54
Henderson, Wade 14
Hobson, Julius W. 44
Hollowell, Donald L. 57
Hooks, Benjamin L. 2, 85
Houston, Charles Hamilton 4
Jackson, Vera 40
Jealous, Benjamin 70
Johnson, James Weldon 5
Jordan, Vernon E. 3, 35
Kidd, Mae Street 39
Lampkin, Daisy 19
Madison, Joseph E. 17
Marshall, Thurgood 1, 44
McKissick, Floyd B. 3
McPhail, Sharon 2
Meredith, James H. 11
Mfume, Kweisi 6, 41
Mitchell, Clarence M., Jr. 88
Mitchell, Sharon 36
Moore, Harry T. 29
Morgan, Irene 65
Moses, Robert Parris 11
Motley, Constance Baker 10, 55
Moyo, Yvette Jackson 36
Owens, Major 6
Payton, John 48
Richardson, Rupert 67
Rustin, Bayard 4
Sutton, Percy E. 42, 82
Talbert, Mary B. 77
Terrell, Mary Church 9
Tobias, Channing H. 79
Tucker, C. Delores 12, 56
Van Lierop, Robert 53
White, Walter F. 4
Wilkins, Roy 4
Williams, Hosea Lorenzo 15, 31
Williams, Robert F. 11

Wilson, Margaret Bush 79
Wright, Louis Tompkins 4

National Association of Black Journalists (NABJ)
Curry, George E. 23
Dawkins, Wayne 20
Harris, Jay T. 19
Jarrett, Vernon D. 42
Lowe, Herbert 57
Madison, Paula 37
Payne, Les 89
Pressley, Condace L. 41
Rice, Linda Johnson 9, 41
Shipp, E. R. 15
Stone, Chuck 9
Washington, Laura S. 18

National Association of Colored Women (NACW)
Bethune, Mary McLeod 4
Cooper, Margaret J. 46
Harper, Frances Ellen Watkins 11
Lampkin, Daisy 19
Ruffin, Josephine St. Pierre 75
Stewart, Ella 39
Talbert, Mary B. 77
Terrell, Mary Church 9

National Association of Negro Business and Professional Women's Clubs
Vaughns, Cleopatra 46

National Association of Negro Musicians
Bonds, Margaret 39
Brown, Uzee 42

National Association of Regulatory Utility Commissioners
Colter, Cyrus, J. 36

National Association of Social Workers
Jackson, Judith D. 57
McMurray, Georgia L. 36

National Association for Stock Car Auto Racing
Lester, Bill 42, 85

National Baptist Convention USA
Bradley, J. Robert 65
Jones, E. Edward, Sr. 45
Lyons, Henry 12
Shaw, William J. 30
Thurston, Stephen J. 49

National Bar Association
Alexander, Joyce London 18
Alexander, Sadie Tanner Mossell 22
Archer, Dennis 7, 36
Bailey, Clyde 45
Hubbard, Arnette 38
McPhail, Sharon 2
Pincham, R. Eugene, Sr. 69
Quince, Peggy A. 69
Ray, Charlotte E. 60
Robinson, Malcolm S. 44
Thompson, Larry D. 39

Walker, Cora T. 68

National Basketball Players Association
Erving, Julius 18, 47
Ewing, Patrick 17, 73
Gourdine, Simon 11
Hunter, Billy 22

National Black Arts Festival (NBAF)
Borders, James 9
Brooks, Avery 9

National Black College Hall of Fame
Dortch, Thomas W., Jr. 45

National Black Farmers Association (NBFA)
Boyd, John W., Jr. 20, 72

National Black Fine Art Show
Wainwright, Joscelyn 46

National Black Gay and Lesbian Conference
Wilson, Phill 9

National Black Gay and Lesbian Leadership Forum (NB-GLLF)
Boykin, Keith 14
Carter, Mandy 11
Wilson, Phill 9

National Black Women's Health Project
Avery, Byllye Y. 66

National Book Award
Ellison, Ralph 7
Haley, Alex 4
Johnson, Charles 1, 82
Mackey, Nathaniel 75
Patterson, Orlando 4

National Broadcasting Company (NBC)
Allen, Byron 3, 24
Gumbel, Bryant 14, 80
Hinderas, Natalie 5
Holt, Lester 66
Ifill, Gwen 28
Johnson, Rodney Van 28
Madison, Paula 37
Reynolds, Star Jones 10, 27, 61
Roker, Al 12, 49
Simpson, Carole 6, 30
Thomas-Graham, Pamela 29
Williams, Montel 4, 57

National Brotherhood of Skiers (NBS)
Horton, Andre 33
Horton, Suki 33

National Center for Neighborhood Enterprise (NCNE)
Woodson, Robert L. 10

National Coalition of 100 Black Women (NCBW)
Mays, Leslie A. 41
McCabe, Jewell Jackson 10

National Coalition to Abolish the Dealth Penalty (NCADP)
Hawkins, Steven 14

National Council of Churches
Howard, M. William, Jr. 26

National Council of Negro Women (NCNW)
Bethune, Mary McLeod 4
Blackwell, Unita 17
Cole, Johnnetta B. 5, 43
Hamer, Fannie Lou 6
Height, Dorothy I. 2, 23, 78
Lampkin, Daisy 19
Sampson, Edith S. 4
Smith, Jane E. 24
Staupers, Mabel K. 7

National Council of Nigeria and the Cameroons (NCNC)
Azikiwe, Nnamdi 13

National Council of Teachers of Mathematics
Granville, Evelyn Boyd 36

National Council on the Arts
Robinson, Cleo Parker 38

National Cowboys of Color Museum and Hall of Fame
Austin, Gloria 63
Austin, Jim 63
Pickett, Bill 11
Pride, Charley 26
Sampson, Charles 13

National Dental Association
Madison, Romell 45

National Earthquake Information Center
Person, Waverly 9, 51

National Education Association (NEA)
Futrell, Mary Hatwood 33

National Endowment for the Arts (NEA)
Barthé, Earl 78
Bradley, David Henry, Jr. 39
Brown, Chuck 78
Hall, Arthur 39
Hemphill, Essex 10
Pope.L, William 72
Serrano, Andres 3
Williams, John A. 27
Williams, William T. 11

National Endowment for the Arts Jazz Hall of Fame
Terry, Clark 39

National Endowment for the Humanities
Gibson, Donald Bernard 40

National Equal Rights League
Trotter, Monroe 9

National Football League (NFL)
Alexander, Shaun 58
Allen, Marcus 20
Anderson, Jamal 22

Barber, Ronde **41**
Barber, Tiki **57**
Barney, Lem **26**
Bettis, Jerome **64**
Briscoe, Marlin **37**
Brooks, Aaron **33**
Brooks, Derrick **43**
Brown, Jim **11**
Bruce, Isaac **26**
Bryant, Cullen **81**
Bush, Reggie **59, 88**
Butler, Leroy, III **17**
Caldwell, Jim **81**
Cherry, Deron **40**
Cox, Bryan **83**
Crennel, Romeo **54**
Croom, Sylvester **50**
Culpepper, Daunte **32, 85**
Cunningham, Randall **23**
Davis, Milt **74**
Davis, Terrell **20**
Delaney, Joe **76**
Dickerson, Eric **27**
Duerson, Dave **93**
Dunn, Warrick **90**
Edwards, Herman **51**
Farr, Mel **24**
Faulk, Marshall **35**
Fowler, Reggie **51**
George, Eddie **80**
Gilliam, Frank **23**
Gilliam, Joe **31**
Green, Darrell **39, 74**
Green, Dennis **5, 45**
Greene, Joe **10**
Harris, James **79**
Hill, Calvin **19**
Holmes, Santonio **87**
Howard, Desmond **16, 58**
Irvin, Michael **64**
Jackson, Rickey **88**
Jackson, Tom **70**
Johnson, Chris **92**
Johnson, Keyshawn **91**
Johnson, Levi **48**
Jones, Deacon **92**
Ladd, Ernie **64**
Lane, Dick **92**
Little, Floyd **86**
Little, Larry **90**
Lofton, James **42**
Lott, Ronnie **9**
Matson, Ollie **93**
Mayhew, Martin R. **76**
McDaniel, Randall Cornell **81**
McNair, Steve **22, 47, 79**
Monk, Art **38, 73**
Moon, Warren **8, 66**
Moss, Randy **23, 90**
Motley, Marion **26**
Newsome, Ozzie **26**
Oliver, Pam **54**
Owens, Terrell **53**
Pace, Orlando **21**
Page, Alan **7**
Payton, Walter **11, 25**
Peete, Rodney **60**
Pryce, Trevor **89**
Randle, John **87**
Rashad, Ahmad **18**
Rhodes, Ray **14**
Rice, Jerry **5, 55, 89**
Sanders, Barry **1, 53**

Sanders, Bob **72**
Sanders, Deion **4, 31**
Sapp, Warren **38**
Sayers, Gale **28**
Sharper, Darren **32**
Shell, Art **1, 66**
Simpson, O.J. **15**
Singletary, Mike **4, 76**
Smith, Bruce **80**
Smith, DeMaurice **92**
Smith, Emmitt **7, 87**
Smith, Rick **72**
Stewart, Kordell **21**
Stingley, Darryl **69**
Strahan, Michael **35, 81**
Stringer, Korey **35**
Swann, Lynn **28**
Tatum, Jack **87**
Taylor, Jason **70**
Taylor, Lawrence **25**
Thomas, Derrick **25**
Thomas, Emmitt **71**
Thomas, Thurman **75**
Thrower, Willie **35**
Toler, Burl **80**
Tomlinson, LaDainian **65**
Tunnell, Emlen **54**
Upshaw, Gene **18, 47, 72**
Vick, Michael **39, 65**
Vincent, Troy **91**
Walker, Herschel **1, 69**
Ward, Hines **84**
Ware, Andre **37**
Ware, DeMarcus **92**
Washington, Kenny **50**
White, Reggie **6, 50**
Williams, Doug **22**
Williams, J. Mayo **83**
Williams, Ricky **85**
Williamson, Fred **67**
Winslow, Kellen **83**
Wright, Rayfield **70**

National Heritage "Living Treasure" Fellowship
Jackson, John **36**

National Hockey League (NHL)
Brashear, Donald **39**
Brathwaite, Fred **35**
Brown, Sean **52**
Doig, Jason **45**
Fuhr, Grant **1, 49**
Grand-Pierre, Jean-Luc **46**
Grier, Mike **43**
Iginla, Jarome **35**
Laraque, Georges **48**
Mayers, Jamal **39**
McBride, Bryant **18**
McCarthy, Sandy **64**
McKegney, Tony **3**
O'Ree, Willie **5**
Salvador, Bryce **51**
Weekes, Kevin **67**

National Information Infra-structure
Lewis, Delano **7**

National Institute of Arts & Letters
Lewis, Norman **39**
White, Charles **39**

National Institute of Education
Baker, Gwendolyn Calvert **9**

National Institutes of Health (NIH)
Anderson, Norman B. **45**
Cargill, Victoria A. **43**
Dunston, Georgia Mae **48**
Pinn, Vivian Winona **49**

National Inventors Hall of Fame
Carruthers, George R. **40**

National Lawn & Garden Distributor Association
Donald, Arnold Wayne **36**

National Medical Association
Cole, Lorraine **48**
Giles, Roscoe C. **93**
Maxey, Randall **46**
Ojikutu, Bisola **65**

National Minority Business Council
Leary, Kathryn D. **10**

National Museum of American History
Crew, Spencer R. **55**
Reagon, Bernice Johnson **7**

National Negro Congress
Bunche, Ralph J. **5**

National Negro Suffrage League
Trotter, Monroe **9**

National Newspaper Publishers Association
Cooper, Andrew W. **36**
Jealous, Benjamin **70**
Oliver, John J., Jr. **48**

National Oceanic and Atmospheric Administration
Bacon-Bercey, June **38**
Fields, Evelyn J. **27**

National Organization for Women (NOW)
Hernandez, Aileen Clarke **13**
Kennedy, Florynce **12, 33**
Murray, Pauli **38**

National Political Congress of Black Women
Chisholm, Shirley **2, 50**
Tucker, C. Delores **12, 56**
Waters, Maxine **3, 67**

National Public Radio (NPR)
Abu-Jamal, Mumia **15**
Bates, Karen Grigsby **40**
Drummond, William J. **40**
Early, Gerald **15**
Lewis, Delano **7**
Mitchell, Elvis **67**
Norris, Michele **83**
Smiley, Tavis **20, 68**
Williams, Juan **35, 80**

Zook, Kristal Brent **62**

National Resistance Army (Uganda; NRA)
Museveni, Yoweri **4**

National Resistance Movement
Museveni, Yoweri **4**

National Revolutionary Movement for Development
See Mouvement Revolutionnaire National pour le Developpement

National Rifle Association (NRA)
Williams, Robert F. **11**

National Science Foundation (NSF)
Massey, Walter E. **5, 45**

National Security Council
Frazer, Jendayi **68**
Powell, Colin **1, 28, 75**
Rice, Condoleezza **3, 28, 72**
Rice, Susan E. **74**
Sutphen, Mona **77**

National Society of Black Engineers
Donald, Arnold Wayne **36**
Price, Richard **51**

National Union for the Total Independence of Angola (UNITA)
Roberto, Holden **65**
Savimbi, Jonas **2, 34**

National Union of Mineworkers (South Africa)
Motlanthe, Kgalema **74**
Ramaphosa, Cyril **3**

National Urban Coalition (NUC)
Edelin, Ramona Hoage **19**

National Urban League
Barrow, Willie T. **85**
Berry, Edwin C. **81**
Brown, Ron **5**
Gordon, Bruce S. **41, 53, 82**
Granger, Lester B. **75**
Greely, M. Gasby **27**
Haynes, George Edmund **8**
Jacob, John E. **2**
Jones, Eugene Kinckle **79**
Jordan, Vernon E. **3, 35**
Price, Hugh B. **9, 54**
Spriggs, William **67**
Young, Whitney M., Jr. **4**

National War College
Clemmons, Reginal G. **41**

National Wildlife Federation
Osborne, Na'taki **54**

National Women's Hall of Fame
Cary, Mary Ann Shadd **30**
Kelly, Leontine **33**

Talbert, Mary B. **77**

National Youth Administration (NYA)
Bethune, Mary McLeod **4**
Primus, Pearl **6**

Nationwide
James, Donna A. **51**

Naval Research Laboratory (NRL)
Carruthers, George R. **40**

NBAF
See National Black Arts Festival

NBC
See National Broadcasting Company

NBGLLF
See National Black Gay and Lesbian Leadership Forum

NCBL
See National Conference on Black Lawyers

NCBW
See National Coalition of 100 Black Women

NCCK
See Kenya National Council of Churches

NCNE
See National Center for Neighborhood Enterprise

NCNW
See National Council of Negro Women

NEA
See National Education Association; National Endowment for the Arts

Nebula awards
Butler, Octavia **8, 43, 58**
Delany, Samuel R., Jr. **9**

Négritude
Césaire, Aimé **48, 69**
Damas, Léon-Gontran **46**
Ndiaye, Iba **74**

Negro American Political League
Trotter, Monroe **9**

Negro Ensemble Company
Cash, Rosalind **28**
Gordon, Carl **87**
Hooks, Robert **76**
Rolle, Esther **13, 21**
Schultz, Michael A. **6**
Ward, Douglas Turner **42**

Negro Leagues
Banks, Ernie **33**
Barnhill, David **30**
Bell, James "Cool Papa" **36**
Black, Joe **75**
Brown, Willard **36**
Campanella, Roy **25**
Charleston, Oscar **39**

Dandridge, Ray **36**
Davis, Piper **19**
Day, Leon **39**
Foster, Andrew **79**
Gibson, Josh **22**
Hairston, Sam **88**
Hyde, Cowan F. "Bubba" **47**
Irvin, Monte **31**
Johnson, Clifford "Connie" **52**
Johnson, Mamie "Peanut" **40**
Kaiser, Cecil **42**
Kimbro, Henry A. **25**
Leonard, Buck **67**
Lloyd, John Henry "Pop" **30**
Mackey, Biz **82**
Morton, Ferdinand Q. **90**
O'Neil, Buck **19, 59**
Paige, Satchel **7**
Pride, Charley **26**
Radcliffe, Ted **74**
Smith, Hilton **29**
Stearnes, Norman "Turkey" **31**
Stone, Toni **15**

Netherlands Antilles government
Liberia-Peters, Maria Philomena **12**

Neurosurgery
Black, Keith Lanier **18, 84**
Canady, Alexa **28**
Carson, Benjamin **1, 35, 76**
Dennis, Gary C. **91**

Neustadt International Prize for Literature
Brathwaite, Kamau **36**

Nevada state government
Horsford, Steven **88**

New Jersey state government
Bryant, Wayne R. **6**
Payne, William D. **60**

New Life Community Choir
Kee, John P. **43**

New Negro movement
See Harlem Renaissance

New Orleans city government
Henry, Troy **85**
Mason, Ronald **27**
Nagin, Ray **42, 57, 88**
Perry, James **83**

New Orleans Saints football team
Brooks, Aaron **33**
Mills, Sam **33**

New York City government
Campbell, Mary Schmidt **43**
Crew, Rudolph F. **16**
Davis, Gordon J. **76**
Dinkins, David **4**
Farrell, Herman D., Jr. **81**
Fields, C. Virginia **25**
Ford, Wallace **58**
Hageman, Hans **36**
Paterson, Basil A. **69**
Spigner, Archie **81**
Sutton, Percy E. **42**
Thompson, William **35**

Tolbert, Terence **74**

New York Coalition of 100 Black Woman
Wein, Joyce **62**

New York Daily News
Cose, Ellis **5, 50**

New York Drama Critics Circle Award
Hansberry, Lorraine **6**

New York Giants baseball team
Dandridge, Ray **36**
Mays, Willie **3**
Tunnell, Emlen **54**

New York Giants football team
Barber, Tiki **57**
Strahan, Michael **35, 81**
Taylor, Lawrence **25**

New York Jets football team
Lott, Ronnie **9**

New York Knicks basketball team
Ewing, Patrick **17, 73**
Johnson, Larry **28**
Reed, Willis, Jr. **86**
Sprewell, Latrell **23**
Stith, Tom **93**

New York Mets baseball team
Clendenon, Donn **26, 56**

New York Philharmonic
DePreist, James **37**

New York Public Library
Baker, Augusta **38**
Dodson, Howard, Jr. **7, 52**
Schomburg, Arthur Alfonso **9**

New York Shakespeare Festival
Browne, Roscoe Lee **66**
Gunn, Moses **10**
Wolfe, George C. **6, 43**

New York state government
Brown, Byron W. **72**
Farrell, Herman D., Jr. **81**
McCall, H. Carl **27**
Meeks, Gregory **25**
Motley, Constance Baker **10, 55**
Owens, Major **6**
Paterson, Basil A. **69**
Paterson, David A. **59**
Smith, Malcolm A. **75**

New York State Supreme Court
Dudley, Edward R. **58**
Wright, Bruce McMarion **3, 52**

New York Stock Exchange
Doley, Harold, Jr. **26**

New York Times
Blair, Jayson **50**
Blow, Charles M. **73**
Boyd, Gerald M. **32, 59**
Broyard, Anatole **68**
Caldwell, Earl **60**

Cooper, Helene **74**
Davis, George **36**
Hunter-Gault, Charlayne **6, 31**
Ifill, Gwen **28**
Mabry, Marcus **70**
Price, Hugh B. **9, 54**
Rhoden, William C. **67**
Wilkins, Roger **2, 84**

New York University
Brathwaite, Kamau **36**
Campbell, Mary Schmidt **43**
Newkirk, Pamela **69**

New York Yankees baseball team
Baylor, Don **6**
Bonds, Bobby **43**
Jackson, Reggie **15**
Jeter, Derek **27, 93**
Sabathia, CC **74**
Strawberry, Darryl **22**
Watson, Bob **25**
Winfield, Dave **5, 91**

Newark (NJ) city government
Booker, Cory Anthony **68**
Gibson, Kenneth Allen **6**
James, Sharpe **23, 69**

Newark Housing Authority
Gibson, Kenneth Allen **6**

The News Hour with Jim Lehrer TV series
Ifill, Gwen **28**

Newsday
Olojede, Dele **59**

Newsweek
Mabry, Marcus **70**

NFL
See National Football League

NHL
See National Hockey League

Niagara movement
Du Bois, W. E. B. **3**
Hope, John **8**
Talbert, Mary B. **77**
Trotter, Monroe **9**

Nickelodeon
Thompson, Kenan **52**

Nigerian Armed Forces
Abacha, Sani **11, 70**
Abiola, Moshood **70**
Babangida, Ibrahim **4**
Obasanjo, Olusegun **5, 22**

Nigerian Association of Patriotic Writers and Artists
Barrett, Lindsay **43**

Nigerian government
Abiola, Moshood **70**
Abubakar, Abdulsalami **66**
Akunyili, Dora Nkem **58**
Jonathan, Goodluck **83**
Obasanjo, Olusegun **5**

Yar'Adua, Umaru **69, 89**

Nigerian literature
Achebe, Chinua **6**
Akpan, Uwem **70**
Amadi, Elechi **40**
Bandele, Biyi **68**
Barrett, Lindsay **43**
Ekwensi, Cyprian **37**
Onwueme, Tess Osonye **23**
Rotimi, Ola **1**
Saro-Wiwa, Kenule **39**
Soyinka, Wole **4, 93**

Nigerien government
Tandja, Mamadou **33, 78**

NIH
See National Institutes of Health

Nike, Inc.
Edwards, Trevor **54**
Miller, Larry G. **72**

Nobel Peace Prize
Annan, Kofi Atta **15, 48**
Bunche, Ralph J. **5**
King, Martin Luther, Jr. **1**
Luthuli, Albert **13**
Tutu, Desmond Mpilo **6, 44**

Nobel Prize for Literature
Morrison, Toni **2, 15, 86**
Soyinka, Wole **4, 93**
Walcott, Derek **5**

Noma Award for Publishing in African
Ba, Mariama **30**

Nonfiction
Abrahams, Peter **39**
Adams-Ender, Clara **40**
Ali, Hana Yasmeen **52**
Allen, Debbie **13, 42**
Allen, Robert L. **38**
Andrews, Tina **74**
Atkins, Cholly **40**
Baisden, Michael **66**
Ballard, Allen Butler, Jr. **40**
Bashir, Halima **73**
Beah, Ishmael **69**
Blassingame, John Wesley **40**
Blockson, Charles L. **42**
Bogle, Donald **34**
Brown, Cecil M. **46**
Brown, Lloyd Louis **42**
Broyard, Bliss **68**
Buckley, Gail Lumet **39**
Carby, Hazel **27**
Carter, Joye Maureen **41**
Carter, Stephen L. **4**
Cashin, Sheryll **63**
Cobb, William Jelani **59**
Cole, Johnnetta B. **5, 43**
Cook, Mercer **40**
Cox, Joseph Mason Andrew **51**
Crew, Spencer R. **55**
Cruse, Harold **54**
Danquah, Meri Nana Ama **93**
Datcher, Michael **60**
Davis, Angela J. **88**
Davis, Arthur P. **41**
Davis, Thulani **61**
Dickerson, Debra J. **60**

Dunnigan, Alice Allison **41**
Edelman, Marian Wright **5, 42**
Elliott, Lorris **37**
Fax, Elton **48**
Fine, Sam **60**
Finner-Williams, Paris Michele **62**
Fisher, Antwone **40**
Fletcher, Bill, Jr. **41**
Ford, Clyde W. **40**
Foster, Cecil **32**
Gayle, Addison, Jr. **41**
Gibson, Donald Bernard **40**
Gladwell, Malcolm **62**
Greenwood, Monique **38**
Harrison, Alvin **28**
Harrison, Calvin **28**
Henderson, David **53**
Henries, A. Doris Banks **44**
Henriques, Julian **37**
Hercules, Frank **44**
Hernton, Calvin C. **51**
Hill, Errol **40**
Hobson, Julius W. **44**
Horne, Frank **44**
Ilibagiza, Immaculée **66**
Jakes, Thomas "T. D." **17, 43**
Johnson, William **91**
Jolley, Willie **28**
Jordan, Vernon E. **7, 35**
Kayira, Legson **40**
Kearney, Janis **54**
Kennedy, Randall **40**
Knight, Etheridge **37**
Kobia, Samuel **43**
Ladner, Joyce A. **42**
Lampley, Oni Faida **43, 71**
Lane, Lunsford **93**
Lincoln, C. Eric **38**
Mabuza-Suttle, Felicia **43**
Malveaux, Julianne **32, 70**
Manley, Ruth **34**
Matthews Shatteen, Westina **51**
McKenzie, Vashti M. **29**
McKinney Hammond, Michelle **51**
McWhorter, John **35**
Mossell, Gertrude Bustill **40**
Murray, Pauli **38**
Myers, Walter Dean **8, 20**
Naylor, Gloria **10, 42**
Neal, Mark Anthony **74**
Newkirk, Pamela **69**
Nissel, Angela **42**
Norton, Meredith **72**
Parks, Rosa **1, 35, 56**
Pitts, Leonard, Jr. **54, 85**
Run **31, 73**
Rusesabagina, Paul **60**
Sadlier, Rosemary **62**
Shakur, Yusef **85**
Smith, Jessie Carney **35**
Steele, Shelby **13, 82**
Thornton, Yvonne S. **69**
Tillis, Frederick **40**
Wade-Gayles, Gloria Jean **41**
Walker, Rebecca **50**
Wambugu, Florence **42**
Wilkens, J. Ernest, Jr. **43**
Williams, Terrie **35**
Williams, Wendy **62**
Wiwa, Ken **67**
Wright, Nathan, Jr. **56**

Zook, Kristal Brent **62**

North Carolina state government
Ballance, Frank W. **41**
Fuller, Thomas O. **90**

North Carolina State University
Lowe, Sidney **64**

North Pole
Counter, S. Allen **74**
Delany, Martin R. **27**
Henson, Matthew **2**
Hillary, Barbara **65**
McLeod, Gus **27**

NOW
See National Organization for Women

NPR
See National Public Radio

NRA
See National Resistance Army (Uganda); National Rifle Association

NRL
See Naval Research Laboratory

NSF
See National Science Foundation

Nuclear energy
O'Leary, Hazel **6**
Packer, Daniel **56**
Quarterman, Lloyd Albert **4**

Nuclear Regulatory Commission
Jackson, Shirley Ann **12**

Nucleus
King, Yolanda **6**
Shabazz, Attallah **6**

Nursing
Adams-Ender, Clara **40**
Auguste, Rose-Anne **13**
Hillary, Barbara **65**
Hughes, Ebony **57**
Hunter, Alberta **42**
Johnson, Hazel **22**
Johnson, Mamie "Peanut" **40**
Larsen, Nella **10**
Lewis, Daurene **72**
Lyttle, Hulda Margaret **14**
Richards, Hilda **49**
Riley, Helen Caldwell Day **13**
Robinson, Rachel **16**
Robinson, Sharon **22**
Seacole, Mary **54**
Shabazz, Betty **7, 26**
Staupers, Mabel K. **7**
Taylor, Susie King **13**

Nutrition
Clark, Celeste **15**
Gregory, Dick **1, 54**
Smith, Ian **62**
Watkins, Shirley R. **17**

Nuwaubianism
York, Dwight D. **71**

NYA
See National Youth Administration

Nyasaland African Congress (NAC)
Banda, Hastings Kamuzu **6, 54**

Oakland Athletics baseball team
Baylor, Don **6**
Henderson, Rickey **28, 78**
Jackson, Reggie **15**

Oakland Raiders football team
Howard, Desmond **16, 58**
Tatum, Jack **87**
Upshaw, Gene **18, 47, 72**

Oakland Tribune
Bailey, Chauncey **68**
Maynard, Nancy Hicks **73**
Maynard, Robert C. **7**

OAU
See Organization of African Unity

Obie awards
Browne, Roscoe Lee **66**
Carter, Nell **39**
De Shields, André **72**
Freeman, Yvette **27**
Orlandersmith, Dael **42**
Sands, Diana **87**
Thigpen, Lynne **17, 41**

Office of Civil Rights
See U.S. Department of Education

Office of Management and Budget
Raines, Franklin Delano **14**

Ohio state government
Brown, Les **5**
Ford, Jack **39**
Stokes, Carl **10, 73**
White, Michael R. **5**
Williams, George Washington **18**

Ohio Women's Hall of Fame
Craig-Jones, Ellen Walker **44**
Stewart, Ella **39**

OKeh record label
Brooks, Hadda **40**
Mo', Keb' **36**

Oklahoma Eagle
Ross, Don **27**

Oklahoma Hall of Fame
Mitchell, Leona **42**

Oklahoma state government
Ross, Don **27**

Olatunji Center for African Culture
Olatunji, Babatunde **36**

Olympics
Ali, Muhammad **2, 16, 52**
Beamon, Bob **30**
Bekele, Kenenisa **75**
Bolt, Usain **73**
Bonaly, Surya **7**
Bonheur, Yannick **84**
Bowe, Riddick **6**

Christie, Linford **8**
Clay, Bryan **57, 74**
Coachman, Alice **18**
Davis, Shani **58, 84**
Dawes, Dominique **11**
DeFrantz, Anita **37**
DeGale, James **74**
Devers, Gail **7, 87**
Dibaba, Tirunesh **73**
Edwards, Teresa **14**
Ervin, Anthony **66**
Eto'o, Samuel **73**
Felix, Allyson **48**
Flowers, Vonetta **35**
Freeman, Cathy **29**
Garrison, Zina **2**
Gebrselassie, Haile **70**
Gourdin, Edward O. **93**
Gourdine, Meredith **33**
Greene, Maurice **27, 77**
Griffith, Yolanda **25**
Griffith-Joyner, Florence **28**
Harrison, Alvin **28**
Harrison, Calvin **28**
Harris-Stewart, Lusia **90**
Hayes, Bob **77**
Hines, Garrett **35**
Holmes, Kelly **47**
Holyfield, Evander **6**
Howard, Sherri **36**
Iginla, Jarome **35**
James, G. Larry **74**
James, Vanessa **84**
Johnson, Ben **1**
Johnson, Michael **13**
Johnson, Rafer **33**
Jones, Cullen **73**
Jones, Lou **64**
Jones, Randy **35**
Joyner-Kersee, Jackie **5**
Keflezighi, Meb **49**
Kidd, Jason **86**
Lewis, Carl **4**
Malone, Karl **18, 51, 90**
Matson, Ollie **93**
Metcalfe, Ralph **26**
Miller, Cheryl **10, 74**
Montgomery, Tim **41**
Moses, Edwin **8**
Mutola, Maria **12**
Owens, Jesse **2**
Powell, Mike **7**
Quirot, Ana **13**
Richards, Sanya **66**
Rudolph, Wilma **4**
Scurry, Briana **27**
Thomas, Debi **26**
Thugwane, Josia **21**
Vanessa James and Yannick Bonheur **84**
Ward, Andre **62**
Ward, Lloyd **21, 46**
Westbrook, Peter **20**
Whitaker, Pernell **10, 89**
White, Willye **67**
Whitfield, Mal **60**
Williams, Lauryn **58**
Woodruff, John **68**

***On a Roll* Radio**
Smith, Greg **28**

Oncology
Leffall, Lasalle **3, 64**

100 Black Men of America
Dortch, Thomas W., Jr. **45**
Llewellyn, J. Bruce **13, 85**

Ontario Legislature
Curling, Alvin **34**

Opera
Adams, Leslie **39**
Allen, Betty **83**
Anderson, Marian **2, 33**
Arroyo, Martina **30**
Battle, Kathleen **70**
Brooks, Avery **9**
Brown, Angela M. **54**
Brown, Anne **76**
Brown, Uzee **42**
Brownlee, Lawrence **88**
Bumbry, Grace **5**
Collins, Janet **33, 64**
Conrad, Barbara Smith **90**
Davis, Anthony **11**
Dobbs, Mattiwilda **34**
Duncan, Todd **76**
Estes, Simon **28**
Freeman, Paul **39**
Graves, Denyce Antoinette **19, 57**
Greely, M. Gasby **27**
Grist, Reri **84**
Hendricks, Barbara **3, 67**
Joplin, Scott **6**
Joyner, Matilda Sissieretta **15**
Lister, Marquita **65**
Matthews, Benjamin **93**
Maynor, Dorothy **19**
McDonald, Audra **20, 62**
Mitchell, Leona **42**
Norman, Jessye **5**
Phillips, Helen L. **63**
Price, Leontyne **1**
Ragin, Derek Lee **84**
Simpson-Hoffman, N'kenge **52**
Still, William Grant **37**
Three Mo' Tenors **35**
Verrett, Shirley **66, 91**
White, Willard **53**

Operation Desert Shield/Operation Desert Storm
Powell, Colin **1, 28, 75**

Operation HOPE
Bryant, John **26**

Ophthalmology
Bath, Patricia E. **37**

Oracle Corporation
Phillips, Charles E., Jr. **57**
Woods, Jacqueline **52**

Organ
McGriff, Jimmy **72**

Organization of African States
Museveni, Yoweri **4**

Organization of African Unity (OAU)
Diouf, Abdou **3**
Haile Selassie **7**
Kaunda, Kenneth **2**

Kenyatta, Jomo **5**
Nkrumah, Kwame **3**
Nujoma, Samuel **10**
Nyerere, Julius **5**
Touré, Sekou **6**

Organization of Women Writers of African Descent
Cortez, Jayne **43**

Organization Us
Karenga, Maulana **10, 71**

Orlando Magic basketball team
Erving, Julius **18, 47**
O'Neal, Shaquille **8, 30**

Osteopathy
Allen, Ethel D. **13**
Anderson, William G(ilchrist) **57**
Ross-Lee, Barbara **67**

Overbrook Entertainment
Pinkett Smith, Jada **10, 41**

Painting
Alston, Charles **33**
Amos, Emma **63**
Andrews, Benny **22, 59**
Bailey, Radcliffe **19**
Bannister, Edward Mitchell **88**
Barnes, Ernie **16, 78**
Barthe, Richmond **15**
Basquiat, Jean-Michel **5**
Bearden, Romare **2, 50**
Beasley, Phoebe **34**
Biggers, John **20, 33**
Bradford, Mark **89**
Campbell, E. Simms **13**
Colescott, Robert **69**
Collins, Paul **61**
Cortor, Eldzier **42**
Cowans, Adger W. **20**
Crichlow, Ernest **75**
Crite, Alan Rohan **29**
Davis, Bing **84**
Delaney, Beauford **19**
Delaney, Joseph **30**
Delsarte, Louis **34**
Douglas, Aaron **7**
Driskell, David C. **7**
Ferguson, Amos **81**
Freeman, Leonard **27**
Gilliam, Sam **16**
Goodnight, Paul **32**
Green, Jonathan **54**
Guyton, Tyree **9**
Harkless, Necia Desiree **19**
Hayden, Palmer **13**
Holder, Geoffrey **78**
Honeywood, Varnette P. **54, 88**
Hunter, Clementine **45**
Jackson, Earl **31**
Johnson, William Henry **3**
Jones, Lois Mailou **13**
Knight, Gwendolyn **63**
Knox, Simmie **49**
Lawrence, Jacob **4, 28**
Lee, Annie Frances **22**
Lee-Smith, Hughie **5, 22**
Lewis, Norman **39**
Lewis, Samella **25**
Ligon, Glenn **82**
Loving, Alvin, Jr. **35, 53**

Major, Clarence **9**
Marshall, Kerry James **59**
Mayhew, Richard **39**
McGee, Charles **10**
Mehretu, Julie **85**
Mitchell, Corinne **8**
Motley, Archibald, Jr. **30**
Mutu, Wangechi **44**
Nascimento, Abdias do **93**
Ndiaye, Iba **74**
Neals, Otto **73**
Nugent, Richard Bruce **39**
Ouattara **43**
Pierre, Andre **17**
Pindell, Howardena **55**
Pippin, Horace **9**
Porter, James A. **11**
Ransome, James E. **88**
Reid, Senghor **55**
Ringgold, Faith **4, 81**
Ruley, Ellis **38**
Sallee, Charles **38**
Sebree, Charles **40**
Smith, Vincent D. **48**
Sudduth, Jimmy Lee **65**
Tanksley, Ann **37**
Tanner, Henry Ossawa **1**
Thomas, Alma **14**
Thomas, Mickalene **61**
Tolliver, Mose **60**
Tolliver, William **9**
Verna, Gelsy **70**
Wagner, Albert **78**
Washington, James, Jr. **38**
Wells, James Lesesne **10**
White, Charles **39**
Wiley, Kehinde **62**
Williams, Billy Dee **8**
Williams, William T. **11**
Wilson, Ellis **39**
Woodruff, Hale **9**

Pan African Orthodox Christian Church
Agyeman, Jaramogi Abebe **10, 63**

Pan-Africanism
Carmichael, Stokely **5, 26**
Clarke, John Henrik **20**
Du Bois, David Graham **45**
Du Bois, W. E. B. **3**
Garvey, Marcus **1**
Haile Selassie **7**
Kenyatta, Jomo **5**
Logan, Rayford W. **40**
Madhubuti, Haki **7, 85**
Marshall, Paule **7, 77**
Nkrumah, Kwame **3**
Nyerere, Julius **5**
Touré, Sekou **6**
Turner, Henry McNeal **5**

Papal Medal
Hampton, Lionel **17, 41**

Parti Démocratique de la Côte d'Ivoire (Democratic Party of the Ivory Coast; PDCI)
Bedie, Henri Konan **21**
Houphouët-Boigny, Félix **4, 64**

PATC
See Performing Arts Training Center

Pathology
Fuller, Solomon Carter, Jr. 15

PBS
See Public Broadcasting Service

PDCI
See Parti Démocratique de la Côte d'Ivoire (Democratic Party of the Ivory Coast)

PDP
See People's Democratic Party

Peace Corps
See U.S. Peace Corps

Peck School of the Fine Arts
Tyson, Andre 40

Pediatrics
Carson, Benjamin 1, 35, 76
Elders, Joycelyn 6
Fennoy, Ilene 72
Witt, Edwin T. 26
Zuma, Nkosazana Dlamini 34

PEN/Faulkner award
Bradley, David Henry, Jr. 39
Mayhew, Richard 39
Wideman, John Edgar 5, 87

Pennsylvania state government
Allen, Ethel D. 13
Brown, Homer S. 47
Fattah, Chaka 11, 70
Irvis, K. Leroy 67
Nix, Robert N. C., Jr. 51

Pennsylvania State University
Dunn, Jerry 27

Pennsylvania Supreme Court
Baldwin, Cynthia A. 74

Pentecostal church
DuBois, Joshua 88
Patterson, Gilbert Earl 41
Patterson, J. O., Jr. 80
Rivers, Eugene F., III 81
Sapp, Marvin 74
Wright, Timothy 74

People United to Serve Humanity (PUSH)
Barrow, Willie T. 85
Jackson, Jesse 1, 27, 72
Jackson, Jesse, Jr. 14, 45, 81

People's Democratic Party (Nigeria; PDP)
Jonathan, Goodluck 83
Obasanjo, Stella 32
Yar'Adua, Umaru 69, 89

People's National Party (Jamaica; PNP)
Patterson, P. J. 6, 20

People's Progressive Party (Gambia; PPP)
Jagan, Cheddi 16
Jawara, Dawda Kairaba 11

PepsiCo Inc.
Banks, Paula A. 68
Boyd, Edward 70

Harvey, William R. 42

Performing Arts Training Center (PATC)
Dunham, Katherine 4, 59

Perkins Prize
Jones, Thomas W. 41

PGA
See Professional Golfers' Association

Pharmaceutical research
Pickett, Cecil 39

Pharmaceuticals
Flowers, Sylester 50
Potter, Myrtle 40

Pharmacist
Akunyili, Dora Nkem 58
Flowers, Sylester 50
Pickett, Cecil 39
Stewart, Ella 39

Phelps Stokes Fund
Patterson, Frederick Douglass 12

Phi Beta Sigma Fraternity
Thomas, Arthur Ray 52

Philadelphia city government
Allen, Ethel D. 13
Goode, W. Wilson 4
Nutter, Michael 69
Street, John F. 24

Philadelphia Eagles football team
Cunningham, Randall 23
McNabb, Donovan 29
Rhodes, Ray 14
White, Reggie 6, 50

Philadelphia Flyers hockey team
Brashear, Donald 39
Charleston, Oscar 39

Philadelphia Phillies baseball team
Howard, Ryan 65
Rollins, Jimmy 70

Philadelphia public schools
Clayton, Constance 1

Philadelphia 76ers basketball team
Barkley, Charles 5, 66
Bol, Manute 1
Chamberlain, Wilt 18, 47
Erving, Julius 18, 47
Iverson, Allen 24, 46
Stackhouse, Jerry 30

Philadelphia Warriors
Chamberlain, Wilt 18, 47

Philanthropy
Banks, Paula A. 68
Brown, Eddie C. 35
Cooper, Evern 40
Cosby, Bill 7, 26, 59
Cosby, Camille 14, 80
Dawson, Matel, Jr. 39
Edley, Christopher 2, 48

Gardner, Chris 65
Golden, Marita 19
Gray, Willie 46
Johnson, Kevin 70
Johnson, Sheila Crump 48
Jones, Paul R. 76
Lavizzo-Mourey, Risa 48
Malone, Annie 13
McCarty, Osceola 16
Millines Dziko, Trish 28
Pleasant, Mary Ellen 9
Reeves, Rachel J. 23
Thomas, Franklin A. 5, 49
Waddles, Charleszetta "Mother" 10, 49
Walker, Madame C. J. 7
Washington, Pauletta Pearson 86
Wein, Joyce 62
White, Reggie 6, 50
Williams, Fannie Barrier 27
Wonder, Stevie 11, 53

Philosophy
Appiah, Kwame Anthony 67
Baker, Houston A., Jr. 6
Hall, Stuart 78
Piper, Adrian 71
Toomer, Jean 6
West, Cornel 5, 33, 80

Phoenix Suns basketball team
Barkley, Charles 5, 66
Heard, Gar 25
Johnson, Kevin 70

Photography
Andrews, Bert 13
Barboza, Anthony 10
Cowans, Adger W. 20
Cox, Renée 67
DeCarava, Roy 42, 81
Hansen, Austin 88
Harris, Lyle Ashton 83
Hinton, Milt 30
Jackson, Vera 40
Lester, Julius 9
Moutoussamy-Ashe, Jeanne 7
Parks, Gordon 1, 35, 58
Pinderhughes, John 47
Robeson, Eslanda Goode 13
Roble, Abdi 71
Serrano, Andres 3
Simpson, Lorna 4, 36
Sleet, Moneta, Jr. 5
Smith, Marvin 46
Smith, Morgan 46
Tanner, Henry Ossawa 1
Thomas, Mickalene 61
VanDerZee, James 6
Weems, Carrie Mae 63
White, John H. 27
Williams, Clarence 70
Willis, Deborah 85

Photojournalism
Ashley-Ward, Amelia 23
du Cille, Michel 74
Jackson, Vera 40
Moutoussamy-Ashe, Jeanne 7
Parks, Gordon 1, 35, 58
Sleet, Moneta, Jr. 5
Van Lierop, Robert 53
Wallace, William 75
White, John H. 27

Williams, Clarence 70
Withers, Ernest C. 68, 88
Yette, Samuel F. 63

Physical therapy
Elders, Joycelyn 6
Griffin, Bessie Blout 43

Physics
Adkins, Rutherford H. 21
Branson, Herman 87
Carruthers, George R. 40
Gates, Sylvester James, Jr. 15
Gourdine, Meredith 33
Imes, Elmer Samuel 39
Jackson, Shirley Ann 12
Johnson, Anthony M. 92
Massey, Walter E. 5, 45
Tyson, Neil deGrasse 15, 65

Piano
Adams, Leslie 39
Allen, Geri 92
Austin, Lovie 40
Basie, Count 23
Bonds, Margaret 39
Brooks, Hadda 40
Cartiér, Xam Wilson 41
Cole, Nat "King" 17
Coltrane, Alice 70
Cook, Charles "Doc" 44
Domino, Fats 20
Donegan, Dorothy 19
Duke, George 21
Ellington, Duke 5
Flanagan, Tommy 69
Garner, Erroll 76
Hancock, Herbie 20, 67
Hardin Armstrong, Lil 39
Harris, Barry 68
Hayes, Isaac 20, 58, 73
Hinderas, Natalie 5
Hines, Earl "Fatha" 39
Horn, Shirley 32, 56
Jamal, Ahmad 69
Johnson, Johnnie 56
Jones, Hank 57, 86
Joplin, Scott 6
Keys, Alicia 32, 68
Lee, Consuela 84
Marsalis, Ellis 90
McRae, Carmen 77
Monk, Thelonious 1
Moran, Jason 89
Perkins, Pinetop 70
Peterson, Oscar 52
Powell, Bud 24
Pratt, Awadagin 31
Preston, Billy 39, 59
Price, Florence 37
Pritchard, Robert Starling 21
Roberts, Marcus 19
Robinson, Reginald R. 53
Sample, Joe 51
Schuyler, Philippa 50
Scott, Hazel 66
Silver, Horace 26
Simone, Nina 15, 41
Sun Ra 60
Swann, Lynn 28
Southern, Eileen 56
Sykes, Roosevelt 20
Taylor, Billy 23, 92
Taylor, Cecil 70

Turner, Ike 68
Tyner, McCoy 92
Valdés, Bebo 75
Valdés, Chucho 89
Vaughan, Sarah 13
Walker, George 37
Waller, Fats 29
Watts, Andre 42
Webster, Katie 29
Williams, Mary Lou 15

Pittsburgh Pirates baseball team
Bonds, Barry 6, 34, 63
Clendenon, Donn 26, 56
Ellis, Dock 78
Stargell, Willie 29

Pittsburgh Steelers football team
Dungy, Tony 17, 42, 59
Gilliam, Joe 31
Greene, Joe 10
Perry, Lowell 30
Stargell, Willie 29
Stewart, Kordell 21
Swann, Lynn 28
Ward, Hines 84
Woodson, Rod 79

Planned Parenthood Federation of America Inc.
Wattleton, Faye 9

Playboy
Brown, Robert 65
Taylor, Karin 34

Playwright
Anthony, Trey 63
Arkadie, Kevin 17
Armah, Esther 87
Baldwin, James 1
Bandele, Biyi 68
Barrett, Lindsay 43
Beckham, Barry 41
Branch, William Blackwell 39
Brown, Cecil M. 46
Brown, Oscar, Jr. 53
Bullins, Ed 25
Caldwell, Benjamin 46
Carroll, Vinnette 29
Césaire, Aimé 48, 69
Chenault, John 40
Childress, Alice 15
Clark-Bekedermo, J. P. 44
Clarke, George 32
Cleage, Pearl 17, 64
Corthron, Kia 43
Cotter, Joseph Seamon, Sr. 40
Cox, Joseph Mason Andrew 51
Dadié, Bernard 34
Davis, Eisa 68
De Veaux, Alexis 44
Dent, Thomas C. 50
Dodson, Owen 38
Elder, Larry, III 38
Evans, Mari 26
Farah, Nuruddin 27
Franklin, J. E. 44
Glover, Keith 79
Gordone, Charles 15
Gurira, Danai 73
Hansberry, Lorraine 6

Harris, Bill 72
Hayes, Teddy 40
Hill, Errol 40
Hill, Leslie Pinckney 44
Holder, Laurence 34
Hughes, Langston 4
Johnson, Georgia Douglas 41
Johnson, Je'Caryous 63
Jones, Sarah 39
Kennedy, Adrienne 11
Kente, Gibson 52
King, Woodie, Jr. 27
Kwei-Armah, Kwame 84
Lampley, Oni Faida 43, 71
Lee, Leslie 85
Long, Richard Alexander 65
Marechera, Dambudzo 39
McClinton, Marion Isaac 77
Milner, Ron 39
Mitchell, Loften 31
Moss, Carlton 17
Mugo, Micere Githae 32
Nottage, Lynn 66
Onwueme, Tess Osonye 23
Orlandersmith, Dael 42
Parks, Suzan-Lori 34, 85
Perry, Tyler 40, 54
Rahman, Aishah 37
Redwood, John Henry 78
Rhone, Trevor 80
Salter, Nikkole 73
Sanchez, Sonia 17, 51
Santiago-Hudson, Ruben 85
Schuyler, George Samuel 40
Sebree, Charles 40
Smith, Anna Deavere 6, 44
Talbert, David E. 34, 93
Taylor, Regina 9, 46
Teer, Barbara Ann 81
Thurman, Wallace 17
Tolson, Melvin B. 37
Walcott, Derek 5
Ward, Douglas Turner 42
Wesley, Richard 73
Williams, Roy 89
Williams, Samm-Art 21
Wilson, August 7, 33, 55
Wilson, Tracey Scott 777
Wolfe, George C. 6, 43
Youngblood, Shay 32

PNP
See People's National Party (Jamaica)

Poet laureate (U.S.)
Dove, Rita 6, 78

Poetry
Abani, Chris 77
Adams, Jenoyne 60
Alexander, Elizabeth 75
Alexander, Margaret Walker 22
Allen, Samuel L. 38
Angelou, Maya 1, 15
Atkins, Russell 45
Aubert, Alvin 41
Baiocchi, Regina Harris 41
Bandele, Asha 36
Barrax, Gerald William 45
Barrett, Lindsay 43
Bell, James Madison 40
Bennett, Gwendolyn B. 59
Bennett, Louise 69

Berry, James 41
Bontemps, Arna 8
Boyd, Melba Joyce 86
Braithwaite, William Stanley 52
Brand, Dionne 32
Breeze, Jean "Binta" 37
Brooks, Gwendolyn 1, 28
Brown, Cecil M. 46
Brutus, Dennis 38
Burgess, Marjorie L. 55
Carter, Martin 49
Cartey, Wilfred 47
Césaire, Aimé 48, 69
Chenault, John 40
Cheney-Coker, Syl 43
Clark-Bekedermo, J. P. 44
Clarke, Cheryl 32
Clarke, George 32
Cleage, Pearl 17, 64
Cliff, Michelle 42
Clifton, Lucille 14, 64, 91
Coleman, Wanda 48
Cooper, Afua 53
Cornish, Sam 50
Cortez, Jayne 43
Cotter, Joseph Seamon, Sr. 40
Cox, Joseph Mason Andrew 51
Cuney, William Waring 44
Dabydeen, David 48
Dadié, Bernard 34
D'Aguiar, Fred 50
Damas, Léon-Gontran 46
Dandridge, Raymond Garfield 45
Danner, Margaret Esse 49
Datcher, Michael 60
Davis, Charles T. 48
Davis, Frank Marshall 47
De Veaux, Alexis 44
Dent, Thomas C. 50
Dodson, Owen 38
Dove, Rita 6, 78
Draper, Sharon Mills 16, 43
Dumas, Henry 41
Dunbar-Nelson, Alice Ruth Moore 44
Dungy, Camille 86
Emanuel, James A. 46
Evans, Mari 26
Fabio, Sarah Webster 48
Fair, Ronald L. 47
Figueroa, John J. 40
Fisher, Antwone 40
Fleming, Raymond 48
Forbes, Calvin 46
Ford, Nick Aaron 44
Frazier, Oscar 58
Gabre-Medhin, Tsegaye 64
Gilbert, Christopher 50
Goings, Russell 59
Goodison, Lorna 71
Harkless, Necia Desiree 19
Harper, Frances Ellen Watkins 11
Harper, Michael S. 34
Harris, Bill 72
Harris, Claire 34
Hayden, Robert 12
Henderson, David 53
Hernton, Calvin C. 51
Hill, Leslie Pinckney 44
Hoagland, Everett H. 45
Horne, Frank 44
Hughes, Langston 7
Jackson, Fred James 25

Joachim, Paulin 34
Johnson, Fenton 91
Johnson, Georgia Douglas 41
Johnson, Linton Kwesi 37
Jones, Sarah 39
Kay, Jackie 37
Keene, John 73
Knight, Etheridge 37
Laraque, Paul 67
Letson, Al 39
Lorde, Audre 6
Mackey, Nathaniel 75
Manley, Ruth 34
Marechera, Dambudzo 39
Matejka, Adrian 87
McClellan, George Marion 91
Moore, Jessica Care 30
Mugo, Micere Githae 32
Mullen, Harryette 34
Naylor, Gloria 10, 42
Neto, António Agostinho 43
Nugent, Richard Bruce 39
Okara, Gabriel 37
Parker, Pat 19
Peters, Lenrie 43
Philip, Marlene Nourbese 32
Powell, Kevin 31, 74
Quigless, Helen G. 49
Randall, Dudley 8, 55
Redmond, Eugene 23
Richards, Beah 30
Sanchez, Sonia 17, 51
Sapphire 14
Senghor, Léopold Sédar 12
Senior, Olive 37
Smith, Mary Carter 26
Spencer, Anne 27
Sundiata, Sekou 66
Tillis, Frederick 40
Tolson, Melvin B. 37
Touré, Askia (Muhammad Abu Bakr el) 47
Troupe, Quincy 83
van Sertima, Ivan 25
Walker, Margaret 29
Washington, James, Jr. 38
Weaver, Afaa Michael 37
Williams, Saul 31
Williams, Sherley Anne 25
Woods, Scott 55
Young, Al 82

Poetry Slam, Inc.
Woods, Scott 55

Political science
Ake, Claude 30
Cohen, Cathy J. 88
Dawson, Michael C. 63
Harris-Lacewell, Melissa 81
Skinner, Kiron K. 65
Walters, Ronald 83
Watson, Carlos 50

Politics
Adebari, Rotimi 83
Alexander, Archie Alphonso 14
Ali, Ayaan Hirsi 58, 92
Allen, Claude 68
Arthur, Owen 33
Austin, Junius C. 44
Avant, Clarence 19, 86
Baker, Thurbert 22
Ballance, Frank W. 41

Barnes, Melody **75**
Barrow, Dean **69**
Bass, Charlotta Spears **40**
Belton, Sharon Sayles **9, 16**
Bishop, Sanford D., Jr. **24**
Blackwell, Unita **17**
Boateng, Paul Yaw **56**
Booker, Cory Anthony **68**
Boye, Madior **30**
Brazile, Donna **25, 70**
Brown, Oscar, Jr. **53**
Buckley, Victoria (Vikki) **24**
Burris, Chuck **21**
Burris, Roland W. **25, 75**
Butler, Jerry **26**
Cain, Herman **15, 92**
Césaire, Aimé **48, 69**
Chideya, Farai **14, 61**
Christian-Green, Donna M. **17**
Clayton, Eva M. **20**
Coleman, Mary **46**
Compton, John **65**
Connerly, Ward **14**
Cummings, Elijah E. **24**
Curling, Alvin **34**
Currie, Betty **21**
Davis, Artur **41**
Davis, James E. **50**
Dixon, Julian C. **24**
Dixon, Sheila **68**
dos Santos, José Eduardo **43**
Dymally, Mervyn **42**
Edmonds, Terry **17**
Ellison, Keith **59**
Fields, C. Virginia **25**
Fields, Julia **45**
Fleming, Erik R. **75**
Ford, Jack **39**
Frazier, Ryan **89**
Gordon, Pamela **17**
Greenlee, Sam **48**
Hatcher, Andrew T. **90**
Hatcher, Richard G. **55**
Henry, Aaron **19**
Hilliard, Earl F. **24**
Hobson, Julius W. **44**
Holmes, Amy **69**
Ingraham, Hubert A. **19**
Isaac, Julius **34**
Jackson, Mae **57**
Jackson Lee, Sheila **20**
James, Sharpe **23, 69**
Jammeh, Yahya **23**
Jarrett, Valerie **73**
Jarvis, Charlene Drew **21**
Jefferson, William J. **25, 72**
Kabbah, Ahmad Tejan **23**
Kabila, Joseph **30**
Kariuki, J. M. **67**
Kelley, Cliff **75**
Lee, Barbara **25**
Lumumba, Patrice **33**
Maathai, Wangari **43**
Magloire, Paul Eugène **68**
Majette, Denise **41**
McGlowan, Angela **64, 86**
Metcalfe, Ralph **26**
Millender-McDonald, Juanita **21, 61**
Moore, Gwendolynne S. **55**
Moore, Harry T. **29**
Morial, Ernest "Dutch" **26**
Morial, Marc H. **20, 51**
Morton, Ferdinand Q. **90**

Nelson, Sophia A. **93**
Pereira, Aristides **30**
Perry, Ruth **15**
Pitta, Celso **17**
Powell, Debra A. **23**
Sankoh, Foday **74**
Scott, David **41**
Scott, Robert C. **23**
Simmons, E. Denise **79**
Simmons, Jamal **72**
Sisulu, Sheila Violet Makate **24**
Smith, Jennifer **21**
Smith, Princella **86**
Spencer, Winston Baldwin **68**
Thompson, Bennie G. **26**
Thurston, Baratunde **79**
Touré, Amadou Toumani **18**
Watkins, Joe **86**
Watt, Melvin **26**
Watts, J. C., Jr. **14, 38**
Wheat, Alan **14**
Williams, Anthony **21**
Williams, Eddie N. **44**
Williams, Eric Eustace **65**
Williams, George Washington **18**
Yar'Adua, Umaru **69, 89**

Pop music
Ashanti **37**
Ashford, Nickolas **21**
Babyface **10, 31, 82**
Bailey Rae, Corinne **83**
Barrino, Fantasia **53**
Bassey, Shirley **25**
Bleu, Corbin **65**
Blige, Mary J. **20, 34, 60**
Brown, Bobby **58**
Brown, Melanie **73**
Butler, Jonathan **28**
Cannon, Nick **47, 73**
Carey, Mariah **32, 53, 69**
Cee-Lo **70**
Chanté, Keshia **50**
Checker, Chubby **28**
Cole, Nat "King" **17**
Coppola, Imani Francesca **82**
Cox, Deborah **28**
David, Craig **31, 53**
Derülo, Jason **93**
Duke, George **21**
Ferrell, Rachelle **29**
Franklin, Aretha **11, 44**
Franklin, Kirk **15, 49**
Gray, Macy **29**
Hailey, JoJo **22**
Hailey, K-Ci **22**
Hawkins, Screamin' Jay **30**
Hayes, Isaac **20, 58, 73**
Hill, Lauryn **20, 53**
Holmes, Clint **57**
Horton, Gladys **92**
Houston, Whitney **7, 28, 83**
Hudson, Jennifer **63, 83**
Humphrey, Bobbi **20**
Isley, Ronald **25, 56**
Jackson, Janet **6, 30, 68**
Jackson, Jermaine **79**
Jackson, Michael **19, 53, 76**
James, Rick **17**
Jarreau, Al **21, 65**
Jones, Booker T. **84**
Jones, Quincy **8, 30**
Jordan, Montell **23**

Kelis **58**
Kendricks, Eddie **22**
Keys, Alicia **32, 68**
Khan, Chaka **12, 50**
LaBelle, Patti **13, 30**
Lewis, Leona **75**
Luckett, Letoya **61**
Martelly, Michel **90**
Massenburg, Kedar **23**
Mathis, Johnny **20**
McFerrin, Bobby **68**
Monica **21**
Moore, Chante **26**
Mumba, Samantha **29**
Mya **35**
Neville, Aaron **21**
Ne-Yo **65**
Noah, Yannick **4, 60**
Osborne, Jeffrey **26**
Otis, Clyde **67**
Palmer, Keke **68**
P.M. Dawn **54**
Preston, Billy **39, 59**
Prince **18, 65**
Reid, Antonio "L.A." **28**
Reid, Vernon **34**
Richie, Lionel **27, 65**
Rihanna **65**
Robinson, Smokey **3, 49**
Rucker, Darius **34, 74**
Seal **14, 75**
Senghor, Léopold Sédar **12**
Short, Bobby **52**
Simpson, Valerie **21**
Sisqo **30**
Smith, Myrna **92**
Smith, Willow **92**
Staton, Candi **27**
Summer, Donna **25**
Supremes, The **33**
Sweat, Keith **19**
Temptations, The **33**
The-Dream **74**
Thomas, Irma **29**
TLC **34**
Turner, Tina **6, 27**
Usher **23, 56**
Vanity **67**
Washington, Dinah **22**
Washington, Grover, Jr. **17, 44**
Washington, Val **12**
Welch, Elisabeth **52**
White, Barry **13, 41**
White, Josh, Jr. **52**
White, Maurice **29**
will.i.am **64**
Williams, Vanessa L. **4, 17**
Wilson, Jackie **60**
Wilson, Mary **28**
Wilson, Nancy **10**
Withers-Mendes, Elisabeth **64**
Wonder, Stevie **11, 53**

Portland (OR) Police Department
Moose, Charles **40**

Portland Trail Blazers basketball team
Drexler, Clyde **4, 61**
Miller, Larry G. **72**

Porter, Terry **75**

PPP
See People's Progressive Party (Gambia)

Pratt Institute
Mayhew, Richard **39**

Presbyterianism
Cannon, Katie **10**

Pride Economic Enterprises
Barry, Marion S. **7, 44**

Princeton University
Blanks, Deborah K. **69**
Harris-Lacewell, Melissa **81**
Rouse, Cecilia **93**
Simmons, Ruth **13, 38**

Printmaking
Blackburn, Robert **28**
Crichlow, Ernest **75**
Neals, Otto **73**
Tanksley, Ann **37**
Thrash, Dox **35**
Wells, James Lesesne **10**

Prison ministry
Bell, Ralph S. **5**

Prison reform
Betts, R. Dwayne **86**

Professional Golfers' Association (PGA)
Bramlett, Joseph **91**
Elder, Lee **6**
Powell, Renee **34**
Sifford, Charlie **4, 49**
Woods, Tiger **14, 31, 81**

Professional Women's Club of Chicago
Gray, Ida **41**

Progressive Labour Party
Smith, Jennifer **21**

Progressive Party
Bass, Charlotta Spears **40**

Pro-Line Corp.
Cottrell, Comer **11**

Proposition 209
Connerly, Ward **14**

Prosecution
Darden, Christopher **13**
Worthy, Kym **84**

Provincial Freeman
Cary, Mary Ann Shadd **30**

Psychiatry
Cobbs, Price M. **9**
Comer, James P. **6**
Fanon, Frantz **44**
Fuller, Solomon Carter, Jr. **15**
Hamburg, Beatrix **84**
Poussaint, Alvin F. **5, 67**
Welsing, Frances Cress **5**

Psychic health
Ford, Clyde W. **40**

Psychology
Anderson, Norman B. **45**
Archie-Hudson, Marguerite **44**

Brown, Joyce F. 25
Clark, Mamie Phipps 79
Edwards, Harry 2
Finner-Williams, Paris Michele 62
Fulani, Lenora 11
Gardere, Jeffrey 76
Gilbert, Christopher 50
Hale, Lorraine 8
Hare, Nathan 44
Hilliard, Asa Grant, III 66
Staples, Brent 8
Steele, Claude Mason 13
Tatum, Beverly Daniel 42, 84

Psychotheraphy
Berrysmith, Don Reginald 49
Ford, Clyde W. 40

Public Broadcasting Service (PBS)
Brown, Les 5
Brown, Tony 3
Creagh, Milton 27
Davis, Ossie 5, 50
Duke, Bill 3
Hampton, Henry 6
Hunter-Gault, Charlayne 6, 31
Ifill, Gwen 28
Lawson, Jennifer 1, 50
Long, Loretta 58
Lynch, Shola 61
Riggs, Marlon 5, 44
Roker, Al 12, 49

Public housing
Hamer, Fannie Lou 6
Lane, Vincent 5
Perry, James 83
Reems, Ernestine Cleveland 27

Public policy
Douglas, Derek 88

Public relations
Barrett, Andrew C. 12
Calhoun, Lillian Scott 87
Compton-Rock, Malaak 86
Edmonds, Terry 17
Graham, Stedman 13
Hedgeman, Anna Arnold 22
Jones, Robert G. 81
McCabe, Jewell Jackson 10
Perez, Anna 1
Pritchard, Robert Starling 21
Rowan, Carl T. 1, 30
Taylor, Kristin Clark 8
Tobin, Patricia 75
Williams, Maggie 7, 71

Public speaking
Bell, James Madison 40
Douglass, Frederick 87
Kennedy, Randall 40

Publishing
Abbott, Robert Sengstacke 27
Achebe, Chinua 6
Ames, Wilmer 27
Ashley-Ward, Amelia 23
Aubert, Alvin 41
Auguste, Arnold A. 47
Baisden, Michael 25, 66
Bass, Charlotta Spears 40
Bates, Daisy 13
Boston, Lloyd 24

Boyd, T. B., III 6
Brown, Jamie Foster 91
Brown, Marie Dutton 12
Cary, Mary Ann Shadd 30
Coombs, Orde M. 44
Cox, William E. 68
Dawkins, Wayne 20
Driver, David E. 11
Ducksworth, Marilyn 12
Dumas, Henry 41
Fuller, Hoyt 44
Giddings, Paula 11
Goodlett, Carlton B. 91
Graves, Butch 77
Graves, Earl G. 1, 35
Harris, Jay 19
Harris, Monica 18
Hill, Bonnie Guiton 20
Hudson, Cheryl 15
Hudson, Wade 15
James, Juanita 13
Jones, Quincy 8, 30
Kunjufu, Jawanza 3, 50
Lawson, Jennifer 1, 50
Leavell, Dorothy R. 17
Lewis, Edward T. 21
Lorde, Audre 6
Madhubuti, Haki 7, 85
Maynard, Nancy Hicks 73
Maynard, Robert C. 7
McDonald, Erroll 1
Moore, Jessica Care 30
Morgan, Garrett 1
Murphy, John H. 42
Myers, Walter Dean 8, 20
Parks, Gordon 1, 35, 58
Perez, Anna 1
Randall, Dudley 8, 55
Scott, C. A. 29
Sengstacke, John 18
Smith, Clarence O. 21
Stinson, Denise L. 59
Stringer, Vickie 58
Tyree, Omar Rashad 21
Vanzant, Iyanla 17, 47
Walker, Alice 1, 43
Washington, Alonzo 29
Washington, Laura S. 18
Wells-Barnett, Ida B. 8
Williams, Armstrong 29
Woods, Teri 69

Pulitzer Prize
Brooks, Gwendolyn 1, 28
Dove, Rita 6, 78
Fuller, Charles 8
Givhan, Robin Deneen 72
Gordone, Charles 15
Haley, Alex 4
Komunyakaa, Yusef 9
Lewis, David Levering 9
McPherson, James Alan 70
Morrison, Toni 2, 15, 86
Newkirk, Pamela 69
Page, Clarence 4
Parks, Suzan-Lori 34, 85
Payne, Les 89
Pitts, Leonard, Jr. 54, 85
Robinson, Eugene 77
Shipp, E. R. 15
Sleet, Moneta, Jr. 5
Walker, Alice 1, 43
Walker, George 37

White, John H. 27
Wilkins, Roger 2, 84
Wilson, August 7, 33, 55

Puppetry
Clash, Kevin 14, 93

PUSH
See People United to Serve Humanity

Quiltmaking
Benberry, Cuesta 65
Ringgold, Faith 4, 81

Qwest Records
Jones, Quincy 8, 30

Race car driving
Brown, Antron 85
Hamilton, Lewis 66
Lester, Bill 42, 85
Ribbs, Willy T. 2
Scott, Wendell Oliver, Sr. 19

Race relations
Abbott, Diane 9
Achebe, Chinua 6
Alexander, Clifford 26
Anthony, Wendell 25
Asante, Molefi Kete 3
Baker, Ella 5
Baker, Houston A., Jr. 6
Baldwin, James 1
Beals, Melba Patillo 15
Bell, Derrick 6
Bethune, Mary McLeod 4
Bobo, Lawrence 60
Booker, Simeon 23
Bosley, Freeman, Jr. 7
Boyd, T. B., III 6
Bradley, David Henry, Jr. 39
Branch, William Blackwell 39
Brown, Elaine 8
Bunche, Ralph J. 5
Butler, Paul D. 17
Cary, Lorene 3
Cashin, Sheryll 63
Cayton, Horace 26
Chavis, Benjamin 6
Clark, Kenneth B. 5, 52
Clark, Septima 7
Cobbs, Price M. 9
Cochran, Johnnie 11, 39, 52
Cole, Johnnetta B. 5, 43
Comer, James P. 6
Cone, James H. 3, 82
Conyers, John, Jr. 4, 45
Cook, Suzan D. Johnson 22
Cook, Toni 23
Cosby, Bill 7, 26, 59
Davis, Angela 5
Davis, Benjamin O., Jr. 2, 43
Davis, Benjamin O., Sr. 4
Dee, Ruby 8, 50, 68
Delany, Martin R. 27
Diallo, Amadou 27
Dickerson, Debra J. 60
Divine, Father 7
DuBois, Shirley Graham 21
Dunbar, Paul Laurence 8
Dunbar-Nelson, Alice Ruth Moore 44
Dyson, Michael Eric 11, 40
Edelman, Marian Wright 5, 42

Elder, Lee 6
Ellison, Ralph 7
Farmer, James 2, 64
Farmer-Paellmann, Deadria 43
Farrakhan, Louis 2
Fauset, Jessie 7
Franklin, John Hope 5, 77
Fuller, Charles 8
Gaines, Ernest J. 7
Gibson, William F. 6
Goode, W. Wilson 4
Graham, Lawrence Otis 12
Gregory, Dick 1, 54
Grimké, Archibald H. 9
Guy, Rosa 5
Haley, Alex 4
Hall, Elliott S. 24
Hampton, Henry 6
Hansberry, Lorraine 6
Harris, Alice 7
Hastie, William H. 8
Haynes, George Edmund 8
Hedgeman, Anna Arnold 22
Henry, Aaron 19
Henry, Lenny 9, 52
Hill, Oliver W. 24, 63
Hope, John 8
Howard, M. William, Jr. 26
Hunt, Darnell 92
Ingram, Rex 5
Innis, Roy 5
Jeffries, Leonard 8
Johnson, James Weldon 5
Jones, Elaine R. 7, 45
Jordan, Vernon E. 3, 35
Khanga, Yelena 6
King, Bernice 4, 81
King, Coretta Scott 3, 57
King, Martin Luther, Jr. 1
King, Yolanda 6
Lane, Charles 3
Lee-Smith, Hughie 5, 22
Lorde, Audre 6
Mabuza-Suttle, Felicia 43
Mandela, Nelson 1, 14, 77
Martin, Louis E. 16
Mathabane, Mark 5
Maynard, Robert C. 7
Mays, Benjamin E. 7
McDougall, Gay J. 11, 43
McKay, Claude 6
Meredith, James H. 11
Micheaux, Oscar 7
Moore, Harry T. 29
Mosley, Walter 5, 25, 68
Muhammad, Khallid Abdul 10, 31
Page, Clarence 4
Perkins, Edward 5
Pitt, David Thomas 10
Poussaint, Alvin F. 5, 67
Price, Frederick K. C. 21
Price, Hugh B. 9, 54
Robeson, Paul 2
Robinson, Spottswood W., III 22
Sampson, Edith S. 4
Shabazz, Attallah 6
Sifford, Charlie 4, 49
Simpson, Carole 6, 30
Sister Souljah 11
Sisulu, Sheila Violet Makate 24
Smith, Anna Deavere 6, 44
Sowell, Thomas 2
Spaulding, Charles Clinton 9

Staples, Brent **8**
Steele, Claude Mason **13**
Steele, Shelby **13, 82**
Taulbert, Clifton Lemoure **19**
Till, Emmett **7**
Tutu, Desmond Mpilo **6, 44**
Tutu, Nontombi Naomi **57**
Tyree, Omar Rashad **21**
Walcott, Derek **5**
Walker, Maggie **17**
Washington, Booker T. **4**
Washington, Harold **6**
Wells-Barnett, Ida B. **8**
Welsing, Frances Cress **5**
Wiley, Ralph **8, 78**
Wilkins, Roy **4**
Williams, Fannie Barrier **27**
Williams, Gregory **11**
Williams, Hosea Lorenzo **15, 31**
Williams, Walter E. **4**
Wilson, Sunnie **7, 55**
Wright, Richard **5**
Young, Whitney M., Jr. **4**

Radio
Abrahams, Peter **39**
Abu-Jamal, Mumia **15**
Alert, Kool DJ Red **33**
Anderson, Eddie "Rochester" **30**
Ashong, Derrick **86**
Banks, William **11**
Bates, Karen Grigsby **40**
Beasley, Phoebe **34**
Blayton, Jesse B., Sr. **55**
Booker, Simeon **23**
Branch, William Blackwell **39**
CoCo Brother **93**
Crocker, Frankie **29**
Dee, Ruby **8, 50, 68**
Dre, Dr. **10, 14, 30**
Elder, Larry **25**
Fuller, Charles **8**
Gibson, Truman K., Jr. **60**
Goode, Mal **13**
Greene, Petey **65**
Gumbel, Greg **8**
Hamblin, Ken **10**
Haynes, Trudy **44**
Holt, Nora **38**
Hughes, Cathy **27**
Jackson, Hal **41**
Jarrett, Vernon D. **42**
Joe, Yolanda **21**
Joyner, Tom **19, 90**
Kelley, Cliff **75**
Keyes, Alan L. **11**
Lewis, Delano **7**
Lewis, Ramsey **35, 70**
Ligging, Alfred, III **43**
Love, Ed **58**
Lover, Ed **10**
Ludacris **37, 60**
Madison, Joseph E. **17**
Majors, Jeff **41**
Michaux, Solomon Lightfoot **91**
Mickelbury, Penny **28**
Moss, Carlton **17**
Parr, Russ **51**
Pressley, Condace L. **41**
Pugh, Charles **81**
Quivers, Robin **61**
Samara, Noah **15**
Smiley, Rickey **59**

Smiley, Tavis **20, 68**
Smith, Greg **28**
Steinberg, Martha Jean "The Queen" **28**
Stuart, Moira **82**
Tirico, Mike **68**
Whack, Rita Coburn **36**
Williams, Armstrong **29**
Williams, Nat D. **91**
Williams, Ted **91**
Williams, Wendy **62**
Woods, Georgie **57**
Yarbrough, Camille **40**

Ragtime
Blake, Eubie **29**
Europe, James Reese **10**
Joplin, Scott **6**
Robinson, Reginald R. **53**
Sissle, Noble **29**

Rainbow Coalition
Chappell, Emma **18**
Jackson, Jesse **1, 27, 72**
Jackson, Jesse, Jr. **14, 45, 81**
Moore, Minyon **45**

Rap music
Alert, Kool DJ Red **33**
Baker, Houston A., Jr. **6**
Bambaataa, Afrika **34**
Banner, David **55**
Benjamin, Andre **45**
Big Daddy Kane **79**
Black Thought **63**
Blackman, Toni **86**
Blow, Kurtis **31**
B.o.B. **91**
Bow Wow **35**
Brown, Foxy **25**
Cee-Lo **70**
Chamillionaire **82**
Chuck D. **9**
Combs, Sean **17, 43, 92**
Common **31, 63**
Da Don, Polow **86**
Deezer D **53**
DJ Jazzy Jeff **32**
DMX **28, 64**
Drake **86**
Dre, Dr. **10, 14, 30**
Dupri, Jermaine **13, 46**
Dyson, Michael Eric **11, 40**
Elliott, Missy **31, 90**
Eve **29**
Fabolous **93**
Fat Boys **92**
50 Cent **46, 83**
Flavor Flav **67**
Flo Rida **78**
Ghostface Killah **90**
Gotti, Irv **39**
Grae, Jean **51**
Grandmaster Flash **33, 60**
Gray, F. Gary **14, 49**
Harrell, Andre **9, 30**
Heavy D **58**
Hill, Lauryn **20, 53**
Ice Cube **8, 30, 60**
Ice-T **6, 31**
Ja Rule **35, 91**
Jay-Z **27, 69**
Jones, Quincy **8, 30**
Kid Cudi **83**

K'naan **76**
Knight, Suge **11, 30**
KRS-One **34**
Kweli, Talib **93**
Lil' Kim **28**
Lil Wayne **66, 84**
Liles, Kevin **42**
Lopes, Lisa "Left Eye" **36**
Lover, Ed **10**
Ludacris **37, 60**
Madlib **88**
Mane, Gucci **91**
Mase **24**
Master P **21**
MC Breed **75**
M.C. Hammer **20, 80**
MC Lyte **34**
McDaniels, Ralph **79**
Method Man **81**
Mos Def **30**
Nate Dogg **92**
Nelly **32, 90**
Notorious B.I.G. **20**
Ol' Dirty Bastard **52**
OutKast **35**
Peterson, James **81**
Queen Latifah **1, 16, 58**
?uestlove **74**
Ray J **86**
Redman **81**
Rhymes, Busta **31**
Riley, Boots **89**
Roberts, Kimberly Rivers **72**
Ross, Rick **79**
Run-DMC **31, 75**
RZA **80**
Sermon, Erick **81**
Shakur, Afeni **67**
Shakur, Tupac **14**
Simmons, Russell **1, 30**
Sir Mix-A-Lot **82**
Sister Souljah **11**
Slick Rick **93**
Slim Thug **86**
Smith, Will **8, 18, 53**
Snoop Dogg **35, 84**
Speech **82**
Sticky Fingaz **86**
Sugarhill Gang, The **79**
Timbaland **32**
T-Pain **73**
Wale **92**
Xzibit **78**
Yarbrough, Camille **40**
Young Jeezy **63**

Rassemblement Démocratique Africain (African Democratic Rally; RDA)
Houphouët-Boigny, Félix **4, 64**
Touré, Sekou **6**

Rastafarianism
Burning Spear **79**
Dube, Lucky **77**
Haile Selassie **7**
Marley, Bob **5**
Marley, Rita **32, 70**
Tosh, Peter **9**

RDA
See Rassemblement Démocratique Africain (African Democratic

Rally)

Reader's Choice Award
Holton, Hugh, Jr. **39**

Reading Is Fundamental
Trueheart, William E. **49**

Real estate development
Amoudi, Mohammed al- **88**
Lane, Vincent **5**
Marshall, Bella **22**
Nail, John E. **92**
Payton, Philip A., Jr. **88**
Russell, Herman Jerome **17**
Toote, Gloria E. A. **64**

Record producer
Albright, Gerald **23**
Ayers, Roy **16**
Babyface **10, 31, 82**
Bambaataa, Afrika **34**
Barnes, Lloyd **77**
Bivins, Michael **72**
Butler, George, Jr. **70**
Coleman, Ornette **39, 69**
Da Don, Polow **86**
Danjah, Terror **91**
de Passe, Suzanne **25**
DJ Jazzy Jeff **32**
Dre, Dr. **10, 14, 30**
Duke, George **21**
Dupri, Jermaine **13, 46**
Elliott, Missy **31, 90**
Fuqua, Harvey **90**
Gotti, Irv **39**
Hailey, JoJo **22**
Hailey, K-Ci **22**
Hammond, Fred **23**
Hawkins, Walter **87**
Hill, Lauryn **20, 53**
Huff, Leon **86**
Ice Cube **8, 30, 60**
Ja Rule **35, 91**
Jackson, George **19**
Jackson, Joe **78**
Jackson, Michael **19, 53, 76**
Jackson, Randy **40**
Jean, Wyclef **20, 86**
Jerkins, Rodney **31**
Jimmy Jam **13**
Jones, Quincy **8, 30**
Kelly, R. **18, 44, 71**
Lewis, Terry **13**
Liles, Kevin **42**
Marley, Rita **32, 70**
Master P **21**
Mayfield, Curtis **2, 43**
Minott, Sugar **86**
Osborne, Jeffrey **26**
Prince **18, 65**
Queen Latifah **1, 16, 58**
Reid, Antonio "L.A." **28**
Robinson, Sylvia **79**
Sermon, Erick **81**
Sweat, Keith **19**
Timbaland **32**
Turner, Ike **68**
Vandross, Luther **13, 48, 59**
White, Barry **13, 41**
Whitfield, Norman **73**
Williams, J. Mayo **83**
Williams, Pharrell **47, 82**
Yabby You **83**

Young, Lee **72**

Recording executives
Busby, Jheryl **3, 74**
Butler, George, Jr. **70**
de Passe, Suzanne **25**
Dupri, Jermaine **13, 46**
Gordy, Berry, Jr. **1**
Gotti, Irv **39**
Harrell, Andre **9, 30**
Jackson, George **19**
Jackson, Randy **40**
Jimmy Jam **13**
Jones, Quincy **8, 30**
Knight, Suge **11, 30**
Lewis, Terry **13**
Liles, Kevin **42**
Massenburg, Kedar **23**
Master P **21**
Mayfield, Curtis **2, 43**
Reid, Antonio "L.A." **28**
Rhone, Sylvia **2**
Sanders, Angelia **86**
Simmons, Russell **1, 30**
Williams, J. Mayo **83**

Reform Party
Foster, Ezola **28**

Reggae
Afro, Teddy **78**
Banton, Buju **93**
Barnes, Lloyd **77**
Beenie Man **32**
Blondy, Alpha **30**
Burning Spear **79**
Cliff, Jimmy **28, 92**
Dube, Lucky **77**
Ellis, Alton **74**
Ford, Vincent **75**
Griffiths, Marcia **29**
Hammond, Lenn **34**
Isaacs, Gregory **89**
Johnson, Linton Kwesi **37**
Marley, Bob **5**
Marley, Rita **32, 70**
Marley, Ziggy **41**
Minott, Sugar **86**
Mowatt, Judy **38**
Perry, Ruth **19**
Rhoden, Wayne **70**
Shaggy **31**
Sly & Robbie **34**
Steely **80**
Tosh, Peter **9**
Yabby You **83**

Republic of New Afrika (RNA)
Williams, Robert F. **11**

Republican Party
Allen, Ethel D. **13**
Fisher, Ada M. **76**
Scott, Tim **87**
Steele, Michael **38, 73, 91**
Toote, Gloria E. A. **64**

Restaurants/Catering/Cooking
Armstrong, Govind **81**
Cain, Herman **15, 92**
Calabrese, Karyn **89**
Daniels-Carter, Valerie **23**
Dorsey, Thomas J. **90**
Downing, George T. **91**
Ford, Barney **90**

Garvin, Gerry **78**
Hawkins, La-Van **17, 54**
Howell, Ayinde **91**
James, Charles H., III **62**
Lewis, Aylwin B. **51, 88**
Otis, Clarence, Jr. **55**
Ouattara, Morou **74**
Pierce, Harold **75**
Rodriguez, Jimmy **47**
Samuelsson, Marcus **53**
Sbraga, Kevin **88**
Smith, B(arbara) **11**
Thompson, Don **56**
Washington, Regynald G. **44**
Williams, Lindsey **75**

Rhode Island School of Design
Bannister, Edward Mitchell **88**
Prophet, Nancy Elizabeth **42**

Rhodes scholar
Braxton, Brad **77**
Kennedy, Randall **40**
Locke, Alain **10**
Rice, Susan E. **74**

Rhythm and blues/soul music
Aaliyah **30**
Ace, Johnny **36**
Adams, Johnny **39**
Adams, Oleta **18**
Akon **68**
Amerie **52**
Ashanti **37**
Ashford, Nickolas **21**
Austin, Patti **24**
Ayers, Roy **16**
Babyface **10, 31, 82**
Badu, Erykah **22**
Bailey, Philip **63**
Baker, Anita **21, 48**
Baker, LaVern **26**
Ballard, Hank **41**
Baylor, Helen **36**
Belgrave, Marcus **77**
Belle, Regina **1, 51**
Benét, Eric **28, 77**
Berry, Chuck **29**
Beverly, Frankie **25**
Beyoncé **39, 70**
Bivins, Michael **72**
Blige, Mary J. **20, 34, 60**
Boyz II Men **82**
Brandy **14, 34, 72**
Braxton, Toni **15, 61, 91**
Brooks, Hadda **40**
Brown, Bobby **58**
Brown, Charles **23**
Brown, Chris **74**
Brown, Chuck **78**
Brown, Clarence Gatemouth **59**
Brown, James **15, 60**
Brown, Nappy **73**
Brown, Oscar, Jr. **53**
Brown, Ruth **90**
Burke, Solomon **31, 86**
Busby, Jheryl **3, 74**
Butler, Jerry **26**
Carey, Mariah **32, 53, 69**
Charles, Ray **16, 48**
Ciara **56**
Clinton, George **9, 93**
Cole, Keyshia **63**

Cole, Natalie **17, 60, 84**
Cooke, Sam **17**
Cox, Deborah **28**
Crawford, Hank **77**
D'Angelo **27**
David, Craig **31, 53**
Davis, Tyrone **54**
DeBarge, El **89**
Derülo, Jason **93**
DeVaughn, Raheem **91**
Diddley, Bo **39, 72**
Domino, Fats **20**
Dorsey, Lee **65**
Downing, Will **19**
Dre, Dr. **14, 30**
Dupri, Jermaine **13, 46**
Escobar, Damien **56**
Escobar, Tourie **56**
Evans, Faith **22**
Feemster, Herbert **72**
Fiona, Melanie **84**
Franklin, Aretha **11, 44**
Fuqua, Harvey **90**
Gamble, Kenny **85**
Garrett, Sean **57**
Gaye, Marvin **2**
Gaynor, Gloria **36**
Gibson, Tyrese **27, 62**
Gill, Johnny **51**
Ginuwine **35**
Goapele **55**
Goodman, Al **87**
Gotti, Irv **39**
Gray, Macy **29**
Green, Al **13, 47, 74**
Hailey, JoJo **22**
Hailey, K-Ci **22**
Hall, Aaron **57**
Hamilton, Anthony **61**
Harris, Corey **39, 73**
Hart, Alvin Youngblood **61**
Hathaway, Donny **18**
Hathaway, Lalah **57, 88**
Hayes, Isaac **20, 58, 73**
Hendryx, Nona **56**
Henry, Clarence "Frogman" **46**
Hill, Lauryn **20, 53**
Hilson, Keri **84**
Holloway, Brenda **65**
Houston, Cissy **20, 83**
Houston, Whitney **7, 28, 83**
Huff, Leon **86**
Hyman, Phyllis **19**
India.Arie **34**
Ingram, James **84**
Isley, Marvin **87**
Isley, Ronald **25, 56**
Jackson, Janet **6, 30, 68**
Jackson, Michael **19, 53, 76**
Jackson, Millie **25**
Jackson, Tito **81**
Jaheim **58**
Jamelia **51**
James, Etta **13, 52**
James, Rick **17**
Jarreau, Al **21, 65**
Jennings, Lyfe **56, 69**
Johnson, Robert **2**
Johnson-George, Tamara **79**
Jones, Booker T. **84**
Jones, Donell **29**
Jones, Quincy **8, 30**
Jones, Sharon **86**

Jordan, Montell **23**
Kandi **83**
Kelly, R. **18, 44, 71**
Kem **47**
Kendricks, Eddie **22**
Keys, Alicia **32, 68**
King Curtis **92**
Knight, Gladys **16, 66**
Knight, Marie **80**
LaBelle, Patti **13, 30**
Larrieux, Amel **63**
Lattimore, Kenny **35**
LaVette, Bettye **85**
Ledisi **73**
Legend, John **67**
Levert, Eddie **70**
Levert, Gerald **22, 59**
Little Richard **15**
Lopes, Lisa "Left Eye" **36**
Love, Darlene **23, 92**
Luckett, Letoya **61**
Maitreya, Sananda **85**
Mario **71**
Massenburg, Kedar **23**
Master P **21**
Maxwell **20, 81**
Mayfield, Curtis **2, 43**
McCoo, Marilyn **53**
McKnight, Brian **18, 34**
Miles, Buddy **69**
Monáe, Janelle **86**
Monica **21**
Moore, Chante **26**
Moore, Melba **21**
Musiq **37, 84**
Mya **35**
Nash, Johnny **40**
Ndegeocello, Meshell **15, 83**
Neale, Haydain **52**
Neville, Aaron **21**
Ne-Yo **65**
Notorious B.I.G. **20**
Otis, Clyde **67**
Parker, Maceo **72**
Parker, Ray, Jr. **85**
Pendergrass, Teddy **22, 83**
Pinkney, Fayette **80**
Pleasure P **84**
Preston, Billy **39, 59**
Price, Kelly **23**
Prince **18, 65**
Reagon, Toshi **76**
Record, Eugene **60**
Redding, Otis **16**
Reed, A. C. **36**
Reeves, Martha **85**
Richard, Dawn **92**
Richie, Lionel **27, 65**
Rihanna **65**
Riperton, Minnie **32**
Robinson, Smokey **3, 49**
Ross, Diana **8, 27**
Russell, Brenda **52**
Sade **15, 92**
Sample, Joe **51**
Scott, Jill **29, 83**
Scott, "Little" Jimmy **48**
Siji **56**
Simpson, Valerie **21**
Sisqo **30**
Sledge, Percy **39**
Songz, Trey **88**
Sparks, Jordin **66**

Staton, Candi **27**
Steinberg, Martha Jean "The Queen" **28**
Stone, Angie **31**
Strong, Barrett **89**
Studdard, Ruben **46**
Sullivan, Jazmine **81**
Supremes, The **33**
Sweat, Keith **19**
Tamia **24, 55**
Temptations, The **33**
Terrell, Tammi **32**
The-Dream **74**
Thomas, Irma **29**
Thomas, Rozonda **34, 78**
Thomas, Rufus **20**
TLC **34**
Tresvant, Ralph **57**
Turner, Ike **68**
Turner, Tina **6, 27**
Ulmer, James **79**
Usher **23, 56**
Valentino, Bobby **62**
Vandross, Luther **13, 48, 59**
Watley, Jody **54**
Watts, Reggie **52**
Wells, Mary **28**
West, Kanye **52, 93**
White, Barry **13, 41**
Williams, Michelle **73**
Williams, Vanessa L. **4, 17**
Wilson, Cassandra **16**
Wilson, Charlie **31, 77**
Wilson, Mary **28**
Wilson, Nancy **10**
Withers, Bill **61**
Womack, Bobby **60, 92**
Wonder, Stevie **11, 53**
Woodson, Ali Ollie **89**

RNA
See Republic of New Afrika

Robert C. Maynard Institute for Journalism Education
Harris, Jay T. **19**
Maynard, Nancy Hicks **73**
Maynard, Robert C. **7**

Roberts Companies, The
Roberts, Mike **57**

Roc-A-Fella
Dash, Damon **31**
Jay-Z **27, 69**

Rock and Roll Hall of Fame
Ballard, Hank **41**
Bennett, Estelle **77**
Berry, Chuck **29**
Bland, Bobby "Blue" **36**
Brown, Charles **23**
Burke, Solomon **31, 86**
Clinton, George **9, 93**
Cole, Nat "King" **17**
Davis, Miles **4**
Diddley, Bo **39, 72**
Franklin, Aretha **11, 44**
Gamble, Kenny **85**
Grandmaster Flash **33, 60**
Green, Al **13, 47, 74**
Guy, Buddy **31**
Hayes, Isaac **20, 58, 73**
Holiday, Billie **1**

Holland-Dozier-Holland **36**
Hooker, John Lee **30**
Isley, Marvin **87**
Isley, Ronald **25, 56**
Jackson, Mahalia **5**
Jackson, Michael **19, 53, 76**
Jackson, Tito **81**
Jamerson, James **59**
James, Etta **13, 52**
Johnson, Johnnie **56**
Jones, Booker T. **84**
Knight, Gladys **16, 66**
Mayfield, Curtis **2, 43**
Morton, Jelly Roll **29**
Prince **18, 65**
Reeves, Martha **85**
Run-DMC **31, 75**
Shider, Garry **87**
Sledge, Percy **39**
Spector, Ronnie **77**
Steinberg, Martha Jean "The Queen" **28**
Stone, Sly **85**
Toussaint, Allen **60**
Turner, Big Joe **92**
Turner, Ike **68**
Turner, Tina **6, 27**
Wilson, Jackie **60**
Wilson, Mary **28**
Wonder, Stevie **11, 53**

Rock music
Adebimpe, Tunde **75**
Ballard, Hank **41**
Bennett, Estelle **77**
Berry, Chuck **29**
Clemons, Clarence **41**
Diddley, Bo **39, 72**
Domino, Fats **20**
Edwards, Esther Gordy **43**
Glover, Corey **34**
Hendrix, Jimi **10**
Ice-T **6, 31**
Johnson, Johnnie **56**
King Curtis **92**
Kravitz, Lenny **10, 34**
Little Richard **15**
Lymon, Frankie **22**
Mayfield, Curtis **2, 43**
Miles, Buddy **69**
Moore, LeRoi **72**
Preston, Billy **39, 59**
Prince **18, 65**
Reagon, Toshi **76**
Reid, Vernon **34**
Run-DMC **31, 75**
Slash **75**
Spector, Ronnie **77**
Stew **69**
Stone, Sly **85**
Tait, Michael **57**
Tamar-kali **63**
Tinsley, Boyd **50**
Toussaint, Allen **60**
Turner, Ike **68**
Turner, Big Joe **92**
Turner, Tina **6, 27**
will.i.am **64**
Wilson, Jackie **60**

Rockefeller Foundation
Price, Hugh B. **9, 54**

Rockets
Williams, O. S. **13**

Rodeo
Nash, Johnny **40**
Pickett, Bill **11**
Sampson, Charles **13**
Whitfield, Fred **23**

Roman Catholic Church
Akpan, Uwem **70**
Arinze, Francis **19**
Aristide, Jean-Bertrand **6, 45**
Chineworth, Mary Alice **79**
Clements, George **2**
DeLille, Henriette **30**
Fabre, Shelton **71**
Gantin, Bernardin **70**
Gregory, Wilton D. **37**
Guy, Rosa **5**
Healy, James Augustine **30**
Jean-Juste, Gérard **78**
Jones, Alex **64**
Marino, Eugene Antonio **30**
Otunga, Maurice Michael **55**
Rugambwa, Laurean **20**
Senghor, Augustin Diamacoune **66**
Stallings, George A., Jr. **6**

Romance fiction
Bunkley, Anita Richmond **39**
Hill, Donna **32**
Jackson, Brenda **87**
Washington, Elsie B. **78**

Royalty
Christophe, Henri **9**
Ka Dinizulu, Mcwayizeni **29**
Mswati III **56**
Mutebi, Ronald **25**

Rugby
Mundine, Anthony **56**

Rutgers University
Davis, George **36**
Gibson, Donald Bernard **40**

Rwandan government
Habyarimana, Juvenal **8**
Kagame, Paul **54**
Mushikiwabo, Louise **88**

SAA
See Syndicat Agricole Africain

Sacramento Kings basketball team
Russell, Bill **8**
Webber, Chris **15, 30, 59**

SADCC
See Southern African Development Coordination Conference

Sailing
Pinckney, Bill **42**

St. Kitts and Nevis government
Douglas, Denzil Llewellyn **53**

St. Louis Blues hockey team
Brathwaite, Fred **35**
Mayers, Jamal **39**

St. Louis Browns baseball team
Brown, Willard **36**
Paige, Satchel **7**

St. Louis Cardinals baseball team
Baylor, Don **6**
Bonds, Bobby **43**
Brock, Lou **18**
Flood, Curt **10, 93**
Gibson, Bob **33**
Lankford, Ray **23**
Smith, Ozzie **77**

St. Louis city government
Bosley, Freeman, Jr. **7**
Harmon, Clarence **26**

St. Louis Hawks basketball team
See Atlanta Hawks basketball team

St. Louis Rams football team
Bruce, Isaac **26**
Faulk, Marshall **35**
Pace, Orlando **21**

Sainte Beuve Prize
Beti, Mongo **36**

Salvation Army
Gaither, Israel L. **65**

Sammy Davis Jr. National Liver Institute University Hospital
Leevy, Carrol M. **42**

San Antonio Spurs basketball team
Duncan, Tim **20, 91**
Elliott, Sean **26**
Gervin, George **80**
Mohammed, Nazr **64**
Parker, Tony **75**
Robinson, David **24, 90**

San Diego Chargers football team
Barnes, Ernie **16, 78**
Lofton, James **42**
Tomlinson, LaDainian **65**
Winslow, Kellen **83**

San Diego Conquistadors
Chamberlain, Wilt **18, 47**

San Diego Padres baseball team
Carter, Joe **30**
Gwynn, Tony **18, 83**
McGriff, Fred **24**
Smith, Ozzie **77**
Winfield, Dave **5, 91**

San Francisco 49ers football team
Green, Dennis **5, 45**
Hayes, Bob **77**
Lott, Ronnie **9**
Rice, Jerry **5, 55, 89**
Simpson, O. J. **15**
Singletary, Mike **4, 76**

Washington, Gene 63

San Francisco Giants baseball team
Baker, Dusty 8, 43, 72
Bonds, Barry 6, 34, 63
Bonds, Bobby 43
Carter, Joe 30
Mays, Willie 3
Morgan, Joe 9
Strawberry, Darryl 22

San Francisco public schools
Coleman, William F., III 61

Saturday Night Live
Meadows, Tim 30
Morgan, Tracy 61
Morris, Garrett 31
Murphy, Eddie 4, 20, 61
Rock, Chris 3, 22, 66
Rudolph, Maya 46
Thompson, Kenan 52

Savoy Ballroom
Johnson, Buddy 36

Saxophone
Adderley, Julian "Cannonball" 30
Albright, Gerald 23
Anderson, Fred 87
Bechet, Sidney 18
Clemons, Clarence 41
Coltrane, John 19
Coltrane, Ravi 71
Crawford, Hank 77
Golson, Benny 37
Gordon, Dexter 25
Greene, Jimmy 74
Griffin, Johnny 71
Hawkins, Coleman 9
Jacquet, Illinois 49
Kay, Ulyssess 37
Kenyatta, Robin 54
King Curtis 92
McLean, Jackie 78
Moody, James 83
Moore, LeRoi 72
Moura, Paulo 87
Newman, David 76
Parker, Charlie 20
Parker, Maceo 72
Redman, Joshua 30
Rollins, Sonny 37
Sanders, Pharoah 64
Shider, Garry 87
Shorter, Wayne 75
Washington, Grover, Jr. 17, 44
Waters, Benny 26
Whalum, Kirk 37, 64
York, Vincent 40
Young, Lester 37

Schomburg Center for Research in Black Culture
Andrews, Bert 13
Dodson, Howard, Jr. 7, 52
Hutson, Jean Blackwell 16
Morrison, Sam 50
Reddick, Lawrence Dunbar 20
Schomburg, Arthur Alfonso 9

School desegregation
Bridges, Ruby 77
Chestnut, J. L., Jr. 73

Fortune, T. Thomas 6
Hamer, Fannie Lou 6
Hobson, Julius W. 44
Holmes, Hamilton E. 82

Science fiction
Barnes, Steven 54
Butler, Octavia 8, 43, 58
Delany, Samuel R., Jr. 9

SCLC
See Southern Christian Leadership Conference

Scotland Yard
Griffin, Bessie Blout 43

Screenplay writing
Akil, Mara Brock 60, 82
Brown, Cecil M. 46
Clack, Zoanne 73
Davis, Thulani 61
Elder, Lonne, III 38
Fisher, Antwone 40
Fletcher, Geoffrey 85
Greaves, William 38
Jones, Orlando 30
Lumet, Jenny 80
McMillan, Tracy 93
Nissel, Angela 42
Prince-Bythewood, Gina 31, 77
Pryce, Trevor 89
Rhimes, Shonda Lynn 67
Rhone, Trevor 80
Ridley, John 69
Robinson, Matt 69
Singleton, John 2, 30
Talbert, David E. 34, 93
Wesley, Richard 73

Sculpture
Allen, Tina 22, 75
Amos, Emma 63
Bailey, Radcliffe 19
Barthe, Richmond 15
Biggers, John 20, 33
Biggers, Sanford 62
Billops, Camille 82
Brown, Donald 19
Burke, Selma 16
Catlett, Elizabeth 2
Chanticleer, Raven 91
Chase-Riboud, Barbara 20, 46
Cortor, Eldzier 42
Dwight, Edward 65
Edwards, Melvin 22
Fuller, Meta Vaux Warrick 27
Guyton, Tyree 9
Hammons, David 69
Hathaway, Isaac Scott 33
Hunt, Richard 6
Lewis, Edmonia 10
Lewis, Samella 25
Manley, Edna 26
Marshall, Kerry James 59
McCullough, Geraldine 58, 79
McGee, Charles 10
Moody, Ronald 30
Neals, Otto 73
Perkins, Marion 38
Pierce, Elijah 84
Prophet, Nancy Elizabeth 42
Puryear, Martin 42
Ringgold, Faith 4, 81

Saar, Alison 16
Saar, Betye 80
Savage, Augusta 12
Scott, John T. 65
Shabazz, Attallah 6
Simmons, Gary 58
Stout, Renee 63
Washington, James, Jr. 38

Seattle city government
Rice, Norm 8

Seattle Mariners baseball team
Griffey, Ken, Jr. 12, 73
Reynolds, Harold 77

Seattle Supersonics basketball team
Bickerstaff, Bernie 21
Durant, Kevin 76
Silas, Paul 24

Security and defense services
Garrett, James F. 78

Seismology
Person, Waverly 9, 51

Senegalese government
Senghor, Léopold Sédar 66
Wade, Abdoulaye 66

Sesame Street
Byrd, Eugene 64
Clash, Kevin 14, 93
Glover, Savion 14
Long, Loretta 58
Orman, Roscoe 55
Reed Hall, Alaina 83
Robinson, Matt 69

Sexual harassment
Gomez-Preston, Cheryl 9
Hill, Anita 5, 65
McCauley, Gina 76
Thomas, Clarence 2, 39, 65

Share
Auguste, Arnold A. 47

Sheila Bridges Design Inc.
Bridges, Sheila 36

Shell Oil Company
Mays, Leslie A. 41

Shrine of the Black Madonna
Agyeman, Jaramogi Abebe 10, 63

Sickle cell anemia
Edwards, Willarda V. 59
Pace, Betty 59
Satcher, David 7, 57

Sierra Leone government
Kabbah, Ahmad Tejan 23
Koroma, Ernest Bai 84

Silicon Graphics Incorporated
Coleman, Ken 57
Hannah, Marc 10

Siméus Foods International
Siméus, Dumas M. 25

Skateboarding
Williams, Stevie 71

Sketches
Crite, Alan Rohan 29
Sallee, Charles 38

Skiing
Horton, Andre 33
Horton, Suki 33

Skillman Foundation
Goss, Carol A. 55

Slavery
Asante, Molefi Kete 3
Bibb, Henry and Mary 54
Blackshear, Leonard 52
Blassingame, John Wesley 40
Chase-Riboud, Barbara 20, 46
Cooper, Anna Julia 20
Douglas, Aaron 7
Du Bois, W. E. B. 3
Dunbar, Paul Laurence 8
Durham, James 90
Easton, Hosea 91
Equiano, Olaudah 78
Farmer-Paellmann, Deadria 43
Gaines, Ernest J. 7
Gordon-Reed, Annette 74
Haley, Alex 4
Harper, Frances Ellen Watkins 11
Henson, Josiah 90
Huggins, Nathan Irvin 52
Johnson, Charles 1, 82
Jones, Edward P. 43, 67
Keckley, Elizabeth 90
Lane, Lunsford 93
Mason, Biddy 89
McWorter, Free Frank 91
Montgomery, Isaiah T. 91
Muhammad, Elijah 4
Patterson, Orlando 4
Pleasant, Mary Ellen 9
Stephens, Charlotte Andrews 14
Stewart, Maria W. Miller 19
Tancil, Gladys Quander 59
Taylor, Susie King 13
Tubman, Harriet 9
Wall, Orindatus S. B. 92

Smithsonian Institution
Bunch, Lonnie G., III 91

Smith College
Mayhew, Richard 39
Simmons, Ruth 13, 38

SNCC
See Student Nonviolent Coordinating Committee

Soccer
Adu, Freddy 67
Anderson, Viv 58
Barnes, John 53
Beasley, Jamar 29
Crooks, Garth 53
dos Santos, Manuel Francisco 65
Drogba, Didier 78
Eto'o, Samuel 73
Ferdinand, Rio 82
Gyan, Asamoah 87
Henry, Thierry 66
Ince, Paul 83
James, David 84
Jones, Cobi N'Gai 18
Kanouté, Fred 68

Mello, Breno **73**
Mensah, John **87**
Milla, Roger **2**
Nakhid, David **25**
Onyewu, Oguchi **60**
Pelé **7**
Regis, Cyrille **51**
Ronaldinho **69**
Scurry, Briana **27**
Sono, Jomo **86**
Weah, George **58**

Social science/social criticism
Berry, Mary Frances **7**
Black, Albert **51**
Bobo, Lawrence **60**
Bunche, Ralph J. **5**
Cayton, Horace **26**
Clark, Kenneth B. **5, 52**
Cobbs, Price M. **9**
Collins, Patricia Hill **67**
Frazier, E. Franklin **10**
George, Zelma Watson **42**
Hall, Stuart **78**
Hare, Nathan **44**
Harris, Eddy L. **18**
Haynes, George Edmund **8**
hooks, bell **5, 90**
Hunt, Darnell **92**
Ladner, Joyce A. **42**
Lawrence-Lightfoot, Sara **10**
Marable, Manning **10**
Steele, Claude Mason **13**
Williams, David Rudyard **50**
Woodson, Robert L. **10**

Social work
Auguste, Rose-Anne **13**
Berry, Bertice **8, 55**
Berrysmith, Don Reginald **49**
Brown, Cora **33**
Canada, Geoffrey **23**
Coles, Alice **80**
Colston, Hal **72**
Compton-Rock, Malaak **86**
Dunham, Katherine **4, 59**
Fields, C. Virginia **25**
Finner-Williams, Paris Michele **62**
Gbowee, Leymah **76**
Granger, Lester B. **75**
Hale, Clara **16**
Hale, Lorraine **8**
Harris, Alice **7**
Haynes, George Edmund **8**
Jackson, Judith D. **57**
Jackson, Mae **57**
King, Barbara **22**
Lewis, Thomas **19**
Little, Robert L. **2**
Robinson, Rachel **16**
Sears, Stephanie **53**
Smith, Damu **54**
Vaughn, Viola **70**
Waddles, Charleszetta "Mother" **10, 49**
Walker, Bernita Ruth **53**
Wallace, Joaquin **49**
Wells, Henrietta Bell **69**
White-Hammond, Gloria **61**
Williams, Fannie Barrier **27**
Thrower, Willie **35**

Young, Whitney M., Jr. **4**

Socialist Party of Senegal
Diouf, Abdou **3**

Sociology
Edwards, Harry **2**

Soledad Brothers
Jackson, George Lester **14**

Somalian government
Ahmed, Sharif **80**

Soul City, NC
McKissick, Floyd B. **3**

Soul food
Williams, Lindsey **75**
Woods, Sylvia **34**

Soul Train
Baylor, Helen **36**
Cornelius, Don **4**
D'Angelo **27**
Lil' Kim **28**
Winans, CeCe **14, 43**

South African Communist Party
Hani, Chris **6**
Mhlaba, Raymond **55**

South African government
Dandala, Mvume **77**
Mhlaba, Raymond **55**
Motlanthe, Kgalema **74**
Sisulu, Walter **47**
Zuma, Jacob **33, 75**
Zuma, Nkosazana Dlamini **34**

South African literature
Abrahams, Peter **39**
Brutus, Dennis **38**
Head, Bessie **28**
Mathabane, Mark **5**
Mofolo, Thomas **37**
Mphalele, Es'kia **40**

South Carolina state government
Cardozo, Francis L. **33**
Scott, Tim **87**

Southeastern University
Jarvis, Charlene Drew **21**

Southern African Development Coordination Conference (SADCC)
Masire, Quett **5**
Nujoma, Samuel **10**

Southern Christian Leadership Conference (SCLC)
Abernathy, Ralph **1**
Angelou, Maya **1, 15**
Baker, Ella **5**
Barrow, Willie T. **85**
Brooks, Tyrone **59**
Chavis, Benjamin **6**
Dee, Ruby **8, 50, 68**
Fauntroy, Walter E. **11**
Hooks, Benjamin L. **2, 85**
Jackson, Jesse **1, 27, 72**
Jones, William A., Jr. **61**
King, Bernice **4, 81**

King, Martin Luther, Jr. **1**
King, Martin Luther, III **20**
Lawson, James M., Jr. **90**
Lee, Eric P. **79**
Lowery, Joseph **2**
Moses, Robert Parris **11**
Moss, Otis, Jr. **72**
Nash, Diane **72**
Orange, James **74**
Rustin, Bayard **4**
Shuttlesworth, Fred **47**
Walker, Wyatt Tee **80**
Williams, Hosea Lorenzo **15, 31**
Young, Andrew **3, 48**

Southern Syncopated Orchestra
Cook, Will Marion **40**

Space shuttle
Gregory, Frederick **8, 51**
Jemison, Mae C. **1, 35**
McNair, Ronald **3, 58**
Wilson, Stephanie **72**

Special Olympics
Clairborne, Loretta **34**

Speedskating
Davis, Shani **58, 84**

Spelman College
Cobb, William Jelani **59**
Cole, Johnnetta B. **5, 43**
Falconer, Etta Zuber **59**
Price, Glenda **22**
Simmons, Ruth **13, 38**
Tatum, Beverly Daniel **42, 84**
Wade-Gayles, Gloria Jean **41**

Sphinx Organization
Dworkin, Aaron P. **52**

Spingarn medal
Aaron, Hank **5**
Ailey, Alvin **8**
Anderson, Marian **2, 33**
Angelou, Maya **1, 15**
Bates, Daisy **13**
Bethune, Mary McLeod **4**
Bradley, Thomas **2, 20**
Brooke, Edward W. **8, 88**
Bunche, Ralph J. **5**
Carver, George Washington **4**
Chesnutt, Charles **29**
Clark, Kenneth B. **5, 52**
Cosby, Bill **7, 26, 59**
Davis, Sammy, Jr. **18**
Drew, Charles Richard **7**
Du Bois, W. E. B. **3**
Ellington, Duke **5**
Evers, Medgar **3**
Franklin, John Hope **5, 77**
Grimké, Archibald H. **9**
Haley, Alex **4**
Hastie, William H. **8**
Hayes, Roland **4**
Height, Dorothy I. **2, 23, 78**
Higginbotham, A. Leon, Jr. **13, 25**
Hinton, William Augustus **8**
Hooks, Benjamin L. **2, 85**
Horne, Lena **5, 86**
Houston, Charles Hamilton **4**
Hughes, Langston **4**
Jackson, Jesse **1, 27, 72**

Johnson, James Weldon **5**
Jordan, Barbara **4, 78**
Julian, Percy Lavon **6**
Just, Ernest Everett **3**
Keith, Damon J. **16, 74**
King, Martin Luther, Jr. **1**
Lawless, Theodore K. **8**
Lawrence, Jacob **4**
Logan, Rayford **40**
Marshall, Thurgood **1, 44**
Mays, Benjamin E. **7**
Moore, Harry T. **29**
Parks, Gordon **1, 35, 58**
Parks, Rosa **1, 35, 56**
Powell, Colin **1, 28, 75**
Price, Leontyne **1**
Randolph, A. Philip **3**
Robeson, Paul **2**
Robinson, Jackie **6**
Staupers, Mabel K. **7**
Sullivan, Leon H. **3, 30**
Tobias, Channing H. **79**
Weaver, Robert C. **8, 46**
White, Walter F. **4**
Wilder, L. Douglas **3, 48**
Wilkins, Roy **4**
Williams, Paul R. **9**
Woodson, Carter G. **2**
Wright, Louis Tompkins **4**
Wright, Richard **5**
Young, Andrew **3, 48**
Young, Coleman **1, 20**

Spirituals
Anderson, Marian **2, 33**
Carr, Kurt **56**
Fisher, Miles Mark **91**
Hairston, Jester **88**
Hayes, Roland **4**
Jackson, Mahalia **5**
Johnson, Hall **90**
Joyner, Matilda Sissieretta **15**
Norman, Jessye **5**
Reese, Della **6, 20**
Williams, Denise **40**

Sports administration
Fuller, Vivian **33**
Kerry, Leon G. **46**
Lee, Bertram M., Sr. **46**
Mills, Steve **47**
Phillips, Teresa L. **42**
Randolph, Willie **53**
Ussery, Terdema, II **29**

Sports agent
Holland, Kimberly N. **62**

Stanford University
Bobo, Lawrence **60**
Rice, Condoleezza **3, 28, 72**
Walker, Arthur, II **87**
Washington, Gene **63**
Willingham, Tyrone **43**

State University of New York
Ballard, Allen Butler, Jr. **40**
Baraka, Amiri **1**
Butts, Calvin O., III **9, 90**
Clemente, Rosa **74**
Wharton, Clifton R., Jr. **7**

Stellar Awards
Baylor, Helen **36**
Hawkins, Walter **87**

Sapp, Marvin **74**
Tribbett, Tye **81**
Walker, Hezekiah **34**

Stonewall 25
Norman, Pat **10**

Stop the Violence Movement
KRS-One **34**
MC Lyte **34**

Storytelling
Baker, Augusta **38**
Bennett, Louise **69**
Hill, Hugh Morgan **83**

Student Nonviolent Coordinating Committee (SNCC)
Al-Amin, Jamil Abdullah **6**
Anderson, William G(ilchrist) **57**
Baker, Ella **5**
Barry, Marion S. **7, 44**
Blackwell, Unita **17**
Bond, Julian **2, 35**
Carmichael, Stokely **5, 26**
Clark, Septima **7**
Davis, Angela **5**
Forman, James **7, 51**
Hamer, Fannie Lou **6**
Holland, Endesha Ida Mae **3, 57**
Lester, Julius **9**
Lewis, John **2, 46, 83**
Moses, Robert Parris **11**
Nash, Diane **72**
Poussaint, Alvin F. **5, 67**
Reagon, Bernice Johnson **7**
Touré, Askia (Muhammad Abu Bakr el) **47**

Sudan government
Bashir, Omar al- **77**
Cham, Adongo Agada Akway **77**
Kiir, Salva **85**

Sun Microsystems
Tademy, Lalita **36**

Sundance Film Festival
Harris, Leslie **6**
Nelson, Stanley **92**

Sunny Alade Records
Ade, King Sunny **41**

Supreme Court
See U.S. Supreme Court

Surfing
Corley, Tony **62**

Surrealism
Ellison, Ralph **7**
Lee-Smith, Hughie **5, 22**

Swaziland government
Mswati III **56**

Sweet Honey in the Rock
Reagon, Bernice Johnson **7**

Swimming
Jones, Cullen **73**

Sylvia's Restaurant
Washington, Regynald G. **44**
Woods, Sylvia **34**

Syndicat Agricole Africain (SAA)
Houphouët-Boigny, Félix **4, 64**

Talk Soup
Tyler, Aisha N. **36**

Talladega College
Archie-Hudson, Marguerite **44**

Tampa Bay Buccaneers football team
Barber, Ronde **41**
Brooks, Derrick **43**
Dungy, Tony **17, 42, 59**
McDaniel, Randall Cornell **81**
Morris, Raheem **77**
Sapp, Warren **38**
Williams, Doug **22**

Tanganyikan African National Union (TANU)
Kikwete, Jakaya Mrisho **73**
Nyerere, Julius **5**

TANU
See Tanganyikan African National Union

Tanzanian African National Union (TANU)
See Tanganyikan African National Union

Tap dancing
Atkins, Cholly **40**
Bates, Peg Leg **14**
Brown, Ernest **80**
Glover, Savion **14**
Hines, Gregory **1, 42**
Lane, William Henry **90**
Robinson, LaVaughn **69**
Sims, Howard "Sandman" **48**
Slyde, Jimmy **70**
Walker, Dianne **57**

TBS
See Turner Broadcasting System

Teacher of the Year Award
Draper, Sharon Mills **16, 43**
Oliver, Kimberly **60**

Teachers Insurance and Annuity Association and the College Retirement Equities Fund (TIAA-CREF)
Wharton, Clifton R., Jr. **7**

Teaching
Abani, Chris **77**
Adams-Ender, Clara **40**
Alexander, Margaret Walker **22**
Amadi, Elechi **40**
Archie-Hudson, Marguerite **44**
Aubert, Alvin **41**
Baiocchi, Regina Harris **41**
Ballard, Allen Butler, Jr. **40**
Belgrave, Marcus **77**
Bibb, Henry and Mary **54**
Blassingame, John Wesley **40**
Branch, William Blackwell **39**
Brawley, Benjamin **44**
Brown, Uzee **42**
Brown, Willa **40**
Bryan, Ashley F. **41**

Campbell, Mary Schmidt **43**
Cardozo, Francis L. **33**
Carruthers, George R. **40**
Carter, Joye Maureen **41**
Chenault, John **40**
Cheney-Coker, Syl **43**
Clarke, John Henrik **20**
Clemmons, Reginal G. **41**
Cobb, Jewel Plummer **42**
Cobb, W. Montague **39**
Cole, Johnnetta B. S. **5, 43**
Colescott, Robert **69**
Collins, Patricia Hill **67**
Cook, Mercer **40**
Cooper Cafritz, Peggy **43**
Cortez, Jayne **43**
Cortor, Eldzier **42**
Cotter, Joseph Seamon, Sr. **40**
Dailey, Ulysses Grant **87**
Davis, Arthur P. **41**
Davis, Gary **41**
Davis, Milt **74**
De Veaux, Alexis **44**
Dennard, Brazeal **37**
Draper, Sharon Mills **16, 43**
Drummond, William J. **40**
Dumas, Henry **41**
Dunnigan, Alice Allison **41**
Dymally, Mervyn **42**
Early, Gerald **15**
Everett, Percival **93**
Falconer, Etta Zuber **59**
Feelings, Muriel **44**
Ferguson, Ronald F. **75**
Figueroa, John J. **40**
Fletcher, Bill, Jr. **41**
Ford, Nick Aaron **44**
Forrest, Leon **44**
Fuller, A. Oveta **43**
Fuller, Arthur **27**
Fuller, Howard L. **37**
Gates, Sylvester James, Jr. **15**
Gayle, Addison, Jr. **41**
George, Zelma Watson **42**
Gibson, Donald Bernard **40**
Gill, Gerald **69**
Hall, Arthur **39**
Hamburg, Beatrix **84**
Hammonds, Evelynn **69**
Harding, Vincent **67**
Hare, Nathan **44**
Harris, Barry **68**
Harvey, William R. **42**
Henries, A. Doris Banks **44**
Hill, Errol **40**
Hill, Leslie Pinckney **44**
Horne, Frank **44**
Humphries, Frederick **20**
Imes, Elmer Samuel **39**
Jackson, Fred James **25**
Jarrett, Vernon D. **42**
Jarvis, Erich **67**
Kennedy, Randall **40**
Ladner, Joyce A. **42**
Leevy, Carrol M. **42**
Lewis, Norman **39**
Lindsey, Tommie **51**
Logan, Rayford W. **40**
Maathai, Wangari **43**
McCullough, Geraldine **58, 79**
Mitchell, Parren J. **42, 66**
Moore, Harry T. **29**
Mphalele, Es'kia **40**

Naylor, Gloria **10, 42**
Norman, Maidie **20**
Oliver, Kimberly **60**
Owens, Helen **48**
Palmer, Everard **37**
Patterson, Mary Jane **54**
Peters, Margaret and Matilda **43**
Player, Willa B. **43**
Prophet, Nancy Elizabeth **42**
Puryear, Martin **42**
Putney, Martha S. **75**
Querino, Manuel Raimundo **84**
Ray, Charlotte E. **60**
Redmond, Eugene **23**
Reid, Senghor **55**
Rhodes, Jewell Parker **84**
Ross-Lee, Barbara **67**
Shockley, Ann Allen **84**
Simpson-Hoffman, N'kenge **52**
Smith, Anna Deavere **6, 44**
Smith, John L. **22**
Tillis, Frederick **40**
Toler, Burl **80**
Tutu, Nontombi Naomi **57**
Tyson, Andre **40**
Wambugu, Florence **42**
Watson, Diane **41**
Wells, Henrietta Bell **69**
Wesley, Richard **73**
Wilkens, J. Ernest, Jr. **43**
Yancy, Dorothy Cowser **42**
Yarbrough, Camille **40**
York, Vincent **40**

Teatro Experimental do Negro
Nascimento, Abdias do **93**

Techno music
Atkins, Juan **50**
Craig, Carl **31, 71**
May, Derrick **41**

TEF
See Theological Education Fund

Telecommunications
Clyburn, Mignon **78**
Gordon, Bruce S. **41, 53, 82**
Ibrahim, Mo **67**
Irvin, Vernon **65**
Wilkins, Ray **47**

Television
Akil, Mara Brock **60, 82**
Anderson, Eddie "Rochester" **30**
Andrews, Tina **74**
Arkadie, Kevin **17**
Arnold, Tichina **63**
Banks, Tyra **11, 50**
Barclay, Paris **37**
Barrino, Fantasia **53**
Beach, Michael **26**
Bentley, Lamont **53**
Blacque, Taurean **58**
Blake, Asha **26**
Bonet, Lisa **58**
Bowser, Yvette Lee **17**
Brady, Wayne **32, 71**
Branch, William Blackwell **39**
Bridges, Todd **37**
Brooks, Golden **62**
Brooks, Hadda **40**
Brooks, Mehcad **62**
Brown, Bobby **58**

Brown, James **22**
Brown, Joe **29**
Brown, Vivian **27**
Burnett, Charles **16, 68**
Carson, Lisa Nicole **21**
Carter, Nell **39**
Cash, Rosalind **28**
Cedric the Entertainer **29, 60**
Cheadle, Don **19, 52**
Clack, Zoanne **73**
CoCo Brother **93**
Coleman, Gary **35, 86**
Corbi, Lana **42**
Cosby, Bill **7, 26, 59**
Creagh, Milton **27**
Curtis-Hall, Vondie **17**
Davis, Viola **34, 76**
de Passe, Suzanne **25**
Deezer D **53**
Diggs, Taye **25, 63**
Dourdan, Gary **37**
Dungey, Merrin **62**
Earthquake **55**
Elba, Idris **49, 89**
Elder, Larry **25**
Ephriam, Mablean **29**
Eubanks, Kevin **15**
Evans, Harry **25**
Faison, Donald **50**
Falana, Lola **42**
Fales-Hill, Susan **88**
Fields, Kim **36**
Flavor Flav **67**
Fox, Rick **27**
Frazier, Kevin **58**
Freeman, Yvette **27**
Gardere, Jeffrey **76**
Gibbs, Marla **86**
Givens, Robin **4, 25, 58**
Gray, Willie **46**
Greely, M. Gasby **27**
Greene, Petey **65**
Grier, David Alan **28**
Griffin, Angela **80**
Hall, Arsenio **58**
Hardison, Kadeem **22**
Harewood, David **52**
Hatchett, Glenda **32**
Haynes, Trudy **44**
Haysbert, Dennis **42**
Hemsley, Sherman **19**
Henriques, Julian **37**
Hill, Lauryn **20, 53**
Hill, Marc Lamont **80**
Hughley, D. L. **23, 76**
Hyman, Earle **25, 79**
Jackson, George **19**
Jackson, Randy **40**
Jackson, Tom **70**
Jarrett, Vernon D. **42**
Jean-Louis, Jimmy **76**
Joe, Yolanda **21**
Johnson, Rodney Van **28**
Jones, Bobby **20**
Kandi **83**
Kodjoe, Boris **34, 89**
Lathan, Sanaa **27**
Lesure, James **64**
Lewis, Emmanuel **36**
Long, Loretta **58**
Lomax, Louis E. **90**
Lumbly, Carl **47**
Mabuza-Suttle, Felicia **43**

Mac, Bernie **29, 61, 72**
Mahorn, Rick **60**
Manigault-Stallworth, Omarosa **69**
Mann, Tamela **92**
Marsalis, Branford **34**
Martin, Helen **31**
Martin, Jesse L. **31**
Mathis, Greg **26**
McCrary Anthony, Crystal **70**
McFarland, Roland **49**
McGlowan, Angela **64, 86**
McKenzie, Vashti M. **29**
McKinney, Nina Mae **40**
Meadows, Tim **30**
Mercado-Valdes, Frank **43**
Michele, Michael **31**
Miller, Wentworth **75**
Mitchell, Brian Stokes **21**
Mitchell, Russ **21, 73**
Moss, Carlton **16**
Nash, Johnny **40**
Nash, Niecy **66**
Neal, Elise **29**
Neville, Arthel **53**
Nicholas, Denise **82**
Nissel, Angela **42**
Norman, Christina **47**
Orman, Roscoe **55**
Palmer, Keke **68**
Parker, Nicole Ari **52**
Perry, Tyler **40, 54**
Phifer, Mekhi **25**
Pickens, James, Jr. **59**
Pitts, Byron **71**
Poussaint, Renee **78**
Pratt, Kyla **57**
Premice, Josephine **41**
Price, Frederick K. C. **21**
Prince-Bythewood, Gina **31, 77**
Quarles, Norma **25**
Ray, Gene Anthony **47**
Reddick, Lance **52**
Reynolds, Star Jones **10, 27, 61**
Rhimes, Shonda Lynn **67**
Richards, Beah **30**
Richardson, Salli **68**
Ridley, John **69**
Roberts, Deborah **35**
Robinson, Shaun **36**
Rock, Chris **3, 22, 66**
Rodrigues, Percy **68**
Roker, Al **12, 49**
Roker, Roxie **68**
Rollins, Howard E., Jr. **17**
Russell, Nipsey **66**
St. Patrick, Mathew **48**
Salters, Lisa **71**
Sanford, Isabel **53**
Shepherd, Sherri **55**
Simmons, Henry **55**
Simmons, Kimora Lee **51, 83**
Smiley, Tavis **20, 68**
Snipes, Wesley **3, 24, 67**
Stewart, Nzingha **89**
Stuart, Moira **82**
Sykes, Wanda **48, 81**
Taylor, Jason **70**
Taylor, Karin **34**
Taylor, Regina **9, 46**
Thigpen, Lynne **17, 41**
Thompson, Kenan **52**
Torres, Gina **52**
Tyler, Aisha N. **36**

Union, Gabrielle **31, 92**
Usher **23, 56**
Vaughn, Countess **53**
Wainwright, Joscelyn **46**
Warner, Malcolm-Jamal **22, 36**
Warren, Michael **27**
Washington, Hayma **86**
Watson, Carlos **50**
Wayans, Damien **78**
Wayans, Damon **8, 41**
Wayans, Marlon **29, 82**
Wayans, Shawn **29**
Whitaker, Forest **2, 49, 67**
Williams, Armstrong **29**
Williams, Clarence, III **26**
Williams, Serena **20, 41, 73**
Williams, Vanessa A. **32, 66**
Williams, Wendy **62**
Williamson, Mykelti **22**
Wilson, Chandra **57**
Wilson, Dorien **55**

Television direction
Barclay, Paris **37**
Warner, Malcolm-Jamal **22, 36**
Whack, Rita Coburn **36**

Tennessee state government
Ford, Harold E(ugene) **42**

Tennessee State University
Phillips, Teresa L. **42**

Tennessee Supreme Court
Birch, Adolpho A., Jr. **85**

Tennessee Titans football team
George, Eddie **80**
McNair, Steve **22, 47, 79**

Tennis
Ashe, Arthur **1, 18**
Blake, James **43**
Garrison, Zina **2**
Gibson, Althea **8, 43**
Jackson, Jamea **64**
McNeil, Lori **1**
Noah, Yannick **4, 60**
Peters, Margaret and Matilda **43**
Rubin, Chanda **37**
Washington, MaliVai **8**
Williams, Samm-Art **21**
Williams, Serena **20, 41, 73**
Williams, Venus **17, 34, 62**
Young, Donald, Jr. **57**

Texas Rangers baseball team
Bonds, Bobby **43**
Cottrell, Comer **11**

Texas state government
Delco, Wilhemina **33**
Johnson, Eddie Bernice **8, 90**
Jordan, Barbara **4, 78**

Theater administration/ownership
Austin, Lovie **40**
Banks, Michelle **59**
Borders, James **9**
Cortez, Jayne **43**
Cox, Ida **42**
Gibson, John Trusty **87**
Hamlin, Larry Leon **49, 62**

Leggs, Kingsley **62**
LeNoire, Rosetta **37**
Leon, Kenny **10**
Marsalis, Delfeayo **41**
Spears, Warren **52**

Theatrical direction/production
Belgrave, Cynthia **75**
Glover, Keith **79**
Hall, Juanita **62**
Hayes, Teddy **40**
McClinton, Marion Isaac **77**
Milner, Ron **39**
Perry, Tyler **40, 54**
Scott, Harold Russell, Jr. **61**
Teer, Barbara Ann **81**
Thompson, Tazewell **13**
Wolfe, George C. **6, 43**

Thelonius Monk Institute of Jazz Performance
Blanchard, Terence **43**

Theological Education Fund (TEF)
Gordon, Pamela **17**
Tutu, Desmond Mpilo **6, 44**

Theology
Cone, James H. **3, 82**
Franklin, Robert M. **13**
Harding, Vincent **67**
Wright, Jeremiah A., Jr. **45, 69**

Threads 4 Life
Jones, Carl **7**
Kani, Karl **10**
Walker, T. J. **7**

Three Fifths Productions
Marsalis, Delfeayo **41**

TIAA-CREF
See Teachers Insurance and Annuity Association and the College Retirement Equities Fund

Time Warner Inc.
Ames, Wilmer **27**
Parsons, Richard Dean **11, 33**

TLC Beatrice International Holdings, Inc.
Lewis, Reginald F. **6**

Togolese government
Eyadéma, Gnassingbé **7, 52**
Gnassingbé, Faure **67**

Toledo Civic Hall of Fame
Stewart, Ella **39**

The Tonight Show
Eubanks, Kevin **15**

Tony awards
Allen, Debbie **13, 42**
Belafonte, Harry **4, 65**
Carroll, Diahann **9**
Carter, Nell **39**
Clarke, Hope **14**
Davis, Viola **34, 76**
Faison, George **16**
Falana, Lola **42**
Fishburne, Laurence **4, 22, 70**
Hall, Juanita **62**

Horne, Lena **5, 86**
Hyman, Phyllis **19**
Jones, James Earl **3, 49, 79**
LaChanze **93**
McDonald, Audra **20, 62**
Mokae, Zakes **80**
Moore, Melba **21**
Premice, Josephine **41**
Richards, Lloyd **2**
Rose, Anika Noni **70**
Santiago-Hudson, Ruben **85**
Thigpen, Lynne **17, 41**
Uggams, Leslie **23**
Vereen, Ben **4**
Wilson, August **7, 33, 55**
Wolfe, George C. **6, 43**

Toronto Blue Jays baseball team
Carter, Joe **30**
Gaston, Cito **71**
McGriff, Fred **24**

Toronto Raptors basketball team
Carter, Butch **27**
Carter, Vince **26**
Olajuwon, Hakeem **2, 72**
Thomas, Isiah **7, 26, 65**

Tourism
Edmunds, Gladys **48**

Track and field
Ashford, Evelyn **63**
Beamon, Bob **30**
Bekele, Kenenisa **75**
Bolt, Usain **73**
Christie, Linford **8**
Clay, Bryan **57, 74**
Devers, Gail **7, 87**
Dibaba, Tirunesh **73**
Felix, Allyson **48**
Freeman, Cathy **29**
Gebrselassie, Haile **70**
Graham, Trevor **84**
Greene, Maurice **27, 77**
Griffith-Joyner, Florence **28**
Harrison, Alvin **28**
Harrison, Calvin **28**
Hayes, Bob **77**
Holmes, Kelly **47**
Jacobs, Regina **38**
James, G. Larry **74**
Johnson, Michael **13**
Johnson, Rodney Van **28**
Jones, Lou **64**
Jones, Marion **21, 66**
Joyner-Kersee, Jackie **5**
Keflezighi, Meb **49**
Lewis, Carl **4**
Matson, Ollie **93**
Metcalfe, Ralph **26**
Montgomery, Tim **41**
Moses, Edwin **8**
Mutola, Maria **12**
Owens, Jesse **2**
Pollard, Fritz **53**
Powell, Mike **7**
Quirot, Ana **13**
Richards, Sanya **66**
Rudolph, Wilma **4**
Thugwane, Josia **21**
White, Willye **67**

Whitfield, Mal **60**
Williams, Lauryn **58**
Woodruff, John **68**

TransAfrica Forum, Inc.
Fletcher, Bill, Jr. **41**
Robinson, Randall **7, 46**

Transplant surgery
Callender, Clive O. **3**
Kountz, Samuel L. **10**

Transport and General Workers' Union
Morris, William "Bill" **51**

"Trial of the Century"
Cochran, Johnnie **11, 39, 52**
Darden, Christopher **13**
Simpson, O. J. **15**

Trombone
Marsalis, Delfeayo **41**
Powell, Benny **87**

Trumpet
Adderley, Nat **29**
Armstrong, Louis **2**
Belgrave, Marcus **77**
Blanchard, Terence **43**
Brown, Clifford **86**
Dara, Olu **35**
Davis, Miles **4**
Dixon, Bill **87**
Eldridge, Roy **37**
Ellison, Ralph **7**
Farmer, Art **38**
Gillespie, Dizzy **1**
Hubbard, Freddie **75**
Jones, Jonah **39**
Jones, Thad **68**
Marsalis, Wynton **16, 90**
Smith, Cladys "Jabbo" **32**
Terry, Clark **39**
Wilson, Gerald **49**

Turner Broadcasting System (TBS)
Clayton, Xernona **3, 45**

Tuskegee Airmen
Archer, Lee, Jr. **79**
Bromery, Randolph Wilson **85**
Brown, Willa **40**
Davis, Benjamin O., Jr. **2, 43**
Haysbert, Raymond V., Sr. **87**
James, Daniel, Jr. **16**
Patterson, Frederick Douglass **12**

Tuskegee University
Carver, George Washington **4**
Dawson, William Levi **39**
Gomillion, Charles **90**
Harvey, William R. **42**
Moton, Robert Russa **83**
Payton, Benjamin F. **23**
Taylor, Robert Robinson **80**

TV One
Ligging, Alfred, III **43**

UAW
See United Auto Workers

UCC
See United Church of Christ

UFBL
See Universal Foundation for Better Living

UGA
See United Golf Association

Ugandan government
Amin, Idi **42**
Museveni, Yoweri **4**
Obote, Milton **63**

Ultraviolet camera/spectrograph (UVC)
Carruthers, George R. **40**

Umkhonto we Sizwe
Hani, Chris **6**
Mandela, Nelson **1, 14, 77**
Motlanthe, Kgalema **74**
Zuma, Jacob **33, 75**

UN
See United Nations

UNCF
See United Negro College Fund

Underground Railroad
Blockson, Charles L. **42**
Cohen, Anthony **15**
Crew, Spencer R. **55**
DeBaptiste, George **32**
Shadd, Abraham D. **81**

Unemployment and Poverty Action Committee
Forman, James **7, 51**

UNESCO
See United Nations Educational, Scientific, and Cultural Organization

UNIA
See Universal Negro Improvement Association

UNICEF
See United Nations Children's Fund

Unions
Brown, Lloyd Louis **42**
Clay, William Lacy **8**
Crockett, George W., Jr. **10, 64**
Ellis-Lamkins, Phaedra **88**
Europe, James Reese **10**
Farmer, James **2, 64**
Fletcher, Benjamin **90**
Fletcher, Bill, Jr. **41**
Hilliard, David **7**
Holt Baker, Arlene **73**
Lucy, William **50**
Morris, William "Bill" **51**
Ramaphosa, Cyril **3**
Randolph, A. Philip **3**
Roberts, Lillian **83**
Smith, Nate **49**
Touré, Sekou **6**
Wyatt, Addie L. **56**

UNIP
See United National Independence Party

UFBL
See Universal Foundation for Better Living

UNITA
See National Union for the Total Independence of Angola

United Auto Workers (UAW)
Fletcher, Bill, Jr. **41**

United Church of Christ (UCC)
Chavis, Benjamin **6**
Forbes, James A., Jr. **71**
Moss, Otis, III **72**

United Democratic Front (UDF; Malawi)
Muluzi, Bakili **14, 76**

United Golf Association (UGA)
Elder, Lee **6**
Sifford, Charlie **4, 49**

United Methodist Church
Caldwell, Kirbyjon **55**
Lawson, James M., Jr. **90**
Lewis, Shirley A. R. **14**
Muzorewa, Abel **85**
Stith, Charles R. **73**

United National Independence Party (UNIP)
Kaunda, Kenneth **2**

United Nations (UN)
Annan, Kofi Atta **15, 48**
Bunche, Ralph J. **5**
Cleaver, Emanuel **4, 45, 68**
Diouf, Abdou **3**
Juma, Calestous **57**
Lafontant, Jewel Stradford **3, 51**
McDonald, Gabrielle Kirk **20**
McHenry, Donald F. **83**
Mongella, Gertrude **11**
Perkins, Edward **5**
Sampson, Edith S. **4**
Young, Andrew **3, 48**

United Nations Children's Fund (UNICEF)
Baker, Gwendolyn Calvert **9**
Belafonte, Harry **4, 65**
Machel, Graca Simbine **16**
Weah, George **58**

United Nations Educational, Scientific, and Cultural Organization (UNESCO)
Diop, Cheikh Anta **4**
Frazier, E. Franklin **10**
Machel, Graca Simbine **16**
Smythe Haith, Mabel **61**

United Negro College Fund (UNCF)
Boyd, T. B., III **6**
Bunkley, Anita Richmond **39**
Creagh, Milton **27**
Dawson, Matel, Jr. **39**
Edley, Christopher **2, 48**
Gray, William H., III **3**
Jordan, Vernon E. **3, 35**
Lomax, Michael L. **58**
Mays, Benjamin E. **7**
Patterson, Frederick Douglass **12**
Tillis, Frederick **40**

United Parcel Service
Cooper, Evern **40**
Darden, Calvin **38**

Washington, Patrice Clarke 12

United Parcel Service Foundation
Cooper, Evern 40

United Somali Congress
Ali Mahdi Mohamed 5

United States Delegations
Shabazz, Ilyasah 36

United States Football League (USFL)
White, Reggie 6, 50
Williams, Doug 22

United Way
Donald, Arnold Wayne 36

United Workers Union of South Africa (UWUSA)
Buthelezi, Mangosuthu Gatsha 9

Universal Foundation for Better Living (UFBL)
Colemon, Johnnie 11
Reese, Della 6, 20

Universal Negro Improvement Association (UNIA)
Austin, Junius C. 44
Garvey, Marcus 1
McGuire, George Alexander 80

University administration
See College and university administration

University of Alabama
Davis, Mike 41
Lucy Foster, Autherine 35

University of California–Berkeley
Blackwell, David 79
Drummond, William J. 40
Edley, Christopher F., Jr. 48

University of Cape Town
Ramphele, Maphela 29

University of Chicago Hospitals
Lee, Raphael C. 87

University of Colorado
Berry, Mary Frances 7

University of Delaware
Mitchell, Sharon 36

University of Florida
Haskins, James 36, 54

University of Michigan
Amaker, Tommy 62
Dillard, Godfrey J. 45
Fuller, A. Oveta 43
Goss, Tom 23
Gray, Ida 41
Imes, Elmer Samuel 39

University of Missouri
Anderson, Mike 63
Floyd, Elson S. 41

University of North Carolina
Floyd, Elson S. 41

University of Notre Dame
Willingham, Tyrone 43

University of Texas
Granville, Evelyn Boyd 36

University of the West Indies
Brathwaite, Kamau 36
Hill, Errol 40

University of Virginia
Littlepage, Craig 35

Upscale magazine
Bronner, Nathaniel H., Sr. 32

Urban League (regional)
Adams, Sheila J. 25
Clayton, Xernona 3, 45
Jacob, John E. 2
Layton, William 87
Mays, Benjamin E. 7
Young, Whitney M., Jr. 4

Urban planning/renewal
Allen, Will 74
Archer, Dennis 7, 36
Blakely, Edward J. 88
Bosley, Freeman, Jr. 7
Carter, Majora 77
Harris, Alice 7
Lane, Vincent 5
Waters, Maxine 3, 67

U.S. Air Force
Anderson, Michael P. 40
Carter, Joye Maureen 41
Davis, Benjamin O., Jr. 2, 43
Drew, Alvin, Jr. 67
Dwight, Edward 65
Gregory, Frederick 8, 51
Harris, Marcelite Jordan 16
James, Daniel, Jr. 16
Johnson, Lonnie G. 32, 93
Jones, Wayne 53
Lyles, Lester 31

U.S. Army
Adams-Ender, Clara 40
Baker, Vernon Joseph 65, 87
Brown, Anthony G. 72
Cadoria, Sherian Grace 14
Clemmons, Reginal G. 41
Davis, Benjamin O., Sr. 4
Delany, Martin R. 27
Flipper, Henry O. 3
Greenhouse, Bunnatine "Bunny" 57
Honoré, Russel L. 64
Jackson, Fred James 25
Johnson, Hazel 22
Johnson, Shoshana 47
King, Teresa 80
Matthews, Mark 59
Perry, Herman 89
Poindexter, Hildrus A. 87
Powell, Colin 1, 28, 75
Rogers, Alan G. 72
Snow, Samuel 71
Stanford, John 20
Watkins, Perry 12
West, Allen 89
West, Togo D., Jr. 16

Young, Charles 77

U.S. Army Air Corps
Anderson, Charles Edward 37

U.S. Atomic Energy Commission
Nabrit, Samuel Milton 47

U.S. Attorney's Office
Jordan, Eddie 82
Lafontant, Jewel Stradford 3, 51

U.S. Bureau of Engraving and Printing
Felix, Larry R. 64

U.S. Cabinet
Brown, Ron 5
Elders, Joycelyn 6
Espy, Mike 6
Harris, Patricia Roberts 2
Herman, Alexis M. 15
Kirk, Ron 11, 75
O'Leary, Hazel 6
Powell, Colin 1, 28, 75
Rice, Condoleezza 3, 28, 72
Slater, Rodney E. 15
Sullivan, Louis 8
Weaver, Robert C. 8, 46

U.S. Coast Guard
Brown, Erroll M. 23
Healy, Michael 90
Rochon, Stephen W. 78

U.S. Commission on Civil Rights
Berry, Mary Frances 7
Edley, Christopher 2, 48
Fletcher, Arthur A. 63

U.S. Conference of Catholic Bishops
Gregory, Wilton D. 37

U.S. Court of Appeals
Hastie, William H. 8
Higginbotham, A. Leon, Jr. 13, 25
Kearse, Amalya Lyle 12
Keith, Damon J. 16, 74
Rawlinson, Johnnie B. 79
Williams, Ann Claire 82

U.S. Department of Agriculture (USDA)
Espy, Mike 6
Layton, William 87
Sherrod, Shirley 87
Vaughn, Gladys Gary 47
Watkins, Shirley R. 17
Williams, Hosea Lorenzo 15, 31

U.S. Department of Commerce
Brown, Ron 5
Irving, Larry, Jr. 12
Person, Waverly 9, 51
Shavers, Cheryl 31

U.S. Department of Defense
Greenhouse, Bunnatine "Bunny" 57
Johnson, Jeh C. 76
Tribble, Israel, Jr. 8

U.S. Department of Education
Ali, Russlynn H. 92
Hill, Anita 5, 65

Hill, Bonnie Guiton 20
Paige, Rod 29
Purnell, Silas 59
Thomas, Clarence 2, 39, 65
Tribble, Israel, Jr. 8
Velez-Rodriguez, Argelia 56

U.S. Department of Energy
O'Leary, Hazel 6

U.S. Department of Health and Human Services (HHS)
See also U.S. Department of Health, Education, and Welfare
Gaston, Marilyn Hughes 60
Hamburg, Margaret 78
Hughes, Dora 88

U.S. Department of Health, Education, and Welfare (HEW)
Bell, Derrick 6
Berry, Mary Frances 7
Harris, Patricia Roberts 2
Randolph, Linda A. 52
Spearman, Leonard H. O., Sr. 81
Sullivan, Louis 8

U.S. Department of Housing and Urban Development (HUD)
Blackwell, J. Kenneth, Sr. 61
Gaines, Brenda 41
Harris, Patricia Roberts 2
Jackson, Alphonso R. 48
Weaver, Robert C. 8, 46

U.S. Department of Justice
Bell, Derrick 6
Campbell, Bill 9, 76
Days, Drew S., III 10
Guinier, Lani 7, 30
Harris, Maya Lakshmi 88
Holder, Eric H., Jr. 9, 76
Lafontant, Jewel Stradford 3, 51
Lewis, Delano 7
Patrick, Deval 12, 61
Payton, John 48
Thompson, Larry D. 39
Williams, Michael L. 86

U.S. Department of Labor
Crockett, George W., Jr. 10, 64
Fletcher, Arthur A. 63
Herman, Alexis M. 15

U.S. Department of State
Baltimore, Richard Lewis, III 71
Bethune, Mary McLeod 4
Bunche, Ralph J. 5
Davis, Ruth 37
Dougherty, Mary Pearl 47
Frazer, Jendayi 68
Ervin, Clark Kent 82
Garrett, Joyce Finley 59
Grimké, Archibald H. 9
Haley, George Williford Boyce 21
Harris, Patricia Roberts 2
Keyes, Alan L. 11
Lafontant, Jewel Stradford 3, 51
McGee, James D. 74
Perkins, Edward 5
Powell, Colin 1, 28, 75
Rice, Condoleezza 3, 28, 72
Rice, Susan E. 74
Stokes, Carl 10, 73

Sutphen, Mona 77
Van Lierop, Robert 53
Wharton, Clifton R., Jr. 7
Wharton, Clifton Reginald, Sr. 36

U.S. Department of the Interior
Person, Waverly 9, 51

U.S. Department of the Treasury
Morton, Azie Taylor 48

U.S. Department of Transportation
Coleman, William T. 76
Davis, Benjamin O., Jr. 2, 43

U.S. Department of Veterans Affairs
Brown, Jesse 6, 41

U.S. Diplomatic Corps
See U.S. Department of State

U.S. District Attorney
Harris, Kamala D. 64
Lloyd, Reginald 64

U.S. District Court judge
Bryant, William Benson 61
Carter, Robert L. 51
Cooke, Marcia 60
Diggs-Taylor, Anna 20
Henderson, Thelton E. 68
Keith, Damon J. 16, 74
Parker, Barrington D. 92
Parsons, James 14
Williams, Ann Claire 82

U.S. Dream Academy
Phipps, Wintley 59

U.S. Environmental Protection Agency
Jackson, Lisa 77

U.S. Foreign Service
See U.S. Department of State

U.S. Geological Survey
Bromery, Randolph Wilson 85
Person, Waverly 9, 51

U.S. House of Representatives
Archie-Hudson, Marguerite 44
Ballance, Frank W. 41
Bishop, Sanford D., Jr. 24
Brown, Corrine 24, 90
Burke, Yvonne Brathwaite 42
Carson, André 69
Carson, Julia 23, 69
Chisholm, Shirley 2, 50
Clarke, Yvette 92
Clay, William Lacy 8
Clayton, Eva M. 20
Cleaver, Emanuel 4, 45, 68
Clyburn, James E. 21, 71
Collins, Barbara-Rose 7, 87
Collins, Cardiss 10, 80
Conyers, John, Jr. 4, 45
Crockett, George W., Jr. 10, 64
Cummings, Elijah E. 24
Davis, Artur 41
Davis, Danny K. 24, 79

De Priest, Oscar Stanton 80
Dellums, Ronald 2, 81
Diggs, Charles C. 21
Dixon, Julian C. 24
Dymally, Mervyn 42
Edwards, Donna 77
Ellison, Keith 59
Espy, Mike 6
Fattah, Chaka 11, 70
Fauntroy, Walter E. 11
Fields, Cleo 13
Flake, Floyd H. 18
Ford, Harold E(ugene) 42
Ford, Harold E(ugene), Jr. 16, 70
Franks, Gary 2
Fudge, Marcia L. 76
Gray, William H., III 3
Hastings, Alcee L. 16
Hawkins, Augustus F. 68
Hilliard, Earl F. 24
Jackson, Jesse, Jr. 14, 45, 81
Jackson Lee, Sheila 20
Jefferson, William J. 25, 72
Johnson, Eddie Bernice 8, 90
Johnson, Hank, Jr. 80
Jordan, Barbara 4, 78
Kilpatrick, Carolyn Cheeks 16
Lee, Barbara 25
Leland, Mickey 2
Lewis, John 2, 46, 83
Majette, Denise 41
McKinney, Cynthia 11, 52, 74
Meek, Carrie 6, 36
Meek, Kendrick 41, 89
Meeks, Gregory 25
Menard, John Willis 90
Metcalfe, Ralph 26
Mfume, Kweisi 6, 41
Millender-McDonald, Juanita 21, 61
Mitchell, Arthur Wergs 91
Mitchell, Parren J. 42, 66
Moore, Gwendolynne S. 55
Norton, Eleanor Holmes 7, 93
Owens, Major 6
Payne, Donald M. 2, 57
Pinchback, P. B. S. 9
Powell, Adam Clayton, Jr. 3
Rangel, Charles B. 3, 52, 85
Rapier, James T. 82
Richardson, Laura 81
Richmond, Cedric 93
Rush, Bobby 26, 76
Scott, David 41
Scott, Robert C. 23
Sewell, Terri 93
Smalls, Robert 82
Stokes, Louis 3
Towns, Edolphus 19, 75
Tubbs Jones, Stephanie 24, 72
Washington, Harold 6
Waters, Maxine 3, 67
Watson, Diane 41
Watt, Melvin 26
Watts, J. C., Jr. 14, 38
West, Allen 89
Wheat, Alan 14
Wilson, Frederica 92
Wynn, Albert R. 25, 77
Young, Andrew 3, 48

U.S. Information Agency
Allen, Samuel 38

U.S. Joint Chiefs of Staff
Howard, Michelle 28
Powell, Colin 1, 28, 75
Rice, Condoleezza 3, 28, 72

U.S. Marines
Bolden, Charles Frank, Jr. 7, 78
Brown, Jesse 6, 41
Petersen, Franke E. 31
Von Lipsey, Roderick K. 11

U.S. Navy
Black, Barry C. 47
Brashear, Carl 29
Brown, Jesse Leroy 31
Doby, Lawrence Eugene, Sr. 16, 41
Fields, Evelyn J. 27
Gravely, Samuel L., Jr. 5, 49
Howard, Michelle 28
Miller, Dorie 29
Pinckney, Bill 42
Reason, J. Paul 19
Wright, Lewin 43

U.S. Open tennis tournament
Williams, Venus 17, 34, 62

U.S. Peace Corps
Days, Drew S., III 10
Johnson, Rafer 33
Lewis, Delano 7

U.S. presidency
Obama, Barack 49, 74, 91

U.S. Register of the Treasury
Bruce, Blanche Kelso 33

U.S. Senate
Black, Barry C. 47
Bowman, Bertie 71
Braun, Carol Moseley 4, 42
Brooke, Edward W. 8, 88
Bruce, Blanche Kelso 33
Burris, Roland W. 25, 75
Obama, Barack 49, 74, 91
Pinchback, P. B. S. 9

U.S. State Department
See U.S. Department of State

U.S. Supreme Court
Marshall, Thurgood 1, 44
Thomas, Clarence 2, 39, 65

U.S. Surgeon General
Elders, Joycelyn 6
Satcher, David 7, 57

U.S. Virgin Islands government
DeJongh, John, Jr. 85
Evans, Melvin H. 88
Hastie, William H. 8
Turnbull, Charles Wesley 62

USDA
See U.S. Department of Agriculture

USFL
See United States Football League

U.S.S. *Constitution*
Wright, Lewin 43

UVC
See Ultraviolet camera/spectrograph

UWUSA
See United Workers Union of South Africa

Vancouver Canucks hockey team
Brashear, Donald 39

Vancouver Grizzlies basketball team
Abdur-Rahim, Shareef 28

Vaudeville
Anderson, Eddie "Rochester" 30
Austin, Lovie 40
Bates, Peg Leg 14
Cox, Ida 42
Davis, Sammy, Jr. 18
Gilpin, Charles Sidney 81
Johnson, Jack 8
Martin, Sara 38
McDaniel, Hattie 5
Mills, Florence 22
Robinson, Bill "Bojangles" 11
Waters, Ethel 7

Veterans's issues
Carr, Keela 74

Veterinary science
Jawara, Dawda Kairaba 11
Lushington, Augustus Nathaniel 56
Maathai, Wangari 43
Patterson, Frederick Douglass 12
Thomas, Vivien 9

Vibe
Jones, Quincy 8, 30
Smith, Danyel 40
Wilbekin, Emil 63

Vibraphone
Hampton, Lionel 17, 41

Victim's Bill of Rights
Dee, Merri 55

Video gaming
Croal, N'Gai 76
Fils-Aimé, Reggie 74

Vietnam Veterans of America
Duggins, George 64

Village Voice
Cooper, Andrew W. 36
Crouch, Stanley 11

Violin
Bridgetower, George 78
Daemyon, Jerald 64
Dworkin, Aaron P. 52
Escobar, Damien 56
Escobar, Tourie 56
Murray, Tai 47
Smith, Stuff 37
Tinsley, Boyd 50
Williams, Claude 80

VIP Memphis magazine
McMillan, Rosalynn A. 36

Virgin Records
Brooks, Hadda **40**
Sledge, Percy **39**

Virginia state government
Marsh, Henry **32**
Martin, Ruby Grant **49**
Wilder, L. Douglas **3, 48**

Virginia State Supreme Court
Hassell, Leroy Rountree, Sr. **41**

Virology
Fuller, A. Oveta **43**

Vogue magazine
Talley, André Leon **56**

Volleyball
Blanton, Dain **29**

Voodoo
Beauvoir, Max **74**
Dunham, Katherine **4, 59**
Guy, Rosa **5**
Hurston, Zora Neale **3**
Pierre, Andre **17**

Voting rights
Cary, Mary Ann Shadd **30**
Chestnut, J. L., Jr. **73**
Clark, Septima **7**
Forman, James **7, 51**
Hamer, Fannie Lou **6**
Harper, Frances Ellen Watkins **11**
Hill, Jesse, Jr. **13**
Lampkin, Daisy **19**
Mandela, Nelson **1, 14, 77**
Moore, Harry T. **29**
Moses, Robert Parris **11**
Terrell, Mary Church **9**
Touré, Faya Ora Rose **56**
Trotter, Monroe **9**
Tubman, Harriet **9**
Wells-Barnett, Ida B. **8**
Williams, Fannie Barrier **27**
Williams, Hosea Lorenzo **15, 31**
Woodard, Alfre **9**

**WAAC (Women's Auxiliary
Army Corps)**
See Women's Army Corps (WAC)

WAC
See Women's Army Corps

Wall Street
Lewis, William M., Jr. **40**
McGuire, Raymond J. **57**
Phillips, Charles E., Jr. **57**

War criminals
Sankoh, Foday **74**

**Washington, D.C., city govern-
ment**
Barry, Marion S. **7, 44**
Brown, Kwame R. **91**
Cooper Cafritz, Peggy **43**
Dixon, Sharon Pratt **1**
Fauntroy, Walter E. **11**
Fenty, Adrian **60, 88**
Gray, Vincent C. **88**
Hobson, Julius W. **44**
Jarvis, Charlene Drew **21**
Norton, Eleanor Holmes **7, 93**

Washington, Walter **45**
Williams, Anthony **21**

**Washington, D.C., Commis-
sion on the Arts and Humanities**
Neal, Larry **38**

Washington Post
Britt, Donna **28**
Davis, George **36**
Givhan, Robin Deneen **72**
Haygood, Wil **83**
Ifill, Gwen **28**
King, Colbert I. **69**
Maynard, Robert C. **7**
McCall, Nathan **8**
Nelson, Jill **6, 54**
Raspberry, William **2**

**Washington Redskins football
team**
Green, Darrell **39, 74**
Monk, Art **38, 73**
Sanders, Deion **4, 31**

**Washington State Higher Edu-
cation Coordinating Board**
Floyd, Elson S. **41**

Washington Week in Review
TV series
Ifill, Gwen **28**

**Washington Wizards basket-
ball team**
Bickerstaff, Bernie **21**
Heard, Gar **25**
Howard, Juwan **15**
Unseld, Wes **23**
Webber, Chris **15, 30, 59**

WCC
See World Council of Churches

Weather
Brown, Vivian **27**
Christian, Spencer **15**
McEwen, Mark **5**
Roker, Al **12, 49**

Welfare reform
Bryant, Wayne R. **6**
Carson, Julia **23, 69**
Parker, Star **70**
Wallace, Joaquin **49**
Williams, Walter E. **4**

West Indian folk songs
Belafonte, Harry **4, 65**
Rhoden, Wayne **70**

West Indian literature
Coombs, Orde M. **44**
Guy, Rosa **5**
Kincaid, Jamaica **4**
Markham, E. A. **37**
Marshall, Paule **7, 77**
McKay, Claude **6**
Walcott, Derek **5**

West Point
Davis, Benjamin O., Jr. **2, 43**
Flipper, Henry O. **3**

Young, Charles **77**

West Side Preparatory School
Collins, Marva **3, 71**

Western Michigan University
Floyd, Elson S. **41**

White House
Allen, Eugene **79**
Butts, Cassandra **78**
Christie, Ron **83**
Gaspard, Patrick **84**
Hatcher, Andrew T. **90**
Jarvis, Kristen **85**
Keckley, Elizabeth **90**
Love, Reggie **77**
Obama, Michelle **61, 90**
Rochon, Stephen W. **78**
Rogers, Desirée **88**
Rouse, Cecilia **93**
Strautmanis, Michael **87**

**Whitney Museum of American
Art**
Golden, Thelma **10, 55**
Simpson, Lorna **4, 36**

Wimbledon
Williams, Venus **17, 34, 62**

Wine and winemaking
Allen-Buillard, Melba **55**
Rideau, Iris **46**

**Wisconsin State Supreme
Court**
Butler, Louis **70**

Women Helping Offenders
Holland, Endesha Ida Mae **3, 57**

Women's Army Corps (WAC)
Adams Earley, Charity **13, 34**
Cadoria, Sherian Grace **14**

**Women's Auxiliary Army
Corps**
See Women's Army Corps

Women's issues
Allen, Ethel D. **13**
Angelou, Maya **1, 15**
Avery, Byllye Y. **66**
Ba, Mariama **30**
Baker, Ella **5**
Bashir, Halima **73**
Berry, Mary Frances **7**
Brown, Elaine **8**
Campbell, Bebe Moore **6, 24, 59**
Cannon, Katie **10**
Carby, Hazel **27**
Cary, Mary Ann Shadd **30**
Charles, Mary Eugenia **10, 55**
Chinn, May Edward **26**
Christian, Barbara T. **44**
Christian-Green, Donna M. **17**
Clark, Septima **7**
Cole, Johnnetta B. **5, 43**
Cooper, Anna Julia **20**
Davis, Angela **5**
De Veaux, Alexis **44**
Edelman, Marian Wright **5, 42**
Edwards, Lena Frances **76**
Elders, Joycelyn **6**
Evans, Diana **72**

Fauset, Jessie **7**
Giddings, Paula **11**
Gomez, Jewelle **30**
Grimké, Archibald H. **9**
Guy-Sheftall, Beverly **13, 92**
Hale, Clara **16**
Hale, Lorraine **8**
Hamer, Fannie Lou **6**
Harper, Frances Ellen Watkins **11**
Harris, Leslie **6**
Harris, Patricia Roberts **2**
Height, Dorothy I. **2, 23, 78**
Hernandez, Aileen Clarke **13**
Hill, Anita **5, 65**
Hine, Darlene Clark **24**
Holland, Endesha Ida Mae **3, 57**
hooks, bell **5, 90**
Hughes, Ebony **57**
Hull, Akasha Gloria **45**
Hussein, Lubna **80**
Jackson, Alexine Clement **22**
Joe, Yolanda **21**
Jordan, June **7, 35**
Lampkin, Daisy **19**
Larsen, Nella **10**
Lorde, Audre **6**
Maathai, Wangari **43**
Marshall, Paule **7, 77**
Mbaye, Mariétou **31**
McCabe, Jewell Jackson **10**
McCauley, Gina **76**
McKenzie, Vashti M. **29**
McMillan, Terry **4, 17, 53**
Millender-McDonald, Juanita **21, 61**
Millner, Denene **76**
Mongella, Gertrude **11**
Mossell, Gertrude Bustill **40**
Naylor, Gloria **10, 42**
Nelson, Jill **6, 54**
Niane, Katoucha **70**
Nichols, Nichelle **11**
Norman, Pat **10**
Ormes, Jackie **73**
Parker, Pat **19**
Rawlings, Nana Konadu Agyeman **13**
Ruffin, Josephine St. Pierre **75**
Shange, Ntozake **8, 89**
Sherrod, Shirley **87**
Simpson, Carole **6, 30**
Smith, Barbara **28**
Smith, Jane E. **24**
Talbert, Mary B. **77**
Terrell, Mary Church **9**
Tubman, Harriet **9**
Vanzant, Iyanla **17, 47**
Walker, Alice **1, 43**
Walker, Rebecca **50**
Wallace, Michele Faith **13**
Waters, Maxine **3, 67**
Wattleton, Faye **9**
Williams, Fannie Barrier **27**
Xuma, Madie Hall **59**

Women's Leadership Forum
Shabazz, Ilyasah **36**

**Women's National Basketball
Association (WNBA)**
Bolton-Holifield, Ruthie **28**
Cash, Swin **59**
Catchings, Tamika **43**
Cooper, Cynthia **17**

Edwards, Teresa **14**
Ford, Cheryl **45**
Griffith, Yolanda **25**
Holdsclaw, Chamique **24**
Jones, Merlakia **34**
Lennox, Betty **31**
Leslie, Lisa **16, 73**
McCray, Nikki **18**
Miller, Cheryl **10, 74**
Milton, DeLisha **31**
Palmer, Violet **59**
Parker, Candace **74**
Peck, Carolyn **23**
Perrot, Kim **23**
Staley, Dawn **57**
Swoopes, Sheryl **12, 56**
Thompson, Tina **25, 75**
Williams, Natalie **31**
Woodard, Lynette **67**

Workplace equity
Clark, Septima **7**
Hill, Anita **5, 65**
Nelson, Jill **6, 54**
Simpson, Carole **6, 30**

**Works Progress (Projects)
Administration (WPA)**
Alexander, Margaret Walker **22**
Baker, Ella **5**
Blackburn, Robert **28**
DeCarava, Roy **42, 81**
Douglas, Aaron **7**
Dunham, Katherine **4, 59**
Hall, Juanita **62**
Lawrence, Jacob **4, 28**
Lee-Smith, Hughie **5, 22**
Murray, Pauli **38**
Sallee, Charles **38**
Sebree, Charles **40**
Winkfield, Jimmy **42**
Wright, Richard **5**

**World African Hebrew Israelite
Community**
Ben-Israel, Ben Ami **11**

World Bank
Soglo, Nicéphore **15**

World beat
Belafonte, Harry **4, 65**
Fela **1, 42**
Maal, Baaba **66**
N'Dour, Youssou **1, 53, 79**
Okosuns, Sonny **71**
Ongala, Remmy **9, 91**

**World Council of Churches
(WCC)**
Kobia, Samuel **43**
Mays, Benjamin E. **7**
Tutu, Desmond Mpilo **6, 44**

World Cup
dos Santos, Manuel Francisco **65**
Gyan, Asamoah **87**
Mensah, John **87**
Milla, Roger **2**
Pelé **7**
Scurry, Briana **27**

World hunger
Belafonte, Harry **4, 65**
Iman **4, 33, 87**
Jones, Quincy **8, 30**
Leland, Mickey **2**
Masire, Quett **5**

**World Wrestling Entertain-
ment (WWE) Hall of Fame**
Ladd, Ernie **64**

**World Wrestling Federation
(WWF)**
Ladd, Ernie **64**
Lashley, Bobby **63**
Rock, The **29, 66**

WPA
See Works Progress (Projects) Administration

Wrestling
Ladd, Ernie **64**
Lashley, Bobby **63**

Rock, The **29, 66**

WWF
See World Wrestling Federation

Xavier University of Louisiana
Francis, Norman (C.) **60**

Xerox Corp.
Burns, Ursula **60**
Rand, A. Barry **6**

Yale Repertory Theater
Dutton, Charles S. **4, 22**
Richards, Lloyd **2**
Wilson, August **7, 33, 55**

Yale University
Blassingame, John Wesley **40**
Carby, Hazel **27**
Davis, Charles T. **48**
Hill, Errol **40**
Neal, Larry **38**

YMCA
See Young Men's Christian Association

Yoruban folklore
Soyinka, Wole **4, 93**
Vanzant, Iyanla **17, 47**

Young adult literature
Anderson, Ho Che **54**
Bolden, Tonya **32**
Ekwensi, Cyprian **37**
Johnson, Angela **52**
Millner, Denene **76**

**Young Men's Christian Asso-
ciation (YMCA)**
Goode, Mal **13**
Hope, John **8**
Mays, Benjamin E. **7**

Tobias, Channing H. **79**

**Young Women's Christian As-
sociation (YWCA)**
Baker, Ella **5**
Baker, Gwendolyn Calvert **9**
Clark, Septima **7**
Claytor, Helen **14, 52**
Hedgeman, Anna Arnold **22**
Height, Dorothy I. **2, 23, 78**
Jackson, Alexine Clement **22**
Jenkins, Ella **15**
Sampson, Edith S. **4**
Stewart, Ella **39**
Xuma, Madie Hall **59**

YWCA
See Young Women's Christian Association

Zairian government
Mobutu Sese Seko **1, 56**

Zambian government
Chiluba, Frederick **56, 80**
Mwanawasa, Levy **72**

ZCTU
See Zimbabwe Congress of Trade
Unions

**Zimbabwe Congress of Trade
Unions (ZCTU)**
Tsvangirai, Morgan **26, 72**
Young, Roger Arliner **29**

Zimbabwean government
Moyo, Lovemore **76**
Mugabe, Robert **10, 71**
Mukoko, Jestina **75**
Muzorewa, Abel **85**
Nkomo, Joshua **4, 65**

ZTA
See Zululand Territorial Authority

**Zululand Territorial Authority
(ZTA)**
Buthelezi, Mangosuthu Gatsha **9**

Cumulative Name Index

Volume numbers appear in **bold**

Aaliyah 1979–2001 **30**

Aaron, Hank 1934— **5**

Aaron, Henry Louis *See Aaron, Hank*

Aaron, Quinton 1984— **82**

Abacha, Sani 1943–1998 **11, 70**

Abani, Chris 1966— **77**

Abbott, Diane (Julie) 1953— **9**

Abbott, Robert Sengstacke 1868–1940 **27**

Abdul-Jabbar, Kareem 1947— **8**

Abdullah, Imaam Isa *See York, Dwight D.*

Abdulmajid, Iman Mohamed *See Iman*

Abdur-Rahim, Shareef 1976— **28**

Abele, Julian 1881–1950 **55**

Abernathy, Ralph David 1926–1990 **1**

Aberra, Amsale 1954— **67**

Abiola, Moshood 1937–1998 **70**

Abrahams, Peter 1919— **39**

Abubakar, Abdulsalami 1942— **66**

Abu-Jamal, Mumia 1954— **15**

Ace, Johnny 1929–1954 **36**

Achebe, (Albert) Chinua(lumogu) 1930— **6**

Acogny, Germaine 1944— **55**

Adams, Eula L. 1950— **39**

Adams, Floyd, Jr. 1945— **12**

Adams, Grantley 1898–1971 **82**

Adams, H. Leslie *See Adams, Leslie*

Adams, Jenoyne (?)— **60**

Adams, Johnny 1932–1998 **39**

Adams, Leslie 1932— **39**

Adams, Oleta 19(?)(?)— **18**

Adams, Osceola Macarthy 1890–1983 **31**

Adams, Paul 1977— **50**

Adams, Sheila J. 1943— **25**

Adams, Yolanda 1961— **17, 67**

Adams-Campbell, Lucille L. 1953— **60**

Adams Earley, Charity (Edna) 1918– **13, 34**

Adams-Ender, Clara 1939— **40**

Adderley, Julian "Cannonball" 1928–1975 **30**

Adderley, Nat 1931–2000 **29**

Adderley, Nathaniel *See Adderley, Nat*

Ade, Sunny King 1946— **41**

Adebari, Rotimi 1963(?)— **83**

Adebimpe, Tunde 1975— **75**

Adeniyi, Sunday *See Ade, Sunny King*

Adichie, Chimamanda Ngozi 1977— **64**

Adjaye, David 1966— **38, 78**

Adkins, Rod 1958— **41**

Adkins, Rutherford H. 1924–1998 **21**

Adu, Freddy 1989— **67**

Adu, Fredua Koranteng *See Adu, Freddy*

Adu, Helen Folasade *See Sade*

Afro, Teddy 1976— **78**

Agyeman, Jaramogi Abebe 1911–2000 **10, 63**

Agyeman Rawlings, Nana Konadu 1948— **13**

Ahidjo, Ahmadou 1924–1989 **81**

Ahmed, Sharif 1964— **80**

Aidoo, Ama Ata 1942— **38**

Aiken, Loretta Mary *See Mabley, Jackie "Moms"*

Ailey, Alvin 1931–1989 **8**

Ake, Claude 1939–1996 **30**

Akil, Mara Brock 1970— **60, 82**

Akinnuoye-Agbaje, Adewale 1967— **56**

Akinola, Peter Jasper 1944— **65**

Akintimehin, Olubowale Victor *See Wale*

Akomfrah, John 1957— **37**

Akon 1973(?)— **68**

Akpan, Uwem 1971— **70**

Akunyili, Dora Nkem 1954— **58**

Al-Amin, Jamil Abdullah 1943— **6**

Albright, Gerald 1947— **23**

Alcindor, Ferdinand Lewis *See Abdul-Jabbar, Kareem*

Alcorn, George Edward, Jr. 1940— **59**

Alert, Kool DJ Red 19(?)(?)— **33**

Alexander, Archie Alphonso 1888–1958 **14**

Alexander, Clifford 1933— **26**

Alexander, Elizabeth 1962— **75**

Alexander, John Marshall *See Ace, Johnny*

Alexander, Joyce London 1949— **18**

Alexander, Khandi 1957— **43**

Alexander, Margaret Walker 1915–1998 **22**

Alexander, Sadie Tanner Mossell 1898–1989 **22**

Alexander, Shaun 1977— **58**

Ali, Ayaan Hirsi 1969— **58, 92**

Ali, Hana Yasmeen 1976— **52**

Ali, Laila 1977— **27, 63**

Ali, Mohammed Naseehu 1971— **60**

Ali, Muhammad 1942— **2, 16, 52**

Ali, Rashied 1935–2009 **79**

Ali, Russlynn H. 1971(?)— **92**

Ali, Tatyana 1979— **73**

Ali Mahdi Mohamed 1940— **5**

Allain, Stephanie 1959— **49**

Allen, Betty 1927–2009 **83**

Allen, Byron 1961— **3, 24**

Allen, Claude 1960— **68**

Allen, Debbie 1950— **13, 42**

Allen, Dick 1942— **85**

Allen, Ethel D. 1929–1981 **13**

Allen, Eugene 1919— **79**

Allen, Fulton *See Fuller, Blind Boy*

Allen, Geri 1957— **92**

Allen, Lucy 1932— **85**

Allen, Marcus 1960— **20**

Allen, Ray 1975— **82**

Allen, Richard 1760–1831 **14**

Allen, Robert L. 1942— **38**

Allen, Samuel W. 1917— **38**

Allen, Tina 1949–2008 **22, 75**

Allen, Will 1949— **74**

Allen-Buillard, Melba 1960— **55**

Alonso, Laz 1974— **87**

Alston, Charles Henry 1907–1997 **33**

Amadi, Elechi 1934— **40**

Amaker, Harold Tommy, Jr. *See Amaker, Tommy*

Amaker, Norman 1935–2000 **63**

Amaker, Tommy 1965— **62**

Amaki, Amalia 1949— **76**

Amerie 1980— **52**

Ames, Wilmer 1950–1993 **27**

Amin, Idi 1925–2003 **42**

Ammons, James H. 1952(?)— **81**

Amos, Emma 1938— **63**

Amos, John 1941— **8, 62**

Amos, Valerie 1954— **41**

Amos, Wally 1937— **9**

Amoudi, Mohammed al- 1946— **88**

Anderson, Anthony 1970— **51, 77**

Anderson, Carl 1945–2004 **48**

Anderson, Charles Edward 1919–1994 **37**

Anderson, Eddie "Rochester" 1905–1977 **30**

Anderson, Elmer 1941— **25**

Anderson, Fred 1929–2010 **87**

Anderson, Ho Che 1969— **54**

Anderson, Jamal 1972— **22**

Anderson, Lauren 1965— **72**

Anderson, Marian 1902— **2, 33**

Anderson, Michael P. 1959–2003 **40**

Anderson, Mike 1959— **63**

Anderson, Norman B. 1955— **45**

Anderson, Reuben V. 1942— **81**

Anderson, Viv 1956— **58**

Anderson, William G(ilchrist) 1927— **57**

Andre 3000 *See Benjamin, Andre*

Andrews, Benny 1930–2006 **22, 59**

Andrews, Bert 1929–1993 **13**

Andrews, Mark *See Sisqo*

Andrews, Raymond 1934–1991 **4**

Andrews, Tina 1951— **74**

Angelou, Maya 1928— **1, 15**

Anna Marie *See Lincoln, Abbey*

Annan, Kofi Atta 1938— **15, 48**

Ansa, Tina McElroy 1949— **14**

Anthony, Carmelo 1984— **46**

Anthony, Crystal *See McCrary Anthony, Crystal*

Anthony, Michael 1930(?)— **29**

Anthony, Trey 1974— **63**

Anthony, Wendell 1950— **25**

apl.de.ap 1974— **84**

Appiah, Kwame Anthony 1954— **67**

Arac de Nyeko, Monica 1979— **66**

Arach, Monica *See Arac de Nyeko, Monica*

Archer, Dennis (Wayne) 1942— **7, 36**

Archer, Lee, Jr. 1919— **79**

Archer, Michael D'Angelo *See D'Angelo*

Archer, Osceola *See Adams, Osceola Macarthy*

Archibald, Nathaniel *See Archibald, Tiny*

Archibald, Tiny 1948— **90**

Archie-Hudson, Marguerite 1937— **44**

Ardoin, Alphonse 1915–2007 **65**

Arenas, Gilbert 1982— **84**

Arinze, Francis 1932— **19**

Aristide, Jean-Bertrand 1953— **6, 45**

Arkadie, Kevin 1957— **17**

Armah, Ayi Kwei 1939— **49**

Armah, Esther 1963— **87**

Armatrading, Joan 1950— 32
Armstrong, Govind 1968— 81
Armstrong, (Daniel) Louis 1900–1971 2
Armstrong, Robb 1962— 15
Armstrong, Vanessa Bell 1953— 24
Arnez J, 1966(?)— 53
Arnold, Monica See Monica
Arnold, Tichina 1971— 63
Arnwine, Barbara 1951(?)— 28
Arrington, Richard 1934— 24
Arroyo, Martina 1936— 30
Artest, Ron 1979— 52
Arthur, Owen 1949— 33
Asante, Molefi Kete 1942— 3
Ashanti 1980— 37
Ashe, Arthur Robert, Jr. 1943–1993 1, 18
Ashford, Calvin, Jr. 1935(?)–2008 74
Ashford, Emmett 1914–1980 22
Ashford, Evelyn 1957— 63
Ashford, Nickolas 1942— 21
Ashley, Maurice 1966— 15, 47
Ashley-Ward, Amelia 1957— 23
Ashong, Derrick 1975— 86
Asim, Jabari 1962— 71
Astatke, Mulatu 1942(?)— 81
Atim, Julian 1980(?)— 66
Atkins, Cholly 1930–2003 40
Atkins, David See Sinbad
Atkins, Erica 1972— See Mary Mary
Atkins, Jeffrey See Ja Rule
Atkins, Juan 1962— 50
Atkins, Russell 1926— 45
Atkins, Tina 1974— See Mary Mary
Atta Mills, John 1944— 75
Atyam, Angelina 1946— 55
Aubert, Alvin 1930— 41
Auguste, Arnold A. 1946— 47
Auguste, Donna 1958— 29
Auguste, (Marie Carmele) Rose-Anne 1963— 13
Augustine, Jean 1937— 53
Austin, Gloria 1956— 63
Austin, Jim 1951— 63
Austin, Junius C. 1887–1968 44
Austin, Lovie 1887–1972 40
Austin, Patti 1948— 24
Autrey, Wesley 1956— 68
Avant, Clarence 1931— 19, 86
Avant, Nicole A. 1968— 90
Avery, Byllye Y. 1937— 66
Awoonor, Kofi 1935— 37
Awoonor-Williams, George See Awoonor, Kofi
Awoyinka, Adesiji See Siji
Ayers, Roy 1940— 16
Azikiwe, Nnamdi 1904–1996 13
Ba, Mariama 1929–1981 30
Babangida, Ibrahim (Badamasi) 1941— 4
Babatunde, Obba 19(?)(?)— 35
Babyface 1959— 10, 31, 82
Baca, Susana 1954— 80
Bacon-Bercey, June 1942— 38
Badu, Erykah 1971(?)— 22
Bahati, Wambui 1950(?)— 60
Bailey, Buster 1902–1967 38
Bailey, Chauncey 1949–2007 68
Bailey, Clyde 1946— 45
Bailey, DeFord 1899–1982 33

Bailey, Pearl Mae 1918–1990 14
Bailey, Philip 1951— 63
Bailey, Preston 1948(?)— 64
Bailey, Radcliffe 1968— 19
Bailey, William C. See Bailey, Buster
Bailey, Xenobia 1955(?)— 11
Bailey Rae, Corinne 1979— 83
Baines, Harold 1959— 32
Baiocchi, Regina Harris 1956— 41
Baisden, Michael 1963— 25, 66
Baker, Anita 1957— 21, 48
Baker, Arlene Holt See Holt Baker, Arlene
Baker, Augusta 1911–1998 38
Baker, Constance See Motley, Constance Baker
Baker, Dusty 1949— 8, 43, 72
Baker, Ella 1903–1986 5
Baker, George See Divine, Father
Baker, Gwendolyn Calvert 1931— 9
Baker, Houston A(lfred), Jr. 1943— 6
Baker, Johnnie B., Jr. See Baker, Dusty
Baker, Josephine 1906–1975 3
Baker, LaVern 1929–1997 26
Baker, Matt 1921–1959 76
Baker, Maxine 1952— 28
Baker, Thurbert 1952— 22
Baker, Vernon Joseph 1919–2010 65, 87
Balance, Frank W. 1942— 41
Baldwin, Cynthia A. 1945— 74
Baldwin, James 1924–1987 1
Ballard, Allen B(utler), Jr. 1930— 40
Ballard, Hank 1927–2003 41
Baltimore, Richard Lewis, III 1946— 71
Bambaataa, Afrika 1958— 34
Bambara, Toni Cade 1939— 10
Banda, Hastings Kamuzu 1898(?)–1997 6, 54
Bandele, Asha 1970(?)— 36
Bandele, Biyi 1967— 68
Bandele-Thomas, Biyi See Bandele, Biyi
Banks, A. Doris See Henries, A. Doris Banks
Banks, Ernie 1931— 33
Banks, Jeffrey 1953— 17
Banks, Michelle 1968(?)— 59
Banks, Paula A. 1950— 68
Banks, Tyra 1973— 11, 50
Banks, William (Venoid) 1903–1985 11
Banneker, Benjamin 1731–1806 93
Banner, David 1975(?)— 55
Bannister, Edward Mitchell 1828–1901 88
Banton, Buju 1973— 93
Baquet, Dean 1956— 63
Baraka, Amiri 1934— 1, 38
Barbee, Lloyd Augustus 1925–2002 71
Barber, Atiim Kiambu See Barber, Tiki
Barber, Ronde 1975— 41
Barber, Tiki 1975— 57
Barboza, Anthony 1944— 10
Barclay, Paris 1957— 37
Barden, Donald H. 1943— 9, 20, 89

Barker, Danny 1909–1994 32
Barkley, Charles 1963— 5, 66
Barlow, Roosevelt 1917–2003 49
Barnes, Ernie 1938–2009 16, 78
Barnes, John 1963— 53
Barnes, Lloyd 1944— 77
Barnes, Melody 1964— 75
Barnes, Roosevelt "Booba" 1936–1996 33
Barnes, Steven 1952— 54
Barnett, Amy Du Bois 1969— 46
Barnett, Etta Moten 1901–2004 18, 56
Barnett, Marguerite 1942–1992 46
Barney, Lem 1945— 26
Barnhill, David 1914–1983 30
Barrax, Gerald William 1933— 45
Barrett, Andrew C. 1942(?)— 12
Barrett, Jacqueline 1950— 28
Barrett, Lindsay 1941— 43
Barrett, Mario Dewar See Mario
Barrino, Fantasia 1984— 53
Barrow, Dean 1951— 69
Barrow, Joseph Louis See Louis, Joe
Barrow, Willie T. 1924— 85
Barry, Marion S(hepilov, Jr.) 1936— 7, 44
Bartels, Peggielene 1953(?)— 80
Barthé, Earl 19(?)(?)— 78
Barthe, Richmond 1901–1989 15
Bashir, Halima 1979— 73
Bashir, Omar al- 1944— 77
Basie, William James See Count Basie
Basquiat, Jean-Michel 1960–1988 5
Bass, Charlotta Amanda Spears 1874–1969 40
Bass, Karen 1953— 70
Bassett, Angela 1958— 6, 23, 62
Bassey, Shirley 1937— 25
Baszile, Jennifer 1969(?)— 79
Bates, Clayton See Bates, Peg Leg
Bates, Daisy (Lee Gatson) 1914(?)— 13
Bates, Elias See Diddley, Bo
Bates, Karen Grigsby 19(?)(?)— 40
Bates, Peg Leg 1907— 14
Bath, Patricia E. 1942— 37
Batiste, Alvin 1932–2007 66
Battle, Kathleen 1948— 70
Baugé, Grégory 1985— 86
Baugh, David 1947— 23
Baylor, Don(ald Edward) 1949— 6
Baylor, Elgin 1934— 93
Baylor, Helen 1953— 36
Beach, Michael 1963— 26
Beah, Ishmael 1980— 69
Beal, Bernard B. 1954(?)— 46
Beals, Jennifer 1963— 12
Beals, Melba Patillo 1941— 15
Beamon, Bob 1946— 30
Bearden, Romare 1912–1988 2, 50
Beasley, Jamar 1979— 29
Beasley, Myrlie See Evers, Myrlie
Beasley, Phoebe 1943— 34
Beaton, Norman Lugard 1934–1994 14
Beatty, Talley 1923(?)–1995 35
Beauvais, Garcelle 1966— 29
Beauvoir, Max 1936(?)— 74
Bebey, Francis 1929–2001 45
Bechet, Sidney 1897–1959 18

Beck, Robert See Iceberg Slim
Beckford, Tyson 1970— 11, 68
Beckham, Barry 1944— 41
Bedie, Henri Konan 1934— 21
Beenie Man 1973— 32
Bekele, Kenenisa 1982— 75
Belafonte, Harold George, Jr. See Belafonte, Harry
Belafonte, Harry 1927— 4, 65
Belgrave, Cynthia 1920–1997 75
Belgrave, Marcus 1936— 77
Bell, Darrin 1975— 77
Bell, Derrick (Albert, Jr.) 1930— 6
Bell, James "Cool Papa" 1901–1991 36
Bell, James A. 1948— 50
Bell, James Madison 1826–1902 40
Bell, Michael 1955— 40
Bell, Ralph S. 1934— 5
Bell, Robert Mack 1943— 22
Bellamy, Bill 1967— 12
Bellamy, Terry 1972— 58
Belle, Albert (Jojuan) 1966— 10
Belle, Regina 1963— 1, 51
Belton, Sharon Sayles 1951— 9, 16
Benberry, Cuesta 1923–2007 65
Benét, Eric 1966— 28, 77
Benham, Robert 1946— 78
Ben-Israel, Ben Ami 1940(?)— 11
Benjamin, Andre 1975— 45
Benjamin, Andre (3000) 1975(?)— See OutKast
Benjamin, Regina 1956— 20, 75
Benjamin, Tritobia Hayes 1944— 53
Bennett, Estelle 1941–2009 77
Bennett, George Harold "Hal" 1930— 45
Bennett, Gwendolyn B. 1902–1981 59
Bennett, Lerone, Jr. 1928— 5, 84
Bennett, Louise 1919–2006 69
Benson, Angela 19(?)(?)— 34
Bentley, Lamont 1973–2005 53
Berrien, Jacqueline A. 1961— 93
Berry, Bertice 1960— 8, 55
Berry, Bill See Berry, Edwin C.
Berry, Charles Edward Anderson See Berry, Chuck
Berry, Chuck 1926— 29
Berry, Edwin C. 1910–1987 81
Berry, Fred "Rerun" 1951–2003 48
Berry, Halle 1966— 4, 19, 57, 91
Berry, James 1925— 41
Berry, Mary Frances 1938— 7
Berry, Moses 1950(?)— 84
Berry, Theodore M. 1905–2000 31
Berrysmith, Don Reginald 1936— 49
Best, Carrie 1903–2001 80
Betha, Mason Durrell 1977(?)— 24
Bethune, Mary (Jane) McLeod 1875–1955 4
Beti, Mongo 1932–2001 36
Betsch, MaVynee 1935— 28
Bettis, Jerome 1972— 64
Betts, Keter 1928–2005 85
Betts, R. Dwayne 1979(?)— 86
Bevel, James L. 1936–2008 75
Beverly, Frankie 1946— 25
Beyoncé 1981— 39, 70
Beze, Dante Terrell See Mos Def

Bibb, Eric 1951— 49

Bibb, Henry 1815–1854 54

Bibb, Mary 1820–1877 54

Bickerstaff, Bernard Tyrone 1944— 21

Big Bank Hank See Sugarhill Gang, The

Big Boi See Patton, Antwan

Big Daddy Kane 1968— 79

Biggers, John 1924–2001 20, 33

Biggers, Sanford 1970— 62

Biko, Stephen See Biko, Steven (Bantu)

Biko, Steven (Bantu) 1946–1977 4

Billops, Camille 1933— 82

bin Wahad, Dhoruba 1943— 85

Bing, Dave 1943— 3, 59, 78

Birch, Adolpho A., Jr. 1932— 85

Birch, Glynn R. 195(?)— 61

Bishop, Eric See Foxx, Jamie

Bishop, Maurice 1944–1983 39

Bishop, Sanford D. Jr. 1947— 24

Bivins, Michael 1968— 72

Biya, Chantal 1970— 89

Biya, Paul 1933— 28

Biyidi-Awala, Alexandre See Beti, Mongo

Bizimungu, Pasteur 1951— 19

Black, Albert 1940— 51

Black, Barry C. 1948— 47

Black, Joe 1924–2002 75

Black, Keith Lanier 1957— 18, 84

Black Kold Madina See Roberts, Kimberly Rivers

Black Thought 1972— 63

Blackburn, Robert 1920— 28

Blackman, Toni 1968— 86

Blackmon, Brenda 1952— 58

Blackshear, Leonard 1943— 52

Blackwell, David 1919— 79

Blackwell, Kenneth, Sr. 1948— 61

Blackwell, Robert D., Sr. 1937— 52

Blackwell, Unita 1933— 17

Blackwood, Maureen 1960— 37

Blacque, Taurean 1941— 58

Blade, Brian 1970— 88

Blair, Jayson 1976— 50

Blair, Maxine See Powell, Maxine

Blair, Paul 1944— 36

Blake, Asha 1961(?)— 26

Blake, Charles E. 1940— 82

Blake, Eubie 1883–1983 29

Blake, James 1979— 43

Blake, James Hubert See Blake, Eubie

Blakely, Edward J. 1938— 88

Blakey, Art(hur) 1919–1990 37

Blanchard, Terence 1962— 43

Bland, Bobby "Blue" 1930— 36

Bland, Eleanor Taylor 1944— 39

Bland, Robert Calvin See Bland, Bobby "Blue"

Blanks, Billy 1955(?)— 22

Blanks, Deborah K. 1958— 69

Blanton, Dain 1971— 29

Blassingame, John Wesley 1940–2000 40

Blaylock, Ronald 1960(?)— 86

Blayton, Jesse B., Sr. 1897–1977 55

Bleu, Corbin 1989— 65

Blige, Mary J. 1971— 20, 34, 60

Blockson, Charles L. 1933— 42

Blondy, Alpha 1953— 30

Bloomer, George 1963— 86

Blow, Charles M. 1968(?)— 73

Blow, Kurtis 1959— 31

Bluford, Guion Stewart, Jr. See Bluford, Guy

Bluford, Guy 1942— 2, 35

Bluitt, Juliann Stephanie 1938— 14

Boateng, Ozwald 1968— 35

Boateng, Paul Yaw 1951— 56

B.o.B. 1988— 91

Bobb, Robert C. 1945— 83

Bobo, Lawrence 1958— 60

Bogle, Donald 19(?)(?)— 34

Bogues, Tyrone "Muggsy" 1965— 56

Bol, Manute 1963— 1

Bolden, Buddy 1877–1931 39

Bolden, Charles Frank, Jr. 1946— 7, 78

Bolden, Charles Joseph See Bolden, Buddy

Bolden, Frank E. 1913–2003 44

Bolden, Tonya 1959— 32

Bolin, Jane 1908–2007 22, 59

Bolt, Usain 1986— 73

Bolton, Terrell D. 1959(?)— 25

Bolton-Holifield, Ruthie 1967— 28

Bonaly, Surya 1973— 7

Bond, Beverly 1970— 53

Bond, J. Max, Jr. 1935— 76

Bond, (Horace) Julian 1940— 2, 35

Bonds, Barry 1964— 6, 34, 63

Bonds, Bobby 1946— 43

Bonds, Margaret 1913–1972 39

Bonet, Lisa 1967— 58

Boney, Lisa Michelle See Bonet, Lisa

Bonga, Kuenda 1942— 13

Bongo, Albert-Bernard See Bongo, Omar

Bongo, Ali Ben 1959— 80

Bongo, Omar 1935–2009 1, 79

Bonheur, Yannick 1982— 84

Bontemps, Arna(ud Wendell) 1902–1973 8

Booker, Cory Anthony 1969— 68

Booker, Simeon 1918— 23

Borders, James (Buchanan, IV) 1949— 9

Bosh, Chris 1984— 85

Bosley, Freeman (Robertson), Jr. 1954— 7

Boston, Kelvin E. 1955(?)— 25

Boston, Lloyd 1970(?)— 24

Bow Wow 1987— 35

Bowe, Riddick (Lamont) 1967— 6

Bowen, John W. E., Sr. 1855–1933 89

Bowen, Ruth 1924–2009 83

Bowman, Bertie 1931— 71

Bowman, Herbert See Bowman, Bertie

Bowser, Yvette Lee 1965(?)— 17

Boyd, Edward 1914–2007 70

Boyd, Gerald M. 1950–2006 32, 59

Boyd, Gwendolyn 1955— 49

Boyd, John W., Jr. 1965— 20, 72

Boyd, Melba Joyce 1950— 86

Boyd, Suzanne 1963— 52

Boyd, T(heophilus) B(artholomew), III 1947— 6

Boye, Madior 1940— 30

Boykin, Keith 1965— 14

Boykin, Otis 1920–1982 92

Boyz II Men 82

Bradford, Mark 1961— 89

Bradley, David Henry, Jr. 1950— 39

Bradley, Ed 1941–2006 2, 59

Bradley, J. Robert 1919–2007 65

Bradley, Jennette B. 1952— 40

Bradley, Thomas 1917— 2, 20

Brady, Wayne 1972— 32, 71

Brae, C. Michael 1963(?)— 61

Braithwaite, William Stanley 1878–1962 52

Bramlett, Joseph 1988— 91

Branch, William Blackwell 1927— 39

Brand, Dionne 1953— 32

Brand, Elton 1979— 31

Brandon, Barbara 1960(?)— 3

Brandon, Thomas Terrell 1970— 16

Brandy 1979— 14, 34, 72

Branham, George, III 1962— 50

Branson, Herman 1914–1995 87

Brashear, Carl Maxie 1931— 29

Brashear, Donald 1972— 39

Brathwaite, Fred 1972— 35

Brathwaite, Kamau 1930— 36

Brathwaite, Lawson Edward See Kamau Brathwaite

Braugher, Andre 1962— 13, 58, 91

Braun, Carol Moseley 1947— 4, 42

Brawley, Benjamin 1882–1939 44

Braxton, Brad 1969(?)— 77

Braxton, Gene See Herndon, Angelo

Braxton, Toni 1967— 15, 61, 91

Brazile, Donna 1959— 25, 70

Breed, Eric T. See MC Breed

Breed, MC See MC Breed

Breedlove, Sarah See Walker, Madame C. J.

Breeze, Jean "Binta" 1956— 37

Bridges, Christopher See Ludacris

Bridges, Ruby 1954— 77

Bridges, Sheila 1964— 36

Bridges, Todd 1965— 37

Bridgetower, George 1780(?)–1860 78

Bridgewater, Dee Dee 1950— 32, 92

Bridgforth, Glinda 1952— 36

Briggs, Curtis 1952(?)— 84

Brimmer, Andrew F. 1926— 2, 48

Briscoe, Connie 1952— 15

Briscoe, Marlin 1946(?)— 37

Britt, Donna 1954(?)— 28

Broadbent, Hydeia 1984— 36

Brock, Lou 1939— 18

Brock, Roslyn McCallister 1965— 86

Bromery, Randolph Wilson 1926— 85

Bronner, Nathaniel H., Sr. 1914–1993 32

Brooke, Edward W. 1919— 8, 88

Brooks, Aaron 1976— 33

Brooks, Avery 1949— 9

Brooks, Derrick 1973— 43

Brooks, Golden 1970— 62

Brooks, Gwendolyn 1917–2000 1, 28

Brooks, Hadda 1916–2002 40

Brooks, Mehcad 1980— 62

Brooks, Tyrone 1945— 59

Broonzy, Big Bill 1893—1958 82

Brother Blue See Hill, Hugh Morgan

Brower, William 1916–2004 49

Brown, Andre See Dre, Dr.

Brown, Angela M. 1964(?)— 54

Brown, Anne 1912–2009 76

Brown, Anthony G. 1961— 72

Brown, Antron 1976— 85

Brown, Bobby 1969— 58

Brown, Buck See Brown, Robert

Brown, Byrd 1930–2001 49

Brown, Byron W. 1958— 72

Brown, Carlinhos 1962— 81

Brown, Cecil M. 1943— 46

Brown, Charles 1922–1999 23

Brown, Chris 1989— 74

Brown, Chuck 1939— 78

Brown, Clarence Gatemouth 1924–2005 59

Brown, Claude 1937–2002 38

Brown, Clifford 1930–1956 86

Brown, Cora 1914–1972 33

Brown, Corrine 1946— 24, 90

Brown, Cupcake 1964— 63

Brown, Donald 1963— 19

Brown, Eddie C. 1940— 35

Brown, Elaine 1943— 8

Brown, Ernest 1916–2009 80

Brown, Erroll M. 1950(?)— 23

Brown, Foxy 1979— 25

Brown, George Leslie 1926–2006 62

Brown, H. Rap See Al-Amin, Jamil Abdullah

Brown, Homer S. 1896–1977 47

Brown, Hubert Gerold See Al-Amin, Jamil Abdullah

Brown, James 1933–2006 15, 60

Brown, James 1951— 22

Brown, James Nathaniel See Brown, Jim

Brown, James Willie, Jr. See Komunyakaa, Yusef

Brown, Jamie Foster 19(?)(?)— 91

Brown, Janice Rogers 1949— 43

Brown, Jesse 1944–2003 6, 41

Brown, Jesse Leroy 1926–1950 31

Brown, Jim 1936— 11

Brown, Joe 19(?)(?)— 29

Brown, Joyce F. 1946— 25

Brown, Kwame R. 1970— 91

Brown, Lee P(atrick) 1937— 1, 24

Brown, Les(lie Calvin) 1945— 5

Brown, Lloyd Louis 1913–2003 42

Brown, Melanie 1975— 73

Brown, Mike 1970— 77

Brown, Nappy 1929–2008 73

Brown, Oscar, Jr. 1926–2005 53

Brown, Patrick "Sleepy" 1970— 50

Brown, Robert 1936–2007 65

Brown, Ron(ald Harmon) 1941–1996 5

Brown, Ronald K. 1966— 91

Brown, Rosemary 1930–2003 62

Brown, Ruth 1928–2006 90

Brown, Sean 1976— 52

Brown, Sterling Allen 1901–1989 10, 64

Brown, Tony 1933— 3

Brown, Uzee 1950— 42

Brown, Vivian 1964— 27

Brown, Warren 1971(?)— 61

Brown, Wesley 1945— **23**

Brown, Willa Beatrice 1906–1992 **40**

Brown, Willard 1911(?)–1996 **36**

Brown, William Anthony *See Brown, Tony*

Brown, Willie 1934— **7, 85**

Brown, Zora Kramer 1949— **12**

Brown Bomber, The *See Louis, Joe*

Browne, Roscoe Lee 1925–2007 **66**

Brownlee, Lawrence 1972(?)— **88**

Broyard, Anatole 1920–1990 **68**

Broyard, Bliss 1966— **68**

Bruce, Blanche Kelso 1849–1898 **33**

Bruce, Bruce 19(?)(?)— **56**

Bruce, Isaac 1972— **26**

Brunson, Dorothy 1938— **1, 87**

Brutus, Dennis 1924— **38**

Bryan, Ashley F. 1923— **41**

Bryant, Cullen 1951–2009 **81**

Bryant, John 1966— **26**

Bryant, John R. 1943— **45**

Bryant, Kobe 1978— **15, 31, 71**

Bryant, Wayne R(ichard) 1947— **6**

Bryant, William Benson 1911–2005 **61**

Bryant, William Cullen *See Bryant, Cullen*

Buchanan, Ray 1971— **32**

Buckley, Gail Lumet 1937— **39**

Buckley, Victoria (Vikki) 1947–1999 **24**

Buff Love *See Fat Boys*

Bullard, Eugene Jacques 1894–1961 **12**

Bullins, Ed 1935— **25**

Bullock, Anna Mae *See Turner, Tina*

Bullock, Steve 1936— **22**

Bully-Cummings, Ella 1957(?)— **48**

Bumbry, Grace (Ann) 1937— **5**

Bunch, Lonnie G., III 1952— **91**

Bunche, Ralph J(ohnson) 1904–1971 **5**

Bunkley, Anita Richmond 19(?)(?)— **39**

Burgess, John 1909–2003 **46**

Burgess, Marjorie L. 1929— **55**

Burke, Selma Hortense 1900–1995 **16**

Burke, Solomon 1940— **31, 86**

Burke, Yvonne Brathwaite 1932— **42**

Burks, Mary Fair 1920–1991 **40**

Burleigh, Henry Thacker 1866–1949 **56**

Burley, Mary Lou *See Williams, Mary Lou*

Burnett, Charles 1944— **16, 68**

Burnett, Chester Arthur *See Howlin' Wolf*

Burnett, Dorothy 1905–1995 **19**

Burnham, Forbes 1923–1985 **66**

Burnim, Mickey L. 1949— **48**

Burning Spear 194(?)— **79**

Burns, Eddie 1928— **44**

Burns, Jesse Louis *See Jackson, Jesse*

Burns, Ursula 1958— **60**

Burnside, R. L. 1926–2005 **56**

Burrell, Orville Richard *See Shaggy*

Burrell, Stanley Kirk *See M.C. Hammer*

Burrell, Tom 1939— **21, 51**

Burris, Chuck 1951— **21**

Burris, Roland W. 1937— **25, 75**

Burroughs, Margaret Taylor 1917— **9**

Burrows, Stephen 1943— **31**

Burrus, William Henry "Bill" 1936— **45**

Burrus, Kandi *See Kandi*

Burt-Murray, Angela 1970— **59**

Burton, LeVar 1957— **8**

Burwell, Bryan 1955— **83**

Busby, Jheryl 1949–2008 **3, 74**

Bush, Gordon 1942— **82**

Bush, Reggie 1985— **59, 88**

Buthelezi, Mangosuthu Gatsha 1928— **9**

Butler, George, Jr. 1931–2008 **70**

Butler, Jerry 1939— **26**

Butler, Jonathan 1961— **28**

Butler, Leroy, III 1968— **17**

Butler, Louis 1952— **70**

Butler, Octavia 1947–2006 **8, 43, 58**

Butler, Paul D. 1961— **17**

Butts, Calvin O, III 1949— **9, 90**

Butts, Cassandra 1965— **78**

Bynoe, Peter C. B. 1951— **40**

Bynum, Juanita 1959— **31, 71**

Byrd, Donald 1949— **10**

Byrd, Eugene 1975— **64**

Byrd, Michelle 1965— **19**

Byrd, Robert (Oliver Daniel, III) 1952— **11**

Byron, JoAnne Deborah *See Shakur, Assata*

Cade, Toni *See Bambara, Toni Cade*

Cadoria, Sherian Grace 1940— **14**

Caesar, Shirley 1938— **19**

Cage, Byron 1965(?)— **53**

Cain, Herman 1945— **15, 92**

Calabrese, Karyn 1947— **89**

Caldwell, Benjamin 1937— **46**

Caldwell, Earl 1941(?)— **60**

Caldwell, Jim 1955— **81**

Caldwell, Kirbyjon 1953(?)— **55**

Calhoun, Cora *See Austin, Lovie*

Calhoun, Lillian Scott 1923–2006 **87**

Callaway, Thomas DeCarlo *See Cee-Lo*

Callender, Clive O(rville) 1936— **3**

Calloway, Cab 1907–1994 **14**

Camara, Moussa Dadis 1964— **76**

Cameron, Earl 1917— **44**

Cameron, James 1914–2006 **80**

Camp, Georgia Blanche Douglas *See Johnson, Georgia Douglas*

Camp, Kimberly 1956— **19**

Campanella, Roy 1921–1993 **25**

Campbell, Bebe Moore 1950–2006 **6, 24, 59**

Campbell, Bill 1954— **9, 76**

Campbell, Charleszetta Lena *See Waddles, Charleszetta (Mother)*

Campbell, Donald J. 1935— **66**

Campbell, E(lmer) Simms 1906–1971 **13**

Campbell, Mary Schmidt 1947— **43**

Campbell, Milton *See Little Milton*

Campbell, Naomi 1970— **1, 31**

Campbell, Tisha *See Campbell-Martin, Tisha*

Campbell-Martin, Tisha 1969— **8, 42**

Canada, Geoffrey 1954— **23**

Canady, Alexa 1950— **28**

Canegata, Leonard Lionel Cornelius *See Lee, Canada*

Cannon, Katie 1950— **10**

Cannon, Nick 1980— **47, 73**

Cannon, Reuben 1946— **50**

Cara, Irene 1959— **77**

Carby, Hazel 1948— **27**

Cardozo, Francis L. 1837–1903 **33**

Carew, Rod 1945— **20**

Carey, Mariah 1970— **32, 53, 69**

Cargill, Victoria A. 19(?)(?)— **43**

Carmichael, Stokely 1941–1998 **5, 26**

Carnegie, Herbert 1919— **25**

Carr, Johnnie 1911–2008 **69**

Carr, Keela 1973— **74**

Carr, Kurt 196(?)— **56**

Carr, Leroy 1905–1935 **49**

Carroll, Diahann 1935— **9**

Carroll, L. Natalie 1950— **44**

Carroll, Rocky 1963— **74**

Carroll, Vinnette 1922— **29**

Carruthers, George R. 1939— **40**

Carson, André 1974— **69**

Carson, Benjamin 1951— **1, 35, 76**

Carson, Johnnie 1943— **85**

Carson, Josephine *See Baker, Josephine*

Carson, Julia 1938–2007 **23, 69**

Carson, Lisa Nicole 1969— **21**

Carter, Anson 1974— **24**

Carter, Ben *See Ben-Israel, Ben Ami*

Carter, Benny 1907–2003 **46**

Carter, Betty 1930— **19**

Carter, Butch 1958— **27**

Carter, Cris 1965— **21**

Carter, Dwayne Michael, Jr. *See Lil Wayne*

Carter, Joe 1960— **30**

Carter, Joye Maureen 1957— **41**

Carter, Kenneth 1959(?)— **53**

Carter, Majora 1966— **77**

Carter, Mandy 1946— **11**

Carter, Martin 1927–1997 **49**

Carter, Nell 1948–2003 **39**

Carter, Pamela Lynn 1949— **67**

Carter, Regina 1966(?)— **23**

Carter, Robert L. 1917— **51**

Carter, Rubin 1937— **26**

Carter, Shawn *See Jay-Z*

Carter, Stephen L(isle) 1954— **4**

Carter, Vince 1977— **26**

Carter, Warrick L. 1942— **27**

Cartey, Wilfred 1931–1992 **47**

Cartiér, Xam Wilson 1949— **41**

Carver, George Washington 1861(?)–1943 **4**

Cary, Lorene 1956— **3**

Cary, Mary Ann Shadd 1823–1893 **30**

Cash, Rosalind 1938–1995 **28**

Cash, Swin 1979— **59**

Cashin, Sheryll 1962— **63**

CasSelle, Malcolm 1970— **11**

Catchings, Tamika 1979— **43**

Catlett, Elizabeth 1919— **2**

Catto, Octavius V. 1839–1871 **83**

Caymmi, Dorival 1914–2008 **72**

Cayton, Horace 1903–1970 **26**

Cedric the Entertainer 1964— **29, 60**

Cee-Lo 1974— **70**

Césaire, Aimé 1913–2008 **48, 69**

Chadiha, Jeffri 1970— **57**

Cham, Adongo Agada Akway 1954(?)— **77**

Chamberlain, Wilt 1936–1999 **18, 47**

Chambers, James *See Cliff, Jimmy*

Chambers, Julius (LeVonne) 1936— **3**

Chamillionaire 1979— **82**

Chaney, John 1932— **67**

Channer, Colin 1963— **36**

Chanté, Keshia 1988— **50**

Chanticleer, Raven 1928–2002 **91**

Chapman, Nathan A., Jr. 1957— **21**

Chapman, Tracy 1964— **26**

Chappell, Emma C. 1941— **18**

Chappelle, Dave 1973— **50**

Charlemagne, Emmanuel *See Charlemagne, Manno*

Charlemagne, Manno 1948— **11**

Charles, Mary Eugenia 1919–2005 **10, 55**

Charles, Pierre 1954–2004 **52**

Charles, Ray 1930–2004 **16, 48**

Charleston, Oscar 1896–1954 **39**

Chase, Debra Martin 1956(?)— **49**

Chase, Leah 1923— **57**

Chase-Riboud, Barbara 1939— **20, 46**

Chatard, Peter 1936— **44**

Chavis, Benjamin (Franklin, Jr.) 1948— **6**

Cheadle, Don 1964— **19, 52**

Cheatham, Doc 1905–1997 **17**

Checker, Chubby 1941— **28**

Cheeks, Maurice 1956— **47**

Chenault, John 1952— **40**

Chenault, Kenneth I. 1952— **4, 36**

Cheney-Coker, Syl 1945— **43**

Cherry, Deron 1959— **40**

Cheruiyot, Robert 1978— **69**

Chesimard, JoAnne (Deborah) *See Shakur, Assata*

Chesnutt, Charles 1858–1932 **29**

Chestnut, J. L., Jr. 1930–2008 **73**

Chestnut, Morris 1969— **31**

Chideya, Farai 1969— **14, 61**

Chief Black Thunderbird Eagle *See York, Dwight D.*

Childress, Alice 1920–1994 **15**

Chiluba, Frederick 1943— **56, 80**

Chineworth, Mary Alice 1917— **79**

Chinn, May Edward 1896–1980 **26**

Chisholm, Daquan 1993— **93**

Chisholm, Samuel J. 1942— **32**

Chisholm, Shirley 1924–2005 **2, 50**

Chissano, Joaquim 1939— **7, 55, 67**

Chong, Rae Dawn 1961— **62**

Christian, Barbara T. 1946–2000 **44**

Christian, Spencer 1947— **15**

Christian-Green, Donna M. 1945— **17**

Christie, Angella **36**

Christie, Linford 1960— **8**

Christie, Perry Gladstone 1944— **53**

Christie, Ron 1969(?)— **83**

Christophe, Henri 1767–1820 **9**

Chuck D 1960— **9**

Church, Bruce *See Bruce, Bruce*

Churchwell, Robert, Sr. 1917–2009 **76**

Chweneyagae, Presley 1984— **63**

Ciara 1985— **56**

Ciara, Barbara 195(?)— **69**

Cissé, Souleymane *See Souleymane, Mahamane*

Clack, Zoanne 1968(?)— **73**

Claiborne, Loretta 1953— **34**

Clark, Celeste (Clesteen) Abraham 1953— **15**

Clark, Joe 1939— **1**

Clark, John Pepper *See Clark-Bekedermo, J. P.*

Clark, Kenneth B. 1914–2005 **5, 52**

Clark, Kristin *See Taylor, Kristin Clark*

Clark, Mamie Phipps 1917–1983 **79**

Clark, Mattie Moss 1925–1994 **61**

Clark, Patrick 1955— **14**

Clark, Septima (Poinsette) 1898–1987 **7**

Clark-Bekedermo, J. P. 1935— **44**

Clark-Cole, Dorinda 1957— **66**

Clarke, Austin C. 1934— **32**

Clarke, Cheryl 1947— **32**

Clarke, George Elliott 1960— **32**

Clarke, Hope 1943(?)— **14**

Clarke, John Henrik 1915–1998 **20**

Clarke, Kenny 1914–1985 **27**

Clarke, Patrice Francise *See Washington, Patrice Clarke*

Clarke, Yvette 1964— **92**

Clark-Sheard, Karen 19(?)(?)— **22**

Clash, Kevin 1960— **14, 93**

Clay, Bryan 1980— **57, 74**

Clay, Cassius Marcellus, Jr. *See Ali, Muhammad*

Clay, William Lacy 1931— **8**

Clayton, Constance 1937— **1**

Clayton, Eva M. 1934— **20**

Clayton, Mayme Agnew 1923–2006 **62**

Clayton, Xernona 1930— **3, 45**

Claytor, Helen 1907–2005 **14, 52**

Cleage, Albert B., Jr. *See Agyeman, Jaramogi Abebe*

Cleage, Pearl 1948— **17, 64**

Cleaver, (Leroy) Eldridge 1935— **5, 45**

Cleaver, Emanuel (II) 1944— **4, 68**

Cleaver, Kathleen Neal 1945— **29**

Clemente, Rosa 1972— **74**

Clements, George (Harold) 1932— **2**

Clemmons, Reginal G. 19(?)(?)— **41**

Clemons, Clarence 1942— **41**

Clemons, Michael "Pinball" 1965— **64**

Clendenon, Donn 1935–2005 **26, 56**

Cleveland, James 1932(?)–1991 **19**

Cliff, Jimmy 1948— **28, 92**

Cliff, Michelle 1946— **42**

Clifton, Lucille 1936–2010 **14, 64, 91**

Clifton, Nathaniel "Sweetwater" 1922(?)–1990 **47**

Clinton, George 1941— **9, 93**

Clyburn, James E. 1940— **21, 71**

Clyburn, Mignon 1962— **78**

Coachman, Alice 1923— **18**

Coates, Ta-Nehisi 1975— **76**

Cobb, Jewel Plummer 1924— **42**

Cobb, Monty *See Cobb, W. Montague*

Cobb, W. Montague 1904–1990 **39**

Cobb, William Jelani 1969— **59**

Cobbs, Price M(ashaw) 1928— **9**

Cochran, Johnnie 1937–2005 **11, 39, 52**

Cockrel, Kenneth V., Jr. 1965— **79**

Cockrel, Kenneth Vern, Sr. 1938–1989 **79**

CoCo Brother 19(?)(?)— **93**

Cohen, Anthony 1963— **15**

Cohen, Cathy J. 1962— **88**

Colbert, Virgis William 1939— **17**

Cole, Johnnetta B(etsch) 1936— **5, 43**

Cole, Keyshia 1983— **63**

Cole, Lorraine 195(?)— **48**

Cole, Nat "King" 1919–1965 **17**

Cole, Natalie 1950— **17, 60, 84**

Cole, Rebecca 1846–1922 **38**

Coleman, Bessie 1892–1926 **9**

Coleman, Donald 1952— **24, 62**

Coleman, Gary 1968–2010 **35, 86**

Coleman, James E., Jr. 1948(?)— **79**

Coleman, Ken 1942— **57**

Coleman, Leonard S., Jr. 1949— **12**

Coleman, Mary 1946— **46**

Coleman, Michael B. 1954— **28, 79**

Coleman, Ornette 1930— **39, 69**

Coleman, Troy *See Cowboy Troy*

Coleman, Wanda 1946— **48**

Coleman, William F., III 1955(?)— **61**

Coleman, William T. 1920— **76**

Colemon, Johnnie 1921(?)— **11**

Coleridge-Taylor, Samuel 1875–1912 **75**

Coles, Alice 1951(?)— **80**

Coles, Dennis *See Ghostface Killah*

Colescott, Robert 1925— **69**

Collins, Albert 1932–1993 **12**

Collins, Barbara-Rose 1939— **7, 87**

Collins, Bootsy 1951— **31**

Collins, Cardiss 1931— **10, 80**

Collins, Janet 1917–2003 **33, 64**

Collins, Lyn 1948–2005 **53**

Collins, Marva 1936— **3, 71**

Collins, Patricia Hill 1948— **67**

Collins, Paul 1936— **61**

Collins, William *See Collins, Bootsy*

Colston, Hal 1953(?)— **72**

Colter, Cyrus J. 1910–2002 **36**

Coltrane, Alice 1937–2007 **70**

Coltrane, John William 1926–1967 **19**

Coltrane, Ravi 1965— **71**

Combs, Sean 1969— **17, 43, 92**

Comer, James P(ierpont) 1934— **6**

Common 1972— **31, 63**

Compaore, Blaise 1951— **87**

Compton, John 1925–2007 **65**

Compton-Rock, Malaak 1969— **86**

Condrey, Cory *See CoCo Brother*

Cone, James H. 1938— **3, 82**

Coney, PonJola 1951— **48**

Conneh, Sekou Damate, Jr. 1960— **51**

Connerly, Ward 1939— **14**

Conrad, Barbara Smith 1940(?)— **90**

Conté, Lansana 1934(?)–2008 **7, 76**

Contee, Cheryl 1971— **88**

Conyers, John, Jr. 1929— **4, 45**

Conyers, Monica 1964— **85**

Conyers, Nathan G. 1932— **24**

Cook, Charles "Doc" 1891–1958 **44**

Cook, (Will) Mercer 1903–1987 **40**

Cook, Sam 1931–1964 **17**

Cook, Samuel DuBois 1928— **14**

Cook, Suzan D. Johnson 1957— **22**

Cook, Toni 1944— **23**

Cook, Victor Trent 19(?)(?)— *See Three Mo' Tenors*

Cook, Wesley *See Abu-Jamal, Mumia*

Cook, Will Marion 1869–1944 **40**

Cooke, Charles L. *See Cook, Charles "Doc"*

Cooke, Marvel 1901(?)–2000 **31**

Cooks, Patricia 1944–1989 **19**

Cool Papa Bell *See Bell, James "Cool Papa"*

Cools, Anne 1943— **64**

Coombs, Orde M. 1939–1984 **44**

Cooper, Afua 1957— **53**

Cooper, Andrew Lewis *See Cooper, Andy "Lefty"*

Cooper, Andrew W. 1928–2002 **36**

Cooper, Andy "Lefty" 1898–1941 **63**

Cooper, Anna Julia 1858–1964 **20**

Cooper, Barry 1956— **33**

Cooper, Charles "Chuck" 1926–1984 **47**

Cooper, Chuck 1954— **75**

Cooper, Cynthia *See Cooper-Dyke, Cynthia*

Cooper, Edward S(awyer) 1926— **6**

Cooper, Evern 19(?)(?)— **40**

Cooper, Helene 1966— **74**

Cooper, J. California 1932(?)— **12, 85**

Cooper, Lisa 1963— **73**

Cooper, Marcus *See Pleasure P*

Cooper, Margaret J. 194(?)— **46**

Cooper, Michael 1956— **31**

Cooper Cafritz, Peggy 1947— **43**

Cooper-Dyke, Cynthia 1963— **17, 89**

Copeland, Michael 1954— **47**

Coppola, Imani Francesca 1978— **82**

Corbi, Lana 1955— **42**

Corley, Tony 1949— **62**

Cornelius, Don 1936— **4**

Cornish, Sam 1935— **50**

Cornwell, Edward E., III 1956— **70**

Correia, Antoné De'Jaun *See Correia, De'Jaun*

Correia, De'Jaun 1994— **93**

Cortez, Jayne 1936— **43**

Corthron, Kia 1961— **43**

Cortor, Eldzier 1916— **42**

Cosby, Bill 1937— **7, 26, 59**

Cosby, Camille 1945— **14, 80**

Cosby, William Henry, Jr. *See Cosby, Bill*

Cose, Ellis 1951— **5, 50**

Cotter, Joseph Seamon, Sr. 1861–1949 **40**

Cottrell, Comer 1931— **11**

Count Basie 1904–1984 **23**

Counter, S. Allen 1944— **74**

Couto, Mia 1955— **45**

Coverley, Louise Bennett *See Bennett, Louise*

Cowans, Adger W. 1936— **20**

Cowboy Troy, 1970— **54**

Cox, Bryan 1968— **83**

Cox, Deborah 1974(?)— **28**

Cox, Donald Lee 1936–2011 **93**

Cox, Ida 1896–1967 **42**

Cox, Joseph Mason Andrew 1930— **51**

Cox, Renée 1960— **67**

Cox, William E. 1942— **68**

Craig, Carl 1969— **31, 71**

Craig-Jones, Ellen Walker 1906–2000 **44**

Crawford, Carl 1981— **90**

Crawford, Hank 1934–2009 **77**

Crawford, Randy 1952— **19**

Crawford, Veronica *See Crawford, Randy*

Cray, Robert 1953— **30**

Creagh, Milton 1957— **27**

Crennel, Romeo 1947— **54**

Crenshaw, Kimberlé Williams 1959— **88**

Crew, Rudolph F. 1950(?)— **16**

Crew, Spencer R. 1949— **55**

Crichlow, Ernest 1914–2005 **75**

Crite, Alan Rohan 1910— **29**

Croal, N'Gai 1972— **76**

Crocker, Frankie 1937–2000 **29**

Crockett, George W., Jr. 1909–1997 **10, 64**

Crooks, Garth 1958— **53**

Croom, Sylvester 1954— **50**

Cross, Dolores E. 1938— **23**

Crosthwait, David 1892–1976 **93**

Crothers, Benjamin Sherman *See Crothers, Scatman*

Crothers, Scatman 1910–1986 **19**

Crouch, Andraé 1942— **27**

Crouch, Stanley 1945— **11, 87**

Crowder, Henry 1895–1954(?) **16**

Crump, Lavell *See Banner, David*

Crumpler, Rebecca Lee 1831–1895 **89**

Cruse, Harold 1916–2005 **54**

Crutchfield, James N. 1947— **55**

Cullen, Countee 1903–1946 **8**

Cullers, Vincent T. 1924(?)–2003 **49**

Culp, Napoleon Brown Goodson *See Brown, Nappy*

Culpepper, Daunte 1977— **32, 85**

Cummings, Elijah E. 1951— **24**

Cuney, William Waring 1906–1976 **44**

Cunningham, Evelyn 1916–2010 **23, 85**

Cunningham, Randall 1963— **23**

Curling, Alvin 1939— **34**

Currie, Betty 1939(?)— **21**

Currie, Ulysses 1937— **73**

Curry, George E. 1947— **23**

Curry, Mark 1964— **17**

Curry, Michael 1968— **85**

Curtis, Christopher Paul 1954(?)— **26**

Curtis-Hall, Vondie 1956— **17**
Da Don, Polow 1978— **86**
da Silva, Benedita 1942— **5**
da Silva, Jorge Mário *See Jorge, Seu*
Dabiri, John 1980(?)— **93**
Dabydeen, David 1956— **48**
Dadié, Bernard 1916— **34**
Daemyon, Jerald 1970(?)— **64**
D'Aguiar, Fred 1960— **50**
Dailey, Ulysses Grant 1885–1961 **87**
Daly, Marie Maynard 1921— **37**
Damas, Léon-Gontran 1912–1978 **46**
Dance, Kelvin *See Kitwana, Bakari*
Dandala, Mvume 1951— **77**
Dandridge, Dorothy 1922–1965 **3**
Dandridge, Ray 1913–1994 **36**
Dandridge, Raymond Garfield 1882–1930 **45**
D'Angelo 1974— **27**
Daniels, Gertrude *See Haynes, Trudy*
Daniels, Lee 1959— **36, 76**
Daniels-Carter, Valerie 19(?)(?)— **23**
Danjah, Terror 1977— **91**
Danner, Margaret Esse 1915–1986 **49**
Danquah, Meri Nana Ama 1967— **93**
Danticat, Edwidge 1969— **15, 68**
Dantley, Adrian 1956— **72**
Dara, Olu 1941— **335**
D'Arby, Terence Trent *See Maitreya, Sananda*
Darden, Calvin 1950— **38**
Darden, Christopher 1957— **13**
Darego, Agbani 1982— **52**
Dash, Damon 19(?)(?)— **31**
Dash, Darien 1972(?)— **29**
Dash, Julie 1952— **4**
Dash, Leon 1944— **47**
Datcher, Michael 1967— **60**
Dathorne, O. R. 1934— **52**
Davenport, Arthur *See Fattah, Chaka*
David, Craig 1981— **31, 53**
David, Keith 1954— **27**
Davidson, Jaye 1967(?)— **5**
Davidson, Tommy 1963(?)— **21**
Davis, Allison 1902–1983 **12**
Davis, Altovise 1943–2009 **76**
Davis, Angela (Yvonne) 1944— **5**
Davis, Angela J. 1956— **88**
Davis, Anthony 1951— **11**
Davis, Anthony Moses *See Beenie Man*
Davis, Arthur P. 1904–1996 **41**
Davis, Artur 1967— **41**
Davis, Belva 1932— **61**
Davis, Benjamin O(liver), Jr. 1912–2002 **2, 43**
Davis, Benjamin O(liver), Sr. 1877–1970 **4**
Davis, Bing 1937— **84**
Davis, Charles T. 1918–1981 **48**
Davis, Chuck 1937— **33**
Davis, Danny K. 1941— **24, 79**
Davis, Douglas E. *See Fresh, Doug E.*
Davis, Ed 1911–1999 **24**
Davis, Eisa 1971— **68**

Davis, Ernie 1939–1963 **48**
Davis, Erroll B., Jr. 1944— **57**
Davis, Frank Marshall 1905–1987 **47**
Davis, Gary 1896–1972 **41**
Davis, George 1939— **36**
Davis, Gordon J. 1941— **76**
Davis, Guy 1952— **36**
Davis, Jamelia Niela *See Jamelia*
Davis, James E. 1962–2003 **50**
Davis, Lorenzo "Piper" 1917–1997 **19**
Davis, Mike 1960— **41**
Davis, Miles (Dewey, III) 1926–1991 **4**
Davis, Milt 1929–2008 **74**
Davis, Nolan 1942— **45**
Davis, Ossie 1917–2005 **5, 50**
Davis, Ruth 1943— **37**
Davis, Sammy, Jr. 1925–1990 **18**
Davis, Shani 1982— **58, 84**
Davis, Terrell 1972— **20**
Davis, Thulani 1948— **61**
Davis, Tyrone 1938–2005 **54**
Davis, Viola 1965— **34, 76**
Dawes, Dominique (Margaux) 1976— **11**
Dawkins, Wayne 1955— **20**
Dawn, Marpessa 1934–2008 **75**
Dawson, Andre 1954— **85**
Dawson, Matel "Mat," Jr. 1921–2002 **39**
Dawson, Michael C. 1951— **63**
Dawson, Rosario 1979— **72**
Dawson, William Levi 1899–1900 **39**
Day, Leon 1916–1995 **39**
Days, Drew S(aunders, III) 1941— **10**
De' Alexander, Quinton 19??— **57**
de Assís Moreira, Ronaldo *See Ronaldinho*
De Bankolé, Isaach 1957— **78**
de Carvalho, Barcelo *See Bonga, Kuenda*
de Lavallade, Carmen 1931— **78**
de Passe, Suzanne 1948(?)— **25**
De Priest, Oscar Stanton 1871–1951 **80**
De Shields, André 1946— **72**
De Veaux, Alexis 1948— **44**
"Deadwood Dick" *See Love, Nat*
Dean, Mark E. 1957— **35**
Deas, Gerald 1931— **85**
DeBaptiste, George 1814(?)–1875 **32**
DeBarge, El 1961— **89**
Déby, Idriss 1952— **30**
DeCarava, Roy 1919–2009 **42, 81**
Deconge-Watson, Lovenia 1933— **55**
Dee, Merri 1936— **55**
Dee, Ruby 1924— **8, 50, 68**
Deezer D 1965— **53**
DeFrantz, Anita 1952— **37**
DeGale, James 1986— **74**
Deggans, Eric 1965— **71**
DeJongh, John, Jr. 1957— **85**
Delaney, Beauford 1901–1979 **19**
Delaney, Joe 1958–1983 **76**
Delaney, Joseph 1904–1991 **30**
Delany, Annie Elizabeth 1891–1995 **12**
Delany, Martin R. 1812–1885 **27**

Delany, Samuel R(ay), Jr. 1942— **9**
Delany, Sarah (Sadie) 1889— **12**
Delco, Wilhemina R. 1929— **33**
Delice, Ronald 1966— **48**
Delice, Rony 1966— **48**
DeLille, Henriette 1813–1862 **30**
Dellums, Ronald 1935— **2, 81**
DeLoach, Nora 1940–2001 **30**
Delsarte, Louis 1944— **34**
Demby, William 1922— **51**
Dennard, Brazeal 1929— **37**
Dennis, Gary C. 1950— **91**
Dent, Thomas C. 1932–1998 **50**
Dent, Tom *See Dent, Thomas C.*
DePreist, James 1936— **37**
Derham, James *See Durham, James*
Derülo, Jason 1989— **93**
Desrouleaux, Jason *See Derülo, Jason*
DeVard, Jerri 1957(?)— **61**
DeVaughn, Raheem 1975— **91**
Devers, Gail 1966— **7, 87**
Devine, Loretta 1953— **24**
Devine, Major J. *See Divine, Father*
DeWese, Mohandas *See Kool Moe Dee*
Diallo, Amadou 1976–1999 **27**
Dibaba, Tirunesh 1985— **73**
Dickens, Helen Octavia 1909–2001 **14, 64**
Dickenson, Vic 1906–1984 **38**
Dickerson, Debra J. 1959— **60**
Dickerson, Eric 1960— **27**
Dickerson, Ernest 1952(?)— **6, 17**
Dickey, Eric Jerome 1961— **21, 56**
Diddley, Bo 1928–2008 **39, 72**
Diesel, Vin 1967(?)— **29**
Dieudonné 1966— **67**
Diggs, Charles C. 1922–1998 **21**
Diggs, Robert Fitzgerald *See RZA*
Diggs, Scott *See Diggs, Taye*
Diggs, Taye 1972— **25, 63**
Diggs-Taylor, Anna 1932— **20**
Dillard, Godfrey J. 1948— **45**
Dillard, Tramar *See Flo Rida*
Dinkins, David (Norman) 1927— **4**
Diogo, Luisa Dias 1958— **63**
Diop, Birago 1906–1989 **53**
Diop, Cheikh Anta 1923–1986 **4**
Diouf, Abdou 1935— **3**
Dirie, Waris 1965(?)— **56**
Divine, Father 1877(?)–1965 **7**
Dixon, Bill 1925–2010 **87**
Dixon, Dean 1915–1976 **68**
Dixon, George 1870–1909 **52**
Dixon, Ivan 1931–2008 **69**
Dixon, Julian C. 1934— **24**
Dixon, Margaret 192(?)— **14**
Dixon, Rodrick 19(?)(?)— *See Three Mo' Tenors*
Dixon, Sharon Pratt 1944— **1**
Dixon, Sheila 1953— **68**
Dixon, Willie (James) 1915–1992 **4**
DJ Jazzy Jeff 1965— **32**
DJ Red Alert *See Alert, Kool DJ Red*
DMC *See Run-DMC*
DMX 1970— **28, 64**
do Nascimento, Edson Arantes *See Pelé*
Dobbs, John Wesley 1882–1961 **89**
Dobbs, Mattiwilda 1925— **34**

Doby, Larry *See Doby, Lawrence Eugene, Sr.*
Doby, Lawrence Eugene, Sr. 1924–2003 **16, 41**
Dodson, Howard, Jr. 1939— **7, 52**
Dodson, Owen 1914–1983 **38**
Dogan, Matthew Winifred 1863–1947 **91**
Doig, Jason 1977— **45**
Doley, Harold, Jr. 1947— **26**
Domini, Rey *See Lorde, Audre (Geraldine)*
Domino, Fats 1928— **20**
Donald, Arnold Wayne 1954— **36**
Donaldson, Jeff 1932–2004 **46**
Donegan, Dorothy 1922–1998 **19**
Donovan, Kevin *See Bambaataa, Afrika*
Dorrell, Karl 1963— **52**
Dorsey, Lee 1926–1986 **65**
Dorsey, Thomas Andrew 1899–1993 **15**
Dorsey, Thomas J. 1812(?)–1875 **90**
Dortch, Thomas W., Jr. 1950— **45**
dos Santos, José Eduardo 1942— **43**
dos Santos, Manuel Francisco 1933 **65**
Dougherty, Mary Pearl 1915–2003 **47**
Douglas, Aaron 1899–1979 **7**
Douglas, Ashanti *See Ashanti*
Douglas, Denzil Llewellyn 1953— **53**
Douglas, Derek 1971— **88**
Douglas, Emory 1943— **89**
Douglas, Lizzie *See Memphis Minnie*
Douglass, Frederick 1817(?)–1895 **87**
Dourdan, Gary 1966— **37**
Dove, Rita 1952— **6, 78**
Dove, Ulysses 1947— **5**
Downing, George T. 1819–1903 **91**
Downing, Will 19(?)(?)— **19**
Dozier, Lamont *See Holland-Dozier-Holland*
Dr. J *See Erving, Julius*
Drake 1986— **86**
Draper, Sharon Mills 1952— **16, 43**
Drayton, William Jonathan, Jr. *See Flavor Flav*
Dre, Dr. 1965(?)— **10, 14, 30**
Dream, The *See The-Dream*
Drew, Alvin, Jr. 1962— **67**
Drew, Charles Richard 1904–1950 **7**
Drexler, Clyde 1962— **4, 61**
Driskell, David C(lyde) 1931— **7**
Driver, David E. 1955— **11**
Drogba, Didier 1978— **78**
Drummond, William J. 1944— **40**
Du Bois, David Graham 1925— **45**
Du Bois, W(illiam) E(dward) B(urghardt) 1868–1963 **3**
du Cille, Michel 1955(?)— **74**
Dube, Lucky 1964–2007 **77**
DuBois, Joshua 1982— **88**
DuBois, Shirley Graham 1907–1977 **21**
Duchemin, Alamaine *See Maxis, Theresa*

Duchemin, Marie *See Maxis, Theresa*

Duchemin, Theresa Maxis *See Maxis, Theresa*

Ducksworth, Marilyn 1957— **12**

Dudley, Edward R. 1911–2005 **58**

Due, Tananarive 1966— **30**

Duerson, Dave 1960–2011 **93**

Duggins, George 1943–2005 **64**

Duke, Bill 1943— **3**

Duke, George 1946— **21**

Dukes, Hazel Nell 1932— **56**

Dumars, Joe 1963— **16, 65**

Dumas, Henry 1934–1968 **41**

Dunbar, Alice *See Dunbar-Nelson, Alice Ruth Moore*

Dunbar, Paul Laurence 1872–1906 **8**

Dunbar, Sly 1952— *See Sly & Robbie*

Dunbar-Nelson, Alice Ruth Moore 1875–1935 **44**

Duncan, Michael Clarke 1957— **26**

Duncan, Tim 1976— **20, 91**

Duncan, Todd 1903–1998 **76**

Dungey, Merrin 1971— **62**

Dungy, Camille 1972— **86**

Dungy, Tony 1955— **17, 42, 59**

Dunham, Katherine 1910–2006 **4, 59**

Dunlap, Ericka 1982(?)— **55**

Dunn, Jerry 1953— **27**

Dunn, Warrick 1975— **90**

Dunner, Leslie B. 1956— **45**

Dunnigan, Alice Allison 1906–1983 **41**

Dunston, Georgia Mae 1944— **48**

Duplechan, Larry 1956— **55**

Dupri, Jermaine 1972— **13, 46**

Durant, Kevin 1988— **76**

Durham, Bobby 1937–2008 **73**

Durham, James 1762–1834(?) **90**

Durham, Robert Joseph *See Durham, Bobby*

Dutton, Charles S. 1951— **4, 22**

Dutton, Marie Elizabeth 1940— **12**

Dwight, Edward 1933— **65**

Dworkin, Aaron P. 1970— **52**

Dye, Jermaine 1974— **58**

Dymally, Mervyn 1926— **42**

Dyson, Michael Eric 1958— **11, 40**

Eagleson, William Lewis 1835–1899 **90**

Early, Deloreese Patricia *See Reese, Della*

Early, Gerald (Lyn) 1952— **15**

Earthquake, 1963— **55**

Easley, Annie J. 1933— **61**

Easton, Hosea 1798–1837 **91**

Ebanks, Michelle 1962— **60**

Ebanks, Selita 1983— **67**

Eckstein, William Clarence *See Eckstine, Billy*

Eckstine, Billy 1914–1993 **28**

Edelin, Ramona Hoage 1945— **19**

Edelman, Marian Wright 1939— **5, 42**

Edgerton, Khia Danielle *See K-Swift*

Edley, Christopher 1928–2003 **2, 48**

Edley, Christopher F., Jr. 1953— **48**

Edmonds, Kenneth *See Babyface*

Edmonds, Terry 1950(?)— **17**

Edmonds, Tracey 1967— **16, 64**

Edmunds, Gladys 1951(?)— **48**

Edwards, Donna 1958— **77**

Edwards, Eli *See McKay, Claude*

Edwards, Esther Gordy 1920(?)— **43**

Edwards, Harry 1942— **2**

Edwards, Herman 1954— **51**

Edwards, Lena Frances 1900–1986 **76**

Edwards, Melvin 1937— **22**

Edwards, Teresa 1964— **14**

Edwards, Trevor 1962— **54**

Edwards, Willarda V. 1951— **59**

Eikerenkoetter, Frederick J., II *See Reverend Ike*

Ejiofor, Chiwetal 1977(?)— **67**

Ekwensi, Cyprian 1921— **37**

El Wilson, Barbara 1959— **35**

Elam, Keith *See Guru*

Elba, Idris 1972— **49, 89**

Elder, Larry 1952— **25**

Elder, (Robert) Lee 1934— **6**

Elder, Lonne, III 1931–1996 **38**

Elders, Joycelyn (Minnie) 1933— **6**

Eldridge, Roy 1911–1989 **37**

El-Hajj Malik El-Shabazz *See X, Malcolm*

Elise, Kimberly 1967— **32**

Ellerbe, Brian 1963— **22**

Ellington, Duke 1899–1974 **5**

Ellington, E. David 1960— **11**

Ellington, Edward Kennedy *See Ellington, Duke*

Ellington, Mercedes 1939— **34**

Elliott, Lorris 1931–1999 **37**

Elliott, Missy 1971— **31, 90**

Elliott, Sean 1968— **26**

Ellis, Alton 1938–2008 **74**

Ellis, Charles H., III 1958(?)— **79**

Ellis, Clarence A. 1943— **38**

Ellis, Dock 1945–2008 **78**

Ellis, Jimmy 1940— **44**

Ellis-Lamkins, Phaedra 1976— **88**

Ellison, Keith 1963— **59**

Ellison, Ralph (Waldo) 1914–1994 **7**

Elmore, Ronn 1957— **21**

El-Shabazz, El-Hajj Malik *See X, Malcolm*

Emanuel, James A. 1921— **46**

Emeagwali, Dale 1954— **31**

Emeagwali, Philip 1954— **30**

Emecheta, Buchi 1944— **30**

Emmanuel, Alphonsia 1956— **38**

Ensley, Carol Denis *See Nash, Niecy*

Ephriam, Mablean 1949(?)— **29**

Epperson, Sharon 1969(?)— **54**

Epps, Archie C., III 1937–2003 **45**

Epps, Mike 1970— **60**

Epps, Omar 1973— **23, 59**

Equiano, Olaudah 1745(?)–1797 **78**

Ericsson-Jackson, Aprille 19(?)(?)— **28**

Ervin, Anthony 1981— **66**

Ervin, Clark Kent 1959— **82**

Erving, Julius 1950— **18, 47**

Escobar, Damien 1987— **56**

Escobar, Tourie 1985— **56**

Esposito, Giancarlo (Giusseppi Alessandro) 1958— **9**

Espy, Alphonso Michael *See Espy, Mike*

Espy, Mike 1953— **6**

Estelle 1980— **75**

Esters, Monica Ann *See Conyers, Monica*

Estes, Rufus 1857–19(?)(?) **29**

Estes, Simon 1938— **28**

Estes, Sleepy John 1899–1977 **33**

Eto'o, Samuel 1981— **73**

Eubanks, Kevin 1957— **15**

Eugene-Richard, Margie 1941— **63**

Europe, (William) James Reese 1880–1919 **10**

Evans, Darryl 1961— **22**

Evans, Diana 1972(?)— **72**

Evans, Ernest *See Checker, Chubby*

Evans, Etu 1969— **55**

Evans, Faith 1973(?)— **22**

Evans, Harry 1956(?)— **25**

Evans, Mari 1923— **26**

Evans, Melvin H. 1917–1984 **88**

Evans, Warren C. 1948— **76**

Eve 1979— **29**

Everett, Francine 1917–1999 **23**

Everett, Percival 1956— **93**

Everett, Ronald McKinley *See Karenga, Maulana*

Evers, Medgar (Riley) 1925–1963 **3**

Evers, Myrlie 1933— **8**

Evora, Cesaria 1941— **12**

Ewing, Patrick 1962— **17, 73**

Eyadéma, Gnassingbé 1937–2005 **7, 52**

Fabio, Sarah Webster 1928–1979 **48**

Fabolous 1977— **93**

Fabre, Shelton 1963— **71**

Fagan, Garth 1940— **18**

Fair, Ronald L. 1932— **47**

Faison, Donald 1974— **50**

Faison, Frankie 1949— **55**

Faison, George William 1946— **16**

Falana, Lola 1942— **42**

Falconer, Etta Zuber 1933–2002 **59**

Fales-Hill, Susan 1962— **88**

Fanon, Frantz 1925–1961 **44**

Farah, Nuruddin 1945— **27**

Fargas, Antonio 1946(?)— **50**

Farley, Christopher John 1966— **54**

Farmer, Art(hur Stewart) 1928–1999 **38**

Farmer, Forest J(ackson) 1941— **1**

Farmer, James 1920–1999 **2, 64**

Farmer-Paellmann, Deadria 1966— **43**

Farr, Mel 1944— **24**

Farrakhan, Louis 1933— **2, 15**

Farrell, Herman D., Jr. 1932— **81**

Farris, Isaac Newton, Jr. 1962— **63**

Fat Boys **92**

Father Goose *See Rhoden, Wayne*

Fattah, Chaka 1956— **11, 70**

Faulk, Marshall 1973— **35**

Fauntroy, Walter E(dward) 1933— **11**

Fauset, Jessie (Redmon) 1882–1961 **7**

Favors, Steve 1948— **23**

Fax, Elton 1909–1993 **48**

Feaster, Robert Franklin *See Sundiata, Sekou*

Feelings, Muriel 1938— **44**

Feelings, Tom 1933–2003 **11, 47**

Feemster, Herbert 1942— **72**

Fela 1938–1997 **1, 42**

Felix, Allyson 1985— **48**

Felix, Larry R. (?)— **64**

Fennoy, Ilene 1947— **72**

Fenton, Kevin 1966(?)— **87**

Fentry, Robyn *See Rihanna*

Fenty, Adrian 1970— **60, 88**

Ferdinand, Rio 1978— **82**

Ferguson, Amos 1920–2009 **81**

Ferguson, Kevin *See Slice, Kimbo*

Ferguson, Roger W. 1951— **25**

Ferguson, Ronald F. 1950(?)— **75**

Ferrell, Rachelle 1961— **29**

Ferrer, Ibrahim 1927— **41**

Fetchit, Stepin 1892–1985 **32**

Fiasco, Lupe 1982— **64**

Fielder, Cecil (Grant) 1963— **2**

Fielder, Prince Semien 1984— **68**

Fields, C. Virginia 1946— **25**

Fields, Cleo 1962— **13**

Fields, Evelyn J. 1949— **27**

Fields, Felicia P. (?)— **60**

Fields, Julia 1938— **45**

Fields, Kim 1969— **36**

50 Cent 1976— **46, 83**

Figueroa, John J. 1920–1999 **40**

Files, Lolita 1964(?)— **35**

Fils-Aimé, Reggie 1961— **74**

Fine, Sam 1969— **60**

Finner-Williams, Paris Michele 1951— **62**

Fiona, Melanie 1983— **84**

Fishburne, Larry *See Fishburne, Laurence*

Fishburne, Laurence 1961— **4, 22, 70**

Fisher, Ada Lois Sipuel 1924–1995 **76**

Fisher, Ada M. 1947— **76**

Fisher, Antwone Quenton 1959— **40**

Fisher, Gail 1935–2000 **85**

Fisher, Miles Mark 1899–1970 **91**

Fisher, Rudolph John Chauncey 1897–1934 **17**

Fitzgerald, Ella 1918–1996 **8, 18**

Flack, Roberta 1940— **19**

Flake, Floyd H. 1945— **18**

Flanagan, Tommy 1930–2001 **69**

Flash, Grandmaster *See Grandmaster Flash*

Flavor Flav 1959— **67**

Fleming, Erik R. 1965— **75**

Fleming, Raymond 1945— **48**

Fletcher, Alphonse, Jr. 1965— **16**

Fletcher, Arthur A. 1924–2005 **63**

Fletcher, Benjamin 1890–1949 **90**

Fletcher, Bill, Jr. 1954— **41**

Fletcher, Geoffrey 1970— **85**

Flipper, Henry O(ssian) 1856–1940 **3**

Flo Rida 1979— **78**

Flood, Curt 1938–1997 **10, 93**

Flowers, Sylester 1935— **50**

Flowers, Vonetta 1973— **35**

Floyd, Elson S. 1956— **41**

Folks, Byron *See Allen, Byron*

Forbes, Audrey Manley 1934— **16**

Forbes, Calvin 1945— **46**

Forbes, James A., Jr. 1935— **71**

Ford, Barney 1822–1902 **90**

Ford, Cheryl 1981— **45**
Ford, Clyde W. 1951— **40**
Ford, Harold E(ugene) 1945— **42**
Ford, Harold E(ugene), Jr. 1970— **16, 70**
Ford, Jack 1947— **39**
Ford, James Lewis Carter See Ford, T-Model
Ford, Johnny 1942— **70**
Ford, Nick Aaron 1904–1982 **44**
Ford, T-Model 1920(?)— **91**
Ford, Vincent 1940(?)–2008 **75**
Ford, Wallace 1950— **58**
Foreman, George 1948— **1, 15**
Forman, James 1928–2005 **7, 51**
Forman, James, Jr. 1967— **89**
Forrest, Leon 1937–1997 **44**
Forrest, Vernon 1971–2009 **40, 79**
Forté, John 1975— **74**
Forte, Linda Diane 1952— **54**
Fortune, James 1977(?)— **92**
Fortune, T(imothy) Thomas 1856–1928 **6**
Foster, Andrew 1879–1930 **79**
Foster, Cecil (A.) 1954— **32**
Foster, Ezola 1938— **28**
Foster, George "Pops" 1892–1969 **40**
Foster, Henry W., Jr. 1933— **26**
Foster, Jylla Moore 1954— **45**
Foster, Marie 1917–2003 **48**
Foster, Rube See Foster, Andrew
Foster, William P. 1919–2010 **88**
Fowler, Reggie 1959— **51**
Fowles, Gloria See Gaynor, Gloria
Fox, Rick 1969— **27**
Fox, Ulrich Alexander See Fox, Rick
Fox, Vivica A. **15, 53**
Foxx, Anthony 1971— **81**
Foxx, Jamie 1967— **15, 48**
Foxx, Redd 1922–1991 **2**
Francis, Norman (C.) 1931— **60**
Francis, Thais 1980— **93**
Franklin, Aretha 1942— **11, 44**
Franklin, C. L. 1915–1984 **68**
Franklin, Carl 1949— **11**
Franklin, Hardy R. 1929–2004 **9, 87**
Franklin, J. E. 1937— **44**
Franklin, John Hope 1915–2009 **5, 77**
Franklin, Kirk 1970(?)— **15, 49**
Franklin, Robert M(ichael) 1954— **13**
Franklin, Shirley 1945— **34, 80**
Franks, Gary 1954(?)— **2**
Franti, Michael 1966— **93**
Frazer, Jendayi 196(?)— **68**
Frazier, Edward Franklin 1894–1962 **10**
Frazier, Joe 1944— **19**
Frazier, Kevin 1964— **58**
Frazier, Oscar 1956–2005 **58**
Frazier, Ryan 1977— **89**
Frazier, Walt 1945— **91**
Frazier-Lyde, Jacqui 1961— **31**
Fredericks, Henry Saint Claire See Mahal, Taj
Freelon, Nnenna 1954— **32**
Freeman, Aaron 1956— **52**
Freeman, Al(bert Cornelius), Jr. 1934— **11**
Freeman, Cathy 1973— **29**

Freeman, Charles Eldridge 1933— **19**
Freeman, Harold P. 1933— **23**
Freeman, Leonard 1950— **27**
Freeman, Marianna 1957— **23**
Freeman, Morgan 1937— **2, 20, 62**
Freeman, Paul 1936— **39**
Freeman, Yvette **27**
French, Albert 1943— **18**
Fresh, Doug E. 1966— **93**
Fresh Prince, The See Smith, Will
Friday, Jeff 1964(?)— **24**
Fryer, Roland G. 1977— **56**
Fudge, Ann (Marie) 1951— **11, 55**
Fudge, Marcia L. 1952— **76**
Fuhr, Grant 1962— **1, 49**
Fulani, Lenora (Branch) 1950— **11**
Fuller, A. Oveta 1955— **43**
Fuller, Arthur 1972— **27**
Fuller, Blind Boy 1907(?)–1941 **86**
Fuller, Charles (Henry) 1939— **8**
Fuller, Howard L. 1941— **37**
Fuller, Hoyt 1923–1981 **44**
Fuller, Meta Vaux Warrick 1877–1968 **27**
Fuller, S. B. 1895–1988 **13**
Fuller, Solomon Carter, Jr. 1872–1953 **15**
Fuller, Thomas O. 1867–1942 **90**
Fuller, Vivian 1954— **33**
Funderburg, I. Owen 1924–2002 **38**
Funnye, Capers C., Jr. 1952(?)— **73**
Fuqua, Antoine 1966— **35**
Fuqua, Harvey 1927–2010 **90**
Futch, Eddie 1911–2001 **33**
Gabre-Medhin, Tsegaye 1936–2006 **64**
Gaines, Brenda 19(?)(?)— **41**
Gaines, Clarence E., Sr. 1923–2005 **55**
Gaines, Ernest J(ames) 1933— **7**
Gaines, Grady 1934— **38**
Gaines, Lloyd 1911–19(?)(?) **79**
Gairy, Eric Matthew 1922–1997 **83**
Gaiter, Dorothy J. 1950(?)— **80**
Gaither, Israel L. 1944— **65**
Gaither, Jake 1903–1994 **14**
Gamble, Kenny 1943— **85**
Gans, Joe 1874–1910 **91**
Gantin, Bernardin 1922–2008 **70**
Gantt, Harvey (Bernard) 1943— **1**
Gardere, Jeffrey 1956— **76**
Gardner, Chris 1954— **65**
Gardner, Edward G. 1925— **45**
Garner, Erroll 1921–1977 **76**
Garnett, Kevin (Maurice) 1976— **14, 70**
Garrett, James F. 1942— **78**
Garrett, Joyce Finley 1931–1997 **59**
Garrett, Sean 1979— **57**
Garrincha See dos Santos, Manuel Francisco
Garrison, Zina 1963— **2**
Garvey, Marcus 1887–1940 **1**
Garvin, Gerry 1967(?)— **78**
Gary, Willie Edward 1947— **12**
Gaskins, Eric 1958— **64**
Gaskins, Rudy 1960(?)— **74**
Gaspard, Patrick 1967— **84**
Gaston, Arthur George 1892–1996 **3, 38, 59**
Gaston, Cito 1944— **71**

Gaston, Clarence Edwin See Gaston, Cito
Gaston, Marilyn Hughes 1939— **60**
Gates, Henry Louis, Jr. 1950— **3, 38, 67**
Gates, Sylvester James, Jr. 1950— **15**
Gay, Marvin Pentz, Jr. See Gaye, Marvin
Gaye, Marvin 1939–1984 **2**
Gaye, Nona 1974— **56**
Gayle, Addison, Jr. 1932–1991 **41**
Gayle, Helene D. 1955— **3, 46**
Gaynor, Gloria 1947— **36**
Gbagbo, Laurent 1945— **43, 90**
Gbowee, Leymah 1971(?)— **76**
Gebrselassie, Haile 1973— **70**
Gentry, Alvin 1954— **23**
George, Eddie 1973— **80**
George, Nelson 1957— **12**
George, Zelma Watson 1903–1994 **42**
Gerima, Haile 1946— **38, 80**
Gervin, George 1952— **80**
Ghostface Killah 1970— **90**
Gibbs, Marla 1931— **86**
Gibson, Althea 1927–2003 **8, 43**
Gibson, Bob 1935— **33**
Gibson, Donald Bernard 1933— **40**
Gibson, John Trusty 1878–1937 **87**
Gibson, Johnnie Mae 1949— **23**
Gibson, Josh 1911–1947 **22**
Gibson, Kenneth Allen 1932— **6**
Gibson, Ted 1965— **66**
Gibson, Truman K., Jr. 1912–2005 **60**
Gibson, Tyrese 1978— **27, 62**
Gibson, William F(rank) 1933— **6**
Giddings, Paula (Jane) 1947— **11**
Gidron, Richard D. 1939–2007 **68**
Gil, Gilberto 1942— **53**
Gilbert, Christopher 1949— **50**
Gilbert, John Wesley 1864–1923 **91**
Giles, Roscoe C. 1890–1970 **93**
Gill, Gerald 1948–2007 **69**
Gill, Johnny 1966— **51**
Gill, Turner 1962— **83**
Gilles, Ralph 1970— **61**
Gillespie, Dizzy 1917–1993 **1**
Gillespie, John Birks See Gillespie, Dizzy
Gilliam, Frank 1934(?)— **23**
Gilliam, Joe, Jr. 1950–2000 **31**
Gilliam, Sam 1933— **16**
Gilliard, Steve 1964–2007 **69**
Gilmore, Marshall 1931— **46**
Gilpin, Charles Sidney 1878–1930 **81**
Ginuwine 1975(?)— **35**
Giovanni, Nikki 1943— **9, 39, 85**
Gist, Carole 1970(?)— **1**
Givens, Adele 19(?)(?)— **62**
Givens, Robin 1964— **4, 25, 58**
Givhan, Robin Deneen 1964— **72**
Gladwell, Malcolm 1963— **62**
Glanville, Douglas Metunwa 1970— **82**
Gloster, Hugh Morris, Sr. 1911–2002 **90**
Glover, Corey 1964— **34**
Glover, Danny 1948— **1, 24**
Glover, Donald 1983— **85**
Glover, Keith 1966— **79**
Glover, Nathaniel, Jr. 1943— **12**

Glover, Savion 1974— **14**
Gnassingbé, Faure 1966— **67**
Goapele 1977— **55**
"The Goat" See Manigault, Earl "The Goat"
Godbolt, James Titus See Slyde, Jimmy
Goines, Donald 1937(?)–1974 **19**
Goings, Russell 1932(?)— **59**
Goldberg, Whoopi 1955— **4, 33, 69**
Golden, Marita 1950— **19**
Golden, Thelma 1965— **10, 55**
Golding, Bruce 1947— **78**
Goldsberry, Ronald 1942— **18**
Golson, Benny 1929— **37**
Golston, Allan C. 1967(?)— **55**
Gomes, Peter J. 1942–2011 **15, 93**
Gomez, Jewelle 1948— **30**
Gomez-Preston, Cheryl 1954— **9**
Gomillion, Charles 1900–1995 **90**
Goode, Mal(vin Russell) 1908–1995 **13**
Goode, W(oodrow) Wilson 1938— **4**
Gooden, Dwight 1964— **20**
Gooden, Lolita See Roxanne Shante
Gooding, Cuba, Jr. 1968— **16, 62**
Goodison, Lorna 1947— **71**
Goodlett, Carlton B. 1914–1997 **91**
Goodman, Al 1943–2010 **87**
Goodnight, Paul 1946— **32**
Gorden, W. C. 1930— **71**
Gorden, William C. See Gorden, W. C.
Gordon, Bruce S. 1946— **41, 53, 82**
Gordon, Carl 1932–2010 **87**
Gordon, Dexter 1923–1990 **25**
Gordon, Ed 1960— **10, 53**
Gordon, Pamela 1955— **17**
Gordone, Charles 1925–1995 **15**
Gordon-Reed, Annette 1958— **74**
Gordy, Berry, Jr. 1929— **1**
Goreed, Joseph See Williams, Joe
Goss, Carol A. 1947— **55**
Goss, Tom 1946— **23**
Gossett, Louis, Jr. 1936— **7**
Gotti, Irv 1971— **39**
Gourdin, Edward O. 1897–1966 **93**
Gourdine, Meredith 1929–1998 **33**
Gourdine, Simon (Peter) 1940— **11**
Grace, George H. 1948— **48**
Grae, Jean 1976— **51**
Graham, Aubrey Drake See Drake
Graham, Lawrence Otis 1962— **12**
Graham, Lorenz 1902–1989 **48**
Graham, Stedman 1951(?)— **13**
Graham, Trevor 1962(?)— **84**
Granderson, Curtis 1981— **66**
Grandmaster Flash 1958— **33, 60**
Grand-Pierre, Jean-Luc 1977— **46**
Granger, Lester B. 1896–1976 **75**
Grant, Augustus O. 1946(?)— **71**
Grant, Bernie 1944–2000 **57**
Grant, Gwendolyn Goldsby 19(?)(?)— **28**
Granville, Evelyn Boyd 1924— **36**
Gravely, Samuel L., Jr. 1922–2004 **5, 49**
Graves, Butch 1962— **77**
Graves, Denyce Antoinette 1964— **19, 57**

Graves, Earl G(ilbert) 1935— **1, 35**

Graves, Earl Gilbert, Jr. *See Graves, Butch*

Gray, Darius 1945— **69**

Gray, F. Gary 1969— **14, 49**

Gray, Farrah 1984— **59**

Gray, Fred Sr. 1930— **37**

Gray, Frizzell *See Mfume, Kweisi*

Gray (Nelson Rollins), Ida 1867–1953 **41**

Gray, Macy 1970— **29**

Gray, Vincent C. 1942— **88**

Gray, William H., III 1941— **3**

Gray, Willie 1947— **46**

Gray, Yeshimbra "Shimmy" 1972— **55**

Greaves, William 1926— **38**

Greely, M. Gasby 1946— **27**

Greely, Margaret Gasby *See Greely, M. Gasby*

Green, A. C. 1963— **32**

Green, Al 1946— **13, 47, 74**

Green, Cee-Lo *See Cee-Lo*

Green, Darrell 1960— **39, 74**

Green, Dennis 1949— **5, 45**

Green, Grant 1935–1979 **56**

Green, Isaac H. 1959— **79**

Green, Jonathan 1955— **54**

Greene, Jimmy 1975— **74**

Greene, Joe 1946— **10**

Greene, Maurice 1974— **27, 77**

Greene, Petey 1931–1984 **65**

Greene, Ralph Waldo *See Greene, Petey*

Greene, Richard Thaddeus, Sr. 1913–2006 **67**

Greene, Talib Kweli *See Kweli, Talib*

Greenfield, Eloise 1929— **9**

Greenfield, Ronnie Spector *See Spector, Ronnie*

Greenhouse, Bunnatine "Bunny" 1944— **57**

Greenlee, Sam 1930— **48**

Greenwood, Monique 1959— **38**

Greer, Hal 1936— **92**

Gregg, Eric 1951— **16**

Gregory, Ann 1912–1990 **63**

Gregory, Dick 1932— **1, 54**

Gregory, Frederick 1941— **8, 51**

Gregory, Wilton 1947— **37**

Grier, David Alan 1955— **28**

Grier, Eliza Ann 1863(?)–1902 **90**

Grier, Mike 1975— **43**

Grier, Pam 1949— **9, 31, 86**

Grier, Roosevelt (Rosey) 1932— **13**

Griffey, Dick 1938–2010 **89**

Griffey, Ken, Jr. 1969— **12, 73**

Griffin, Angela 1976— **80**

Griffin, Anthony 1960— **71**

Griffin, Bessie Blout 1914— **43**

Griffin, John Arnold, III *See Griffin, Johnny*

Griffin, Johnny 1928–2008 **71**

Griffin, LaShell 1967— **51**

Griffith, Mark Winston 1963— **8**

Griffith, Patrick A. 1944— **64**

Griffith, Yolanda 1970— **25**

Griffith-Joyner, Florence 1959–1998 **28**

Griffiths, Marcia 1948(?)— **29**

Grimké, Archibald H(enry) 1849–1930 **9**

Grist, Reri 1932— **84**

Grooms, Henry R(andall) 1944— **50**

Guarionex *See Schomburg, Arthur Alfonso*

Guebuza, Armando 1943— **81**

Guéï, Robert 1941–2002 **66**

Guillaume, Robert 1927— **3, 48**

Güines, Tata 1930–2008 **69**

Guinier, (Carol) Lani 1950— **7, 30**

Gumbel, Bryant 1948— **14, 80**

Gumbel, Greg 1946— **8**

Gunn, Moses 1929–1993 **10**

Gurira, Danai 1978(?)— **73**

Guru 1961–2010 **84**

Guy, (George) Buddy 1936— **31**

Guy, Jasmine 1964(?)— **2**

Guy, Rosa 1925(?)— **5**

Guy-Sheftall, Beverly 1946— **13, 92**

Guyton, Tyree 1955— **9**

Gwynn, Tony 1960— **18, 83**

Gyan, Asamoah 1985— **87**

Habré, Hissène 1942— **6**

Habyarimana, Juvenal 1937–1994 **8**

Haddon, Dietrick 1973(?)— **55**

Hageman, Hans 19(?)(?)— **36**

Hageman, Ivan 19(?)(?)— **36**

Haile Selassie 1892–1975 **7**

Hailey, JoJo 1971— **22**

Hailey, K-Ci 1969— **22**

Hairston, Jester 1901–2000 **88**

Hairston, Sam 1920–1997 **88**

Hale, Clara 1902–1992 **16**

Hale, Lorraine 1926(?)— **8**

Hale, Nathaniel Dawayne *See Nate Dogg*

Haley, Alex (Palmer) 1921–1992 **4**

Haley, George Williford Boyce 1925— **21**

Hall, Aaron 1963— **57**

Hall, Alvin D. 1952— **86**

Hall, Arsenio 1955— **58**

Hall, Arthur 1943–2000 **39**

Hall, Elliott S. 1938(?)— **24**

Hall, Juanita 1901–1968 **62**

Hall, Kevan 19(?)(?)— **61**

Hall, Lloyd A(ugustus) 1894–1971 **8**

Hall, Syren *See Fiona, Melanie*

Hall, Stuart 1932— **78**

Halliburton, Warren J. 1924— **49**

Hallim, Melanie Fiona *See Fiona, Melanie*

Ham, Cynthia Parker 1970(?)— **58**

Hamblin, Ken 1940— **10**

Hamburg, Beatrix 1923— **84**

Hamburg, Margaret 1955— **78**

Hamer, Fannie Lou (Townsend) 1917–1977 **6**

Hamilton, Anthony 1971— **61**

Hamilton, Lewis 1985— **66**

Hamilton, Lisa Gay 1964— **71**

Hamilton, Samuel C. 19(?)(?)— **47**

Hamilton, Tanya 1968— **93**

Hamilton, Virginia 1936— **10**

Hamlin, Larry Leon 1948–2007 **49, 62**

Hammer, M. C. *See M.C. Hammer*

Hammond, Fred 1960— **23**

Hammond, Lenn 1970(?)— **34**

Hammonds, Evelynn 1953— **69**

Hammons, David 1943— **69**

Hampton, Fred 1948–1969 **18**

Hampton, Henry (Eugene, Jr.) 1940— **6**

Hampton, Lionel 1908(?)–2002 **17, 41**

Hancock, Herbie 1940— **20, 67**

Handy, W(illiam) C(hristopher) 1873–1937 **8**

Haney, Lee 1959— **77**

Hani, Chris 1942–1993 **6**

Hani, Martin Thembisile *See Hani, Chris*

Hannah, Marc (Regis) 1956— **10**

Hansberry, Lorraine (Vivian) 1930–1965 **6**

Hansberry, Tony, II 1994— **93**

Hansberry, William Leo 1894–1965 **11**

Hansen, Austin 1910–1996 **88**

Hardaway, Anfernee (Penny) 1971— **13**

Hardaway, Penny *See Hardaway, Anfernee (Penny)*

Hardaway, Tim 1966— **35**

Hardin Armstrong, Lil 1898–1971 **39**

Hardin, Lillian Beatrice *See Hardin Armstrong, Lil*

Harding, Vincent 1931— **67**

Hardison, Bethann 19(?)(?)— **12**

Hardison, Kadeem 1966— **22**

Hardy, Antonio *See Big Daddy Kane*

Hardy, Nell *See Carter, Nell*

Hare, Nathan 1934— **44**

Harewood, David 1965— **52**

Harkless, Necia Desiree 1920— **19**

Harmon, Clarence 1940(?)— **26**

Harold, Erika 1980(?)— **54**

Harper, Ben 1969— **34, 62**

Harper, Frances E(llen) W(atkins) 1825–1911 **11**

Harper, Frank *See Harper, Hill*

Harper, Hill 1966— **32, 65**

Harper, Michael S. 1938— **34**

Harper, Rachel M. 1972— **92**

Harrell, Andre (O'Neal) 1962(?)— **9, 30**

Harrington, Oliver W(endell) 1912— **9**

Harris, Alice 1934— **7**

Harris, Barbara 1930— **12**

Harris, Barry 1929— **68**

Harris, Bernard A. 1956— **90**

Harris, Bill 1941— **72**

Harris, Carla A. 1962— **67**

Harris, Ciara Princess *See Ciara*

Harris, Claire 1937— **34**

Harris, Corey 1969— **39, 73**

Harris, E. Lynn 1957— **12, 33**

Harris, Eddy L. 1956— **18**

Harris, Gary L. 1953— **87**

Harris, James 1947— **79**

Harris, James, III *See Jimmy Jam*

Harris, Jay **19**

Harris, Jessica B. 1948— **91**

Harris, Kamala D. 1964— **64**

Harris, Leslie 1961— **6**

Harris, Lyle Ashton 1965— **83**

Harris, Marcelite Jordan 1943— **16**

Harris, Mary Styles 1949— **31**

Harris, Maya Lakshmi 1966— **88**

Harris, Monica 1968— **18**

Harris, Naomie 1976— **55**

Harris, Patricia Roberts 1924–1985 **2**

Harris, Richard E. 1912(?)— **61**

Harris, Robin 1953–1990 **7**

Harris, Shack *See Harris, James*

Harris, "Sweet" Alice *See Harris, Alice*

Harris, Sylvia 1967(?)— **70**

Harris, Wesley L. 1941— **92**

Harris, William Anthony *See Harris, Bill*

Harris-Lacewell, Melissa 1973— **81**

Harrison, Alvin 1974— **28**

Harrison, Calvin 1974— **28**

Harrison, Charles 1931— **72**

Harrison, Mya *See Mya*

Harris-Stewart, Lusia 1955— **90**

Harsh, Vivian Gordon 1890–1960 **14**

Hart, Alvin Youngblood 1963— **61**

Hart, Gregory Edward *See Hart, Alvin Youngblood*

Harvard, Beverly (Joyce Bailey) 1950— **11**

Harvey, Steve 1956— **18, 58**

Harvey, William R. 1941— **42**

Haskins, Clem 1943— **23**

Haskins, James 1941–2005 **36, 54**

Hassell, Leroy Rountree, Sr. 1955— **41**

Hastie, William H(enry) 1904–1976 **8**

Hastings, Alcee Lamar 1936— **16**

Hatcher, Andrew T. 1923–1990 **90**

Hatcher, Richard G. 1933— **55**

Hatchett, Glenda 1951(?)— **32**

Hathaway, Donny 1945–1979 **18**

Hathaway, Isaac Scott 1874–1967 **33**

Hathaway, Lalah 1968— **57, 88**

Haughton, Aaliyah *See Aaliyah*

Hawkins, Adrienne Lita *See Kennedy, Adrienne*

Hawkins, Augustus F. 1907–2007 **68**

Hawkins, Coleman 1904–1969 **9**

Hawkins, Connie 1942— **91**

Hawkins, Erskine Ramsey 1914–1993 **14**

Hawkins, Jamesetta *See James, Etta*

Hawkins, La-Van 1960— **17, 54**

Hawkins, "Screamin'" Jay 1929–2000 **30**

Hawkins, Steven Wayne 1962— **14**

Hawkins, Tramaine Aunzola 1951— **16**

Hawkins, Walter 1949–2010 **87**

Hayden, Carla D. 1952— **47**

Hayden, Palmer 1890–1973 **13**

Hayden, Robert Earl 1913–1980 **12**

Haye, David 1980— **82**

Hayes, Bob 1942–2002 **77**

Hayes, Cecil N. 1945— **46**

Hayes, Dennis 1951— **54**

Hayes, Elvin 1945— **93**

Hayes, Isaac 1942–2008 **20, 58, 73**

Hayes, James C. 1946— **10**

Hayes, Robert Lee *See Hayes, Bob*

Hayes, Roland 1887–1977 **4**

Hayes, Teddy 1951— **40**

Haygood, Wil 1954— **83**

Haynes, Cornell, Jr. *See Nelly*

Haynes, George Edmund 1880–1960 **8**

Haynes, Marques 1926— **22**

Haynes, Roy 1925— **87**

Haynes, Trudy 1926— **44**

Haysbert, Dennis 1955— **42**

Haysbert, Raymond V., Sr. 1920–2010 **87**

Haywood, Gar Anthony 1954— **43**

Haywood, Jimmy 1993(?)— **58**

Haywood, Margaret A. 1912— **24**

Hazel, Darryl B. 1949— **50**

Head, Bessie 1937–1986 **28**

Healy, James Augustine 1830–1900 **30**

Healy, Michael 1839–1904 **90**

Heard, Gar 1948— **25**

Heard, Nathan C. 1936–2004 **45**

Hearne, John Edgar Caulwell 1926–1994 **45**

Hearns, Thomas 1958— **29**

Heavy D 1967— **58**

Hedgeman, Anna Arnold 1899–1990 **22**

Hedgeman, Peyton Cole See Hayden, Palmer

Height, Dorothy I. 1912— **2, 23, 78**

Hemphill, Essex 1957— **10**

Hemphill, Jessie Mae 1923–2006 **33, 59**

Hemsley, Sherman 1938— **19**

Henderson, Cornelius Langston 1888(?)–1976 **26**

Henderson, David 1942— **53**

Henderson, Fletcher 1897–1952 **32**

Henderson, Gordon 1957— **5**

Henderson, Henry Fairfax, Jr. 1928— **89**

Henderson, Jeff 1964— **72**

Henderson, Natalie Leota See Hinderas, Natalie

Henderson, Rickey 1958— **28, 78**

Henderson, Stephen E. 1925–1997 **45**

Henderson, Thelton E. 1933— **68**

Henderson, Wade 1944(?)— **14**

Henderson, Zelma 1920–2008 **71**

Hendricks, Barbara 1948— **3, 67**

Hendrix, James Marshall See Hendrix, Jimi

Hendrix, Jimi 1942–1970 **10**

Hendrix, Johnny Allen See Hendrix, Jimi

Hendryx, Nona 1944— **56**

Hendy, Francis 195(?)— **47**

Henries, A. Doris Banks 1913–1981 **44**

Henriques, Julian 1955(?)— **37**

Henry, Aaron Edd 1922–1997 **19**

Henry, Clarence "Frogman" 1937— **46**

Henry, Lenny 1958— **9, 52**

Henry, Richard Bullock See Obadele, Imari

Henry, Thierry 1977— **66**

Henry, Troy 1960(?)— **85**

Henson, Darrin 1970(?)— **33**

Henson, Josiah 1789–1883 **90**

Henson, Matthew (Alexander) 1866–1955 **2**

Henson, Taraji P. 1970— **58, 77**

Herbert, Bob 1945— **63**

Hercules, Frank 1911–1996 **44**

Herenton, Willie W. 1940— **24, 81**

Herman, Alexis Margaret 1947— **15**

Hernandez, Aileen Clarke 1926— **13**

Herndon, Alonzo Franklin 1858–1927 **89**

Herndon, Angelo 1913–1997 **90**

Hernton, Calvin C. 1932–2001 **51**

Hickman, Fred(erick Douglass) 1951— **11**

Hicks Maynard, Nancy See Maynard, Nancy Hicks

Higginbotham, A(loyisus) Leon, Jr. 1928–1998 **13, 25**

Higginbotham, Jack See Higginbotham, Jay C.

Higginbotham, Jay C. 1906–1973 **37**

Higginsen, Vy 1945(?)— **65**

Hightower, Dennis F(owler) 1941— **13**

Hill, Andrew 1931–2007 **66**

Hill, Anita 1956— **5, 65**

Hill, Beatrice See Moore, Melba

Hill, Bonnie Guiton 1941— **20**

Hill, Calvin 1947— **19**

Hill, Donna 1955— **32**

Hill, Dulé 1975(?)— **29**

Hill, Errol 1921— **40**

Hill, Grant (Henry) 1972— **13**

Hill, Hugh Morgan 1921–2009 **83**

Hill, Janet 1947— **19**

Hill, Jesse, Jr. 1927— **13**

Hill, Lauryn 1975— **20, 53**

Hill, Leslie Pinckney 1880–1960 **44**

Hill, Marc Lamont 1978— **80**

Hill, Oliver W. 1907–2007 **24, 63**

Hill, Peter 1767–1829 **92**

Hill, Tamia See Tamia

Hillard, Terry 1954— **25**

Hillary, Barbara 1923(?)— **65**

Hilliard, Asa Grant, III 1933–2007 **66**

Hilliard, David 1942— **7**

Hilliard, Earl F. 1942— **24**

Hilliard, Wendy 196(?)— **53**

Hilson, Keri 1982— **84**

Himes, Chester 1909–1984 **8**

Hinderas, Natalie 1927–1987 **5**

Hine, Darlene Clark 1947— **24**

Hines, Earl "Fatha" 1905–1983 **39**

Hines, Garrett 1969— **35**

Hines, Gregory (Oliver) 1946–2003 **1, 42**

Hinton, Milt 1910–2000 **30**

Hinton, William Augustus 1883–1959 **8**

Hoagland, Everett H. 1942— **45**

Hoagland, Jaheim See Jaheim

Hobson, Julius W. 1919–1977 **44**

Hobson, Mellody 1969— **40**

Hogan, Beverly Wade 1951— **50**

Holder, Eric H., Jr. 1951— **9, 76**

Holder, Geoffrey 1930— **78**

Holder, Laurence 1939— **34**

Holdsclaw, Chamique 1977— **24**

Holiday, Billie 1915–1959 **1**

Holland, Brian See Holland-Dozier-Holland

Holland, Eddie See Holland-Dozier-Holland

Holland, Endesha Ida Mae 1944–2006 **3, 57**

Holland, Kimberly N. 19(?)(?)— **62**

Holland, Robert, Jr. 1940— **11**

Holland-Dozier-Holland **36**

Holloway, Brenda 1946— **65**

Hollowell, Donald L. 1917–2004 **57**

Holmes, Amy 1973— **69**

Holmes, Clint 1946— **57**

Holmes, Hamilton E. 1941–1995 **82**

Holmes, Kelly 1970— **47**

Holmes, Larry 1949— **20, 68**

Holmes, Santonio 1984— **87**

Holmes, Shannon 1973(?)— **70**

Holsey, Lucius Henry 1842–1920 **92**

Holstein, Casper 1876–1944 **89**

Holt, Lester 1959— **66**

Holt, Nora 1885(?)–1974 **38**

Holt Baker, Arlene 1951— **73**

Holte, Patricia Louise See LaBelle, Patti

Holton, Hugh, Jr. 1947–2001 **39**

Holyfield, Evander 1962— **6**

Honeywood, Varnette P. 1950–2010 **54, 88**

Honoré, Russel L. 1947— **64**

Hood, James Walker 1831–1918 **91**

Hooker, John Lee 1917–2000 **30**

hooks, bell 1952— **5, 90**

Hooks, Benjamin L. 1925–2010 **2, 85**

Hooks, Robert 1937— **76**

Hope, John 1868–1936 **8**

Hope, Lugenia Burns 1871–1947 **89**

Hopgood, Hadda See Brooks, Hadda

Hopkins, Bernard 1965— **35, 69**

Hopkins, Donald R. 1941— **89**

Hopkins, Lightnin' 1912–1982 **83**

Hopkins, Sam See Hopkins, Lightnin'

Horn, Shirley 1934–2005 **32, 56**

Horne, Frank 1899–1974 **44**

Horne, Lena 1917–2010 **5, 86**

Horsford, Steven 1973— **88**

Horton, Andre 1979— **33**

Horton, Gladys 1945–2011 **92**

Horton, James Oliver 1943— **58**

Horton, (Andreana) "Suki" 1982— **33**

Houghton, Israel 1971— **92**

Hounsou, Djimon 1964— **19, 45**

Houphouët, Dia See Houphouët-Boigny, Félix

Houphouët-Boigny, Félix 1905–1993 **4, 64**

House, Eddie James, Jr. See House, Son

House, Eugene See House, Son

House, Son 1902–1988 **8**

Houston, Charles Hamilton 1895–1950 **4**

Houston, Cissy 1933— **20, 83**

Houston, Whitney 1963— **7, 28, 83**

Howard, Ayanna 1972— **65**

Howard, Corinne See Mitchell, Corinne

Howard, Desmond 1970— **16, 58**

Howard, Juwan Antonio 1973— **15**

Howard, M. William, Jr. 1946— **26**

Howard, Michelle 1960— **28**

Howard, Ryan 1979— **65**

Howard, Sherri 1962— **36**

Howard, Terrence Dashon 1969— **59**

Howell, Ayinde 1978— **91**

Howlin' Wolf 1910–1976 **9**

Howroyd, Janice Bryant 1953— **42**

Hoyte, Lenon 1905–1999 **50**

Hrabowski, Freeman A., III 1950— **22**

Hubbard, Arnette 19(?)(?)— **38**

Hubbard, Freddie 1948–2008 **75**

Hubbard, Frederick DeWayne See Hubbard, Freddie

Huddleston, William Emanuel See Lateef, Yusef

Hudlin, Reginald 1961— **9, 86**

Hudlin, Warrington, Jr. 1953(?)— **9**

Hudson, Cheryl 19(?)(?)— **15**

Hudson, Ernie 1945— **72**

Hudson, Jennifer 1981— **63, 83**

Hudson, Saul See Slash

Hudson, Wade 1946— **15**

Huff, Leon 1942— **86**

Huggins, Edie 1935–2008 **71**

Huggins, Larry 1950— **21**

Huggins, Nathan Irvin 1927–1989 **52**

Hughes, Albert 1972— **7**

Hughes, Allen 1972— **7**

Hughes, Cathy 1947(?)— **27**

Hughes, Dora 1970(?)— **88**

Hughes, Ebony 1948— **57**

Hughes, (James Mercer) Langston 1902–1967 **4**

Hughley, D. L. 1963— **23, 76**

Hughley, Darryl Lynn See Hughley, D. L.

Hull, Akasha Gloria 1944— **45**

Humphrey, Bobbi 1950— **20**

Humphries, Frederick 1935— **20**

Hunt, Darnell 1962— **92**

Hunt, Richard (Howard) 1935— **6**

Hunter, Alberta 1895–1984 **42**

Hunter, Billy 1943— **22**

Hunter, Charlayne See Hunter-Gault, Charlayne

Hunter, Clementine 1887–1988 **45**

Hunter, George William See Hunter, Billy

Hunter, Torii 1975— **43**

Hunter-Gault, Charlayne 1942— **6, 31**

Hurston, Zora Neale 1891–1960 **3**

Hurt, Byron 1970— **61**

Hurt, Mississippi John 1892(?)–1966 **84**

Hurtt, Harold 1947(?)— **46**

Hussein, Lubna 1970(?)— **80**

Hutch, Willie 1944–2005 **62**

Hutcherson, Hilda Yvonne 1955— **54**

Hutchinson, Earl Ofari 1945— **24**

Hutson, Jean Blackwell 1914— **16**

Hyde, Cowan F. "Bubba" 1908–2003 **47**

Hyman, Earle 1926— **25, 79**

Hyman, Phyllis 1949(?)–1995 **19**

Ibrahim, Mo 1946— **67**

Ice Cube 1969— **8, 30, 60**

Iceberg Slim 1918–1992 **11**

Ice-T 1958(?)— **6, 31**

Ifill, Gwen 1955— **28**

Iginla, Jarome 1977— **35**

Ilibagiza, Immaculée 1972(?)— **66**

Iman 1955— **4, 33, 87**

Iman, Chanel 1989— **66**

Imes, Elmer Samuel 1883–1941 **39**

Ince, Paul 1967— **83**

India.Arie 1975— **34**
Ingraham, Hubert A. 1947— **19**
Ingram, James 1952— **84**
Ingram, Rex 1895–1969 **5**
Innis, Roy (Emile Alfredo) 1934— **5**
Irvin, Michael 1966— **64**
Irvin, (Monford Merrill) Monte 1919— **31**
Irvin, Vernon 1961— **65**
Irving, Clarence (Larry) 1955— **12**
Irvis, K. Leroy 1917(?)–2006 **67**
Isaac, Julius 1928— **34**
Isaacs, Gregory 1951–2010 **89**
Isaacs, John 1915–2009 **76**
Isley, Marvin 1953–2010 **87**
Isley, Ronald 1941— **25, 56**
Iverson, Allen 1975— **24, 46**
Ivey, Phil 1976— **72**
Ja Rule 1976— **35, 91**
Jackson, Alexine Clement 1936— **22**
Jackson, Alphonso R. 1946— **48**
Jackson, Brenda 1953— **87**
Jackson, Earl 1948— **31**
Jackson, Edison O. 1943(?)— **67**
Jackson, Frank G. 1946— **76**
Jackson, Fred James 1950— **25**
Jackson, George 1960(?)— **19**
Jackson, George Lester 1941–1971 **14**
Jackson, Hal 1915— **41**
Jackson, Isaiah (Allen) 1945— **3**
Jackson, Jamea 1986— **64**
Jackson, James A. 1878–1960 **90**
Jackson, James Curtis, III *See 50 Cent*
Jackson, Janet 1966— **6, 30, 68**
Jackson, Jermaine 1954— **79**
Jackson, Jesse 1941— **1, 27, 72**
Jackson, Jesse, Jr. 1965— **14, 45, 81**
Jackson, Joe 1929— **78**
Jackson, John 1924–2002 **36**
Jackson, John David *See Fabolous*
Jackson, Judith D. 1950— **57**
Jackson, Lisa 1962— **77**
Jackson, Mae 1941–2005 **57**
Jackson, Mahalia 1911–1972 **5**
Jackson, Mannie 1939— **14**
Jackson, Mary 1945— **73**
Jackson, Maynard (Holbrook, Jr.) 1938–2003 **2, 41**
Jackson, Michael 1958–2009 **19, 53, 76**
Jackson, Millie 1944— **25**
Jackson, Milt 1923–1999 **26**
Jackson, O'Shea *See Ice Cube*
Jackson, Otis, Jr. *See Madlib*
Jackson, Quinton *See Jackson, Rampage*
Jackson, Rampage 1978— **83**
Jackson, Randy 1956— **40**
Jackson, Reginald Martinez 1946— **15**
Jackson, Rickey 1958— **88**
Jackson, Samuel 1948— **8, 19, 63**
Jackson, Sheneska 1970(?)— **18**
Jackson, Shirley Ann 1946— **12**
Jackson, Tito 1953— **81**
Jackson, Tom 1951— **70**
Jackson, Vera 1912— **40**
Jackson, Vivian *See Yabby You*

Jackson, Zelda Mavin *See Ormes, Jackie*
Jackson Lee, Sheila 1950— **20**
Jaco, Wasalu Muhammad *See Fiasco, Lupe*
Jacob, John E(dward) 1934— **2**
Jacobs, Marion Walter *See Little Walter*
Jacobs, Regina 1963— **38**
Jacquet, Illinois 1922(?)–2004 **49**
Jagan, Cheddi 1918–1997 **16**
Jaheim 1978— **58**
Jakes, Thomas "T.D." 1957— **17, 43**
Jam, Jimmy *See Jimmy Jam*
Jam Master Jay *See Run-DMC*
Jamal, Ahmad 1930— **69**
Jamelia 1981— **51**
Jamerson, James 1936–1983 **59**
James, Charles H., III 1959(?)— **62**
James, Daniel "Chappie," Jr. 1920–1978 **16**
James, David 1970— **84**
James, Donna A. 1957— **51**
James, Etta 1938— **13, 52**
James, G. Larry 1947–2008 **74**
James, Juanita (Therese) 1952— **13**
James, LeBron 1984— **46, 78**
James, Marlon 1970— **85**
James, Sharpe 1936— **23, 69**
James, Skip 1902–1969 **38**
James, Vanessa 1987— **84**
Jamison, Judith 1943— **7, 67**
Jammeh, Yahya 1965— **23**
Jarreau, Al 1940— **21, 65**
Jarrett, Valerie 1956— **73**
Jarrett, Vernon D. 1921— **42**
Jarvis, Charlene Drew 1941— **21**
Jarvis, Erich 1965— **67**
Jarvis, Kristen 1981(?)— **85**
Jasper, John J. 1812–1901 **91**
Jasper, Kenji 1976(?)— **39**
Jawara, Dawda Kairaba 1924— **11**
Jay-Z 1970— **27, 69**
Jealous, Benjamin 1973— **70**
Jean, Michaëlle 1957— **70**
Jean, Wyclef 1970— **20, 86**
Jean-Baptiste, Marianne 1967— **17, 46**
Jean-Juste, Gérard 1946–2009 **78**
Jean-Louis, Jimmy 1968— **76**
Jeffers, Eve Jihan *See Eve*
Jefferson, Blind Lemon 1893(?)–1929 **81**
Jefferson, Denise 1944–2010 **87**
Jefferson, Mildred Fay 1927–2010 **89**
Jefferson, William J. 1947— **25, 72**
Jeffries, Leonard 1937— **8**
Jemison, Mae C. 1957— **1, 35**
Jemison, Major L. 1955(?)— **48**
Jenifer, Franklyn G(reen) 1939— **2**
Jenkins, Beverly 1951— **14**
Jenkins, Ella (Louise) 1924— **15**
Jenkins, Fergie 1943— **46**
Jenkins, Jay *See Young Jeezy*
Jenkins, Ray 1920–2009 **77**
Jennings, Chester *See Jennings, Lyfe*
Jennings, Lyfe 1973— **56, 69**
Jerkins, Rodney 1978(?)— **31**
Jeter, Claude 1914–2009 **75**

Jeter, Derek 1974— **27, 93**
Jimmy Jam 1959— **13**
Joachim, Paulin 1931— **34**
Joe, Yolanda 19(?)(?)— **21**
John, Daymond 1969(?)— **23**
Johns, Vernon 1892–1965 **38**
Johnson, Angela 1961— **52**
Johnson, Anthony M. 1954— **92**
Johnson, Arnez *See Arnez J*
Johnson, Avery 1965— **62**
Johnson, Ben 1961— **1**
Johnson, Beverly 1952— **2**
Johnson, Buddy 1915–1977 **36**
Johnson, Carol Diann *See Carroll, Diahann*
Johnson, Caryn E. *See Goldberg, Whoopi*
Johnson, Charles 1948— **1, 82**
Johnson, Charles Arthur *See St. Jacques, Raymond*
Johnson, Charles Spurgeon 1893–1956 **12**
Johnson, Chris 1985— **92**
Johnson, Clifford "Connie" 1922–2004 **52**
Johnson, Dennis 1954–2007 **89**
Johnson, Dwayne *See Rock, The*
Johnson, Earvin "Magic" 1959— **3, 39**
Johnson, Eddie Bernice 1935— **8, 90**
Johnson, Eunice W. 1916–2010 **83**
Johnson, Fenton 1888–1958 **91**
Johnson, George E. 1927— **29**
Johnson, Georgia Douglas 1880–1966 **41**
Johnson, Gus 1938–1987 **92**
Johnson, Hall 1888–1970 **90**
Johnson, Hank, Jr. 1954— **80**
Johnson, Harry E. 1954— **57**
Johnson, Harvey, Jr. 1947(?)— **24, 82**
Johnson, Hazel 1927— **22**
Johnson, J. J. 1924–2001 **37**
Johnson, Jack 1878–1946 **8**
Johnson, James Louis *See Johnson, J. J.*
Johnson, James Weldon 1871–1938 **5**
Johnson, James William *See Johnson, James Weldon*
Johnson, Je'Caryous 1977— **63**
Johnson, Jeh C. 1957— **76**
Johnson, Jeh Vincent 1931— **44**
Johnson, John Arthur *See Johnson, Jack*
Johnson, John H. 1918–2005 **3, 54**
Johnson, Johnnie 1924–2005 **56**
Johnson, Katherine (Coleman Goble) 1918— **61**
Johnson, Kevin 1966— **70**
Johnson, Keyshawn 1972— **91**
Johnson, Larry 1969— **28**
Johnson, Leroy R. 1928— **89**
Johnson, Levi 1950— **48**
Johnson, Linton Kwesi 1952— **37**
Johnson, Lonnie 1899(?)–1970 **85**
Johnson, Lonnie G. 1949— **32, 93**
Johnson, "Magic" *See Johnson, Earvin "Magic"*
Johnson, Mamie "Peanut" 1932— **40**
Johnson, Marguerite *See Angelou, Maya*

Johnson, Mat 1971(?)— **31**
Johnson, Michael (Duane) 1967— **13**
Johnson, Michelle *See Ndegeocello, Meshell*
Johnson, Mordecai Wyatt 1890–1976 **79**
Johnson, Norma L. Holloway 1932— **17**
Johnson, R. M. 1968— **36**
Johnson, Rafer 1934— **33**
Johnson, Robert 1911–1938 **2**
Johnson, Robert L. 1946(?)— **3, 39**
Johnson, Robert T. 1948— **17**
Johnson, Rodney Van 19(?)(?)— **28**
Johnson, Sheila Crump 1949(?)— **48**
Johnson, Shoshana 1973— **47**
Johnson, Taalib *See Musiq*
Johnson, Virginia (Alma Fairfax) 1950— **9**
Johnson, William 1809–1851 **91**
Johnson, William Henry 1901–1970 **3**
Johnson, Woodrow Wilson *See Johnson, Buddy*
Johnson, Wycliffe *See Steely*
Johnson-Brown, Hazel W. *See Johnson, Hazel*
Johnson-George, Tamara 1971— **79**
Joiner, Alvin Nathaniel *See Xzibit*
Jolley, Willie 1956— **28**
Jonathan, Goodluck 1957— **83**
Jones, Absalom 1746–1818 **52**
Jones, Alex 1941— **64**
Jones, Anthony *See Jones, Van*
Jones, Bill T. 1952— **1, 46, 80**
Jones, Bob *See Jones, Robert G.*
Jones, Bobby 1939(?)— **20**
Jones, Booker T. 1944— **84**
Jones, Carl 1955(?)— **7**
Jones, Caroline R. 1942— **29**
Jones, Clara Stanton 1913— **51**
Jones, Cobi N'Gai 1970— **18**
Jones, Cullen 1984— **73**
Jones, Deacon 1938— **92**
Jones, Donell 1973— **29**
Jones, Doris W. 1914(?)–2006 **62**
Jones, E. Edward, Sr. 1931— **45**
Jones, Ed "Too Tall" 1951— **46**
Jones, Edith Mae Irby 1927— **65**
Jones, Edward P. 1950— **43, 67**
Jones, Elaine R. 1944— **7, 45**
Jones, Elvin 1927–2004 **14, 68**
Jones, Emil, Jr. 1935— **74**
Jones, Etta 1928–2001 **35**
Jones, Eugene Kinckle 1885–1954 **79**
Jones, Frederick McKinley 1893–1961 **68**
Jones, Frederick Russell *See Jamal, Ahmad*
Jones, Gayl 1949— **37**
Jones, Hank 1918–2010 **57, 86**
Jones, Ingrid Saunders 1945— **18**
Jones, James Earl 1931— **3, 49, 79**
Jones, John 1816–1879 **89**
Jones, Jonah 1909–2000 **39**
Jones, K. C. 1932— **83**
Jones, Kelis *See Kelis*

Jones, Kimberly Denise *See Lil' Kim*

Jones, Kirk *See Sticky Fingaz*

Jones, Le Roi *See Baraka, Amiri*

Jones, Lillie Mae *See Carter, Betty*

Jones, Lois Mailou 1905— 13

Jones, Lou 1932–2006 64

Jones, Marion 1975— 21, 66

Jones, Merlakia 1973— 34

Jones, Monty 1951(?)— 66

Jones, Nasir *See Nas*

Jones, Orlando 1968— 30

Jones, Paul R. 1928— 76

Jones, Quincy (Delight) 1933— 8, 30

Jones, Randy 1969— 35

Jones, Robert Elijah 1872–1960 90

Jones, Robert Elliott *See Jones, Jonah*

Jones, Robert G. 1936–2008 81

Jones, Roy Jr. 1969— 22

Jones, Russell *See Ol' Dirty Bastard*

Jones, Ruth Lee *See Washington, Dinah*

Jones, Sam 1933— 85

Jones, Sarah 1974— 39

Jones, Sharon 1955(?)— 86

Jones, Sissieretta *See Joyner, Matilda Sissieretta*

Jones, Star *See Reynolds, Star Jones*

Jones, Thad 1923–1986 68

Jones, Thomas W. 1949— 41

Jones, Van 1968— 70

Jones, Wayne 1952— 53

Jones, William A., Jr. 1934–2006 61

Joplin, Scott 1868–1917 6

Jordan, Barbara 1936–1996 4, 78

Jordan, Eddie 1952— 82

Jordan, Eddie 1955— 83

Jordan, Eric Benét *See Benét, Eric*

Jordan, June 1936— 7, 35

Jordan, Michael (Jeffrey) 1963— 6, 21

Jordan, Montell 1968(?)— 23

Jordan, Ronny 1962— 26

Jordan, Vernon E(ulion, Jr.) 1935— 3, 35

Jorge, Seu 1970— 73

Joseph, Kathie-Ann 1970(?)— 56

Josey, E. J. 1924— 10

Joyce, Dru 1955— 81

Joyner, Jacqueline *See Joyner-Kersee, Jackie*

Joyner, Marjorie Stewart 1896–1994 26

Joyner, Matilda Sissieretta 1869(?)–1933 15

Joyner, Tom 1949(?)— 19, 90

Joyner-Kersee, Jackie 1962— 5

Julian, Hubert 1897–1983 90

Julian, Percy Lavon 1899–1975 6

Julien, Isaac 1960— 3

July, William II 19(?)(?)— 27

Juma, Calestous 1953— 57

Just, Ernest Everett 1883–1941 3

Justice, David Christopher 1966— 18

Ka Dinizulu, Israel *See Ka Dinizulu, Mcwayizeni*

Ka Dinizulu, Mcwayizeni 1932–1999 29

Kabbah, Ahmad Tejan 1932— 23

Kabila, Joseph 1968(?)— 30

Kabila, Laurent 1939— 20

Kagame, Paul 1957— 54

Kaigler, Denise 1962— 63

Kaiser, Cecil 1916— 42

Kalbani, Adil 1959(?)— 77

Kamau, Johnstone *See Kenyatta, Jomo*

Kamau, Kwadwo Agymah 1960(?)— 28

Kandi 1976— 83

Kani, Karl 1968(?)— 10

Kanouté, Fred 1977— 68

Karenga, Maulana 1941— 10, 71

Karim, Benjamin 1932–2005 61

Kariuki, J. M. 1929–1975 67

Kassahun, Tewodros *See Afro, Teddy*

Katoucha *See Niane, Katoucha*

Kaufman, Monica 1948(?)— 66

Kaunda, Kenneth (David) 1924— 2

Kay, Jackie 1961— 37

Kay, Ulysses 1917–1995 37

Kayira, Legson 1942— 40

Kearney, Janis 1953— 54

Kearse, Amalya Lyle 1937— 12

Kebede, Liya 1978— 59

Keckley, Elizabeth 1818–1907 90

Kee, John P. 1962— 43

Keene, John 1965— 73

Keflezighi, Meb 1975— 49

Keita, Salif 1949— 83

Keith, Damon J. 1922— 16, 74

Keith, Floyd A. 1948— 61

Keith, Rachel Boone 1924–2007 63

Kelis 1979— 58

Kelley, Cliff 1941— 75

Kelley, Elijah 1986— 65

Kelley, Malcolm David 1992— 59

Kellogg, Clark 1961— 64

Kelly, Leontine 1920— 33

Kelly, Patrick 1954(?)–1990 3

Kelly, R. 1967— 18, 44, 71

Kelly, Robert Sylvester *See Kelly, R.*

Kelly, Sharon Pratt *See Dixon, Sharon Pratt*

Kem 196(?)— 47

Kendrick, Erika 1975— 57

Kendricks, Eddie 1939–1992 22

Kennard, William Earl 1957— 18

Kennedy, Adrienne 1931— 11

Kennedy, Florynce Rae 1916–2000 12, 33

Kennedy, Lelia McWilliams Robinson 1885–1931 14

Kennedy, Randall 1954— 40

Kennedy-Overton, Jayne Harris 1951— 46

Kenney, John A., Jr. 1914–2003 48

Kenoly, Ron 1944— 45

Kente, Gibson 1932–2004 52

Kenyatta, Jomo 1891(?)–1978 5

Kenyatta, Robin 1942–2004 54

Kerekou, Ahmed (Mathieu) 1933— 1

Kerry, Leon G. 1949(?)— 46

Keyes, Alan L(ee) 1950— 11

Keys, Alicia 1981— 32, 68

Khan, Chaka 1953— 12, 50

Khanga, Yelena 1962— 6

Khumalo, Leleti 1970— 51

Kibaki, Mwai 1931— 60

Kid Cudi 1984— 83

Kidd, Jason 1973— 86

Kidd, Mae Street 1904–1995 39

Kidjo, Angelique 1960— 50

Kiir, Salva 1951— 85

Kikwete, Jakaya Mrisho 1950— 73

Killens, John O. 1967–1987 54

Killings, Debra 196(?)— 57

Killingsworth, Cleve, Jr. 1952— 54

Kilpatrick, Carolyn Cheeks 1945— 16

Kilpatrick, Kwame 1970— 34, 71

Kimbro, Dennis (Paul) 1950— 10

Kimbro, Henry A. 1912–1999 25

Kimbro, Warren 1934–2009 76

Kincaid, Bernard 1945— 28

Kincaid, Jamaica 1949— 4

King, Alonzo 19(?)(?)— 38

King, B. B. 1925— 7

King, Barbara 19(?)(?)— 22

King, Bernice 1963— 4, 81

King, Colbert I. 1939— 69

King, Coretta Scott 1927–2006 3, 57

King, Dexter (Scott) 1961— 10

King, Don 1931— 14

King, Freddie 1934–1976 92

King, Gayle 1956— 19

King, Martin Luther, III 1957— 20

King, Martin Luther, Jr. 1929–1968 1

King, Martin Luther, Sr. 1899–1984 89

King, Oona 1967— 27

King, Preston 1936— 28

King, Reatha Clark 1938— 65

King, Regina 1971— 22, 45

King, Riley B. *See King, B. B.*

King, Robert Arthur 1945— 58

King, Robert Hillary 1942— 84

King, Teresa 1961— 80

King, Woodie Jr. 1937— 27

King, Yolanda (Denise) 1955— 6

King Curtis 1934–1971 92

Kintaudi, Leon 1949(?)— 62

Kintaudi, Ngoma Miezi *See Kintaudi, Leon*

Kirby, George 1924–1995 14

Kirk, Ron 1954— 11, 75

Kitt, Eartha 1927–2008 16, 75

Kitt, Sandra 1947— 23

Kittles, Rick 1976(?)— 51

Kitwana, Bakari 19(?)(?)— 86

Klugh, Earl 1953— 59

K'naan 1978— 76

Knight, Etheridge 1931–1991 37

Knight, Gladys 1944— 16, 66

Knight, Gwendolyn 1913–2005 63

Knight, Marie 1925(?)–2009 80

Knight, Marion, Jr. *See Knight, Suge*

Knight, Suge 1966— 11, 30

Knowles, Beyoncé *See Beyoncé*

Knowles, Tina 1954(?)— 61

Knowling, Robert Jr. 1955(?)— 38

Knox, Simmie 1935— 49

Knuckles, Frankie 1955— 42

Kobia, Samuel 1947— 43

Kodjoe, Boris 1973— 34, 89

Kolosoy, Wendo 1925–2008 73

Komunyakaa, Yusef 1941— 9

Kone, Seydou *See Blondy, Alpha*

Kong, B. Waine 1943— 50

Kool DJ Red Alert *See Alert, Kool DJ Red*

Kool Moe Dee 1963— 37

Kool Rock Ski *See Fat Boys*

Koroma, Ernest Bai 1953— 84

Kotto, Yaphet (Fredrick) 1944— 7

Kountz, Samuel L(ee) 1930–1981 10

Kravitz, Lenny 1964— 10, 34

Kravitz, Leonard *See Kravitz, Lenny*

KRS-One 1965— 34

Krute, Fred *See Alert, Kool DJ Red*

K-Swift 1978–2008 73

Kufuor, John Agyekum 1938— 54, 82

Kunjufu, Jawanza 1953— 3, 50

Kuti, Fela Anikulapo *See Fela*

Kuti, Femi 1962— 47

Kuzwayo, Ellen 1914–2006 68

Kwei-Armah, Kwame 1967— 84

Kweli, Talib 1975— 93

Kyles, Cedric *See Cedric the Entertainer*

La Menthe, Ferdinand Joseph *See Morton, Jelly Roll*

La Salle, Eriq 1962— 12

LaBelle, Patti 1944— 13, 30

LaChanze 1961— 93

Lacy, Sam 1903–2003 30, 46

Ladd, Ernie 1938–2007 64

Ladner, Joyce A. 1943— 42

Laferriere, Dany 1953— 33

Lafontant, Jewel Stradford 1922–1997 3, 51

Lafontant-MANkarious, Jewel Stradford *See Lafontant, Jewel Stradford*

LaGuma, Alex 1925–1985 30

Lamming, George 1927— 35

Lampkin, Daisy 1883(?)–1965 19

Lampley, Oni Faida 1959–2008 43, 71

Lampley, Vera *See Lampley, Oni Faida*

Lane, Charles 1953— 3

Lane, Dick 1927–2002 92

Lane, Lunsford 1803–18(?)(?)(?) 93

Lane, Vincent 1942— 5

Lane, William Henry 1825(?)–1852(?) 90

Langford, Larry P. 1948— 74

Langhart Cohen, Janet 1941— 19, 60

Lanier, Bob 1948— 47

Lanier, Willie 1945— 33

Lankford, Raymond Lewis 1967— 23

Laraque, Georges 1976— 48

Laraque, Paul 1920–2007 67

Larkin, Barry 1964— 24

Laroche, Joseph Philippe Lemercier 1889–1912 85

Larrieux, Amel 1973(?)— 63

Lars, Byron 1965— 32

Larsen, Nella 1891–1964 10

Laryea, Thomas Davies III 1979— 67

Lashley, Bobby 1976— 63

Lashley, Franklin Roberto *See Lashley, Bobby*

Lassiter, Roy 1969— 24

Lateef, Yusef 1920— 91

Lathan, Sanaa 1971— **27**

Latimer, Lewis H(oward) 1848–1928 **4**

Lattany, Kristin Hunter 1931–2008 **88**

Lattimore, Kenny 1970(?)— **35**

LaVette, Bettye 1946— **85**

Lavizzo-Mourey, Risa 1954— **48**

Lawal, Kase L. 19(?)(?)— **45**

Lawless, Theodore K(enneth) 1892–1971 **8**

Lawrence, Jacob (Armstead) 1917–2000 **4, 28**

Lawrence, Martin 1965— **6, 27, 60**

Lawrence, Robert Henry, Jr. 1935–1967 **16**

Lawrence-Lightfoot, Sara 1944— **10**

Laws, Hubert 1939— **90**

Lawson, James M., Jr. 1928— **90**

Lawson, Jennifer 1946— **1, 50**

Layton, William 1915–2007 **87**

Leadbelly 1885–1949 **82**

Leary, Kathryn D. 1952— **10**

Leavell, Dorothy R. 1944— **17**

Ledbetter, Hudson William *See Leadbelly*

Ledisi 197(?)— **73**

Lee, Annie Frances 1935— **22**

Lee, Barbara 1946— **25**

Lee, Bertram M., Sr. 1939–2003 **46**

Lee, Canada 1907–1952 **8**

Lee, Consuela 1926–2009 **84**

Lee, Debra L. 1954— **62**

Lee, Don Luther *See Madhubuti, Haki R.*

Lee, Eric P. 1958— **79**

Lee, Gabby *See Lincoln, Abbey*

Lee, Joe A. 1946(?)— **45**

Lee, Joie 1962(?)— **1**

Lee, Leslie 1935— **85**

Lee, Malcolm D. 1970— **75**

Lee, Raphael C. 1949— **87**

Lee, Shelton Jackson *See Lee, Spike*

Lee, Spike 1957— **5, 19, 86**

Lee-Smith, Hughie 1915— **5, 22**

Leevy, Carrol M. 1920— **42**

Lefel, Edith 1963–2003 **41**

Leffall, Lasalle, Jr. 1930— **3, 64**

Legend, John 1978— **67**

Leggs, Kingsley 196(?)— **62**

Leland, George Thomas *See Leland, Mickey*

Leland, Mickey 1944–1989 **2**

Lemmons, Kasi 1961— **20**

Lennox, Betty 1976— **31**

LeNoire, Rosetta 1911–2002 **37**

Lenox, Adriane 1956— **59**

Leon, Kenny 1957(?)— **10**

León, Tania 1943— **13**

Leonard, Buck 1907— **67**

Leonard, Sugar Ray 1956— **15**

Leonard, Walter Fenner *See Leonard, Buck*

Leslie, Lisa 1972— **16, 73**

Lester, Adrian 1968— **46**

Lester, Bill 1961— **42, 85**

Lester, Julius 1939— **9**

Lesure, James 1975— **64**

LeTang, Henry 1915–2007 **66**

Letson, Al 1972— **39**

Levert, Eddie 1942— **70**

Levert, Gerald 1966–2006 **22, 59**

Lewis, Aylwin B. 1954— **51, 88**

Lewis, Butch 1946— **71**

Lewis, Byron E(ugene) 1931— **13**

Lewis, (Frederick) Carl(ton) 1961— **4**

Lewis, Daurene 194(?)— **72**

Lewis, David Levering 1936— **9**

Lewis, Delano (Eugene) 1938— **7**

Lewis, Denise 1972— **33**

Lewis, (Mary) Edmonia 1845(?)–1911(?) **10**

Lewis, Edward T. 1940— **21**

Lewis, Emmanuel 1971— **36**

Lewis, Henry 1932–1996 **38**

Lewis, John 1940— **2, 46, 83**

Lewis, Lennox 1965— **27**

Lewis, Leona 1985— **75**

Lewis, Marvin 1958— **51, 87**

Lewis, Norman 1909–1979 **39**

Lewis, Oliver 1856–1924 **56**

Lewis, Ramsey 1935— **35, 70**

Lewis, Ray 1975— **33**

Lewis, Reginald F. 1942–1993 **6**

Lewis, Ronald *See Lewis, Butch*

Lewis, Samella 1924— **25**

Lewis, Shirley Ann Redd 1937— **14**

Lewis, Terry 1956— **13**

Lewis, Thomas 1939— **19**

Lewis, William Henry 1868–1949 **89**

Lewis, William M., Jr. 1956— **40**

Lewis-Thornton, Rae 1962— **32**

Ligging, Alfred III 1965— **43**

Ligon, Glenn 1960— **82**

Lil' Bow Wow *See Bow Wow*

Lil' Kim 1975— **28**

Lil Wayne 1982— **66, 84**

Lilakoi Moon *See Bonet, Lisa*

Liles, Kevin 1968— **42**

Lincoln, Abbey 1930–2010 **3, 88**

Lincoln, C(harles) Eric 1924–2000 **38**

Lindo, Allen Pineda *See apl.de.ap*

Lindo, Delroy 1952— **18, 45**

Lindsey, Tommie 1951— **51**

Lipscomb, Mance 1895–1976 **49**

LisaRaye 1967— **27**

Lister, Marquita 1965(?) **65**

Liston, (Charles) Sonny 1928(?)–1970 **33**

Little, Benilde 1958— **21**

Little, Floyd 1942— **86**

Little, Larry 1945— **90**

Little, Malcolm *See X, Malcolm*

Little, Robert L(angdon) 1938— **2**

Little Milton 1934–2005 **36, 54**

Little Richard 1932— **15**

Little Walter 1930–1968 **36**

Little Warrior *See Barrow, Willie T.*

Littlepage, Craig 1951— **35**

LL Cool J 1968— **16, 49**

Llewellyn, J. Bruce 1927–2010 **13, 85**

Lloyd, Earl 1928(?)— **26**

Lloyd, John Henry "Pop" 1884–1965 **30**

Lloyd, Reginald 1967— **64**

Locke, Alain (LeRoy) 1886–1954 **10**

Locke, Attica 1974— **85**

Locke, Eddie 1930— **44**

Lofton, James 1956— **42**

Lofton, Kenneth 1967— **12**

Lofton, Ramona 1950— **14**

Logan, Onnie Lee 1910(?)–1995 **14**

Logan, Rayford W. 1897–1982 **40**

Loguen, J. W. 1813–1872 **91**

Lomax, Louis E. 1922–1970 **90**

Lomax, Michael L. 1947— **58**

Long, Eddie L. 1953— **29, 89**

Long, Huey 1904–2009 **79**

Long, Loretta 1940— **58**

Long, Nia 1970— **17**

Long, Richard Alexander 1927— **65**

Lopes, Davey 1945— **92**

Lopes, Lisa " Left Eye" 1971–2002 **36**

Lord Pitt of Hampstead *See Pitt, David Thomas*

Lorde, Audre (Geraldine) 1934–1992 **6**

Lorenzo, Irving *See Gotti, Irv*

Loroupe, Tegla 1973— **59**

Lott, Ronnie 1959— **9**

Loueke, Lionel 1973(?)— **88**

Louis, Errol T. 1962— **8**

Louis, Joe 1914–1981 **5**

Loury, Glenn 1948— **36**

Love, Darlene 1941— **23, 92**

Love, Ed 1932(?)— **58**

Love, Laura 1960— **50**

Love, Nat 1854–1921 **9**

Love, Reggie 1982— **77**

Lovell, Whitfield 1959— **74**

Lover, Ed **10**

Loving, Alvin, Jr., 1935–2005 **35, 53**

Loving, Mildred 1939–2008 **69**

Lowe, Herbert 1962— **57**

Lowe, Sidney 1960— **64**

Lowery, Joseph E. 1924— **2**

Lowery, Myron 1946(?)— **80**

Lowry, A. Leon 1913–2005 **60**

Lucas, John 1953— **7**

Lucie, Lawrence 1907–2009 **80**

Lucien, Jon 1942–2007 **66**

Luckett, Letoya 1981— **61**

Lucy, William 1933— **50**

Lucy Foster, Autherine 1929— **35**

Ludacris, 1978— **37, 60**

Luke, Derek 1974— **61**

Lumbly, Carl 1952— **47**

Lumet, Jenny 1967— **80**

Lumpkin, Elgin Baylor *See Ginuwine*

Lumumba, Patrice 1925–1961 **33**

Luna, Donyale 1946–1979 **88**

Lushington, Augustus Nathaniel 1869–1939 **56**

Luthuli, Albert (John Mvumbi) 1898(?)–1967 **13**

Lyfe *See Jennings, Lyfe*

Lyle, Marcenia *See Stone, Toni*

Lyles, Lester Lawrence 1946— **31**

Lymon, Frankie 1942–1968 **22**

Lynch, Shola 1969— **61**

Lynn, Lonnie Rashid *See Common*

Lyons, Henry 1942(?)— **12**

Lyttle, Hulda Margaret 1889–1983 **14**

Maal, Baaba 1953— **66**

Maathai, Wangari 1940— **43**

Mabley, Jackie "Moms" 1897(?)–1975 **15**

Mabrey, Vicki 1957(?)— **26**

Mabry, Marcus 1967— **70**

Mabuza, Lindiwe 1938— **18**

Mabuza-Suttle, Felicia 1950— **43**

Mac, Bernie 1957–2008 **29, 61, 72**

Maceo, Antonio 1845–1896 **82**

Machado de Assis 1839–1908 **74**

Machel, Graca Simbine 1945— **16**

Machel, Samora Moises 1933–1986 **8**

Mackey, Biz 1897–1965 **82**

Mackey, Nathaniel 1947— **75**

Madhubuti, Haki R. 1942— **7, 85**

Madikizela, Nkosikazi Nobandle Nomzamo Winifred *See Mandela, Winnie*

Madison, Joseph E. 1949— **17**

Madison, Paula 1952— **37**

Madison, Romell 1952— **45**

Madlib 1973— **88**

Magan, Ayaan Hirsi *See Ali, Ayaan Hirsi*

Magloire, Paul Eugène 1907–2001 **68**

Mahal, Taj 1942— **39**

Mahlasela, Vusi 1965— **65**

Mahorn, Rick 1958— **60**

Mainor, Dorothy Leigh 1910(?)–1996 **19**

Maitreya, Sananda 1962— **85**

Majette, Denise 1955— **41**

Major, Clarence 1936— **9**

Majors, Jeff 1960(?)— **41**

Makeba, Miriam 1932–2008 **2, 50, 74**

Malco, Romany 1968— **71**

Malcolm X *See X, Malcolm*

Mallett, Conrad, Jr. 1953— **16**

Mallory, Mark 1962— **62**

Malone, Annie (Minerva Turnbo Pope) 1869–1957 **13**

Malone, Karl 1963— **18, 51, 90**

Malone, Maurice 1965— **32**

Malone, Moses 1955— **79**

Malone Jones, Vivian 1942–2005 **59**

Malveaux, Floyd 1940— **54**

Malveaux, Julianne 1953— **32, 70**

Malveaux, Suzanne 1966— **88**

Mandela, Nelson 1918— **1, 14, 77**

Mandela, Winnie 1934— **2, 35**

Mane, Gucci 1980— **91**

Manigat, Mirlande 1940— **90**

Manigault, Earl "The Goat" 1943— **15**

Manigault-Stallworth, Omarosa 1974— **69**

Manley, Audrey Forbes 1934— **16**

Manley, Edna 1900–1987 **26**

Manley, Ruth 1947— **34**

Mann, Tamela 1966— **92**

Manning, Frankie 1914–2009 **78**

Marable, Manning 1950— **10**

March, William Carrington 1923–2002 **56**

Marchand, Inga *See Foxy Brown*

Marechera, Charles William *See Marechera, Dambudzo*

Marechera, Dambudzo 1952–1987 **39**

Marechera, Tambudzai *See Marechera, Dambudzo*

Mariner, Jonathan 1954(?)— **41**

Marino, Eugene Antonio 1934–2000 **30**

Mario 1986— **71**

Markham, E(dward) A(rchibald) 1939— **37**

Marley, Bob 1945–1981 **5**

Marley, David See Marley, Ziggy

Marley, Rita 1947— **32, 70**

Marley, Robert Nesta See Marley, Bob

Marley, Ziggy 1968— **41**

Marrow, Queen Esther 1943(?)— **24**

Marrow, Tracey See Ice-T

Marsalis, Branford 1960— **34**

Marsalis, Delfeayo 1965— **41**

Marsalis, Ellis 1934— **90**

Marsalis, Wynton 1961— **16, 90**

Marsh, Henry L., III 1934(?)— **32**

Marshall, Bella 1950— **22**

Marshall, Gloria See Sudarkasa, Niara

Marshall, Kerry James 1955— **59**

Marshall, Paule 1929— **7, 77**

Marshall, Thurgood 1908–1993 **1, 44**

Marshall, Valenza Pauline Burke See Marshall, Paule

Martelly, Michel 1961— **90**

Martha Jean "The Queen" See Steinberg, Martha Jean

Martin, Darnell 1964— **43, 78**

Martin, Helen 1909–2000 **31**

Martin, Jesse L. 19(?)(?)— **31**

Martin, Louis Emanuel 1912–1997 **16**

Martin, Roberta 1907–1969 **58**

Martin, Roland S. 1968— **49, 84**

Martin, Ruby Grant 1933–2003 **49**

Martin, Sara 1884–1955 **38**

Martinez, Pedro 1971— **81**

Marvin X See X, Marvin

Mary Mary **34, 92**

Mase 1977(?)— **24**

Masekela, Barbara 1941— **18**

Masekela, Hugh (Ramopolo) 1939— **1**

Masire, Quett (Ketumile Joni) 1925— **5**

Mason, Biddy 1818–1891 **89**

Mason, Felicia 1963(?)— **31**

Mason, Herman, Jr. 1962— **83**

Mason, Ronald 1949— **27**

Massaquoi, Hans J. 1926— **30**

Massenburg, Kedar 1964(?)— **23**

Massey, Brandon 1973— **40**

Massey, Walter E(ugene) 1938— **5, 45**

Massie, Samuel Proctor, Jr. 1919— **29**

Master Gee See Sugarhill Gang, The

Master P 1970— **21**

Matejka, Adrian 1971(?)— **87**

Mathabane, Johannes See Mathabane, Mark

Mathabane, Mark 1960— **5**

Mathis, Greg 1960— **26**

Mathis, Johnny 1935— **20**

Matson, Ollie 1930–2011 **93**

Matthews, Benjamin 1932–2006 **93**

Matthews, Denise See Vanity

Matthews, Mark 1894–2005 **59**

Matthews Shatteen, Westina 1948— **51**

Matzeliger, Jan 1852–1889 **93**

Mauldin, Jermaine Dupri See Dupri, Jermaine

Maupin, John E., Jr. 1946— **92**

Maxey, Randall 1941— **46**

Maxis, Theresa 1810–1892 **62**

Maxwell 1973— **20, 81**

May, Derrick 1963— **41**

Mayers, Jamal 1974— **39**

Mayfield, Curtis (Lee) 1942–1999 **2, 43**

Mayhew, Martin R. 1965— **76**

Mayhew, Richard 1924— **39**

Maynard, Nancy Hicks 1946–2008 **73**

Maynard, Robert C(lyve) 1937–1993 **7**

Maynor, Dorothy 1910–1996 **19**

Mayo, Whitman 1930–2001 **32**

Mays, Benjamin E(lijah) 1894–1984 **7**

Mays, Leslie A. 19(?)(?)— **41**

Mays, William G. 1946— **34**

Mays, William Howard, Jr. See Mays, Willie

Mays, Willie 1931— **3**

Mayweather, Floyd, Jr. 1977— **57**

Mazrui, Ali Al'Amin 1933— **12**

M'bala M'bala, Dieudonné See Dieudonné

Mbatha-Raw, Gugu 1983— **89**

Mbaye, Mariétou 1948— **31**

Mbeki, Govan A. 1910–2001 **80**

Mbeki, Thabo 1942— **14, 73**

Mboup, Souleymane 1951— **10**

Mbuende, Kaire Munionganda 1953— **12**

MC Breed 1971–2008 **75**

M.C. Hammer 1963— **20, 80**

MC Lyte 1971— **34**

McAdoo, Bob 1951— **75**

McAnulty, William E., Jr. 1947–2007 **66**

McBay, Henry C. 1914–1995 **91**

McBride, Bryant Scott 1965— **18**

McBride, Chi 1961— **73**

McBride, James 1957— **35, 87**

McCabe, Jewell Jackson 1945— **10**

McCall, H. Carl 1938(?)— **27**

McCall, Nathan 1955— **8**

McCann, Renetta 1957(?)— **44**

McCarthy, Sandy 1972— **64**

McCarty, Osceola 1908— **16**

McCary, Michael S. See Boyz II Men

McCauley, Gina 1976(?)— **76**

McClellan, George Marion 1860–1934 **91**

McClendon, Lisa 1975(?)— **61**

McClinton, Marion Isaac 1954— **77**

McClurkin, Donnie 1961— **25**

McCoo, Marilyn 1943— **53**

McCoy, Elijah 1844–1929 **8**

McCrary, Crystal See McCrary Anthony, Crystal

McCrary Anthony, Crystal 1969— **70**

McCray, Nikki 1972— **18**

McCullough, Bernard Jeffrey See Mac, Bernie

McCullough, Geraldine 1917–2008 **58, 79**

McDaniel, Hattie 1895–1952 **5**

McDaniel, Randall Cornell 1964— **81**

McDaniels, Darryl See DMC

McDaniels, Ralph 19(?)(?)— **79**

McDonald, Audra 1970— **20, 62**

McDonald, Erroll 1954(?)— **1**

McDonald, Gabrielle Kirk 1942— **20**

McDougall, Gay J. 1947— **11, 43**

McDuffie, Dwayne 1962— **62**

McEwen, Mark 1954— **5**

McFadden, Bernice L. 1966— **39**

McFarlan, Tyron 1971(?)— **60**

McFarland, Roland 1940— **49**

McFerrin, Bobby 1950— **68**

McFerrin, Robert, Jr. See McFerrin, Bobby

McGee, Charles 1924— **10**

McGee, James D. 1949— **74**

McGee, James Madison 1940— **46**

McGill, Anthony 1979— **76**

McGlowan, Angela 1970— **64, 86**

McGrady, Tracy 1979— **80**

McGrath, Pat 1970— **72**

McGriff, Fred 1963— **24**

McGriff, James Harrell See McGriff, Jimmy

McGriff, Jimmy 1936–2008 **72**

McGruder, Aaron 1974— **28, 56**

McGruder, Robert 1942— **22, 35**

McGuire, George Alexander 1866–1934 **80**

McGuire, Raymond J. 1957(?)(—) **57**

McHenry, Donald F. 1936— **83**

McIntosh, Winston Hubert See Tosh, Peter

McIntyre, Natalie See Gary, Macy

McJunkin, George 1851–1922 **93**

McKay, Claude 1889–1948 **6**

McKay, Festus Claudius See McKay, Claude

McKay, Nellie Yvonne 19(?)(?)–2006 **17, 57**

McKee, Lonette 1952— **12**

McKegney, Tony 1958— **3**

McKenzie, Jaunel 1986— **73**

McKenzie, Vashti M. 1947— **29**

McKinney, Cynthia 1955— **11, 52, 74**

McKinney, Nina Mae 1912–1967 **40**

McKinney Hammond, Michelle 1957— **51**

McKinney-Whetstone, Diane 1954(?)— **27**

McKinney, Ike See McKinnon, Isaiah

McKinnon, Isaiah 1943— **9**

McKissack, Leatrice 1930— **80**

McKissick, Floyd B(ixler) 1922–1981 **3**

McKnight, Brian 1969— **18, 34**

McLean, Jackie 1931–2006 **78**

McLendon, John B., Jr. 1915–1999 **89**

McLeod, Gus 1955(?)— **27**

McMillan, Rosalynn A. 1953— **36**

McMillan, Terry 1951— **4, 17, 53**

McMillan, Tracy 1964— **93**

McMurray, Georgia L. 1934–1992 **36**

McNabb, Donovan 1976— **29**

McNair, Ronald 1950–1986 **3, 58**

McNair, Steve 1973–2009 **22, 47, 79**

McNeil, Lori 1964(?)— **1**

McPhail, Sharon 1948— **2**

McPherson, David 1968— **32**

McPherson, James Alan 1943— **70**

McQueen, Butterfly 1911–1995 **6, 54**

McQueen, Steve 1969— **84**

McRae, Carmen 1920–1994 **77**

McRae, Hal 1945— **84**

McTell, Blind Willie 1901–1959 **89**

McWhorter, John 1965— **35**

McWorter, Free Frank 1777–1854 **91**

Meadows, Tim 1961— **30**

Meek, Carrie (Pittman) 1926— **6, 36**

Meek, Kendrick 1966— **41, 89**

Meeks, Gregory 1953— **25**

Meeks, James T. 1956— **92**

Mehretu, Julie 1970— **85**

Meles Zenawi 1955(?)— **3**

Mell, Patricia 1953— **49**

Mello, Breno 1931–2008 **73**

Melton, Frank 1949–2009 **81**

Melton, Harold D. 1966— **79**

Memmi, Albert 1920— **37**

Memphis Minnie 1897–1973 **33**

Menard, John Willis 1838–1893 **90**

Mengestu, Dinaw 1978— **66**

Mengistu, Haile Mariam 1937— **65**

Mensah, John 1982— **87**

Mensah, Thomas 1950— **48**

Mercado-Valdes, Frank 1962— **43**

Meredith, James H(oward) 1933— **11**

Merkerson, S. Epatha 1952— **47, 83**

Mescudi, Scott Ramon Seguro See Kid Cudi

Messenger, The See Divine, Father

Metcalfe, Ralph 1910–1978 **26**

Method Man 1971— **81**

Meyer, June See Jordan, June

Mfume, Kweisi 1948— **6, 41**

Mhlaba, Raymond 1920–2005 **55**

Michaux, Solomon Lightfoot 1884–1968 **93**

Micheaux, Oscar (Devereaux) 1884–1951 **7**

Michele, Michael 1966— **31**

Mickelbury, Penny 1948— **28**

Miles, Buddy 1947–2008 **69**

Miles, George Allen, Jr. See Miles, Buddy

Milla, Roger 1952— **2**

Millender-McDonald, Juanita 1938–2007 **21, 61**

Miller, Bebe 1950— **3**

Miller, Cheryl 1964— **10, 74**

Miller, Dorie 1919–1943 **29**

Miller, Doris See Miller, Dorie

Miller, Larry G. 1950(?)— **72**

Miller, Marcus 1959— **84**

Miller, Maria 1803–1879 **19**

Miller, Omar Benson 1978— **93**

Miller, Percy See Master P

Miller, Reggie 1965— **33**

Miller, Rice See Williamson, Sonny Boy

Miller, Warren F., Jr. 1943— **53**

Miller, Wentworth 1972— **75**

Miller-Travis, Vernice 1959— **64**

Millines Dziko, Trish 1957— **28**

Millner, Denene 1969(?)— **76**

Mills, Dylan Kwabena *See Rascal, Dizzee*

Mills, Florence 1896–1927 **22**

Mills, Joseph C. 1946— **51**

Mills, Sam 1959— **33**

Mills, Stephanie 1957— **36**

Mills, Steve 1960(?)— **47**

Milner, Ron 1938— **39**

Milton, DeLisha 1974— **31**

Minaj, Nicki 1984— **86**

Mingo, Frank L. 1939–1989 **32**

Mingus, Charles Jr. 1922–1979 **15**

Minor, DeWayne 1956— **32**

Minoso, Minnie 1925— **89**

Minott, Sugar 1956–2010 **86**

Mitchell, Arthur 1934— **2, 47**

Mitchell, Arthur Wergs 1883–1968 **91**

Mitchell, Brian Stokes 1957— **21**

Mitchell, Clarence M., Jr. 1911–1984 **88**

Mitchell, Corinne 1914–1993 **8**

Mitchell, Elvis 1958— **67**

Mitchell, Keith 1946— **82**

Mitchell, Kel 1978— **66**

Mitchell, Leona 1949— **42**

Mitchell, Loften 1919–2001 **31**

Mitchell, Nicole 1967(?)— **66**

Mitchell, Parren J. 1922–2007 **42, 66**

Mitchell, Russ 1960— **21, 73**

Mitchell, Sam 1963— **82**

Mitchell, Sharon 1962— **36**

Mitchell, Shireen 1970— **89**

Mizell, Jason *See Run-DMC*

Mo', Keb' 1952— **36**

Mobutu Sese Seko 1930–1997 **1, 56**

Mofolo, Thomas (Mokopu) 1876–1948 **37**

Mogae, Festus Gontebanye 1939— **19, 79**

Mohamed, Ali Mahdi *See Ali Mahdi Mohamed*

Mohammed, Nazr 1977— **64**

Mohammed, W. Deen 1933— **27**

Mohammed, Warith Deen *See Mohammed, W. Deen*

Mohlabane, Goapele *See Goapele*

Moi, Daniel Arap 1924— **1, 35**

Mokae, Zakes 1934–2009 **80**

Mollel, Tololwa 1952— **38**

Monáe, Janelle 1985— **86**

Mongella, Gertrude 1945— **11**

Monica 1980— **21**

Mo'Nique 1967— **35, 84**

Monk, Art 1957— **38, 73**

Monk, Thelonious (Sphere, Jr.) 1917–1982 **1**

Monroe, Bryan 1965— **71**

Monroe, Earl 1944— **89**

Monroe, Mary 19(?)(?)— **35**

Montgomery, Isaiah T. 1847–1924 **91**

Montgomery, Tim 1975— **41**

Montgomery, Wes 1923–1968 **88**

Moody, James 1925— **83**

Moody, Ronald 1900–1984 **30**

Moody-Adams, Michele 1956— **76**

Moon, Warren 1956— **8, 66**

Mooney, Paul 19(?)(?)— **37**

Moore, Alice Ruth *See Dunbar-Nelson, Alice Ruth Moore*

Moore, Barbara C. 1949— **49**

Moore, Bobby *See Rashad, Ahmad*

Moore, Chante 1970(?)— **26**

Moore, Dorothy Rudd 1940— **46**

Moore, Gwendolynne S. 1951— **55**

Moore, Harry T. 1905–1951 **29**

Moore, Jessica Care 1971— **30**

Moore, Johnny B. 1950— **38**

Moore, Juanita 1922— **83**

Moore, Kevin *See Mo', Keb'*

Moore, LeRoi 1961–2008 **72**

Moore, Melba 1945— **21**

Moore, Minyon 19(?)(?)— **45**

Moore, Richard *See bin Wahad, Dhoruba*

Moore, Shemar 1970— **21**

Moore, Undine Smith 1904–1989 **28**

Moore, Wes 1978— **86**

Moorer, Lana *See MC Lyte*

Moorer, Michael 1967— **19**

Moose, Charles 1953— **40**

Morales, Mark 1960— *See Fat Boys*

Moran, Jason 1975— **89**

Morgan, Garrett (Augustus) 1877–1963 **1**

Morgan, Gertrude 1900–1986 **63**

Morgan, Irene 1917–2007 **65**

Morgan, Joe Leonard 1943— **9**

Morgan, Rose (Meta) 1912(?)— **11**

Morgan, Tracy 1968— **61**

Morganfield, McKinley *See Muddy Waters*

Morial, Ernest "Dutch" 1929–1989 **26**

Morial, Marc H. 1958— **20, 51**

Morón, Alonzo G. 1909–1971 **91**

Morris, Garrett 1937— **31**

Morris, Greg 1934–1996 **28**

Morris, Nathan *See Boyz II Men*

Morris, Raheem 1976— **77**

Morris, Wanya *See Boyz II Men*

Morris, William "Bill" 1938— **51**

Morris, Stevland Judkins *See Wonder, Stevie*

Morrison, Keith 1942— **13**

Morrison, Mary Thelma *See Washington, Mary T.*

Morrison, Sam 1936— **50**

Morrison, Toni 1931— **2, 15, 86**

Morrison, Vanessa 1969(?)— **84**

Morton, Azie Taylor 1936–2003 **48**

Morton, Ferdinand Q. 1881–1949 **90**

Morton, Frederick A., Jr. 1967(?)— **93**

Morton, Jelly Roll 1885(?)–1941 **29**

Morton, Joe 1947— **18**

Mos Def 1973— **30**

Moseley-Braun, Carol *See Braun, Carol Moseley*

Moses, Edwin 1955— **8**

Moses, Gilbert, III 1942–1995 **12**

Moses, Robert Parris 1935— **11**

Mosley, "Sugar" Shane 1971— **32**

Mosley, Tim *See Timbaland*

Mosley, Walter 1952— **5, 25, 68**

Moss, Bryant *See Moss, Preacher*

Moss, Carlton 1909–1997 **17**

Moss, J. (?)— **64**

Moss, Otis, Jr. 1935— **72**

Moss, Otis, III 1971(?)— **72**

Moss, Preacher 1967— **63**

Moss, Randy 1977— **23, 90**

Moss, Shad Gregory *See Lil' Bow Wow*

Mossell, Gertrude Bustill 1855–1948 **40**

Mossell, Nathan Francis 1856–1946 **91**

Moten, Etta *See Barnett, Etta Moten*

Motlanthe, Kgalema 1949— **74**

Motley, Archibald, Jr. 1891–1981 **30**

Motley, Constance Baker 1921–2005 **10, 55**

Motley, Marion 1920–1999 **26**

Moton, Robert Russa 1867–1940 **83**

Moura, Paulo 1932–2010 **87**

Mourning, Alonzo 1970— **17, 44**

Moutoussamy-Ashe, Jeanne 1951— **7**

Mowatt, Judy 1952(?)— **38**

Mowry, Jess 1960— **7**

Mowry, Tamera 1978— **79**

Mowry, Tia 1978— **78**

Moyo, Dambisa 1970(?)— **76**

Moyo, Karega Kofi 19(?)(?)— **36**

Moyo, Lovemore 1965— **76**

Moyo, Yvette Jackson 1953— **36**

Mphalele, Es'kia (Ezekiel) 1919— **40**

Mswati III 1968— **56**

Mudimbe, V. Y. 1941— **61**

Mugabe, Robert 1924— **10, 71**

Mugo, Madeleine *See Mugo, Micere Githae*

Mugo, Micere Githae 1942— **32**

Muhajir, El *See X, Marvin*

Muhammad, Ava 1951— **31**

Muhammad, Elijah 1897–1975 **4**

Muhammad, Jabir Herbert 1929–2008 **72**

Muhammad, Khallid Abdul 1951(?)— **10, 31**

Mukoko, Jestina 1957(?)— **75**

Mullen, Harryette 1953— **34**

Mullen, Nicole C. 1967— **45**

Muluzi, Bakili 1943— **14, 76**

Mumba, Samantha 1983— **29**

Mundine, Anthony 1975— **56**

Murphy, Eddie 1961— **4, 20, 61**

Murphy, Edward Regan *See Murphy, Eddie*

Murphy, John H. 1916— **42**

Murphy, Laura M. 1955— **43**

Murphy McKenzie, Vashti *See McKenzie, Vashti M.*

Murray, Albert L. 1916— **33**

Murray, Cecil 1929— **12, 47**

Murray, Eddie 1956— **12**

Murray, Lenda 1962— **10**

Murray, Pauli 1910–1985 **38**

Murray, Tai 1982— **47**

Murrell, Sylvia Marilyn 1947— **49**

Muse, Clarence Edouard 1889–1979 **21**

Museveni, Yoweri (Kaguta) 1944(?)— **4**

Mushikiwabo, Louise 1961— **88**

Musiq 1977— **37, 84**

Mutebi, Ronald 1956— **25**

Mutola, Maria de Lurdes 1972— **12**

Mutombo, Dikembe 1966— **7**

Mutu, Wangechi 19(?)(?)— **44**

Muzorewa, Abel 1925–2010 **85**

Mwanawasa, Levy 1948–2008 **72**

Mwangi, Meja 1948— **40**

Mwinyi, Ali Hassan 1925— **1, 77**

Mya 1979— **35**

Myers, Dwight *See Heavy D*

Myers, Walter Dean 1937— **8, 70**

Myers, Walter Milton *See Myers, Walter Dean*

Myles, Kim 1974— **69**

Myrie, Mark Anthony *See Banton, Buju*

Nabrit, Samuel Milton 1905–2003 **47**

Nagin, Ray 1956— **42, 57, 88**

Nail, John E. 1883–1947 **92**

Najm, Faheem Rasheed *See T-Pain*

Nakhid, David 1964— **25**

Naki, Hamilton 1926–2005 **63**

Nance, Cynthia 1958— **71**

Nanula, Richard D. 1960— **20**

Napoleon, Benny N. 1956(?)— **23**

Nas 1973— **33**

Nascimento, Abdias do 1914–2011 **93**

Nascimento, Milton 1942— **2, 64**

Nash, Diane 1938— **72**

Nash, Joe 1919–2005 **55**

Nash, Johnny 1940— **40**

Nash, Niecy 1970— **66**

Nash, Shannon King 1971— **84**

Nash, Terius Youngdell *See The-Dream*

Nate Dogg 1969–2011 **92**

Naylor, Gloria 1950— **10, 42**

Nazario, Zoe Yadira Zaldaña *See Saldana, Zoe*

Ndadaye, Melchior 1953–1993 **7**

Ndegeocello, Meshell 1968— **15, 83**

Ndiaye, Iba 1928–2008 **74**

N'Dour, Youssou 1959— **1, 53, 79**

Ndungane, Winston Njongonkulu 1941— **16**

Neal, Elise 1970— **29**

Neal, Larry 1937–1981 **38**

Neal, Mark Anthony 1965(?)— **74**

Neal, Raful 1936— **44**

Neale, Haydain 1970— **52**

Neals, Otto 1930— **73**

Nelly 1974— **32, 90**

Nelson, Jill 1952— **6, 54**

Nelson, Prince Rogers *See Prince*

Nelson, Sophia A. 1967— **93**

Nelson, Stanley 1951— **92**

Nelson Meigs, Andrea 1968— **48**

Neto, António Agostinho 1922— **43**

Nettles, Marva Deloise *See Collins, Marva*

Neverson, Tremaine Aldon *See Songz, Trey*

Neville, Aaron 1941— **21**

Neville, Arthel 1962— **53**

Newcombe, Don 1926— **24**

Newkirk, Pamela 1957— **69**

Newman, David 1933–2009 **76**

Newman, Lester C. 1952— **51**

Newsome, Ozzie 1956— **26**

Newton, Huey (Percy) 1942–1989 **2**

Newton, Thandie 1972— **26**

Ne-Yo 1982— **65**

Ngaujah, Sahr 1976— **86**

Ngengi, Kamau wa See Kenyatta, Jomo
Ngilu, Charity 1952— 58
Ngubane, (Baldwin Sipho) Ben 1941— 33
Ngugi wa Thiong'o 1938— 29, 61
Ngugi, James wa Thiong'o See Ngugi wa Thiong'o
Niane, Katoucha 1960–2008 70
Nicholas, Denise 1944— 82
Nicholas, Fayard 1914–2006 20, 57, 61
Nicholas, Harold 1921— 20
Nichols, Grace See Nichols, Nichelle
Nichols, James Thomas See Bell, James "Cool Papa"
Nichols, Nichelle 1933(?)— 11
Nissel, Angela 1974— 42
Nix, Robert N. C., Jr. 1928–2003 51
Njawe, Pius 1957–2010 87
Njongonkulu, Winston Ndungane 1941— 16
Nkoli, Simon 1957–1998 60
Nkomo, Joshua 1917–1999 4, 65
Nkosi, Lewis 1936— 46
Nkrumah, Kwame 1909–1972 3
Nkunda, Laurent 1967— 75
Nkurunziza, Pierre 1963— 78
N'Namdi, George R. 1946— 17
Noah, Yannick 1960— 4, 60
Noble, Gil 1932— 76
Noble, Reginald See Redman
Noble, Ronald 1957— 46
Norman, Christina 1960(?)— 47
Norman, Jessye 1945— 5
Norman, Maidie 1912–1998 20
Norman, Pat 1939— 10
Norris, Michele 1961— 83
Norton, Eleanor Holmes 1937— 7, 93
Norton, Meredith 1970(?)— 72
Norwood, Brandy See Brandy
Norwood, William Raymond, Jr. See Ray J
Notorious B.I.G. 1972–1997 20
Nottage, Cynthia DeLores See Tucker, C. DeLores
Nottage, Lynn 1964— 66
Nour, Nawal M. 1965(?)— 56
Ntaryamira, Cyprien 1955–1994 8
Ntshona, Winston 1941— 52
Nugent, Richard Bruce 1906–1987 39
Nujoma, Samuel 1929— 10
Nunez, Elizabeth 1944(?)— 62
Nunn, Annetta 1959— 43
Nutter, Michael 1958— 69
Nuttin' but Stringz See Escobar, Tourie, and Escobar, Damien
Nyanda, Siphiwe 1950— 21
Nyerere, Julius (Kambarage) 1922— 5
Nzo, Alfred (Baphethuxolo) 1925— 15
Obadele, Imari 1930–2010 84
Obama, Barack 1961— 49, 74, 91
Obama, Michelle 1964— 61, 90
Obasanjo, Olusegun 1937— 5, 22
Obasanjo, Stella 1945–2005 32, 56
Obote, Milton 1925–2005 63
O'Brien, Soledad 1966— 88
ODB See Ol' Dirty Bastard

Odetta 1930— 37, 74
Odinga, Raila 1945— 67
Odom, Lamar 1979— 81
Oglesby, Zena 1947— 12
Ogletree, Charles, Jr. 1952— 12, 47
O'Grady, Lorraine 1934— 73
Ogunlesi, Adebayo O. 19(?)(?)— 37
Ojikutu, Bayo 1971— 66
Ojikutu, Bisola 1974— 65
Okaalet, Peter 1953— 58
Okara, Gabriel 1921— 37
Okonedo, Sophie 1969— 67
Okosuns, Sonny 1947–2008 71
Ol' Dirty Bastard 1968–2004 52
Olajuwon, Akeem See Olajuwon, Hakeem
Olajuwon, Hakeem 1963— 2, 72
Olatunji, Babatunde 1927— 36
Olden, Georg(e) 1920–1975 44
O'Leary, Hazel (Rollins) 1937— 6
Oliver, Jerry 1947— 37
Oliver, Joe "King" 1885–1938 42
Oliver, John J., Jr. 1945— 48
Oliver, Kimberly 1976— 60
Oliver, Pam 1961— 54
Olojede, Dele 1961— 59
Olopade, Olufunmilayo Falusi 1957(?)— 58
O'Neal, Rodney 1954— 88
O'Neal, Ron 1937–2004 46
O'Neal, Shaquille (Rashaun) 1972— 8, 30
O'Neal, Stanley 1951— 38, 67
O'Neil, Buck 1911–2006 19, 59
O'Neil, John Jordan See O'Neil, Buck
Ongala, Ramadhani Mtoro See Ongala, Remmy
Ongala, Remmy 1947–2010 9, 91
Onwueme, Tess Osonye 1955— 23
Onwurah, Ngozi 1966(?)— 38
Onyewu, Oguchi 1982— 60
Orange, James 1942–2008 74
O'Ree, William Eldon See O'Ree, Willie
O'Ree, Willie 1935— 5
Orlandersmith, Dael 1959— 42
Orman, Roscoe 1944— 55
Ormes, Jackie 1911–1985 73
Ortiz, David 1975— 52, 82
Osborne, Jeffrey 1948— 26
Osborne, Na'taki 1974— 54
Otis, Clarence, Jr. 1956— 55
Otis, Clyde 1924— 67
Otunga, Maurice Michael 1923–2003 55
Ouattara 1957— 43
Ouattara, Alassane 1942— 90
Ouattara, Morou 1966— 74
Ousley, Curtis See King Curtis
Ousmane, Sembène See Sembène, Ousmane
OutKast 35
Owens, Dana See Queen Latifah
Owens, Helen 1937— 48
Owens, J. C. See Owens, Jesse
Owens, Jack 1904–1997 38
Owens, James Cleveland See Owens, Jesse
Owens, Jesse 1913–1980 2
Owens, Major (Robert) 1936— 6

Owens, Terrell 1973— 53
Oyelowo, David 1976— 82
Oyono, Ferdinand 1929— 38
P. Diddy See Combs, Sean
Pace, Betty 1954— 59
Pace, Orlando 1975— 21
Packer, Daniel 1947— 56
Packer, Will 1974(?)— 71
Packer, Z. Z. 1973— 64
Page, Alan (Cedric) 1945— 7
Page, Clarence 1947— 4
Page, Greg 1958–2009 78
Page, Inman 1853–1935 82
Paige, Leroy Robert See Paige, Satchel
Paige, Rod 1933— 29
Paige, Satchel 1906–1982 7
Painter, Nell Irvin 1942— 24, 88
Palmer, Everard 1930— 37
Palmer, Keke 1993— 68
Palmer, Rissi 1981— 65
Palmer, Violet 1964— 59
Papa Wendo See Kolosoy, Wendo
Parham, Marjorie B. 1918— 71
Parish, Robert 1953— 43
Parker, Barrington D. 1915–1993 92
Parker, Candace 1986— 74
Parker, Charlie 1920–1955 20
Parker, Jim 1934–2005 64
Parker, Kellis E. 1942–2000 30
Parker, (Lawrence) Kris(hna) See KRS-One
Parker, LarStella Irby See Parker, Star
Parker, Maceo 1943— 72
Parker, Nicole Ari 1970— 52
Parker, Ray, Jr. 1954— 85
Parker, Star 1956— 70
Parker, Tony 1982— 75
Parks, Bernard C. 1943— 17
Parks, Gordon 1912–2006 1, 35, 58
Parks, Henry Green, Jr. 1916–1989 89
Parks, Rosa 1913–2005 1, 35, 56
Parks, Suzan-Lori 1963— 34, 85
Parr, Russ 196(?)— 51
Parsons, James Benton 1911–1993 14
Parsons, Richard Dean 1948— 11, 33
Pascal-Trouillot, Ertha 1943— 3
Paterson, Basil A. 1926— 69
Paterson, David A. 1954— 59
Patillo, Melba Joy 1941— 15
Patrick, Deval 1956— 12, 61
Patterson, Floyd 1935–2006 19, 58
Patterson, Frederick Douglass 1901–1988 12
Patterson, Gilbert Earl 1939— 41
Patterson, J. O., Jr. 1935— 80
Patterson, Louise 1901–1999 25
Patterson, Mary Jane 1840–1894 54
Patterson, Orlando 1940— 4
Patterson, P(ercival) J(ames) 1936(?)— 6, 20
Patterson, Robert, Jr. See Ali, Rashied
Patton, Antwan 1975— 45
Patton, Antwan "Big Boi" 1975(?)— See OutKast
Patton, Paula 1975— 62

Paul, Chris 1985— 84
Payne, Allen 1962(?)— 13
Payne, Donald M. 1934— 2, 57
Payne, Ethel L. 1911–1991 28
Payne, Freda 1942— 58
Payne, Les 1941— 89
Payne, Ulice 1955— 42
Payne, William D. 1932— 60
Payton, Benjamin F. 1932— 23
Payton, John 1946— 48
Payton, Philip A., Jr. 1876–1917 88
Payton, Walter (Jerry) 1954–1999 11, 25
Pearman, Raven-Symone Christina See Raven
Peck, Carolyn 1966(?)— 23
Peck, Raoul 1953— 32
Peete, Calvin 1943— 11
Peete, Holly Robinson 1965— 20
Peete, Rodney 1966— 60
Pelé 1940— 7
Pena, Paul 1950–2005 58
Pendergrass, Teddy 1950–2010 22, 83
Penniman, Richard Wayne See Little Richard
Peoples, Dottie 19(?)(?)— 22
Pereira, Aristides 1923— 30
Perez, Anna 1951— 1
Perkins, Anthony 1959(?)— 24
Perkins, Edward (Joseph) 1928— 5
Perkins, James, Jr. 1953(?)— 55
Perkins, Joe Willie See Perkins, Pinetop
Perkins, Marion 1908–1961 38
Perkins, Pinetop 1913— 70
Perren, Freddie 1943–2004 60
Perrineau, Harold, Jr. 1968— 51
Perrot, Kim 1967–1999 23
Perry, Emmitt, Jr. See Perry, Tyler
Perry, Herman 1922–1945 89
Perry, James 1975— 83
Perry, Laval 195(?)— 64
Perry, Lee "Scratch" 1936— 19
Perry, Lincoln See Fetchit, Stepin
Perry, Lowell 1931–2001 30
Perry, Rainford Hugh See Perry, Lee "Scratch"
Perry, Ruth 1936— 19
Perry, Ruth Sando 1939— 15
Perry, Tyler 1969— 40, 54
Perry, Warren 1942(?)— 56
Person, Waverly 1927— 9, 51
Peters, Lenrie 1932— 43
Peters, Margaret 1915— 43
Peters, Maria Philomena 1941— 12
Peters, Matilda 1917— 43
Petersen, Frank E. 1932— 31
Peterson, Hannibal See Peterson, Marvin
Peterson, James 19(?)(?)— 81
Peterson, James 1937— 38
Peterson, Jesse Lee 1949— 81
Peterson, Karen Carter 1969— 90
Peterson, Marvin 1948— 27
Peterson, Oscar 1925— 52
Petry, Ann 1909–1997 19
Phifer, Mekhi 1975— 25
Philip, M. Nourbese See Philip, Marlene Nourbese
Philip, Marlene Nourbese 1947— 32
Phillips, Charles E., Jr. 1959— 57

Phillips, Helen L. 1919–2005 **63**
Phillips, Joseph C. 1962— **73**
Phillips, Teresa L. 1958— **42**
Phipps, Wintley 1955— **59**
Pickens, James, Jr. 1954— **59**
Pickett, Bill 1870–1932 **11**
Pickett, Cecil 1945— **39**
Pierce, Elijah 1892–1984 **84**
Pierce, Harold 1917-1988 **75**
Pierce, Paul 1977— **71**
Pierce, Wendell 1962— **90**
Pierre, Andre 1915— **17**
Pierre, Percy Anthony 1939— **46**
Pierre-Louis, Michèle 1947— **75**
Pincham, R. Eugene, Sr. 1925–2008 **69**
Pinchback, P(inckney) B(enton) S(tewart) 1837–1921 **9**
Pinckney, Bill 1935— **42**
Pinckney, Sandra 194(?)— **56**
Pindell, Howardena 1943— **55**
Pinder, Jefferson 1970— **77**
Pinderhughes, John 1946— **47**
Pindling, Lynden 1930–2000 **81**
Pinkett, Jada See Pinkett Smith, Jada
Pinkett, Randal 1971— **61**
Pinkett Smith, Jada 1971— **10, 41**
Pinkney, Fayette 1948–2009 **80**
Pinkney, Jerry 1939— **15**
Pinkston, W. Randall 1950— **24**
Pinn, Vivian Winona 1941— **49**
Piper, Adrian 1948— **71**
Pippen, Scottie 1965— **15, 89**
Pippin, Horace 1888–1946 **9**
Pitt, David Thomas 1913–1994 **10**
Pitta (do Nascimento), Celso (Roberto) 19(?)(?)— **17**
Pitts, Byron 1960— **71**
Pitts, Derrick 1956(?)— **77**
Pitts, Leonard, Jr. 1957— **54, 85**
Pitts, Robb 1941— **84**
Pitts, Robert Lee See Pitts, Robb
Plaatje, Sol. T. 1876–1932 **80**
Player, Willa B. 1909–2003 **43**
Pleasant, Mary Ellen 1814–1904 **9**
Pleasure P 1984— **84**
Plessy, Homer Adolph 1862–1925 **31**
P.M. Dawn, **54**
Poindexter, Hildrus A. 1901–1987 **87**
Poitier, Sidney 1927— **11, 36**
Poitier, Sydney Tamiia 1973— **65**
Polite, Carlene Hatcher 1932–2009 **82**
Pollard, Fritz 1894–1986 **53**
Pollard, William L. 1945(?)— **91**
Pomare, Eleo 1937–2008 **72**
Poole, Elijah See Muhammad, Elijah
Pope.L, William 1955— **72**
Porter, Countee Leroy See Cullin, Countee
Porter, Dorothy See Wesley, Dorothy Porter
Porter, James A(mos) 1905–1970 **11**
Porter, Terry 1963— **75**
Portuondo, Omara 1930— **53**
Potter, Myrtle 1958— **40**
Pough, Terrell 1987(?)–2005 **58**

Pounder, Carol Christine Hilaria See Pounder, CCH
Pounder, CCH 1952— **72**
Poussaint, Alvin F. 1934— **5, 67**
Poussaint, Renee 1944— **78**
Powell, Adam Clayton, Jr. 1908–1972 **3**
Powell, Benny 1930–2010 **87**
Powell, Bud 1924–1966 **24**
Powell, Colin 1937— **1, 28, 75**
Powell, Debra A. 1964— **23**
Powell, Kevin 1966— **31, 74**
Powell, Maxine 1924— **8**
Powell, Michael Anthony See Powell, Mike
Powell, Michael K. 1963— **32**
Powell, Mike 1963— **7**
Powell, Renee 1946— **34**
Powell, William J. 1916–2009 **82**
Power, Will 1970— **83**
Pratt, Awadagin 1966— **31**
Pratt, Geronimo 1947— **18**
Pratt, Kyla 1986— **57**
Pratt Dixon, Sharon See Dixon, Sharon Pratt
Preer, Evelyn 1896–1932 **82**
Premice, Josephine 1926–2001 **41**
Pressley, Condace L. 1964— **41**
Preston, Billy 1946–2006 **39, 59**
Preston, William Everett See Preston, Billy
Préval, René 1943— **87**
Price, Florence 1887–1953 **37**
Price, Frederick K.C. 1932— **21**
Price, Glenda 1939— **22**
Price, Hugh B. 1941— **9, 54**
Price, Kelly 1973(?)— **23**
Price, Leontyne 1927— **1**
Price, Richard 1930(?)— **51**
Pride, Charley 1938(?)— **26**
Primus, Pearl 1919— **6**
Prince 1958— **18, 65**
Prince, Richard E. 1947— **71**
Prince, Ron 1969— **64**
Prince, Tayshaun 1980— **68**
Prince Markie Dee See Fat Boys
Prince-Bythewood, Gina 1969— **31, 77**
Pritchard, Robert Starling 1927— **21**
Procope, Ernesta 19(?)(?)— **23**
Procope, John Levy 1925–2005 **56**
Prophet, Nancy Elizabeth 1890–1960 **42**
Prothrow, Deborah Boutin See Prothrow-Stith, Deborah
Prothrow-Stith, Deborah 1954— **10**
Pryce, Trevor 1975— **89**
Pryor, Rain 1969— **65**
Pryor, Richard 1940–2005 **3, 24, 56**
Puckett, Kirby 1960–2006 **4, 58**
Puff Daddy See Combs, Sean
Pugh, Charles 197199— **81**
Purdie, Bernard 1939— **77**
Purnell, Silas 1923–2003 **59**
Puryear, Martin 1941— **42**
Putney, Martha S. 1916–2008 **75**
Quarles, Benjamin Arthur 1904–1996 **18**
Quarles, Norma 1936— **25**
Quarterman, Lloyd Albert 1918–1982 **4**
Queen Latifah 1970— **1, 16, 58**

Querino, Manuel Raimundo 1851–1923 **84**
?uestlove 1971— **74**
Quigless, Helen G. 1944–2004 **49**
Quince, Peggy A. 1948— **69**
Quirot, Ana (Fidelia) 1963— **13**
Quivers, Robin 1952— **61**
Rabb, Maurice F., Jr. 1932–2005 **58**
Rabia, Aliyah See Staton, Dakota
Radcliffe, Ted 1902–2005 **74**
Radcliffe, Theodore Roosevelt See Radcliffe, Ted
Ragin, Derek Lee 1958— **84**
Rahman, Aishah 1936— **37**
Raines, Franklin Delano 1949— **14**
Rainey, Ma 1886–1939 **33**
Ralph, Sheryl Lee 1956— **18**
Ramaphosa, (Matamela) Cyril 1952— **3**
Rambough, Lori Ann See Sommore
Ramphele, Mamphela 1947— **29**
Ramsey, Charles H. 1948— **21, 69**
Rand, A(ddison) Barry 1944— **6**
Randall, Alice 1959— **38**
Randall, Dudley 1914–2000 **8, 55**
Randle, John 1967— **87**
Randle, Theresa 1967— **16**
Randolph, A(sa) Philip 1889–1979 **3**
Randolph, Linda A. 1941— **52**
Randolph, Willie 1954— **53**
Rangel, Charles B. 1930— **3, 52, 85**
Ranglin, Ernest 1932— **78**
Rankin Don See Rhoden, Wayne
Ransome, James E. 1961— **88**
Raoul, Kwame 1964— **55**
Rapier, James T. 1837–1883 **82**
Ras Tafari See Haile Selassie
Rascal, Dizzee 1985— **82**
Rashad, Ahmad 1949— **18**
Rashad, Phylicia 1948— **21**
Raspberry, William 1935— **2**
Raven, 1985— **44**
Raven-Symone See Raven
Rawlings, Jerry (John) 1947— **9**
Rawlings-Blake, Stephanie 1970— **93**
Rawlinson, Johnnie B. 1952— **79**
Rawls, Lou 1936–2006 **17, 57**
Ray, Charlotte E. 1850–1911 **60**
Ray, Gene Anthony 1962–2003 **47**
Ray J 1981— **86**
Raymond, Usher, IV See Usher
Razaf, Andy 1895–1973 **19**
Razafkeriefo, Andreamentania Paul See Razaf, Andy
Ready, Stephanie 1975— **33**
Reagon, Bernice Johnson 1942— **7**
Reagon, Toshi 1964— **76**
Reason, Joseph Paul 1943— **19**
Record, Eugene 1940–2005 **60**
Redd, Dana 1968— **93**
Reddick, Lance 19(?)(?)— **52**
Reddick, Lawrence Dunbar 1910–1995 **20**
Redding, Ann Holmes 1951— **77**
Redding, J. Saunders 1906–1988 **26**
Redding, Louis L. 1901–1998 **26**
Redding, Otis, Jr. 1941— **16**
Redman 1970— **81**
Redman, Joshua 1969— **30**

Redmond, Eugene 1937— **23**
Redwood, John Henry 1942–2003 **78**
Reece, E. Albert 1950— **63**
Reed, A. C. 1926— **36**
Reed, Alaina See Reed Hall, Alaina
Reed, Ishmael 1938— **8**
Reed, Jimmy 1925–1976 **38**
Reed, Kasim 1969— **82**
Reed, Willis, Jr. 1942— **86**
Reed Amini, Alaina See Reed Hall, Alaina
Reed Hall, Alaina 1946–2009 **83**
Reems, Ernestine Cleveland 1932— **27**
Reese, Calvin See Reese, Pokey
Reese, Della 1931— **6, 20**
Reese, Milous J., Jr. 1904— **51**
Reese, Pokey 1973— **28**
Reese, Tracy 1964— **54**
Reeves, Dianne 1956— **32**
Reeves, Gregory 1952— **49**
Reeves, Martha 1941— **85**
Reeves, Rachel J. 1950(?)— **23**
Reeves, Triette Lipsey 1963— **27**
Regis, Cyrille 1958— **51**
Reid, Antonio "L.A." 1958(?)— **28**
Reid, Irvin D. 1941— **20**
Reid, L.A. See Reid, Antonio "L.A."
Reid, Senghor 1976— **55**
Reid, Tim 1944— **56**
Reid, Vernon 1958— **34**
Reivers, Corbin Bleu See Corbin Bleu
Reuben, Gloria 19(?)(?)— **15**
Rev Run See Run; Run-DMC
Reverend Ike 1935–2009 **79**
Reynolds, Harold 1960— **77**
Reynolds, Star Jones 1962(?)— **10, 27, 61**
Rhames, Ving 1959— **14, 50**
Rhimes, Shonda Lynn 1970— **67**
Rhoden, Dwight 1962— **40**
Rhoden, Wayne 1966— **70**
Rhoden, William C. 1950(?)— **67**
Rhodes, Jewell Parker 1954— **84**
Rhodes, Ray 1950— **14**
Rhone, Sylvia 1952— **2**
Rhone, Trevor 1940–2009 **80**
Rhymes, Busta 1972— **31**
Ribbs, William Theodore, Jr. See Ribbs, Willy T.
Ribbs, Willy T. 1956— **2**
Ribeau, Sidney 1947(?)— **70**
Ribeiro, Alfonso 1971— **17**
Rice, Condoleezza 1954— **3, 28, 72**
Rice, Constance LaMay 1956— **60**
Rice, Jerry 1962— **5, 55, 89**
Rice, Jim 1953— **75**
Rice, Linda Johnson 1958— **9, 41**
Rice, Louise Allen 1941— **54**
Rice, Norm(an Blann) 1943— **8**
Rice, Susan E. 1964— **74**
Richard, Dawn 1983— **92**
Richard, J. R. 1950— **87**
Richards, Beah 1926–2000 **30**
Richards, Hilda 1936— **49**
Richards, Lloyd 1923(?)— **2**
Richards, Sanya 1985— **66**
Richardson, Desmond 1969— **39**
Richardson, Donna 1962— **39**

Richardson, Elaine Potter See Kincaid, Jamaica
Richardson, Julieanna 1954— 81
Richardson, LaTanya 1949— 71
Richardson, Laura 1962— 81
Richardson, Nolan 1941— 9
Richardson, Pat See Norman, Pat
Richardson, Rupert 1930–2008 67
Richardson, Salli 1967— 68
Richie, Leroy C. 1941— 18
Richie, Lionel 1949— 27, 65
Richmond, Cedric 1973— 93
Richmond, Mitchell James 1965— 19
Rideau, Iris 1940(?)— 46
Ridenhour, Carlton See Chuck D.
Ridley, John 1965— 69
Riggs, Marlon 1957–1994 5, 44
Rihanna 1988— 65
Riles, Wilson C. 1917–1999 79
Riley, Boots 1971— 89
Riley, Helen Caldwell Day 1926— 13
Riley, Rochelle 1959(?)— 50
Rillieux, Norbert 1806–1894 92
Ringgold, Faith 1930— 4, 81
Riperton, Minnie 1947–1979 32
Rivers, Doc 1961— 25, 81
Rivers, Eugene F., III 1950— 81
Rivers, Glenn See Rivers, Doc
Rivers, Kim See Roberts, Kimberly Rivers
Roach, Max 1924–2007 21, 63
Roberto, Holden 1923–2007 65
Roberts, Darryl 1962(?)— 70
Roberts, Deborah 1960— 35
Roberts, Ian See Kwei-Armah, Kwame
Roberts, James See Lover, Ed
Roberts, Kimberly Rivers 1981(?)— 72
Roberts, Kristina LaFerne See Zane
Roberts, Lillian 1928— 83
Roberts, Marcus 1963— 19
Roberts, Marthaniel See Roberts, Marcus
Roberts, Mike 1948— 57
Roberts, Robin 1960— 16, 54
Roberts, Roy S. 1939(?)— 14
Roberts, William Leonard, II See Ross, Rick
Robertson, Gil L., IV 1964— 85
Robertson, Oscar 1938— 26
Robeson, Eslanda Goode 1896–1965 13
Robeson, Paul (Leroy Bustill) 1898–1976 2
Robinson, Aminah 1940— 50
Robinson, Bill "Bojangles" 1878–1949 11
Robinson, Bishop L. 1927— 66
Robinson, Cleo Parker 1948(?)— 38
Robinson, Darren 1967–1995 See Fat Boys
Robinson, David 1965— 24, 90
Robinson, Eddie G. 1919–2007 10, 61
Robinson, Eugene 1955— 77
Robinson, Fatima 19(?)(?)— 34
Robinson, Fenton 1935–1997 38
Robinson, Frank 1935— 9, 87

Robinson, Jack Roosevelt See Robinson, Jackie
Robinson, Jackie 1919–1972 6
Robinson, LaVaughn 1927–2008 69
Robinson, Luther See Robinson, Bill "Bojangles"
Robinson, Malcolm S. 1948— 44
Robinson, Matt 1937–2002 69
Robinson, Matthew, Jr. See Robinson, Matt
Robinson, Max 1939–1988 3
Robinson, Patrick 1966— 19, 71
Robinson, Rachel 1922— 16
Robinson, Randall 1941— 7, 46
Robinson, Reginald R. 1972— 53
Robinson, Sharon 1950— 22
Robinson, Shaun 19(?)(?)— 36
Robinson, Smokey 1940— 3, 49
Robinson, Spottswood W., III 1916–1998 22
Robinson, Sugar Ray 1921— 18
Robinson, Sylvia 1936— 79
Robinson, Will 1911–2008 51, 69
Robinson, William, Jr. See Robinson, Smokey
Roble, Abdi 1964— 71
Roby, Kimberla Lawson 1965— 86
Roche, Joyce M. 1947— 17
Rochester See Anderson, Eddie "Rochester"
Rochon, Lela 1965(?)— 16
Rochon, Stephen W. 1950(?)— 78
Rock, Chris 1967(?)— 3, 22, 66
Rock, The 1972— 29, 66
Rodgers, Johnathan 1946— 6, 51
Rodgers, Rod 1937–2002 36
Rodman, Dennis 1961— 12, 44
Rodney, Winston See Burning Spear
Rodrigues, Percy 1918–2007 68
Rodríguez, Arsenio 1911–1970 87
Rodriguez, Jimmy 1963(?)— 47
Rodriguez, Cheryl 1952— 64
Rogers, Alan G. 1967–2008 72
Rogers, Desirée 1959— 88
Rogers, Jimmy 1924–1997 38
Rogers, Joe 1964— 27
Rogers, Joel Augustus 1883(?)–1996 30
Rogers, John W., Jr. 1958— 5, 52
Rogers, Kelis See Kelis
Rojas, Don 1949— 33
Roker, Al 1954— 12, 49
Roker, Roxie 1929–1995 68
Rolle, Esther 1920–1998 13, 21
Rollins, Charlemae Hill 1897–1979 27
Rollins, Howard E., Jr. 1950–1996 16
Rollins, Ida Gray Nelson See Gray (Nelson Rollins), Ida
Rollins, James Calvin, III See Rollins, Jimmy
Rollins, Jimmy 1978— 70
Rollins, Sonny 1930— 37
Ronaldinho 1980— 69
Rooakhptah, Amunnubi See York, Dwight D.
Rose, Anika Noni 1972— 70
Rose, Derrick 1988— 82
Rose, Lionel 1948— 56
Ross, Araminta See Tubman, Harriet
Ross, Charles 1957— 27

Ross, Diana 1944— 8, 27
Ross, Don 1941— 29
Ross, Isaiah "Doc" 1925–1993 40
Ross, Rick 1976— 79
Ross, Tracee Ellis 1972— 35
Ross-Lee, Barbara 1942— 67
Rotimi, (Emmanuel Gladstone) Ola-(wale) 1938— 1
Roundtree, Dovey 1914— 80
Roundtree, Richard 1942— 27
Rouse, Cecilia 1963— 93
Rowan, Carl T(homas) 1925— 1, 30
Rowell, Victoria 1960— 13, 68
Roxanne Shante 1969— 33
Roy, Kenny 1990(?)— 51
Rubin, Chanda 1976— 37
Rucker, Darius 1966— 34, 74
Rudder, David 1953— 79
Rudolph, Maya 1972— 46
Rudolph, Wilma (Glodean) 1940— 4
Ruffin, Joseph Lee See Shakur, Yusef
Ruffin, Josephine St. Pierre 1842–1924 75
Ruffins, Kermit 1964— 85
Rugambwa, Laurean 1912–1997 20
Ruley, Ellis 1882–1959 38
Run 1964— 31, 73, 75
Run-DMC 31, 75
RuPaul 1960— 17, 91
Rusesabagina, Paul 1954— 60
Rush, Bobby 1940— 78
Rush, Bobby 1946— 26, 76
Rush, Otis 1934— 38
Rushen, Patrice 1954— 12
Rushing, Jimmy 1903–1972 37
Russell, Bill 1934— 8
Russell, Brenda 1944(?)— 52
Russell, Herman Jerome 1931(?)— 17
Russell, Nipsey 1924–2005 66
Russell, William Felton See Russell, Bill
Russell-McCloud, Patricia 1946— 17
Rust, Art, Jr. 1927–2010 83
Rustin, Bayard 1910–1987 4
RZA 1969— 80
Saar, Alison 1956— 16
Saar, Betye 1926— 80
Sabathia, Carsten Charles, Jr. See Sabathia, CC
Sabathia, CC 1980— 74
Sade 1959— 15, 92
Sadler, Joseph See Grandmaster Flash
Sadlier, Rosemary 19(?)(?)— 62
St. Jacques, Raymond 1930–1990 8
Saint James, Synthia 1949— 12
St. John, Kristoff 1966— 25
St. Julien, Marlon 1972— 29
St. Patrick, Mathew 1969— 48
Saldana, Zoe 1978— 72
Salih, Al-Tayyib 1929— 37
Sallee, Charles 1911— 38
Salter, Nikkole 1979(?)— 73
Salters, Alisia See Salters, Lisa
Salters, Lisa 1966(?)— 71
Salvador, Bryce 1976— 51
Samara, Noah 1956— 15

SAMO See Basquiat, Jean-Michel
Sample, Joe 1939— 51
Sampson, Charles 1957— 13
Sampson, Edith S(purlock) 1901–1979 4
Samuel, Sealhenry Olumide See Seal
Samuelsson, Marcus 1970— 53
Sanchez, Sonia 1934— 17, 51
Sanders, Angelia 1961(?)— 86
Sanders, Barry 1968— 1, 53
Sanders, Bob 1981— 72
Sanders, Deion (Luwynn) 1967— 4, 31
Sanders, Demond See Sanders, Bob
Sanders, Dori(nda) 1935— 8
Sanders, Joseph R(ichard, Jr.) 1954— 11
Sanders, Malika 1973— 48
Sanders, Pharoah 1940— 64
Sanders, Rose M. See Touré, Faya Ora Rose
Sanders, Satch 1938— 77
Sanders, Thomas Ernest See Sanders, Satch
Sands, Diana 1934–1973 87
Sané, Pierre Gabriel 1948–1998 21
Sanford, Isabel 1917–2004 53
Sanford, John Elroy See Foxx, Redd
Sangare, Oumou 1968— 18
Sanhá Malam Bacai 1947— 84
Sankara, Thomas 1949–1987 17
Sankoh, Foday 1937–2003 74
Santamaria, Mongo 1917–2003 81
Santiago-Hudson, Ruben 1956— 85
Santos de Freitas, Antonio Carlos See Brown, Carlinhos
Sapp, Marvin 1966(?)— 74
Sapp, Rhonda LaChanze See LaChanze
Sapp, Warren 1972— 38
Saro-Wiwa, Kenule 1941–1995 39
Satcher, David 1941— 7, 57
Satchmo See Armstrong, (Daniel) Louis
Savage, Augusta Christine 1892(?)–1962 12
Savimbi, Jonas (Malheiro) 1934–2002 2, 34
Sawyer, Amos 1945— 2
Sawyer, Eugene 1934–2008 81
Sayers, Gale 1943— 28
Sayles Belton, Sharon 1952(?)— 9, 16
Sbraga, Kevin 1979(?)— 88
Scantlebury, Janna 1984(?)— 47
Scantlebury-White, Velma 1955— 64
Scarlett, Millicent 1971— 49
Schmoke, Kurt 1949— 1, 48
Schomburg, Arthur Alfonso 1874–1938 9
Schomburg, Arturo Alfonso See Schomburg, Arthur Alfonso
Schultz, Michael A. 1938— 6
Schuyler, George Samuel 1895–1977 40
Schuyler, Philippa 1931–1967 50
Scott, C. A. 1908–2000 29
Scott, Coretta See King, Coretta Scott

Scott, Cornelius Adolphus *See Scott, C. A.*
Scott, David 1946— **41**
Scott, George 1929–2005 **55**
Scott, Harold Russell, Jr. 1935–2006 **61**
Scott, Hazel 1920–1981 **66**
Scott, Jill 1972— **29, 83**
Scott, John T. 1940–2007 **65**
Scott, "Little" Jimmy 1925— **48**
Scott, Milton 1956— **51**
Scott, Robert C. 1947— **23**
Scott, Stuart 1965— **34**
Scott, Tim 1965— **87**
Scott, Wendell Oliver, Sr. 1921–1990 **19**
Scruggs, Mary Elfrieda *See Williams, Mary Lou*
Scurry, Briana 1971— **27**
Seacole, Mary 1805–1881 **54**
Seal **14, 75**
Seale, Bobby 1936— **3**
Seale, Robert George *See Seale, Bobby*
Seals, Frank *See Seals, Son*
Seals, Son 1942–2004 **56**
Sears, Leah Ward 1955— **5, 79**
Sears, Stephanie 1964— **53**
Sears-Collins, Leah J(eanette) *See Sears, Leah Ward*
Sebree, Charles 1914–1985 **40**
Seele, Pernessa 1954— **46**
Selassie, Haile *See Haile Selassie*
Sembène, Ousmane 1923–2007 **13, 62**
Senghor, Augustin Diamacoune 1928–2007 **66**
Senghor, Léopold Sédar 1906–2001 **12, 66**
Sengstacke, John Herman Henry 1912–1997 **18**
Senior, Olive 1941— **37**
Senna, Danzy 1970— **93**
Sentamu, John 1949— **58**
Sermon, Erick 1968— **81**
Serrano, Andres 1951(?)— **3**
Sewell, Terri 1965— **93**
Shabazz, Attallah 1958— **6**
Shabazz, Betty 1936–1997 **7, 26**
Shabazz, Ilyasah 1962— **36**
Shadd, Abraham D. 1801–1882 **81**
Shaggy 1968— **31**
Shakespeare, Robbie 1953— *See Sly & Robbie*
Shakur, Afeni 1947— **67**
Shakur, Assata 1947— **6**
Shakur, Meshell Suihailia Bashir *See Ndegeocello, Meshell*
Shakur, Tupac Amaru 1971–1996 **14**
Shakur, Yusef 1973— **85**
Shange, Ntozake 1948— **8, 89**
Shank, Suzanne F. 1962(?)— **77**
Shannon, Randy 1966— **82**
Sharper, Darren 1975— **32**
Sharpton, Al 1954— **21**
Shavers, Cheryl 19(?)(?)— **31**
Shaw, Bernard 1940— **2, 28**
Shaw, William J. 1934— **30**
Sheard, Kierra "Kiki" 1987— **61**
Sheffey, Asa Bundy *See Hayden, Robert Earl*
Sheffield, Gary Antonian 1968— **16**
Shell, Art 1946— **1, 66**

Shelton, Paula Young 1961— **86**
Shepherd, Sherri 1970— **55**
Sherrod, Clayton 1944— **17**
Sherrod, Shirley 1948— **87**
Shider, Garry 1953–2010 **87**
Shinhoster, Earl 1950(?)–2000 **32**
Shipp, E. R. 1955— **15**
Shippen, John 1879–1968 **43**
Shirley, George I. 1934— **33**
Shockley, Ann Allen 1927— **84**
Shonibare, Yinka 1962— **58**
Short, Bobby 1924–2005 **52**
Short, Columbus 1982— **79**
Shorter, Wayne 1933— **75**
Shorty, Ras, I 1941–2000 **47**
Showers, Reggie 1964— **30**
Shropshire, Thomas B. 1925–2003 **49**
Shuttlesworth, Fred 1922— **47**
Sidibe, Gabourey 1983— **84**
Sifford, Charlie 1922— **4, 49**
Sigur, Wanda 1958— **44**
Siji 1971(?)— **56**
Silas, Paul 1943— **24**
Silva, Marina 1958— **80**
Silver, Horace 1928— **26**
Siméus, Dumas M. 1940— **25**
Simmons, Bob 1948— **29**
Simmons, E. Denise 19(?)(?)— **79**
Simmons, Gary 1964— **58**
Simmons, Henry 1970— **55**
Simmons, Jamal 1971— **72**
Simmons, Joseph *See Run; Run-DMC*
Simmons, Kimora Lee 1975— **51, 83**
Simmons, Russell 1957(?)— **1, 30**
Simmons, Ruth J. 1945— **13, 38**
Simone, Nina 1933–2003 **15, 41**
Simpson, Carole 1940— **6, 30**
Simpson, Lorna 1960— **4, 36**
Simpson, O. J. 1947— **15**
Simpson, Valerie 1946— **21**
Simpson-Hoffman, N'kenge 1975(?)— **52**
Simpson-Miller, Portia 1945— **62**
Sims, Howard "Sandman" 1917–2003 **48**
Sims, Lowery Stokes 1949— **27**
Sims, Naomi 1948–2009 **29, 79**
Sinbad 1957(?)— **1, 16**
Sinclair, Madge 1938–1995 **78**
Singletary, Mike 1958— **4, 76**
Singleton, John 1968— **2, 30**
Sinkford, Jeanne C. 1933— **13**
Sir Mix-A-Lot 1963— **82**
Sirleaf, Ellen Johnson 1938— **71**
Sisqo 1976— **30**
Sissle, Noble 1889–1975 **29**
Sister Souljah 1964— **11**
Sisulu, Albertina 1918— **57**
Sisulu, Sheila Violet Makate 1948(?)— **24**
Sisulu, Walter 1912–2003 **47**
Sizemore, Barbara A. 1927— **26**
Skerrit, Roosevelt 1972— **72**
Skinner, Kiron K. 1962(?) **65**
Sklarek, Norma Merrick 1928— **25**
Slash 1975— **75**
Slater, Rodney Earl 1955— **15**
Slaughter, John Brooks 1934— **53**
Sledge, Percy 1940— **39**
Sleet, Moneta (J.), Jr. 1926— **5**

Slice, Kimbo 1974— **73**
Slick Rick 1965— **93**
Slim Thug 1980— **86**
Slocumb, Jonathan 19(?)(?)— **52**
Sly & Robbie **34**
Slyde, Jimmy 1927–2008 **70**
Smalls, Robert 1839–1915 **82**
Smaltz, Audrey 1937(?)— **12**
Smiley, Rickey 1968— **59**
Smiley, Tavis 1964— **20, 68**
Smith, Anjela Lauren 1973— **44**
Smith, Anna Deavere 1950— **6, 44**
Smith, Arthur Lee, *See Asante, Molefi Kete*
Smith, B. *See Smith, B(arbara)*
Smith, B(arbara) 1949(?)— **11**
Smith, Barbara 1946— **28**
Smith, Bessie 1894–1937 **3**
Smith, Bruce 1984— **80**
Smith, Bruce W. 19(?)(?)— **53**
Smith, Cladys "Jabbo" 1908–1991 **32**
Smith, Clarence O. 1933— **21**
Smith, Clifford *See Method Man*
Smith, Damu 1951— **54**
Smith, Danyel 1966(?)— **40**
Smith, DeMaurice 1964— **92**
Smith, Dr. Lonnie 1942— **49**
Smith, Emmitt 1969— **7, 87**
Smith, Greg 1964— **28**
Smith, Hezekiah Leroy Gordon *See Smith, Stuff*
Smith, Hilton 1912–1983 **29**
Smith, Ian 1970(?)— **62**
Smith, Jabbo *See Smith, Cladys "Jabbo"*
Smith, Jaden 1998— **82**
Smith, Jane E. 1946— **24**
Smith, Jennifer 1947— **21**
Smith, Jessie Carney 1930— **35**
Smith, John L. 1938— **22**
Smith, Joshua (Isaac) 1941— **10**
Smith, Kemba 1971— **70**
Smith, Lonnie Liston 1940— **49**
Smith, Lovie 1958— **66**
Smith, Malcolm A. 1956— **75**
Smith, Mamie 1883–1946 **32**
Smith, Marie F. 1939— **70**
Smith, Marvin 1910–2003 **46**
Smith, Mary Carter 1919— **26**
Smith, Morgan 1910–1993 **46**
Smith, Myrna 1941–2010 **92**
Smith, Nate 1929— **49**
Smith, Orlando *See Smith, Tubby*
Smith, Ozzie 1954— **77**
Smith, Princella 1983— **86**
Smith, Randy 1948–2009 **81**
Smith, Richard 1957— **51**
Smith, Rick 1969— **72**
Smith, Roger Guenveur 1960— **12**
Smith, Shaffer Chimere *See Ne-Yo*
Smith, Stephen A. 1967— **69**
Smith, Stuff 1909–1967 **37**
Smith, Tasha 1971— **73**
Smith, Trevor, Jr. *See Rhymes, Busta*
Smith, Trixie 1895–1943 **34**
Smith, Tubby 1951— **18, 83**
Smith, Vincent D. 1929–2003 **48**
Smith, Walker, Jr. *See Robinson, Sugar Ray*
Smith, Will 1968— **8, 18, 53**
Smith, Willi (Donnell) 1948–1987 **8**

Smith, Willow 2000— **92**
Smith, Zadie 1975— **51**
Smyre, Calvin 1947— **90**
Smythe Haith, Mabel 1918–2006 **61**
Sneed, Paula A. 1947— **18**
Snipes, Wesley 1962— **3, 24, 67**
Snoop Dogg 1971— **35, 84**
Snow, Samuel 1923–2008 **71**
Snowden, Frank M., Jr. 1911–2007 **67**
Soglo, Nicéphore 1935— **15**
Solomon, Jimmie Lee 1947(?)— **38**
Somé, Malidoma Patrice 1956— **10**
Somi 1979— **85**
Sommore, 1966— **61**
Songz, Trey 1984— **88**
Sono, Jomo 1955— **86**
Sosa, Sammy 1968— **21, 44**
Soto Alejo, Federico Arístides *See Güines, Tata*
Soulchild, Musiq *See Musiq*
Souleymane, Mahamane 1940— **78**
Southern, Eileen 1920–2002 **56**
Southgate, Martha 1960(?)— **58**
Sowande, Fela 1905–1987 **39**
Sowande, Olufela Obafunmilayo *See Sowande, Fela*
Sowell, Thomas 1930— **2**
Soyinka, Wole 1934— **4, 93**
Sparks, Corinne Etta 1953— **53**
Sparks, Jordin 1989— **66**
Spaulding, Charles Clinton 1874–1952 **9**
Spearman, Leonard H. O., Sr. 1929–2008 **81**
Spears, Warren 1954–2005 **52**
Spector, Ronnie 1943— **77**
Speech 1968— **82**
Spence, Joseph 1910–1984 **49**
Spencer, Anne 1882–1975 **27**
Spencer, Michael G. 1952— **87**
Spencer, Winston Baldwin 1948— **68**
Spigner, Archie 1928— **81**
Spikes, Dolores Margaret Richard 1936— **18**
Spiller, Bill 1913–1988 **64**
Sprewell, Latrell 1970— **23**
Spriggs, William 195(?)— **67**
Stackhouse, Jerry 1974— **30**
Staley, Dawn 1970— **57**
Stallings, George A(ugustus), Jr. 1948— **6**
Stampley, Micah 1971— **54**
Stanford, John 1938— **20**
Stanford, Olivia Lee Dilworth 1914–2004 **49**
Stanton, Alysa 1963— **78**
Stanton, Robert 1940— **20**
Staples, Brent 1951— **8**
Staples, Mavis 1939(?)— **50, 88**
Staples, "Pops" 1915–2000 **32**
Staples, Roebuck *See Staples, "Pops"*
Stargell, Willie 1940(?)–2001 **29**
Staton, Candi 1940(?)— **27**
Staton, Dakota 1930(?)–2007 **62**
Staupers, Mabel K(eaton) 1890–1989 **7**
Stearnes, Norman "Turkey" 1901–1979 **31**
Steave-Dickerson, Kia 1970— **57**

Steele, Claude Mason 1946— **13**
Steele, Lawrence 1963— **28**
Steele, Michael 1958— **38, 73, 91**
Steele, Shelby 1946— **13, 82**
Steely 1962–2009 **80**
Steinberg, Martha Jean
  1930(?)–2000 **28**
Stephens, Charlotte Andrews
  1854–1951 **14**
Stephens, John *See Legend, John*
Stephens, Myrtle *See Potter, Myrtle*
Stevens, Yvette *See Khan, Chaka*
Stew 1961— **69**
Steward, David L. 19(?)(?)— **36**
Steward, Emanuel 1944— **18**
Stewart, Alison 1966(?)— **13**
Stewart, Ella 1893–1987 **39**
Stewart, James "Bubba," Jr. 1985—
  60
Stewart, Kordell 1972— **21**
Stewart, Mark *See Stew*
Stewart, Nzingha 1974— **89**
Stewart, Paul Wilbur 1925— **12**
Stewart, Sylvester *See Stone, Sly*
Stewart, Tonea Harris 1947— **78**
Sticky Fingaz 1970— **86**
Still, William Grant 1895–1978 **37**
Stingley, Darryl 1951–2007 **69**
Stinson, Denise L. 1954— **59**
Stith, Charles R. 1949— **73**
Stith, Tom 1939–2010 **93**
Stockman, Shawn *See Boyz II Men*
Stokes, Carl 1927–1996 **10, 73**
Stokes, Louis 1925— **3**
Stone, Angie 1965(?)— **31**
Stone, Charles Sumner, Jr. *See
  Stone, Chuck*
Stone, Chuck 1924— **9**
Stone, Sly 1943— **85**
Stone, Toni 1921–1996 **15**
Stoney, Michael 1969— **50**
Stott, Dorothy M. *See Stout, Renee*
Stott, Dot *See Stout, Renee*
Stoudemire, Amaré 1982— **59**
Stout, Juanita Kidd 1919–1998 **24**
Stout, Renee 1958— **63**
Stoute, Steve 1971(?)— **38**
Stoutt, H. Lavity 1929–1995 **83**
Strahan, Michael 1971— **35, 81**
Strautmanis, Michael 1969— **87**
Strawberry, Darryl 1962— **12**
Strayhorn, Billy 1915–1967 **31**
Street, John F. 1943(?)— **24**
Streeter, Sarah 1953— **45**
Stringer, C. Vivian 1948— **13, 66**
Stringer, Korey 1974–2001 **35**
Stringer, Vickie 196(?)— **58**
Stroman, Nathaniel *See Earth-
  quake*
Strong, Barrett 1941— **89**
Stuart, Moira 1949— **82**
Studdard, Ruben 1978— **46**
Sudarkasa, Niara 1938— **4**
Sudduth, Jimmy Lee 1910–2007 **65**
Sugarhill Gang, The **79**
Sullivan, Jazmine 1987— **81**
Sullivan, Leon H(oward) 1922— **3,
  30**
Sullivan, Louis (Wade) 1933— **8**
Sullivan, Maxine 1911–1987 **37**
Summer, Donna 1948— **25**
Sun Ra, 1914–1993 **60**
Sundiata, Sekou 1948–2007 **66**

Supremes, The **33**
Sutphen, Mona 1967— **77**
Sutton, Percy E. 1920–2009 **42, 82**
Swann, Lynn 1952— **28**
Swaray, Fanta Estelle *See Estelle*
Sweat, Keith 1961(?)— **19**
Sweet, Ossian 1895–1960 **68**
Swoopes, Sheryl 1971— **12, 56**
Swygert, H. Patrick 1943— **22**
Sy, Oumou 1952— **65**
Sykes, Roosevelt 1906–1984 **20**
Sykes, Wanda 1964— **48, 81**
Syler, Rene 1963— **53**
Tademy, Lalita 1948— **36**
Tafari Makonnen *See Haile Se-
  lassie*
Tait, Michael 1966— **57**
Talbert, David E. 1966(?)— **34, 93**
Talbert, Mary B. 1866–1923 **77**
Talley, André Leon 1949(?)— **56**
Tamar-kali 1973(?)— **63**
Tamia 1975— **24, 55**
Tampa Red 1904(?)–1980 **63**
Tancil, Gladys Quander 1921–2002
  59
Tandja, Mamadou 1938— **33, 78**
Tanksley, Ann (Graves) 1934— **37**
Tanner, Henry Ossawa 1859–1937
  1
Tate, Eleanora E. 1948— **20, 55**
Tate, Larenz 1975— **15**
Tatum, Art 1909–1956 **28**
Tatum, Beverly Daniel 1954— **42,
  84**
Tatum, Elinor R. 197(?)— **78**
Tatum, Jack 1948— **87**
Tatum, Wilbert 1933–2009 **76**
Taulbert, Clifton Lemoure 1945—
  19
Taylor, Billy 1921–2010 **23, 92**
Taylor, Bo 1966–2008 **72**
Taylor, Cecil 1929— **70**
Taylor, Charles 1948— **20**
Taylor, Darren *See Taylor, Bo*
Taylor, Ephren W., II 1982— **61**
Taylor, Gardner C. 1918— **76**
Taylor, Helen (Lavon Hollingshed)
  1942–2000 **30**
Taylor, Jason 1974— **70**
Taylor, Jermain 1978— **60**
Taylor, John (David Beckett)
  1952— **16**
Taylor, Karin 1971— **34**
Taylor, Koko 1928–2009 **40, 80**
Taylor, Kristin Clark 1959— **8**
Taylor, Lawrence 1959— **25**
Taylor, Marshall Walter "Major"
  1878–1932 **62**
Taylor, Meshach 1947(?)— **4**
Taylor, Mildred D. 1943— **26**
Taylor, Natalie 1959— **47**
Taylor, Recy 1919— **92**
Taylor, Regina 1959(?)— **9, 46**
Taylor, Robert Robinson
  1868–1942 **80**
Taylor, Ron 1952–2002 **35**
Taylor, Susan C. 1957— **62**
Taylor, Susan L. 1946— **10, 86**
Taylor, Susie King 1848–1912 **13**
Teasley, Lisa 1962— **92**
Teer, Barbara Ann 1937–2008 **81**
Tergat, Paul 1969— **59**

Terrell, Dorothy A. 1945— **24**
Terrell, Mary (Elizabeth) Church
  1863–1954 **9**
Terrell, Tammi 1945–1970 **32**
Terrell-Kearney, Kim 1965— **83**
Terrill, Saunders *See Terry, Sonny*
Terry, Clark 1920— **39**
Terry, Sonny 1911–1986 **88**
Tharpe, Rosetta 1915–1973 **65**
The Artist *See Prince*
The-Dream 1982— **74**
Thiam, Aliaune Akon *See Akon*
Thigpen, Lynne 1948–2003 **17, 41**
Thomas, Alma Woodsey
  1891–1978 **14**
Thomas, Arthur Ray 1951— **52**
Thomas, Clarence 1948— **2, 39, 65**
Thomas, Claudia Lynn 1950— **64**
Thomas, Debi 1967— **26**
Thomas, Derrick 1967–2000 **25**
Thomas, Emmitt 1943— **71**
Thomas, Frank 1968— **12, 51**
Thomas, Franklin A. 1934— **5, 49**
Thomas, Irma 1941— **29**
Thomas, Isiah 1961— **7, 26, 65**
Thomas, Jefferson 1942–2010 **88**
Thomas, Michael 1967— **69**
Thomas, Mickalene 1971— **61**
Thomas, Rozonda 1971— **34, 78**
Thomas, Rufus 1917— **20**
Thomas, Sean Patrick 1970— **35**
Thomas, Stayve Jerome *See Slim
  Thug*
Thomas, Thurman 1966— **75**
Thomas, Todd *See Speech*
Thomas, Trisha R. 1964— **65**
Thomas, Vivien (T.) 1910–1985 **9**
Thomas-Graham, Pamela
  1963(?)— **29**
Thomason, Marsha 1976— **47**
Thompson, Ahmir *See ?uestlove*
Thompson, Bennie G. 1948— **26**
Thompson, Cynthia Bramlett
  1949— **50**
Thompson, Dearon *See Deezer D*
Thompson, Don 1963— **56**
Thompson, John Douglas 1964—
  81
Thompson, John W. 1949— **26**
Thompson, Kenan 1978— **52**
Thompson, Larry D. 1945— **39**
Thompson, Tazewell (Alfred, Jr.)
  1954— **13**
Thompson, Tina 1975— **25, 75**
Thompson, William C. 1953(?)— **35**
Thoms, Tracie 1975— **61**
Thornton, Big Mama 1926–1984 **33**
Thornton, Yvonne S. 1947— **69**
Thrash, Dox 1893–1965 **35**
Three Mo' Tenors **35**
Thrower, Willie 1930–2002 **35**
Thugwane, Josia 1971— **21**
Thurman, Howard 1900–1981 **3**
Thurman, Wallace Henry
  1902–1934 **16**
Thurmond, Nate 1941— **88**
Thurston, Baratunde 1977— **79**
Thurston, Stephen J. 1952— **49**
Till, Emmett (Louis) 1941–1955 **7**
Tillard, Conrad 1964— **47**
Tillis, Frederick 1930— **40**
Tillman, Dorothy 1947— **76**
Tillman, George, Jr. 1968— **20**

Timbaland 1971— **32**
Tinsley, Boyd 1964— **50**
Tirico, Michael *See Tirico, Mike*
Tirico, Mike 1966— **68**
Tisdale, Wayman 1964— **50**
TLC **34**
Tobias, Channing H. 1882–1961 **79**
Tobin, Patricia 1943–2008 **75**
Todman, Terence A. 1926— **55**
Tolbert, Terence 1964— **74**
Toler, Burl 1928–2009 **80**
Tolliver, Mose 1915(?)–2006 **60**
Tolliver, William (Mack) 1951— **9**
Tolson, Melvin B(eaunorus)
  1898–1966 **37**
Tolton, Augustine 1854–1897 **62**
Tomlinson, LaDainian 1979— **65**
Tonex, 1978(?)— **54**
Toney, James 1968— **89**
Tooks, Lance 1962— **62**
Toomer, Jean 1894–1967 **6**
Toomer, Nathan Pinchback *See
  Toomer, Jean*
Toote, Gloria E. A. 1931— **64**
Torres, Gina 1969— **52**
Torry, Guy 19(?)(?)— **31**
Tosh, Peter 1944–1987 **9**
Touré, Amadou Toumani 1948(?)—
  18
Touré, Askia (Muhammad Abu Bakr
  el) 1938— **47**
Touré, Faya Ora Rose 1945— **56**
Touré, Sekou 1922–1984 **6**
Toussaint, Allen 1938— **60**
Toussaint, Lorraine 1960— **32**
Townes, Jeffrey Allan *See DJ Jazzy
  Jeff*
Towns, Edolphus 1934— **19, 75**
Townsend, Robert 1957— **4, 23**
T-Pain 1985— **73**
Trammell, Kimberly N. *See Holland,
  Kimberly N.*
Tresvant, Ralph 1968— **57**
Tribbett, Tye 1977— **81**
Tribble, Israel, Jr. 1940— **8**
Trotter, Donne E. 1950— **28**
Trotter, Lloyd G. 1945(?)— **56**
Trotter, (William) Monroe
  1872–1934 **9**
Trotter, Tariq Luqmaan *See Black
  Thought*
Trouillot, Ertha Pascal *See Pascal-
  Trouillot, Ertha*
Troupe, Quincy 1943— **83**
Trouppe, Quincy Thomas, Sr.
  1912–1993 **84**
True, Rachel 1966— **82**
Trueheart, William E. 1942— **49**
Tsvangirai, Morgan 1952— **26, 72**
Tubbs Jones, Stephanie
  1949–2008 **24, 72**
Tubman, Harriet 1820(?)–1913 **9**
Tucker, C. Delores 1927–2005 **12,
  56**
Tucker, Chris 1972— **13, 23, 62**
Tucker, Cynthia 1955— **1561**
Tucker, Rosina Budd Harvey Cor-
  rothers 1881–1987 **14**
Tuckson, Reed V. 1951(?)— **71**
Tunie, Tamara 1959— **63**
Tunnell, Emlen 1925–1975 **54**
Ture, Kwame *See Carmichael,
  Stokely*

Turnbull, Charles Wesley 1935— 62

Turnbull, Walter 1944— 13, 60

Turner, Big Joe 1911–1985 92

Turner, Henry McNeal 1834–1915 5

Turner, Ike 1931–2007 68

Turner, Izear See Turner, Ike

Turner, Tina 1939— 6, 27

Tutu, Desmond (Mpilo) 1931— 6, 44

Tutu, Nontombi Naomi 1960— 57

Tutuola, Amos 1920–1997 30

Tyler, Aisha N. 1970— 36

Tyner, McCoy 1938— 92

Tyree, Omar Rashad 1969— 21

Tyrese See Gibson, Tyrese

Tyson, Andre 1960— 40

Tyson, Asha 1970— 39

Tyson, Cicely 1933— 7, 51

Tyson, Mike 1966— 28, 44, 93

Tyson, Neil deGrasse 1958— 15, 65

Uggams, Leslie 1943— 23

Ukpabio, Helen 1969— 86

Ulmer, James 1942— 79

Underwood, Blair 1964— 7, 27, 76

Union, Gabrielle 1972— 31, 92

Unseld, Wes 1946— 23

Upshaw, Gene 1945–2008 18, 47, 72

Usher 1978— 23, 56

Usry, James L. 1922— 23

Ussery, Terdema Lamar, II 1958— 29

Utendahl, John 1956— 23

Valdés, Bebo 1918— 75

Valdés, Chucho 1941— 89

Valdés, Dionisio Ramón Emilio See Valdés, Bebo

Valentino, Bobby 1980— 62

Van Lierop, Robert 1939— 53

Van Peebles, Mario 1957— 2, 51

Van Peebles, Melvin 1932— 7

van Sertima, Ivan 1935— 25

Vance, Courtney B. 1960— 15, 60

VanDerZee, James (Augustus Joseph) 1886–1983 6

Vandross, Luther 1951–2005 13, 48, 59

Vanessa James and Yannick Bonheur 84

Vanity 1959— 67

Vann, Harold Moore See Muhammad, Khallid Abdul

Vanzant, Iyanla 1953— 17, 47

Vaughan, Sarah (Lois) 1924–1990 13

Vaughn, Countess 1978— 53

Vaughn, Gladys Gary 1942(?)— 47

Vaughn, Mo 1967— 16

Vaughn, Viola 1947— 70

Vaughns, Cleopatra 1940— 46

Vega, Marta Moreno 1942(?)— 61

Velez-Rodriguez, Argelia 1936— 56

Vera, Yvonne 1964— 32

Verdelle, A. J. 1960— 26

Vereen, Ben(jamin Augustus) 1946— 4

Verna, Gelsy 1961–2008 70

Verrett, Shirley 1931–2010 66, 91

Vick, Michael 1980— 39, 65

Vieira, João Bernardo 1939–2009 14, 84

Villarosa, Clara 1930(?)— 85

Vincent, Marjorie Judith 1965(?)— 2

Vincent, Mark See Diesel, Vin

Vincent, Troy 1971— 91

Virgil, Ozzie 1933— 48

Von Lipsey, Roderick 1959— 11

wa Ngengi, Kamau See Kenyatta, Jomo

Waddles, Charleszetta "Mother" 1912–2001 10, 49

Waddles, Mother See Waddles, Charleszetta "Mother"

Wade, Abdoulaye 1926— 66

Wade, Dwyane 1982— 61

Wade-Gayles, Gloria Jean 1937(?)— 41

Wagner, Albert 1924–2006 78

Wagner, Annice 1937— 22

Wainwright, Joscelyn 1941— 46

Walcott, Derek (Alton) 1930— 5

Walcott, Louis Eugene 1933— 2, 15

Wale 1984— 92

Walker, Albertina 1929–2010 10, 58, 89

Walker, Alice 1944— 1, 43

Walker, Arthur, II 1936–2001 87

Walker, Bernita Ruth 1946— 53

Walker, Cedric "Ricky" 1953— 19

Walker, Cora T. 1922–2006 68

Walker, Dianne 1951— 57

Walker, Eamonn 1961(?)— 37

Walker, George 1922— 37

Walker, Herschel 1962— 1, 69

Walker, Hezekiah 1962— 34

Walker, John T. 1925–1989 50

Walker, Kara 1969— 16, 80

Walker, Kurt See Blow, Kurtis

Walker, Lucius, Jr. 1930–2010 88

Walker, Madame C. J. 1867–1919 7

Walker, Maggie Lena 1867(?)–1934 17

Walker, Margaret 1915–1998 29

Walker, Nellie Marian See Larsen, Nella

Walker, Rebecca 1969— 50

Walker, T. J. 1961(?)— 7

Walker, Thomas "T. J." See Walker, T. J.

Walker, Wyatt Tee 1929— 80

Wall, Orindatus S. B. 1825–1891 92

Wallace, Ben 1974— 54

Wallace, Joaquin 1965— 49

Wallace, Michele Faith 1952— 13

Wallace, Perry E. 1948— 47

Wallace, Phyllis A(nn) 1920(?)–1993 9

Wallace, Rasheed 1974— 56

Wallace, Ruby Ann See Dee, Ruby

Wallace, Sippie 1898–1986 1

Wallace, William 1939–2008 75

Waller, Fats 1904–1943 29

Waller, Thomas Wright See Waller, Fats

Walters, Richard See Slick Rick

Walters, Ronald 1938— 83

Walton, Cora See Taylor, Koko

Wambugu, Florence 1953— 42

Wamutombo, Dikembe Mutombo Mpolondo Mukamba Jean Jacque See Mutombo, Dikembe

Ward, Andre 1984— 62

Ward, Benjamin 1926–2002 68

Ward, Douglas Turner 1930— 42

Ward, Hines 1976— 84

Ward, Lloyd 1949— 21, 46

Ware, Andre 1968— 37

Ware, Carl H. 1943— 30

Ware, DeMarcus 1982— 92

Warfield, Marsha 1955— 2

Warner, Malcolm-Jamal 1970— 22, 36

Warren, Michael 1946— 27

Warren, Mike See Warren, Michael

Warsame, Keinan Abdi See K'naan

Warwick, Dionne 1940— 18

Washington, Alonzo 1967— 29

Washington, Booker T(aliaferro) 1856–1915 4

Washington, Denzel 1954— 1, 16, 93

Washington, Dinah 1924–1963 22

Washington, Ebonya 1973(?)— 79

Washington, Elsie B. 1942–2009 78

Washington, Fred(er)i(cka Carolyn) 1903–1994 10

Washington, Gene 1947— 63

Washington, Grover, Jr. 1943–1999 17, 44

Washington, Harold 1922–1987 6

Washington, Harriet A. 1951— 69

Washington, Hayma 19(?)(?)— 86

Washington, Isaiah 1963— 62

Washington, James, Jr. 1909(?)–2000 38

Washington, James Melvin 1948–1997 50

Washington, Kenny 1918–1971 50

Washington, Kerry 1977— 46

Washington, Laura S. 1956(?)— 18

Washington, MaliVai 1969— 8

Washington, Mary T. 1906–2005 57

Washington, Patrice Clarke 1961— 12

Washington, Pauletta Pearson 1950— 86

Washington, Regynald G. 1954(?)— 44

Washington, Tamia Reneé See Tamia

Washington, Valores James 1903–1995 12

Washington, Walter 1915–2003 45

Washington Wylie, Mary T. See Washington, Mary T.

Wasow, Omar 1970— 15

Waters, Benny 1902–1998 26

Waters, Ethel 1895–1977 7

Waters, Maxine 1938— 3, 67

Waters, Muddy 1915–1983 34

Watkins, Donald 1948— 35

Watkins, Frances Ellen See Harper, Frances Ellen Watkins

Watkins, Gloria Jean See hooks, bell

Watkins, Joe 1953— 86

Watkins, Levi, Jr. 1945— 9

Watkins, Perry James Henry 1948–1996 12

Watkins, Shirley R. 1938— 17

Watkins, Tionne "T-Boz" 1970— See TLC

Watkins, Walter C. 1946— 24

Watley, Jody 1959— 54

Watson, Bob 1946— 25

Watson, Carlos 1970— 50

Watson, Diane 1933— 41

Watson, Johnny "Guitar" 1935–1996 18

Watt, Melvin 1945— 26

Wattleton, (Alyce) Faye 1943— 9

Watts, Andre 1946— 42

Watts, J(ulius) C(aesar), Jr. 1957— 14, 38

Watts, Reggie 1972(?)— 52

Watts, Rolonda 1959— 9

Wayans, Damien 198(?)— 78

Wayans, Damon 1961— 8, 41

Wayans, Keenen Ivory 1958— 18

Wayans, Kim 1961— 80

Wayans, Marlon 1972— 29, 82

Wayans, Shawn 1971— 29

Waymon, Eunice Kathleen See Simone, Nina

Weah, George 1966— 58

Weathers, Carl 1948— 10

Weaver, Afaa Michael 1951— 37

Weaver, Michael S. See Weaver, Afaa Michael

Weaver, Robert C. 1907–1997 8, 46

Webb, Veronica 1965— 10

Webb, Wellington 1941— 3, 81

Webber, Chris 1973— 15, 30, 59

Webster, Katie 1936–1999 29

Wedgeworth, Robert W. 1937— 42

Weekes, Kevin 1975— 67

Weeks, Thomas, III 1967— 70

Weems, Carrie Mae 1953— 63

Weems, Renita J. 1954— 44

Wein, Joyce 1928–2005 62

Wek, Alek 1977— 18, 63

Welburn, Edward T. 1950— 50

Welch, Elisabeth 1908–2003 52

Welles, Rosalind See Washington, Elsie B.

Wells, Henrietta Bell 1912–2008 69

Wells, James Lesesne 1902–1993 10

Wells, Mary 1943–1992 28

Wells, Vernon 1978— 91

Wells-Barnett, Ida B(ell) 1862–1931 8

Welsing, Frances (Luella) Cress 1935— 5

Wendo See Kolosoy, Wendo

Wesley, Dorothy Porter 1905–1995 19

Wesley, Richard 1945— 73

Wesley, Valerie Wilson 194(?)— 18

West, Allen 1961— 89

West, Cornel 1953— 5, 33, 80

West, Dorothy 1907–1998 12, 54

West, James E. 1931— 87

West, Kanye 1977— 52, 93

West, Togo Dennis, Jr. 1942— 16

Westbrook, Kelvin 1955— 50

Westbrook, Peter 1952— 20

Westbrooks, Bobby 1930(?)–1995 51

Whack, Rita Coburn 1958— 36

Whalum, Kirk 1958— 37, 64

Wharton, Clifton R(eginald), Jr. 1926— 7

Wharton, Clifton Reginald, Sr. 1899–1990 36

Wheat, Alan Dupree 1951— 14

Whitaker, Forest 1961— 2, 49, 67

Whitaker, Mark 1957— 21, 47

Whitaker, Pernell 1964— 10, 89

Whitaker, "Sweet Pea" See Whitaker, Pernell
White, Armond 1954(?)— **80**
White, Barry 1944–2003 **13, 41**
White, Bill 1933(?)— **1, 48**
White, Charles 1918–1979 **39**
White, (Donald) Dondi 1961–1998 **34**
White, Jesse 1934— **22, 75**
White, Jessica 1984— **83**
White, John H. 1945— **27**
White, Josh 1914(?)–1969 **86**
White, Josh, Jr. 1940— **52**
White, Linda M. 1942— **45**
White, Lois Jean 1938— **20**
White, Maurice 1941— **29**
White, Michael Jai 1967— **71**
White, Michael R(eed) 1951— **5**
White, Reggie 1961–2004 **6, 50**
White, Reginald Howard See White, Reggie
White, Terri 1948— **82**
White, Walter F(rancis) 1893–1955 **4**
White, Willard 1946— **53**
White, William DeKova See White, Bill
White, Willye 1939— **67**
White-Hammond, Gloria 1951(?)— **61**
Whitehead, Colson 1969— **77**
Whitfield, Fred 1967— **23**
Whitfield, LeRoy 1969–2005 **84**
Whitfield, Lynn 1954— **18**
Whitfield, Mal 1924— **60**
Whitfield, Norman 1940–2008 **73**
Whitfield, Van 1960(?)— **34**
Whitlock, Jason 1967— **78**
Whittaker, Hudson See Tampa Red
Wideman, John Edgar 1941— **5, 87**
Wilbekin, Emil 1968— **63**
Wilbon, Michael 1958— **68**
Wilder, L. Douglas 1931— **3, 48**
Wiley, Kehinde 1977— **62**
Wiley, Ralph 1952–2004 **8, 78**
Wilkens, J. Ernest, Jr. 1923— **43**
Wilkens, Lenny 1937— **11, 88**
Wilkens, Leonard Randolph See Wilkens, Lenny
Wilkerson, Isabel 1961— **71**
Wilkerson, Robert King See King, Robert Hillary
Wilkins, David 1956— **77**
Wilkins, Dominique 1960— **74**
Wilkins, Ray 1951— **47**
Wilkins, Roger 1932— **2, 84**
Wilkins, Roy 1901–1981 **4**
Wilkins, Thomas Alphonso 1956— **71**
will.i.am 1975— **64**
Williams, Alice Faye See Shakur, Afeni
Williams, Ann Claire 1949— **82**
Williams, Anthony 1951— **21**
Williams, Anthony Charles See Tonex
Williams, Armstrong 1959— **29**
Williams, Bert 1874–1922 **18**
Williams, Billy 1938— **86**
Williams, Billy Dee 1937— **8**
Williams, Carl See Kani, Karl
Williams, Clarence 1893(?)–1965 **33**

Williams, Clarence 1967— **70**
Williams, Clarence, III 1939— **26**
Williams, Claude 1908–2004 **80**
Williams, Daniel Hale (III) 1856–1931 **2**
Williams, David Rudyard 1954— **50**
Williams, Deniece 1951— **36**
Williams, Denise 1958— **40**
Williams, Deron 1984— **92**
Williams, Doug 1955— **22**
Williams, Dudley 1938— **60**
Williams, Eddie N. 1932— **44**
Williams, Eric Eustace 1911–1981 **65**
Williams, Evelyn 1922(?)— **10**
Williams, Fannie Barrier 1855–1944 **27**
Williams, Frederick (B.) 1939–2006 **63**
Williams, George Washington 1849–1891 **18**
Williams, Gertrude See Morgan, Gertrude
Williams, Gregory (Howard) 1943— **11**
Williams, Hosea Lorenzo 1926— **15, 31**
Williams, J. Mayo 1894–1980 **83**
Williams, Joe 1918–1999 **5, 25**
Williams, John A. 1925— **27**
Williams, Juan 1954— **35, 80**
Williams, Ken 1964— **68**
Williams, Lauryn 1983— **58**
Williams, Lindsey 1966— **75**
Williams, Maggie 1954— **7, 71**
Williams, Malinda 1975— **57**
Williams, Marco 1956— **53**
Williams, Margaret Ann See Williams, Maggie
Williams, Mary Lou 1910–1981 **15**
Williams, Michael L. 1953— **86**
Williams, Michelle 1980— **73**
Williams, Montel 1956— **4, 57**
Williams, Nat D. 1907–1983 **91**
Williams, Natalie 1970— **31**
Williams, O(swald) S. 1921— **13**
Williams, Patricia 1951— **11, 54**
Williams, Paul R(evere) 1894–1980 **9**
Williams, Paulette Linda See Shange, Ntozake
Williams, Pharrell 1973— **47, 82**
Williams, Preston Warren, II 1939(?)— **64**
Williams, Rhonda Y. 1967(?)— **86**
Williams, Ricky 1977— **85**
Williams, Robert F(ranklin) 1925— **11**
Williams, Robert Peter See Guillaume, Robert
Williams, Ronald A. 1949— **57**
Williams, Roy 1968— **89**
Williams, Russell, II 1952— **70**
Williams, Samuel Arthur 1946— **21**
Williams, Saul 1972— **31**
Williams, Serena 1981— **20, 41, 73**
Williams, Sherley Anne 1944–1999 **25**
Williams, Stanley "Tookie" 1953–2005 **29, 57**
Williams, Stevie 1979— **71**
Williams, Ted 1957— **91**
Williams, Terrie M. 1954— **35**
Williams, Tony 1945–1997 **67**

Williams, Vanessa A. 1963— **32, 66**
Williams, Vanessa L. 1963— **4, 17**
Williams, Venus 1980— **17, 34, 62**
Williams, Walter E(dward) 1936— **4**
Williams, Wendy 1964— **62**
Williams, William December See Williams, Billy Dee
Williams, William T(homas) 1942— **11**
Williams, Willie L(awrence) 1943— **4**
Williamson, Fred 1938— **67**
Williamson, Lisa See Sister Souljah
Williamson, Mykelti 1957— **22**
Williamson, Sonny Boy 1899(?)–1965 **84**
Willie, Louis, Jr. 1923–2007 **68**
Willingham, Tyrone 1953— **43**
Willis, Bill 1921–2007 **68**
Willis, Cheryl See Hudson, Cheryl
Willis, Deborah 1948— **85**
Willis, Dontrelle 1982— **55**
Willis, William Karnet See Willis, Bill
Wills, Harry 1889(?)–1958 **80**
Wills, Maury 1932— **73**
Wilson, August 1945–2005 **7, 33, 55**
Wilson, Cassandra 1955— **16**
Wilson, Chandra 1969— **57**
Wilson, Charlie 1953— **31, 77**
Wilson, Debra 1970(?)— **38**
Wilson, Donald E. 1936(?)— **88**
Wilson, Dorien 1962(?)— **55**
Wilson, Ellis 1899–1977 **39**
Wilson, Frederica 1942— **92**
Wilson, Flip 1933–1998 **21**
Wilson, Gerald 1918— **49**
Wilson, Jackie 1934–1984 **60**
Wilson, Jimmy 1946— **45**
Wilson, Margaret Bush 1919–2009 **79**
Wilson, Mary 1944 **28**
Wilson, Nancy 1937— **10**
Wilson, Natalie 1972(?)— **38**
Wilson, Phill 1956— **9**
Wilson, Stephanie 1966— **72**
Wilson, Sunnie 1908–1999 **7, 55**
Wilson, Tracey Scott 1967(?)— **77**
Wilson, William Julius 1935— **22**
Wilson, William Nathaniel See Wilson, Sunnie
Wimbley, Damon 1966— See Fat Boys
Winans, Angie 1968— **36**
Winans, Benjamin 1962— **14**
Winans, CeCe 1964— **14, 43**
Winans, David 1934–2009 **77**
Winans, Debbie 1972— **36**
Winans, Marvin L. 1958— **17**
Winans, Ronald 1956–2005 **54**
Winans, Vickie 1953(?)— **24**
Winfield, Dave 1951— **5, 91**
Winfield, David Mark See Winfield, Dave
Winfield, Paul (Edward) 1941–2004 **2, 45**
Winfrey, Oprah 1954— **2, 15, 61**
Winkfield, Jimmy 1882–1974 **42**
Winslow, Kellen 1957— **83**
Wisdom, Kimberlydawn 1956— **57**
Withers, Bill 1938— **61**
Withers, Ernest C. 1922–2007 **68, 88**

Withers-Mendes, Elisabeth 1973(?)— **64**
Witherspoon, John 1942— **38**
Witt, Edwin T. 1920— **26**
Wiwa, Ken 1968— **67**
Wofford, Chloe Anthony See Morrison, Toni
Wolfe, Ann 1971— **82**
Wolfe, George C. 1954— **6, 43**
Womack, Bobby 1944— **60, 92**
Wonder, Stevie 1950— **11, 53**
Wonder Mike See Sugarhill Gang, The
Woodard, Alfre 1953— **9**
Woodard, Lynette 1959— **67**
Woodbridge, Hudson See Tampa Red
Woodruff, Hale (Aspacio) 1900–1980 **9**
Woodruff, John 1915–2007 **68**
Woods, Abraham, Jr. 1928–2008 **74**
Woods, Eldrick See Woods, Tiger
Woods, Georgie 1927–2005 **57**
Woods, Granville T. 1856–1910 **5**
Woods, Jacqueline 1962— **52**
Woods, Mattiebelle 1902–2005 **63**
Woods, Scott 1971— **55**
Woods, Sylvia 1926— **34**
Woods, Teri 1968— **69**
Woods, Tiger 1975— **14, 31, 81**
Woodson, Ali Ollie 1951–2010 **89**
Woodson, Carter G(odwin) 1875–1950 **2**
Woodson, Mike 1958— **78**
Woodson, Robert L. 1937— **10**
Woodson, Rod 1965— **79**
Wooldridge, Anna Marie See Lincoln, Abbey
Worrill, Conrad 1941— **12**
Worthy, James 1961— **49**
Worthy, Kym 1956— **84**
Wright, Antoinette 195(?)— **60**
Wright, Bruce McMarion 1918–2005 **3, 52**
Wright, Charles H. 1918–2002 **35**
Wright, Deborah C. 1958— **25**
Wright, Jeffrey 1966— **54**
Wright, Jeremiah A., Jr. 1941— **45, 69**
Wright, Lewin 1962— **43**
Wright, Louis Tompkins 1891–1952 **4**
Wright, Nathan, Jr. 1923–2005 **56**
Wright, Rayfield 1945— **70**
Wright, Richard 1908–1960 **5**
Wright, Timothy 1947— **74**
Wyatt, Addie L. 1924— **56**
Wynn, Albert R. 1951— **25, 77**
X, Malcolm 1925–1965 **1**
X, Marvin 1944— **45**
Xuma, Madie Hall 1894–1982 **59**
Xzibit 1974— **78**
Yabby You 1946–2010 **83**
Yancy, Dorothy Cowser 1944— **42**
Yar'Adua, Umaru 1951–2010 **69, 89**
Yarbrough, Camille 1938— **40**
Yarbrough, Cedric 1971— **51**
Yayi, Boni T. 1952— **84**
Yeboah, Emmanuel Ofosu 1977— **53**

Yette, Samuel F. 1929— **63**

Yoba, (Abdul-)Malik (Kashie) 1967— **11**

York, Dwight D. 1945— **71**

York, Malachi Z. *See York, Dwight D.*

York, Vincent 1952— **40**

Young, Al 1939— **82**

Young, Andre Ramelle *See Dre, Dr.*

Young, Andrew 1932— **3, 48**

Young, Charles 1864–1922 **77**

Young, Coleman 1918–1997 **1, 20**

Young, Donald, Jr. 1989— **57**

Young, Jean Childs 1933–1994 **14**

Young, Jimmy 1948–2005 **54**

Young, Ledisi Anibade *See Ledisi*

Young, Lee 1914–2008 **72**

Young, Leonidas Raymond *See Young, Lee*

Young, Roger Arliner 1899–1964 **29**

Young, Thomas 194(?)— *See Three Mo' Tenors*

Young, Whitney M(oore), Jr. 1921–1971 **4**

Young Jeezy 1977— **63**

Youngblood, Johnny Ray 1948— **8**

Youngblood, Shay 1959— **32**

Zane 1967(?)— **71**

Zollar, Alfred 1955(?)— **40**

Zollar, Jawole Willa Jo 1950— **28**

Zook, Kristal Brent 1966(?)— **62**

Zulu, Princess Kasune 1977— **54**

Zuma, Jacob 1942— **33, 75**

Zuma, Nkosazana Dlamini 1949— **34**